Frommer's

Virginia
7th Edition

by Bill Goodwin

Here's what the critics say about Frommer's:

"Amazingly easy to use. Very portable, very complete."

—*Booklist*

"Detailed, accurate, and easy-to-read information for all price ranges."
—*Glamour Magazine*

"Hotel information is close to encyclopedic."
—*Des Moines Sunday Register*

"Frommer's Guides have a way of giving you a real feel for a place."
—*Knight Ridder Newspapers*

WILEY

Wiley Publishing, Inc.

About the Author

Born and raised in North Carolina near Hampton Roads, **Bill Goodwin** has lived in northern Virginia since 1979. He was an award-winning newspaper reporter for the *Atlanta Journal* before becoming a legal counsel and speechwriter for two U.S. Senators, Sam Nunn of Georgia and the late Sam J. Ervin Jr. of North Carolina. Now a full-time travel writer, Goodwin also is the author of *Frommer's South Pacific*.

Published by:

Wiley Publishing, Inc.

111 River St.
Hoboken, NJ 07030-5774

ISBN 0-7645-4341-5

Editor: Kathleen Warnock
Production Editor: Tammy Ahrens
Cartographer: John Decamillis
Photo Editor: Richard Fox
Production by Wiley Indianapolis Composition Services

Front cover photo: Residents of Colonial Williamsburg
Back cover photo: Mabry Mill on the Blue Ridge Parkway

For information on our other products and services or to obtain technical support, please contact our Customer Care Department within the U.S. at 800/762-2974, outside the U.S. at 317/572-3993 or fax 317/572-4002.

Wiley also publishes its books in a variety of electronic formats. Some content that appears in print may not be available in electronic formats.

Manufactured in the United States of America

5   4   3   2

Contents

List of Maps

An Invitation to the Reader

In researching this book, we discovered many wonderful places—hotels, restaurants, shops, and more. We're sure you'll find others. Please tell us about them, so we can share the information with your fellow travelers in upcoming editions. If you were disappointed with a recommendation, we'd love to know that, too. Please write to:

Frommer's Virginia, 7th Edition
Wiley Publishing, Inc. • 111 River St. • Hoboken, NJ 07030-5774

An Additional Note

Please be advised that travel information is subject to change at any time—and this is especially true of prices. We therefore suggest that you write or call ahead for confirmation when making your travel plans. The authors, editors, and publisher cannot be held responsible for the experiences of readers while traveling. Your safety is important to us, however, so we encourage you to stay alert and be aware of your surroundings. Keep a close eye on cameras, purses, and wallets, all favorite targets of thieves and pickpockets.

Other Great Guides for Your Trip:

Frommer's Maryland & Delaware

Frommer's Exploring America by RV

Frommer's The Carolinas & Georgia

The Unofficial Guide to Bed & Breakfasts and Country Inns in the Mid-Atlantic

The Unofficial Guide to the Mid-Atlantic with Kids

Frommer's Star Ratings, Icons & Abbreviations

Every hotel, restaurant, and attraction listing in this guide has been ranked for quality, value, service, amenities, and special features using a **star-rating system.** In country, state, and regional guides, we also rate towns and regions to help you narrow down your choices and budget your time accordingly. Hotels and restaurants are rated on a scale of zero (recommended) to three stars (exceptional). Attractions, shopping, nightlife, towns, and regions are rated according to the following scale: zero stars (recommended), one star (highly recommended), two stars (very highly recommended), and three stars (must-see).

In addition to the star-rating system, we also use **seven feature icons** that point you to the great deals, in-the-know advice, and unique experiences that separate travelers from tourists. Throughout the book, look for:

Finds	Special finds—those places only insiders know about
Fun Fact	Fun facts—details that make travelers more informed and their trips more fun
Kids	Best bets for kids and advice for the whole family
Moments	Special moments—those experiences that memories are made of
Overrated	Places or experiences not worth your time or money
Tips	Insider tips—great ways to save time and money
Value	Great values—where to get the best deals

The following **abbreviations** are used for credit cards:

AE	American Express	DISC	Discover	V	Visa
DC	Diners Club	MC	MasterCard		

Frommers.com

Now that you have the guidebook to a great trip, visit our website at **www.frommers.com** for travel information on more than 3,000 destinations. With features updated regularly, we give you instant access to the most current trip-planning information available. At Frommers.com, you'll also find the best prices on airfares, accommodations, and car rentals—and you can even book travel online through our travel booking partners. At Frommers.com, you'll also find the following:

- Online updates to our most popular guidebooks
- Vacation sweepstakes and contest giveaways
- Newsletter highlighting the hottest travel trends
- Online travel message boards with featured travel discussions

What's New in Virginia

NORTHERN VIRGINIA Old Town Alexandria continues to see explosive development around its King Street Metrorail station, with new office buildings going up all the time. Among them are the **Hampton Inn-King Street Metro,** 1616 King St. (© **800/ HAMPTON** or 703/299-9900; www. hamptoninn.com), and the luxurious **Hilton Alexandria Old Town,** 1767 King St. (© **800/HILTONS** or 703/ 837-0440; www.hiltonalexandria.com).

New restaurants have come on line, too, including **Cafe Salsa,** 703 King St. (© **703/684-4100**), offering tastes of various Latin American cuisines.

Mount Vernon, George Washington's home, has opened **Washington's Gristmill,** a 1933 reconstruction 3 miles south of the plantation on Mount Vernon Memorial Parkway. Nearby, archaeologists have discovered the foundation of Washington's whiskey still.

For complete information on this region, see chapter 4.

FREDERICKSBURG & THE NORTHERN NECK Historic artifacts including the 1668 Bible on which George Washington took his obligation are no longer on display at **Masonic Lodge #4.** You might be able to see them at the **Fredericksburg Area Museum and Cultural Center.**

The new **Feast-O-Rama,** 1008 Sophia St. (© **540/373-9040**), between William and Amelia streets, has supplies for a gourmet picnic by the Rappahannock River. Open Tuesday to Saturday, 10am to 6pm.

Rappahannock River Cruises (© **804/453-2628;** www.tangiercruise. com) sends the stern-wheel *City of Fredericksburg* on cruises down the river, including a 2-hour lunch trip which stops at Ingleside Vineyards for wine tastings.

On **the Northern Neck,** the venerable **Tides Inn** in Irvington has undergone a major renovation and is now one of a handful of outstanding resorts in Virginia. Old-timers may be surprised to find a British raj decor instead of the Old Virginia style the inn had worn since 1947. It now has a full-service spa.

Also in Irvington, **The Hope and Glory Inn,** one of Virginia's most unusual country inns, has added two new town house–style cottages with upstairs bedrooms.

For complete information on this region, see chapter 5.

CHARLOTTESVILLE The new **Courtyard by Marriott University/ Medical Center,** 1201 W. Main St. (© **800/321-2211** or 434/977-1700; www.courtyard.com), brings modern, well-equipped accommodations to the university area. The **Omni Charlottesville Hotel,** 235 W. Main St. (© **434/971-5500;** www.omnihotels. com), has redesigned its atrium restaurant and added a sports bar. Out in the rolling countryside, **The Foxfield Inn,** 2280 Garth Rd. (© **800/369-3536** or 434/923-8892; www.foxfield-inn. com), offers 5 romantic rooms and an eight-person hot tub 7 miles northwest of Charlottesville.

On the Downtown Mall, **Blue Light Bar & Grill,** 120 E. Main St. (© 434/295-1223), provides four types of oysters among Charlottesville's freshest seafood.

North of Charlottesville, James Madison's **Montpelier** is undergoing a major 4-year restoration, which will reduce it from its current 55 rooms to the 22-room version James and wife Dolley occupied in the 1820s. The mansion remains open, with special guided tours of the construction areas.

And a perennial "Best of," **The Clifton Inn,** an 18th-century inn on the National Register of Historic Places, was seriously damaged in a fire, and is closed indefinitely.

For complete information on Charlottesville, see chapter 6.

THE SHENANDOAH VALLEY Near Front Royal, the super-luxe **Inn at Little Washington,** Middle and Main streets (© 540/675-3800; fax 540/675-3100; www.relaischateaux. com/washington), has converted a 1790s farmhouse into its Presidential Retreat. It's 17 miles away from the inn, but the butler will bring you to the inn for dinner.

In Winchester, the new **Old Court House Civil War Museum,** 20 N. Loudoun St. (© 540/542-1145; www. civilwarmuseum.org), has a fascinating display of graffiti that prisoners of war carved into its upstairs walls.

Near Middletown, Belle Grove Plantation and the Cedar Creek Battlefield Visitors Center across U.S. 11 are partners in the new **Cedar Creek & Belle Grove National Historical Park,** P.O. Box 229, Strasburg, VA 22657 (© 540/ 868-9176; www.nps.gov/cebe). Call or check the website for developments.

There's a new **Staunton Visitors Center** at 35 S. New St. in downtown Staunton (© 540/332-3971; www. stauntonva.org). The free **Downtown Staunton Trolley** now stops there every 25 minutes during its around-town tours, Monday to Saturday from

10am to 10pm. The town's most famous attraction, Woodrow Wilson's Birthplace, has changed its name to **The Woodrow Wilson Presidential Library at His Birthplace.**

The marvelous dining room at Staunton's **Belle Grae Inn,** 515 W. Frederick St. (© 888/541-5151 or 540/886-5151), no longer has set seating times at dinner; it's strictly a la carte. The **Frederick House,** 28 N. New St. (© 800/334-5575 or 540/885-4220), had added a restaurant to its repertoire. A former Travelodge, the **Regency Inn,** 268 N. Central Ave. (© 540/886-5330), has been renovated and now offers a viable downtown budget option.

The success of Staunton's **Blackfriars Playhouse** has spurred downtown development, including new restaurants such as the **Clock Tower Tavern,** 27 W. Beverly St. (© 540/213-2403), and **The Pampered Palate Café,** 26–28 E. Beverly St. (© 540/886-9463). **L'Italia Restaurant,** 23 E. Beverley St. (© 540/ 885-0102), has added the swank **Pompeii Lounge** upstairs.

In Lexington, Ghost Tour of Lexington has changed its name and phone number to **Haunting Tales of Historic Lexington** (© 540/463-5647) but still conducts 1¼-hour nighttime walks through the streets, alleys, and Stonewall Jackson Cemetery. The **Stonewall Jackson House** and **Virginia Military Institute Museum** are slated for renovation in 2004 but will remain open.

In downtown Lexington, **A Joyful Spirit Cafe,** 26 S. Main St. (© 540/ 463-4191), now provides a joyful combination of flavors at breakfast and lunch, and vegetarians will love the **Blue Heron Cafe,** 4 E. Washington St. (© 540/463-2800).

For complete information on this region, see chapter 7.

ROANOKE & THE SOUTHWEST HIGHLANDS The **Roanoke Convention and Visitors Bureau** has moved to new quarters at 101 Shenandoah Ave. NE, Roanoke, VA 24016 (© 800/635-5535 or 540/342-6025; fax 540/342-7119; www.visitroanoke va.com), in the recently restored Norfolk & Western train station across the tracks from trendy Market Square. The center shares the station with the new **O. Winston Link Museum** (© 540/ 857-4394; www.linkmuseum.org) that displays the remarkable railroad photography of the late O. Winston Link. A pathway follows the railroad to the **Virginia Museum of Transportation,** which has opened the Claytor Pavilion covering its collection of vintage locomotives, passenger cars, and cabooses.

Market Square, Roanoke's prime dining and nightlife area, has received a dose of big-city sophistication with the opening of **Metro!** (© 540/345-6645), a restaurant-lounge offering a mix of exciting flavors and dancing after 11pm. Meanwhile, **Carlos Brazilian International Cuisine** has fled Market Square for the suburbs, and **Buck Mountain Grille** has moved from its former perch near the Blue Ridge Parkway to 3603 Franklin Rd., north of I-581/U.S. 220 (© 540/348-6455).

In Wytheville, **The Clinic,** 95 W. Main St. (© 276/228-9111), has opened in a storefront once used as a clinic. Adorned with crutches and big, one-blip neon electrocardiograms, it offers billiards, inexpensive meals, and medicinal whiskey.

In Abingdon, the new **Café at Barter Theater Stage II,** 110 Main St. (© 276/619-5462), serves coffee, pastries, and sandwiches in a delightful room attached to the theater's auxiliary stage. For fine dining, **Caroline's** has replaced the gourmet deli and bakery of The Abingdon General Store and Gallery at 301 E. Main St. (© 276/739-0042).

For complete information on this region, see chapter 8.

RICHMOND   The Jefferson Hotel has added a greenhouselike extension to **Lemaire,** one of Virginia's top restaurants. Slated for further improvement, **Linden Row Inn** has been designated a Historic Hotel of America. The **Richmond Marriott** has undergone a renovation.

On the dining front, **The Old Original Bookbinder's,** the first branch of the Philadelphia institution, is now Richmond's most popular seafood restaurant. For well-heeled beefeaters, here's a new **Morton's of Chicago** in Shockoe Slip at 111 Virginia St. (© 804/648-1662).

Richmond National Battlefield Park has added "Richmond Speaks"— an exhibit telling the city's Civil War story with photos, artifacts, and readings from letters soldiers wrote to their families—to **Richmond Civil War Visitor Center at Tredegar Iron Works,** the new name of its main visitor center. Outside the center, a touching statue of President Abraham Lincoln and son Todd depicts their visit to Richmond shortly after the city fell in 1865. Out on the battlefields, a visitor center is now open at **Glendale/ Malvern Hill,** just off Va. 5.

At **The Valentine Richmond History Center,** visitors can look inside the **Edward Valentine Sculpture Studio** and see the sculptor's personal effects and plaster models of his work, including an early version of his "Lee Recumbent."

The **Virginia State Capitol** now requires casual visitors to take a guided tour in order to see inside the building. The capitol complex also is scheduled for renovation between 2004 and 2006.

The **Virginia Holocaust Museum** has moved to new quarters at 2000 E. Cary St. (© 804/257-5400; www. va-holocaust.com) and has added the Survivors' Room, a moving exhibit in which local survivors tell their Holocaust stories.

For complete information on Richmond, see chapter 9.

WILLIAMSBURG, JAMESTOWN & YORKTOWN Cash-strapped Colonial Williamsburg has raised its admission fees and closed **Carter's Grove** plantation and **The Rockefeller Archeology Museum** for the time being.

Plans have been announced to combine Colonial Williamsburg's two museums—the Abbey Aldrich Rockefeller Folk Art Museum and the DeWitt Wallace Decorative Arts Museum—into one facility occupied at present by the Wallace museum. They will maintain their separate identities but collectively will be known as The Museums at Colonial Williamsburg. A museum cafe is also on the drawing board. Other scheduled changes include the conversion of the building adjacent to the super-luxe Williamsburg Inn, now housing the Craft House shop, into a spa and health evaluation center.

Busch Gardens Williamsburg has added a barbecue restaurant, and a 4-D movie, "R. L. Stine's Haunted Lighthouse" is now part of its fun-filled repertoire. It also offers a "Night Time Pass," which permits unlimited visits after 4pm in summer; it costs the same as a 1-day ticket. Sister parks Busch Gardens and **Water Country USA** are offering discounted "Bounce" tickets permitting unlimited admissions to both over 2- to 4-day periods.

Josiah Chowning's Tavern, one of Colonial Williamsburg's restored "ordinaries," has switched from Colonial fare to timeless Virginia-style pit-cooked barbecue. Unlike the other historic taverns, where bookings are a must, it no longer accepts reservations. **Shields Tavern** has added an all-you-can-eat feast in its cellar. It's a good value compared to prices at the other taverns. In Merchant's Square, **The Cheese Shop** has moved its gourmet deli into quarters vacated by **A Good Place to Eat,** which has gone out of business.

At Jamestown, National Park Service has changed the name of its Jamestown Island site to **Historic Jamestowne.** Both it and the state-run **Jamestown Settlement** are being expanded and upgraded in preparation for Jamestown's big 400th anniversary celebration in 2007.

At **Yorktown** in February of 2004, the National Park Service opened the Poor Potter on the site of the town's original pottery factory. While touring the historic town, you can now have breakfast or lunch at the **Carrot Tree** (© 757/246-9559), the Cole Diggs House on Main Street at Reed Street. The town itself is undertaking a $40-million renovation of its waterfront, which will add a new boardwalk, shops, and a pier. Already on the waterfront, the **Watermen's Museum** (© 757/887-2641) displays work boats, oyster-harvesting tools, and other examples of how the Chesapeake's "watermen" earn their livelihoods. From the museum you can venture out on the water with **Yorktown Lady Cruises** (© 757/229-6244; www.yorktowncruises.com).

On the James River, **Sherwood Forest Plantation** is no longer open to visitors.

The **Hampton Visitors Center** has relocated to 1919 Commerce Dr., Hampton, VA 23666 (© 800/800-2202 or 757/727-1102; fax 757/727-6712; www.hamptoncvb.com), where it shares space with the new **Hampton History Museum.**

In Newport News, the **Mariners' Museum** now has the turret, engine, propeller and hundreds of other artifacts recovered from the Union ironclad USS *Monitor,* which sank off Cape Hatteras in 1862.

For complete information on this region, see chapter 10.

NORFOLK, VIRGINIA BEACH & THE EASTERN SHORE Downtown Norfolk has a new free trolley service—**Norfolk Electric Transit**—operated by the city's parking department (© 757/441-2661; www.norfolk.gov/visitors/net.asp). It's the easiest way to get around. The area's public transportation system, Hampton Roads Transit, has resumed its popular trolley tours of **Naval Station Norfolk,** the U.S. Navy's largest base, which were suspended after the September 11, 2001, terrorist attacks.

If you're walking, volunteer **Public Safety Ambassadors** now patrol Norfolk's downtown streets; call © **757/ 478-7233** if you need an escort.

Town Point Park, between The Waterside and NAUTICUS, is now home to **The Homecomer,** a touching statue of a returning sailor greeted by his wife and child, and the **Armed Forces Memorial,** where bronze replicas of letters written home by sailors litter the ground.

The **Virginia Zoo** has opened its long-awaited Okavango Delta African plains exhibit, which has added zebras, lions, giraffes, and meerkats to the nearly 400 animals already there.

Downtown Norfolk now has a modern, moderately priced hotel in the **Courtyard by Marriott,** 520 Plume St. (© **800/321-2211** or 757/963-6000; www.courtyard.com), which opened in 2002 almost across the street from the MacArthur Center.

In Virginia Beach, the new **Courtyard by Marriott Oceanfront North,** 3737 Atlantic Ave., at 37th Street (© **800/321-2211** or 757/437-0098; www.courtyardoceanfrontnorth.com), boasts the oceanfront's largest swimming pool, with rocks, waterfalls, a lifeguard, and its own bar). It's the sister of

the Courtyard by Marriott Oceanfront South, at Atlantic Avenue and 25th Street, a virtually identical property except for the outdoor pool.

Already loaded with amenities, the **Comfort Inn–Virginia Beach,** a block off the oceanfront at 2800 Pacific Ave. (© **800/441-0684** or 757/428-2203), has added cable-modem speed Internet access to every room.

Now more B&B than hostel, **Angie's Guest Cottage** has added two family units equipped with TVs and kitchens. It's still an official hostel, however, now affiliated with **Hosteling International-USA.**

Barclay Cottage has new owners— Stephen and Marie-Louise LaFonde— and is open year-round.

On the Eastern Shore, quaint and remote **Tangier Island** now has 15-minute island tours via enlarged golf carts, and two bed-and-breakfasts have joined Hilda Crockett's Chesapeake House: **Shirley's Bay View Inn,** P.O. Box 183 (© **757/891-2396;** www. tangierisland.net), and **Sunset Inn Bed & Breakfast,** 16650 W. Ridge Rd. (© **757/891-2535;** www.tangier islandsunset.com).

Chincoteague has a new **Hampton Inn & Suites,** 4179 Main St. (© **800/ HAMPTON** or 757/336-1616; www. hamptoninnsuiteschincoteague.com), on the waterfront next to the existing Comfort Suites.

For complete information on this region, see chapter 11.

1

The Best of Virginia

America's first permanent English-speaking colonists had a rough start at Jamestown in 1607, but within a few years the beautiful and bountiful land they called Virginia had greatly rewarded them for their courageous efforts. They first set foot on a sandy Atlantic Ocean beach at Cape Charles, at the mouth of one of the world's great estuaries, the Chesapeake Bay. Beyond them lay a varied, rich, and highly scenic land. They settled beside one of the great tidal rivers whose tributaries led their descendants through the rolling hills of the Piedmont, over the Blue Ridge Mountains, and into the great valleys beyond.

Almost 400 years later, the history-loving Commonwealth of Virginia abounds with historic homes and plantations, buildings that rang with revolutionary oratory, museums that recall the storied past, and small towns that seem little changed since colonial times.

Fortunately, preservation hasn't been limited to historical landmarks. Conservation efforts have kept a great deal of Virginia's wilderness looking much as it did in 1607, making the state a prime destination for lovers of the great outdoors. Whether you like to hike, bike, bird watch, fish, canoe, or boat—or just lie on a sandy beach—Virginia has a place to indulge your passion.

This chapter describes some of the best experiences Virginia has to offer. Bear in mind that it's just an overview, and you'll surely come up with your own "bests" as you travel through the state. Be sure to see the destination chapters later in this book for full details on the places mentioned below.

1 The Best of Colonial Virginia

- **Old Town Alexandria:** Although Alexandria is very much part of metropolitan Washington, D.C., the historic district known as "Old Town" evokes the time when the nation's early leaders strolled its streets and partook of grog at Gadsby's Tavern. See "Alexandria," in chapter 4.

- **Mount Vernon:** When he wasn't off surveying, fighting in the French and Indian Wars, leading the American Revolution, or serving as our first president, George Washington made his home at a plantation 8 miles south of Alexandria. Restored to look as it was in Washington's day, Mount Vernon is America's second most visited historic home. See "Mount Vernon & the Potomac Plantations," in chapter 4.

- **Fredericksburg & the Northern Neck:** Not only did the Fredericksburg area play a role in the birth of a nation, it was the birthplace of George Washington, father of the new nation. Also born here was James Monroe, who as president kept European powers out of the Americas by promulgating the Monroe Doctrine. The great Confederate leader Robert E. Lee was born here a generation later. Fredericksburg still retains much of the charm it possessed in those early

Virginia

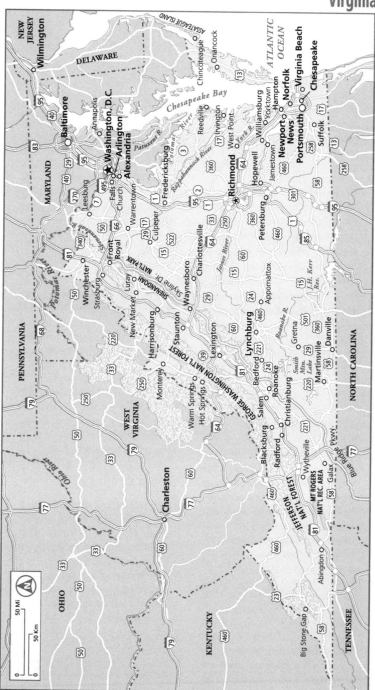

days, and the birthplaces of Washington and Lee stand not far from town on the Northern Neck. See chapter 5.

- **Charlottesville:** If Washington was the father of the United States, then Thomas Jefferson was its intellectual genius. This scholar, lawyer, writer, and architect built two monuments—his lovely hilltop home, Monticello, and the University of Virginia that still evoke memories of this great thinker and patriot. See chapter 6.

- **Williamsburg, Jamestown & Yorktown:** Known as the Historic Triangle, these three towns are the finest examples of colonial America to be found. Thanks to the Rockefeller family, Colonial Williamsburg has been restored and rebuilt as it appeared when it was the capital of Virginia in the 18th century. The site of the original Jamestown settlement is now a national historical park, as is Yorktown, where George Washington bottled up Lord Cornwallis and won the American Revolution. See chapter 10.

- **James River Plantations:** Colonists fanning out from Jamestown hacked huge tobacco plantations out of Virginia's forests creating America's first great wealth. Today, you can visit some of their great manses on the James River between Williamsburg and Richmond. Descendants of the colonial planters still occupy some of these mansions. See "James River Plantations" in chapter 10.

2 The Best of Civil War Virginia

When the Civil War broke out in 1861 and the Confederacy moved its capital to Richmond, the state became the prime target of the Union armies. Virginia saw more battles than any other state, as Robert E. Lee's Army of Northern Virginia turned back one assault after another. Today's visitor can visit the sites of many key battles, all of them national historical parks.

- **Manassas:** The first battle of the war occurred along Bull Run near Manassas in northern Virginia, and it was a shock to the Union (and thousands of spectators who came from Washington to watch), when the rebels engineered a victory over a disorganized Union force. They won again at the Second Battle of Manassas. See "The Hunt Country," in chapter 4.

- **Fredericksburg:** No other town in Virginia has as many significant battlefields as Fredericksburg. Lee used the Rappahannock River as a natural line of defense, and he fought several battles against Union armies trying to cross it and advance on Richmond. Today, you can visit the battlefields in town, at Chancellorsville, and the Wilderness in a day. See chapter 5.

- **Appomattox Court House:** After the fall of Petersburg in 1865, Lee fled for little more than a week until realizing that continuing the war was fruitless. On April 9, he met Grant at Wilbur McLean's farmhouse and surrendered his sword. America's bloodiest conflict was over. The farmhouse is preserved as part of Appomattox Court House National Historical Park. See "What to See & Do," in Charlottesville, chapter 6.

- **New Market:** While Lee was fending off the Union near Fredericksburg, the war flowed up and down the Shenandoah Valley, the Confederacy's breadbasket. The town of Winchester changed hands 72 times. Perhaps the war's most poignant battlefield is at New Market, where the corps of cadets from Virginia Military Institute helped stop a larger Union force. Ten of the teenagers were killed, and 47 wounded. See "New Market: A Civil War Battlefield," in chapter 7.

- **Richmond:** The capital of the Confederacy, Richmond is loaded with reminders of the conflict, including the magnificent Museum of the Confederacy and its adjacent White House of the Confederacy, home of Pres. Jefferson Davis. The city's Monument Avenue is lined with statues of the rebel leaders. Now suburbs, the city's eastern outskirts are ringed with battle sites,

part of the Richmond National Battlefield Park. See chapter 9.

- **Petersburg:** After nearly 4 years of frustration trying to capture Richmond, Union Gen. Ulysses S. Grant bypassed the southern capital in 1864 and headed for the railroad junction of Petersburg, the lifeline of the Confederate capital. Even there he was forced into a siege situation, but finally, in April of 1865, Grant broke through and forced Lee into retreat westward. See "An Easy Excursion to Petersburg," in chapter 9.

3 The Best of the Great Outdoors

Virginia has hundreds of thousands of acres of natural beauty preserved in national and state parks, national forests, and recreation areas. Especially in the mountains, you can find more than 1,000 miles of trails for hiking, biking, and horseback riding. The Chesapeake Bay offers boating and fishing, and the Atlantic beaches are among the best on the East Coast.

- **Shenandoah National Park:** Nearly two million visitors a year venture into the Shenandoah National Park, which straddles the Blue Ridge Mountains from Front Royal to Rockfish Gap between Charlottesville and Waynesboro. Many visitors merely drive along the 105-mile Skyline Drive, one of America's most scenic routes. Others come to walk some of the more than 500 miles of hiking trails, including 101 miles of the Appalachian Trail. Many trails start at the Skyline Drive and drop down into hollows and canyons, some of them with waterfalls. Even on the Skyline Drive, you are likely to encounter deer, and you might even see bear, bobcat, and wild turkey. See "Shenandoah National Park & the Skyline Drive," in chapter 7.

- **Running the Rivers** (Front Royal, Luray, Lexington, Richmond): The South Fork of the Shenandoah River twists and turns its way between the valley towns of Front Royal and Luray, making it a perfect place for river rafting, canoeing, and kayaking—or just floating along in an inner tube. The James River can be swift and turbulent as it crosses the Shenandoah Valley, cuts through the Blue Ridge Mountains, and courses its way across the Piedmont to Hampton Roads. Depending on the amount of rain, you can even raft down the James through metropolitan Richmond. See chapters 7 and 8.

- **Mount Rogers National Recreation Area:** While you won't be alone in Shenandoah National Park, you could have a hiking, biking, horseback-riding, or cross-country skiing trail all to yourself in Mount Rogers National Recreation Area. This wild land in the Southwest Highlands occupies some 117,000 acres of forest, and includes its namesake, Virginia's highest peak. Two of Virginia's finest rails-to-trails hiking, biking, and riding paths serve as bookends to the 60-mile-long recreation area: the New River Trail near Wytheville, and the Virginia Creeper Trail, from Abingdon to White Top Mountain. See "Mount Rogers National Recreation Area," in chapter 8.

- **Back Bay National Wildlife Refuge/False Cape State Park** (Virginia Beach): You can't sunbathe or swim on the beach of Back Bay National Wildlife Refuge, but you can hike through the dunes or take a canoe into the marshes, which are on the Atlantic Flyway for migrating birds. You can sunbathe and swim at the adjoining False Cape State Park, but it's so out of the way that you'll have to bring your own drinking water.

See "Parks & Wildlife Refuges" in chapter 11.

- **Assateague Island:** Of all the natural areas in Virginia, none surpasses Assateague, which keeps the Atlantic Ocean from the back bays of Chincoteague. Here you will find the famous wild ponies in Chincoteague National Wildlife Refuge, and relatively tame humans strolling along some 37 miles of pristine beach. Assateague Island is also situated directly on the Atlantic Flyway, making it one of the best bird-watching sites in the country. See "Chincoteague & Assateague Islands," in chapter 11.

4 The Best Scenic Drives

One of the best ways to see Virginia is by car: the Old Dominion has some of America's most beautiful scenic drives.

- **George Washington Memorial Parkway** (Northern Virginia): Stay away during rush hour, when it becomes a major commuter artery into and out of Washington, D.C., But any other time, the "G.W. Parkway" is a great drive along the Potomac River from I-495 at the Maryland line to Mount Vernon. The river views of Washington's monuments are unparalleled. See "A Scenic Drive Along the Potomac River," in chapter 4.

- **Skyline Drive** (Shenandoah National Park): Few roads anywhere can top the Skyline Drive, which twists and turns 105 miles along the Blue Ridge crest in Shenandoah National Park. The views over the rolling Piedmont to the east and Shenandoah Valley to the west are spectacular, especially during spring, when the wildflowers are in bloom, and in fall, when the leaves change from green to brilliant hues of rust, orange, and yellow. See "Shenandoah National

Park & the Skyline Drive," in chapter 7.

- **Lexington to Hot Springs:** While I-81 runs down the floor of Virginia's great valleys, other roads offer a different scenic treat by cutting across the mountains. One of these is Va. 39, which runs from Lexington to Hot Springs via the Goshen Pass, a picturesque gorge cut by the Maury River. You can make a loop by continuing north from Hot Springs via U.S. 220 to the beautiful village of Monterey in "Virginia's Switzerland." From Monterey, you can cross the mountains via U.S. 250 to Staunton and I-81. See chapter 7.

- **Blue Ridge Parkway:** A continuation of the Skyline Drive, this road continues along the Blue Ridge crest south to the Great Smoky Mountains National Park in North Carolina. Of the 218 miles in Virginia, the most scenic are north of Roanoke. You'll find it difficult to keep your eyes on the road, as the parkway often runs right along the ridgeline, with views down both sides of the mountain at once. See "The Blue Ridge Parkway," in chapter 8.

- **Colonial Parkway:** It's not long, but the Colonial Parkway between Jamestown, Williamsburg, and Yorktown has its scenic merits, especially the views of the James River near Jamestown and of the York River near Yorktown. The parkway goes through a tunnel under the heart of Colonial Williamsburg. See chapter 10.

- **Chesapeake Bay Bridge-Tunnel:** A man-made wonder, the Chesapeake Bay Bridge-Tunnel runs for 17 miles over—and under—the mouth of the Chesapeake Bay between Norfolk and the Eastern Shore. You can barely see land when you're in the middle. See chapter 11.

5 The Best Small Towns

Virginia's many lovely small towns capture and nurture the state's history and culture. This is especially true in the Shenandoah Valley, where the Valley Pike, then U.S. 11, and now I-81 string together Winchester, Strasburg, Staunton, and Lexington, all possessed of 18th- and 19th-century brick and stone buildings.

- **Middleburg:** The self-proclaimed capital of Virginia's Hunt Country, Middleburg takes up barely 6 blocks along U.S. 50, small enough to be digested in an afternoon. Some of the world's wealthiest individuals keep their horses near Middleburg, and the town has a host of upscale shops in buildings dating from the 1700s. See "The Hunt Country," in chapter 4.

- **Monterey:** Over Shenandoah and Bull Pasture Mountains from Staunton, the village of Monterey appears more like New England than Virginia, with its white churches and clapboard homes in a picturesque valley. Thousands of visitors make the trek over the mountains to the annual Highland Maple Festival in March. See "Over the Mountains to Monterey," in chapter 7.

- **Staunton:** There's Shakespeare to be seen at the Blackfriars Playhouse in Staunton, an old railroad town that was formerly most famous as President Woodrow Wilson's birthplace. The replica of The Bard's 17th-century indoor theater has spurred a downtown renaissance, with new restaurants and shops opening all the time. A don't-miss for kids, the Frontier Culture Museum is here, too. See "Staunton: A Presidential Birthplace with The Bard's Playhouse," in chapter 7.

- **Lexington:** One of America's best small towns, Lexington has a lively college atmosphere in addition to a host of historical sights. It's home to Virginia Military Institute (VMI), where Gen. Thomas J. "Stonewall" Jackson taught; its students went off to the Civil War at New Market. Afterwards, Robert E. Lee came here as president of Washington College, now Washington and Lee University. VMI was also the alma mater of Gen. George C. Marshall, winner of the Nobel Peace Prize for his plan to rebuild Europe after World War II. Jackson, Lee, and Marshall are buried here, and the town has three museums dedicated to these leaders. Lexington's downtown looks so much like it did when Jackson and Lee were here that only dirt had to be added to Main Street's pavement for the film *Sommersby.* See "Lexington: A College Town with a Slice of American History," in chapter 7.

- **Abingdon:** Daniel Boone opened Virginia's Southwest Highlands to settlement in the 1770s, and a thriving town grew up at Abingdon. Homes and buildings dating to 1779 line Main Street, making it a wonderful place to stroll. The town's beauty has attracted artists, craftspeople, and actors, who perform at the Barter Theatre, where you can still barter for a ticket. See "Abingdon: A Town with Beauty & Charm," in chapter 8.

6 The Best Family Vacations

A vast majority of Virginia's visitors arrive by car, and most of them are families. Accordingly, the state's major attractions and resorts are well equipped to entertain and care for children. It's a great place for kids to learn about American history, while enjoying a good time at the beach or one of three major amusement parks.

- **Shenandoah National Park:** Two lodges in the most popular part of Shenandoah National Park make this a great place for family vacations. The kids can participate in ranger programs, hike to waterfalls, or go for a pony ride in the mountain forests. See "Shenandoah National Park & the Skyline Drive," in chapter 7.
- **Richmond:** The state capital has several attractions of interest to children, including the hands-on Science Museum of Virginia. The big draws, however, are the wild rides and movie and TV characters at the huge Paramount's Kings Dominion amusement park north of the city. See chapter 9.
- **Colonial Williamsburg:** The historic area of Colonial Williamsburg is the best place of all for children to get a quick lesson in American history. On the streets, they might run into Thomas Jefferson (actually, an actor) and have a conversation about the Declaration of Independence, or practice marching and drilling with the 18th-century militia. As soon as they get bored, head for Busch Gardens Williamsburg or Water Country USA, two nearby theme parks. See chapter 10.
- **Virginia Beach:** First there's the beach, 4 miles or so, with lifeguards during summer—but that's not all. Rainy days can be spent at the local Virginia Marine Science Museum—the state's most popular museum. Norfolk's NAUTICUS, Hampton's Virginia Air and Space Center, and Colonial Williamsburg are all just short drives away. See chapter 11.
- **Chincoteague & Assateague Islands:** The fishing village was the setting for Marguerite Henry's classic children's book *Misty of Chincoteague,* and there are plenty of wild horses (called "ponies") in Chincoteague National Wildlife Refuge on Assateague Island, which also has a lifeguarded beach for swimming during the summer. The best time to see the horses is during the annual pony swim the last week in July, but the kids can ride one in a small equestrian center. See "Chincoteague & Assateague Islands," in chapter 11.

7 The Most Unusual Virginia Travel Experiences

A museum devoted to hounds, a stalactite organ, an 18th-century version of today's Jacuzzi, a stuffed horse, and a cruise to Elizabethan times all make for unusual travel in Virginia.

- *Tally Ho!* (Leesburg): The Hunt Country gets its name from the hounds, horses, and very wealthy people who hunt foxes for sport here. You can learn all about the history of this aristocratic pastime at Leesburg's Morven Park, home to the Museum of Hounds and Hunting. See p. 93.
- **Chimes Down Under** (Luray): There are several caverns under the Shenandoah Valley, but one of the most fascinating is at Luray. Through subterranean rooms more than 140 feet high comes beautiful music—in the form of hammers striking million-year-old stalactites. See "Luray: An Underground Organ," in chapter 7.
- **Ancient Hot Tubs** (Warm Springs): Eighteenth-century travelers couldn't climb into the Jacuzzi after a rough day on the road—unless, that is, they pulled into Warm Springs. Since 1761, travelers have slipped their weary bodies into these natural rock pools whose waters range from 94°F to 104°F (34°C–40°C). You can, too. See "Warm Springs & Hot Springs: Taking the Waters," in chapter 7.
- **Mounting Little Sorrel** (Lexington): After he died of wounds accidentally inflicted by his own men at the Battle of Chancellorsville, Gen. Stonewall Jackson was buried in Lexington, where he had taught at Virginia Military Institute. One of the exhibits at VMI's museum is the bullet-pierced raincoat Jackson was wearing that disastrous night. And thanks to taxidermy, there stands the hide of his warhorse, Little Sorrel. Nearby, Robert E. Lee's horse, Traveller, is buried just outside Lee Chapel, his master's resting place. See p. 181.
- *Hoi Toide Tonoit* (Tangier Island): Out in the Chesapeake Bay sits remote Tangier Island, whose residents have been so isolated that they still speak with the Elizabethan brogue of their forebears. Out here, "high tide tonight" is pronounced *hoi toide tonoit*—as in "hoity-toity"—and narrow 17th-century lanes barely can accommodate modern automobiles. Cruises leave from the Northern Neck and the Eastern Shore. See chapters 5 and 11.

8 The Best Country Inns

With all of its old homes and gorgeous countryside, it's no wonder that Virginia is a hotbed of country inns and bed-and-breakfasts. Some have been in business since colonial times, and a few are among the best around. Our picks barely touch the surface.

- **Red Fox Inn** (Middleburg): In the center of tiny Middleburg, this rambling inn maintains the romantic charm of early Virginia in its original 1728 stone structure. There's a cozy dining room downstairs and a lively sports bar across the street. See p. 100.
- **Hope and Glory Inn** (Irvington): The state's most fascinating country

inn occupies a converted 1890s school house, and it has charming cottages in the garden, but what really sets it apart is an outdoor bathroom complete with clawfoot tub. That's right: It's outdoors, albeit surrounded by a stockade fence. See p. 120.

- **Inn at Little Washington** (Washington): For the best, you need look no further than the Blue Ridge foothill village of Washington, which everyone in Virginia calls "Little Washington." An English decorator designed the rooms here, but it's the romantic restaurant that draws the most raves, as co-owner and chef Patrick O'Connell relies on regional products to produce wonderful French cuisine. See p. 160.

- **Fort Lewis Lodge** (Millboro): One of Virginia's most unusual inns, the Fort Lewis Lodge occupies an old mill and rebuilt barn on a farm beside the Cowpasture River, just over the mountain from Warm Springs. A spiral staircase ascends to three rooms inside the old silo, and there are two log cabins with their own fireplaces. It's a great place to show urban kids a bit of farm life in beautiful surroundings. See p. 176.

- **Martha Washington Inn** (Abingdon): Gracing Abingdon's historic district, the center portion of this Greek Revival inn was built as a private home in 1832—and as if to prove it, the plank floors creak loudly as you enter the gracious lobby. You can sit in white-wicker rocking chairs on the front porch and watch the traffic on Main Street—or imagine Daniel Boone's dogs being attacked by wolves nearby. See p. 210.

9 The Best Luxury Accommodations

With deep enough pockets, you can enjoy some of the Mid-Atlantic's best luxury accommodations in Virginia.

- **Relais & Chateau Morrison House** (Alexandria): More like a country inn in the middle of Old Town Alexandria, this small, luxurious hotel isn't that old, but it looks exactly like the Federal period homes surrounding it. The dining is marvelous. See p. 74.

- **The Tides Inn** (Irvington): After a multi-million dollar renovation, The Tides Inn once again stands among Virginia's elite resorts. The style is now more British raj than Old Virginny, but the facilities are first-rate, including a spa with treatment rooms overlooking Carter's Creek. The golf course has been improved, too. See p. 121.

- **The Boar's Head Inn** (Charlottesville): A 19th-century gristmill serves as the centerpiece of this lakeside resort, on the outskirts of Charlottesville, and lends ancient charm to the Old Mill dining room, one of the best places to sample Virginia wines without trekking to the vineyards. Modern amenities include a full-service spa and access to Charlottesville's best-equipped sports club. See p. 126.

- **The Homestead** (Hot Springs): Outstanding service, fine cuisine, and a myriad of activities denote this grand old establishment, in business since Thomas Jefferson's day. In fact, Jefferson was the first of seven presidents to stay here. The Homestead offers accommodations ranging from standard rooms to plush suites. PGA pro Lanny Wadkins presides over its golf course, one of Virginia's finest. See p. 174.

- **Hotel Roanoke & Conference Center** (Roanoke): The grand, Tudor-style Hotel Roanoke stood in a wheat field when the Norfolk & Western Railroad built it in 1882. It was closed in 1989, but a $45-million renovation completely restored its grand public areas to their original appearance and rebuilt all its rooms to modern standards. See p. 197.

- **Jefferson Hotel** (Richmond): A stunning beaux arts landmark with Renaissance-style balconies and an Italian clock tower, the Jefferson was opened in 1895 by a wealthy Richmonder who wanted his city to have one of America's finest hotels. A complete 1980s restoration renewed its original splendor. See p. 220.

- **Williamsburg Inn:** An establishment with three fine golf courses, the Williamsburg Inn was built as part of the Colonial Williamsburg restoration, but looks like it might have been here in 1750. If staying in the main inn with its superb service and cuisine won't do, you can opt for one of the restored houses and taverns that have been converted into accommodations. See p. 261.

10 The Best Moderately Priced Accommodations

Virginia has too many fine, affordable lodgings to mention them all here. The following are some we like best:

- **Holiday Inn Select Old Town** (Alexandria): One of the finest Holiday Inns, this colonial-style brick building occupies an entire block in the heart of Alexandria's historic Old Town. It looks like it's been there forever. See p. 74.
- **Norris House Inn** (Leesburg): Built in 1806, this charming house offers comfortable lodging right in the middle of Leesburg's historic district. See p. 97.
- **Richard Johnston Inn** (Fredericksburg): Elegantly appointed rooms await in these two 18th-century homes across from historic Fredericksburg's visitors center. See p. 111.
- **Belle Grae Inn** (Staunton): Michael Organ gave up teaching at Mary Baldwin College in the 1980s to convert an 1873 hilltop Victorian house into an inn. Today his establishment includes houses ringing an entire block, all of them beautifully restored and furnished with period pieces. The cuisine is the best in town. See p. 169.
- **Hampton Inn Col Alto** (Lexington): No ordinary Hampton Inn, Col Alto is an 1827 manor house converted into a comfortable B&B-type hotel. Even if you stay in the modern motel buildings next door, you'll eat your continental breakfast in the period dining room. See p. 183.
- **Linden Row Inn** (Richmond): This row of Victorian-era town houses in downtown Richmond has been renovated but not restored, which has left the rooms with 12-foot ceilings, a mix of late Empire and Victorian pieces, and marble-top dressers. See p. 221.

11 The Best Inexpensive Accommodations

Virginia has many clean, comfortable motels of the budget chain variety. But for something a little more special, check out the following choices:

- **Big Meadows & Skyland Lodges** (Shenandoah National Park): With stunning views from perches atop the Blue Ridge Mountains, these two rustic but charming inns are surprisingly affordable. Just be sure to reserve as early as possible. See p. 150.
- **Fredericksburg Colonial Inn** (Fredericksburg): Don't be surprised to see Blues and Grays toting Civil War rifles in the lobby; this place is very popular with reenactors. An avid collector, the owner has laden the rooms with antiques. See p. 110.
- **Roseloe Motel** (Hot Springs): You don't have to pay a fortune to stay at the Homestead—head 3 miles north to the Roseloe, a clean family operation across U.S. 220 from the Garth Newel Chamber Music Center. Warm Springs is a short drive, and you can pay much less than the cost of a room to use the Homestead's recreational facilities. See p. 175.

Fun Fact Virginia's Gourmet Contributions

Author William Styron, a native of Newport News, once said that the French consider salt-cured Virginia hams to be America's only gourmet contribution to the world's cuisine. Virginians love their ham (especially stuffed into hot biscuits), and they are also crazy about rockfish (sea bass) and crabs from the Chesapeake Bay and shad and trout from the rivers. Virginia's farms produce a plethora of vegetables, and its orchards are famous for apples. And let's not forget the peanut, one of Virginia's major crops, which has been used in soup since colonial times!

- **Colony House Motor Lodge** (Roanoke): This older, but clean and very well maintained motel, is convenient to both downtown Roanoke and the Blue Ridge Parkway. Doors to the rooms have louvers to let in fresh air but not light—an unusual touch for any inexpensive hotel. See p. 197.

- **Angie's Guest Cottage and HI-USA Hostel** (Virginia Beach): You won't find any luxuries but you will have an interesting mix of guests at one of Virginia's few youth hostels. Those who don't care for dorm-style accommodations can stay in one of the comfortable, spotlessly clean private rooms. See p. 308.

12 The Best Culinary Experiences

You can dine on all types of cuisine in Virginia, but the highlights are produced from recipes handed down since colonial times—dishes such as peanut soup and Sally Lunn bread—or that put a modern spin on fresh local ingredients. Here are some of the best places to sample Virginia's unique and very historic cuisine.

- **Gadsby's Tavern** (Alexandria): George Washington said good-bye to his troops from the door of Gadsby's Tavern in Alexandria's Old Town. This former rooming house and the tavern next door look much as they did then, and a waitstaff in colonial garb still serve chicken roasted on an open fire, buttermilk pie, and other dishes from that period. See p. 76.

- **Inn at Little Washington** (Washington): Chef Patrick O'Connell constantly changes his menu to take advantage of trout, Chesapeake Bay seafood, Virginia hams, and other local delicacies in his romantic dining room. The service

at Virginia's finest restaurant is wonderfully attentive and unobtrusive. See p. 160.

- **Mrs. Rowe's Restaurant and Bakery** (Staunton): Every town has its favorite "local" restaurant, where you can clog your arteries with old Southern favorites like pan-fried chicken, sausage gravy over biscuits, and fresh vegetables seasoned with smoked pork and cooked to smithereens. In business since 1947, Mrs. Rowe's somehow manages to cook the golden oldies without all the lard you'll ingest elsewhere. See p. 171.

- **Roanoker Restaurant** (Roanoke): Another favorite "local," the Roanoaker regularly changes its menu to take advantage of the freshest vegetables available, but every day it serves the best biscuits in Virginia, hot from the oven. See p. 200.

- **The Log House 1776 Restaurant** (Wytheville): The name is appropriate at this restaurant, part of which is contained in a log house built in 1776. Here you can order Thomas Jefferson's favorite, chicken marengo, or a very sweet Confederate beef-and-apple stew like the one Robert E. Lee fed his troops. See p. 204.

- **King's Barbecue** (Petersburg): Like all Southerners, Virginians love their smoked pork barbecue, and it doesn't get any better than at the two branches of King's. Pork, beef, ribs, and chicken roast constantly over an open pit right in the dining rooms, and the sauce is served on the side, not soaking the succulent meat and overpowering its smoked flavor. See p. 242.
- **Trellis Cafe, Restaurant & Grill** (Williamsburg): Chef Marcel Desaulniers has been nationally recognized for his outstanding regional cuisine, all of which emphasizes fresh local produce. Desaulniers has written three cookbooks, including *Death by Chocolate*. They don't raise cocoa in Virginia, but you can definitely die by it here. See p. 268.

- **Old Chickahominy House** (Williamsburg): Named for a nearby river, this reconstructed, antiques-filled 18th-century house is one of the best places to sample traditional Virginia fare, such as Brunswick stew and Virginia ham on hot biscuits. See p. 269.
- **Todd Jurich's Bistro** (Norfolk): Actor Donald Sutherland and other famous folk frequent this bistro, where chef Todd Jurich uses produce from local farms that practice "ecologically sound agriculture." See p. 295.
- **Cora** (Norfolk): Chef Nancy Cobb blends grits, okra, and other local products with more fancy items in her "creative Southern" cuisine. She even offers a version of her father's hearty "fishmuddle" seafood stew. See p. 295.
- **Lynnhaven Fish House** (Virginia Beach): Wonderful water views accompany some of the state's finest seafood at this restaurant built on a fishing pier over the Chesapeake Bay. See p. 311.

2

Planning Your Trip to Virginia

Whether you plan to spend a day, a week, 2 weeks, or longer in Virginia, you'll need to make many "where," "when," and "how" choices *before* you leave home. This chapter explains how best to plan your trip.

1 The Regions in Brief

Virginia has three distinct geographic regions. Along the eastern coast, the **Tidewater** (or coastal plain) is dominated by four rivers—the Potomac, Rappahannock, York, and James— that empty into the Chesapeake Bay, one of the world's largest estuaries. These rivers divide the Tidewater into three peninsulas, or *necks.* To the south, the Chesapeake meets the Atlantic Ocean at the large natural harbor of Hampton Roads.

The rolling hills of the **Piedmont** run through central Virginia, from Richmond, Charlottesville, and Lynchburg to the Hunt Country and suburban sprawl of northern Virginia. This farm country rises to meet the foothills of the **Blue Ridge Mountains.** Between the Blue Ridge and the Allegheny Mountains to the west, gorgeous valleys—including the Shenandoah—extend the length of the state, from the Potomac in the north to the Southwest Highlands near the borders of Tennessee and Kentucky.

NORTHERN VIRGINIA The fastest growing, most densely populated, and wealthiest part of the state, northern Virginia is much more than a suburban bedroom for government workers in Washington, D.C. Areas such as Tysons Corner have become unincorporated cities in their own right, with employment in high tech service industries outstripping that of the federal government. Long known for its cemetery just across the Potomac from the nation's capital, **Arlington** is the gateway to Northern Virginia. Centered on its historic Old Town, **Alexandria** offers fascinating daytime walks as well as lively nighttime entertainment and good restaurants. Beyond are the Potomac plantations, including George Washington's **Mount Vernon.** In Virginia's **Hunt Country,** sightseers can enjoy Virginia's historic inns and fine restaurants. Farther south is **Manassas,** site of the first major battle of the Civil War.

FREDERICKSBURG & THE NORTHERN NECK The quaint cobblestone streets and historic houses of **Fredericksburg** recall America's first heroes—George Washington, James Monroe, John Paul Jones—as does the quiet Northern Neck farmland, where Washington and Robert E. Lee were born. Military buffs love to explore Fredericksburg's Civil War battlefields.

CENTRAL VIRGINIA These rolling Piedmont hills are "Mr. Jefferson's country." **Charlottesville** boasts his magnificent estate, Monticello, as well as the University of Virginia, which he designed. Near **Lynchburg,** you can visit Poplar Forest, his beloved retreat, Patrick Henry's final home at Red Hill, and Appomattox Court House, where the Civil War ended when Robert E. Lee surrendered to Ulysses S. Grant.

THE SHENANDOAH VALLEY

Some of Virginia's most striking scenery is along the **Skyline Drive,** which follows the crest of the Blue Ridge Mountains through magnificent **Shenandoah National Park,** where visitors will find a host of hiking paths, including part of the Maine-to-Georgia Appalachian Trail. Down below, charming towns like **Winchester, Staunton,** and **Lexington** evoke the Civil War, which flowed over the rolling countryside of the Shenandoah Valley, the South's breadbasket. Across the mountains are the famous mineral waters of **Warm Springs** and **Hot Springs.**

THE SOUTHWEST HIGHLANDS

Beyond the vibrant city of **Roanoke** rise the highlands of Virginia's southwestern extremity, a land of untouched forests, waterfalls and streams. Here sits the state's highest point, **Mount Rogers,** surrounded by a national recreation area teeming with trails for hiking, mountain biking, and horseback riding. Down in the Great Valley of Virginia, the crossroads town of **Wytheville** still shows signs of Daniel Boone's famous trail to Kentucky, and the quaint town of **Abingdon** features the famous Barter Theatre, begun during the Great Depression when its company traded tickets for hams.

RICHMOND

The state capital has few rivals among U.S. cities for its historic associations, among them St. John's Church, where Patrick Henry said, "Give me liberty, or give me death." Fine arts and science museums, cafes, lively concerts, and theater add to Richmond's cosmopolitan ambience. Military buffs can tour the Richmond and Petersburg battlefield sites, and children can get their kicks at nearby Paramount's Kings Dominion amusement park.

WILLIAMSBURG, YORKTOWN & JAMESTOWN

Coastal Virginia's "Historic Triangle" is one of the country's most visited areas, and with good reason. **Williamsburg** immaculately recreates Virginia's colonial capital. **Yorktown** commemorates the last battle of the American Revolution. **Jamestown** is where America's first permanent English settlers arrived in 1607. Adding to its allure are theme parks and world-class discount shopping. From here it's an easy excursion to one of the nation's premier maritime museums in the shipbuilding city of **Newport News** and to the air and space museum in historic **Hampton,** the country's oldest continuous English-speaking settlement.

HAMPTON ROADS & THE EASTERN SHORE

At the mouth of the Chesapeake Bay, Hampton Roads is ringed by Virginia's largest metropolitan area, highlighted by the resurgent cities of **Norfolk** and **Portsmouth.** You can play in the surf on **Virginia Beach,** whose boardwalk and 20 miles of white-sand beach are lined with hotels, or commune with nature in Back Bay National Wildlife Refuge and the remote False Cape State Park. You can drive across the 17-mile-long Chesapeake Bay Bridge-Tunnel to Eastern Shore, an unspoiled sanctuary noted for the charming village of **Chincoteague** and nearby **Assateague Island,** whose wildlife refuge and national seashore have protected the famous wild ponies and prevented any development on almost 40 miles of pristine beach.

2 Visitor Information

The **Virginia Tourism Corporation,** 901 E. Byrd St. (P.O. Box 798), Richmond, VA 23219 (© **800/VISIT-VA** or 804/786-2051; fax 804/786-1919; www.virginia.org), is the best source for information about the state. It publishes or distributes a host of information, including a statewide travel planner; official state highway maps; lists of all hotels and motels and those

Destination Virginia—Red Alert Checklist

- Are there any **special requirements** for your destination? Do you need detailed road maps? Bug repellents? Appropriate attire?
- Do any theater, restaurant, or travel reservations need to be booked in advance?
- Did you make sure your favorite attraction is open? In Old Town Alexandria, for example, most attractions are closed on Monday. Some on military posts may be closed for security reasons. Call ahead for opening and closing hours.
- If you purchased traveler's checks, have you recorded the check numbers, and stored the documentation separately from the checks?
- If you packed film in your checked baggage, did you invest in protective pouches to shield film from airport X-rays?
- Do you have a safe, accessible place to store money?
- Did you bring your ID cards that could entitle you to discounts such as AAA and AARP cards, student IDs, etc.?
- Did you bring emergency drug prescriptions and extra glasses and/or contact lenses?
- Do you have your credit card PIN?
- If you have an E-ticket, do you have documentation?
- Did you leave a copy of your itinerary with someone at home?

that accept pets; a list of country inns and bed-and-breakfasts; an outdoor guide to the state; a golf directory; a biking guide; a state park directory; a list of Virginia wineries and wine festivals; and a guide for travelers with disabilities. Most can be ordered on its website.

The corporation also operates an information office in **Washington, D.C.,** at 1629 K St. NW (© **800/934-9184** or 202/872-0523).

In **Canada,** contact Discover the World Marketing, 1599 Hurontario St., Suite 100, Mississauga, Ontario L5G 4S1 (© **905/891-0093;** fax 905/891-8026; www.discovertheworld.com).

If you're driving into Virginia, you can stop at roadside **Welcome Centers** in Bracey, on I-85 near the North Carolina border; Bristol, on I-81 near the Tennessee border; Clear Brook, on I-81 near the West Virginia border; Covington, on I-64 near the West Virginia border; New Church, on U.S. 13 south of the Maryland border; Fredericksburg, on I-95 southbound between U.S. 17 and Va. 3; Lambsburg, on I-77; Manassas, on I-66; Rocky Gap, on I-77 near the North Carolina state line; and Skippers, on I-95 north of the North Carolina border.

3 Money

As you might expect, Virginia is more expensive in its larger cities, and in the Washington, D.C., suburbs of Northern Virginia. It's also hard to find bargains at the beach in the summer. Even so, the state itself is not a particularly expensive destination. While there are

plenty of high-end restaurants, luxury hotels and B&Bs, there are also many smaller independent hotels and motels, as well as representatives of all the major budget chains. It's possible to eat and stay very well in Virginia without spending a fortune, and should you decide to splurge, you can find a lot of luxury for your money.

ATMS

The easiest and best way to get cash away from home is from an ATM (automated teller machine). The **Cirrus** (☎ **800/424-7787;** www.mastercard. com) and **PLUS** (☎ **800/843-7587;** www.visa.com) networks span the globe; look at the back of your bank card to see which network you're on, then call or check online for ATM locations at your destination. Be sure you know your personal identification number (PIN) before you leave home and be sure to find out your daily withdrawal limit before you depart. Also keep in mind that many banks impose a fee every time a card is used at a different bank's ATM. On top of this, the bank from which you withdraw cash may charge its own fee. To compare banks' ATM fees within the U.S., use www.bankrate.com.

You can also get cash advances on your credit card at an ATM. Keep in mind that credit card companies try to protect themselves from theft by limiting the funds someone can withdraw outside their home country, so call your credit card company before you leave home.

TRAVELER'S CHECKS

Traveler's checks are something of an anachronism from the days before the ATM made cash accessible at any time. Traveler's checks used to be the only sound alternative to traveling with dangerously large amounts of cash. They were as reliable as currency, but, unlike cash, could be replaced if lost or stolen.

These days, traveler's checks are less necessary because most cities have 24-hour ATMs that allow you to withdraw small amounts of cash as needed. However, keep in mind that you will likely be charged an ATM withdrawal fee if the bank is not your own, so if you're withdrawing money every day, you

might be better off with traveler's checks—provided that you don't mind showing identification every time you want to cash one.

You can get traveler's checks at almost any bank. **American Express** offers denominations of $20, $50, $100, $500, and (for cardholders only) $1,000. You'll pay a service charge ranging from 1% to 4%. You can also get American Express traveler's checks over the phone by calling ☎ **800/221-7282;** Amex gold and platinum cardholders who use this number are exempt from the 1% fee.

Visa offers traveler's checks at Citibank locations nationwide, as well as at several other banks. The service charge ranges between 1.5% and 2%; checks come in denominations of $20, $50, $100, $500, and $1,000. Call ☎ **800/732-1322** for information. AAA members can obtain Visa checks without a fee at most AAA offices or by calling ☎ **866/339-3378. MasterCard** also offers traveler's checks. Call ☎ **800/ 223-9920** for a location near you.

If you choose to carry traveler's checks, be sure to keep a record of their serial numbers separate from your checks in the event that they are stolen or lost. You'll get a refund faster if you know the numbers.

CREDIT CARDS

Credit cards are a safe way to carry money, they provide a convenient record of all your expenses, and they generally offer good exchange rates. You can also withdraw cash advances from your credit cards at banks or ATMs, provided you know your PIN. If you've forgotten yours, or didn't even know you had one, call the number on the back of your credit card and ask the bank to send it to you. It usually takes 5 to 7 business days, though some banks will provide the number over the phone if you tell them your mother's maiden name or some other personal information.

4 When to Go

Virginia is a gorgeous place in October, during Indian summer when the turning leaves blaze orange, red, and yellow across the state. October also is the most crowded time in the western part of the state, when throngs of visitors mob the mountains during this "leaf season." (You can find out the approximate dates for peak color by calling ℂ 800/434-5323 for the Shenandoah Valley, ℂ 540/999-3500 for Shenandoah National Park and the Skyline Drive, and ℂ 704/298-0398 for Virginia's portion of the Blue Ridge Parkway.)

Otherwise, Virginia is busiest during summer, when the historic sites, theme parks, and beaches draw millions of visitors—and hotel rates are at their highest. The least crowded—and least expensive—time to visit is in spring. Fortunately, that's when the dogwoods, azaleas, and wildflowers are in a riot of bloom from one end of Virginia to the other.

THE CLIMATE

Virginia enjoys four distinct seasons, with some variations from the warmer, more humid coastal areas to the cooler climate in the mountains. Wintertime snows are usually confined to northern Virginia and the mountains. In summer, extremely hot and humid spells can last several weeks, but are normally short-lived. Spring and autumn are long seasons, and in terms of natural beauty and heavenly climate, they're optimum times to visit. Annual rainfall averages 46 inches; annual snowfall, 18 inches.

Virginia's Average Temperatures

	Jan	Feb	Mar	Apr	May	June	July	Aug	Sept	Oct	Nov	Dec
High °F (°C)	44 (6)	46 (8)	56 (13)	68 (20)	75 (24)	84 (29)	90 (32)	88 (31)	81 (27)	69 (21)	57 (14)	47 (8)
Low °F (°C)	26 (-3)	27 (-3)	38 (3)	45 (7)	54 (12)	62 (17)	66 (19)	65 (18)	59 (15)	48 (9)	39 (4)	28 (-2)

VIRGINIA CALENDAR OF EVENTS

January

Lee Birthday Celebrations, Alexandria. Period music, plus house tours at Lee-Fendall House. ℂ 703/548-1789; www.leefendallhouse.org. Fourth Sunday in January. Also, open house at Stratford Hall on the Northern Neck, Lee's birthplace. ℂ 804/493-8038; www.stratford hall.org. January 19.

February

Maymont Flower and Garden Show, Richmond. A breath of spring, with landscape exhibits, vendors, and speakers. ℂ 804/358-7166; www.maymont.org. Mid-February.

George Washington Birthday Events, Alexandria. Black tie or colonial costume Saturday evening dinner, followed by birth-night ball at Gadsby's Tavern, where George and Martha Washington attended balls in 1798 and 1799. On Sunday, Revolutionary War encampment at Fort Ward, featuring a skirmish between British and colonial uniformed troops. There's a parade on Monday. ℂ 800/388-9119 or 703/838-4200; www.funside.com. Presidents' Day weekend.

George Washington's Birthday Party, Fredericksburg. Reduced rates at attractions, celebrations at Belmont Plantation and George Washington's Ferry Farm. ℂ 800/678-4748 or 540/373-1776; www.fredericksburgvirginia.net. Monday of Washington's Birthday weekend.

March

James Madison's Birthday, Montpelier. Ceremony at cemetery and reception at house. ℂ **540/ 672-2728**; www.montpelier.org. March 16.

Patrick Henry Speech Reenactment, St. John's Episcocpal Church, Richmond. "Give me liberty or give me death," resounds once again. Call ℂ **804/648-5015**; www.historic stjohnschurch.org. Closest Sunday to March 23.

Highland Maple Festival, Monterey. See maple syrup produced, pour it over pancakes, and visit one of the state's largest crafts shows. Call ℂ **540/468-2550**; www.highland county.org. Second and third weekends in March.

April

Thomas Jefferson's Birthday Commemoration, Monticello, Charlottesville. Wreath-laying ceremony at gravesite, fife-and-drum corps, and a speaker. ℂ **434/984-9822**; www. monticello.org. April 13.

International Azalea Festival, Norfolk. The brilliant beauty of azaleas in bloom is the backdrop for ceremonies in the Norfolk Botanical Garden saluting NATO countries, including the crowning of a queen who reigns at a parade and other festivities. Also features a military display that includes an air show, visiting of ships, and aircraft ground exhibits. ℂ **800/368-3097** or 757/ 441-1852; www.azaleafestival.com. Second to third week in April.

Virginia International Arts Festival, Williamsburg, Hampton, Newport News, Norfolk, Virginia Beach. Famous performers appear at venues from Williamsburg to Virginia Beach during month-long festival. ℂ **800/VA-BEACH** or 757/282-2800 (Norfolk); www.virginiaarts fest.com. Mid-April to mid-May.

Virginia Horse Festival, Virginia Horse Center, Lexington. All breeds are showcased with demonstrations, events, seminars, sales, and equine art and merchandise. ℂ **540/463-2194**; www.horsecenter.org. Third weekend in April.

Historic Garden Week in Virginia, statewide. The event of the year—a celebration with tours of the grounds and gardens of some 200 Virginia landmarks, including plantations and other sites open only during this week. For information contact the **Garden Club of Virginia,** 12 E. Franklin St., Richmond, VA 23219 (ℂ **804/644-7776** or 804/643-7141; www.vagardenweek.org). Last full week in April.

May

Shenandoah Apple Blossom Festival, Winchester. Acres of orchards in blossom throughout the valley, plus 5 days of music, band competitions, parades, coronation of the queen, footraces, arts and crafts sale, midway amusements, and a carnival, with a celebrity grand marshal. ℂ **800/230-2139** or 540/ 662-3863; www.sabf.org. Usually first weekend in May.

Virginia Gold Cup Race Meet, Great Meadow Course, The Plains. Everyone dresses to the nines for the state's premier steeplechase event. ℂ **800/69RACES** or 540/347-2612; www.vagoldcup.com. First Saturday in May.

Seafood Festival, Chincoteague. All you can eat—a seafood lover's dream come true. Get tickets in advance from **Eastern Shore Chamber of Commerce,** P.O. Box 460, Melfa, VA 23410 (ℂ **757/787-2460**; www.esvatourism.org). First weekend in May.

George Mason Day, Gunston Hall, Lorton. All-day celebration with music and costumed interpreters portraying Mason's daily life and concern for the Bill of Rights. ℂ **703/550-9220**; www.gunston hall.org. May 5.

Jamestown Landing Day, Jamestown. Militia presentations and sailing demonstrations celebrate the first settlers. ⓒ **888/593-4682** or 757/ 253-4838; www.historyisfun.org. Early May.

Reenactment of Battle of New Market, New Market Battlefield State Historical Park, New Market. ⓒ **540/740-3101;** www.vmi.edu/ museum/nm. Second or third weekend in May.

New Market Day, Virginia Military Institute Campus, Lexington. Annual roll call for cadets who died in the battle. ⓒ **540/464-7000;** www.vmi.edu. May 15.

Oatlands Sheepdog Trials, Leesburg. Dogs compete in sheepherding contests. Crafts, food, and house and garden tours. ⓒ **703/777-3174;** www.oatlands.org. Late May.

Virginia Hunt Country Stable Tour, Loudon County. A unique opportunity to view prestigious Leesburg, Middleburg, and Upperville horse farms and private estates. ⓒ 540/592-3711; www.middleburg online.com/stabletour. Late May.

Shenandoah Valley Music Festival, Orkney Springs. Music from classical to country-and-western fills the mountain air. Call **Orkney Springs Hotel** at ⓒ **800/459-3396** or 540/ 459-3396; www.musicfest.org. Concerts start Memorial Day weekend, and run on weekends through August.

June

Vintage Virginia Wine Festival, Great Meadows Steeplechase Course, The Plains. Taste the premium vintages from 35 wineries at this Hunt Country festival. Arts and crafts displays, food, and jazz, reggae, and pop music. ⓒ **800/277-CORK;** www. vintagevirginia.com (for information about this and many other wine festivals statewide). First weekend in June.

Harborfest, Norfolk. Tall ships, sailboat races, air shows, military demonstrations, and fireworks. ⓒ **800/368-3097** or 757/441-1852; www.norfolkcvb.com. First full weekend in June.

Boardwalk Art Show, Virginia Beach. Works in all mediums, between 14th Street and 28th Street on the boardwalk. ⓒ **800/ VA-BEACH;** www.vbfun.com. Mid-June.

Ash Lawn–Highland Summer Festival, Charlottesville. James Monroe's home is the setting for opera, musicals, concerts, and a traditional bonfire finale. ⓒ **434/293-9539;** www. ashlawnhighland.org. End of June to August.

July

Independence Day Celebrations, statewide. Every town parties and shoots fireworks in honor of the nation's birthday. Contact local tourist information offices. July 4.

Pony Swim and Auction, Chincoteague. Famous wild horses swim the Assateague Channel, and are later herded to carnival grounds and auctioned off. Return swim to Assateague on Friday. ⓒ **757/336-6161;** fax 757/336-1241; www. chincoteaguechamber.com. Festival is last 2 weeks in July; swim on last Wednesday in July.

August

Virginia Highlands Festival, Abingdon. Appalachian Mountain culture showcase for musicians, artists, artisans, and writers. Area's largest crafts show has an antiques market and hot air balloons. Call ⓒ **800/676-2282** or 540/676-3440; www.vahighlands festival.org. First 2 weeks in August.

Old Time Fiddlers' Convention, Galax. Dating to 1935, one of the largest and oldest such conventions in the world. It also coincides with the Fiddlefest street festival. Call ℂ **276/236-8541;** www.oldfiddlers convention.com. Early August.

September

American Music Festival, Virginia Beach. Top entertainers perform on the sand. Tickets are first come, first served. Call ℂ **800/VA-BEACH;** www.vbfun.com. Labor Day weekend.

State Fair of Virginia, Richmond Raceway Complex, Richmond. Rides, entertainment, agricultural exhibits, pioneer farmstead, and flower shows. ℂ **800/588-3247** or 804/228-3200; www.statefair.com. Ten days in late September.

October

Chincoteague Oyster Festival, Chincoteague. A feast of oysters— but for advance ticket holders only. ℂ **804/336-6161;** www. chincoteaguechamber.com. Early October.

Waterford Homes Tour and Crafts Exhibit, Waterford Village. The tiny Quaker town grows to some 40,000 on this one weekend. ℂ **540/882-3018;** www.waterfordva.org. First weekend in October.

Virginia Film Festival, Charlottesville. Tribute to all things celluloid. ℂ **800/882-3378** for tickets, 804/924-3376 for information; www.vafilm.com. Starts mid-Oct.

Yorktown Day, Colonial National Historic Park, Yorktown. British surrender in 1781 celebrated with a parade, historic house tours, colonial music and dress, and military drills. ℂ **757/898-2410** or 757/898-3400. www.nps.gov/colo. October 19.

International Gold Cup, Great Meadows Course, The Plains. Fall colors provide a backdrop to one of the most prestigious steeplechase races. ℂ **800/69RACES** or 540/347-2612; www.vagoldcup.com. Third Saturday in October.

Marine Corps Marathon, Arlington. More than 18,000 men and women run a 26-mile course from Arlington through Washington, D.C., and back. The U.S. Marine Corps' "People's Marathon" is open to all (there's even a wheelchair division). Call ℂ **800/786-8762** or 703/784-2225; www.marinemarathon.com. Third or fourth Sunday in October.

November

The First Thanksgiving, Charles City. Reenactment at Berkeley Plantation. ℂ **888/466-6018** or 804/829-6018; www.berkeleyplantation.com. Early November.

Assateague Island Waterfowl Week, Chincoteague. The only time of the year when visitors can drive to the northern end of Chincoteague National Wildlife Refuge on Assateague Island. Guided walks for pedestrians. ℂ **757/336-6122;** http://chinco.fws.gov. Thanksgiving weekend.

December

Mount Vernon by Candlelight, Mount Vernon. See Washington's mansion as he would have, by the light of candles. Tickets required. ℂ **703/780-2000;** www.mount vernon.org. First week in December.

Grand Illumination, Williamsburg. Gala opening of holiday season with fife-and-drum corps, illumination of buildings, caroling, dancing, and fireworks. ℂ **800/HISTORY** or 757/220-7645; www.colonial williamsburg.com. First Saturday in December.

Christmas Candlelight Tour, Fredericksburg. ℂ **800/678-4748** or 540/373-1776; www.fredericks burgvirginia.net. First weekend in December.

Monticello Candlelight Tour, Charlottesville. Call © **804/984-9822;** www.monticello.org. Early December.

Historic Michie Tavern Feast and Open House, Charlottesville. The old tavern puts on two Christmas-time feasts. Reservations required.

Call © **804/977-1234;** www.michie tavern.com. Second weekend in December.

Jamestown Christmas, Jamestown. © **888/593-4682** or 757/253-4838; www.historyisfun.org. Jamestown Settlement is all decked out 17th century–style. Second to fourth week in December.

5 Travel Insurance

Check your existing insurance policies and credit-card coverage before you buy travel insurance. You may already be covered for lost luggage, cancelled tickets or medical expenses. The cost of travel insurance varies widely, depending on the cost and length of your trip, your age, health, and the type of trip you're taking.

TRIP-CANCELLATION INSUR-ANCE Trip-cancellation insurance helps you get your money back if you have to back out of a trip, if you have to go home early, or if your travel supplier goes bankrupt. Allowed reasons for cancellation can range from sickness to natural disasters to the State Department declaring your destination unsafe for travel. (Insurers usually won't cover vague fears, though, as many travelers discovered who tried to cancel their trips in October 2001 because they were wary of flying.) In this unstable world, trip-cancellation insurance is a good buy if you're getting tickets well in advance—who knows what the state of the world, or of your airline, will be in 9 months? Insurance policy details vary, so read the fine print—and especially make sure that your airline or cruise line is on the list of carriers covered in case of bankruptcy. For information, contact one of the following insurers: **Access America** (© 866/807-3982; www.accessamerica.com); **Travel Guard International** (© 800/826-4919; www.travelguard.com); **Travel Insured International** (© 800/243-3174;

www.travelinsured.com); and **Travelex Insurance Services** (© 888/457-4602; www.travelex-insurance.com).

MEDICAL INSURANCE Most health insurance policies cover you if you get sick away from home—but check, particularly if you're insured by an HMO.

LOST-LUGGAGE INSURANCE On domestic flights, checked baggage is covered up to $2,500 per ticketed passenger. On international flights (including U.S. portions of international trips), baggage is limited to approximately $9.07 per pound, up to approximately $635 per checked bag. If you plan to check items more valuable than the standard liability, see if your valuables are covered by your homeowner's policy, get baggage insurance as part of your comprehensive travel-insurance package or buy Travel Guard's "Bag-Trak" product. Don't buy insurance at the airport, as it's usually overpriced. Be sure to take any valuables or irreplaceable items with you in your carry-on luggage, as many valuables (including books, money and electronics) aren't covered by airline policies.

If your luggage is lost, immediately file a lost-luggage claim at the airport, detailing the luggage contents. For most airlines, you must report delayed, damaged, or lost baggage within 4 hours of arrival. The airlines are required to deliver luggage, once found, directly to your house or destination free of charge.

6 Health & Safety

STAYING HEALTHY

Malaria may have been a curse of the colonists who settled Virginia, but today the state poses no unusual health threats. Although they don't carry malaria, mosquitoes are still rampant in the Tidewater during summer, especially in the marshes of Chincoteague and the Eastern Shore, so take plenty of insect repellent if you're going there. Hospitals and emergency care facilities are widespread in the state, so unless you're in the backcountry mountains, help will be close at hand.

WHAT TO DO IF YOU GET SICK AWAY FROM HOME

In most cases, your existing health plan will provide the coverage you need. But double-check; you may want to buy **travel medical insurance** instead. (See the section on insurance, above.) Bring your insurance ID card with you when you travel.

If you suffer from a chronic illness, consult your doctor before your departure. For conditions like epilepsy, diabetes, or heart problems, wear a **Medic Alert Identification Tag** (© 800/825-3785; www.medicalert.org), which will immediately alert doctors to your condition and give them access to your records through Medic Alert's 24-hour hot line.

Pack **prescription medications** in your carry-on luggage, and carry prescription medications in their original containers. Also bring along copies of your prescriptions in case you lose your pills or run out.

And don't forget sunglasses and an extra pair of contact lenses or prescription glasses.

If you get sick, consider asking your hotel concierge to recommend a local doctor—even his or her own. You can also try the emergency room at a local hospital; many have walk-in clinics for emergency cases that are not life threatening. You may not get immediate attention, but you won't pay the high price of an emergency room visit (usually a minimum of $300 just for signing your name).

STAYING SAFE

Most areas of Virginia are relatively free of street crime, but this is not the case in some areas of Richmond, Norfolk, Roanoke, and other cities. Ask your hotel staff or the local visitor information office whether neighborhoods you intend to visit are safe. Avoid deserted streets and alleys, and always be especially alert at night. Never leave anything of value visible in your parked car; it's an invitation to theft.

When heading outdoors, keep in mind that injuries often occur when people fail to follow instructions. Believe the experts who tell you to stay on the established ski trails. Hike only in designated areas, follow the marine charts if piloting your own boat, carry rain gear, and wear a life jacket when rafting. Mountain weather can be fickle at any time. Watch out for summer thunderstorms that can leave you drenched and send bolts of lightning your way.

7 Specialized Travel Resources

TRAVELERS WITH DISABILITIES

Most disabilities shouldn't stop anyone from traveling. There are more options and resources out there than ever before. This is especially true in Virginia, where establishments are required to comply with the federal Americans with Disabilities Act.

The U.S. National Park Service offers a **Golden Access Passport** that gives free lifetime entrance to the Shenandoah National Park, Colonial National Historical Park, Assateague

Island National Seashore, the Civil War battlefields, and other U.S. national parks for persons who are blind or permanently disabled, regardless of age. You may pick up a Golden Access Passport at any NPS entrance fee area by showing proof of medically determined disability and eligibility for receiving benefits under federal law. Besides free entry, the Golden Access Passport also offers a 50% discount on federal-use fees charged for such facilities as camping, swimming, parking, boat launching, and tours. For more information, click onto www.nps.gov/fees_passes. htm or call © **888/467-2757.**

Many travel agencies offer customized tours and itineraries for travelers with disabilities. **Flying Wheels Travel** (© **507/451-5005;** www.flying wheelstravel.com) offers escorted tours and cruises that emphasize sports and private tours in minivans with lifts. **Accessible Journeys** (© **800/846-4537** or 610/521-0339; www.disability travel.com) caters specifically to slow walkers and wheelchair travelers and their families and friends.

Organizations that offer assistance to disabled travelers include the **Moss Rehab Hospital** (www.mossresource net.org), which provides a library of accessible-travel resources online; the **Society for Accessible Travel and Hospitality** (© **212/447-7284;** www. sath.org; annual membership fees: $45 adults, $30 seniors and students), which offers a wealth of travel resources for all types of disabilities and informed recommendations on destinations, access guides, travel agents, tour operators, vehicle rentals, and companion services; and the **American Foundation for the Blind** (© **800/232-5463;** www.afb.org), which provides information on traveling with Seeing Eye dogs.

For more information specifically targeted to travelers with disabilities, the community website **iCan** (www. icanonline.net/channels/travel/index. cfm) has destination guides and several regular columns on accessible travel. Also check out the quarterly magazine **Emerging Horizons** ($14.95 per yr., $19.95 outside the U.S.; www. emerginghorizons.com); **Twin Peaks Press** (© **360/694-2462;** http:// disabilitybookshop.virtualave.net/blist 84.htm), offering travel-related books for travelers with special needs; and *Open World Magazine,* published by the Society for Accessible Travel and Hospitality (see above; subscription: $18 per yr., $35 outside the U.S.).

GAY & LESBIAN TRAVELERS

Virginia has its intolerant contingent, particularly in rural areas, but by and large, the state is a safe, comfortable place for gay and lesbian travelers. There are gay and lesbian communities in most cities here.

The **International Gay & Lesbian Travel Association** (IGLTA) (© **800/ 448-8550** or 954/776-2626; www. iglta.org) is the trade association for the gay and lesbian travel industry, and offers an online directory of gay and lesbian-friendly travel businesses; go to their website and click on "Members."

Many agencies offer tours and travel itineraries specifically for gay and lesbian travelers. **Above and Beyond Tours** (© **800/397-2681;** www.above beyondtours.com) is the exclusive gay and lesbian tour operator for United Airlines. **Now, Voyager** (© **800/255-6951;** www.nowvoyager.com) is a well-known San Francisco–based gay-owned and -operated travel service.

Out and About (© **800/929-2268** or 415/644-8044; www.outandabout. com), offers guidebooks and a newsletter 10 times a year packed with solid information on the global gay and lesbian scene; *Spartacus International Gay Guide* and *Odysseus* are both good, annual English-language guidebooks focused on gay men; the *Damron* guides, with separate, annual books for gay men and lesbians; and *Gay*

Travel A to Z: The World of Gay & Lesbian Travel Options at Your Fingertips, by Marianne Ferrari (Ferrari Publications; Box 35575, Phoenix, AZ 85069), a very good gay and lesbian guidebook series.

SENIOR TRAVEL

Mention the fact that you're a senior citizen when you make your travel reservations. All major airlines and many Virginia hotels offer discounts for seniors. Major airlines also offer coupons for domestic travel for seniors over 60. Typically, a book of four coupons costs less than $700, which means you can fly anywhere in the continental U.S. for under $350 round trip. In most cities, people over the age of 60 qualify for reduced admission to theaters, museums, and other attractions, as well as discounted fares on public transportation.

Members of **AARP** (formerly known as the American Association of Retired Persons), 601 E St. NW, Washington, DC 20049 (© **800/424-3410** or 202/434-2277; www.aarp.org), get discounts on hotels, airfares, and car rentals. AARP offers members a wide range of benefits, including *Modern Maturity* magazine and a monthly newsletter. Anyone over 50 can join.

The **U.S. National Park Service** offers a **Golden Age Passport** that gives seniors 62 years or older lifetime entrance to Virginia's many U.S. national park facilities for a one-time processing fee of $10, which must be purchased in person at any NPS facility that charges an entrance fee. Besides free entry, a Golden Age Passport also offers a 50% discount on federal-use fees charged for such facilities as camping, swimming, parking, boat launching, and tours. For more information, click onto www.nps.gov/fees_passes. htm or call © **888/GO-PARKS.**

Many reliable agencies and organizations target the 50-plus market.

Elderhostel (© **877/426-8056;** www. elderhostel.org) arranges study programs for those aged 55 and over (and a spouse or companion of any age) in the U.S. and in more than 80 countries around the world. Most courses last 5 to 7 days in the U.S., and many include airfare, accommodations in university dormitories or modest inns, meals, and tuition.

Recommended publications offering travel resources and discounts for seniors include: the quarterly magazine *Travel 50 & Beyond* (www.travel50 andbeyond.com); *Travel Unlimited: Uncommon Adventures for the Mature Traveler* (Avalon); *101 Tips for Mature Travelers,* available from Grand Circle Travel (© **800/221-2610** or 617/350-7500; www.gct.com); *The 50+ Traveler's Guidebook* (St. Martin's Press); and *Unbelievably Good Deals and Great Adventures That You Absolutely Can't Get Unless You're Over 50* (McGraw Hill).

FAMILY TRAVEL

Virginia has a host of activities ideal for families with children, from learning American history everywhere to the exciting rides at Busch Gardens Williamsburg and at Paramount's Kings Dominion near Richmond. We won't begin to tell you how to raise your children, but you might give them a stake in your trip by letting them help plan it. And since much of your travel in Virginia is likely to be by car, think about carrying a few games to relieve potential boredom. Many Virginia hotels offer babysitting services, and most resorts have children's programs.

You might also want to pick up a copy of *The Unofficial Guide to the Mid-Atlantic with Kids* (Wiley Publishing, Inc.) for more ideas on itineraries and activities in Virginia.

STUDENT TRAVEL

It's worthwhile to bring along your valid high school or college identification.

Virginia Is for Kids, Too

Virginia will bring history to life for your kids (and you, too) with a myriad of associations involving America's first heroes—Washington, Jefferson, Madison, Monroe, and Patrick Henry among them. Take them to the first English settlement at **Jamestown;** to the picturesque village of **Colonial Williamsburg** and its craft demonstrations, militia reviews, and tours designed especially for kids; and to **Yorktown,** where they can climb the ramparts where Washington defeated Cornwallis.

Especially entertaining for kids are the living history demonstrations at **Jamestown Settlement, Yorktown Victory Center,** the **Frontier Culture Museum** at Staunton, and **Virginia's Explore Park** at Roanoke.

Other possibilities are the presidential homes of **Mount Vernon, Monticello,** and **Ash Lawn–Highland** (Monroe's home). **Civil War battlefield** tours portray crucial events with fascinating exhibits, scenic walks and drives, and multimedia programs.

Theme parks offer thrills and chills, not to mention food, fun, and entertainment, at **Paramount's Kings Dominion, Busch Gardens Williamsburg,** and **Water Country USA.**

Roanoke's **Virginia Museum of Transportation,** with its railroad cars, and **Science Museum,** featuring interactive exhibits, rate high with kids. Richmond's **Children's Museum** and **Science Museum of Virginia** will keep them engaged with activities and "touch me" exhibits.

Virginia's family favorite is the **Marine Science Museum** in Virginia Beach, where computers, exhibits, and the museum's own waterside setting help explain the marine environment. Nearby in Norfolk, the **NAUTICUS** has interactive and "virtual adventures" featuring make-believe U.S. Navy ships. Across the harbor in Hampton, they can see spaceships at the **Virginia Air and Space Center.**

It's not a museum, but after reading the story of *Misty of Chincoteague,* kids will adore a chance to see the action themselves at the **wild ponies' swim across Assateague Channel.** The wildlife refuge also offers hikes, nature programs, and a sandy beach.

Presenting it can mean discounted admission to museums and other attractions. Alcoholic beverages cannot be sold in Virginia to anyone who is under 21, so if you're eligible and intend to imbibe, bring your driver's license or another photo identification with your date of birth.

The Hanging Out Guides (www. frommers.com/hangingout), published by Frommer's, is the top travel series for today's students, covering everything from adrenaline sports to the club and music scenes.

TRAVELING WITH PETS

The **Virginia Tourism Corporation** publishes a list of the state's hotels and motels that accept pets (see "Visitor Information," earlier). You can download and print a copy of the list at the website, www.virginia.org. Policies vary from hotel to hotel, so call ahead to find out the rules. Also, a fee is often charged to allow them into guest rooms. Most B&Bs do not accept pets, but some of their owners have them, so ask before booking if you're allergic to animals.

Pets are allowed on short leashes in Virginia state parks, but restricted in national parks (there is one short trail in Shenandoah National Park on which you can walk Fido). Check with each park's ranger station before setting out.

8 Planning Your Trip Online

SURFING FOR AIRFARES

The "big three" online travel agencies, **Expedia.com, Travelocity.com,** and **Orbitz.com** sell most of the air tickets bought on the Internet. (Canadian travelers should try expedia.ca and Travelocity.ca; U.K. residents can go for expedia.co.uk and opodo.co.uk.) Each has different business deals with the airlines and may offer different fares on the same flights, so it's wise to shop around. Expedia and Travelocity will also send you **e-mail notification** when a cheap fare becomes available to your favorite destination. Of the smaller travel agency websites, **Side-Step** (www.sidestep.com) has gotten the best reviews from Frommer's authors. It's a browser add-on that purports to "search 140 sites at once," but in reality only beats competitors' fares as often as other sites do.

Also remember to check **airline websites,** especially those for low-fare carriers such as Southwest, JetBlue, AirTran, WestJet, or Ryanair, whose fares are often misreported or simply missing from travel agency websites. Even with major airlines, you can often shave a few bucks from a fare by booking directly through the airline and avoiding a travel agency's transaction fee. But you'll get these discounts only by **booking online:** Most airlines now offer online-only fares that even their phone agents know nothing about. For the websites of airlines that fly to and from your destination, go to "Getting There," later in this chapter.

Great **last-minute deals** are available through free weekly e-mail services provided directly by the airlines. Most of these are announced on Tuesday or Wednesday and must be purchased online. Most are only valid for travel that weekend, but some (such as Southwest's) can be booked weeks or months in advance. Sign up for weekly e-mail alerts at airline websites or check mega-sites that compile lists of last-minute specials, such as **Smarter Living** (smarterliving.com). For last-minute trips, **site59.com** in the U.S. and **lastminute.com** in Europe often have better deals than the major-label sites.

If you're willing to give up some control over your flight details, use an **opaque fare service** like **Priceline** (www.priceline.com; www.priceline.co.uk for Europeans) or **Hotwire** (www.hotwire.com). Both offer rock-bottom prices in exchange for travel on a "mystery airline" at a mysterious time of day, often with a mysterious change of planes enroute. The mystery airlines are all major, well-known carriers—and the possibility of being sent from Philadelphia to Chicago via Tampa is remote; the airlines' routing computers have gotten a lot better than they used to be. But your chances of getting a 6am or 11pm flight are pretty high. Hotwire tells you flight prices before you buy; Priceline usually has better deals than Hotwire, but you have to play their "name our price" game. If you're new at this, the helpful folks at **BiddingForTravel** (www.biddingfortravel.com) do a good job of demystifying Priceline's prices. Priceline and Hotwire are great for flights within North America and between the U.S. and Europe. But for flights to other parts of the world, consolidators will almost always beat their fares.

For much more about airfares and savvy air-travel tips and advice, pick up a copy of *Frommer's Fly Safe, Fly Smart* (Wiley Publishing, Inc.).

Frommers.com: The Complete Travel Resource

For an excellent travel-planning resource, we highly recommend Frommers.com (www.frommers.com). We're a little biased, of course, but we guarantee that you'll find the travel tips, reviews, monthly vacation giveaways, and online-booking capabilities thoroughly indispensable. Among the special features are our popular **Message Boards,** where Frommer's readers post queries and share advice (sometimes even our authors show up to answer questions); **Frommers.com Newsletter,** for the latest travel bargains and insider travel secrets; and **Frommer's Destinations Section,** where you'll get expert travel tips, hotel and dining recommendations, and advice on the sights to see for more than 3,000 destinations around the globe. When your research is done, the **Online Reservations System** (www.frommers.com/book_a_trip) takes you to Frommer's preferred online partners for booking your vacation at affordable prices.

SURFING FOR HOTELS

Shopping online for hotels is much easier in the U.S., than it is in the rest of the world. If you try to book a Chinese hotel online, for instance, you'll probably overpay. Also, many smaller hotels and B&Bs don't show up on websites at all. Of the "big three" sites, **Expedia** may be the best choice, thanks to its long list of deals. **Travelocity** runs a close second. Hotel specialist sites **hotels.com** and **hoteldiscounts.com** are also reliable. An excellent free program, **TravelAxe** (www.travelaxe.net), can help you search multiple hotel sites, even ones you may never have heard of.

Priceline and Hotwire are even better for hotels than for airfares; with both, you're allowed to pick the neighborhood and quality level of your hotel before offering up your money. *Note:* Hotwire overrates its hotels by one star—what Hotwire calls a four-star is a three-star anywhere else.

SURFING FOR RENTAL CARS

For booking rental cars online, the best deals are usually found at rental-car company websites, although all the major online travel agencies also offer rental-car reservations services. Priceline and Hotwire work well for rental cars, too; the only "mystery" is which major rental company you get, and for most travelers the difference between Hertz, Avis, and Budget is negligible.

9 The 21st-Century Traveler

INTERNET ACCESS AWAY FROM HOME

Travelers have any number of ways to check their e-mail and access the Internet on the road. Of course, using your own laptop—or even a PDA (personal digital assistant) or electronic organizer with a modem—gives you the most flexibility. But even if you don't have a computer, you can still access your e-mail and even your office computer from cybercafes.

WITHOUT YOUR OWN COMPUTER

Most **public libraries** in Virginia offer Internet access free or for a small charge. **Hotel business centers** have access, too, but often charge exorbitant rates.

To retrieve your e-mail, ask your **Internet Service Provider (ISP)** if it has a Web-based interface tied to your existing e-mail account. If your ISP doesn't have such an interface, you can use the free **mail2web** service (www.mail2web.com) to view (but not reply to) your home e-mail. For more flexibility, you may want to open a free, Web-based e-mail account with **Yahoo! Mail** (mail.yahoo.com). (Microsoft's Hotmail is another popular option, but Hotmail has severe spam problems.) Your home ISP may be able to forward your e-mail to the Web-based account automatically.

If you need to access files on your office computer, look into a service called **GoToMyPC** (www.gotomypc.com). The service provides a Web-based interface for you to access and manipulate a distant PC from anywhere—even a cybercafe—provided your "target" PC is on and has an always-on connection to the Internet (such as with Road Runner cable). The service offers top-quality security, but if you're worried about hackers, use your own laptop rather than a cybercafe to access the GoToMyPC system.

WITH YOUR OWN COMPUTER

Major Internet Service Providers (ISP) have **local access numbers** around Virginia, allowing you to go online by simply placing a local call. Check your ISP's website or call its toll-free number and ask how you can use your current account away from home, and how much it will cost.

If you're traveling outside the reach of your ISP, the **iPass** network has dial-up numbers in most of the world's countries. You'll have to sign up with an iPass provider, who will then tell you how to set up your computer for your destination(s). For a list of iPass providers, go to www.ipass.com and click on "Individuals." One solid provider is **i2roam** (© **866/811-6209** or 920/235-0475; www.i2roam.com).

Most business-class hotels inn Virginia offer dataports for laptop modems, and a few offer high-speed Internet access using an Ethernet network cable. You'll have to bring your own cables either way, so **call your hotel in advance** to find out what the options are.

Some business-class hotels also offer a form of computer-free Web browsing through the room TV set. We've successfully checked Yahoo! Mail, but not Hotmail, on these systems.

If you have an 802.11b/**Wi-fi** card for your computer, **T-Mobile Hotspot** (www.t-mobile.com/hotspot) serves up wireless connections at more than 1,000 Starbucks coffee shops nationwide.

USING A CELLPHONE

Just because your cellphone works at home doesn't mean it'll work in Virginia (thanks to our nation's fragmented cellphone system). It's a good bet that your phone will work in major cities. But take a look at your wireless company's coverage map on its website before heading out—T-Mobile, Sprint, and Nextel can be particularly weak in rural areas. If you need to stay in touch at a destination where you know your phone won't work, **rent** a phone that does from **InTouch USA** (© **800/872-7626**; www.intouchglobal.com) or a rental car location, but beware that you'll pay $1 a minute or more for airtime.

If you're not from the U.S., you'll be appalled at the poor reach of our **GSM (Global System for Mobiles) wireless network,** which is used by much of the rest of the world. Your phone may work, but don't count on it. (To see where GSM phones work in the U.S., check out www.t-mobile.com/coverage/national_popup.asp.) Assume nothing—call your wireless provider and get the full scoop. In a worst-case scenario, you can always rent a phone; InTouch USA delivers to hotels.

Online Traveler's Toolbox

Veteran travelers usually carry some essential items to make their trips easier. Following is a selection of online tools to bookmark and use.

- **Visa ATM Locator** (www.visa.com), for locations of PLUS ATMs worldwide, or **MasterCard ATM Locator** (www.mastercard.com), for locations of Cirrus ATMs worldwide.
- **Foreign Languages for Travelers** (www.travlang.com). Learn basic terms in more than 70 languages and click on any underlined phrase to hear what it sounds like.
- **Intellicast** (www.intellicast.com) and **Weather.com** (www.weather.com). Gives weather forecasts for all 50 states and for cities around the world.
- **Mapquest** (www.mapquest.com). This best of the mapping sites lets you choose a specific address or destination, and in seconds, it will return a map and detailed directions.
- **Universal Currency Converter** (www.xe.com/ucc). See what your dollar or pound is worth in more than 100 other countries.

10 Getting There & Getting Around

BY PLANE

Most international visitors will arrive at **Washington Dulles International Airport** (© 703/661-2700; www.mwaa.com), in northern Virginia about 25 miles west of Washington, D.C. Dulles is also a major regional hub for domestic flights, and fares generally are less to fly in and out of here than other airports in Virginia.

Washington Dulles is served by a number of carriers including **Aeroflot** (© 888/340-6400), **Air Canada** (© 888/247-2262), **Air France** (© 800/321-4538), **AirTran Airlines** (© 800/247-8726), **Alaska Airlines** (© 800/252-7522), **All Nippon Airways** (© 800/235-9262), **American** (© 800/433-7300), **American West** (© 800/2FLY-AWA), **Austrian Airlines** (© 800/843-0002), **British Airways** (© 800/247-9297), **Continental** (© 800/525-0280), **Delta Airlines** (© 800/221-1212), **Korean Airlines** (© 800/438-5000), **Lufthansa Airlines** (© 800/645-3880), **Northwest/KLM Royal Dutch Airlines** (© 800/225-2525), **Qantas Airlines** (© 800/227-4500), **SAS Scandinavian Airlines** (© 800/221-2350), **United Airlines** (© 800/241-6522), **US Airways** (© 800/428-4322), and **Virgin Atlantic Airlines** (© 800/862-8621).

Ronald Reagan Washington National Airport (© 703/685-8000; www.mwaa.com), on the Potomac River midway between Arlington and Alexandria, is served by **Air Canada, Alaska Airlines, America West, American, American Trans Air, Continental, Delta Airlines, Frontier Airlines** (© 800/432-1359), **Midwest Express** (© 800/452-2022), **Northwest/KLM, United,** and **US Airways.**

Other major Virginia gateways are **Richmond International Airport** (© 804/226-3000; www.flyrichmond.com), **Norfolk International Airport** (© 757/857-3351; www.norfolkairport.com), **Newport News/Williamsburg Airport** (© 757/877-0221; www.nnwairport.com),

Charlottesville/Albemarle Airport (② 804/973-8341; www.gocho.com), and **Roanoke Regional Airport** (② 540/362-1999; www.roanoke regionalairport.com).

See the destination chapters for details about these airports. With a few exceptions, most flights to them are of the "commuter" variety, and usually you'll pay higher fares to fly into them than into Washington Dulles.

You can get around Virginia by flying from one of these airports to another, but you are likely to change planes along the way. For example, US Airways offers the most flights around the state, but you may have to fly through its hubs at Ronald Reagan Washington National Airport or Charlotte, North Carolina, to get, say, from Roanoke to Norfolk. Check with the airlines or your travel agent for the most efficient, cost-effective routing.

For more information about getting here from other countries, see "Getting to & Around the U.S." in chapter 3.

GETTING THROUGH THE AIRPORT

With the federalization of airport security, security procedures at U.S. airports are more stable and consistent than ever. Generally, you'll be fine if you arrive at the airport **2 hours** before a domestic flight and at least **3 hours** before an international flight; if you show up late, tell an airline employee and she'll probably whisk you to the front of the line.

Bring a **current, government-issued photo ID** such as a driver's license or passport, and if you've got an E-ticket, print out the **official confirmation page;** you'll need to show your confirmation at the security checkpoint, and your ID at the ticket counter or the gate. (Children under 18 do not need photo IDs for domestic flights, but the adults checking in with them need them.)

Security lines are getting shorter than they were during 2002 and 2003, but some doozies remain. If you have trouble standing for long periods of time, tell an airline employee; the airline will provide a wheelchair. Speed up security by **not wearing metal objects** such as big belt buckles or clanky earrings. If you've got metallic body parts, a note from your doctor can prevent a long chat with the security screeners. Keep in mind that only **ticketed passengers** are allowed past security, except for folks escorting disabled passengers or children.

Federalization has stabilized **what you can carry on** and **what you can't.** The general rule is that sharp things are out, nail clippers are okay, and food and beverages must be passed through the X-ray machine—but that security screeners can't make you drink from your coffee cup. Bring food in your carry-on rather than checking it, as explosive-detection machines used on checked luggage have been known to mistake food (especially chocolate, for some reason) for bombs. Travelers in the U.S. are allowed one carry-on bag, plus a "personal item" such as a purse, briefcase, or laptop bag. Carry-on hoarders can stuff all sorts of things into a laptop bag; as long as it has a laptop in it, it's still considered a personal item. The Transportation Security Administration (TSA) has issued a list of restricted items; check its website (www.tsa.gov/public) for details.

In 2003, the TSA began phasing out **gate check-in** at all U.S. airports. Passengers with E-tickets and without checked bags can still beat the ticket-counter lines by using **electronic kiosks** or even **online check-in.** Ask your airline which alternatives are available, and if you're using a kiosk, bring the credit card you used to book the ticket. If you're checking bags, you will still be able to use most airlines' kiosks; again call your airline for up-to-date

Flying with Film & Video

Never pack film—developed or undeveloped—in checked bags, as the new, more powerful scanners in U.S. airports can fog film. The film you carry with you can be damaged by scanners as well. X-ray damage is cumulative; the slower the film, and the more times you put it through a scanner, the more likely the damage. Film under 800 ASA is usually safe for up to five scans. If you're taking your film through additional scans, U.S. regulations permit you to demand hand inspections.

On international flights, store your film in transparent baggies, so you can remove it easily before you go through scanners. Keep in mind that airports are not the only places where your camera may be scanned: Highly trafficked attractions are X-raying visitors' bags with increasing frequency.

Most photo supply stores sell protective pouches designed to block damaging X-rays. The pouches fit both film and loaded cameras. They should protect your film in checked baggage, but they also may raise alarms and result in a hand inspection.

An organization called **Film Safety for Traveling on Planes (FSTOP)** (© 888/301-2665; www.f-stop.org) can provide additional tips for traveling with film and equipment.

Carry-on scanners will not damage **videotape** in video cameras, but the magnetic fields emitted by the walk-through security gateways and handheld inspection wands will. Always place your loaded camcorder on the screening conveyor belt or have it hand-inspected. Be sure your batteries are charged, as you will probably be required to turn the device on to ensure that it's what it appears to be.

information. **Curbside check-in** is also a good way to avoid lines, although a few airlines still ban curbside check-in entirely; call before you go.

At press time, the TSA is also recommending that you **not lock your checked luggage** so screeners can search it by hand if necessary. The agency says to use plastic "zip ties" instead, which can be bought at hardware stores and can be easily cut off.

FLYING FOR LESS: TIPS FOR GETTING THE BEST AIRFARE

Passengers sharing the same airplane cabin rarely pay the same fare. Travelers who need to purchase tickets at the last minute, change their itinerary at a moment's notice, or fly one-way often get stuck paying the premium rate.

Here are some ways to keep your airfare costs down.

- Passengers who can book their ticket **long in advance,** who can **stay over Saturday night,** or who **fly midweek** or **at less-trafficked hours** will pay a fraction of the full fare. If your schedule is flexible, say so, and ask if you can secure a cheaper fare by changing your flight plans.

- You can also save on airfares by keeping an eye out in local newspapers for **promotional specials** or **fare wars,** when airlines lower prices on their most popular routes. You rarely see fare wars offered for peak travel times, but if you can travel in the off-months, you may snag a bargain.

> ## Tips Cancelled Plans
>
> If your flight is cancelled, don't book a new fare at the ticket counter. Find the nearest phone and call the airline directly to reschedule. You'll be relaxing while other passengers are still standing in line.

- Search **the Internet** for cheap fares (see "Planning Your Trip Online," earlier in the chapter).
- **Consolidators,** also known as bucket shops, are great sources for international tickets, although they usually can't beat the Internet on fares within North America. Start by looking in Sunday newspaper travel sections; U.S. travelers should focus on the *New York Times, Los Angeles Times,* and *Miami Herald.* For less-developed destinations, small travel agents who cater to immigrant communities in large cities often have the best deals. *Beware:* Bucket shop tickets are usually nonrefundable or rigged with stiff cancellation penalties, often as high as 50% to 75% of the ticket price, and some put you on charter airlines with questionable safety records. Several reliable consolidators are worldwide and available on the Net. **STA Travel** is now the world's leader in student travel, thanks to their purchase of Council Travel. It also offers good fares for travelers of all ages. **Flights.com** (© **800/TRAV-800;** www.flights. com) started in Europe and has excellent fares worldwide, but particularly to that continent. It also has "local" websites in 12 countries. **FlyCheap** (© **800/FLY-CHEAP;** www.flycheap.com) is owned by package-holiday megalith MyTravel and so has especially good access to fares for sunny destinations. **Air Tickets Direct** (© **800/778-3447;** www.airticketsdirect.com) is based in Montreal and leverages the currently weak Canadian dollar for low fares; it'll also book trips to places that U.S. travel agents won't touch, such as Cuba.

- Join **frequent-flier clubs.** Accrue enough miles, and you'll be rewarded with free flights and elite status. It's free, and you'll get the best choice of seats, faster response to phone inquiries, and prompter service if your luggage is stolen, your flight is canceled or delayed, or if you want to change your seat. You don't need to fly to build frequent-flier miles—**frequent-flier credit cards** can provide thousands of miles for doing your everyday shopping.

- For many more tips about air travel, including a rundown of the major frequent-flier credit cards, pick up a copy of *Frommer's Fly Safe, Fly Smart* (Wiley Publishing, Inc.).

BY CAR

If you don't drive your own vehicle to Virginia, you should rent one to see the state. You'll have optimum flexibility to visit the rural beauties, including the plantations and Civil War battlefields. And, of course, two of the state's most scenic attractions, the Skyline Drive and Blue Ridge Parkway, are motoring destinations. Only in northern Virginia, Richmond, and Hampton Roads will you encounter heavy rush-hour traffic.

Visitors arriving in Virginia by car from the northeast do so via **I-95,** which runs north-south across the state (note that I-95 is undergoing several major long-term construction projects, especially at the Capital Beltway [I-495] junction in northern Virginia and south of Petersburg near the North Carolina line. From western

---

Tips Driving the Civil War Trails

One advantage of touring by car is that you can follow the state's Civil War Trails. These sign-posted driving tours follow the Shenandoah battles, the Peninsula campaign of 1862, the battles from Manassas to Fredericksburg, Lee vs. Grant as the Union drove south to Richmond in 1864, and Lee's Retreat from Petersburg to Appomattox in 1865. Call © 888/CIVIL-WAR; www.civilwartrails.org.

Maryland and eastern Tennessee, the major highway is **I-81,** which runs north-south the entire length of the state through the Shenandoah Valley and Southwest Highlands. Be aware that both I-95 and I-81 are heavy-duty truck routes, and accidents are common, so be especially careful while driving on them. Major western entrance points are from West Virginia via **I-77** and **I-64.** The latter runs east-west across the state between Covington and Norfolk. In northern Virginia, **I-66** traverses the state east-west between Arlington and I-81 at Strasburg. Be aware that I-66 can slow to a snail's pace during rush hours in northern Virginia.

The **Virginia Department of Transportation,** 1401 E. Broad St., Richmond, VA 23219 (© **804/786-5731;** www.virginiadot.org), publishes a free list of road construction projects, and it maintains a 24-hour-a-day **Highway Helpline** (© **800/367-ROAD**) for information about road conditions and to report emergencies. It has live Web cams of key northern Virginia and Hampton Roads highways and posts road condition maps online. Call © **800/792-2800** to check on conditions in Hampton Roads' often-congested tunnels.

The Virginia Tourism Corporation distributes a detailed **state road map** as well as one that highlights the scenic drives (see "Visitor Information," earlier).

Most **car-rental companies** operate in Virginia's major metropolitan areas and at all but the smallest of airports.

BY TRAIN

Amtrak trains (© **800/USA-RAIL;** www.amtrak.com) are better for getting to and from Virginia than for getting around the state. The high-speed Acela, Metroliner service, and other northeast corridor trains connect New York to Union Station in Washington, D.C., where riders can board the Metrorail subway to Arlington and Alexandria. All Amtrak trains between New York and Florida stop at Washington, D.C., and Richmond; some stop at Alexandria, Quantico, and Fredericksburg. Another train follows this route from New York to Richmond, then heads east to Newport News via Williamsburg. From Newport News, Amtrak's Thruway bus service connects to Norfolk and Virginia Beach. Some east- and westbound trains to and from Washington stop at Charlottesville, Staunton, and Clifton Forge. From Clifton Forge, a Thruway bus connects to Roanoke.

BY ESCORTED BUS TOUR

Several travel companies offer **escorted bus tours** of the historic sites in Virginia and Pennsylvania. These 1-week or longer tours usually start in Washington, D.C, and visit Mount Vernon, Fredericksburg, Williamsburg, Richmond, Charlottesville, the Shenandoah National Park, and Harpers Ferry. From there they go on to Gettysburg and the Amish Country in Pennsylvania before ending in Philadelphia. You'll have to pay extra to get to Washington and home from Philadelphia,

Virginia Driving Times & Distances

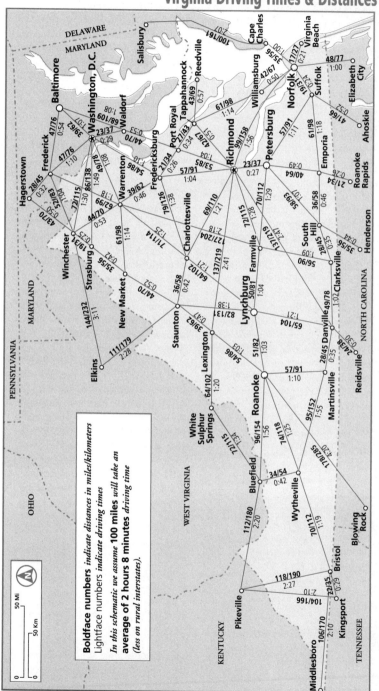

Boldface numbers *indicate distances in miles/kilometers*
Lightface numbers *indicate driving times*

In this schematic we assume **100 miles will take an average of 2 hours 8 minutes** *driving time (less on rural interstates).*

but meals, lodging, and bus transportation are included in the tour prices, which start at $1,000 per person double occupancy.

Most companies prefer that you book through a travel agent, but you can contact **Tauck Tours** (© **800/788-7855;** www.tauck.com) and **Mayflower Tours** (© **800/323-7604;** www.mayflowertours.com) directly to see what they're offering. **Globus and Cosmos Tours** require you to book through a travel agent, but you can order brochures on their website (www.globusandcosmos.com).

You can also make 1-day escorted bus tours from Washington, D.C., to Williamsburg with the venerable **Gray Line** (© **800/862-1400** or 301/386-8300; fax 301/386-2024; www.graylinedc.com). The 14-hour Williamsburg tour is offered 2 days a week from April through October and costs $70 for adults, $60 for children. Overnight trips from Washington to Williamsburg also are available.

11 The Active Vacation Planner

Although Virginia is best known for its multitude of historic sites, it's also home to a host of outdoor activities. You'll find them described in the chapters that follow, but here's a brief overview of the best places to move your muscles, with tips on how to get more detailed information.

The Virginia Tourism Corporation publishes an annual *Virginia Outdoors* magazine that gives a comprehensive rundown of the activities available, a calendar of outdoor events, and a list of the many outfitters and tour companies operating in the state. Call © **800/827-3325** for a copy, or see "Visitor Information," earlier.

BICYCLING & MOUNTAIN BIKING Bicycling is popular throughout Virginia, and with good reason. Most of the state's scenic highways are open to bicycles: the 17-mile **George Washington/Mount Vernon Memorial Parkway** between Arlington and Mount Vernon (see chapter 4), the 105-mile **Skyline Drive** above the Shenandoah Valley (see chapter 7), the 218-mile **Blue Ridge Parkway** in the Southwest Highlands (see chapter 8), and the 22-mile **Colonial Parkway** between Jamestown and Yorktown (see chapter 10), to name the most popular.

The state also has three excellent "rails-to-trails" parks, in which old railroad beds have been turned into biking and hiking avenues. In northern Virginia there's the **Washington & Old Dominion Trail,** which begins in Arlington and ends 45 miles away at Purcellville in the rolling hills of the Hunt Country (see the Arlington section in chapter 4). The Southwest Highlands boasts two dramatic trails through some of the state's finest mountain scenery (see chapter 8). The 34-mile **Virginia Creeper Trail** begins in the Mount Rogers National Recreation Area high up on the flanks of Whitetop Mountain, Virginia's second highest peak, and descends to Abingdon (see the Abingdon section in chapter 8). Near Wytheville, the 55-mile **New River Trail** follows the New River, which actually is one of the world's oldest rivers (see the Wytheville section in chapter 8). Outfitters along both trails rent bikes and provide shuttle services so you don't have to ride both ways—particularly handy on the Virginia Creeper Trail, which drops more than 3,000 feet from Whitetop Mountain to Damascus, near Abingdon.

Down on the coast, bikers can ride along the **Virginia Beach Boardwalk,** through the natural beauty of **First Landing/Seashore State Park** and **Back Bay National Wildlife Refuge,** and along all of the flat Eastern Shore roads (see chapter 11).

Virginia is crossed by sections of three major Interstate Bicycle routes. The Maine-to-Virginia **Route 1** runs 150 miles from Arlington to Richmond and connects to 130 miles of the Virginia-to-Florida **Route 17** from Richmond to the North Carolina line at Suffolk. Some 500 miles of the TransAmerican Bicycle Trail (Route 76) runs from the Kentucky line to Yorktown, including a stretch through Mount Rogers National Recreation Area in the Southwest Highlands. For strip maps of these routes, contact **Adventure Cycling Association,** P.O. Box 8308W, Missoula, MT 59807 (© **800/755-2453** or 406/721-1776; fax 406/721-8754; www.adv-cycling.org).

Mountain bikers can find plenty of trails, especially in Mount Rogers National Recreation Area and in the George Washington and Jefferson National Forests, which occupy parts of the Shenandoah Valley (see chapter 8) and the Southwest Highlands (see chapter 7). For details about the latter, contact the **George Washington and Jefferson National Forests,** 210 Franklin Rd. SW, Roanoke, VA 24004 (© **540/265-6054;** www.southern region.fs.fed.us/gwj). *Mountain Bike Virginia,* by Scott Adams (Beachway Press, 1995), is a very handy atlas to Virginia's best trails, with excellent maps.

The **Virginia Department of Transportation's Bicycle Coordinator,** 1401 E. Broad St., Richmond, VA 23219 (© **800/835-1203** or 804/786-2964; www.virginiadot.org), publishes the annual *Virginia Bicycling Guide,* which describes Virginia's routes and trials and lists local bike clubs and relevant publications. Contact the department or the Virginia Tourism Corporation (see "Visitor Information," earlier) for a free copy.

BIRD-WATCHING The big bird-watching draws in Virginia are waterfowl nesting in the flatlands and marshes along the coast on the Atlantic Flyway. Chincoteague National Wildlife Refuge on Assateague Island and Back Bay National Wildlife Refuge below Virginia Beach offer first-rate bird-watching. Chincoteague is especially good on Thanksgiving weekend, the only time the refuge's back roads are open to vehicles. See chapter 11.

BOATING The Chesapeake Bay and its many tributaries, including the Potomac, Rappahannock, York, and James rivers, are perfect for boating. In fact, you can come away from eastern Virginia with the impression that every other home has a boat and trailer sitting in the yard. Marinas abound on the Northern Neck (see chapter 5), and you can rent boats in Hampton Roads and over on the Eastern Shore, where the back bays of Chincoteague and Wachapreague await to be explored from a fish's-eye view (see chapter 11).

A detailed map showing public access to the Chesapeake and its tributaries is available from the **Virginia Department of Conservation and Recreation,** 203 Governor St., Suite 302, Richmond, VA 23219 (© **804/ 786-1712;** www.dcr.state.va.us).

CANOEING, KAYAKING & RIVER-RAFTING Kayakers and canoeists will find easy, quiet paddling on the backwater creeks of the Northern Neck (see chapter 5) and in Hampton Roads and on the Eastern Shore (see chapter 11). Outfitters in Reedville, Virginia Beach, and Chincoteague rent both canoes and kayaks and offer guided excursions of the creeks and back bays. **Atlantic Kayak Company,** 1201 N. Royal St., Alexandria, VA 22124 (© **703/838-9072;** www.atlantickayak.com), has kayaking packages on the local waters of Northern Virginia and to the Northern Neck and the Eastern Shore.

Up in the hills, the Shenandoah, James, and Maury rivers can be either quiet or raging, depending on how much rain has dropped recently. Depending on the state of the rivers, outfitters in Scottsville near Charlottesville (see chapter 6), near Front Royal, Luray, and Lexington in the Shenandoah Valley (see the "Rafting, Canoeing & Kayaking on the Shenandoah River" box in chapter 7), and in Richmond (the only city in the country with white-water rafting right in town; see chapter 9) provide canoe- or river-rafting excursions. White-water rafting is most likely during spring and late fall. When the water is low during summer, multitudes forget canoes and rafts and lazily float down the rivers in inner tubes.

FISHING The waters that are so great for boating are stocked with a wide array of fish. The best rivers for fishing include the South Fork of the Shenandoah near Front Royal for smallmouth bass and redbreast sunfish; the James between Richmond and Norfolk for smallmouth bass and catfish; the New near Wytheville for walleye, yellow perch, musky, and smallmouth bass; the Rappahannock from Fredericksburg to the Northern Neck for smallmouth bass and catfish; and the Chickahominy near Williamsburg for largemouth bass, chain pickerel, bluegill, white perch, and channel catfish.

The mountains have 2,800 miles of trout streams, many stocked annually. You can go trout fishing in Shenandoah National Park (see chapter 7), and guides are available in Lexington (chapter 7) and Abingdon (chapter 8).

From Virginia Beach and Chincoteague you can go deep-sea fishing on charter and party boats in search of bluefish, flounder, cobia, gray and spotted trout, sharks, and other ocean-dwellers (see chapter 11).

The **Virginia Department of Game and Inland Fisheries,** 4010 W. Broad St., Richmond, VA 23230 (© **804/ 367-1000;** www.dgif.state.va.us), publishes an annual freshwater-fishing guide and regulations pamphlet detailing licensing requirements and regulations. Available at most sporting-goods stores, marinas, and bait shops, licenses are required except on the first Saturday and Sunday in June, which are free fishing days.

GOLF You can play golf almost anytime and anywhere in Virginia, given the state's mild climate and more than 130 courses, but serious duffers head to **Williamsburg** and the Golden Horseshoe, Green, and Gold courses at the Williamsburg Inn, and the links at Kingsmill Resort, home of the annual PGA Michelob Classic in October (see chapter 10). An hour's drive away, the PGA-owned Tournament Players Club in **Virginia Beach** is one of the country's best upscale links (see chapter 11). Up in the mountains, the Homestead's beautiful course in Hot Springs has the nation's oldest first tee, in continuous use since 1890 (see chapter 7). Wintergreen Resort near Charlottesville also has an excellent course (see chapter 6).

The best source for information is the Virginia Tourism Corporation's annual *Virginia Golf Guide,* which lists and describes the state's courses (see "Visitor Information," earlier).

HIKING & BACKPACKING The same trails that make Virginia so popular with bicyclists also make it a hiker's heaven. Both good and easy are the state's rails-to-trails paths along old railroad beds (see "Bicycling & Mountain Biking," above). Some 450 miles of the **Appalachian Trail** snake through Virginia, nearly climbing Mount Rogers and paralleling the Blue Ridge Parkway and the Skyline Drive in many places. The best backcountry trails are in **Shenandoah National Park** (see chapter 7) and **Mount Rogers National Recreation Area** (see chapter 8), with less-traveled trails in the George Washington and Jefferson national forests.

For information and maps of the Appalachian Trail, contact the **Appalachian Trail Conference,** P.O. Box 807, Harpers Ferry, WV 25425-0807 (© **304/535-6331;** www.atconf. org). Three good books give trail-by-trail descriptions. *The Trails of Virginia: Hiking the Old Dominion,* by Allen de Hart (University of North Carolina Press, 1995), is the most comprehensive guide to Virginia's trails. *The Hiker's Guide to Virginia,* by Randy Johnson (Falcon Press, 1992), is a slimmer, easier-to-carry volume, as is *Hiking Virginia's National Forests,* by Karin Wuertz-Schaeffer (Globe Pequot Press, 1994), which covers trails in the George Washington and Jefferson National Forests in the Shenandoah Valley and Southwest Highlands.

HORSEBACK RIDING Equestrians will find stables with horses to rent to ride on hundreds of miles of public horse trails in Virginia, the majority of them in the Shenandoah Valley (chapter 7) and the Southwest Highlands (chapter 8). The granddaddy of all trails, the **Virginia Highlands Horse Trail,** runs the length of Mount Rogers National Recreation Area, which has campgrounds especially for horse owners. Horses are also permitted on the Virginia Creeper Trail and the New River Trail. You can rent horses at the Mount Rogers National Recreation Area and along the New River Trail (see chapter 8). Shenandoah National Park has guided trail rides (see chapter 7). Ironically, few stables rent horses in Northern Virginia's Hunt Country, where just about everyone who rides owns a horse (see chapter 4).

The **Virginia Horse Council,** 2799 Stratford Rd., Richmond, VA 23225 (© **804/330-0345;** www.virginiahorse. com), publishes a list of public horse trails and stables statewide.

WATERSPORTS To indulge your passion for surfing, jet-skiing, waverunning, sailing, or scuba diving, head for Virginia Beach, which has it all in abundance. See chapter 11.

12 Tips on Accommodations

Virginia has a vast array of accommodations, from rock-bottom roadside motels to some of the nation's finest resorts. Whether you spend a pittance or a bundle depends on your budget and tastes. You can enjoy "champagne tastes on a beer budget"—if you plan carefully and possess a little knowledge of how the hotel industry works.

The Virginia Tourism Corporation (see "Visitor Information," earlier in the chapter) publishes a directory of all the state's accommodations.

SAVING ON YOUR HOTEL ROOM

In this book we give each hotel's **rack rate,** which is the maximum rate that it charges for a room. Hardly anybody pays this price, however. To lower the cost of your room:

- **Ask about special rates or other discounts.** Always ask whether a room less expensive than the first one quoted is available, or whether any special rates apply to you. You may qualify for corporate, student, military, senior, or other discounts. Mention membership in AAA, AARP, frequent-flier programs, or trade unions, which may entitle you to special deals as well. Find out the hotel policy on children— do kids stay free in the room or is there a special rate?
- **Dial direct.** When booking a room in a chain hotel, you'll often get a better deal by calling the individual hotel's reservation desk than at the chain's main number.
- **Book online.** Many hotels offer Internet-only discounts, or supply

rooms to Priceline, Hotwire or Expedia at rates much lower than the ones you can get through the hotel itself.

- **Remember the law of supply and demand.** Resort hotels are most crowded and therefore most expensive on weekends, so discounts are usually available for midweek stays. Business hotels in downtown locations are busiest during the week, so you can expect big discounts over the weekend. Many hotels have high-season and low-season prices, and booking the day after high season ends can mean big discounts.
- **Look into group or long-stay discounts.** If you come as part of a large group, you should be able to negotiate a bargain rate, since the hotel can then guarantee occupancy in a number of rooms. Likewise, if you're planning a long stay (at least 5 days), you might qualify for a discount. As a general rule, expect 1 night free after a 7-night stay.
- **Avoid excess charges and hidden costs.** When you book a room, ask whether the hotel charges for parking. Use your own cellphone, pay phones, or prepaid phone cards instead of dialing direct from hotel phones, which usually have exorbitant rates. And don't be tempted by the room's minibar offerings: Most hotels charge through the nose for water, soda, and snacks. Finally, ask about local taxes and service charges, which can increase the cost of a room by 15% or more. If a hotel insists upon tacking on a surprise "energy surcharge" that wasn't mentioned at check-in or a "resort fee" for amenities you didn't use, you can often make a case for getting it removed.
- **Book an efficiency.** A room with a kitchenette allows you to shop for groceries and cook meals. This is a big money saver, especially for families on long stays.

LANDING THE BEST ROOM

Somebody has to get the best room in the house. It might as well be you.

Always ask about a corner room. They're often larger and quieter, with more windows and light, and they often cost the same as standard rooms.

When you make your reservation, ask if the hotel is renovating; if it is, request a room away from the construction. Ask about nonsmoking rooms, rooms with views, rooms with twin, queen- or king-size beds. If you're a light sleeper, request a quiet room away from vending machines, elevators, restaurants, bars, and discos. Ask for one of the rooms that have been most recently renovated or redecorated. If you aren't happy with your room when you arrive, talk to the front desk. If they have another room, they may be willing to accommodate you. Join the hotel's frequent visitor club; you may qualify for upgrades.

BED & BREAKFASTS

Virginia has several hundred bed-and-breakfasts, far too many to mention them all in this book. Most have rooms adorned with antiques or quality reproductions, luxurious touches like fresh flowers and top-drawer linens and toiletries, and gourmet breakfasts. Some even add whirlpool tubs to their bathrooms. All these niceties have a price, so bed-and-breakfasts aren't inexpensive. On the other hand, you don't have to go out for breakfast, and the hosts are usually fonts of information about where to dine and what to see and do in their areas. More than 200 of the best belong to the **Bed & Breakfast Association of Virginia,** P.O. Box 1077, Standardsville, VA 22973 (*©* **888/660-BBAV** or 540/672-6700; www.bbav.org), which publishes an annual directory of its members. The association inspects and approves the establishments it promotes. The Virginia Division of Tourism operates a **reservation service** for country inns and bed-and-breakfasts (© **800/934-9184**). Most local visitor centers will send you a list of bed-and-breakfasts in their area.

13 Suggested Itineraries

How you go about seeing Virginia will depend on your special interests—whether you're into history or into hiking, for example. Here are a few suggestions that will get you expeditiously around the state.

THE GRAND TOUR

Focus: The highlights of Virginia.
Length: 2 weeks.
Highlights: Shenandoah National Park, Staunton, Lexington, Charlottesville, Richmond, Williamsburg, Jamestown, Yorktown, Virginia Beach.
Route and major stops: This comprehensive route will take you to most of the major sites in Virginia. Although you'll need 2 weeks to see everything, it can be done in a week if you really hurry and see only the top attractions.

Start at Washington Dulles International Airport and take I-64 to Front Royal and the northern entrance to the Shenandoah National Park. From there follow the Skyline Drive to the park's Central District, where you can spend 2 nights in the park.

On Day 3 drive through Luray to the famous Civil War battlefield at New Market. Spend the night in Staunton, where you can watch Shakespeare at the outstanding Blackfriers Playhouse. Spend Day 5 exploring Staunton and nearby Lexington, one of America's great small towns.

On Day 6, take I-64 to Charlottesville, where you'll spend Day 7 seeing Monticello and the university town's other sights.

From Charlottesville take I-64 to Richmond, where you will spend Days 8 and 9 exploring the White House of the Confederacy and the state capitol's other Civil War related sites.

You will need Days 10, 11, and part of 12 to explore the colonial sites at Williamsburg, Jamestown, and Yorktown. From there, stop in Norfolk on your way to Virginia Beach, where you can unwind from your whirlwind grand tour of the Old Dominion.

COLONIAL ERA VIRGINIA

Focus: Virginia in Colonial times.
Length: 1 week.
Highlights: Williamsburg, Jamestown, Yorktown, Fredericksburg, Alexandria.
Route and major stops: This route follows the progress of Virginia's colonial settlers from Jamestown in 1607 through the plantations and towns they built along the state's great tidal rivers.

Spend your first 2 days in Williamsburg. You'll need one of them to see the town's beautifully restored Historic Area, the other to visit the original settlement at Jamestown and the great battlefield at Yorktown, where Lord Cornwallis surrendered to George Washington.

Spend Day 3 touring the great James River tobacco on Plantations on Va. 5 between Williamsburg and Richmond, then head up I-295 and I-95 to Fredericksburg. On Day 5 there, you can walk the cobblestone streets tread by Washington, James Monroe, and Thomas Jefferson.

Day 6 will take you to Old Town Alexandria via Washington's plantation home at Mount Vernon.

GREAT CIVIL WAR BATTLES

Focus: Highlights of the Civil War.
Length: 1 week.
Highlights: The major battlefields between Washington, D.C., and Petersburg.

Route and major stops: This route follows two Union attempts to capture the Confederate capital at Richmond, about 100 miles south of Washington, D.C., between 1862 and 1865.

Spend Day 1 at Manassas, site of two battles including the war's first great engagement. Spend Days 2 and 3 exploring Fredericksburg and the nearby Chancellorsville and Wilderness battlefields. Devote Days 4 and 6 to the historic sites in Richmond and the battlefields on its eastern flanks. On Day 6 drive down to Petersburg to see The Crater and other battle sites of Grant's great siege. On Day 7 follow Lee's Retreat to Appomattox, where he surrendered.

A TIPSY WINE TOUR

Focus: Virginia vineyards.
Length: 3 days.
Highlights: A good sampling of Virginia's wines within a relatively concentrated area.
Route and major stops: This trip will take you a few of Virginia's 140-plus vineyards and 50 wineries, which produce moderately good wines at moderate prices. Most are small (if this were beer, we would call them microbreweries), but together they produce enough to make Virginia the nation's fifth largest wine producing state behind California, Washington, Oregon, and New York.

They're all over the state (see "On the Wine Trail" in the following chapters), but there's a concentration of them in Hunt Country of northern Virginia. So spend your first night in Leesburg and take your pick of several vineyards in the surrounding hills.

From Leesburg, drive south on U.S. 15 to Orange County, northeast of Charlottesville, where you can visit two of the state's best: Hortonsville Vineyards, Barboursville Vineyards, and Prince Michel and Rapidan River Vineyards. The latter has a fine restaurant and accommodations, where you can spend your second night.

Spend your third night in Charlottesville, where you can sample the vintages of Jefferson Vineyards after spending a morning touring Thomas Jefferson's Monticello.

SHAKESPEARE IN THE VALLEY

Focus: Good theater in the great towns of the Shenandoah Valley and the Southwest Highlands.
Length: 6 days.
Highlights: You can see a good play every night while touring the Shenandoah Valley and Southwest Highlands. Proceeding from north to south, on Day 1 stay at Middletown's ancient Wayside Inn and see that night's play at the adjoining Wayside Theater. On Day 2 drive to Staunton for a bit of Shakespeare at the outstanding Blackfriar's Playhouse. Day 3 will put in Lexington and a play the al fresco Theater at Lime Kiln. Day 4 will be spent in Roanoke for a show at the Mill Mountain Theater. And on Days 5 and 6 you'll hit two plays in Abingdon, home of The Barter Theater. This trip is best done in summer, when all stages are lighted.

FAST FACTS: **Virginia**

American Express Call customer service (© **800/528-4800**) to report lost or stolen traveler's checks or for locations in Virginia. The main Virginia office is in Richmond at 1412A Starling Dr. (© **804/740-2030**).

Car Rentals See "Getting There & Getting Around" earlier in this chapter and in the destination chapters which follow.

Climate See "When to Go" earlier in this chapter.

Embassies & Consulates See chapter 3, "For International Visitors."

Emergencies Call ✆ **911** (no charge) for police, fire, and ambulance.

Information See "Visitor Information" earlier in this chapter.

Liquor Laws In Virginia, many grocery and convenience stores sell beer and wine, but only state-licensed Alcoholic Beverage Control (ABC) stores are permitted to sell bottles of hard liquor. Any licensed establishment (restaurant or bar) can sell drinks by the glass. The legal drinking age is 21, and photo ID may be requested.

Newspapers/Magazines Each major city in Virginia has its own daily newspaper. The *Washington Post* and *USA Today* are available at newsstands and coin boxes throughout the state.

Police To reach the police, dial ✆ **911** from any phone (no charge).

Taxes The Virginia state sales tax is 4.5% for most purchases, and a few jurisdictions add another .5% to bring the total tax to 5%. Hotel taxes vary from town to town; in most communities it's 5%, which makes the total tax on your hotel bill 9.5% or 10%. Some local jurisdictions also add a restaurant tax, which jacks up the price of food and drink by 8% to 10%.

Time Zone Virginia is on **Eastern Standard Time (EST)**, the same as New York and other East Coast cities. When it's noon in Virginia, it's 11am in Chicago, 10am in Detroit, 9am in Los Angeles, 8am in Anchorage, and 7am in Honolulu. Daylight savings time is in effect from at 2am on the first Sunday of April until 2am on the last Sunday of October (time moves ahead 1 hour in Apr, back 1 hour in Oct).

Weather See "When to Go" earlier this chapter for Virginia's climate. For current conditions in northern Virginia, call ✆ **703/936-1212**; in Richmond, call ✆ **804/268-1212**; in Roanoke, call ✆ **540/982-2303**. Elsewhere, check the front pages of the telephone directory for the local number.

3

For International Visitors

The pervasiveness of American culture around the world may make you feel that you know the USA pretty well, but leaving your own country still requires an additional degree of planning. This chapter will help prepare you for the more common problems that visitors may encounter.

1 Preparing for Your Trip

ENTRY REQUIREMENTS

Check at any U.S. embassy or consulate for current information and requirements. You can also obtain a visa application and other information online at the **U.S. State Department**'s website, at **www.travel.state.gov**.

VISAS The U.S. State Department has a **Visa Waiver Program** allowing citizens of certain countries to enter the United States without a visa for stays of up to 90 days. At press time these included Andorra, Australia, Austria, Belgium, Brunei, Denmark, Finland, France, Germany, Iceland, Ireland, Italy, Japan, Liechtenstein, Luxembourg, Monaco, the Netherlands, New Zealand, Norway, Portugal, San Marino, Singapore, Slovenia, Spain, Sweden, Switzerland, and the United Kingdom. Citizens of these countries need only a valid passport and a round-trip air or cruise ticket in their possession upon arrival. If they first enter the United States, they may also visit Mexico, Canada, Bermuda, and/or the Caribbean islands and return to the United States without a visa. Further information is available from any U.S. embassy or consulate. Canadian citizens may enter the United States without visas; they need only proof of residence.

Citizens of all other countries must have (1) a valid passport that expires at least 6 months later than the end of their visit, and (2) a tourist visa, which may be obtained without charge from any U.S. consulate.

To obtain a visa, the traveler must submit a completed application form (either in person or by mail) with a 1½-inch-square photo, and must demonstrate binding ties to a residence abroad. Usually you can obtain a visa at once or within 24 hours, but it may take longer during the summer rush from June through August. If you cannot go in person, contact the nearest U.S. embassy or consulate for directions on applying by mail. Your travel agent or airline office may also be able to provide you with visa applications and instructions. The U.S. consulate or embassy that issues your visa will determine whether you will be issued a multiple- or single-entry visa and any restrictions regarding the length of your stay.

British subjects can obtain up-to-date visa information by calling the **U.S. Embassy Visa Information Line** (© 0891/200-290) or by visiting the "Consular Services" section of the American Embassy London's website at www.usembassy.org.uk.

DRIVER'S LICENSES Foreign driver's licenses are mostly recognized in the U.S., although you may want to get an international driver's license if your home license is not in English.

Tips **Machine Readable Passports**

All travelers entering the United States under the Visa Waiver Program are now required to have a machine-readable passport. If you don't have one, you will be required to obtain a visa before coming to the United States.

MEDICAL REQUIREMENTS Unless you're arriving from an area known to be suffering from an epidemic (particularly cholera or yellow fever), inoculations or vaccinations are not required for entry into the United States. If you have a medical condition that requires **syringe-administered medications,** carry a valid, signed prescription from your physician—the Federal Aviation Administration (FAA) no longer allows airline passengers to pack syringes in their carry-on baggage without documented proof of medical need. If you have a disease that requires treatment with **narcotics,** you should also carry documented proof with you—smuggling narcotics aboard a plane is a serious offense that carries severe penalties in the U.S.

For **HIV-positive visitors,** requirements for entering the United States are somewhat vague and change frequently. According to the latest publication of *HIV and Immigrants: A Manual for AIDS Service Providers,* the Immigration and Naturalization Service (INS) doesn't require a medical exam for entry into the U.S., but INS officials may stop individuals because they look sick or because they are carrying AIDS/HIV medicine.

If an HIV-positive non-citizen applies for a non-immigrant visa, the question on the application regarding communicable diseases is tricky no matter which way it's answered. If the applicant checks "no," INS may deny the visa on the grounds that the applicant committed fraud. If the applicant checks "yes" or if INS suspects the person is HIV positive, it will deny the visa unless the applicant asks for a special waiver for visitors. This waiver is for people visiting the United States for a short time, to attend a conference, for instance, to visit close relatives, or to receive medical treatment. It can be a confusing situation. For up-to-the-minute information, contact **AIDSinfo** (② **800/448-0440,** or 301/519-6616 outside the U.S.; www. aidsinfo.nih.gov) or the **Gay Men's Health Crisis** (② **212/367-1000;** www.gmhc.org).

PASSPORT INFORMATION

Safeguard your passport in an inconspicuous, inaccessible place like a money belt. Make a copy of the critical pages, including the passport number, and store it in a safe place, separate from the passport. If you lose your passport, visit the nearest consulate of your native country as soon as possible for a replacement.

Note that the International Civil Aviation Organization (ICAO) has recommended a policy requiring that *every* individual who travels by air has his or her own passport. In response, many countries are now requiring that children be issued their own passport to travel internationally, where before those under 16 or so may have been allowed to travel on a parent or guardian's passport.

FOR RESIDENTS OF CANADA

You can pick up a passport application at one of 28 regional passport offices or most travel agencies. Canadian children who travel must have their own passport. However, if you hold a valid Canadian passport issued before December 11, 2001, that bears the name of your child, the passport remains valid for you and your child until it expires. Passports cost C$85 for those 16 years and older (valid 5 yr.), C$35 children 3 to 15 (valid 5 yr.), and C$20, children under 3 (valid for 3 yr.). Applications, which must be accompanied by two identical passport-size photographs and proof of Canadian citizenship, are available at travel agencies throughout Canada or from the central **Passport Office,** Department of Foreign Affairs and International Trade, Ottawa, ON K1A 0G3 (© **800/567-6868;** www.dfait-maeci.gc.ca/passport). Processing takes 5 to 10 days if you apply in person, or about 3 weeks by mail.

FOR RESIDENTS OF THE UNITED KINGDOM

As a member of the European Union, you need only an identity card, not a passport, to travel to other EU countries. However, if you already possess a passport, it's always useful to carry it. To pick up an application for a standard 10-year passport (5-yr. passport for children under 16), visit the nearest Passport Office, major post office, or travel agency. You can also contact the **United Kingdom Passport Service** at © **0870/571-0410** or visit its website at www.passport.gov.uk. Passports are £33 for adults and £19 for children under 16, with an additional £30 fee if you apply in person at a Passport Office. Processing takes about 2 weeks (1 week if you apply at the Passport Office).

CUSTOMS
WHAT YOU CAN BRING IN

Every visitor more than 21 years of age may bring in, free of duty, the following: (1) 1 liter of wine or hard liquor; (2) 200 cigarettes, 100 cigars (but not from Cuba), or 3 pounds of smoking tobacco; and (3) $100 worth of gifts. These exemptions are offered to travelers who spend at least 72 hours in the United States and who have not claimed them within the preceding 6 months. It is altogether forbidden to bring into the country foodstuffs (particularly fruit, cooked meats, and canned goods) and plants (vegetables, seeds, tropical plants, and the like). Foreign tourists may bring in or take out up to $10,000 in U.S. or foreign currency with no formalities; larger sums must be declared to U.S. Customs on entering or leaving, which includes filing form CM 4790. For more specific information regarding U.S. Customs, contact your nearest U.S. embassy or consulate, or the **U.S. Customs** office (© **202/927-1770** or www.customs.ustreas.gov).

WHAT YOU CAN TAKE HOME

U.K. citizens returning from a non-EU country have a customs allowance of: 200 cigarettes; 50 cigars; 250g of smoking tobacco; 2 liters of still table wine; 1 liter of spirits or strong liqueurs (over 22% volume); 2 liters of fortified wine, sparkling wine or other liqueurs; 60cc (ml) perfume; 250cc (ml) of toilet water; and £145 worth of all other goods, including gifts and souvenirs. People under 17 cannot have the tobacco or alcohol allowance. For more information, contact **HM Customs & Excise** at © **0845/010-9000** (from outside the U.K., 020/8929-0152), or consult their website at www.hmce.gov.uk.

For a clear summary of **Canadian** rules, request the booklet *I Declare,* issued by the **Canada Customs and Revenue Agency** (© **800/461-9999** in Canada, or 204/983-3500; www.ccra-adrc.gc.ca). Canada allows its citizens a C$750 exemption, and you're allowed to bring back duty-free one carton of cigarettes, one can of tobacco, 40 imperial ounces of liquor, and 50 cigars. In addition, you're allowed to mail gifts to Canada valued at less than C$60 a day, provided they're unsolicited and don't contain alcohol or tobacco (write on the package "Unsolicited gift, under $60 value"). All valuables should be declared on the Y-38 form before departure from Canada, including serial numbers of valuables you already own, such as expensive foreign cameras. *Note:* The C$750 exemption can only be used once a year and only after an absence of 7 days.

HEALTH INSURANCE

Although it's not required of travelers, health insurance is highly recommended. Unlike many European countries, the United States does not usually offer free or low-cost medical care to its citizens or visitors. Doctors and hospitals are expensive and, in most cases, will require advance payment or proof of coverage before they render their services. Policies can cover everything from the loss or theft of your baggage and trip cancellation to the guarantee of bail in case you're arrested. Good policies will also cover the costs of an accident, repatriation, or death. See "Health & Insurance" in chapter 2 for more information. Packages such as **Europ Assistance's "Worldwide Healthcare Plan"** are sold by European automobile clubs and travel agencies at attractive rates. **Worldwide Assistance Services, Inc.** (© 800/821-2828; www.worldwideassistance.com) is the agent for Europ Assistance in the U.S.

Though lack of health insurance may prevent you from being admitted to a hospital in non-emergencies, don't worry about being left on a street corner to die: The American way is to fix you now and bill the living daylights out of you later.

INSURANCE FOR BRITISH TRAVELERS Most big travel agents offer their own insurance and will probably try to sell you their package when you book a holiday. Think before you sign. **Britain's Consumers' Association** recommends that you insist on seeing the policy and reading the fine print before buying travel insurance. **The Association of British Insurers**

(© **020/7600-3333;** www.abi.org.uk) gives advice by phone and publishes *Holiday Insurance,* a free guide to policy provisions and prices. You might also shop around for better deals: Try **Columbus Direct** (© **020/7375-0011;** www.columbusdirect.net).

INSURANCE FOR CANADIAN TRAVELERS Canadians should check with their provincial health plan offices or call **Health Santé Canada** (© **613/957-2991;** www.hc-sc.gc.ca) to find out the extent of their coverage and what documentation and receipts they must take home in case they are treated in the United States.

MONEY

CURRENCY The U.S. monetary system is very simple: The most common **bills** are the $1 (colloquially, a "buck"), $5, $10, and $20 denominations. There are also $2 bills (seldom encountered), $50 bills, and $100 bills (the last two are usually not welcome as payment for small purchases). All the paper money was recently redesigned, making the famous faces adorning them disproportionately large. The old-style bills are still legal tender.

There are seven denominations of coins: 1¢ (1 cent, or a penny); 5¢ (5 cents, or a nickel); 10¢ (10 cents, or a dime); 25¢ (25 cents, or a quarter); 50¢ (50 cents, or a half-dollar); the gold-colored "Sacagawea" coin worth $1; and, the less common silver dollar.

Note: The "foreign-exchange bureaus" common in Europe are rare even at airports in the U.S., and nonexistent outside major cities. It's best not to change foreign money (or traveler's checks in a currency other than U.S. dollars) at a small-town bank, or even a branch in a big city; in fact, leave any currency other than U.S. dollars at home—it may prove a greater nuisance to you than it's worth.

TRAVELER'S CHECKS Though traveler's checks are widely accepted, make sure that they're denominated in

U.S. dollars, as foreign-currency checks are often difficult to exchange. The three traveler's checks that are most widely recognized—and least likely to be denied—are **Visa, American Express,** and **Thomas Cook.** Be sure to record the numbers of the checks, and keep that information in a separate place in case they get lost or stolen. Most businesses are good about taking traveler's checks, but you're better off cashing them in at a bank (in small amounts) and paying in cash. *Remember:* You'll need identification, such as a driver's license or passport, to change a traveler's check.

CREDIT CARDS & ATMS   Credit cards are the most widely used form of payment in the United States: **Visa** (Barclaycard in Britain), **MasterCard** (Eurocard in Europe, Access in Britain, Chargex in Canada), **American Express, Diners Club, Discover,** and **Carte Blanche.** There are, however, some stores and restaurants that do not take credit cards, so be sure to ask in advance. Most businesses display a sticker near their entrance to let you know which cards they accept. (*Note:* Businesses may require a minimum purchase, usually around $10, to use a credit card.)

It is strongly recommended that you bring at least one major credit card. You must have a credit or charge card to rent a car. Hotels and airlines usually require a credit-card imprint as a deposit, and in an emergency a credit card can be priceless.

You'll find **automated teller machines (ATMs)** on just about every block—at least in almost every town—across the country. Some ATMs will allow you to draw U.S. currency against your bank and credit cards. Check with your bank before leaving, and remember that you will need your personal identification number (PIN) to do so. Most accept Visa, Master-Card, and American Express, as well as ATM cards from other U.S. banks.

Expect to be charged up to $3 per transaction, however, if you're not using your own bank's ATM.

One way around these fees is to ask for cash back at grocery stores that accept ATM cards and don't charge usage fees. Of course, you'll have to purchase something first.

ATM cards with major credit card backing, known as "debit cards," are now a commonly acceptable form of payment in most stores and restaurants. Debit cards draw money directly from your checking account. Some stores enable you to receive "cash back" on your debit-card purchases as well.

SAFETY
GENERAL SUGGESTIONS   Although tourist areas are generally safe, U.S. urban areas tend to be less safe than those in Europe or Japan. You should always stay alert. This is particularly true of large American cities. If you're in doubt about which neighborhoods are safe, don't hesitate to make inquiries with the hotel front desk staff or the local tourist office.

Avoid deserted areas, especially at night, and don't go into parks after dark unless there's a concert or similar occasion that will attract a crowd.

Avoid carrying valuables with you on the street, and keep expensive cameras or electronic equipment bagged up or covered when not in use. If you're using a map, try to consult it inconspicuously—or better yet, study it before you leave your room. Hold onto your pocketbook, and place your billfold in an inside pocket. In theaters, restaurants, and other public places, keep your possessions in sight.

Always lock your room door—don't assume that once you're inside you are automatically safe and no longer need to be aware of your surroundings. Hotels are open to the public, and in a large hotel, security may not be able to screen everyone who enters.

> **Tips   Telephone Tips**
>
> - **To place a direct call from your home country to the United States:** Dial the international access code (0011 in Australia; 00 in Ireland, New Zealand and the U.K.), plus the 3-digit area code and 7-digit local number (for example, 011-804/000-0000). Calls from Canada to the U.S. do not require a country code.
> - **To place a long-distance call within the United States:** Dial "1" followed by the 3-digit area code and the 7-digit local number (for example, when calling Richmond, dial 1-804/000-0000).
> - **To place a direct call from the United States to your home country:** Dial the international access code (011) followed by the country code (Australia 61, Republic of Ireland 353, New Zealand 64, U.K./Northern Ireland 44). For calls from the U.S. to Canada, just dial "1" followed by the area code and local number.
> - **To reach directory assistance ("information"):** Dial ℂ **411** for local numbers. For long distance information, dial 1 followed by the appropriate area code and ℂ **555-1212**.

DRIVING SAFETY   Driving safety is important too, and carjacking is not unprecedented. Question your rental agency about personal safety and ask for a traveler-safety brochure when you pick up your car. Obtain written directions—or a map with the route clearly marked—from the agency showing how to get to your destination. (Many agencies now offer the option of renting a cellphone for the duration of your car rental; check with the agent when you pick up the car. Otherwise, contact **InTouch USA** at ℂ **800/872-7626** or www.intouch usa.com for short-term cellphone rental.) If possible, arrive and depart during daylight hours.

If you drive off a highway and end up in a dodgy-looking neighborhood, leave the area as quickly as possible. If you have an accident, even on the highway, stay in your car with the doors locked until you assess the situation or until the police arrive. If you're bumped from behind on the street or are involved in a minor accident with no injuries, and the situation appears to be suspicious, motion to the other driver to follow you. Never get out of your car in such situations. Go directly to the nearest police precinct, well-lit service station, or 24-hour store.

Park in well-lit and well-traveled areas whenever possible. Always keep your car doors locked, whether the vehicle is attended or unattended. Never leave any packages or valuables in sight. If someone attempts to rob you or steal your car, don't try to resist the thief/carjacker. Report the incident to the police department immediately by calling ℂ **911.**

2 Getting to & Around the U.S.

Most U.S. and several international airlines offer service from Europe to Washington Dulles International Airport (see "Getting There & Getting Around," in chapter 2). You can get here from Australia and New Zealand via **Air New Zealand** (www.airnz.com), **Qantas** (www.qantas.com), **American** (www.americanair.com), and **United** (www.ual.com), with a change of planes in Los Angeles. Call the airlines' local offices or contact your travel agent, and ask about promotional fares and discounts.

From Great Britain, **Virgin Atlantic Airways** (© **800/662-8621** in the U.S. or 01/293-74-77-47 in the U.K.; www.virgin-atlantic.com) has attractive deals on its flights from London and Manchester to Washington Dulles.

Canadians should check with **Air Canada** (© **800/776-3000**; www.air canada.ca), which flies to both Washington Dulles and Washington Reagan National.

AIRFARES Whichever airline you choose, always ask about **advance purchase excursion (APEX)** fares, which represent substantial savings over regular fares. Most require tickets to be bought 21 days prior to departure.

On the Internet, the European Travel Network (ETN) operates a site at **www.discount-tickets.com**, which offers cut-rate prices on international airfares to the United States, accommodations, car rentals, and tours. Another site to click on for discount fares worldwide is **OnlineBookingEngines.com**.

IMMIGRATION & CUSTOMS CLEARANCE Visitors arriving by air, no matter what the port of entry, should cultivate patience and resignation before setting foot on U.S. soil. Getting through immigration control can take as long as 2 hours on some days, especially on summer weekends, so be sure to carry this guidebook or something else to read. This is especially true in the aftermath of the September 11, 2001, terrorist attacks, when security clearances have been considerably beefed up at U.S. airports.

People traveling by air from Canada, Bermuda, and certain countries in the Caribbean can sometimes clear Customs and Immigration at the point of departure, which is much quicker.

GETTING AROUND THE U.S.

BY PLANE Some large airlines (for example, Northwest and Delta) offer travelers on their transatlantic or transpacific flights special discount tickets under the name **Visit USA,** allowing mostly one-way travel from one U.S. destination to another at very low prices. These discount tickets are not on sale in the United States and must be purchased abroad in conjunction with your international ticket. This system is the best, easiest, and fastest way to see the United States at a low cost. You should obtain information well in advance from your travel agent or the office of the airline concerned, since the conditions attached to these discount tickets can be changed without advance notice.

BY TRAIN Long-distance trains in the United States are operated by **Amtrak** (© **800/USA-RAIL**; www. amtrak.com), the national passenger rail corporation, which has a number of stations in Virginia. See "Getting There & Getting Around," in chapter 2, for information about Amtrak's services to and within the state.

International visitors (excluding Canada) can buy a **USA Rail Pass,** good for 15 or 30 days of unlimited travel on Amtrak (© **800/USA-RAIL**; www.amtrak.com). The pass is available through many overseas travel agents. Prices in 2003 for a 15-day pass were $295 off-peak, $440 peak; a

---

(*Tips* **A Paper Trail**

Make copies of all your travel papers (passport, visas, plane tickets), and leave them with someone at home should you need a document faxed in an emergency.

Tips   The Right Side Is the "Right" Side

In the United States we drive on the **right side of the road** as in Europe, not on the left side as in the United Kingdom, Australia, New Zealand, and South Africa.

30-day pass costs $385 off-peak, $550 peak. With a foreign passport, you can also buy passes at some Amtrak offices in the United States, including locations in San Francisco, Los Angeles, Chicago, New York, Miami, Boston, and Washington, D.C. Reservations are generally required and should be made for each part of your trip as early as possible. Regional rail passes are also available.

BY BUS   Although bus travel is often the most economical form of public transit for short hops between U.S. cities, it can also be slow and uncomfortable—certainly not an option for everyone. **Greyhound/Trailways** (© **800/231-2222;** www. greyhound.com), the sole nationwide bus line, offers an **International Ameripass** that must be purchased before coming to the United States, or by phone through the **Greyhound International Office** at the Port Authority Bus Terminal in New York City (© **212/971-0492**). (A slightly more expensive North America Discovery Pass is available at U.S. bus stations.) The Ameripass can be obtained from foreign travel agents or through Greyhound's website (order at least 21 days before your departure to the U.S.). 2004 passes cost as follows: 4 days ($140), 7 days ($199), 10 days ($249), 15 days ($289), 21 days ($339), 30 days ($379), 45 days ($429), or 60 days ($519). You can get more info at the website, or by calling © **402/330-8552.** In addition, special rates are available for seniors and students.

BY CAR   Unless you plan to spend the bulk of your vacation time in a city where walking is the best and easiest way to get around (read: New York City or New Orleans), the most cost-effective, convenient, and comfortable way to travel around the United States is by car. The interstate highway system connects cities and towns all over the country; in addition to these high-speed, limited-access roadways, there's an extensive network of federal, state, and local highways and roads. Some of the national car-rental companies include **Alamo** (© 800/462-5266; www.alamo.com), **Avis** (© 800/230-4898; www.avis.com), **Budget** (© 800/527-0700; www.budget.com), **Dollar** (© 800/800-3665; www.dollar.com), **Hertz** (© 800/654-3131; www.hertz.com), **National** (© 800/227-7368; www.nationalcar.com), and **Thrifty** (© 800/847-4389; www.thrifty.com).

If you plan to rent a car in the United States, you probably won't need the services of an additional automobile organization. If you're planning to buy or borrow a car, automobile-association membership is recommended. **AAA,** the **American Automobile Association** (© **800/222-4357;** www.aaa.com), is the country's largest auto club and supplies its members with maps, insurance, and, most important, emergency road service. The cost of joining runs from $63 for singles to $87 for two members, but if you're a member of a foreign auto club with reciprocal arrangements, you can enjoy free AAA service in America. See "Getting There & Getting Around" in chapter 2 for more information.

3 Shopping Tips

The U.S. government charges very low duties when compared to the rest of the world, so you could get some excellent deals on imported electronic goods, cameras, and clothing. Of course, it all depends on the value of your home currency versus the dollar, and how much duty you'll have to pay on your purchases when you get home.

Many computers and most other electronic equipment here use 110- to 120-volt AC (60-cycle) electricity. You will need a transformer to use them at home if your power is 220 to 240 volts AC (50 cycles). Be sure to ask the salesperson if an item has a universal power adapter.

The national "discount" chain stores consistently offer some of our best shopping deals. For televisions, VCRs, radios, camcorders, computers, and other electronic goods, go to **Best Buy, Circuit City,** and **Radio Shack.** Best Buy also has a wide selection of music. **CompUSA, Computer City,** and **Micro Center** specialize in computer hardware, accessories, and software.

Our major department store chains are **Sears, Macy's, Saks Fifth Avenue, Lord & Taylor,** and **JCPenney.** You get real deals in department stores only during sales, when selected merchandise is marked down 25% or more. The **Marshall's** and **TJ Maxx** chains carry name-brand clothing at department-store sale prices, but their stock tends to vary greatly from store to store.

Another popular source is **outlet malls,** in which manufacturers operate their own shops, selling directly to the consumer. Sometimes you can get very good buys at the outlets, especially when sales are going on. Most lingerie and china outlets have good prices when compared to those at department stores, but that's not necessarily the case with designer clothing. In addition, some manufacturers produce items of lesser quality so that they can charge less at their outlets, so inspect the quality of all merchandise carefully. The main advantage to outlet malls is that if you are looking for a specific brand—Levi's jeans, for example—the company's outlet will have it.

You'll find national chain stores, department stores, and outlet malls throughout Virginia. Many are listed under "Shopping" in the following chapters. You will also find listings in the local telephone directory.

FAST FACTS: For the International Traveler

Automobile Organizations Auto clubs will supply maps, suggested routes, guidebooks, accident and bail-bond insurance, and emergency road service. The **American Automobile Association (AAA)** is the major auto club in the United States. If you belong to an auto club in your home country, inquire about AAA reciprocity before you leave. You may be able to join AAA even if you're not a member of a reciprocal club; to inquire, call AAA (✆ **800/222-4357;** www.aaa.com). AAA has a nationwide emergency road service number: ✆ **800/AAA-HELP.**

Business Hours Offices are usually open weekdays from 9am to 5pm. Banks are open weekdays from 9am to 3pm or later and sometimes Saturday mornings. Stores typically open between 9 and 10am and close between 5 and 6pm from Monday through Saturday. Stores in shopping complexes or malls tend to stay open late: until about 9pm on weekdays and weekends, and many malls and larger department stores are open on Sundays.

Currency & Currency Exchange See "Entry Requirements" and "Money," under "Preparing for Your Trip," earlier.

Drinking Laws The legal age for purchase and consumption of alcoholic beverages is 21; proof of age is required and often requested at bars, nightclubs, and restaurants, so it's always a good idea to bring a picture ID when you go out. Beer and wine often can be purchased in supermarkets, but liquor laws vary from state to state.

Do not carry open containers of alcohol in your car or any public area that isn't zoned for alcohol consumption. The police can fine you on the spot. And nothing will ruin your trip faster than getting a citation for DUI ("driving under the influence"), so don't even think about driving while intoxicated.

Electricity Like Canada, the United States uses 110 to 120 volts AC (60 cycles), compared to 220 to 240 volts AC (50 cycles) in most of Europe, Australia, and New Zealand. If your small appliances use 220 to 240 volts, you'll need a 110-volt transformer and a plug adapter with two flat parallel pins to operate them here. Downward converters that change 220 to 240 volts to 110 to 120 volts are difficult to find in the United States, so bring one with you.

Embassies & Consulates All embassies are located in the national capital, Washington, D.C., which is just across the Potomac River from northern Virginia. Some key embassies are:

Australia: 1601 Massachusetts Ave. NW, Washington, DC 20036 (© 202/797-3000; www.austemb.org). There are Australian consulates in New York, Honolulu, Houston, Los Angeles, and San Francisco.

Canada: 501 Pennsylvania Ave. NW, Washington, DC 20001 (© 202/682-1740; www.cdnemb-washdc.org).

Republic of Ireland: 2234 Massachusetts Ave. NW, Washington, DC 20008 (© 202/462-3939). Irish consulates are in Boston, Chicago, New York, and San Francisco.

New Zealand: 37 Observatory Circle NW, Washington, DC 20008 (© 202/328-4800; www.emb.com/nzemb). New Zealand consulates are in Los Angeles, Salt Lake City, San Francisco, and Seattle.

United Kingdom: 3100 Massachusetts Ave. NW, Washington, DC 20008 (© 202/462-1340). Other consulates are in Atlanta, Boston, Chicago, Cleveland, Dallas, Houston, Los Angeles, and New York.

Emergencies Call © **911** to report a fire, call the police, or get an ambulance anywhere in the United States. This is a toll-free call (no coins are required at public telephones).

If you encounter traveler's problems, check the telephone directory to find the local **Traveler's Aid International** (www.travelersaid.org), a national, nonprofit organization geared to helping travelers in difficult straits. Their services might include reuniting families separated while traveling, providing food and/or shelter to people stranded without cash, or even offering emotional counseling. If you're in trouble, seek them out.

Gasoline (Petrol) Petrol is known as gasoline (or simply "gas"), and petrol stations are known as both gas stations and service stations. Gasoline costs about half as much in the U.S. as it does in Europe. One U.S. gallon equals 3.8 liters or .85 imperial gallons. A majority of gas stations in Virginia are convenience grocery stores with gas pumps outside; they do not service automobiles. All but a few stations have self-service gas pumps.

Holidays Banks, government offices, post offices, and many stores, restaurants, and museums are closed on the following legal national holidays: January 1 (New Year's Day), the third Monday in January (Martin Luther King Jr. Day), the third Monday in February (Presidents' Day, Washington's Birthday), the last Monday in May (Memorial Day), July 4 (Independence Day), the first Monday in September (Labor Day), the second Monday in October (Columbus Day), November 11 (Veterans' Day/Armistice Day), the fourth Thursday in November (Thanksgiving Day), and December 25 (Christmas).

Legal Aid The foreign tourist will probably never become involved with the American legal system. If you are "pulled over" for a minor infraction (for example, speeding), never attempt to pay the fine directly to a police officer; this could be construed as attempted bribery, a serious crime. Pay fines by mail, or directly into the hands of the clerk of the court. If accused of a more serious offense, say and do nothing before consulting a lawyer or your embassy or consulate. Here, the government must prove a person's guilt beyond a reasonable doubt, and everyone has the right to remain silent, whether he or she is suspected of a crime or actually arrested. If arrested, a person can make one telephone call to a party of his or her choice, and non–U.S. citizens have a right to call their embassies or consulates.

Mail Mail is delivered throughout the country by the **United States Postal Service** (www.usps.com). If you aren't sure what your address will be in the United States, mail can be sent to you, in your name, **c/o General Delivery** at the main post office of the city or region where you expect to be. You must pick it up in person and must produce proof of identity (driver's license, passport, and so on).

Generally found at intersections, **mailboxes** are blue with a red-and-white stripe and carry the inscription U.S. MAIL. If your mail is addressed to a U.S. destination, don't forget to add the five-digit postal code, or ZIP code, after the two-letter abbreviation of the state to which the mail is addressed (VA for Virginia).

Domestic postage rates are 23¢ for a postcard and 37¢ for a letter. Airmail postcards to Canada cost 60¢, while letters were 80¢. Airmail letters to other countries were 80¢ for the first ounce.

Newspapers/Magazines All over Virginia, you'll be able to buy *USA Today,* our national daily, and *The Washington Post,* one of the most highly respected dailies in the country. Every city has its own daily paper.

Taxes In the United States there is no value-added tax (VAT) or other indirect tax at the national level. Every state, county, and city has the right to levy its own local tax on all purchases, including hotel and restaurant checks, airline tickets, and so on. For Virginia's sales taxes, see "Fast Facts: Virginia," in chapter 2.

Telephone, Telegraph & Fax The telephone system in the United States is run by private corporations, so rates, especially for long-distance service and operator-assisted calls, can vary widely. Generally, hotel surcharges on long-distance and local calls are astronomical, so you're usually better off using a **public pay telephone,** which you'll find clearly marked in most public buildings and private establishments as well as on the street. Convenience grocery stores and gas stations always have them. Many convenience groceries and packaging services sell **prepaid calling cards** in denominations up to $50; these can be the least expensive way to call home. Many public phones at airports now accept American Express, MasterCard, and Visa credit cards. Local calls made from public pay phones in Virginia cost 50¢.

Calls to area codes **800, 866, 877,** and **888** are toll-free. However, calls to numbers in area codes 700 and 900 (chat lines, bulletin boards, "dating" services, and so on) can be very expensive—usually a charge of 95¢ to $3 or more per minute, and they sometimes have minimum charges that can run as high as $15 or more.

For **reversed-charge** or **collect calls,** and for **person-to-person calls,** dial 0 (zero, *not* the letter O) followed by the area code and number you want; an operator will then come on the line, and you should specify that you are calling collect, or person-to-person, or both. If your operator-assisted call is international, ask for the overseas operator.

Telegraph and telex services are provided primarily by **Western Union** (www.westernunion.com). You can bring your telegram into any Western Union office (there are hundreds across the country) or dictate it over the phone (© **800/325-6000**). You can also send money or have it sent to you, very quickly, over the Western Union system, but the fee for this service can be as much as 15% to 25% of the amount sent.

Most hotels have **fax** machines available for guest use (be sure to ask about the charge to use it), and many hotel rooms are even wired for guests' fax machines. A less expensive way to send and receive faxes may be at copy centers such as **Kinko's** (www.kinkos.com) and **The UPS Store** (formerly Mail Boxes Etc.; www.theupsstore.com), a chain of packing service shops (look in the Yellow Pages directory under "Copying" and "Packing Services," respectively). Some Kinko's and UPS stores have computers with Internet access for sending and receiving e-mail.

There are two kinds of telephone directories in the United States. The so-called **White Pages** list private and business subscribers in alphabetical order. The inside front cover lists emergency numbers for police, fire, ambulance, the coast guard, poison-control center, crime-victims hot line, and so on. The first few pages will tell you how to make long-distance and international calls, complete with country codes and area codes. Government numbers usually are on pages printed on blue paper. Printed on yellow paper, the so-called **Yellow Pages,** list all local services, businesses, industries, and churches and synagogues by type of activity, with an index at the front or back. The Yellow Pages also include city plans or detailed area maps, often showing postal zip codes and public transportation routes.

Time The continental United States is divided into four **time zones:** Eastern Standard Time (EST), Central Standard Time (CST), Mountain Standard

Time (MST), and Pacific Standard Time (PST). Alaska and Hawaii have their own zones. For example, noon in New York City (EST) is 11am in Chicago (CST), 10am in Denver (MST), 9am in Los Angeles (PST), 8am in Anchorage (AST), and 7am in Honolulu (HST). Virginia observes Eastern Standard time.

Daylight savings time is in effect from 1am on the first Sunday in April through 1am on the last Sunday in October. Daylight savings time moves the clock 1 hour ahead of standard time.

Tipping Tipping is so ingrained in the American way of life that the annual income tax of tip-earning personnel is based on how much they should have received based on their employers' gross revenues. Accordingly, they may have to pay tax on a tip you didn't give them.

Here are some rules of thumb: **bartenders,** 10% to 15% of the check; **bellhops,** at least 50¢ per bag, or $2 to $3 for a lot of luggage; **cab drivers,** 10% of the fare; **chambermaids,** $1 per day; **checkroom attendants,** $1 per garment; **hairdressers and barbers,** 15% to 20% of the bill; **waiters and waitresses,** 15% to 20% of the check; **valet parking attendants,** $1 per vehicle; **restroom attendants,** 25¢. We do not tip theater ushers, gas station attendants, or the staff at cafeterias and fast-food restaurants.

Toilets You won't find public toilets (referred to here as "restrooms") on the streets in most U.S. cities, but they can be found in hotel lobbies, bars, restaurants, museums, larger stores, railway and bus stations, or service stations. Note that restaurants and bars in resorts or heavily visited areas may reserve their restrooms for the use of their patrons.

4

Northern Virginia

America's past and present meet in northern Virginia. Linked by bridges and three subway lines to the nation's capital, it is an integral part of the sprawling Washington, D.C., metropolitan area. Yet leaving the District will take you back hundreds of years in just a few minutes and a few miles. In Alexandria, the cobblestone streets of the 18th-century Old Town still ring with the footsteps of George Washington, James Monroe, and Robert E. Lee. Arlington is the final resting place of many of our nation's warriors. South of Old Town on the Potomac, George Washington's Mount Vernon is one of the most visited American homes.

Arlington and other nearby Virginia municipalities were once primarily bedroom communities for D.C. workers, but these days, the federal government employs only 11% of the region's workforce. The 1990s high-tech boom turned northern Virginia into the richest part of the state and an economic dynamo in its own right. Although business slowed considerably following the stock market and Internet bust of 1999 and 2000, the strip running west from the Fairfax area known as Tysons Corner through Reston and Herndon to Washington Dulles International Airport is still one of the nation's major high-tech corridors. Fairfax County, which wraps around Arlington and Alexandria, has more than one million residents, making it the most populous single jurisdiction in Virginia—and almost twice the size of the District of Columbia. Tysons Corner has more office space than downtown Denver. Beyond the airport, Loudoun County is the nation's second fastest growing county despite the economic downturn.

A different picture emerges in the western part of Loudoun County and in all of Fauquier County. Out there, crowded highways eventually give way to the winding country roads, rolling hills, picturesque horse farms, charming country inns, and the villages of Virginia's renowned Hunt Country.

1 Alexandria ★ ★ ★

5 miles S of Washington, D.C.; 95 miles N of Richmond

Founded by a group of Scottish tobacco merchants, the seaport town of Alexandria came into being on a sunny day in July 1749, when a 60-acre tract of land was auctioned off in ½-acre lots. As you stroll the brick sidewalks and cobblestone streets of highly gentrified **Old Town,** the city's official historic district, you'll see more than 2,000 buildings dating from the 18th and 19th centuries. You can visit Gadsby's Tavern, where 2 centuries ago the men who created this nation discussed politics, freedom, and revolution over tankards of ale. You can stand in the doorway of the tavern where George Washington reviewed his troops for the last time, walk past Robert E. Lee's boyhood home, and sit in the pews of Christ Church where both men worshipped.

Today, Old Town Alexandria boasts an abundance of quaint shops, boutiques, art galleries, restaurants, and tourists (not to mention hordes of late-teens hanging out on Fri and Sat nights). But in this history-conscious "mother lode of Americana," the past is being ever-increasingly restored in an ongoing archaeological and historical research program. Indeed, if they weren't instantly shocked back to death by the cars jockeying for prized parking spaces, Washington and Lee would still recognize their old hometown.

ESSENTIALS
VISITOR INFORMATION
The Alexandria Convention & Visitors Association's **Ramsay House Visitor Center,** 221 King St., at Fairfax Street facing Market Square (© **800/388-9119** or 703/838-4200; 703/838-5005 for 24-hr. Alexandria events recording; fax 703/838-4683; www.funside.com), is open daily from 9am to 5pm (closed New Year's Day, Thanksgiving, and Christmas). Here you can pick up maps and brochures, find out about special events during your visit, and get information about accommodations, restaurants, sights, shopping, and whatever else. If you come by car, your first item of business should be to get a **1-day parking permit** here (see the box, below).

Be sure to pick up a free copy of *Old Town Crier* (© **703/836-9132;** www.oldtowncrier.com), a monthly magazine packed with information and news about special events, dining, shopping and entertainment.

GETTING THERE
BY PLANE   **Ronald Reagan Washington National Airport** (© **703/685-8000;** www.metwashairports.com/National) is 2 miles north of Alexandria via the George Washington Memorial Parkway. See "Getting There & Getting Around" in chapter 2 for more information. Washington's **Metrorail** (see below) provides easy transport to Alexandria via its Blue and Yellow lines. **SuperShuttle** (© **800/BLUE-VAN**) operates frequent van service daily from 6am to 10pm.

BY CAR   Going south from Washington, cross the 14th Street Bridge (I-395) and go south on the scenic George Washington Memorial Parkway, which becomes Washington Street, Alexandria's main north-south thoroughfare. A left turn on King Street will take you into the heart of Old Town. I-95 crosses the Potomac River at Alexandria; take Exit 177 (U.S. 1) and go north into Old Town.

On-street **parking** is severely limited, but you can get a 1-day pass from the Alexandria Convention & Visitors Association (see "Visitor Information," above). The passes are good at any 2-hour parking metered space but not at those restricted to Alexandria residents. They may be renewed once. You'll need your driver's license and your license plate number. There's a public garage under Market Square, opposite the visitor center on Fairfax Street north of King Street.

Tips   How to Avoid Gridlock

The Washington, D.C., area officially has the nation's third most congested traffic, behind only Los Angeles and Houston. The best way to avoid the gridlock is to stay off the roads from 6:30 to 9:30am and from 3:30 to 6:30pm on weekdays. Take the area's Metrorail or other public transportation. If you must drive during those hours, tune your car radio to WTOP (1500AM), which gives traffic reports every 10 minutes.

(*Tips* **Your First Item of Business: Free Parking**

If you come by car, your first item of business should be to get a **1-day parking permit** at the Ramsay House Visitor Center, 221 King St., at Fairfax Street facing Market Square; you'll need your driver's license and your license plate number. The permit allows you to park free at any 2-hour meter for up to 24 hours. They do not, however, apply to spaces without meters, especially those reserved for Old Town residents. In other words, park your car in a metered space, put a quarter (25¢) into the meter, go get a pass at the visitor center, then return to your car and place the permit on the dashboard.

BY TRAIN   The **Amtrak** station (© **800/USA-RAIL** or 703/836-4339; www. amtrak.com) is at 110 Callahan Dr., at King Street.

BY WASHINGTON METRORAIL   From Arlington or Washington, take the Blue or Yellow **Metrorail** (© **202/637-7000**; www.wmata.com) lines to the King Street station (it's across the tracks from Amtrak's Alexandria station). Metrorail operates Monday to Thursday from 5:30am to midnight, Friday 5:30am to 2am, Saturday 8am to 3am, and Sunday 8am to midnight. Fares range from $1.20 to $3.60 depending on time of day and length of ride.

From the King Street Station, it's about a 15-minute walk east on King Street through Old Town's rapidly developing western section. Or, you can save your shoe leather for sightseeing by boarding DASH buses numbered AT-2 or AT-5 (or the free weekend shuttle), down King Street to the corner of Fairfax Street and the door of the visitor center (see "Getting Around," below). Base fare is $1.

CITY LAYOUT

Old Town Alexandria is laid out in a simple grid. The original town grew north-south along the Potomac River, but most of what you will want to see and do today is on, or a few blocks off, King Street, the main east-west drag, between the waterfront and the King Street Metrorail station. Until a few years ago, visitors to Old Town seldom wandered west of Washington Street. But the Metro has spurred massive development near the station and an explosion of new stores and restaurants all along King Street.

Going west from the Potomac River, Union to Lee Street is the 100 block, Lee to Fairfax the 200 block, and so on. Numbers on the cross streets (more or less going north and south) are divided north and south by King Street. King to Cameron is the 100 block north, Cameron to Queen the 200 block north, and so on. King to Prince is the 100 block south, and so on.

GETTING AROUND

As a glance at the walking tour map later in this chapter will indicate, Old Town's prime historic sites are contained within several blocks. Park your car for the day, don comfortable shoes, and start walking—it's the easiest way.

From a visitor's standpoint, Alexandria's bus system, known as **DASH** (© **703/ 370-3274**; www.dashbus.com), is primarily useful for getting from the King Street Metro station to the Ramsay House Visitor Center (take buses numbered AT-2 and AT-5). A free weekend shuttle runs along King Street on weekends. DASH provides service from 5:30am to 11pm weekdays, from 7am to 10pm on weekends. There's no service New Year's Day, Thanksgiving, and Christmas. Base fare is $1 with exact fare or tokens required. The visitor center gives away route maps.

All the major **car-rental firms** are based at Ronald Reagan Washington National Airport. For a taxi, call **Alexandria Yellow Cab Company** (📞 703/549-2500) or **Alexandria White Top Cab Company** (📞 703/683-4004).

EXPLORING OLD TOWN

Whenever you come, you're sure to run into some activity or other—a jazz festival, a tea garden or tavern gambol, a quilt exhibit, a wine tasting, or an organ recital. It's all part of Alexandria's *cead mile failte* (100,000 welcomes) to visitors.

The Potomac plantations (described later in this chapter) are 9 to 15 miles south of Alexandria and are most logically visited on day trips from here.

THE TOP ATTRACTIONS

Carlyle House Not only is Carlyle House one of Virginia's most architecturally impressive 18th-century homes, it also figured prominently in American history. Patterned after Scottish-English manor houses, it was completed in 1753 by Scottish merchant John Carlyle for his bride, Sarah Fairfax, who hailed from one of Virginia's most prominent families. Then a waterfront property with its own wharf (landfills have left the house 2 blocks inland), it became a social and political center visited by many great men of the time including George Washington. But, its most important moment in history occurred in April 1755, when Maj. Gen. Edward Braddock, commander-in-chief of His Majesty's forces in North America, met here with five colonial governors and asked them to tax colonists to finance a campaign against the French and Indians. Colonial legislatures refused to comply, one of the first instances of serious friction between America and Britain. Nevertheless, Braddock made Carlyle House his headquarters during the campaign.

The house is furnished with period pieces, and the original large parlor and study have survived intact. An upstairs room houses the exhibit "A Workman's View," which explains 18th-century construction methods with hand-hewn beams and hand-wrought nails. There's seldom a wait for a tour, but if there is, you can explore the gardens or browse the gift shop, which offers jewelry, books, colonial toys, and other items. Call ahead for a schedule of special events and lectures.

121 N. Fairfax St. (near Cameron St.). 📞 703/549-2997. www.carlylehouse.org. Admission $4 adults, $2 children 11–17, free for children 10 and under. Tues–Sat 10am–4:30pm; Sun noon–4:30pm. Mandatory 40-min. tours depart on the hour and half-hour.

Tips Save with a Discounted Attraction Pass

Alexandria's Ramsay House Visitor Center usually sells money-saving **discounted attraction passes** to some of the top sights. A "Very Important Patriot Pass" recently knocked 21% off the combined admission to four museums, a guided walking tour of Old Town, and a Potomac River cruise, while a "Key Pass" included Mount Vernon and the other Potomac River plantations (see section 2, later in this chapter). The passes change from season to season, but it should pay to ask the center or check its website to see if discounts are available. *Note:* Many Alexandria attractions are closed on Monday.

Christ Church ✪ This sturdy redbrick Georgian-style church, in continuous use since 1773, would be an important national landmark even if its two most distinguished members were not George Washington and Robert E. Lee. Washington and other early members fomented revolution in the churchyard, and Lee met here with Richmond representatives, who offered him command of Virginia's army during the Civil War. You can sit in their family pews. There have, of course, been many changes since Washington's day. The bell tower, church bell, galleries, and organ were added by the early 1800s; the "wineglass" pulpit, during an 1891 restoration. The pristine white interior with wood moldings and gold trim is colonially correct, though modern heating has obviated the need for charcoal braziers and hot bricks. For the most part, the original structure remains, including the hand-blown glass in the windows.

The **Old Parish Hall** was restored in 1991 to its original appearance; it now houses a gift shop and an exhibit on the history of the church. Do walk in the weathered graveyard, Alexandria's first and only burial ground until 1805.

118 N. Washington St. (at Cameron St.). ✆ **703/549-1450.** Free admission (contributions accepted). Mon–Sat 9am–4pm; Sun 2–4:30pm. Gift shop Tues–Sat 10am–4pm; Sun 8:45am–1pm. Sun services 8, 9, 11:15am, and 5pm. Closed federal holidays.

Gadsby's Tavern Museum ✪ Alexandria was at the crossroads of early America, and the center of life in Alexandria was Gadsby's Tavern. Consisting of two buildings—a tavern dating from about 1785 and the City Tavern and Hotel (1792)—it's named for a memorable owner, Englishman John Gadsby, whose establishment was a "gentleman's tavern" renowned for elegance and comfort. The rooms have been restored to their 18th-century appearance. The second-floor ballroom, with its musicians' gallery, was the scene of Alexandria's most lavish parties, and, since 1797, George Washington's birthnight ball and banquet have been an annual tradition here. "Lantern Tours" are offered on Friday evenings from March through November. To cap off your colonial experience, you can dine at Gadsby's Tavern, which is still operating (see "Where to Dine," later).

134 N. Royal St. ✆ 703/838-4242. www.gadsbystavern.org. Admission $4 adults, $2 children 11–17, free for children 10 and under. Lantern tours $5 adults, $2 children 2–17. Museum hours Apr–Sept, Tues–Sat 10am–5pm, Sun 1–4:15pm; Oct–Mar, Tues–Sat 11am–3:15pm, Sun 1–3:15pm. Mandatory 30-min. tours begin 15 min. before and after the hour. Lantern tours Mar–Nov, Fri 7–9:15pm.

Lee-Fendall House *Kids* Light-Horse Harry Lee never actually lived in this Greek Revival–style house, although he was a visitor, as was his friend George Washington. Light-Horse Harry sold the original lot to Philip Richard Fendall (a Lee on his mother's side), who built the house in 1785. It was home to 37 Lees of Virginia until 1903. John L. Lewis, the American labor leader, was its last private owner; his estate sold it to the Virginia Trust for Historic Preservation, which opened it as a museum in 1974. Today, it's a treasure of Lee family furniture, heirlooms, and documents. You shouldn't have to wait long for a 30-minute guided tour, which will interpret the home as it was between 1850 and 1870 and offer insight into Victorian family life. You'll also see the award-winning garden with its magnolia and chestnut trees, roses, and boxwood-lined paths.

614 Oronoco St. (at Washington St.). ✆ 703/548-1789. www.leefendallhouse.org. Admission $4 adults, $2 children 11–17, free for children 10 and under. Tues–Sat 10am–4pm; Sun 1–4pm. Closed mid-Dec to Jan. Mandatory 30-min. tours depart on hour and half-hour.

Stabler-Leadbeater Apothecary Museum Beginning in 1792, this landmark drugstore was run for five generations by the same family. Its early patrons included George Washington and Robert E. Lee, who purchased the paint for

---

Fun Fact   **Signing Brothers**

The only brothers to sign the Declaration of Independence were Virginians Richard Henry "Light-Horse Harry" Lee and Francis Lightfoot Lee.

Arlington House here. Gothic Revival decorative elements and Victorian-style doors were added in the 1860s. When it went out of business in 1933, it had been the second-oldest pharmacy in continuous operation in America.

A recording guides you around the displays, which include about 900 of the original hand-blown gold leaf–labeled bottles (the most valuable collection of antique medicinal bottles in the United States), patent medicines, and equipment for bloodletting. Among the shop's documentary records is an 1802 epistle from Mount Vernon: "Mrs. Washington desires Mr. Stabler to send by the bearer a quart bottle of his best Castor Oil and the bill for it."

Note: Extensive renovations are planned through 2004, so call ahead to make sure the museum is open.

105–107 S. Fairfax St. (between King and Prince sts.). ✆ 703/836-3713. www.apothecary.org. Admission $2.50 adults, $2 students 11–17, free for children 10 and under. Mon–Sat 10am–4pm; Sun 1–5pm. Closed New Year's Day, Thanksgiving, and Christmas.

MORE ATTRACTIONS

Alexandria Black History Resource Center   Located in a 1940s building that originally housed the black community's first public library, the Black History Resource Center exhibits historical objects, photographs, documents, and memorabilia relating to African Americans in Alexandria from the 18th century on. In addition to the permanent collection, the museum presents rotating exhibits. Optional guided tours take about 30 minutes.

638 N. Alfred St. ✆ 703/838-4356. www.alexblackhistory.org. Free admission. Tues–Sat 10am–4pm.

The Athenaeum   A handsome Greek Revival building with a classic portico and Doric columns, the Athenaeum is home to the Northern Virginia Fine Arts Association. Art exhibits here run the gamut from Matisse lithographs to shows of East Coast artists. The building, which dates from 1851, originally contained the Bank of the Old Dominion. The bank's operations were interrupted by the Civil War, when Yankee troops used the building as their headquarters. Today, it hosts performances by the Alexandria Ballet. Guided tours are available on request.

201 Prince St. (at Lee St.). ✆ 703/548-0035. Free admission (donations appreciated). Wed–Fri 11am–3pm; Sun 1–4pm. Call for Sat hours. Gallery shows April–Nov.

Fort Ward Museum and Historic Site   If you're a Civil War buff, you will enjoy taking a short drive from Old Town to this 45-acre museum, park, and Union fort that President Lincoln ordered erected as part of a system called the "Defenses of Washington." About 90% of the earthwork walls are preserved, and the Northwest Bastion has been restored, with 6 mounted guns (there were originally 36) facing south waiting for the Confederates who never came. You can explore the fort as well as replicas of the Ceremonial Entrance Gate and an officers' hut. A museum on the premises houses Civil War objects. Give yourself an hour to see all three attractions.

4301 W. Braddock Rd. ✆ 703/838-4848. www.fortward.org. Free admission. Fort, daily 9am–sunset; museum, Tues–Sat 9am–5pm; Sun noon–5pm. From Old Town, follow King St. west, go right on Kenwood St., then left on W. Braddock Rd. Continue for ¾ mile to the entrance on the right.

Friendship Firehouse   Alexandria's first firefighting organization, the Friendship Fire Company, was established in 1774. As the city grew, the company attracted increasing recognition, not only for its firefighting efforts but also for its ceremonial and social presence at parades and other public occasions. Ironically, Friendship's building at 107 S. Alfred St. was destroyed by fire in 1855. Today's museum is in the brick building erected on the same spot in the fashionable Italianate style. Local lore has it that George Washington was a founding member, active firefighter, and purchaser of its first fire engine, although extensive research does not bear out these stories. This museum not only exhibits firefighting paraphernalia dating back to the 18th century, it also documents the Friendship Company's efforts to claim Washington as one of their own. Tours are given by the staff on request; they take about 20 minutes.

107 S. Alfred St. (between King and Prince sts.). ℂ **703/838-3891** or 703/838-4994. Free admission. Fri–Sat 10am–4pm; Sun 1–4pm.

The Lyceum   Another distinguished Greek Revival building, the Lyceum is a museum focusing on Alexandria's history from colonial times through the 20th century. It features changing exhibits and an ongoing series of lectures, concerts, and educational programs. An adjoining nonprofit shop carries books, maps, toys, and gifts. Even without its manifold offerings, the brick-and-stucco Lyceum itself merits a visit. Built in 1839, it was designed in the Doric temple style (with imposing white columns) to serve as a lecture, meeting, and concert hall. The first floor originally contained the Alexandria Library and natural science and historical exhibits. It was an important center of Alexandria's cultural life until the Civil War, when Union forces took it over for use as a hospital.

201 S. Washington St. ℂ **703/838-4994**. www.alexandriahistory.org. Free admission. Mon–Sat 10am–5pm; Sun 1–5pm.

Old Presbyterian Meeting House   Presbyterian congregations have worshipped in Virginia since Jamestown days, when the Rev. Alexander Whittaker converted Pocahontas. Scottish pioneers established this brick church in 1774.

The Boyhood Home of Robert E. Lee

In 1812, American Revolution cavalry hero Gen. Henry "Light-Horse Harry" Lee moved his wife, Ann Hill Carter, and their family from Stratford Hall Plantation on the Northern Neck (see chapter 5) to a Federal-style mansion at 607 Oronoco Street in Alexandria. One of the Lee's children was Robert E. Lee, then a 5-year-old, who grew up to become the commander of the Confederate Army of Northern Virginia.

George Washington was an occasional guest of earlier occupants, Col. and Mrs. William Fitzhugh. In 1804, the Fitzhughs' daughter, Mary Lee, married Martha Washington's grandson, George Washington Parke Custis, in the drawing room. The Custises' daughter later married Robert E. Lee. Years after, the drawing room was named the "Lafayette Room" to commemorate a visit by General Lafayette, a comrade of Light-Horse Harry during the American Revolution, to Ann Hill Carter Lee in October 1824.

Built in 1785, the house once operated as a museum known as "The Boyhood Home of Robert E. Lee." It's now a private residence.

Though it wasn't George Washington's church, the Old Meeting House bell tolled continuously for 4 days after his death in December 1799, and Presbyterian, Episcopal, and Methodist ministers preached memorial services from its pulpit.

Many famous Alexandrians are buried in the church graveyard—John and Sara Carlyle, Dr. James Craik (the surgeon who treated Washington, dressed Lafayette's wounds at Brandywine, and ministered to the dying Braddock at Monongahela), and William Hunter Jr., founder of the St. Andrew's Society of Scottish descendants (bagpipers pay homage to him the first Saturday of each December). It's also the site of the Tomb of an Unknown Revolutionary Soldier. The original parsonage, or *manse,* is still intact. There's no guided tour, but there are recorded narratives in the church and graveyard.

321 S. Fairfax St. (at Duke St.). © **703/549-6670**. www.opmh.org. Free admission. Mon–Fri 9am–4:30pm; services Sun at 8:30 and 11am.

George Washington Masonic National Memorial Visible for miles around, this imposing neoclassical shrine is modeled on the design of the lighthouse at Alexandria, Egypt, and dedicated to the most illustrious member and first Worshipful Master of Alexandria Lodge No. 22. It sits atop Shooter's Hill, overlooking the city and river. Emphasizing the panoramic view is an overlook with a wide-angle photograph pinpointing Civil War battle sites in Alexandria, taken by Matthew Brady during the Civil War. President Coolidge and former president Taft spoke at the cornerstone laying in 1923, and President Hoover assisted in rites dedicating the pink-granite memorial in 1932.

You'll enter through the ornate Memorial Hall, which is dominated by a colossal 17-foot-high bronze of Washington sculpted by Bryant Baker. On either side are 46-foot-long murals by Allyn Cox: One depicts Washington laying the Capitol cornerstone, and the other shows him and his officers in Christ Church, Philadelphia. A stained-glass window in the hall honors 16 patriots associated with Washington. A fourth-floor museum displays many items, including the Washington family Bible, the bedchamber clock stopped by Washington's physician at 10:20pm (the time of his death), and a key to the Paris Bastille presented to the lodge by the Marquis de Lafayette. On the ninth floor, an observatory parapet offers a 360-degree view that takes in the Potomac, Mount Vernon, the Capitol, and the Maryland shore.

101 Callahan Dr. (at King St.). © **703/683-2007**. www.gwmemorial.org. Free admission. Daily 9am–5pm. Closed New Years Day, Thanksgiving, and Christmas. Guided tours available every 45 min. between 9am and 4pm. Metro: King Street.

GUIDED TOURS

Though it's easy to see Alexandria on your own (see "Walking Tour: Old Town Alexandria," below), you may find your experience enhanced by having a knowledgeable local guide. If so, contact **Alexandria's Footsteps to the Past** (© **703/683-3451** or 703/850-7138), **Del Sanderson-Alexandria Tours** (© **703/329-11222**), or **The Old Town Experience** (© **703/836-0694**).

Even if you see everything on your own during the day, you'll enjoy spooking around after dark with **Alexandria Colonial Ghost Tours** (© **703/370-1185** or 703/548-0100; www.alexcolonialtours.com). They usually explore Old Town's streets and back alleys Wednesday to Sunday nights (call for the schedule and to make reservations). They cost $6 for adults, $4 for kids 7 to 12, free for children 6 and under.

You can clop around the town as George Washington did with Ann Crump of **Old Town Horse and Carriage Tours** (© **703/765-8976**). Look for Ann and Hobo the Horse at the corner of King and Lee streets on weekends, but to make sure of a ride, call a day in advance for reservations. The 20-minute rides cost $6 for adults, $3 for children 11 and under.

WALKING TOUR   OLD TOWN ALEXANDRIA

Start:	Ramsay House Visitor Center, King Street and Fairfax Street.
Finish:	Torpedo Factory, Waterfront at Cameron Street.
Time:	Allow approximately 2½ hours, not including museum and shopping stops.
Best Times:	Anytime Tuesday through Sunday.
Worst Times:	Monday, when many historic sites are closed.

You'll get a glimpse into the 18th century as you stroll Alexandria's brick-paved sidewalks, lined with colonial residences, historic houses and churches, museums, shops, and restaurants. This walk ends at the waterfront, no longer a center of commercial shipping but now home to an arts center along the Potomac riverfront.

Begin your walk at the:
❶ Ramsay House Visitor Center
The center is a historic structure, with a Dutch barn roof and an English garden at 221 King St., at Fairfax Street, in the heart of the Historic District. This is a fine place to get your bearings.

Head north on Fairfax Street to:
❷ Carlyle House
This elegant 1753 manor house is set off from the street by a low wall.

Continue north on Fairfax to the corner. Turn left on Cameron, past the back of the old city hall, to the redbrick buildings across Royal Street, known as:
❸ Gadsby's Tavern Museum
The 18th-century tavern complex houses a museum of 18th-century antiques, while the hotel portion is an Early American–style restaurant.

TAKE A BREAK
If you're ready for lunch, the 18th-century atmosphere at **Gadsby's Tavern** is the perfect place for a sandwich or salad (see its restaurant listing on p. 76).

From Gadsby's, continue west on Cameron Street and turn right on St. Asaph Street. At Queen Street, you can see:

❹ No. 523
It's the smallest house in Alexandria. Continuing north on St. Asaph, you'll come to:

❺ Princess Street
The cobble paving stones are original (and you'll see why heavy traffic is banned here).

One block farther north on St. Asaph, turn left at Oronoco Street. The house on your right at number 607 was:
❻ The Boyhood Home of Robert E. Lee
Lee lived in the Federal-style mansion at 607 Oronoco Street from age 5 until he went to West Point in 1825. Once a museum, it's now a private residence.

Across Oronoco Street, at the corner of Washington, is the:
❼ Lee-Fendall House
The gracious white clapboard residence was home to several generations of Lees. Enter through the pretty colonial garden.

Head south (left) on Washington, a busy commercial thoroughfare, to Queen Street and cross over to:
❽ Lloyd House
A beautiful late Georgian home (1797) the house is now part of the Alexandria

Library and holds a fascinating collection of documents, books, and records on the city and state.

From here, proceed south on Washington Street to the quiet graveyard entrance behind:

⑨ Christ Church

The Washingtons and Lees worshipped in this Episcopal church.

Leave by the front entrance, on Columbus Street, and turn left to King Street.

TAKE A BREAK
A cappuccino-and-pastry break at **Bread & Chocolate,** 611 King St. (see "Where to Dine," later), is guaranteed to revive flagging spirits. Sandwiches and salads are also available at this casual spot.

From King Street, turn left on Alfred Street, to the small but historic:

⑩ Friendship Firehouse

You can see an extensive collection of antique fire-fighting equipment here.

Turn left at the corner of Prince Street and proceed to Washington. At the corner is the Greek Revival:

⑪ Lyceum

Built in 1839 as the city's first cultural center, today it's a city historical museum. The museum shop has a lovely selection of crafts, silver, and other gift items.

At the intersection of Washington and Prince stands:

⑫ The Confederate Soldier

The sculptor modeled the sadly dejected bronze figure after one in the painting *Appomattox* by John A. Elder. Confederate-soldier statues in Southern towns traditionally face north (in case the Yankees return), but Alexandria's looks southward.

From here, continue walking east on Prince to Pitt Street, then turn left to King. Turn right and you'll see the fountain in:

⑬ Market Square

This open space along King Street from Royal to Fairfax in front of the modern but Williamsburg-style Town Hall has been used as a town market and meeting ground since 1749. Today, the market is held once a week, on Saturday mornings.

From here, turn right on Fairfax to the quaint:

⑭ Stabler-Leadbeater Apothecary Shop

A remarkable collection of early medical ware and hand-blown glass containers is on display here.

Head south on Fairfax to Duke Street, to the:

⑮ Old Presbyterian Meeting House

George Washington's funeral sermons were preached in 1799 in this 18th-century church. The graveyard has a marker commemorating the Unknown Soldier of the Revolutionary War.

Retrace your steps back to Prince Street and turn right. Between Fairfax Street and Lee Street you'll see:

⑯ Gentry Row

The local leaders who made their homes in these three-story town houses in the 18th and 19th centuries gave their name to the row.

At the corner of Prince and Lee is the:

⑰ Athenaeum

It's a handsome Greek Revival structure that now houses contemporary art shows.

Cross Lee Street to:

⑱ Captain's Row

This is a pretty cobblestone section of Prince Street. You're now in sight of the Potomac riverfront and may want to stroll down to the little waterfront park at the foot of Prince Street for a panoramic view of the river.

Continue north on Union Street, where you can begin your shopping expedition at:

⑲ The Torpedo Factory

You can wander the arts-and-crafts center's studios and galleries open to the public.

Walking Tour: Old Town Alexandria

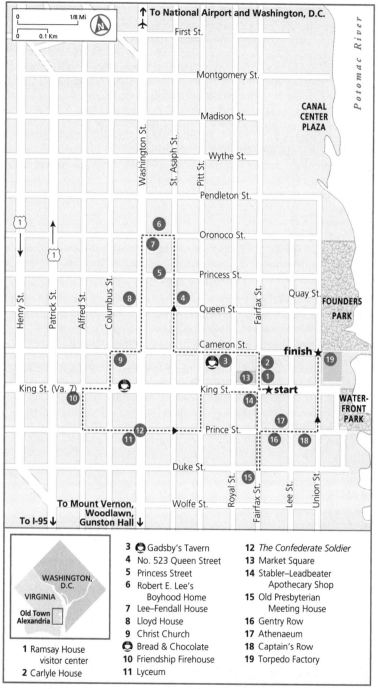

1 Ramsay House visitor center
2 Carlyle House
3 Gadsby's Tavern
4 No. 523 Queen Street
5 Princess Street
6 Robert E. Lee's Boyhood Home
7 Lee–Fendall House
8 Lloyd House
9 Christ Church
Bread & Chocolate
10 Friendship Firehouse
11 Lyceum
12 *The Confederate Soldier*
13 Market Square
14 Stabler–Leadbeater Apothecary Shop
15 Old Presbyterian Meeting House
16 Gentry Row
17 Athenaeum
18 Captain's Row
19 Torpedo Factory

POTOMAC RIVER CRUISES

After you've seen Old Town's attractions on foot, you can get a fish's-eye view of the city on a cruise operated by **Potomac Riverboat Company** (© 877/502-2628 or 703/548-9000; www.potomacriverboatco.com), based at the city dock behind the Torpedo Factory Art Center, 105 N. Union St. The "Alexandria Seaport Tour" will give you a fish's-eye view of Old Town, but the "Washington Monuments Tour" is a better choice since it goes upriver for super views of the capital city. The cruises run from Tuesday to Sunday from June through September, weekends during May and October. Roundtrip fares are $16 for adults, $15 seniors, and $8 children 2 to 12. The schedules change seasonally, so check at the dockside booth or call for information and reservations.

The company also operates full-day cruises to Mount Vernon. See section 3, later, for details.

You can dine on the river aboard the *Dandy* and *Nina's Dandy,* a couple of restaurant cruise ships berthed at the foot of Prince Street (© **703/683-6090;** www.dandydinnerboat.com). They can carry 200 and 250 passengers, respectively, so you'll have lots of company on their 2½-hour luncheon and 3-hour dinner cruises. I've lived in this area for more than 30 years, and I've never been on one of these boats except to attend parties or special functions. Call or check the website for schedules, prices, and reservations.

OUTDOOR ACTIVITIES

This part of northern Virginia has two first-rate hiking, biking, and running trails. A 17-mile paved trail starts at Memorial Bridge and borders the **George Washington Memorial Parkway** south to Mount Vernon, passing through Old Town on the way (see "A Scenic Drive Along the Potomac River," later in this chapter). Beginning in the Shirlington area, on I-395 in neighboring Arlington, the **Washington & Old Dominion (W&OD) Trail** follows Four-Mile Run Drive and Glencarlyn Park northwest to an old railroad bed, which then proceeds 45 miles through Leesburg to Purcellville (see "The Hunt Country," later in this chapter).

Big Wheel Bikes, 2 Prince St., at The Strand (© **703/739-2300;** www.bigwheelbikes.com), rents a wide range of bikes ranging from $5 an hour to $100 a week. Open Monday to Friday 11am to 7pm, Saturday 10am to 6pm, Sunday 11am to 5pm.

You can learn to paddle, explore local waters, or go on guided trips with **Atlantic Kayak,** 1201 N. Royal St. (© **800/297-0066** or 703/838-9072; www.atlantickayak.com). Call or check their website for classes, demonstrations, and day trips along the Potomac River and as far away as the Eastern Shore.

SHOPPING

Old Town has hundreds of boutiques, antiques stores, art galleries, and gift shops selling everything from souvenir T-shirts to 18th-century reproductions. Plan to spend a fair amount of time browsing between visits to historic sites. A guide to the city's 50-plus antiques and collectibles stores is available at the visitor center.

One essential stop is **The Torpedo Factory,** 105 N. Union St., between King and Cameron streets on the Potomac River (© **703/838-4565;** www.torpedofactory.org). This block-long, three-story waterfront structure was built by the U.S. Navy in 1918 and operated as a torpedo shell-case factory until the early 1950s, then used as storage for artifacts from the Smithsonian Institution. Today, it houses more than 150 artists and craftspeople, who create and sell their works on the premises. You can see potters, painters, printmakers, photographers, sculptors, and jewelers at work. The shops and galleries are open daily 10am to 5pm. Closed New Years Day, Easter, July 4, Thanksgiving, and Christmas.

Most of the best stores are interspersed among the multitude of restaurants and offices on King Street all the way from the waterfront to the Metrorail station.

One highlight here is the **Winterthur Museum Store** *GG*, 207 King St., between Lee and Fairfax streets (© **703/684-6092**), an off-site venture of the renowned museum of decorative arts on the country estate of horticulturist Henry Francis du Pont, in Delaware's Brandywine Valley. It's a delightful browse, including the back garden, which features all sorts of garden plants and ornaments. You'll come across fine reproductions from the Winterthur collection, including lamps, prints, ceramics, brassware, jewelry, garden furniture, and statuary. Open Monday to Saturday 10am to 5pm, Sunday 11am to 5pm.

There's also a branch of the interesting **Ten Thousand Villages,** 824 King St. (© **703/684-1435**), at Alfred Street, where you will find handcrafts and other items from more than 30 countries.

WHERE TO STAY

The Alexandria Hotel Association provides a free **reservation service** (© **800/ 296-1000** or 703/836-6653) to help you find a room at the Old Town properties plus several chain motels near I-95 and I-395 and along U.S. 1 south.

The area around the King Street Metrorail station is home to several new hotels, including the Hilton Alexandria Old Town and the Hampton Inn–King Street Metro Station (see below). Another good bet if you want a kitchen is **Embassy Suites Hotel Old Town,** 1900 Diagonal Rd. (© **800/EMBASSY** or 703/684-5900; www.embassysuites.com).

In the less convenient northern end of Old Town are the **Holiday Inn Hotel & Suites,** 625 1st St. (© **800/HOLIDAY** or 703/548-6300); the **Best Western Old Colony,** 615 1st St. (© **800/528-1234** or 703/739-2222), whose rooms are spacious although the baths are dated and small; and the **Executive Club Suites** at 610 Bashford Lane (© **800/535-CLUB** or 703/739-2582), where every unit is an apartment. Nearby, **Sheraton Suites Alexandria,** 801 N. St. Asaph St. (© **800/325-3535** or 703/836-4700), provides nothing but suites, while the high-rise **Radisson Hotel Old Town Alexandria,** 901 N. Fairfax St., at Montgomery Street (© **800/333-3333** or 703/683-6000), stands near the river, giving some of its 258 rooms water views.

Hampton Inn–King Street Metro *(Value*   Less than a block east of the King Street Metro station, this new six-story hotel is a bit more upscale than most of its sisters in this chain. The reasonably spacious rooms are decorated in typical Hampton fashion. The best are those on the upper floors, which have views over the city. Continental breakfast is served in a room off the lobby, which has a 24-hour coffee and juice dispenser. The outdoor pool is open during summer.

1616 King St. (at Harvard St.), Alexandria, VA 22314. © **800/HAMPTON** or 703/299-9900. Fax 703/299-9937. www.hamptoninn.com. 80 units. $109–$154 double. Rates include continental breakfast. AE, DC, DISC, MC, V. Self-parking $8. **Amenities:** Outdoor pool; health club; business center; laundry service; coin-op washers and dryers. *In room:* A/C, TV, dataport, coffeemaker, iron.

Hilton Alexandria Old Town *G*   Although it lacks the pampering services of the Relais & Chateau Morrison House and the colonial charm of the Holiday

Inn Select (see below), this seven-story structure nevertheless is one of Old Town's most luxurious hotels. The spacious rooms are furnished with antique reproductions. Those on the concierge level come equipped with marble bathrooms and feather beds. Off the lobby and with outdoor seating in warm weather, **Seagar's Restaurant & Piano Bar** offers seafood, prime steaks, and a little music to go with it. In addition, you can walk into its soundproof wine room and pick your vintage (couples can reserve a table for private dining), or into the humidor room to select your after-dinner stogie.

1767 King St. (at Diagonal Rd.), Alexandria, VA 22314. ℂ 800/HILTONS or 703/837-0440. Fax 703/837-0454. www.hiltonalexandria.com. 241 units. $179–$269 double. Rates include continental breakfast. AE, DC, DISC, MC, V. Self-parking $14. **Amenities:** Restaurant (seafood/steaks); bar; indoor pool; health club; sauna; business center; limited room service; laundry service; concierge-level rooms. *In room:* A/C, TV, dataport, mini-bar, coffeemaker, iron.

Holiday Inn Select Old Town ★★
The only hotel in the heart of Old Town (just a block from the visitor center), this six-story redbrick building is one of the finest of Holiday Inns; it even feels more like an inn than a hotel. Entered via a quiet brick courtyard and Williamsburg-look lobby, the hotel occupies an entire block. Complimentary morning coffee and Danish and afternoon English tea are served in the lamp lit lobby. Dark antique-look furniture lends colonial ambience to the guest rooms. Rooms with king-size beds have small seating areas with couches and coffee tables. The **101 Royal Restaurant** features seafood and steaks, although you'll find better fare at the plethora of nearby restaurants.

480 King St. (between Pitt and Royal sts.), Alexandria, VA 22314. ℂ 800/368-5047 or 703/549-6080. Fax 703/684-6508. www.oldtownhis.com. 227 units. $159–$249 double. Weekend and other packages available. AE, DC, DISC, MC, V. Self parking $10. **Amenities:** 2 restaurants; bar; indoor pool; health club; concierge; business center; limited room service; laundry service; concierge-level rooms. *In room:* A/C, TV, dataport, coffeemaker, iron, safe.

Relais & Chateau Morrison House ★★★
Although it's of much more recent vintage, Alexandria's finest hotel was designed after the grand manor houses of the Federal period. In fact, it's not a hotel at all but an elegant, comfortable country inn tucked away in Old Town. The enchantment begins the moment you ascend the curving staircase to its white-columned portico, where a butler greets you at the door of the marble foyer and personally registers you— in your room, no less. That's a fitting introduction to the inn's ask-and-it-shall-be-done service, from shining your shoes to bringing dinner to your room in the middle of the night. The residential-style lobby divides into a mahogany-paneled library, a formal parlor, two of Alexandria's finest restaurants (see "Where to Dine," below), and a lounge bar. Locals and guests alike pack the lounge on Thursday, Friday, and Saturday nights to hear a resident pianist on the baby grand accompany would-be opera stars and torch singers.

Each of the spacious, luxuriously appointed guest rooms and suites is individually decorated and furnished with Federal-period reproductions. Some have mahogany four-poster beds, brass chandeliers, and decorative fireplaces. In your room you'll find two phones, fresh flowers, down comforters, and robes. Bathrooms are marble-lined throughout and come equipped with makeup mirrors.

116 S. Alfred St. (between King and Prince sts.), Alexandria, VA 22314. ℂ 800/367-0800 or 703/838-8000. Fax 703/684-6283. www.morrisonhouse.com. 42 units, 3 suites. $150–$400 double; $350–$700 suite. AE, DC, MC, V. Valet parking $20. **Amenities:** 2 restaurants; bar; access to nearby health club; 24-hr. room service; babysitting; laundry service. *In room:* A/C, TV/VCR, dataport, hair dryer, iron.

Old Town Alexandria Accommodations & Dining

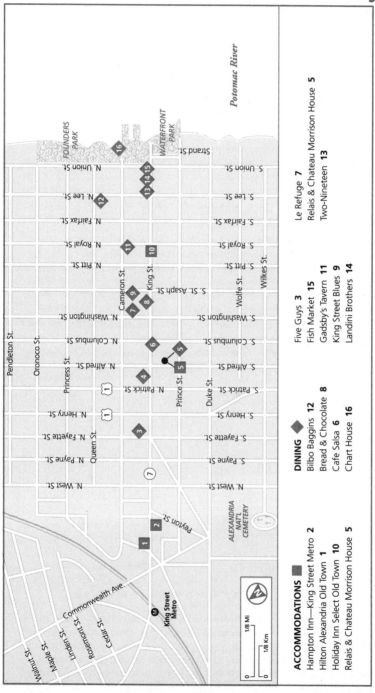

ACCOMMODATIONS ■

Hampton Inn—King Street Metro **2**
Hilton Alexandria Old Town **1**
Holiday Inn Select Old Town **10**
Relais & Chateau Morrison House **5**

DINING ◆

Bilbo Baggins **12**
Bread & Chocolate **8**
Cafe Salsa **6**
Chart House **16**

Five Guys **3**
Fish Market **15**
Gadsby's Tavern **11**
King Street Blues **9**
Landini Brothers **14**

Le Refuge **7**
Relais & Chateau Morrison House **5**
Two-Nineteen **13**

BED & BREAKFASTS

A dozen private Old Town homes, many of them historic properties, offer B&B accommodations under the aegis **Alexandria & Arlington Bed & Breakfast Network,** P.O. Box 25319, Arlington, VA 22202 (✆ **888/549-3415** or 703/ 549-3415; www.aabbn.com), which also represents properties in adjoining Arlington. Old Town rates range from $90 to $250 a night.

WHERE TO DINE

One of the Washington area's most popular dining destinations, Old Town has many more restaurants than it does historic attractions. You'll find cuisines from around the world offered in every price range along King Street and on Union Street south of King Street. The restaurants below will give you a good sampling of the many tastes offered here, but don't be afraid to stroll along and pick one of your own. They all post their menus out front, and you'll know by the number of customers which restaurants get nods from the town's affluent citizenry.

EXPENSIVE

Chart House ✦ AMERICAN   One of the few Washington-area restaurants actually on the Potomac River, this member of the national Chart House chain gives diners a view of the river, with al fresco patio dining in good weather. The ample, straightforward American fare includes seafood and thick, tender steaks and prime rib, supplemented by daily specials. All entrees come with freshly baked breads and unlimited trips to the salad bar, which often features caviar. Serving appetizers all afternoon, the bar and its outdoor tables are the best place to cool down after your walking tour.

1 Cameron St. (on the Potomac River). ✆ **703/684-5080.** Reservations recommended. Sandwiches (lunch only) $8–$13; main courses $14–$37; Sun brunch $24. AE, DC, DISC, MC, V. Mon–Thurs 11:30am–3pm and 5–10pm; Fri 11:30am–3pm and 5–11pm; Sat 11:30am–3pm and 4–11pm; Sun 11am–10pm. Bar open all afternoon.

Gadsby's Tavern ✦✦ AMERICAN   Behind the portals where Washington reviewed his troops for the last time, period furnishings, wood plank floors, fireplace, and gaslight-style lamps recreate an atmosphere for authentic colonial chow, while costumed waitstaff make for a fun time along the lines of Colonial Williamsburg's taverns. You'll dine from the same kind of pewter and china our ancestors used, and Sally Lunn bread is baked daily. Lunch might consist of a Scottish smoked salmon and Surrey bacon club sandwich or a Virginia ham and English cheddar cheese quiche. Dinner entrees usually include one of George Washington's favorites, half a duckling stuffed with fruit and served with Madeira gravy. In winter, warm yourself with drinks like hot buttered rum and Martha's Remedy—coffee, cocoa, and brandy. Entertainers perform 18th-century style during dinner and at Sunday brunch. The courtyard serves as an outdoor dining area during fine weather (you can smoke there, but not inside).

138 N. Royal St. (at Cameron St.). ✆ **703/548-1288.** Reservations recommended. Main courses $18–$26. AE, DISC, MC, V. Mon–Sat 11:30am–3pm and 5:30–10pm; Sun 11am–3pm and 5:30–10pm.

Landini Brothers ✦✦ NORTHERN ITALIAN   Old Town's finest Italian fare—or the classic, delicate cuisine of Tuscany, to be more precise—is featured at this rustic, almost grottolike restaurant with stone walls, a flagstone floor, and rough-hewn beams overhead. It's especially charming at night by candlelight. There's additional seating in a lovely upstairs dining room. Everything is homemade—the pasta, the desserts, and the crusty Italian bread. Things might get underway with prosciutto and melon or Top Neck clams on the half shell, followed by prime aged beef tenderloin medallions sautéed with garlic, mushrooms,

and rosemary in a Barolo wine sauce. Dessert choices include tiramisu and cus-
tard-filled fruit tarts.

115 King St. (between Lee and Union sts.). ⓒ **703/836-8404**. Reservations recommended. Main courses
$15–$24. AE, DC, DISC, MC, V. Mon–Sat 11:30am–11pm; Sun 4–10pm.

Relais & Chateau Morrison House ★★★ INTERNATIONAL Old Town's
top accommodations (see "Where to Stay," above) also is the setting for its finest
dining, especially the inn's showpiece, the **Elysium Dining Room.** Instead of a
waiter handing you a menu, the chef comes to your table and explains what
organic meats, wild-game fish, free-range fowl, and other, mostly natural, ingredients he has on hand. Anything goes in this fixed-price "Flight of Food." You
can make your choices and tell the chef how to prepare it, or leave to his or her
discretion. You can even have it all in one extravagant course, but it's best to order
a variety served in small doses over several courses, each explained when served.
For an extra $38 per person, the maitre d' will choose—and explain—a "custom-
paired" glass of wine for each course. This adventure in dining is well worth the
cost. Meanwhile, the inn's cozy **Grill Room** specializes in grilled steaks, chops,
lamb, fish, and other comfort food offered from a menu. The Elysium also serves
a scrumptious Sunday brunch.

116 S. Alfred St. (between King and Prince sts.), Alexandria, VA 22314. ⓒ **703/838-8000**. Reservations
highly recommended. Elysium Dining Room, fixed-price dinner $67 per person. Grill Room, main courses
$23–$31. AE, DC, MC, V. Elysium Dining Room, Mon 6–10am; Tues–Fri 6–10am and 6–10pm; Sun noon–2pm.
Grill Room, daily 11:30am–11pm.

Two-Nineteen AMERICAN/CREOLE Two-Nineteen is comprised of three
formal Victorian-style dining rooms, a covered sidewalk patio, and the Bayou
Room, a Rathskeller-like basement. Inside the main dining rooms, crystal chandeliers, rose-velvet upholstery, and a floral-patterned carpet re-create Victorian
New Orleans for Creole cuisine, featured here along with less exciting Chesapeake Bay–style seafood (forget it; go to the Fish Market; see below). Begin with
crabmeat royale (with artichoke bottoms and hollandaise sauce) or a version of
creamy she-crab soup that is actually spicier than the otherwise authentic
gumbo. Seafood entrees include blackened gulf-fish with blue crab claws, barbecued shrimp Naw'lins-style, and seafood-stuffed rainbow trout.

219 King St. (between Fairfax and Lee sts.). ⓒ **703/549-1141**. Reservations recommended, especially for
dinner in the formal dining rooms. Main courses $15–$24. AE, DC, DISC, MC, V. Mon–Thurs 11am–10:30pm;
Fri–Sat 11am–11pm; Sun 10am–4pm (brunch) and 5–10:30pm.

MODERATE
Bilbo Baggins ✦ INTERNATIONAL Named for the title character in *The
Hobbit,* this charming two-story restaurant offers fresh homemade fare. The
downstairs has rustic wide-plank floors, wood-paneled walls, oak tables, and a
brick oven centerpiece. Upstairs is another dining room with stained glass windows and seating on old church pews. It adjoins a skylit wine bar with windows
overlooking Queen Street treetops. Candlelit at night, it becomes even cozier.
The menu changes daily to reflect seasonal specialties. At dinner, you'll enjoy
entrees such as a wasabi-tinged salmon filet with a ragout of fresh asparagus and
wild mushrooms, and chicken breast spiced up by an andouille sausage and
jalapeño jack cheese stuffing. An extensive wine list is available (more than 30
boutique wines are offered by the glass and another 150 by the bottle). Homemade desserts like steamed white-chocolate bread pudding topped with
whipped cream provide a delightful finish. Lighter and less expensive fare is
available in the bar.

208 Queen St. (between Fairfax and Lee sts.). ℭ **703/683-0300.** Reservations accepted only for parties of 6 or more. Main courses $15–$19. AE, DC, DISC, MC, V. Mon–Sat 11:30am–2:30pm and 5:30–10:30pm; Sun 11am–2:30pm and 4:30–9pm. Closed Christmas Day.

Cafe Salsa ⭐ *Finds* LATIN AMERICAN   Although it has a limited menu, this chic little bistro offers a wide sampling of Latin America. The chef hails from Puerto Rico, so start with his *alcapurrias*—green bananas stuffed with ground beef sautéed with cilantro and served with a spicy jalapeño salsa. Afterwards you can chose from the likes of Argentine-style marinated and grilled beef, chicken, and chorizo topped with *chimichurri* salsa and served over yellow rice. From Cuba comes *ropa vieja,* the traditional flank steak sautéed with tri-color peppers, tomatoes, and onions and served with yellow rice. Top off with a Nicaraguan version of *tres leches,* a sponge cake enriched by three milks: whole, condensed, and evaporated. The upstairs bar has half-priced appetizers during happy hour Monday to Friday from 4 to 7pm.

703 King St. (between Columbus and Alfred sts.) ℭ **703/684-4100.** Reservations recommended. Main courses $15–$20. AE, DC, DISC, MC, V. Mon and Wed 11:30am–10pm; Tues and Thurs–Sat 11:30am–2am; Sun 11am–9pm.

Fish Market *Value* SEAFOOD   Although the popular Fish Market has grown to include the building next door, its original corner location is a warehouse that's over 200 years old. Heavy beams, terra-cotta tile floors, exposed-brick and stucco walls adorned with nautical antiques, copper pots over a fireplace, copper-topped bars, and saloon doors all lend an old-time ambience. If you're lucky, in fine weather, you might get a table for two on a one-table-wide balcony above King Street. Although not exceptional, the fare is quite passable and reasonably priced Chesapeake-style (broiled, fried, or grilled) fresh fish, shrimp, oysters, and crab. The seafood stew is a wonderful warmer-upper on a cold day. On weekends, there's live entertainment in the Main Dining Room and the Sunquest Room.

105 King St. (at Union St.). ℭ **703/836-5676.** Reservations not accepted. Salads and sandwiches $5–$10; main courses $13–$18. AE, DC, DISC, MC, V. Sun–Thurs 11:15am–1am; Fri–Sat 11:15am–2am (kitchen closes at 12:15am).

Le Refuge ⭐ *Value* FRENCH   A wicker model of the Eiffel Tower sits in the bowfronted window of Jean-François Chaufour's charming little restaurant, a local mainstay since 1983. Reflecting the cooking style, the intimate setting is typically French country—stucco walls adorned with wine labels and provincial ceramics, bentwood chairs, black-leather banquettes, and tables covered with beige-and-brown napery. The special three-course pre- and after-theater dinner is a great buy: It includes soup or salad; fresh catch of the day, leg of lamb, or calf's liver; and crème brûlée or peach Melba for dessert. There's a lunch version

---

Tips **Bags of Burgers**

Everyone from panhandlers to Old Town's gentry can be seen hauling bags of juicy hamburgers, hot dogs, and seasoned french fries out of **Five Guys,** 107 N. Fayette St. (ℭ **703/549-7991**), between King and Cameron streets. This order-at-the-counter joint harkens back to pre-McDonald's days when hamburgers weren't frozen beforehand and fresh potatoes were cut on premises. There's even a hand-lettered sign telling you where today's spuds were grown. The burgers and dogs come with a choice of fixings and cost just $2.70 to $4.70. Open daily 11am to 10pm.

for about $16. Regular house specialties include bouillabaisse, classic rack of lamb, rainbow trout amandine, and chicken Dijonnaise, and nightly specials feature produce fresh from the market.

127 N. Washington St. (at Cameron St.). ⓒ 703/548-4661. Reservations recommended. Main courses $17–$24; fixed-price 3-course dinner $23. AE, DC, MC, V. Mon–Sat 11:30am–2:30pm and 5–10pm (early bird dinner, Mon all evening; Tues–Thurs 5–7pm and 9–10pm).

Majestic Cafe ★★ *Finds* NEW VIRGINIAN   The bright neon sign recalls the 1950s when a small town cafe occupied this King Street storefront, but the building got a thorough makeover before Susan McCreight Lindeborg, former chef at the Morrison-Clark Inn in Washington, D.C., reopened it in 2001. She blends the old with the new in a cuisine that can best be described as New Virginian. In autumn she combines Chesapeake Bay oysters and Virginia ham in au gratin; rockfish with hominy, pickled corn, and mustard greens; and sautéed chicken breast with pecan and bacon-seasoned cornbread dressing. Locals love to do Sunday brunch here.

911 King St. (between Alfred and Patrick sts.). ⓒ 703/837-9117. Reservations recommended. Main courses $15–$22. AE, DC, DISC, MC, V. Tues–Thurs 11:30am–2:30pm and 5–10pm; Fri–Sat 11:30am–2:30pm and 5–11pm; Sun 11am–2:30pm and 5:30–10pm.

INEXPENSIVE

Stalls sell inexpensive eats in the **Food Pavilion** behind the Torpedo Factory, at King and Cameron streets. Open daily from 11am to 9:30pm.

Bread & Chocolate CONTINENTAL/BAKERY   This cheerful European-style place has a counter displaying an array of fresh breads, croissants, napoleons, chocolate truffle cakes, Grand Marnier cakes, Bavarian fruit tarts, and other goodies. The interior features a changing art show on white walls lit by gallery lights. At breakfast, you can get a caffé mocha and an almond croissant or an omelet with potatoes and a slice of melon. The rest of the day, soups, salads, sandwiches, a Greek stew or vegetarian lasagna will keep you walking.

611 King St. (between Washington and St. Asaph sts.). ⓒ 703/548-0992. Reservations not accepted. Breakfast $2.50–$8; sandwiches and salads $6–$8; main courses $7–$8. AE, DC, DISC, MC, V. Mon–Sat 7am–7pm; Sun 8am–6pm.

King Street Blues ★ *Value* AMERICAN/SOUTHERN   This lively, often noisy roadhouse is one of Alexandria's most charming restaurants—and one of its best values. It's easy to find, for it occupies all three floors of a small brick building with windows painted on its exterior brick wall, and has a blue entrance canopy adorned with a pig trumpeting the words "Good Food." Red neon outlines the real windowpanes. Brian McCall, a local artist, has covered almost every inch of the interior walls with papier-mâché figures and murals. His colorful work is reminiscent of Red Grooms's constructions, created with a sly tongue-in-cheek good humor. A young crowd packs the place for the house beef stew (with a memorable accompaniment of garlic mashed potatoes), barbecued pork and chicken in a sweet yet spicy sauce, southern-fried catfish, meatloaf, and house-smoked baby back ribs. For something unusual, order the "American nachos"—they come with cheese, scallions, and either chicken or pork barbecue over potato chips instead of tortilla chips. The blue-plate special is an excellent money-saver.

112 N. St. Asaph St. (between King and Cameron sts.). ⓒ 703/836-8800. Reservations accepted. Salads and sandwiches $7–$9; main courses $10–$13; blue-plate specials $7. AE, DC, DISC, MC, V. Mon–Thurs 11:30am–10pm; Fri–Sat 11:30am–11pm; Sun 11am–10pm; blue-plate specials Mon–Thurs; bar stays open later.

ALEXANDRIA AFTER DARK

Alexandria falls under the aegis of Washington, D.C., when it comes to the performing arts. The monthly free magazine *Old Town Crier* is the one of the best sources of news about the local bar and music scene; pick up a copy at the Ramsay House Visitor Center and in hotel lobbies.

King Street restaurants are the center of Alexandria's ongoing club and bar scene. Especially noteworthy are **Two-Nineteen,** 219 King St. (© **703/549-1141**), which features live jazz Tuesday to Saturday nights in the Basin Street Lounge; the **Fish Market,** 105 King St. (© **703/836-5676**), with either a pianist or a guitarist from Thursday to Saturday nights; and **Murphy's,** 713 King St. (© **703/548-1717**), which has live Irish bands to accompany corned beef and cabbage on weekends.

An older crowd likes to sing along on Thursday, Friday, and Saturday evenings with the resident pianist in the lounge of the **Morrison House,** 116 S. Alfred St. (© **703/838-8000**), between King and Prince streets (see "Where to Stay," earlier). You could hear wannabe professional singers belt out some fine jazz and even an aria or two.

The **Birchmere,** 3901 Mount Vernon Ave., south of Glebe Road (© **703/549-5919;** www.birchmere.com), is the Washington area's prime showcase for nationally known bluegrass, country, and folk stars. Call or check the website for the schedule and reservations, which are absolutely necessary when a top performer is on stage.

A SIDETRIP FROM ALEXANDRIA
ARLINGTON NATIONAL CEMETERY ✦✦✦

For more than a century, this famous cemetery overlooking the Potomac River and Washington, D.C., has been a cherished shrine commemorating the lives given by members of the U.S. armed forces. Its seemingly endless rows of graves mark the mortal remains of the honored dead, both the known and the unknown, who served in conflicts from the Revolutionary War through the Persian Gulf War.

Women in Military Service for America Memorial: At the cemetery's ceremonial entrance, you'll come to a fountain emptying into a reflecting pool backed by an imposing granite wall. This is the Women in Military Service for America Memorial (© **800/222-2294** or 703/533-1155; www.womensmemorial.org), dedicated in 1997 to honor all women who have served in the military, from the Revolution to the present. The memorial's Hall of Honor has a block of Colorado marble virtually identical to that of the Tomb of the Unknowns (see below). On

---

(Tips **Seeing the Cemetery**

Head first for the **Arlington Cemetery Visitor Center,** where you can get a free map—and if you have family buried here, find out where. This quiet expanse of green is a walker's paradise, but you can ride around via the **Tourmobile** (© **888/868-7707** or 202/554-5100; www.tourmobile.com). Service is continuous daily from 9:30am to 4:30pm, and the commentary interesting. Tickets cost $6 for adults, $3 for children 3 to 11. At the visitor center you can also purchase Tourmobile combination tickets that include Arlington and major Washington, D.C., sights, allowing you to stop and re-board when you're ready. Tourmobiles also depart here for Mount Vernon (see below).

Born of Vengeance

On April 20, 1861, Robert E. Lee crossed the Potomac River to a meeting at Blair House, opposite the White House in Washington, D.C. There he was offered command of all Union forces that would fight the Civil War. A distinguished career soldier and patriot, Lee nevertheless turned down Pres. Abraham Lincoln and went home to his Custis-Lee mansion across the Potomac River in Arlington. Two days later, he left for Richmond, where he joined his native Virginia's rebel army.

The Union turned the Custis-Lee estate into a bivouac area for troops. Outraged at Lee's inflicting an unexpected defeat on them at the first Battle of Manassas, Quartermaster General Montgomery Meigs ordered that Union dead be buried in the front yard of Lee's mansion. Thus was America's most hallowed national cemetery born of an act of vengeance.

Robert E. Lee never returned to Arlington. After many years and lengthy litigation, the U.S. Supreme Court returned ownership to his son. In 1883, George Washington Custis Lee sold the estate to the U.S. government for $150,000. Today, you can visit Lee's old home, which has been restored to reflect its appearance during the Lee family's time of residence.

the terrace roof, 11 glass panels are etched with quotations about women who have served, and inside, there's a computerized registry of more than 250,000 women veterans.

The Kennedy Graves: Follow the paved pathways to the John F. Kennedy gravesite, which is marked by an eternal flame. Jacqueline Kennedy Onassis is buried next to her first husband. Nearby stands a simple white cross at the grave of Robert F. Kennedy. Looking north, you'll have a spectacular view of the capital city across the river (during his presidency, Kennedy once remarked of this spot, "I could stay here forever"). A few steps below the gravesite is a wall inscribed with JFK quotations, including the one he's most remembered for: "And so my fellow Americans, ask not what your country can do for you—ask what you can do for your country."

Arlington House: Commanding a gorgeous view of Washington, D.C., from atop the ridge above the Kennedy graves, the Greek Revival Arlington House (© 703/557-0613; www.nps.gov/arho) was built by George Washington Parke Custis, grandson of Martha Washington by her first marriage, after his daughter married a young Virginian named Robert E. Lee. The Lees had lived in the mansion for 30 years when General Lee received word in April 1861 of the dissolution of the Union and Virginia's secession (see the "Born of Vengeance" box, below). Restored to its pre–Civil War appearance and furnished with original pieces (as much as possible) and replicas, it has served as a memorial to Robert E. Lee since 1955, when its official name was changed to "Custis-Lee Mansion." A small Robert E. Lee Museum adjoins. There's a self-guided tour, with volunteers on hand to give an introductory talk, hand out brochures, and answer questions. Admission is free. The mansion is open daily from 9:30am to 4:30pm; the museum from 8am to 4:30pm. Both are closed Christmas and New Year's Day.

Arlington National Cemetery

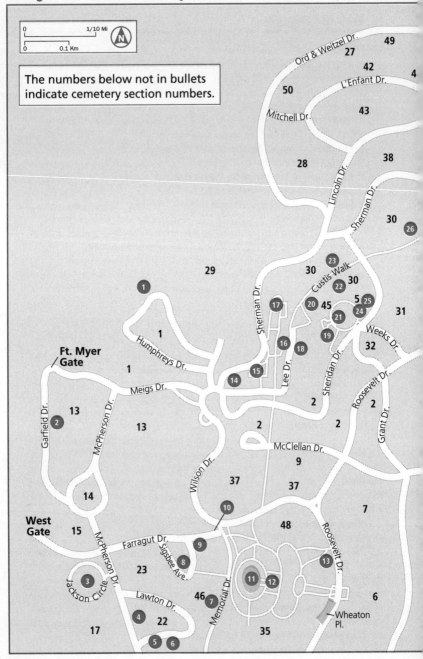

The numbers below not in bullets indicate cemetery section numbers.

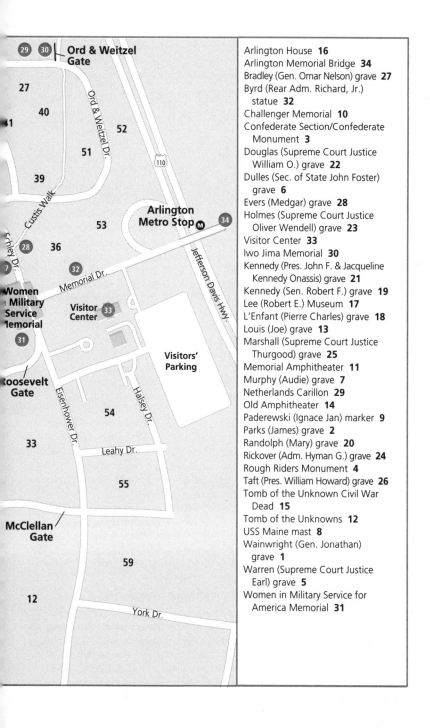

Ord & Weitzel Gate

Ord & Weitzel Dr.

110

Arlington Metro Stop Ⓜ

Custis Walk

Women Military Service Memorial

Memorial Dr.

Visitor Center

Jefferson Davis Hwy.

Visitors' Parking

Roosevelt Gate

Eisenhower Dr.

Halsey Dr.

Leahy Dr.

McClellan Gate

York Dr.

Tomb of the Unknowns: Beyond the mansion, America's most distinguished honor guard slowly marches before the Tomb of the Unknowns, a tribute to all members of the armed forces who have given their lives for their country in war. The 50-ton white-marble tomb rests above the remains of unidentified combatants slain during World War I. Unknowns from World War II and the Korean War are in the crypts on the plaza in front of it. There's also a crypt for an unknown killed in the Vietnam War, but modern forensic science is so sophisticated that the serviceman originally buried there with much ceremony was later identified as a U.S. Air Force pilot. His body was moved to another grave. Plan your visit to coincide with the changing of the guard ceremony—an impressive ritual of rifle maneuvers, heel clicking, and military salutes. It takes place daily every half-hour April through September, every hour on the hour the rest of the year.

Memorial Amphitheater: Adjoining the Tomb is the Greek Revival outdoor Memorial Amphitheater, used for holiday services, particularly on Memorial Day when the sitting president or vice president attends. Free Tourmobile transportation from the visitor center parking lot is provided on these occasions.

U.S. Marine Corps War Memorial: On the northern periphery of Arlington National Cemetery, just off Va. 110 about 1½ miles north of the Kennedy graves, stands the famous U.S. Marine Corps War Memorial, better known as the Iwo Jima Memorial. The statue of Marines raising the American flag over Iwo Jima in February 1945 symbolizes the nation's esteem for the honored dead of the U.S. Marine Corps. News photographer Joe Rosenthal won a Pulitzer Prize for his photo of the flag raising on Mount Suribachi, and sculptor Felix W. de Weldon was moved to create a sculpture based on the image. The sculpture took 3 years to complete and was dedicated in 1954 on the Marines' 179th anniversary. The Memorial grounds are used for military parades in summer, when there is a free shuttle from the visitor center. Call ⓒ **703/289-2500** for the schedule.

Netherlands Carillon: Adjacent to the Iwo Jima statue is the Netherlands Carillon, a gift from the people of Holland, with 50 bells, each carrying an emblem signifying a segment of Dutch society. Poet Ben van Eysselsteijn composed verses inscribed on each bell. Thousands of tulip bulbs are planted on the grounds surrounding 127-foot-high open steel tower, creating a colorful display in spring. Carillon concerts are presented on Easter Sunday and every Saturday thereafter in April, May, and September, from 2 to 4pm. Concerts are held daily from 6 to 8pm June through August. Visitors are permitted into the tower after the carillonneur performs, to enjoy spectacular views of Washington.

Va. 110 at Memorial Circle. ⓒ **703/607-8052**. www.arlingtoncemetery.org. Free admission. Apr–Sept daily 8am–7pm; Oct–Mar daily 8am–5pm. Parking $1.25 per hour first 3 hours, $2 per hour thereafter. Metro: Blue line to Arlington Cemetery. From I-395 or I-66 take Va. 110 to entrance signs.

A SCENIC DRIVE ALONG THE POTOMAC RIVER

Skirting the south bank of the Potomac River for 30 miles between Mount Vernon in the south to the Capital Beltway (I-495) in the northwest, the **George Washington Memorial Parkway** is one of Virginia's most scenic drives. It's also a major commuter route, which means lots of congestion during rush hours. Other times, you can drive the entire route in about 45 minutes without stopping. The parkway runs through Old Town Alexandria via King Street; otherwise, it's a four-lane road with neither traffic signals nor stop signs. Also, with the exception of the Lyndon B. Johnson Memorial Grove, you cannot make a left turn; accordingly, it's best driven from south to north so you can pull off at designated areas (perhaps for a picnic) beside or overlooking the river.

Thrill-seekers congregate at **Gravelly Point,** just north of Ronald Reagan Washington National Airport, where jet planes roar overhead just a few feet off the ground. You'll get a view of the Washington, D.C., monuments across the river from the **Lyndon Baines Johnson Memorial Grove,** north of the Pentagon, where 500 white pines and inscriptions carved into Texas granite commemorate the 36th president. Another good spot is on a hill north of Key Bridge at **Potomac Overlook Regional Park,** where you'll have a great view over the capital city.

As noted in "Outdoor Activities," below, you can also run, hike, or bike along part of the parkway. One of the most pleasant places for a short stroll is on **Theodore Roosevelt Island,** an 88-acre wooded preserve and bird sanctuary connected to the parkway by a footbridge just south of Rosslyn. There's a statute of the Rough Rider in the middle of the island and 2½ miles of hiking trails through its forest.

For more information, contact **Headquarters,** George Washington Memorial Parkway, c/o Turkey Run Park, McLean, VA 22101 (© **703/289-2500;** fax 703/289-2598; www.nps.gov/gwmp).

2 Mount Vernon & the Potomac Plantations ⟨★

Mount Vernon: 9 miles S of Old Town Alexandria

With spacious lawns spread like carpets among the sprawling suburbs south of Alexandria, the Potomac River plantations at Mount Vernon, Woodlawn, and Gunston Hall beckon anyone interested in early American thought, politics, sociology, art, architecture, fashion, and the decorative arts. The Mount Vernon home of George and Martha Washington is one of Virginia's top attractions. The first president gave Woodlawn, on a hilltop 3½ miles down the road, as a 2,000-acre gift to their adopted daughter, who was Martha's actual granddaughter via her first marriage. And at the less imposing but equally fascinating Gunston Hall lived their creative neighbor, George Mason, a revolutionary liberal whose words inspired Thomas Jefferson when he sat down in 1776 to pen the Declaration of Independence.

The plantations are best seen as a day excursion from Washington, D.C., or Old Town Alexandria. Start early and give yourself a morning to explore Mount Vernon, the most extensive and interesting of the plantations and the only one actually overlooking the Potomac River. Have lunch at Mount Vernon and then tour the other plantations. If you have time for just one more, make it Gunston Hall, where you will learn of Mason's valuable but lesser known contributions to the American Revolution and the principles for which it was fought.

GETTING THERE
You will need a car to get to Woodlawn, Gunston Hall, and the other attractions south of Mount Vernon, but you can get to the first president's home by public transportation.

BY CAR It's a pleasant, picturesque drive to Mount Vernon, 9 miles south of Alexandria via the Mount Vernon Memorial Parkway. After passing Mount Vernon, the same highway connects to U.S. 1 and the nearby attractions.

BY SUBWAY, BUS & TAXI It's not the easiest or most efficient way to go, but you can get to Mount Vernon via Washington's Metrorail and connecting bus. Take Metro's Yellow line subway (© **202/637-7000**) to Huntington Station south of Alexandria. Exit to Huntington Avenue and catch the **Fairfax Connector** bus 101 (© **703/339-7200;** www.co.fairfax.va.us). The bus ride from Huntington to

Mount Vernon takes about 20 minutes and costs 50¢ each way. Call for the bus schedules (they don't run on holidays). You can also take a **White Top Cab** (📞 703/644-4500) from the station; fares are about $15 each way.

BY TOURMOBILE From Arlington National Cemetery or from the Washington Monument and Lincoln Memorial in Washington, D.C., you can take the **Tourmobile** (📞 202/554-5100; www.tourmobile.com) to Mount Vernon from April to mid-November daily at 10am, noon and 2pm. The fare is $25 for adults, $12 for children 3 to 11, free for children 2 and under, including admission to Mount Vernon. The trip takes about 4 hours; reservations are required in person at least 30 minutes before departure. Call for off-season departure times.

BY BOAT From April to October, the **Potomac Riverboat Company,** at Union and Cameron streets behind the Torpedo Factory Art Center in Old Town Alexandria (📞 703/548-9000; www.potomacriverboatco.com), offers cruises down the river to Mount Vernon and back. They depart Tuesday to Sunday at 11am from Memorial Day to Labor Day, on weekends during May, September, and October. The return voyage leaves Mount Vernon at 4pm, which means you will have about 3 hours to explore the mansion and grounds. Roundtrip fares are $27 for adults, $26 for seniors, and $15 for children, including admission to Mount Vernon.

THE TOP ATTRACTIONS

Gunston Hall ⭐ Although he shunned public office and thus is not well known outside Virginia, George Mason (1725–92) was a statesman and political thinker who played an important role in founding our nation. He drafted the Virginia Declaration of Rights, model for the Bill of Rights. Thomas Jefferson based his famous first sentence of the Declaration of Independence on Mason's statement that "all men are by nature equally free and independent and have certain inherent rights . . . namely, the enjoyment of life and liberty, with the means of acquiring and possessing property, and pursuing and obtaining happiness and safety." Mason helped write the Constitution but then refused to sign it because it didn't abolish the slave trade or initially contain a Bill of Rights.

A fine example of colonial American architecture, the brick house is unusual hereabouts because it's only one and a half-story tall (the peaked roof has gables to let light into the upstairs rooms). Mason knew what type of house he wanted but couldn't build it, so he asked his brother, who was studying law in England, to find him an architect who would come to America as an indentured servant. The brother found William Buckland, an English craftsman in his early 20s, who worked on the house from 1755 to 1759. Buckland's great achievement was the Palladian Room, whose intricately carved woodwork was inspired by the 16th-century Italian architect Andrea Palladio. Another room features a chinoiserie interior, the rage in London in the mid–18th century.

The formal gardens focus on the 12-foot-high English boxwood *allée* (tree-lined walkway) planted by Mason (that's right: the shrubs are more than 250 years old!). Also on the premises is the family graveyard where George and Ann

---

(*Fun Fact* **Mother of Presidents**

Virginia is known as the "Mother of Presidents" because eight U.S. presidents were born here: George Washington, Thomas Jefferson, James Madison, James Monroe, both William Henry and Benjamin Harrison, John Tyler, and Woodrow Wilson.

Mount Vernon & the Potomac Plantations

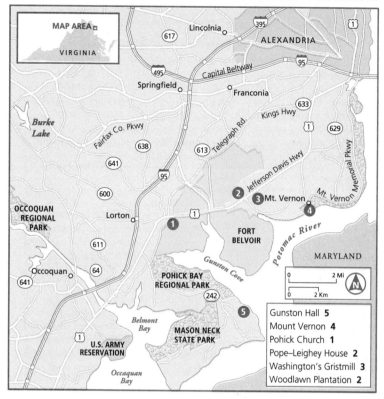

Mason are buried. If you have an extra hour for the round-trip stroll, you can take a nature trail down the Potomac past Mason's Deer Park and woodland area (you cannot see the river from the mansion).

At the reception center, an 11-minute film will introduce you to Mason and his estate. You must then take a 30-minute tour in order to enter the mansion. Allow 45 minutes for the total house tour, 1½ hours to see the house and gardens. En route to the house, you'll pass a small museum of Mason family memorabilia.

10709 Gunston Rd. (Va. 242). © 703/550-9220. www.gunstonhall.org. Admission $8 adults, $7 seniors, $4 students through 12th grade, free for children 5 and under. Daily 9:30am–5pm (30-min. tours on hour and half-hour 9:30am–4:30pm). Closed New Year's Day, Thanksgiving, and Christmas. From Woodlawn, drive 5½ miles south on U.S. 1, turn left on Gunston Rd. (Va. 242), then 3¾ miles to plantation entry on left.

Mount Vernon ★★★   With its tall white columns standing at the top of a lawn sloping down to the Potomac River, the home of George and Martha Washington has been one of America's most-visited shrines since 1858, when a group of women banded together to raise money to rescue the sadly deteriorated mansion. The organization, the Mount Vernon Ladies Association of the Union, purchased the estate from Washington's great-grandnephew, John Augustine Washington Jr., and continues to own and maintain the mansion and its grounds. For more than a century, there's been an ongoing effort to locate and return the estate's scattered contents and memorabilia, thus enhancing its authentic appearance (ca. 1799). About 30% of the contents actually belonged to the Washingtons.

Tips Beating the Crowds at Mount Vernon

The best time to visit is during fall and winter, when the crowds are fewer. If you come in spring or summer, get here by 8am to beat the mobs. Buy your ticket, rent a helpful 40-minute taped audio tour, get a detailed map of the property, and *head straight for the mansion,* the most popular part of the complex. (The ticket office also sells the 132-page, full-color *Mount Vernon Handbook,* which is helpful, inexpensive, and a good souvenir.)

Allow at least 2 hours to tour the house and grounds. There's no formal tour, but attendants stationed throughout the house and grounds offer commentary explaining 18th-century plantation life.

Constructed of beveled pine painted to look like stone, the house is an outstanding example of Georgian architecture. You'll enter by way of the "large dining room," which contains many of the original chairs, Hepplewhite mahogany sideboards, and paintings. Step outside on the long front porch and enjoy the view that prompted Washington to declare, "No estate in United America is more pleasantly situated than this."

A key to the Paris Bastille, which Lafayette presented to Washington in 1790 via messenger Thomas Paine, hangs in the central hall, the social center of the house in Washington's day. The "little parlor" contains the English harpsichord of Martha Washington's granddaughter, Nelly Custis. Martha's china tea service is laid out on the table in the "west parlor." In the "small dining room," the sweetmeat course set up on the original mahogany dining table is based on a description of an actual Mount Vernon dinner in 1799. Washington's study contains its original globe, desk, and dressing table.

Upstairs are five bedchambers, including the "Lafayette Room," named for the Marquis, and George and Martha's bedroom, in which Washington died.

After leaving the house, tour the kitchen, smokehouse, overseer's and slave quarters, the Washingtons' graves, and the slave burial ground marked by two monuments to the African-Americans who lived, worked, and died at the plantation. A museum on the property has interesting exhibits and memorabilia. Down by the river, a 4-acre exhibition area focuses on Washington's accomplishments as a gentleman farmer (he practiced innovative soil conservation and crop-rotation).

In the 1760s, Washington switched his staple crop from tobacco to wheat, which required less labor to produce and had a more reliable market. Three miles south of the plantation on Mount Vernon Memorial Parkway, you can visit **George Washington's Gristmill,** a 1933 reconstruction of the stone mill he built to grind his new crop. Costumed interpreters show how it was done. Nearby, archaeologists have discovered the foundation of Washington's whiskey still (there were no "revenuers" in those days).

There's an ongoing schedule of special activities at Mount Vernon, especially in summer. They run the gamut from special garden and history tours to colonial crafts demonstrations and treasure hunts for children. Call to find out what's going on during your visit. On Washington's Birthday (the federal holiday, not the actual date), admission is free and a wreath-laying ceremony is held at his tomb. Needless to say, the place is mobbed with visitors that day.

End of George Washington Memorial Parkway, 9 miles S of Old Town Alexandria and I-95. © **703/780-2000.** www.mountvernon.org. Admission $11 adults, $10.50 seniors, $5 children 6–11. Gristmill admission $4 adults,

$2 children 6–11. Combination admission $13 adults, $5.50 children 6–11. Taped mansion tour recording rentals $3. Apr–Aug daily 8am–5pm; Sept–Oct daily 9am–5pm; Nov–Mar daily 9am–4pm.

WHERE TO DINE AT MOUNT VERNON   Plan to have lunch at Mount Vernon after touring the mansion and grounds. There's a **food court** in a shopping complex at the traffic circle outside the main gate. Open daily from 9:30am to 5:30pm. Next door, the charming **Mount Vernon Inn** (© 703/780-0011) serves some of the colonial-style fare George and Martha provided their guests. It's not exceptional at lunch (the turkey pie can be on a par with Stouffer's frozen version), but it's inexpensive and the atmosphere is great—period furnishings, working fireplaces, a wait staff in 18th-century costumes. There's a full bar, and Virginia wines are offered by the glass. Lunch is first come, first served, but reservations are highly recommended at dinner (if for no other reason than to find out if the inn is closed for a wedding reception or other event). American Express, Discover, MasterCard, and Visa are accepted. It's open Monday to Friday 11am to 3:30pm and 5 to 9pm, Saturday 11am to 3:30pm and 5 to 9pm, Sunday 11am to 3:30pm.

Pohick Church   The seat of Mount Vernon Parish, Pohick Church was built between 1769 and 1774 from plans drawn up by George Washington. The interior was designed by George Mason, owner of Gunston Hall (see above), with the pulpit to one side and box pews like those prevalent in England at the time. During the Civil War, Union troops stabled their horses in the church and stripped the interior. The east wall was used for target practice. Today, the church is restored to its original appearance and houses an active Episcopal congregation.

9301 Richmond Hwy. (U.S. 1, at Telegraph Rd.). © 703/339-6572. www.pohick.org. Free admission. Mon–Fri 9am–4:30pm; services Sun 8 and 10am. From Woodlawn, drive 5½ miles south on U.S. 1.

Woodlawn Plantation and Pope-Leighey House ★   On a hill overlooking the Potomac River valley (but not the river), Woodlawn was a 2,000-acre section of Mount Vernon, of which some 130 acres remain. George Washington gave it as a wedding gift to his adopted daughter (and Martha's granddaughter), beautiful Eleanor "Nelly" Parke Custis, and her husband, his nephew, Maj. Lawrence Lewis, when they married in 1799. Three years later, they moved into the Georgian-style brick mansion designed by William Thornton, first architect of the U.S. Capitol, and furnished it primarily with pieces from Mount Vernon (everything you see dates to before 1840, with about 30% from the Lewis' time). Now under the auspices of the National Trust for Historic Preservation, the restored Woodlawn mansion and its elegant formal gardens reflect the lives and lifestyles of the plantation's original free and enslaved inhabitants.

On the other side of the parking lot, you leap 150 years ahead architecturally to Frank Lloyd Wright's modernistic **Pope-Leighey House,** designed in 1940

Overrated **River Cruises**

If you have an extra 40 minutes to spare, the cruise boat *Potomac Spirit* (© **866/211-3811** or 202/554-8013; www.spiritcitycruises.com) makes sightseeing trips on the river from Mount Vernon's wharf. The mansion is lovely when seen from out on the river, but you get almost as good a view from the water's edge. The cruises depart daily at 10:30 and 11:30am and at 2:30pm from Memorial Day to the first weekend in October, on weekends during the off season. Available at the main gate or at the wharf, tickets cost $8 for adults, $4 for children.

for the Loren Pope family of Falls Church. Built of cypress, brick, and glass, the flat-roofed house was created as a prototype of well-designed space for middle-income people. "The house of moderate cost," said Wright in 1938 (the house and lot cost $7,000 back then), "is not only America's major architectural problem but the problem most difficult for her major architects." In 1946, the Robert A. Leigheys purchased the house. After living in it for 17 years, Mrs. Leighey donated it to the National Trust, which moved it here.

House tours are provided twice daily during March, when Woodlawn hosts one of the largest annual **needlework exhibits** in the United States.

9000 Richmond Hwy. (U.S. 1, at Mount Vernon Memorial Pkwy. [Va. 235]). ℂ **703/780-4000.** www.woodlawn 1805.org; www.popeleighey1940.org. Admission to each house $7.50 adults, $3 students, free for children 4 and under. Combination tickets $13 adults, $5 students, free for children 4 and under. Admission may be higher during special events. Daily 10am–4pm. Mandatory 35-min. tours on the hour and half-hour. Closed Jan–Feb, Thanksgiving, and Christmas. From Mount Vernon, drive 3 miles west on Mount Vernon Memorial Parkway (Va. 235) to U.S. 1. Entry is straight ahead.

3 The Hunt Country

Leesburg: 35 miles NW of Washington, D.C.; 115 miles NW of Richmond
Middleburg: 45 miles W of Washington, D.C.; 95 miles NW of Richmond

Although horse farms extend southwestward from the Washington suburbs all the way to Charlottesville, the heart of Virginia's Hunt Country beats in the rolling hills of Loudoun and Fauquier counties, between Washington Dulles International Airport and the Blue Ridge Mountains. The colonial tradition of fox hunting still reigns out this way, and steeplechase racing is still something to do on a Saturday. You don't want to be caught dead without your jodhpurs in these parts.

Beyond the rapid suburban development west of Dulles airport, the Hunt Country is studded with horse farms bordered by stone fences, plantations with elegant manses, picturesque villages, country inns, and fine restaurants. Don't be surprised to see rich and famous folk strolling the streets or having a bite of lunch in picturesque towns like Leesburg, Middleburg, Upperville, Purcellville and Hillsboro, for some of the world's wealthiest people keep their thoroughbreds here. The public pavilion and garden next door to Middleburg's tiny information center are dedicated to the late Jacqueline Kennedy Onassis in honor of the contributions she made to the town while residing here.

Others with a little money have started vineyards, and the Hunt Country will introduce you to Virginia's growing wine industry. If you avoid getting tipsy in the tasting rooms, it's easy to wind your way through the farms and hamlets to Manassas, where the North and the South fought two major Civil War battles on the banks of Bull Run, including that conflict's first great contest. You will be following in the horse steps of Col. John Singleton Mosby, the famous Confederate raider who made Hunt Country life miserable for the Yankees.

ESSENTIALS
VISITOR INFORMATION

For advance information, contact the **Loudoun Convention & Visitor Association,** 222 Catoctin Circle SE, Suite 100, Leesburg, VA 22075 (ℂ **800/752-6118** or 703/771-2170; www.visitLoudoun.org). Its offices and **Leesburg Visitor Center** are about ½ mile east of downtown on the first floor of the Jewell Building on Catoctin Circle, just south of Market Street (Va. 7 Business). The center is open daily from 9am to 5pm. Pick up a visitor guidebook, a town map, and a list of

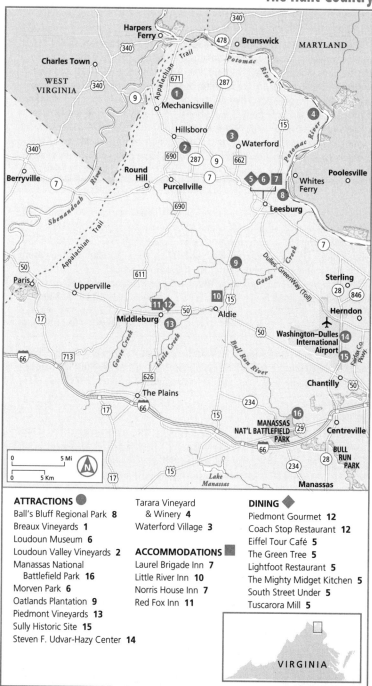

The Hunt Country

ATTRACTIONS ●
Ball's Bluff Regional Park **8**
Breaux Vineyards **1**
Loudoun Museum **6**
Loudoun Valley Vineyards **2**
Manassas National
 Battlefield Park **16**
Morven Park **6**
Oatlands Plantation **9**
Piedmont Vineyards **13**
Sully Historic Site **15**
Steven F. Udvar-Hazy Center **14**

Tarara Vineyard
 & Winery **4**
Waterford Village **3**

ACCOMMODATIONS ■
Laurel Brigade Inn **7**
Little River Inn **10**
Norris House Inn **7**
Red Fox Inn **11**

DINING ◆
Piedmont Gourmet **12**
Coach Stop Restaurant **12**
Eiffel Tour Café **5**
The Green Tree **5**
Lightfoot Restaurant **5**
The Mighty Midget Kitchen **5**
South Street Under **5**
Tuscarora Mill **5**

VIRGINIA

Fun Fact **The Grey Ghost**

The Hunt Country was the stomping ground of the Confederate raider, Col. John Singleton Mosby, whose hit-and-run exploits earned him the nickname "The Grey Ghost." Today, U.S. 50 is the John S. Mosby Highway, and local residents have dubbed it the John Singleton Mosby Heritage Area. You can get a driving tour brochure explaining historic sights from local tourist info offices (see "Visitor Information," above) or directly from the **Mosby Heritage Area**, P.O. Box 1497, Middleburg, VA 20118 (© **540/687-6681;** www.mosbyheritagearea.org). Tour guide Dave Goetz has half-day **Mosby's Confederacy Tours** (© 540/364-9086; www.mosbytours.com) of the area, which can be combined into an all-day outing. Call for prices and reservations.

---

antiques dealers. Also ask for a copy of the walking-tour guide to Waterford Village (see below).

Middleburg has an information center in the Pink Box, 12 Madison St., Middleburg, VA 22117 (© **540/687-8888**). It's open Monday to Friday from 11am to 3pm, Saturday and Sunday from 11am to 4pm.

For Manassas, contact the **Prince William County/Manassas Conference and Visitors Bureau,** 8609 Sudley Rd., Suite 105, Manassas, VA 20112 (© **800/432-1792** or 703/792-4254; www.visitpwc.com). The town of Manassas has a visitors' center in the Railroad Depot, 9431 West St. (© **703/361-6599**), open daily from 9am to 5pm.

For Fauquier County, contact or visit the **Warrenton-Fauquier County Chamber of Commerce,** 183A Keith St., Warrenton, VA 20186 (© **800/820-1021** or 540/347-4414; fax 540/347-7510; www.fauquierchamber.org). It's open daily 9am to 5pm.

GETTING THERE
BY PLANE   Washington Dulles Airport is on the eastern edge of the Hunt Country, 14 miles southeast of Leesburg and 21 miles east of Middleburg. See "Getting There & Getting Around" in chapter 2 for details.

BY CAR   You'll need a vehicle to explore the beautiful back roads of the Hunt Country. Washington Dulles airport has all the major rental firms. There are two routes from the Capital Beltway (I-495) to **Leesburg.** The free but slower way is Va. 7. The faster route is via the Dulles Toll Road (Va. 267) between I-495 and Washington Dulles Airport; it feeds into the Dulles Greenway (© **888/707-8870;** www.dullesgreenway.com), a privately financed toll expressway connecting the airport to Leesburg. The total toll from the I-495 to Leesburg is about $3. Once in downtown Leesburg, you can scout around for an on-street space or leave your vehicle in the **municipal parking garage** on Loudoun Street between King and Wirt streets, where parking cost $4 a day.

To **Middleburg,** you can take U.S. 50 west all the way into town or follow I-66 west to Va. 28 north to U.S. 50 west. U.S. 15 south from Leesburg intersects with U.S. 50 westbound 10 miles east of Middleburg. Park anywhere you can find an on-street space in Middleburg.

LEESBURG
Founded in 1758, Leesburg is the largest town in the Hunt Country and a good base for exploring the region. Although not as picturesque as Middleburg, it has

considerable charm, with architecture ranging from pre-Revolutionary to late 19th century. The center of Leesburg and its historic district is at the intersection of Market Street (Va. 7 Business) and King Street (U.S. 15 Business), where you'll find the brick **Loudoun County Court House,** built in 1895 which contains a mix of Roman Revival and classical elements. Most of what you will want to see is within 2 blocks of this key crossroads, including one of the largest collections of antiques dealers in Virginia.

EXPLORING LEESBURG

One-hour **walking tours** usually depart the Loudoun Museum (see below) on Friday at 1pm and Saturday at 11am and 1pm from mid-May through September, but call the museum to make sure. The tours cost $4 for adults, $2 for seniors and children. The museum sponsors tours of the town's historic homes a few times a year.

Ball's Bluff Regional Park   On the northeastern outskirts of town, this pristine regional park is best known for a little circle of stone markers in **Ball's Bluff National Cemetery,** the nation's second smallest national cemetery. It holds the remains of 54 Union soldiers—only one identified—who fell in the Battle of Ball's Bluff, in October 1861, a Confederate victory. Many more Union troops were shot dead as they scrambled down the bluff toward the Potomac River and safety in Maryland. Many of their corpses slid into the river and floated down to Washington, bringing the grim realities of the war to the nation's capital. The park has hiking trails and interpretive displays, and rangers lead guided tours of the battlefield on weekends from May through October.

Ball's Bluff Rd. (northeast Leesburg off U.S. 15 Bypass). ✆ 703/737-7800. www.nvrpa.org/ballsbluff.html. Free admission. Daily dawn to dusk. Free walking tours May–Oct Sat 11am and 2pm; Sun 1 and 3pm. From U.S. 15 bypass, go east on Battlefield Blvd. to Ball's Bluff Rd.

Loudoun Museum   This small but interesting museum houses memorabilia about the county from American Indian days to the present. It also distributes free visitor information and sells helpful walking and driving tour booklets. A 15-minute video sets the scene for your tour of the country. Allow another 30 minutes to explore the museum and its gift shop.

16 W. Loudoun St., at Wirt St. ✆ 703/777-7427. www.loudounmuseum.org. Admission $2 adults, $1 students, free for children 9 and under. Mon–Sat 10am–5pm; Sun 1–5pm.

Morven Park   On the northwest edge of town, this 1,200-acre estate and its Greek Revival mansion are don't-misses for fox hunting and horse-drawn carriage fans. Seriously renovated in 2003, the original part of the manse was built in the early 18th century as a farmhouse. It's now home to the **Museum of Hounds and Hunting,** while the carriage house holds the impressive **Winmill Carriage Collection.** They are surrounded by rolling pastureland; there are picnic tables under shade trees at the parking lot, so bring the fixings. Allow 1½ hours to take the 45-minute house tour and visit the museums.

17263 Southern Planter Lane, off Old Waterford Rd. ✆ 703/777-2414. www.morvenpark.org. Admission to mansion and carriage collection $7 adults, $6 seniors, $1 children 6–12. Apr–Dec Fri–Mon noon–4pm. Mandatory 45-min. tours departing every hour on the hour from noon–4pm. Call for special events. Take Va. 7 Business west 1 mile from the center of town, turn right onto Morven Park Rd., left onto Old Waterford Rd. to park on right.

Oatlands Plantation   George Carter, a great-grandson of legendary planter Robert "King" Carter of the Northern Neck, built this mansion in the Federal style in 1804 but later converted it the Greek Revival manse we see today. His formal terraced garden and its 1810 propagation greenhouse—it's considered America's second oldest—are as interesting as the mansion itself. The plantation's remaining 330 acres also contain unique tree species. Now operated by the National Trust for Historic Preservation, Oatlands hosts numerous events, such as the Antiques at Oatlands show, sanctioned sheepdog trials, a bridal fair, and an American-crafts show (call for the schedule). From mid-November through December, the mansion is all decked out for its annual holiday candlelight tours. You must take a tour to see the house, but you can wander the gardens on your own.

20850 Oatlands Plantation Lane (on U.S. 15, 6 miles south of Leesburg). © **703/777-3174.** www.oatlands. org. Admission $8 adults, $7 seniors and students, $1 children 5–11, free for children 4 and under. Mar–Dec Mon–Sat 10am–4pm; Sun 1–4pm. Mandatory 40-min. house tours depart on the hour.

Sully Historic Site   Sully Plantation, a two and a half-story farmhouse, was built in 1794 by Richard Bland Lee, northern Virginia's first congressman and uncle of Robert E. Lee, who lived here with his wife, Elizabeth Collins Lee, until 1811 (they are buried here). Now owned and operated by the Fairfax County Parks Authority, the house is furnished with Federal period antiques and looks much as it would have when the Lees lived here. The original plantation had more than 3,000 acres. Washington Dulles International Airport now occupies most of the land, leaving the main house and original stone dairy, smokehouse and kitchen building. A highlight of the site are the representative slave quarters, which demonstrate the harshness of everyday life for the plantation's African-American workers. You must take a tour of the house and slave quarters, but you can wander around the grounds and look into the outbuilding windows on your own. Call for a schedule of events, which include an antique car show in June and a quilt show in September.

3601 Sully Rd. (Va. 28), Chantilly. © **703/437-1794.** www.fairfaxcounty.gov/parks. Admission to house $5 adults, $4 students, $3 seniors and children 5–15; grounds free. Mar–Dec Wed–Mon 11am–4pm. Grounds open until sunset. Mandatory 45-min. house tours depart on the hour. Call for holiday hours. Sully is on Va. 28, ¾ mile north of U.S. 50, 9 miles south of Va. 7 in Leesburg.

WATERFORD VILLAGE ★★

Reached by a marvelous scenic drive, the enchanting hamlet of **Waterford,** with numerous 18th- and 19th-century buildings, is a National Historic Landmark. Surrounded by a rolling landscape of 1,420 acres, it offers vistas of farmland and pasture that unfold behind barns and churches. You'll feel as though you've entered an English country scene painted by Constable. A Quaker from Pennsylvania, Amos Janney, built a mill here in the 1740s. Other Quakers followed, and by 1840, most of the buildings now on Main Street and Second Street were in place. In 1870, the railroad bypassed Waterford, and because the pace of change slowed, much of the town was preserved. Affluent professionals who work in Washington, D.C., and the bustling northern Virginia suburbs now own many of the homes. In other words, it's a real town, not a theme park like Williamsburg, so don't traipse through their front yards.

Usually counted in the few hundreds, the population swells to the many thousands on the first weekend in October, when local residents stage the annual **Waterford Arts and Crafts Fair,** one of the best in the region.

Be sure to get a walking-tour guide booklet from **The Waterford Foundation, Inc.,** P.O. Box 142, Waterford, VA 20197 (© **540/882-3018;** fax 540/882-3921; www.waterfordva.org). The foundation's office is in the Corner Store at Main and Second streets and is open Monday to Friday 9am to 5pm. The booklets are usually available at the Leesburg Visitor Center (see "Visitor Information," above),

---

Tips **New Home for the Enola Gay**

When the Smithsonian Institution's magnificent National Air and Space Museum ran out of space in Washington, D.C., to house its many historic air- and spacecraft, it built the **Steven F. Udvar-Hazy Center** ⭐⭐, 14390 Air and Space Museum Pkwy., Chantilly, Va. (© 202/357-2700; www. nasm.si.edu/udvarhazycenter). That's on Va. 28 between U.S. 50 and the Dulles Toll Road (Va. 267), not far from Sully Historic Site. This huge Quonset hut–like hanger will eventually house more than 200 planes and 135 spacecraft. Already on display: the *Enola Gay,* the B-29 which dropped the first atomic bomb on Japan in 1945; the space shuttle *Enterprise,* which NASA used for approach and landing tests in the late 1970s; and one of Air France's supersonic Concorde jetliners. On the southeastern edge of Washington-Dulles International Airport, the center has a 164-foot high tower for observing modern-day takeoffs and landings. The center is open daily from 10am to 5:30pm except Christmas. Admission is free.

---

and can be downloaded from the website. Ask the foundation about walking tours, which are given on many Sundays.

Waterford is about 6 miles northwest of Leesburg. Don't take Old Waterford Road, which isn't paved. Instead, follow Va. 7 west, turn right onto Va. 9 for about a mile, then right on Clark's Gap Road (C.R. 662) into Waterford.

ON THE WINE TRAIL

You'll pass several "farm" vineyards while driving around Loudoun County. The most interesting is **Tarara Vineyard & Winery,** 13648 Tarara Lane (© 703/771-7100; www.tarara.com), overlooking the Potomac River, where wines are aged in a 6,000-square-foot cave. Try the 2002 viognier, which won the Virginia Governor's Cup gold medal. Tours and tastings are daily 11am to 5pm. If you taste too many glasses of its vino, you can sleep it off at Tarara Vineyards & Winery's bed-and-breakfast. From Leesburg, drive north on U.S. 15 to Lucketts, then east on C.R. 662.

Northwest of Leesburg are **Loudoun Valley Vineyards,** on Va. 9 (© 540/882-3375; www.loudounvalleyvineyards.com), which has tours Friday to Sunday from 11am to 5pm April to December, Saturday and Sunday only in winter, and **Breaux Vineyards,** north of Hillsboro on C.R. 671 (© 800/492-9961 or 540/668-6299; www.breauxvineyards.com), whose Mediterranean-style tasting room is open daily from 11am to 5pm. On C.R. 690 is **Windham Winery** (© 540/688-6464; www.windhamwinery.com), which is open Friday, Saturday, and Sunday from noon to 6pm.

OUTDOOR ACTIVITIES

The Hunt Country's picturesque back roads and its portion of the 45-mile Washington & Old Dominion Railroad (W&OD) Trail bring bicyclists from all over the mid-Atlantic. The W&OD follows an old railroad bed through the heart of the area, crossing South King Street in downtown Leesburg. You can rent wheels in downtown Leesburg from **Plum Grove Cyclery,** 26 W. Market St.

(© **703/777-2252;** www.plumgrovecyclery.com), and from **Bicycle Outfitters,** 19 Catoctin Circle NE, in the Leesburg Plaza Shopping Center (© **703/777-2148;** www.bikeoutfitters.com). Both are 2 blocks north of the W&OD and charge $25 a day.

Although there are many horse trails in the hills, not many stables rent mounts. One that does is **Greenway Stables** (© **703/327-6117;** www.greenwaystables. com), which offers unguided trail rides over its property at 24397 Racefield Road, off U.S. 50 between I-66 and C.R. 629. Reservations are required; let them know your level of experience and whether you prefer English or Western.

Golfers can tee off at the Gary Player–designed **Raspberry Falls Golf & Hunt Club,** 3 miles north of Leesburg on U.S. 15 (© **703/779-2555,** or 703/589-1042 from anywhere in the Washington metropolitan area; www.raspberryfalls.com). East of Leesburg off Va. 7 are the Robert Trent Jones Jr. links at **Lansdowne Resort,** a large, conference-oriented facility at 44050 Woodridge Pkwy. (© **800/541-4801** or 703/729-8400; www.lansdowneresort.com). Less expensive are **Goose Creek Golf Club,** 43001 Golf Club Rd. (© **703/729-2500;** www.goose creekgolf.com), and the municipal **Brambleton Regional Park Golf Course,** 42180 Ryan Rd. in nearby Ashburn (© **703/327-3403;** www.nvrpa.org).

SHOPPING

Leesburg's numerous **antiques shops** are within a block of the Market Street–King Street intersection and easy to find. The visitor center has lists of the shops, both in town and throughout the Hunt Country.

Two miles east of downtown near the intersection of the U.S. 15 bypass and Va. 7, the **Leesburg Corner Premium Outlets,** 241 Fort Evans Rd. (© **703/737-3071;** www.premiumoutlets.com), has more than 50 stores and a food court. Many well-known brands are present, including Banana Republic, Brooks Brothers, Burberry, Bass, Gap, Jockey, Jones New York, Liz Claiborne, Nike, Off 5th-Saks Fifth Avenue, Polo Ralph Lauren, Reebok, Tommy Hilfiger, OshKosh B'Gosh, Rockport, L'eggs/Hanes/Bali/Playtex, Mikasa, Oneida, Pfaltzgraff, and WestPoint Stevens. Open Monday to Saturday 10am to 9pm, Sunday 11am to 6pm.

WHERE TO STAY

A mansion built atop a knoll in 1773 is the centerpiece of the **Holiday Inn at Historic Carradoc Hall,** 1500 E. Market St. (Va. 7), 2 miles east of downtown (© **800/465-4329** or 703/771-9200; www.leesburgvaholidayinn.com). The four suites on the mansion's second floor have country inn–like ambience. The other 122 rooms are in standard motel buildings. The most modern digs in town are at the new **Comfort Suites Leesburg,** 80 Prosperity Ave. (© **866/533-7287** or 540/669-1650; www.comfortsuitesleesburg.com), which has some Jacuzzi-equipped units. It's only ½ mile east of downtown off Market Street (Va. 7 business), east of the U.S. 15 bypass. Nearby on Va. 7 are the **Best Western Leesburg-Dulles** (© **800/528-1234** or 703/777-9400; www.guests-inc.com) and the **Leesburg Days Inn** (© **800/DAYS-INN** or 703/777-6622).

Southeast of Leesburg off Va. 7, **Lansdowne Resort,** 44050 Woodridge Pkwy. (© **800/541-4801** or 703/729-8400; www.lansdowneresort.com) offers a complete resort experience including a full-service spa and Robert Trent Jones golf course. Its large conference wing draws many conventions and groups.

In addition to the inns mentioned below, Loudoun has a dozen **bed-and-breakfasts** scattered around the county, including Tarara Vineyard & Winery (see "On the Wine Trail," above). Most belong to the Loudoun County Bed

& Breakfast Guild (no address or phone; www.vabb.com), which publishes a listing available from the Leesburg Visitor Center (see "Visitor Information," above).

Laurel Brigade Inn   The history of this two-story Federal-period inn goes back to 1766, when town records show that a tavern operator named John Miller became the owner of an "ordinary" (the colonial equivalent of a British pub) on this lot. In 1817, it was purchased by Eleanor and Henry Peers and became the Peers Hotel. The hotel's kitchen was so highly regarded it was chosen to prepare the food when Lafayette visited Leesburg in 1825. The inn and its lovely garden hosts weddings, receptions, and other special events (the restaurant serves only afternoon tea and Sunday brunch). In 1949, the building became Laurel Brigade Inn, named for a Civil War brigade. Dated by today's standards, but nevertheless comfortable, the guest quarters are furnished with wing chairs, chenille spreads, and hooked rugs. Units on the rear garden side are preferable to those on the front, which face the bright lights of the Tally Ho Theatre across Market Street. Window units provide air-conditioning.

20 W. Market St., Leesburg, VA 22075 (between King and Wirt sts.). (© **866/777-1020** or 703/777-1010. Fax 703/777-9001. www.laurelbrigade.com. 5 units. $95–$145 double. AE, DISC, MC, V. **Amenities:** Restaurant (afternoon tea, Sun brunch only). *In room:* A/C, no phones.

Norris House Inn 🖈   A charming three-story red-brick 1806 home, Norris House was renovated in the Eastlake style in the Victorian era. Its facade is bedecked with green shutters and a white-columned entrance porch, the whole capped by three pedimented dormer windows. The common rooms include a parlor and library, both with oak fireplaces. Full breakfasts are served in the formal dining room. Guest-room furnishings are a charming mix of antiques. All share three bathrooms and have non-working fireplaces, stenciled fireplace surrounds, four-poster beds (some with lace canopies), rockers, and framed botanical prints on the walls. Most interesting and private accommodations are in the atticlike third floor. None of the rooms has a telephone. You can have afternoon tea on weekends in the **Stone House Tea Room** next door.

108 Loudoun St. SW, Leesburg, VA 20175 (between Wirt and Liberty sts.). (© **800/644-1806** or 703/777-1806. Fax 703/771-8051. www.norrishouse.com. 6 units (none with private bathroom). $100–$150 double. Rates include full breakfast. AE, DC, DISC, MC, V. **Amenities:** Restaurant (breakfast, afternoon tea); access to nearby health club; business center. *In room:* A/C, no phone.

WHERE TO DINE

Eiffel Tower Café 🖈 FRENCH   An elegant French country ambience reigns in this rambling clapboard house with large windows that let in plenty of sunlight. The menu is traditional French with some interesting Asian, Italian and North African twists, such as pan-fried halibut with a spicy Szechuan pepper sauce and accompanied by lentils cooked with bacon, grilled sea bass with couscous, and scallops with mushroom risotto. Bastille Day (July 14) is a big day here.

107 W. Loudon St. (between Wirt and Liberty sts.). (© **703/777-5242**. Reservations recommended. Main courses $18–$28. AE, DC, MC, V. Tues–Thurs 11:30am–9:30pm; Fri–Sat 11:30am–10pm; Sun 11:30am–3pm.

The Green Tree COLONIAL AMERICAN   Dishes made from 18th-century recipes gathered from the Library of Congress and the National Archives highlight this restaurant. Green-herb soup, Sally Lunn bread, roast prime rib with Yorkshire pudding, and rum-and-black-walnut pie are among the results of this research. Both dining rooms have wide-plank floors, harvest dining tables, ladderback chairs, brass chandeliers, working fireplaces, and walls hung with hunting prints; servers are in period dress. If you dined at Gadsby's Tavern in

Totaled by a Triumph

The best barbecue in Leesburg is at **The Mighty Midget Kitchen,** 202 Harrison St., at Royal Street (℗ **540/777-6406**), one of the country's smallest restaurants at only 8-feet wide by 6-feet deep. The original building, actually part of a World War II bomber, was totaled in 1959 during an unfortunate encounter with a Triumph sports car. The present building is made the aluminum remnants of another B-29, rivets and all. There are a few outdoor tables; otherwise, get your barbecue, smoked kielbasa, fish sandwiches, and hot dogs to go. Open Tuesday to Thursday 11am to 8pm (to 7pm in winter), Friday and Saturday 11am to 8pm (to 7pm in winter), Sunday noon to 6pm (closed Sun in winter). Most items range from $2.50 to $6.50.

Alexandria (see "Where to Dine", earlier in this chapter), don't bother repeating the experience here.

15 S. King St. (between Market and Loudoun sts.), Leesburg. ℗ **703/777-7246.** Reservations recommended, especially for dinner on weekends. Main courses $15–$25. AE, MC, V. Summer daily 11:30am–10pm. Off season Mon–Thurs 11:30am–9:30pm; Fri–Sun 11:30am–10pm.

Lightfoot Restaurant ℗ ECLECTIC   Leesburg's most interesting restaurant occupies an old Romanesque Revival bank building, complete with two-story-high oak-paneled ceiling. A round mezzanine with bar underneath dominates the center of the room, which is too big and thus too noisy for intimate dining. Nevertheless, the chef puts forth an interesting mix of flavors, from lamb chops finished with *rogan josh* curry sauce to seared duck a la Provençal.

11 N. King St. (north of Market St.). ℗ **703/771-2233.** Reservations recommended. Main courses $19–$26. AE, MC, V. Mon–Thurs 11:30am–11pm; Fri and Sat 11:30am–midnight; Sun 11:30am–3:30pm and 5:30–11pm.

South Street Under DELI/BAKERY   Operated by the Tuscarora Mill (see below), this bright bakery and deli is housed in a turn-of-the-20th-century mill, one of the six historic buildings that make up the Market Station shopping and dining complex. It's the best place in town for a breakfast of gourmet coffee and hot-out-of-the-oven pastries, or a lunch of tarragon chicken salad or a made-to-order sandwich on freshly baked ciabatta bread. Order at the counter, and in good weather, grab a table out in the sunny courtyard.

203 Harrison St. (in Market Station, between Loudoun and Harrison sts.), Leesburg. ℗ **703/771-9610.** Reservations not accepted. Most items $2–$6. AE, MC, V. Mon–Fri 7am–6pm; Sat 8am–6pm; Sun 8am–4pm.

Tuscarora Mill ℗ AMERICAN   One of Leesburg's most popular restaurants, "Tuskie's" brings a casual, publike ambience to the old mill. High wood-beamed ceilings, grain bins, belts, pulleys, and a scale evoke the building's past in the main dining room, while plants and skylights brighten another room to the side. Delicious luncheon fare includes sandwiches and hot entrees like sautéed shrimp accompanied by cheese grits and smoked country sausage, which often appears at dinner. The dinner menu changes frequently, but other nighttime standouts might include sesame-roasted salmon.

203 Harrison St. (in Market Station, between Loudoun and Harrison sts.), Leesburg. ℗ **703/771-9300.** Reservations recommended, especially at dinner. Main courses $15–$22. AE, DISC, MC, V. Daily 11:30am–2:30pm and 5:30–9:30pm; bar serves light fare until 11pm Sun–Thurs, until midnight Fri–Sat.

MIDDLEBURG ✦

One of Virginia's most beautiful small towns, Middleburg likes to call itself the unofficial capital of the Hunt Country. Indeed, jodhpurs and riding boots are *de rigeur* in this town that is home to those interested in horses, horse breeding, steeplechase racing, and fox hunting. Look carefully, because the person walking next to you could be very, very famous.

Middleburg is included on the National Register of Historic Villages, and it's about the same size today—600 residents—as when it was settled in 1731. There's so much money here, a lot of it devoted to keeping the town in its original condition, that the village looks almost too real to be true.

You can't get lost in Middleburg, for the entire town occupies just 6 blocks along Washington Street (U.S. 50).

Park anywhere on Washington Street and start your tour at the **Pink Box Visitor Information Center,** on Madison Street a block north of Washington Street (see "Visitor Information," earlier). Then stroll along Middleburg's shady brick sidewalks, poke your head into upscale shops with names like Crème de la Crème that sell "home embellishments," have lunch at one of several restaurants, or stop for a cone at Scruffy's Ice Cream Parlor. Note the small Gothic Revival **Emmanuel Episcopal Church** (1842) at Liberty Street; it was the first example of mid-19th-century architecture in the village.

NEARBY ATTRACTIONS

Manassas National Battlefield Park ✦✦   The first massive clash of the Civil War took place along a stream known as Bull Run on July 21, 1861. A well-equipped but poorly trained Union army of 35,000 under Gen. Irvin McDowell had marched from Washington, where cheering crowds expected them to return victorious within days. Most of the men were 90-day volunteers who had little knowledge of what war would mean. Their goal was Richmond, but to meet the oncoming army, Gen. P. G. T. Beauregard deployed his Confederate troops along Bull Run to the north of the railroad junction of Manassas. The 10 hours of heavy fighting stunned soldiers on both sides as well as onlookers who had ridden out from Washington to watch. A Confederate victory shattered any hopes that the war would end quickly. Historians later conjectured that had the Confederates followed the fleeing Union troops, an even more decisive victory perhaps could have ended the war, with the South victorious.

Union and Confederate armies met here again on August 28 through 30, 1862. The Second Battle of Manassas secured Gen. Robert E. Lee's place in history as his 55,000 men soundly defeated the Union army under Gen. John Pope.

Start your tour at the visitor center, where a museum, a 45-minute film and a 6-minute battle map program tell the story. These rolling hills are excellent for hiking, and there are a number of self-guided walking tours that highlight Henry Hill, Stone Bridge, and the other critical areas of the two battles. Allow about 2 hours to take in the visitors' center and the First Battle walking tour (it's about 1 mile long). The tour of the entire First Battle area is 6½ miles long. A

Fun Fact **"Like a Stone Wall"**

Stonewall Jackson got his nickname in the first Battle of Manassas when Confederate Gen. Bernard Bee, marveling at his persistence in standing his ground, marveled: "There stands Jackson, like a stone wall!"

12-mile driving tour covers Second Manassas, which raged over a much larger area, will take about 1½ hours if you get out of your car to examine the sites.

6511 Sudley Rd. (Va. 234), Manassas. © 703/361-1339. www.nps.gov/mana. Admission (good for 3 days) $3 adults, free for children 16 and under. National Park Service passes accepted. Battlefield, daily dawn to dusk. Visitor center 8:30am–5pm. From Middleburg (about 11 miles), take U.S. 50 east, turn right onto U.S. 15 south, turn left at Va. 234, and continue southeast to Manassas. From I-66, take Exit 47B and go a ½ mile north on Va. 234.

ON THE WINE TRAIL

The more interesting of the local wineries is **Piedmont Vineyards,** on Halfway Road (C.R. 626) about 3 miles south of town (© 540/687-5528; www.piedmont wines.com), a former dairy farm whose barn now houses a tasting room and gift shop. The tasting room is open daily 11am to 6pm.

Off U.S. 50, a mile east of the village, **Swedenburg Estate Vineyard,** 23595 Winery Lane (© 540/687-5219; www.swedenburgwines.com), occupies part of Valley View Farm, founded about 1762. It's open daily from 10am to 4pm. Farther east on Champe Ford Rd. (C.R. 629), between Middleburg and Aldie, is **Chrysalia Vineyards** (© 800/235-8804 or 540/687-8222; www.chrysaliawine. com), which is open daily from 10am to 5pm.

The wineries are closed New Year's Day, Thanksgiving, and Christmas.

WHERE TO STAY

Red Fox Inn ★★   The historic Red Fox Inn in the center of Middleburg maintains the romantic charm of early Virginia in its original 1728 stone structure. Later additions include the Stray Fox Inn building, so called because a misfired cannonball struck its foundation in the Civil War; and the McConnell House Inn building. The Red Fox has three rooms and three suites, all with wide-plank floors and 18th-century furnishings; several have working fireplaces. Rooms in the other building also preserve a traditional character with hand-stenciled walls, canopy beds, hooked rugs, and original fireplace mantels. Continental breakfast is served in the rooms, and extra amenities include terry bathrobes, bedside sweets, fresh flowers, and a morning newspaper.

The dark, cozy **Red Fox Inn Restaurant** occupies the first floor of the inn. It features a Hunt Country ambience—low beamed ceilings, pewter dishes, and equestrian prints lining the walls. The seasonal menus feature heavy regulars like filet mignon, crab cakes, rack of lamb and grilled fish. Across the back street, **Mosby's Tavern** serves as the town's drinking establishment. It offers a mixed menu for lunch and dinner, which you can enjoy at one of the wooden booths or, in good weather, on the small outdoor patio.

Tips Grist for the Aldie Mill

Most of the quaint hamlet of **Aldie**, 5 miles east of Middleburg on John Mosby Highway (U.S. 50), has been on the National Register of Historic Places since 1970, which has helped protect it from development. On a Sunday afternoon from April to October, you can take a tour of **Aldie Mill** (© 703/327-9777; www.virginiaoutdoorsfoundation.org), the only gristmill in Virginia powered by twin water wheels. Built in 1807, the mill is being restored by the Virginia Outdoors Foundation, which in 2003 got its two big wheels going for the first time in 50 years. Antiques stores and other shops along the highway merit browsing, and the annual Aldie Harvest Festival is worth a stop on the third Saturday in October.

2 E. Washington St. (P.O. Box 385), Middleburg, VA 20118. ⓒ **800/223-1728** or 540/687-6301. Fax 540/687-6053. www.redfox.com. 21 units and suites. $150–$325 double. Rates include continental breakfast. AE, DC, DISC, MC, V. **Amenities:** 2 restaurants (American); bar. *In room:* A/C, TV, dataport, hair dryer, iron.

A NEARBY BED & BREAKFAST

Little River Inn ★ The peaceful setting here is so appealing, it's almost worth coming to Aldie just to stay. Farm animals, a small garden, and a patio are behind the main building, an early-19th-century farmhouse. The living room has polished wide-plank floors; in front of the fireplace are two wing chairs and a sofa, all upholstered in colonial-print fabrics. Fresh flowers, a basket of magazines, and a few decorative pieces of china add warmth to the setting. Accommodations range from one room to a cottage of your own (none of them with telephones). The main house has five bedrooms, all charmingly furnished with antique pieces and pretty quilts; one has a working fireplace. Three small houses are also on the property—both the log cabin and the Patent House, a small late 1700s domicile, have working fireplaces. Hill House (ca. 1870) sits on 2 acres of landscaped gardens and can be rented in its entirety, or its two bedrooms may be rented separately. For breakfast, innkeepers Tucker and Mary Ann Withers offer home-baked goodies like poppyseed muffins and giant popovers filled with cooked apples, raisins, and cinnamon sauce.

39307 John Mosby Hwy. (U.S. 50; P.O. Box 116), Aldie, VA 22001. ⓒ **703/327-6742.** www.aldie.com. 5 units (4 with private bathroom), 3 cottages. $95–$225 double. Rates include full breakfast. AE, MC, V. **Amenities:** Outdoor pool. *In room:* A/C.

WHERE TO DINE

You may want to buy the fixings for a picnic before you set out for the day in Hunt Country. Try **Piedmont Gourmet,** 20 E. Washington St. (ⓒ **540/687-6833**), or the **Upper Crust Bakery,** 2 N. Pendleton St. (ⓒ **540/687-5666**).

Coach Stop Restaurant (Value) AMERICAN Locals have been flocking to this country-style restaurant (albeit one with racks of fine wine behind the counter and lots of horse photos on the walls) since 1958 for old-fashioned American fare. The menu offers everything from a breakfast of Virginia country ham and eggs or creamed chipped beef on buttermilk biscuits to a dinner of honey-dipped fried chicken. Seating is at the counter or at tables and booths. Ceiling fans keep the breezes moving as you tuck into a hearty meal. You can order sandwiches served with french fries or pasta salad. Dinner entrees—comfort foods like pork chops or roast turkey with stuffing and gravy—are served with two vegetables.

9 E. Washington St., Middleburg. ⓒ **540/687-5515.** Reservations accepted. Breakfast $4–$8.50; sandwiches and salads $5–$10; main courses $14–$20. AE, DC, DISC, MC, V. Mon–Sat 7am–9pm; Sun 8am–9pm.

5

Fredericksburg & the Northern Neck

Like Alexandria, Richmond, Williamsburg and other early Virginia towns, Fredericksburg is steeped in American history. It came into being in 1728 as a 500-acre frontier settlement on the banks of the Rappahannock River, and its heritage spans colonial, Revolutionary, and Civil War events. George Washington, James Monroe, Thomas Jefferson, and George Mason are among the great men who walked Fredericksburg's cobblestone streets.

For Civil War buffs, Fredericksburg is almost a holy shire. Heroes such as Robert E. Lee and Stonewall Jackson fought a major battle in town and others nearby at Chancellorsville, the Wilderness, and Spotsylvania Court House. Jackson was shot (mistakenly) by his own men at Chancellorsville; his amputated arm is buried at Ellwood Plantation, where the Battle of the Wilderness would be fought a year later. Each year, hundreds of thousands of visitors come to the battlefields, now part of a national military park.

Both George Washington and Robert E. Lee were born on the bucolic Northern Neck, a peninsula set apart by the broad Potomac on one side and the winding Rappahannock River on the other. At the end of it is the fishing village of Reedville, built in the Victorian era and still making its living from the Chesapeake Bay, and Irvington, home to The Tides Inn, one of the state's finest golf resorts. Large and small creeks crisscross the neck, and bald eagles, blue heron, flocks of waterfowl, and an occasional wild turkey inhabit the unspoiled marshland.

1 Fredericksburg

50 miles S of Washington, D.C.; 45 miles S of Alexandria; 50 miles N of Richmond

Though George Washington always called Alexandria his hometown, he spent his formative years across the Rappahannock River from Fredericksburg at Ferry Farm, where he supposedly never told a lie about chopping down the cherry tree. His mother later lived in a house he purchased for her on Charles Street, and she is buried on the former Kenmore estate, home of his sister, Betty Washington Lewis.

The town was a hotbed of revolutionary zeal in the 1770s. Troops drilled on the courthouse green on Princess Anne Street, and Thomas Jefferson, George Mason, and other founding fathers met in Fredericksburg in 1777 to draft what later became the Virginia Statute of Religious Freedoms, the basis for the First Amendment guaranteeing separation of church and state. James Monroe began his law career in Fredericksburg in 1786.

During the Civil War, its strategic location—equidistant from two rival capitals, Richmond and Washington—turned Fredericksburg into a fierce battlefield, scene of one of the war's bloodiest conflicts. Clara Barton and Walt Whitman nursed wounded Federal soldiers in Chatham mansion, just across the river. Cannonballs embedded in the walls of some prominent buildings, as well as the graves of 17,000 Civil War soldiers are grim reminders of that tragic era.

Although rapid growth is beginning to absorb Fredericksburg within the Washington, D.C., suburban megalopolis, a 40-block area of the town is a National Register Historic District. Most visitors come here either to see the buildings in which Washington, Jefferson, Lee, Mason, Monroe and their families lived and worked, or to explore the Civil War battlefields. Among the highlights are the Hugh Mercer Apothecary Shop and The Rising Sun Tavern, two of the more entertaining historic sites in Virginia.

ESSENTIALS
VISITOR INFORMATION
The **Fredericksburg Visitor Center,** 706 Caroline St. (at Charlotte St.), Fredericksburg, VA 22401 (© **800/678-4748** or 540/373-1776; fax 540/372-587; www.fredericksburgvirginia.net), offers free maps, many restaurant menus, and a walking tour brochure following the 1862 Battle of Fredericksburg. It also shows a 14-minute video which will get you oriented, gives out free all-day parking passes (you can leave your car in the center's lot all day), and sells a block ticket to the major sites (see "Exploring Fredericksburg," below). The center is open Memorial Day to Labor Day, daily from 9am to 7pm; the rest of the year, 9am to 5pm. Closed New Year's Day, Thanksgiving and Christmas.

Value **A Money-Saving Pass & a Trolley Tour**

Make your first stop in town the **Fredericksburg Visitor Center** (see "Essentials," above), which is housed in a historic 1824 house on Caroline Street at Charlotte Street. Here you can see a 14-minute video on Fredericksburg's colonial history and get a pass for free parking anywhere in the city (including lots beside the center and across the street). Except for Belmont and Chatham, which are across the river, the historic sights are within walking distance of the visitor center.

The visitor center sells a **Pass to Historic Fredericksburg** which includes admission to Belmont, Fredericksburg Area Museum and Cultural Center, Hugh Mercer Apothecary Shop, James Monroe Museum and Memorial Library, Kenmore, Mary Washington House, The Rising Sun Tavern, and the Civil War battlefields. It's $24 for adults, $8 for students 6 to 18. That's a 40% savings off individual admissions. *Note:* Most of the block-ticket attractions are closed New Year's Day, Thanksgiving, and December 24, 25, and 31.

You can sit and get an entertaining overview of the town with **Trolley Tours** of Fredericksburg (© 540/898-0737), which passes 35 historic sights. The 1¼-hour narrated tours usually leave the visitor center at 10:30am, noon, 1:30, and 3:30pm from June through September. During April, May, and October, they depart at 10:30am and 1:30pm. Fares are $14 for adults, $5 for children under 18. Buy your tickets at the trolley stop at the visitor center.

Note: The admission prices given in the listings below are to the individual properties without a block ticket.

GETTING THERE

BY CAR   Fredericksburg is about an hour from Richmond or Arlington, a little less from Alexandria via I-95. From I-95, take Exit 130A and follow Va. 3 east. Bear left on William Street (Va. 3 Business), to the heart of town. There are no parking meters in Fredericksburg but many on-street spaces are limited to 2 hours, so be sure to get a free all-day pass from the visitor center.

BY PLANE   The nearest airports are Ronald Reagan Washington National, Washington Dulles International (see "Getting There" in chapter 4) and Richmond International (see chapter 9, "Richmond.")

BY TRAIN   Fredericksburg's **Amtrak** station (© **800/872-7245;** www.amtrak. com) is at Lafayette Boulevard and Princess Anne Street, 3 blocks south of the visitor center. Several trains arrive daily from Washington, D.C., and New York City to the north, Richmond and Newport News to the south.

   Virginia Railway Express (© **800/743-3843** or 703/497-7777; www.vre. org) operates early-morning, mid-day, and late-afternoon rail links between the Fredericksburg Amtrak station and Union Station in Washington, D.C., with stops at Arlington (Crystal City), Alexandria, Lorton, Woodbridge, Quantico, and Stafford. The fare from Alexandria to Fredericksburg is about $6.50 (with discounts for children, seniors, and people with disabilities).

EXPLORING FREDERICKSBURG

Washington Avenue north of Kenmore Plantation & Gardens is the site of several notable monuments. Mary Ball Washington is buried at Meditation Rock, a spot where she often came to pray and meditate; there's a monument there in her honor. Just across the way is the Thomas Jefferson Religious Freedom Monument, commemorating Jefferson's Fredericksburg meeting with George Mason, Edmond Pendleton, George Wythe, and Thomas Ludwell Lee in 1777 to draft the Virginia Statute of Religious Freedom. The Hugh Mercer Monument, off Fauquier Street, honors the doctor and Revolutionary War general whose apothecary shop is now a museum (see below).

THE TOP ATTRACTIONS

Belmont: The Gari Melchers Estate & Memorial Gallery ★   Situated on 27 hillside acres overlooking the falls of the Rappahannock River, Belmont began as an 18th-century farmhouse (the central 6 rooms of the house date to the 1790s) and was enlarged to a 22-room estate by a later owner. The house is furnished with the art treasures, family heirlooms, and European antiques of famed American artist Gari Melchers, who lived here from 1916 until his death in 1932. His wife, Corinne, gave Belmont to the Commonwealth of Virginia in 1955. In addition to Melchers's own works, there are many wonderful paintings in the house—a watercolor sketch by Jan Brueghel, 19th-century paintings by Morisot, and works by Rodin. Tours begin in the Stroh Visitor Center (Melchers's former carriage house), where you can also view an orientation video. It'll take about an hour to see the video and tour the house. You can explore the gardens on your own. Call for a schedule of special exhibitions and lectures.

224 Washington St. (Va. 1001), Falmouth. © **540/654-1015.** www.mwc.edu/belmont. Admission $6 adults, $1 children 6–18, free for children 5 and under. Mar–Nov Mon–Sat 10am–5pm, Sun 1–5pm; Dec–Feb Mon–Sat 10am–4pm, Sun 1–4pm. Mandatory 30-min. house tours depart on hour and half-hour (last tour 4:30pm). From the visitor center, take U.S. 1 north across the Falmouth Bridge, turn left at the traffic light in Falmouth, and go ¼ mile up the hill; turn left on Washington St. (C.R. 1001) to Belmont.

Old Town Fredericksburg

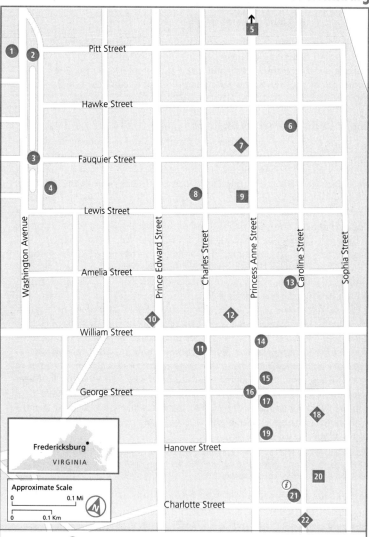

Fun Fact **A Sawbones at Work**

In Dr. Hugh Mercer's Apothecary Shop you can see how he used a heated cup to remove boils and carbuncles, a knife to cut out cataracts, an ominous-looking key to extract teeth, and a saw for amputating limbs. The latter instrument gave rise to the early slang term for doctors: sawbones.

Hugh Mercer Apothecary Shop ★★ Although he was a noted physician, Dr. Hugh Mercer was better known as a warrior. Born in Scotland in 1726, he fled to Pennsylvania after choosing the wrong side in the "Bonnie Prince Charlie" rebellion of 1745–46. He met and became friends with George Washington when they were colonels during the French and Indian Wars of the 1750s. At Washington's urging, he opened this apothecary shop in 1761 and practiced here until the American Revolution broke out. He returned to service as a brigadier-general and was with Washington during the famous crossing of the Delaware River on Christmas night of 1776, which led to the Americans' surprise victory the next morning. Had he not been bayoneted at the Battle of Princeton a few days later, he may well have become one of our Founding Fathers. (The warrior tradition continued in his family—Gen. George S. Patton was his great-great-great-grandson.)

Today, this is one of the most entertaining colonial attractions in Virginia. Hostesses in period dress explain how the doctor operated in those days. Patients didn't read magazines while waiting to see this doctor, for Mercer's waiting room doubled as his operating room. Since opium, the only known anesthesia, was too expensive and difficult to obtain, those waiting for treatment were often put to work holding down the screaming wretch under the knife. Even minor treatment seems ghoulish by today's standards. Leeches and other devices were used to bleed patients (Washington may well have bled to death while undergoing treatment).

Optional tours run continuously, so you can join one when you get here and see what you missed on the next.

1020 Caroline St. (at Amelia St.). © 540/373-3362. www.apva.org/apva/hugh.html. Admission $5 adults, free for students and children. Mar–Nov Mon–Sat 9am–5pm, Sun 11am–5pm; Dec–Feb Mon–Sat 10am–4pm, Sun noon–4pm. Half-hour tours run continuously.

James Monroe Museum and Memorial Library ★ One of the most distinguished Americans of his time, James Monroe served as a U.S. senator; minister to France, England, and Spain; governor of Virginia; secretary of state; secretary of war; and fifth president of the United States (1817–25). As president, he promulgated the Monroe Doctrine, which kept European powers from meddling in the Western Hemisphere.

Monroe practiced law in Fredericksburg from 1786 until 1789, when he moved to Charlottesville to be near his close friend, Thomas Jefferson, and build his home, Highland (now known as Ash Lawn–Highland; see chapter 6), within 2 miles of Jefferson's magnificent Monticello. His great-granddaughter established this museum in 1927 on the site of his Fredericksburg office. Now administered by Mary Washington College, its interior captures the essence of an 18th-century attorney's quarters. The furnishings are originals from either the Monroes' White House years or their retirement home. You can peruse correspondence from Jefferson (don't miss the letter written partially in code), James Madison, and Benjamin Franklin. Here, too, are the gun and canteen Monroe used in the American Revolution. Other than Washington, Monroe was the only president to fight in the War of Independence.

Also on display are two Rembrandt Peale portraits of Monroe, the outfits the Monroes wore at the court of Napoleon, silhouettes of the Monroes by Charles Willson Peale, his wife's teensy wedding slippers, his dueling pistols, and other memorabilia. The library of some 10,000 books is a reconstruction of Monroe's own personal collection. You must take a 30-minute guided tour, which have no fixed schedule but are given throughout the day as demand dictates.

908 Charles St. (between William and George sts.). (C) 540/654-1043. www.mwc.edu/jmmu. Admission $5 adults, $1 children 6–18, free for children 5 and under. Mar–Nov daily 10am–5pm; Dec–Feb daily 10am–4pm. Mandatory 30-min. tours given throughout the day.

Kenmore Plantation & Gardens ☆☆ This stately Georgian mansion was built in the 1770s for George Washington's only sister, Betty Washington, and her husband, Fielding Lewis, one of the wealthiest planters in Fredericksburg. According to legend, Washington involved himself closely in the building, decoration, and furnishings of the estate. During the Revolution, Lewis financed a gun factory and built vessels for the Virginia navy. As a result of his large expenditures in the cause of patriotism, he had to sell Kenmore to liquidate his debts. He died soon after the victory at Yorktown.

Today, the house is undergoing a 3- to 5-year renovation, which will restore it to its colonial elegance. In the meantime, some of the paintings and furniture are on display in the gallery at the visitor center, and tours concentrate on its architectural features, of which the exquisitely molded plaster ceilings and cornices are the most outstanding. Much of the flooring and all the woodwork and paneling are also original.

Either before or after the tour, spend another 15 to 30 minutes on your own exploring the famous gardens, restored and maintained according to the original plans by the Garden Club of Virginia, and the excellent museum shop.

1201 Washington Ave. (between Lewis and Fauquier sts.). (C) 540/373-3381. www.kenmore.org. Admission $6 adults, $3 children 6–18, free for children 5 and under. Mar–Dec daily 11am–5pm. Jan–Feb Sat 11am–5pm. Mandatory 30-min. house tours depart on hour and half-hour (last tour 4:30pm).

The Rising Sun Tavern ☆ The Rising Sun was originally a residence, built in 1760 by Charles Washington, George's youngest brother, but beginning in the early 1790s it served as a tavern for some 30 years. The building is preserved, not reconstructed, though the 17th- and 18th-century furnishings are not all originals. You'll be thoroughly entertained during the 30-minute tours led by a tavern wench—an indentured servant sentenced to 7 years for stealing a loaf of bread in

---

Moments **Down a Lazy River**

Operated by the same company that goes to Tangier Island from Reedville on the Northern Neck, **Rappahannock River Cruises** ((C) 804/ 453-2628; www.tangiercruise.com) sends the stern-wheel _City of Fredericksburg_ down the river. The 2-hour lunch trips, which stop at Ingleside Vineyards (see "The Northern Neck," later in this chapter) for wine tastings, are the most popular. They depart at noon Tuesday to Saturday from the City Dock on Sophia Street. Fares are $25 for adults, $16 for children. The company also has dinner and Sunday brunch cruises.

England. The Rising Sun Tavern was a proper high-class tavern, she explains, not for riffraff. The gentlemen congregated over Madeira and cards in the Great Room or had a rollicking good time in the Taproom over multicourse meals and many tankards of ale. Meanwhile, ladies were consigned to the Retiring Room, where they would spend the entire day gossiping and doing needlework. You must take a tour, but as at Hugh Mercer Apothecary Shop, they run continuously so you can join the one in progress when you get here and see what you missed on the next.

1306 Caroline St. (at Fauquier St.). ⓒ 540/371-1494. Admission (without the block ticket) $5 adults, $1.50 children 6–18, free for children 5 and under. Mar–Nov Mon–Sat 9am–5pm; Sun 11am–5pm; Dec–Feb Mon–Sat 10am–4pm; Sun noon–4pm. Mandatory 30-min. tours run continuously.

MORE ATTRACTIONS

Chatham This pre-Revolutionary mansion built between 1768 and 1771 by wealthy planter William Fitzhugh has figured prominently in American history. Fitzhugh was a fourth-generation American who supported the Revolution politically and financially. In the 18th century, Chatham was a center of Southern hospitality, often visited by George Washington. During the Civil War, the house, which belonged to J. Horace Lacy, served as headquarters for Federal commanders and as a Union field hospital. Lincoln visited his Union generals at the house, and volunteers Clara Barton, founder of the American Red Cross, and poet Walt Whitman helped nurse the wounded here. Exhibits tell about the families who have owned Chatham and detail the role the estate played during the war. Plaques on the grounds identify battle landmarks. You can tour five rooms and the grounds on your own. The dining room and hallway have exhibits on Chatham's owners and its role in the Civil War. National Park Service employees are on hand to answer questions. There is a picnic area on the premises. The mansion is headquarters of the Fredericksburg and Spotsylvania National Military Park, so your admission here will include the Civil War battlefields (see section 2, "Civil War Battlefields").

120 Chatham Lane. ⓒ 540/371-0802. www.nps.gov/frsp. Admission $4 per person, good for 7 days (includes Fredericksburg and Spotsylvania National Military Park). Daily 9am–5pm. Closed Christmas and New Year's Day. Take William St. (Va. 3) east across the river and follow the signs.

The Courthouse If you're interested in architecture, see this Gothic Revival courthouse, built in 1853. Its architect, James Renwick, also designed St. Patrick's Cathedral in New York and the original Smithsonian "Castle" and Renwick Gallery in Washington, D.C. Exhibits in the lobby include copies of Mary Ball Washington's will and George Washington's address to the city council in 1784.

Princess Anne and George sts. ⓒ 540/372-1066. Free admission. Mon–Fri 9am–4pm.

Fredericksburg Area Museum and Cultural Center This very good local museum occupies the 1816 Town Hall in Market Square. In existence since 1733, Market Square was the center of trade and commerce in Fredericksburg for more than a century, while Town Hall served as the city's social and legal center. Lafayette was entertained here in 1824 with lavish parties and balls, and the building continued to serve its original function until 1982. The first level is a changing exhibit area for displays relating to regional and cultural history. If it's still on display, don't miss the collection of Masonic artifacts, including a Gilbert Stuart portrait of Washington in its original gilt Federalist frame, and the 1668 Bible on which Washington took his Masonic obligation (oath) when joining Masonic Lodge No. 4. The second floor houses permanent exhibits about the area's history, from Native American settlements and pre–English explorers to the present. The Civil War exhibit graphically depicts the reality of the war as experienced by the local citizenry. The hall's 19th-century Council Chamber on the third floor is also used for changing exhibits.

907 Princess Anne St. (at William St.). ✆ **540/371-3037**. www.famcc.org. Admission $4 adults, $1.50 children 6–18, free for children 5 and under. Mar–Nov Mon–Sat 10am–5pm, Sun 1–5pm; Dec–Feb Mon–Sat 10am–4pm, Sun 1–4pm.

George Washington's Ferry Farm

The first president was 6 years old when his family moved to this farm of about 600 acres across the river from Fredericksburg in 1738. It was here that George purportedly confessed to chopping down the cherry tree. He, sister Betty, and brothers Samuel, John and Charles took a ferry across the river to school in Fredericksburg. After their father, Augustine Washington, died in 1743, their mother Mary Ball Washington stayed on the farm until 1772, when George bought her a house in town (see below). Union soldiers camped on the farm during the Civil War. Archaeological digs have uncovered the remains of what appears to be the Washingtons' first house, and relics are on display in the visitor center. You can watch the archaeologists at work Wednesday to Sunday during summer. The grounds make for a pleasant stroll.

268 Kings Hwy. (Va. 3). ✆ **540/370-0732**. Admission $3 adults, $1.50 children 6–17, free for children 5 and under. Jan–Feb Sat only, 10am–4pm; Mar–Dec 10am–4pm daily. Closed New Year's Day, Thanksgiving, Christmas Eve, Christmas, and New Year's Eve. Take Va. 3 east across Rappahannock River, turn right after 3rd traffic signal.

Mary Washington House

George Washington purchased this house for his mother in 1772, and added a two-story extension. She was then 64 years old and had been living at nearby Ferry Farm since 1738. Lafayette visited during the Revolution to pay respects to the mother of the greatest living American, and Washington came in 1789 to receive her blessing before going to New York for his inauguration as president. He never saw her again, for she died later that year.

1200 Charles St. (at Lewis St.). ✆ **540/373-1569**. Admission $5 adults, $1.50 children 6–18, free for children 5 and under. Mar–Nov Mon–Sat 9am–5pm, Sun 11am–5pm; Dec–Feb Mon–Sat 10am–4pm; Sun noon–4pm. Mandatory 30-min. tours run continuously.

Masonic Lodge No. 4

Not only is this the mother lodge of the father of our country, it's also one of the oldest Masonic lodges in America, established around 1735. Although the original building was down the street, Masons have been meeting at this address since 1812. The lodge owns many historic artifacts, including the Gilbert Stuart portrait of Washington and the Bible on which Washington took his Masonic oath, which have been on display at the Fredericksburg Area Museum and Cultural Center (see above). The lodge is open only by appointment, which Masons should definitely make. The rest of us can see the building from the street.

803 Princess Anne St. (at Hanover St.). ✆ **540/373-5885**. Open by appointment only.

The Presbyterian Church

This church dates to the early 1800s, although the present Greek Revival building was completed in 1855—just in time to be shelled during the Civil War, and, like St. George's (below), to serve as a hospital where Clara Barton nursed Union wounded. Cannonballs in the front left pillar and scars on the walls of the loft and belfry remain. The present church bell replaced one that was given to the Confederacy to be melted down for making cannons.

810 Princess Anne St. (at George St.). ✆ **540/373-7057**. Free admission. Services Labor Day to June Sun 8:30 and 11am; June–Aug Sun 8:30 and 10am (go to church office at other times).

St. George's Episcopal Church Martha Washington's father and John Paul Jones's brother are buried in the graveyard of this church, and members of the first parish congregation included Mary Washington and Revolutionary War generals Hugh Mercer and George Weedon. The original church on this site was built in 1732; the current Romanesque structure, in 1849. During the Battle of Fredericksburg, the church was hit at least 25 times, and in 1863, it was used by General Lee's troops for religious revival meetings. In 1864, when wounded Union soldiers filled every available building in town, it served as a hospital. Note the three, signed Tiffany windows.

905 Princess Anne St. (between George and William sts.). ℭ 540/373-4133. www.stgeorgesepiscopal.net. Free admission. Mon–Sat 9am–5pm (unless a wedding is taking place Sat); Sun services 8 and 10am.

SHOPPING

Fredericksburg is a treasure trove for antiques and collectibles shoppers, with more than 40 stores in the historic area. The selection is good here, and the prices are reasonable when compared to those in metropolitan areas such as Alexandria, Richmond, and Norfolk.

You'll pass most of the shops along Caroline Street, the city's main drag, north of the visitor center. Others are on Sophia and William streets. The center has brochures describing each store's specialty (see "Essentials," earlier).

WHERE TO STAY

Every major chain has motels off I-95. The strip along Va. 3 at Exit 130 is Fredericksburg's major shopping area, with the Spotsylvania Mall, and a host of family restaurants. You'll find the **Best Western Fredericksburg** (ℭ 800/528-1234 or 540/371-5050), the **Best Western Thunderbird** (ℭ 800/528-1234 or 540/786-7404), the **Econo Lodge Central** (ℭ 800/55-ECONO or 540/786-8374), a **Hampton Inn** (ℭ 800/HAMPTON or 540/371-0330), a **Ramada Inn** (ℭ 800/2RAMADA or 540/786-8361), the **Sheraton Fredericksburg Inn & Conference Center** (ℭ 800/682-1049 or 540/786-8321), and a **Super 8** (ℭ 800/800-8000 or 540/786-8881).

The following inns are located in the historic area.

Fredericksburg Colonial Inn _(Value_ Victorian furnishings from the Civil War era make this attractive spot a hub for Civil War buffs, and people participating in Civil War reenactments often drop by; don't be surprised to see musket-toting Blues and Grays in the lobby. In the Conference Room, you'll find a display of Civil War weaponry and Confederate dollars. The rooms are furnished with some reproductions but mostly with antiques (the owner is an avid collector), such as marble-top walnut dressers, rag rugs, canopied beds, Victorian sofas, and a bed that belonged to George Mason's son. The spacious lobby is furnished with wicker rocking chairs and a player piano. This is a non-smoking hotel.

1707 Princess Anne St. (at Herndon St.), Fredericksburg, VA 22401. ℭ 540/371-5666. Fax 540/371-5884. www.fci1.com. 28 units. $70–$120 double. Rates include light continental breakfast. AE, MC, V. **Amenities:** Access to nearby health club. _In room:_ A/C, TV, fridge.

Kenmore Inn ⚝ An elegant white pediment supported by fluted columns and a front porch with wicker chairs welcome you to this late 1700s mansion in Old Town on property originally owned by George Washington's brother-in-law, Fielding Lewis. Crystal chandeliers, Oriental rugs, Georgian side tables, and an enormous gold-framed mirror enhance the foyer. A sweeping staircase leads to the guest rooms—a handsome assortment of both cozy and spacious accommodations furnished with a mix of antiques, many in Regency style. Expect to find four-poster beds with pretty coverlets and lacy canopies, draperies framing lou-ver-shuttered windows, antique chests, and walls hung with botanical prints and engravings. The house has eight working fireplaces, four in the bedrooms. The inn serves lunch and dinner Tuesday through Saturday and brunch on Sunday. The Pub offers live jazz and blues Friday and Saturday nights.

1200 Princess Anne St. (at Lewis St.), Fredericksburg, VA 22401. ℂ 540/371-7622. Fax 540/371-5480. www. kenmoreinn.com. 12 units. $95–$200 double. Rates include continental breakfast. Packages available. AE, DC, MC, V. **Amenities:** Restaurant; bar; access to nearby health club. *In room:* A/C, TV (deluxe units only).

Richard Johnston Inn ✰✰   Two 18th-century brick row houses have been joined to form this elegantly restored inn across the street from the visitor center. The downstairs sitting rooms and dining room, where continental breakfast is served, are invitingly furnished. The Oriental rugs and mahogany furniture in the second-floor rooms in one house create a more formal atmosphere; while in the other, braided rugs, rockers, oak dressers, and four-poster beds lend a country charm. Third-floor dormer rooms are charming, with low ceilings. The inn's orig-inal summer kitchen exudes charm, with brick floors, two queen beds, and a pri-vate entrance off the courtyard. The spacious, comfortable suites each offer a private courtyard entrance as well as a separate living room with TV, wet bar, and refrigerator. One of these has a king bed in a loft. The innkeeper has a dog in the house, and two rooms here are pet-friendly. There are no phones in the rooms.

711 Caroline St. (between Hanover and Charlotte sts.), Fredericksburg, VA 22401. ℂ 877/577-0770 or 540/ 899-7606. Fax 540/899-6837. www.therichardjohnstoninn.com. 9 units. $90–$175 double. Rates include con-tinental breakfast weekdays, full breakfast on weekends. AE, MC, V. **Amenities:** Free wireless Internet access. *In room:* A/C, TV.

WHERE TO DINE

La Petite Auberge ✰ FRENCH TRADITIONAL   Christian Etienne Rean-ult's delightful restaurant was designed to look like a garden, an effect enhanced by white latticework and garden furnishings. Unpainted brick walls are hung with copper pots and cheerful oil paintings, and candlelit tables are adorned with fresh flowers. A cozy lounge adjoins. The menu changes daily. The menu might offer salade Niçoise, soft-shell crab amandine, poached salmon with hol-landaise sauce, and sirloin steak with béarnaise sauce. The early-bird dinner here is an attractive offering—soup, salad, a choice of seven entrees from the regular dinner menu, and ice cream.

311 William St. (between Princess Anne and Charles sts.). ℂ 540/371-2727. Reservations recommended, especially at dinner. Main courses $10–$26; early-bird dinner $17. AE, DC, MC, V. Mon–Fri 11:30am–2:30pm and 5:30–10pm; Sat 11:20am–2:15pm and 5:30–10pm; early-bird dinner Mon–Thurs 5:30–7pm.

Ristorante Renato *Value* SOUTHERN ITALIAN   This very good, reasonably priced Italian eatery offers homey decor—candlelit (at night) white-linened tables adorned with fresh flowers, ceramic candelabra chandeliers, oil paintings of Italy lining the walls, and a working fireplace. The booths in a small room to one side are especially cozy. In addition to its regular menu, Renato offers a complete lunch

---

Tips **A Picnic by the River**

A picnic by the Rappahannock River is a good idea here, and **Feast-O-Rama,** 1008 Sophia St. (ℂ 540/373-9040), between William and Amelia streets, has all the supplies, including gourmet meats and cheeses, hearth-baked breads, wine, and micro-brewed beers. Open Tuesday to Saturday 10am to 6pm.

featuring salad, home-baked bread, and entrees like eggplant parmigiana, fettuc-cine Alfredo, or steamed mussels in white sauce. A similar early-bird dinner adds dessert and a demi-carafe of wine; a three-course meal with a bottle of wine is available anytime Monday through Thursday evenings for $50 for two people.

422 William St. (at Prince Edward St.). ℭ 540/317-8228. Reservations recommended, especially on week-ends. Main courses $10–$25; early-bird dinner $24 for 2 people. AE, DISC, MC, V. Mon–Fri 11:30am–2pm and 4:30–10pm; Sat–Sun 4:30–10pm; early-bird dinner Mon–Fri 4:30–6pm.

Sammy T's AMERICAN/VEGETARIAN Located in the middle of the his-toric business district, this popular, inexpensive pub offers a relaxed, tasteful set-ting and a creative health-food orientation. It has a rustic feel, with large overhead fans, a pressed-tin ceiling, knotty-pine booths, a long oak bar, and painted wood walls adorned with framed art posters. Everything on the menu is made from scratch, with an emphasis on natural ingredients. The lunch and dinner menu offer many vegetarian items, such as a lentil burger and a spicy black-bean cake. Entrees like broiled salmon steak, vegetarian lasagna, and chicken Parmesan over fettuccine are other possibilities.

801 Caroline St. (at Hanover St.). ℭ 540/371-2008. Reservations not accepted. Sandwiches $5–$7.50; main courses $5.50–$9. AE, DISC, MC, V. Mon–Sat 11am–10pm; Sun 11am–8pm.

623 Restaurant COMTEMPORARY AMERICAN/TAPAS A restored Geor-gian-style private home built about 1769 houses this bistro-style restaurant offer-ing Spanish tapas and contemporary American main courses. The interior retains much of its colonial character, with original wide-plank flooring, paneling, and dining-room fireplaces. The tapas definitely are Iberian, while the main courses range from chili-and-brown-sugar-cured salmon to a New York strip steak served with warm applewood smoked bacon and red bliss potato salad.

623 Caroline St. (at Charlotte St.). ℭ 540/361-2640. www.sixtwentythree.com. Reservations recom-mended. Main courses $16–$20; tapas $4–$8. AE, DC, DISC, MC, V. Wed–Sat 5–10pm (bar open to midnight on weekends, 2am on weekends in summer); Sun 11am–3pm and 5–10pm.

The Smythe's Cottage and Tavern ☆ TRADITIONAL SOUTHERN Fredericksburg's answer to Williamsburg's colonial taverns, this quaintly charming cottage is an appropriate stop for lunch during your walking tour of the historic sites. Although the current building dates to 1840, it's on the site of a blacksmith's stable once operated by George Washington's brother. The low-ceilinged interior is cozy, decorated with colonial-style furnishings, oil portraits, and family memo-rabilia. The restaurant's original owner hailed from an old Virginia clan, hence the back-room photograph of General Grant upside down next to a photo of her great-great-grandfather, who was hanged by the Union army in the Civil War. There's dining in a bright sunroom, and alfresco in a flower-bordered garden when the weather's clear and warm. Waiters dressed in colonial attire serve good Virginia fare like creamy peanut soup and a delicious chicken or seafood potpie under a flaky crust. The wine list features vintages from the Northern Neck's Ingleside Vineyards (p. 119).

303 Fauquier St. (at Princess Anne St.). ℭ 540/373-1645. Reservations suggested on weekends. Lunch $4–$7; main courses $12–$20. MC, V. Mon and Wed–Thurs 11am–9pm; Fri–Sat 11am–10pm; Sun noon–9pm.

2 The Civil War Battlefields ☆☆

Fredericksburg has never forgotten its Civil War victories and defeats in the bat-tles of Fredericksburg and at Chancellorsville, The Wilderness, and Spotsylvania Court House, 12 to 15 miles west of the city. The battles were part of three different Union attempts to advance from Washington, D.C., to Richmond between December 1862 and May 1864. Only the last one succeeded. Today, the sites are beautifully preserved in the National Park Service's **Fredericksburg & Spotsylvania National Military Park,** which also includes the Stonewall Jackson Shrine, where the great Confederate general died after being mistakenly shot by his own men.

SEEING THE BATTLEFIELDS

Start at the **Fredericksburg Battlefield Visitor Center,** 1013 Lafayette Blvd. (U.S. 1 Business), at Sunken Road (© **540/373-6122**), where you can get detailed tour brochures and buy or rent the 3-hour auto-tour tapes or CDs ($4.95 to rent, $7.95 to purchase). The center offers a short slide-show orientation and has related exhibits. Be sure to pick up the park service's main brochure, which has a detailed map, and pamphlets for each of the sites. If you want more detailed information, a bookstore across the parking lot is packed with Civil War literature. The visitor center is open daily from 9am to 5pm, to 6pm on fall weekends.

The actual battlefields are open daily from sunrise to sunset.

There's also a visitor center at **Chancellorsville** (see below). The Wilderness and Spotsylvania Court House battlefields have shelters with exhibits explaining what happened. Park rangers give **guided tours** of each battlefield daily during summer and on autumn weekends. Call the visitor centers for the schedule.

Admission to the park is $4 per person, payable at the Fredericksburg or Chancellorsville battlefields or at Chatham plantation (see "More Attractions" in "Exploring Fredericksburg," earlier). It's good for 7 days and includes Chatham. National Park Service passports are accepted.

For advance **information,** contact the Superintendent, Fredericksburg and Spotsylvania National Military Park, 120 Chatham Lane, Fredericksburg, VA 22405 (© **540/371-0802;** www.nps.gov/frsp).

⟨Tips A Battle Plan for Seeing the Battlefields

Although you can drive around the battlefields in less than a day, you'll need 2 days to take the full 75-mile audio-guided auto tours of the Fredericksburg and Spotsylvania battlefields. Allow a minimum of 30 minutes at each of the two visitor centers and 3 hours for each of the four battlefield audio tours, plus driving times in between.

I strongly recommend the audio tour tapes and CDs available at the Fredericksburg and Chancellorsville visitor centers. Renting a player along with them will allow you to get out of your car and still hear the informative commentary.

Although you can start at the Chancellorsville visitor center, it will make more sense to tour the battlefields in the order in which the conflicts occurred: Fredericksburg (Dec 11–12, 1862), Chancellorsville (Apr 27–May 6, 1863), The Wilderness (May 5–6, 1864), and Spotsylvania Court House (May 8–21, 1864). Spend the first day at Fredericksburg and Chancellorsville; the second, at The Wilderness and Spotsylvania Court House, where the battles happened within days of each other. The Stonewall Jackson Shrine at Guinea Station is 18 miles southeast of Spotsylvania Court House; go there last.

BATTLE OF FREDERICKSBURG

Lee used the Rappahannock River as a natural line of defense for much of the war, while the Union army's goal was to cross it and head for Richmond. The Battle of Fredericksburg took place from December 11 to 13, 1862, when the Union army under Gen. Ambrose E. Burnside crossed the river into Fredericksburg via pontoon bridges. Burnside made a huge mistake when he sent the body of his 100,000 men uphill against Lee's 75,000 troops, most of them dug in behind a stone wall along Sunken Road at the base of Marye's Heights. The ground below the heights became a bloody killing field as Lee's cannon, firing from the hill, mowed down the Yankees. The stone wall—some parts original, some reconstructed—stands beside the visitor center at the base of Marye's Heights. Before setting out on the driving tour, examine the wall and follow the gently sloping pathway up the 40-foot-high heights for a fine view over the town. The stroll takes about 30 minutes.

BATTLE OF CHANCELLORSVILLE

President Lincoln fired Burnside after the Marye's Heights massacre. Under Gen. Joseph Hooker, Burnside's replacement, the Union forces crossed the river north of Fredericksburg in late April 1863, and advanced to Chancellorsville, a crossroads 10 miles west of Fredericksburg on the Orange Turnpike (now Va. 3). When Lee rushed westward to meet him, Hooker dug in. In a surprise attack, Stonewall Jackson flanked Hooker's line on May 2 and won a spectacular victory. Jackson was inadvertently shot by his own men that same night. He was taken 5 miles west to Ellwood Plantation, where doctors amputated his arm (which is buried in the family cemetery). Then they moved him to Guinea Station, 27 miles away, to be evacuated by train. Pneumonia set in, however, and Jackson died there on May 10 (see "Stonewall Jackson Shrine," below). By then, Lee had driven the Union army back across the Rappahannock.

Stop at the **Chancellorsville Visitor Center** (© **540/786-2880**), 12 miles east of Fredericksburg on Va. 3, to see another audiovisual orientation and related exhibits. Once again, auto-tour tapes and CDs are available. The center is open daily from 9am to 5pm, with extended hours on autumn weekends. Closed New Year's Day and Christmas.

BATTLE OF THE WILDERNESS

A year later under the direction of the aggressive Ulysses S. Grant, Union forces once again crossed the Rappahannock and advanced south to Wilderness Tavern, 5 miles west of Chancellorsville near what is now the junction of Va. 3 and Va. 20. Lee advanced to meet him, thus setting up the first battle between these two great generals. For the 2 days of May 5 and 6, 1864, the armies fought in the tangled thickets of The Wilderness. The battle was a stalemate, but instead of retreating as his predecessors had, Grant backed off and went around Lee toward his ultimate target, Richmond, via the shortest road south (now Va. 208).

The battle raged around Ellwood plantation, which had served as a Confederate hospital during the Battle of Chancellorsville. You can see the grave of Stonewall Jackson's arm in the old family cemetery, which is open to the public Saturday and Sunday from 11am to 5pm between Memorial Day and Columbus Day.

BATTLE OF SPOTSYLVANIA COURTHOUSE

Lee quickly regrouped and tried to stop Grant 2 days later at Spotsylvania Court House, about 18 miles southeast of The Wilderness. Taking advantage of thick

Civil War Battlefields & the Northern Neck

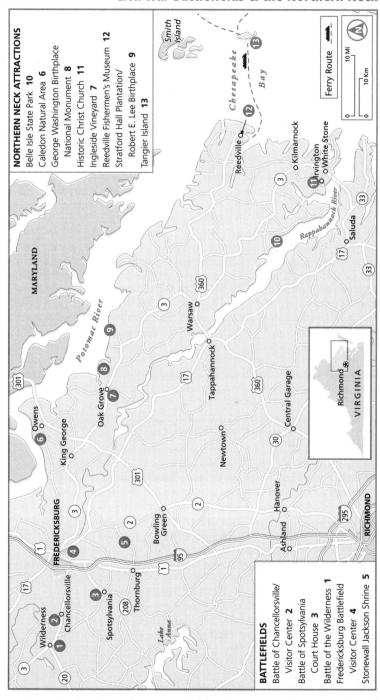

NORTHERN NECK ATTRACTIONS

Belle Isle State Park **10**
Caledon Natural Area **6**
George Washington Birthplace
  National Monument **8**
Historic Christ Church **11**
Ingleside Vineyard **7**
Reedville Fishermen's Museum **12**
Stratford Hall Plantation/
  Robert E. Lee Birthplace **9**
Tangier Island **13**

BATTLEFIELDS

Battle of Chancellorsville/
  Visitor Center **2**
Battle of Spotsylvania
  Court House **3**
Battle of the Wilderness **1**
Fredericksburg Battlefield
  Visitor Center **4**
Stonewall Jackson Shrine **5**

Smith Island

Chesapeake Bay

Ferry Route

10 Mi
10 Km

MARYLAND

Potomac River

Rappahannock River

Reedville

Kilmarnock
Irvington
White Stone

Saluda

Warsaw

Tappahannock

Central Garage

Newtown

Oak Grove

King George

Owens

FREDERICKSBURG

Bowling Green

Hanover

Ashland

RICHMOND

Chancellorsville
Wilderness

Spotsylvania

Thornburg

Lake Anna

Richmond
VIRGINIA

301

360

360

30

17

33

33

3

3

3

3

2

2

1

1

95

295

208

20

17

17

1

115

fog and wet Confederate gunpowder, Union troops breached the Southerners' line. When Lee's reinforcements arrived, the sides spent 20 hours in the war's most intense hand-to-hand combat at a site known as Bloody Angle. During the fighting, Lee built new fortifications to the rear, which he successfully defended. Instead of pushing the fight to the finish, however, Grant again backed off, flanked his entire army around Lee's, and resumed his unrelenting march toward Richmond. It was the end of major fighting in the Fredericksburg area, as the war moved south to its ultimate conclusion 11 months later at Appomattox.

There's an exhibit shelter on Grant Drive, where park rangers lead walking tours daily during summer, weekends in spring and fall. Call the Fredericksburg or Chancellorsville visitor centers for details.

STONEWALL JACKSON SHRINE

Now part of the park, the **Stonewall Jackson Shrine** (© **804/633-6076**) is in the plantation office where the general spent the last 6 days of his life after being shot and mortally wounded by his own men at Chancellorsville. The wood-frame office was one of the outbuildings on Fairfield Plantation. Jackson's doctors chose it because it was quieter and more private than the manor house. They hoped that he would recover sufficiently to board a train at nearby Guinea Station for the ride to Richmond, but it was not to be. Jackson's body was taken to Lexington, where he was buried with full honors (see chapter 7, "The Shenandoah Valley").

The office is the only structure remaining at the plantation and appears as it did when Jackson died. About 45% of its contents are original.

The shrine is open 9am to 5pm, daily from Memorial Day to Labor Day, Friday to Tuesday in spring and fall, Saturday to Monday in winter. It's at the junction of C.R. 606 and C.R. 607, about 27 miles southeast of Chancellorsville, 18 miles southeast of Spotsylvania Court House. From I-95, take Exit 118 at Thornburg and follow the signs east on C.R. 606.

3 The Northern Neck

A peninsula between the Potomac and Rappahannock rivers, the Northern Neck stretches 90 miles east from Fredericksburg to the Chesapeake Bay. A popular weekend getaway and retirement retreat for residents of nearby metropolitan areas, this rural land of rolling hills serrated by quiet tidal creeks is the ancestral home of the Washingtons and the Lees, who created large plantations on the riverbanks. Its hills are still punctuated by agricultural and small fishing villages (they speak in terms of counties here, not towns).

From a visitor's standpoint, the Northern Neck has three areas of interest. Heading east from Fredericksburg on Va. 3, you first come to George Washington's Birthplace National Monument, where the first president was born in 1732 on Pope's Creek Plantation, and Stratford Hall, the magnificently restored Lee plantation. Nearby, the Ingleside Plantation Vineyards offer tours and tastings.

A left turn on Va. 202 will take you northeast to the end of the Northern Neck, at Smith Point on the Chesapeake. Here you can explore the quaint town of Reedville, founded as a menhaden fishing port in 1867 by Capt. Elijah Reed, a New England seafarer. Reedville soon became rich, and its captains and plant owners built magnificent Victorian-style homes. One plant still processes the small, toothless fish, which is of little use for human consumption but extremely valuable as meal, oil, and protein supplements used in everything from Pepperidge Farm cookies to Rustoleum paint. You can learn all about the menhaden at the local fishing museum. From Reedville you can depart on cruises to remote Tangier Island out in the bay.

Va. 200 will take you south to the genteel riverfront hamlet of Irvington, home of Christ Church, perhaps the nation's best example of colonial church architecture; The Tides Inn, one of Virginia's premier resorts; and The Hope and Glory Inn, one of its most unusual bed-and-breakfasts. Irvington and its neighboring villages of White Stone and Kilmarnock constitute one of Virginia's most affluent retirement communities.

ESSENTIALS

VISITOR INFORMATION   For advance information about the area, contact the **Northern Neck Tourism Council,** P.O. Box 1707, Warsaw, VA 22572 (© **800/393-6180** or 804/333-1919; www.northernneck.org). The council's offices are at 479 Main St. (Va. 3 Business) in the McKinley Office Park. The walk-in **Virginia's Potomac Gateway Welcome Center** (© **540/633-3205**) is on U.S. 301 just south of the Potomac River Bridge. It's open daily from 9am to 5pm. The **Reedville Fishermen's Museum** (see "Exploring the Northern Neck," below) has information about Reedville and the Smith Point area. For the Irvington area, check with the **Lancaster County Chamber of Commerce & Visitor Center,** P.O. Box 1868, Kilmarnock, VA 22482 (© **804/435-6092**), which is in the Chesapeake Commons Shopping Center on Va. 3 west of Kilmarnock. Open Monday to Thursday 9am to 4pm.

GETTING THERE   You'll need a **car** to get here. From Fredericksburg, go east on Va. 3, which traverses the length of the peninsula. From Fredericksburg, Washington's Birthplace is 40 miles; Irvington, 95 miles. You can make a scenic loop tour of the peninsula by taking Va. 3 past Montross, Va. 202 to Reedville, Va. 200 to Irvington, then Va. 3 back to Fredericksburg. The "fast" route from Fredericksburg to Reedville and Irvington is via U.S. 17 and U.S. 360. You can get here from Richmond via U.S. 360 and from Williamsburg on U.S. 17 and Va. 3.

EXPLORING THE NORTHERN NECK

George Washington Birthplace National Monument ⋆   Although it's a
re-creation of Popes Creek Plantation, this national monument shows you what 18th-century farm life was like when Washington's father, Augustine, established a tobacco plantation here in 1718. The first president was born on February 22, 1732, and lived here until here until he was 3½ years old. The manor house burned on Christmas Day in 1779 and was never rebuilt. There are no records detailing what it looked like, but the outline of the foundation is marked on the lawn of Memorial House. Built in 1930–31 and furnished with period antiques, Memorial House is an accurate reproduction of a plantation home of that era. The kitchen, workshop, and other outbuildings have also been reconstructed.

You can see the site in 1½- to 2 hours. Start at the visitor center, where a 14-minute film explains plantation life, and a display case holds Washington family

---

Tips   How to See the Northern Neck

You can easily see George Washington's Birthplace, Stratford Hall Plantation, and the Ingleside Vineyards as a day trip from Fredericksburg or as stops on the way to Irvington. Plan on at least 2 days if you go on to Reedville and Irvington, 3 days if taking an all-day cruise to Tangier or Smith Islands.

artifacts uncovered during archaeological digs here. A slightly uphill walk of some 300 yards along Popes Creek leads to the actual birthplace (transportation is provided if you can't walk that distance). You'll first pass the outlines of the main house and then the kitchen building and Memorial House (a guide will take you through). Beyond are the spinning shed, workshop, vegetable gardens, hog pen, and paddocks holding cows, bullocks, horses, sheep, geese, and ducks. Park ranger programs are offered hourly, and rangers conduct guided tours from the visitor center. The graves of 32 Washington-family members, including George's father, are in a small burial ground on the property.

Admission is free on the Monday of Washington's Birthday weekend in February (gingerbread and hot cider are served), and a multitude of activities take place on February 22, George's actual birthday.

1732 Popes Creek Rd. (Va. 204, off Va. 3). © 804/224-1732. www.nps.gov/gewa. Admission $3 adults, free for children 16 and under (good for 7 days). National Park Service passports accepted. Daily 9am–5pm. Closed New Year's Day, Thanksgiving, and Christmas.

Historic Christ Church ★★★ Elegant in its simplicity and virtually unchanged since 1735, Christ Church was the gift of Robert "King" Carter, who offered to finance it if his parents' graves remained interred in the chancel. His father, John Carter, four of his five wives, and two infant children are still here. Robert Carter's tomb is on the grounds. Among the descendants of the Carters are eight governors of Virginia; two United States presidents (the Harrisons); Gen. Robert E. Lee; and Edward D. White, a chief justice of the U.S. Supreme Court.

Listed on the National Register of Historic Places, the church is cruciform in shape, its brick facade laid in a pleasing Flemish bond pattern, with a three-color design that saves the expanse of brick from monotony. Inside, the three-tiered pulpit is in excellent condition, and all 26 original pews remain (they're like box seats, with more important families occupying the larger boxes). A marble baptismal font dates to the 1660s. The building has no artificial heat or light. Its only electrical outlet is in the Carter family pew, and that's to power the organ used for services only during the summer.

Begin your visit in the museum, where there's a 10-minute video, then take a 30-minute guided tour through the church. The guides are particularly good at children's tours. Allow 30 minutes or so to poke among the gravestones.

C.R. 646, off Va. 200, 1 mile north of Irvington. © 804/438-6855. www.christchurch1735.org. Free admission (donations accepted). Church, daily 9am–5pm. Museum and 30-min. guided tours, Apr–Nov Mon–Sat 10am–4pm; Sun 2–5pm. Worship services held in the church Sun at 8am from Memorial to Labor Day. Closed December.

Reedville Fishermen's Museum On Cockrell's Creek, an inlet of Chesapeake Bay, the fishing village of Reedville provides a living image of the past with its Victorian mansions and seafaring atmosphere. The Fishermen's Museum consists of the 1875 William Walker House, the town's oldest building, which has been restored to appear as it did in 1900. The Covington Building houses a permanent collection and special exhibits commemorating the watermen who participate in the town's leading industry, menhaden fishing, which dates to 1874 when Capt. Elijah Reed arrived here. There's an 11-minute video about the industry, and guides lead 10-minute tours of the Walker House.

504 Main St., Reedville. © 540/453-6529. www.rfmuseum.com. Admission $3 adults, free for children 11 and under. Mar–Apr Sat–Sun 10:30am–4:30pm; May–Oct daily 10:30am–4:30pm; Nov–Jan Fri–Mon 10:30am–4:30pm; closed Feb. From Va. 3 east, take U.S. 360 east to Reedville.

(*Tips* **Taking a Lunch Break**

There aren't many places to dine here, so have lunch in the log cabin-style **Plantation Dining Room** at Stratford Hall Plantation. It offers worthy Virginia-style cream of crab soup, crab cake and fried oyster sandwiches, salads topped with chicken or cured ham, ham biscuits, and meals of fried chicken, crab cakes, flounder, or ham, all at reasonable prices. Chardonnay and cabernet sauvignon wines from Ingleside Vineyards are served by the glass or bottle. Open daily from 11:30am to 3pm except Thanksgiving and December 23 to January 4.

Stratford Hall Plantation ★★★   This is one of the great houses of the South, magnificently set on 1,600 acres above the Potomac, renowned for its distinctive architectural style and for the illustrious members of the Lee family who lived here. Thomas Lee (1690–1750), a planter who later served as governor of the Virginia colony, built Stratford in the 1730s. Five of his sons played major roles in the forming of the new nation, most notably Richard Henry Lee, who made the motion for independence in the Continental Congress in 1776. He and Francis Lightfoot Lee were the only brothers to sign the Declaration. Cousin Henry "Light-Horse Harry" Lee, a hero of the Revolution, was a friend of George Washington and father of Robert E. Lee, who was born here in 1807.

The H-shaped manor house, its four dependencies, coach house, and stables have been brilliantly restored. Brick chimney groupings that flank the roofline are some of the mansion's most striking features. The paneled Great Hall, one of the finest rooms to have survived from colonial times, runs the depth of the house and has an inverted tray ceiling. On the same floor are bedrooms and a nursery, where you can see Robert E. Lee's crib. The fireplace in the nursery is trimmed with sculpted angels' heads.

Start at the reception center, where tours begin. You can go inside the mansion and its dependencies only on 30-minute tours led by costumed guides, who will meet you at one of the outbuildings. You can easily spend another 2 hours strolling the gardens, meadows, and nature trails on this 1,600-acre estate, still operated as a working farm.

Va. 214, 2 miles north of Va. 3, Stratford. (804/493-8038. www.stratfordhall.org. Admission $9 adults, $8 seniors, $5 children 6–11, free for children under 6. Daily 9:30am–4pm (tours 10am–4pm). Dining room daily 11:30am–3pm. Stratford Hall Plantation closed New Year's Day, Thanksgiving, and Christmas. Plantation dining room closed Dec 23–Jan 4.

ON THE WINE TRAIL

Ingleside Vineyards   On the Rappahannock River side of the peninsula, Ingleside Vineyards has winery tours, tastings, a gift shop selling wine-related items, and a small exhibit area displaying colonial wine bottles, Chesapeake waterfowl carvings, and Native American artifacts. If you're coming from Fredericksburg, you'll get here before Washington's birthplace and Stratford Hall, so go easy on tasting the chardonnay and cabernet sauvignon.

5872 Leedstown Rd., Oak Grove. (804/224-8687. www.ipwine.com. Free admission. Mon–Sat 10am–5pm; Sun noon–5pm (to 6pm daily June–Oct). Closed Thanksgiving, Christmas, New Year's, and Easter. From Va. 3, turn right in Oak Grove on Leedstown Rd. (C.R. 638) and go about 2½ miles south.

BIKING, BIRDING, GOLFING, FISHING & KAYAKING

Country roads winding through gentling rolling hills and crossing picturesque creeks make the Northern Neck a great place to ride your bicycle. One excellent route makes a loop from Reedville via U.S. 360 and county roads 652 and 644. On C.R. 644, you'll cross the Little Wicomico River via the free Sunnybank Ferry. Some bed-and-breakfasts and campgrounds provide bikes for the guests, but there are no places to rent them here, so bring your own.

The Northern Neck has more than 1,100 miles of shoreline and 6,500 acres of nature preserves, making it an important stop for birds migrating along the Atlantic Flyway. It also has a substantial population of bald eagles. One of the best places to view the migratory birds is at **Belle Isle State Park** (© **804/462-5030;** www.dcr.state.va.us/parks/bellisle.htm), off C.R. 354 on the Rappahannock River northwest of Irvington, which has guided canoe trips. To see the eagles, head to the **Caledon Natural Area,** on Va. 218 near King George (© **540/663-3861;** www.dcr.state.va.us/parks/caledon.htm), which has observation tours along the Potomac River. The **Northern Neck Audubon Society,** P.O. Box 991, Kilmarnock, VA 22482 (www.northernneckaudubon.org), organizes field trips.

Golfers come here to play the Golden Eagle course at The Tides Inn (see "Where to Stay," below), one of Virginia's best. Other less challenging—and less expensive—links are **Quinton Oaks Golf Course** near Callao (© **804/529-5367;** www.quintonoaks.com); and a nine-holer at **Bushfield Golf Course** on Va. 202 at Mt. Holly (© **804/472-2602**).

Reedville is the jumping-off point for fishing charters on the Chesapeake Bay, where you might hook a fighting bluefish or snag a succulent rockfish (sea bass). In Reedville call Capt. Jim Hardy of *The Ranger II* (© **804/453-6635**), or **Pittman's Charters** (© **804/453-3643**). The latter operates the *Mystic Lady II*, a 25-passenger party boat.

You can learn to sail at **Premier Sailing School** (© and fax **804/438-9300;** www.sailingschool.net) which is based at The Tides Inn.

A CRUISE TO TANGIER ISLAND

Out in the Chesapeake Bay lies the quaint and still relatively remote **Tangier Island** ✧✧. It is so remote, in fact, that you can still hear an Elizabethan brogue on the tongues of its 650 residents. See "Onancock" under "Chincoteague & the Eastern Shore" in chapter 11 for more information.

Tangier Island Cruises (© **800/598-2628** or 804/453-2628) leave from Buzzards Point Marina, off U.S. 360 east of Reedville at 10am daily from May to mid-October. The narrated voyages take 90 minutes each way, leaving daytrippers 2½ hours to have lunch on Tangier and poke around the island. You can also go all the way across the bay by connecting with the Onancock-Tangier ferry in the afternoon. Fares are $22 for adults, $12 for children 4 to 13, $15 for bicycles. Reservations are required.

WHERE TO STAY

The only chain motels on the Northern Neck are a new **Holiday Inn Express,** 599 N. Main St., Kilmarnock (© **800/HOLIDAY** or 804/436-1500), and the older **Best Western Warsaw,** on U.S. 360 at Warsaw (© **800/528-1234** or 804/333-1700). Although the Best Western is centrally located, it's not particularly convenient to any of the major sights.

The Hope and Glory Inn ✧✧✧ Virginia's most fascinating country inn occupies a three-story schoolhouse built in the 1890s. Unusual for its time, it was

Travel Tip: He who finds the best hotel deal has more to spend on facials involving knobbly vegetables.

Hello, the Roaming Gnome here. I've been nabbed from the garden and taken round the world. The people who took me are so terribly clever. They find the best offerings on Travelocity. For very little cha-ching. And that means I get to be pampered and exfoliated till I'm pink as a bunny's doodah.

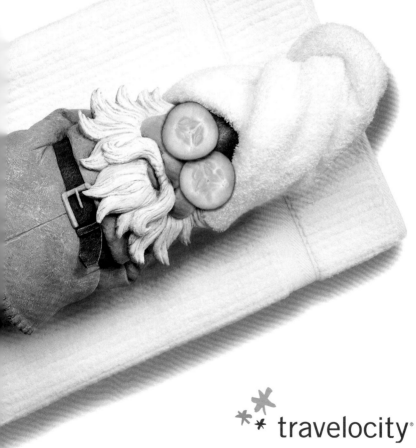

travelocity®

1-888-TRAVELOCITY / travelocity.com / America Online Keyword: Travel

Plan your vacation

- flights, hotels, car rentals
- cruises & vacation packages
- destination guides
- fare alerts
- go to yahoo.com, click travel

DO YOU YAHOO!?

co-educational, albeit with separate front doors for boys and girls. Today, those doors lead from the front porch into a large main lounge with a comfy TV-fireplace nook to one side of a broad center staircase leading to seven guest rooms plus a sitting room (the latter opens to a large deck). Out back, in a beautifully landscaped yard, are six light and airy clapboard cottages, the best accommodations here. The two largest cottages are town house–style; their upstairs bedrooms have Romeo-and-Juliet balconies overlooking the gardens. Although every room has its own bathroom, guests with an exhibitionist streak can use an extraordinary outdoor bathroom complete with clawfoot tub, large shower, and lavatory—all surrounded by a wooden privacy fence. An eclectic mix of furniture and lots of whimsical folk art add to the charm. Gourmet breakfasts are served in the school building, and guests have free use of bicycles. Note that some cottages have telephones, while rooms in the school do not.

65 Tavern Rd. (at King Carter Dr.; P.O. Box 425), Irvington, VA 22480. © 800/497-8228 or 804/438-6053. Fax 804/438-5362. www.hopeandgloryinn.com. 13 units (all with bathroom). $175–$235 double; $225–$325 cottage. Rates include full breakfast. AE, DISC, MC, V. **Amenities:** Access to nearby health club and tennis courts; free bicycles. *In room:* A/C.

The Tides Inn ★★★

Renown for its exceptional Golden Eagle golf course The Tides has been one of Virginia's top golf resorts since 1947, and it has gotten a lot better in recent years under its new owner, the Arizona-based Sedona Resorts Management. In addition, making it even more luxurious in terms of services and amenities, a complete renovation has resulted in a big change of style. A British raj theme now dominates, replacing the inn's traditional Old Virginny touches. For example, ceiling fans and Indian mahogany furniture now adorn the rooms, and wooden floor-to-ceiling plantation shutters have replaced most of the draperies. There's a full-service spa here now, including six treatment rooms with water views and little patios for cooling down with a glass of wine.

The sprawling inn consists of several low-rise buildings on the banks of Carter's Creek. In the clapboard Main Building, the exceptional dining room and Chesapeake Club lounge both have outstanding views down the creek to the Rappahannock River. Rooms in the Main Building have fine views, too, but those in the cottagelike Windsor or Lancaster Houses are more spacious and feature large bathrooms, living areas, and, in some cases, balconies overlooking the creek. Other hotel-style rooms are in the East, Garden, and Terrace Wings, where the preferable ground floor units have patios. All rooms have CD and DVD players and marble bathrooms.

The dining room serves gourmet fare, while the semi-circular **Chesapeake Club** lounge offers burgers and sandwiches. (Note the exquisite wood paneling in the Chesapeake Club: It includes bottle lockers left from the days before Virginia allowed liquor-by-the-drink.) The club has a pianist during the week and a band on weekends for dancing. Men must wear jackets at dinner in the main dining room (they'll lend you one), and "resort casual" attire is required except in the pool, marina, and tennis areas. All facilities, including the spa, the marina and the golf course, are open to the public. Families will especially like it here during the summer when the very good "Crab Net" program keeps the kids occupied. The Premier Sailing School operates here, and a 127-foot yacht *Miss Ann* takes guests cruising. Your small pets can enjoy the luxuries, too, including a pet-sitter.

480 King Carter Dr. (P.O. Box 480), Irvington, VA 22480. © 800/843-3746 or 804/438-5000. Fax 804/438-5552. www.thetides.com. 106 units. $295–$325 double; $495 suite. $8 per room daily resort fee. Golf packages available. Valet parking free 1st night, $5 thereafter; free self-parking. Pets $25 per animal (in some rooms). AE, DC, DISC, MC, V. Closed early Jan to mid-Mar. From Va. 3, take Va. 200 south 2 miles to Irvington, turn right at the

sign to end of King Carter Dr. **Amenities:** 4 restaurants; 3 bars; 3 heated outdoor pools; 2 golf courses; 4 tennis courts; spa; watersports/equipment rentals; bike rentals; children's programs; concierge; business center; shopping arcade; 24-hr. room service; massage; babysitting; laundry service; coin-op washers and dryers. *In room:* A/C, TV, dataport, minibar, coffeemaker, iron, safe.

WHERE TO DINE

Overlooking Crockrell Creek near Reedville, **Fairport Marina** (ℂ 804/453-5002) is one of several Northern Neck marinas with low-key restaurants, where you can have your fill of steamed crabs, spiced shrimp, and broiled or fried fish from the Chesapeake Bay. It's open daily for lunch and dinner. Take U.S. 360 west and follow the signs at the turn-off to Tangier Island Cruises.

The Crazy Crab SEAFOOD   You can look out across the Reedville harbor to the menhaden processing plants from inside or outside this cafe-style restaurant. Best bets are the finely seasoned crab cakes made with premium back fin meat (I found not a shred of shell in mine—unusual at even expensive restaurants), which are available as sandwiches at lunch, main courses at dinner. Other temptations include soft-shell crabs, shrimp, and fried, broiled, or stuffed fresh flounder. Light eaters can turn to large salads, especially the shrimp or crabmeat versions.

902 Main St., Reedville (end of U.S. 360, at Reedville Marina). ℂ 804/453-6789. Reservations not accepted. Main courses $9.50–$21. MC, V. Mid-March to Apr and Nov to mid-Dec, Fri 5–9pm; Sat–Sun noon–9pm. May to Labor Day, Tues–Sun 11am–9pm. Labor Day to Oct, Tues–Fri 5–9pm; Sat–Sun noon–9pm. Closed Dec to mid-Mar.

Sandpiper Restaurant SEAFOOD   This popular restaurant has been serving Chesapeake Bay seafood to locals and visitors alike since 1982. Start with chargrilled bacon-wrapped shrimp and proceed to the star attraction, crab cakes made mostly of back fin meat. Other favorites include oysters fried in a delicate batter, or a platter of fried or broiled seafood. Chargrilled kabobs of shrimp, scallops, filet mignon cubes and vegetables offer variety, as does shrimp in a fresh tomato basil sauce over linguini. Landlubbers can opt for steaks or pork chops.

Rappahannock Dr. (Va. 3), White Stone. ℂ 804/435-6176. Reservations not accepted. Main courses $14–$22. DISC, MC, V. Tues–Thurs 5–9pm; Fri–Sat 5–10pm.

Trick Dog Cafe ★★ *Finds* INTERNATIONAL   The Northern Neck's best and most sophisticated restaurant—a cross between SoHo and South Beach—is named for a sooty statue of little black dog which survived the Great Irvington Fire of 1917. A local man gave the statue to his son, telling him it was a "trick dog" because he didn't need to be fed, and he would always sit and stay. The dog now resides here, where you pet it for good luck. You won't need any luck to enjoy the food here, which leans heavily on local vegetables, wild game such as venison and quail, and seafood flown in from overseas—as if the Chesapeake Bay doesn't provide enough. Veal, crab cakes, and steaks are regulars, too. You can dine under the patio's glass roof in warm weather, and drink with the locals at the bar all year.

4357 Irvington Rd. (Va. 200), Irvington. ℂ 804/438-1055. Reservations recommended. Main courses $17–$25. AE, MC, V. Tues–Thurs 5–10pm; Fri–Sat 5–11pm; Sun 11am–2pm.

6

Charlottesville

With the serene Blue Ridge Mountains on the horizon to the west, the rolling hills of central Virginia reveal a scenic pastoral landscape. No wonder Peter Jefferson, coming here to survey the land, decided to settle and amassed hundreds of acres. His son, Thomas Jefferson, America's third president, inherited not only his father's property but an abiding attachment to the land where he, too, spent much of his life, and where his friends included James Madison and James Monroe, two other future presidents. His presence is very much felt today in what the locals call "Mr. Jefferson's Country."

It was in Charlottesville that Thomas Jefferson built his famous mountaintop home, Monticello; selected the site for and helped plan James Monroe's Ash Lawn–Highland house near Monticello; designed his "academical village," the University of Virginia; and died at home. "All my wishes end where I hope my days will end," he wrote, "at Monticello."

Established in 1762 as the county seat for Albemarle, Charlottesville had its Court Square complete with courthouse, jail, whipping post, pillory, and stocks to keep fractious citizens in line. The courthouse doubled as marketplace and served as a church as well, with rotating services for different denominations (Jefferson called it the "Common Temple"). Elections were held in Court Square followed by raucous political celebrations. Needless to say, the taverns across the street were well patronized.

Along with Madison, who lived at Montpelier 25 miles north of Charlottesville, Jefferson and Monroe were instrumental in developing the emerging nation. In addition to writing the Declaration of Independence, Jefferson advocated freedom of religion and public education. And though he never freed his own slaves (it's now established through DNA testing that he sired a child with Sally Hemings, his slave mistress), he believed slavery should be abolished.

Charlottesville today is a growing cosmopolitan center, attracting an increasing number of rich and famous folks like author John Grisham. But its prime attractions are still Thomas Jefferson and his magnificent creations.

1 Orientation & Getting Around

VISITOR INFORMATION

For information, contact the **Monticello Visitor Center,** P.O. Box 178, Charlottesville, VA 22902 (© **877/386-1102** or 434/977-1783; fax 434/295-2176; www.SoVeryVirginia.org). The center is on Va. 20 at Exit 121 off I-64. The center sells block tickets to Monticello and other attractions (see "What to See & Do" later). It also provides maps and literature about local and state attractions, and can make same-day, discounted hotel/motel reservations for you. The center is open

March through October, daily from 9am to 5:30pm; the rest of the year, daily until 5pm. Closed New Year's Day, Thanksgiving and Christmas.

Be sure to pick up copies of *The Charlottesville Guide* (www.charlottesville guide.com), a slick, advertiser-supported booklet containing maps and information about the area's attractions, hotels, restaurants, and shops; and *Charlottesville Arts & Entertainment* (www.artsmonthly.com), a monthly mini-magazine concentrating on the town's cultural life. Two free weekly alternative newspapers, *C-Ville* (www.c-ville.com) and *The Hook* (www.readthehook.com), are packed with news about what's happening.

GETTING THERE

BY CAR   Charlottesville is on I-64 from east or west and U.S. 29 from north or south. I-64 connects with I-81 at Staunton and with I-95 at Richmond.

BY PLANE   US Airways, Delta, and United fly commuter planes to **Charlottesville-Albemarle Airport,** 201 Bowen Loop (© **434/973-8341;** www. gocho.com), north of town off U.S. 29. Taxis are available, and **Van on the Go** (© **877/973-7667** or 434/975-8267) provides shuttle service into town.

BY TRAIN   The **Amtrak** station is at 810 W. Main St. (© **800/872-7245;** www.amtrak.com), about halfway between the town's commercial district and the University of Virginia.

CITY LAYOUT

Charlottesville has not one but two commercial centers, one catering to college students, the other to grownups. Both are on Main Street (U.S. 250 Business), about a mile apart. On West Main Street, opposite the University of Virginia between 13th Street and Elliewood Avenue, the **Corner** neighborhood is a typical campus enclave, with student-dominated restaurants, bookstores and clothing stores, and a dearth of parking spaces. A mile to the east, **Historic Downtown Charlottesville** is centered on the **Downtown Mall,** an 8-block, pedestrian-only strip of Main Street between 2nd Street West and 8th Street East. The major suburban growth is along U.S. 29 north, which is lined with shopping centers, chain motels, restaurants, and traffic signals.

GETTING AROUND

The easiest way to get between the campus and the Downtown Mall is on the **free trolley** operated by the Charlottesville Transit Service (CTA) (© **434/296-RIDE**). It runs along Main Street every 10 to 15 minutes Monday to Saturday from 6:30am to midnight.

CTA also has bus service Monday through Saturday from 6:30am to 6:30pm throughout the city (but not to Monticello).

PARKING   On-street parking is extremely limited. In the historic downtown area, you can park free for 2 hours with merchant validation (take your ticket with you and get it stamped) in the garage on Market Street between 1st and 2nd streets, or in any of the lots and two garages along Water Street. The university's visitor parking garage is on the western side of the campus, on Emmet Street (U.S. 29 Business) a block south of University Avenue (which is the continuation of West Main Street). On the eastern side of campus, two public garages are located opposite the University Hospital on Lee Street, off Jefferson Park Avenue. The Corner has public parking on Elliewood Avenue, Wertland Street at 14th Street, and down the alleys behind the businesses fronting West Main Street.

Charlottesville

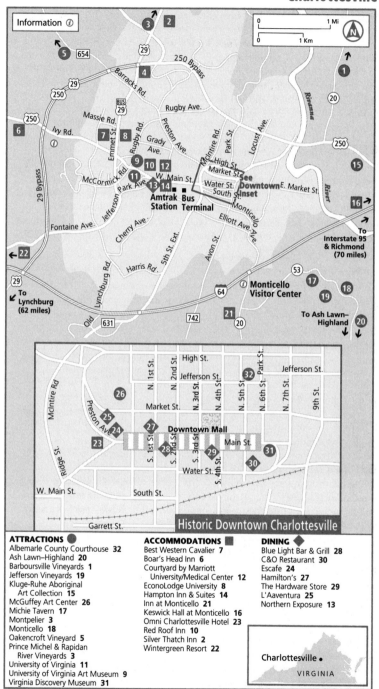

Historic Downtown Charlottesville

ATTRACTIONS ●
Albemarle County Courthouse **32**
Ash Lawn–Highland **20**
Barboursville Vineyards **1**
Jefferson Vineyards **19**
Kluge-Ruhe Aboriginal
    Art Collection **15**
McGuffey Art Center **26**
Michie Tavern **17**
Montpelier **3**
Monticello **18**
Oakencroft Vineyard **5**
Prince Michel & Rapidan
    River Vineyards **3**
University of Virginia **11**
University of Virginia Art Museum **9**
Virginia Discovery Museum **31**

ACCOMMODATIONS ■
Best Western Cavalier **7**
Boar's Head Inn **6**
Courtyard by Marriott
    University/Medical Center **12**
EconoLodge University **8**
Hampton Inn & Suites **14**
Inn at Monticello **21**
Keswick Hall at Monticello **16**
Omni Charlottesville Hotel **23**
Red Roof Inn **10**
Silver Thatch Inn **2**
Wintergreen Resort **22**

DINING ◆
Blue Light Bar & Grill **28**
C&O Restaurant **30**
Escafe **24**
Hamilton's **27**
The Hardware Store **29**
L'Aaventura **25**
Northern Exposure **13**

Charlottesville ●
VIRGINIA

2 Where to Stay

The most convenient chain hotels to Monticello, Ash Lawn–Highland, and Michie Tavern are the **Holiday Inn Monticello** (© **800/HOLIDAY** or 434/977-5100), a full-service hotel with restaurant and bar, and a **Sleep Inn and Suites** (© **800/4CHOICE** or 434/244-9969). Both are on 5th Street Extended just north of I-64. It's an easy drive to downtown.

The traffic-signal encrusted commercial strip along U.S. 29 north of the U.S. 250 bypass has an abundance of chain properties, including the **Doubletree Hotel Charlottesville** (© **800/494-7596** or 434/973-2121), the area's best suburban hotel; a comfortable **Courtyard by Marriott** (© **800/321-2211** or 434/973-7100), which abuts the Fashion Square Mall. Others along U.S. 29 north include **Best Western Mount Vernon** (© **800/528-1234** or 434/296-5501), **Comfort Inn** (© **800/228-5150** or 434/293-6188), **Econo Lodge North** (© **800/55-ECONO** or 434/295-3185), **Hampton Inn** (© **800/HAMPTON** or 434/978-7888), **Holiday Inn North** (© **800/HOLIDAY** or 434/293-9111), **Sheraton Inn Charlottesville** (© **800/325-3535** or 434/973-2121), and **Super 8** (© **800/800-8000** or 434/973-0888).

EXPENSIVE

Boar's Head Inn ★★   Standing beside a picturesque lake and named for the traditional symbol of hospitality in Shakespeare's England, this university-owned property is one of the best all-around resorts in Virginia. The focal point is a 19th-century gristmill that was dismantled and brought here in the early 1960s. It is loaded with antiques and art, and its plank flooring and huge old ceiling beams give ancient charm to the **Old Mill Room,** the resort's signature restaurant offering fine dining accompanied by an excellent selection of Virginia wines (ask about the weekend tasting events). The adjoining Bistro 1834 pub offers lighter fare and outdoor seating by the lake. The innlike guest rooms upstairs in the mill are charming and romantic, but if you want more space and a balcony, opt for a unit in one of the other lakeside structures, especially the Hunt Club building between the old mill and the resort's full-service spa. Guest quarters throughout are furnished with colonial reproductions. Some units in the Ednam Hall, which does not face the lake, have kitchenettes. In addition to the spa and the resort's own tennis courts, guests can use the adjacent Boar's Head Sports Club (17 tennis courts, two pools, state-of-the-art fitness center) and the university's Birdwood Golf Course nearby. The Boar's Head also is one of the best places in the region to take off on a hot-air balloon ride.

200 Ednam Dr. (P.O. Box 5307), Charlottesville, VA 22905. © **800/476-1988** or 434/296-2181. Fax 434/972-6019. www.boarsheadinn.com. 171 units. $189–$325 double. Weekend, spa, and golf packages available. AE, DC, DISC, MC, V. Resort is on U.S. 250 1 mile west of U.S. 29/250 bypass. **Amenities:** 2 restaurants; bar; 4 outdoor pools (1 heated); golf course; 6 tennis courts; health club; spa; Jacuzzi; free bicycles; children's programs;

⌒Tips Avoiding the Crowds in Charlottesville

The town is packed and every accommodations is full during University of Virginia events such as football games, graduation, and parents' weekends. You may want to avoid being in Charlottesville then—or make your reservations as far in advance as possible. You will also pay premium rates at these times. Check the schedules at www.virginia.edu.

concierge; business center; shopping arcade; limited room service; massage; babysitting; laundry service. *In room:* A/C, TV, dataport, kitchen (11 units), fridge (stocked on request), coffeemaker, iron, safe.

MODERATE

Courtyard by Marriott University/Medical Center ⚘   Sitting at the eastern edge of the university, this modern yet colonial-style brick building fits in with the ancient campus structures nearby. Like all Courtyards, it's designed with business travelers in mind, offering well-equipped rooms and a restaurant serving a breakfast buffet daily, dinner and libation Monday to Thursday. For the romantically inclined, six units have two-person Jacuzzi tubs almost surrounded by floor-to-ceiling mirrors. Northern Exposure restaurant (see p. 132) is across Main Street.

1201 W. Main St. (at 12th St. NW), Charlottesville, VA 22903. ✆ **800/321-2211** or 434/977-1700. Fax 434/977-2600. www.courtyard.com. 137 units. $99–$199 double. AE, DC, DISC, MC, V. **Amenities:** Restaurant; bar, indoor pool, health club, Jacuzzi, limited room service, laundry service. *In room:* A/C, TV, dataport, fridge, coffeemaker, iron.

Hampton Inn & Suites *Value*   Also well-situated, this five-story brick structure is 3 blocks east of the Courtyard—far enough away from The Corner to avoid the crowds. The city's free trolley runs along Main Street, so it's easy to get from here to the campus and the Downtown Mall without having to drive. Murals of Monticello, the Rotunda, and other local scenes overlook a gas fireplace in the center of an elegant, two-story lobby. Eight of the suites here also have gas fireplaces, and all have separate bedrooms, VCRs, and kitchens with microwave ovens and dishwashers. The medium-size rooms also come well equipped. Guests are treated to an extensive continental breakfast in a room off the lobby.

900 W. Main St. (at 10th St.), Charlottesville, VA 22903. ✆ **800/HAMPTON** or 434/923-8600. Fax 434/923-8601. www.hamptonsuites.com. 100 units. $93–$108 double; $128–$143 suites. Rates include continental breakfast. AE, DC, DISC, MC, V. **Amenities:** Health club; coin-op washers and dryers. *In room:* A/C, TV, dataport, coffeemaker, iron.

The Omni Charlottesville Hotel ⚘⚘   You can't miss this seven-story, brick-and-glass structure with a soaring atrium lobby, since its triangular shape towers above the western end of the Downtown Mall. The location is ideal, since you can walk to the mall's many restaurants and shops and ride the free trolley to the university. All of the medium-size rooms have Internet access through their TVs, and those on the upper floors have views over the city. At the street level, a fountain bubbles amid a tropical forest in the atrium lobby. With a view of the mall, a contemporary-style restaurant specializes in regional cuisine and local wines. It shares atrium space with a bistro-style sports bar. The Omni has extensive meeting space and draws more conventions and groups than most hotels here. Your small pet can share your room for a fee.

235 W. Main St. (at McIntire St.), Charlottesville, VA 22901. ✆ **800/THE-OMNI** or 434/971-5500. Fax 434/979-4456. www.omnihotels.com. 204 units. $129–$169 double. Small pets accepted ($50 fee). AE, DC, DISC, MC, V. From I-64, take Exit 120 and follow Fifth Ridge St. (C.R. 631) north to McIntire St.; hotel on the right. **Amenities:** Restaurant; bar; 2 pools (indoor and outdoor); health club; Jacuzzi; concierge; limited room service; laundry service; concierge-level rooms. *In room:* A/C, TV, dataport, minibar, coffeemaker, iron.

INEXPENSIVE

Best Western Cavalier   Half a mile west of the Rotunda, this five-story, glass-and-steel motel is popular with visiting athletic teams, since it's close to Scott Stadium and University Hall, the major sports venues. Although it has been around for more than 3 decades, it received a major face-lift a few years ago. The spacious motel-style rooms are entered through external walkways bordered by wrought-iron railings. A continental breakfast is served in a charming room off the lobby

---

Tips **Walk-ins Get Discounted Rates**

If you are willing to risk not getting a room at all, the **Monticello Visitor Center** makes same-day hotel reservations at discounted rates for walk-in visitors. Don't try it on a football weekend or during graduation and other special university events. See "Visitor Information," above.

---

which doubles as the guest lounge. During summer you can cool off in a small outdoor pool. The hotel provides complimentary shuttle service to and from the airport and the Amtrak and bus stations. Small pets are accepted.

105 Emmet St. (P.O. Box 5647) (at W. Main St.), Charlottesville, VA 22905. ℂ **888/882-2129** or 434/296-8111. Fax 434/296-3523. www.cavalierinn.com. 118 units. $69–$99 double. Rates include continental breakfast. Small pets accepted ($50 fee). AE, DC, DISC, MC, V. From U.S. 29 bypass, go east on Ivy Rd. (U.S. 250 Business) 1 mile to hotel on the left. **Amenities:** Outdoor pool; access to nearby health club; business center; laundry service. *In room:* A/C, TV, dataport, coffeemaker, iron.

Econo Lodge University   This Econo Lodge is 2 blocks north of West Main Street and across Emmet Street from University Hall, the sports arena. The rooms are small but comfortable, and 15 are equipped for seniors (with special phones with oversized buttons, grab-bars in the bathtubs, and so forth). The best rooms, in the rear of the L-shaped building, face a hillside and get less street noise than those in the front. Some units have microwave ovens and refrigerators. There's a reasonably good Italian restaurant next door. Small pets are accepted.

400 Emmet St. (U.S. 29 Business), Charlottesville, VA 22903. ℂ **800/55-ECONO** or 434/296-2104. Fax 434/977-5591. 60 units. $49–$140 double. Rates include continental breakfast. Small pets accepted ($10 fee). AE, DC, DISC, MC, V. **Amenities:** Outdoor pool. *In room:* A/C, TV, dataport, fridge, coffeemaker.

Red Roof Inn   If you want to stay in the middle of the action, this clean, comfortable seven-story hotel is on the eastern edge of The Corner and across West Main Street from the university. Interior hallways lead to medium-size guest rooms, which contain cherrywood furniture. Despite being a bit small, the bathrooms have surprisingly ample vanity space. The Corner's many food outlets are steps away.

1309 W. Main St. (at 13th St.), Charlottesville, VA 22903. ℂ **800/THE-ROOF** or 434/295-4333. Fax 434/295-2021. 135 units. $59–$135 double. AE, DC, DISC, MC, V. From U.S. 29 bypass, go east on Ivy Rd. (U.S. 250 Business) 1½ miles to hotel on the left. **Amenities:** Access to nearby health club; laundry service; coin-op washers and dryers. *In room:* A/C, TV, dataport.

BED & BREAKFAST ACCOMMODATIONS

Guesthouses Reservation Service, Inc., P.O. Box 5737, Charlottesville, VA 22905 (ℂ **434/979-7264;** www.va-guesthouses.com), handles bed-and-breakfast accommodations in elegant homes and private cottages. You can write or visit the website for information and reservations. The office is open Monday through Friday from noon to 5pm.

If you want to stay out in the rolling countryside, **The Foxfield Inn,** 2280 Garth Rd., Charlottesville, VA 22901 (ℂ **800/369-3536** or 434/923-8892; fax 434/923-0963; www.foxfield-inn.com), off Barracks Road about 7 miles northwest of Charlottesville, has five romantic rooms and an eight-person hot tub. Rates range from $150 to $190 double, with discounts during the week.

The Inn at Monticello ⭐   The most convenient accommodations to Monticello, Ash Lawn–Highland, and Michie Tavern, this beautiful two-story white-clapboard country house sits on 5 acres well back from Va. 20. The manicured lawn is ornamented in spring with blooming dogwood trees and azaleas. Box-woods, tall shade and evergreen trees, shrubs, and a bubbling brook provide a lovely setting. Guests enter via the front porch into a sitting room with two fire-places and a handsome collection of antiques. Guest rooms are individually dec-orated and have such special features as a working fireplace, private porch, or four-poster canopy bed—but no phones. Guests can relax outdoors on the ham-mock or on the front verandah lined with wicker rockers. Afternoon snacks are accompanied by Virginia wine.

1188 Scottsville Rd. (Va. 20), Charlottesville, VA 22902. © **434/979-3593.** Fax 434/296-1344. www.innat monticello.com. 5 units. $110–$175 double. Rates include full breakfast. AE, MC, V. From I-64, take Va. 20 south and continue past the visitor center for about ¼ mile. The inn is on your right. *In room:* A/C, iron, no phone.

NEARBY COUNTRY INNS

Keswick Hall at Monticello Although it's now owned and operated by Orient Express Hotels, this super-luxury estate was the creation of Sir Bernard Ashley, widower of famed designer Laura Ashley. Many of the 1912 vintage Ital-ianate Crawford villa's rooms and suites have fireplaces, clawfoot tubs, and views over a golf course redesigned by Arnold Palmer, but don't expect to find these in the 14 least expensive "house rooms." All guests can roam around the vast pub-lic rooms on the main level, including a lounge with fireplace and terrace with golf-course view. The dining room is quite good, offering a mix of cuisine and excellent service. English afternoon tea is free to guests, who can have lunch or dinner at the adjoining Keswick Club's bistro. Guests here get free use of the pri-vate Keswick Club with spa, fitness center, and indoor and outdoor pools.

701 Country Club Dr., Keswick, VA 22947. © **800/274-5391** or 434/979-3440. Fax 434/977-4171. www .keswick.com. 48 units. $495–$850 double. Rates include afternoon tea. AE, DC, MC, V. From Charlottesville take U.S. 250 or I-64 east to Shadwell (Exit 124), then Va. 22 east and follow signs to Keswick. **Amenities:** Restaurant; bar; 4 pools (1 indoor); golf course; 5 tennis courts; health club; spa; Jacuzzi; sauna; concierge; 24-hr. room service; massage; babysitting; laundry service. *In room:* A/C, TV, dataport, iron.

Silver Thatch Inn Occupying a rambling white-clapboard house, a sec-tion of which dates back to Revolutionary days, this charming hostelry is located on a quiet road set on nicely landscaped grounds. Attractively decorated with authentic 18th-century pieces, the original part of the building now serves as a cozy common room, where guests are invited for afternoon refreshments. The 1812 center part of the house is now one of the dining rooms. Three guest rooms are upstairs in the main house, while four others are in the President's Cottage. Named for Virginia's seven presidents, all are lovely, with down com-forters on four-poster canopied beds, antique pine dressers, carved walnut-and-mahogany armoires, and exquisite quilts. Several rooms have working fireplaces. Telephones and TVs are available in the common areas. Offering contemporary cuisine, the dining room is open to the public for lunch and dinner (inn guests should reserve a table in advance, since this is one of the area's most popular din-ing venues). The list of Virginia and California wines is excellent.

3001 Hollymead Dr., Charlottesville, VA 22911. © **800/261-0720** or 434/978-4686. Fax 434/973-6156. www.silverthatch.com. 7 units. $125–$170 double. Rates include full breakfast. AE, DC, MC, V. Take U.S. 29 about 8 miles north of town, turn right at traffic signal onto Hollymead Dr. to inn on the right. **Amenities:** Restaurant; bar; outdoor pool; access to nearby health club; massage. *In room:* A/C, iron.

A MOUNTAIN GETAWAY

Wintergreen Resort With 6,700 of its 11,000 acres dedicated to the remaining undisturbed forest, this recreational real estate development offers year-round vacation activities in a Blue Ridge Mountain setting. The big draws here include skiing, golf (the short, narrow fairways of Devil's Knob course follow the cool summit of a 4,000-ft.-high mountain), horseback riding, mountain biking, swimming in the lake, canoeing, and an adventure center with rock climbing, skateboarding, wintertime snow tubing, and other activities. Wintergreen also has a Nature Foundation that offers guided hikes, seminars, and camps for children. There's music in the cool air, too, since **Wintergreen Performing Arts, Inc.** (© **434/325-8292;** www.wintergreenmusic.com) sponsors the Wintergreen Summer Music Festival in July and weekend concerts throughout the summer.

The resort's focal point is the tastefully lodgelike Inn, which has a huge gristmill wheel occupying the two-story registration area. Most accommodations are in small enclaves scattered throughout the property, but there are also two- to seven-bedroom homes, one- to four-bedroom condos, and studios and lodge rooms. Since the homes and condos are privately owned, furnishings are highly individual, ranging from country quaint to sleek and sophisticated. Each condo is appointed with a modern kitchen, living area, bathroom for each bedroom, and balcony or patio (the mountain views are superb); most have working fireplaces.

P.O. Box 706, Wintergreen, VA 22958. © **800/266-2444** or 434/325-2200. Fax 434/325-8004. www. wintergreenresort.com. 300 units. $154–$189 double; $179–$749 condos and homes. Weekly rates and packages available. AE, MC, V. Take I-64 west to Exit 107 and follow U.S. 250 west; turn left onto C.R. 151 south, then right on C.R. 644 for 4½ miles to resort. It's about 43 miles from Charlottesville. **Amenities:** 5 restaurants; 3 bars; 6 pools (5 outdoor pools, 1 indoor); 2 golf courses; 24 tennis courts (3 indoor); health club; spa; watersports equipment/rentals; bike rentals; children's programs; concierge (winter only); activities desk; business center; shopping arcade; babysitting; laundry service. In room: A/C, TV, kitchen, coffeemaker, iron.

3 Where to Dine

This area's most exceptional dining is at its country inns The Country Inn and the Silver Thatch Inn (see "Nearby Country Inns," above).

Charlottesville has more than 200 restaurants—an enormous number for such a small city. For a complete rundown, pick up a copy of *Bites,* a free restaurant guide at the Monticello Visitor Center (see "Visitor Information," earlier). There're also lists and reviews in *C-Ville* (www.c-ville.com) and *The Hook* (www.readthehook.com), the two free newspapers found in boxes all over town.

It's great fun to stroll along the Downtown Mall and check out its many restaurants serving a wide array of cuisine, especially during warm weather when most offer outdoor seating under the shade trees. They all post their menus outside, too, so you can pick and choose depending on your tastes. For a caffeine fix, drop into **The Mudhouse,** 213 W. Main St. (© **434/984-6833**), a quintessential college-town coffeehouse.

Likewise, the Corner opposite the university has several restaurants catering to the college crowd (the best are on Elliewood Avenue, a block-long, alleylike street off University Avenue). Just stroll these neighborhoods and pick your place. You can tell by the crowds which are "in" and which aren't.

Blue Light Bar & Grill ⭐ SEAFOOD   You'll get the freshest seafood in town at this storefront restaurant on the Downtown Mall. Atop a mound of ice behind the long bar to the left as you enter wait four types of oysters—from Chincoteague, Long Island, NY, and the Pacific Northwest—waiting to be consumed raw or steamed on the half shell. If they won't do for an appetizer, order the crab cocktail with huge chunks of blue crab meat served with drawn butter. Among the Asian-influenced main courses, many of them creative, the best bet is the monkfish coated with crushed citrus, lightly fried, and served under a slightly spicy Thai-style basil sauce and under a mound of rice. Finish with Key lime pie.

120 E. Main St. (at 2nd St.). ℭ **434/295-1223**. Reservations recommended on weekends. Main courses $12–$20. AE, DISC, MC, V. Tues–Fri 11:30am–2:30pm and 5:30–10pm; Sat 11:30am–4pm and 5:30–10pm.

C&O Restaurant ⚘ INTERNATIONAL   A block south of the Downtown Mall's eastern end, this unprepossessing brick front, complete with a faded Pepsi sign, might make you think twice, but don't be deterred, for the C&O provides the town's most unusual setting for acclaimed fare. From all appearances, the creaky floors in this charming old building were around in Jefferson's day. Changing monthly, the menu is basically country French but ranges across the globe—from Thailand to New Mexico and Louisiana—for additional inspiration. Many patrons stop in the downstairs Bistro, a rustic setting of exposed brick and rough-hewn barnwood, while others proceed upstairs to a more formal venue or to the covered garden. All three dining areas have candlelight, tables adorned with attractive flower arrangements, and the same excellent menu choices. The C&O's list has won a *Wine Spectator* award for excellence.

515 E. Water St. (at 5th St. E.). ℭ **434/971-7044**. Reservations recommended (not accepted in downstairs Bistro). Main courses $13–$25. MC, V. Daily 5:30–11:30pm. Closed July 4th and first week in Jan.

Escafe ⚘⚘ INTERNATIONAL   This lively bistro is one of the town's most popular spots for an inexpensive yet fine meal, especially in warm-weather when the front wall rolls up and the entire joint opens to seating on the Mall. The constantly changing menu features salads and sandwiches, and the stellar main courses always feature a spicy Thai green- and red-chili bowl of vegetables and noodles, to which you can add the meat or seafood of your choice.

102 Old Preston Ave. (western end of the Downtown Mall). ℭ **434/295-8668**. Reservations accepted only for groups. Main courses $8–$17. AE, DC, DISC, MC, V. Tues–Wed 5:30pm–midnight; Thurs–Sat 5:30pm–2am; Sun 4:30pm–midnight.

The Hardware Store *Value* AMERICAN   Old rolling ladders; stacks of oak drawers that once held screws, nuts and bolts; and vintage advertising signs—all display the old-time origins of this fun, high-energy spot popular with town and gown alike. A long, narrow space with an upstairs gallery, it provides comfortable seating in leather-upholstered booths. Specialties include quiches and crepes, crab cakes, salads, an enormous variety of hamburgers, sandwiches, platters of pasta, and barbecued ribs. There are soda-fountain treats, and pastries and cakes run the gamut from dense double-chocolate truffle cake to Southern pecan pie. The Hardware Store has a fully stocked bar.

316 E. Main St. (Downtown Mall). ℭ **434/977-1518**. Sandwiches and salads $5–$10; main courses $10–$19. AE, DC, MC, V. Mon–Thurs 11am–9pm; Fri–Sat 11am–10pm.

Hamilton's ⚘⚘ CONTEMPORARY AMERICAN   Marble-top tables, crisp linen napkins, and fresh flowers let you know you're in for some high style at the urbane bistro in the Downtown Mall. It's the kind of place you'd take a special date, but not necessarily propose marriage. The menu changes frequently, but offered, the pan roasted crab cakes on Jasmine rice and red pepper purée, will demonstrate the chef's prowess. There is usually a dish or two with Asian influences, such as an Indian masala-style rice stir-fry with chicken and shrimp and a tomato–coconut milk sauce. The daily vegetarian blue-plate special is very tasty, too. In fine weather you can dine on the mall.

101 W. Main St. (at 1st St., midway along the Downtown Mall). ℭ **434/295-6649**. Reservations recommended. Main courses $18–$28. AE, DC, DISC, MC, V. Mon–Sat 11:30am–3pm and 5:30–10pm.

L'Avventura ⚘⚘ ITALIAN   This casually elegant little spot with natural wood booths offers this area's most creative Italian cuisine. There are just 41 seats inside, plus patio dining in good weather, at which to enjoy the likes of grilled shrimp with arugula, artichoke *trifolati,* and sautéed sea scallops with capers, sage, and potato gnocchi. The menu changes seasonally, but a grilled pizza is offered every night. The extraordinary wine list, which features out-of-the-way Italian vintages, has recently won *Wine Spectator* magazine awards for excellence. The kitchen produces its own deserts, including four flavors of gelato.

220 Market St. (between McIntire Rd. and High St.). (C) **434/977-1912.** Reservations recommended on weekends. Pizza $11; main courses $14–$21. AE, MC, V. Wed–Sat 5:30–10pm. From western end of Downtown Mall, go through small parking lot next to Escafe, turn left on Market St.

Northern Exposure 🕊 ITALIAN/NEW AMERICAN   You may have to wait for a table at this sophisticated bistro 2 blocks east of The Corner, for it's one of Charlottesville's most popular dining spots. Patrons sit in one of four areas: a dining room decorated with old photos of New York City and a huge map of Gotham's subway system (guess where the owners are from); an enclosed patio; an open-air, heated patio; and a rooftop deck. Both lunch and dinner feature individual-size pizzas, either "red" with tomato sauce or "white" with olive oil, garlic, and cheese, with a choice of toppings both traditional and inventive. You can order pasta with standard sauces like marinara, but the emphasis is on creative concoctions like shrimp or chicken and peppers sautéed with Tabasco butter and served over angel hair pasta. Big salads and burgers are available at all hours.

1202 W. Main St. (at 12th St.). (C) **434/977-6002.** Reservations accepted only for groups. Pizzas $10–$13; main courses $10–$19. AE, DC, DISC, MC, V. Sun 10am–10pm; Mon–Thurs 11am–10pm; Fri–Sat 11am–11pm.

4 What to See & Do

The Monticello Visitor Center (see "Visitor Information," earlier) sells a **Presidents' Pass,** a discount block ticket combining admission to Monticello, Michie Tavern, and Ash Lawn–Highland. It costs $24 for adults, and is not available for children. The attractions validate the tickets when you show up, so there's no time limit on when you must use the pass. They don't advertise the fact, but the three attractions also sell the Presidents' Pass. See the box, "Getting the Most out of Charlottesville," later, for advice on how best to use your time.

THE TOP ATTRACTIONS

Ash Lawn–Highland 🕊🕊   Fifth president James Monroe fought in the Revolution, was wounded in Trenton, and went on to hold more public offices than any other president. Monroe's close friendship with Thomas Jefferson brought him to Charlottesville from Fredericksburg, where he practiced law (see chapter 5). Monroe purchased 1,000 acres adjacent to Monticello in 1793 and built an estate he called "Highland." (The name *Ash Lawn* was added in 1838, and a later owner built a two-story addition to the main house in 1882).

Before Monroe could settle in, Washington named him minister to France and sent him to Paris for 3 years. During his absence, Jefferson sent gardeners over to start orchards, and the Madisons made agricultural contributions as well. By the time Monroe returned, he was suffering financial difficulties, and his "cabin castle" developed along more modest lines than originally intended. When Monroe left the presidency in 1825, his debts totaled $75,000, and he was forced to sell his farm. He spent his final years near Leesburg and in New York City.

Today, Monroe's 535-acre estate is owned and maintained as a working farm by his alma mater, the College of William and Mary in Williamsburg. Livestock, vegetable and herb gardens, and colonial crafts demonstrations recall the elements of

⌒Tips Getting the Most Out of Charlottesville

Monticello, Ash Lawn–Highland, and Michie Tavern are within 2 miles of each other near the visitor center, on the southeastern outskirts of town. You'll need a full day to fully take in all three.

You will want to arrive at Monticello before it opens at 8am, especially on spring and summer weekends and during the October "leaf season," when you can expect long lines to go through Jefferson's home. The **Monticello Visitor Center** (see "Visitor Information" earlier), however, doesn't open until 9am. Accordingly, go to the center at least a day before you plan to tour Monticello, Ash Lawn–Highland, and Michie Tavern and buy a Presidents' Pass ticket to the three attractions ($24 per adult, not available to children). You should also take in the center's marvelous "Thomas Jefferson at Monticello" exhibit and see a free 30-minute video about Jefferson, which shows at 11am and 2pm daily. Both will add to your visit.

If you can't spend that much time at the visitor center, you can buy a Presidents' Pass when you arrive at Monticello.

Timed passes to Monticello are given out when the wait exceeds 30 to 40 minutes; you can spend the time exploring Monticello's gardens and outbuildings on your own.

Next, head to nearby **Michie Tavern,** where you can spend 30 minutes touring the tavern and the Virginia Wine Museum, and then have a colonial-style lunch in the dining room (again, expect a wait on weekends and in October). In the afternoon, head for Monroe's **Ash Lawn–Highland,** 2½ miles away, which will take about an hour to see.

If you have time left over, head for the **University of Virginia.** Otherwise, plan to tour the campus and see the town's other sights the next day.

daily life on the Monroe plantation. Horses, sheep, and cattle graze in the fields, while peacocks roam the boxwood gardens. The original rooms were redecorated recently based on new research. The basement kitchen, the plantation office, the overseer's cottage, restored slave quarters, and the old smokehouse also remain. On a 30-minute house tour, you'll see some of the family's original furnishings and artifacts and learn a great deal about the fifth president. Allow another 30 minutes to explore the grounds and gift shop on your own.

Among many special events taking place at Ash Lawn–Highland, the outdoor **Summer Music Festival** features opera and contemporary music, while **Plantation Days,** held monthly during summer, showcases dozens of 18th-century crafts, historic reenactments, period music performances, and dressage.

C.R. 795. ⌘ 434/293-9539. www.ashlawnhighland.org. Admission $10 adults, $9 seniors, $5 children 6–11, free for children 5 and under. Apr–Oct daily 9am–6pm; Nov–Mar daily 10am–5pm. Mandatory 30-min. house tours depart every 10–15 min. From Va. 20, follow the directions to Monticello. Ash Lawn–Highland is 2½ miles past Monticello on James Monroe Parkway (C.R. 795).

Michie Tavern ca. 1784 ✸✸   In 1746, Scotsman "Scotch John" Michie (pronounced "Mickey") purchased 1,152 acres of land from Patrick Henry's father, and in 1784, Michie's son, William, built this tavern on a well-traveled stagecoach route at Earlysville, 17 miles northwest of Charlottesville. A wealthy business-woman, Josephine Henderson, saw its value as a historic structure and in 1927 had it moved to its present location and reconstructed. Michie Tavern stands today as a tribute to early preservationists.

Included in the 30-minute living-history tours are the **Virginia Wine Museum** and reproductions of the "dependencies"—log kitchen, dairy, smokehouse, ice-house, root cellar, and "necessary" (note the not-so-soft corncobs). The general store has been re-created, along with an excellent crafts shop and the **Printer's Market,** offering newspapers, money, and other early American printed items. Behind the store is a gristmill that has operated continuously since 1797.

Plan your visit to Michie Tavern to coincide with lunchtime, when an all-you-can-eat buffet is served to weary travelers for reasonable pence in the "Ordinary," a converted log cabin with original hand-hewn walls and beamed ceilings. The fare is based on recipes from the 18th century, when travelers would "fill up" because they never knew when they would get their next meal. Expect a short wait on summer weekends and during all of October.

683 Thomas Jefferson Pkwy. (Va. 683). ℭ 434/977-1234. www.michietavern.com. Admission $8 adults, $7 seniors, $3 children 6–11, free for children 5 and under. Meals $14 adults, $7 children. Daily 9am–5pm (last tour 4:20pm). Restaurant daily 11:30am–3pm. 30-min. tavern-museum tours during dining room hours, Apr–Oct. Self-guided tours, Nov–Mar. Closed New Year's Day and Christmas. From the visitor center, go south on Va. 20, turn left at Thomas Jefferson Pkwy. (Va. 683); Michie Tavern is about 1 mile on right.

Monticello ✶✶✶ Pronounced "Mon-ti-*chel*-lo," the home Thomas Jefferson built over 40 years from 1769 to 1809 is a highlight of any visit to Virginia. This architectural masterpiece was the first Virginia plantation manse to sit atop a mountain rather than beside a river. Because it was British, Jefferson rejected the

The Legacy of Thomas Jefferson

The phrase "Renaissance man" might have been coined to describe Thomas Jefferson. Perhaps our most important founding father, he was a lawyer, architect, scientist, musician, writer, educator, and horti-culturist.

After writing the Declaration of Independence, Jefferson served as governor of Virginia, ambassador to France, secretary of state, and president for two terms, during which he nearly doubled the size of the United States by engineering the Louisiana Purchase from France. He also helped found one of America's first political parties.

Yet despite all his achievements, Jefferson ordered that his grave-stone be inscribed: "Here Was Buried Thomas Jefferson/Author Of The Declaration Of American Independence/Of The Statute Of Virginia For Religious Freedom/And Father Of The University Of Virginia."

Jefferson was 83 when he died at Monticello on July 4, 1826, 50 years to the day after his Declaration of Independence was signed at Philadelphia.

Ironically, his fellow revolutionary—but later heated political enemy—John Adams lay on his own deathbed in Massachusetts. Unaware that Jefferson had died earlier, Adams's last words were: "Jefferson survives."

Georgian architecture that characterized his time, opting instead for the 16th-century Italian style of Andrea Palladio. Later, during his 5-year term as minister to France, he was influenced by the homes of nobles at the court of Louis XVI, and after returning home in 1789, he enlarged Monticello, incorporating features of the Parisian buildings he so admired.

Today, the house has been restored as closely as possible to its appearance during Jefferson's retirement years. Jefferson or his family owned nearly all its furniture and other household objects. The garden has been extended to its original 1,000-foot length, and Mulberry Row—where slaves and free artisans lived and labored in light industrial shops such as a joinery, smokehouse-dairy, blacksmith shop-nailery, and carpenter's shop—has been excavated. Guided tours of the gardens and Mulberry Row are available from April through October.

Jefferson's grave is in the family burial ground, which is still in use. After visiting the graveyard, you can take a shuttle bus to the visitor parking lot or walk through the woods via a delightful path. There is a lovely wooded picnic area with tables and grills on the premises, and, in summer, lunch fare can be purchased.

Traffic is heaviest on spring and summer weekends and during October, when you can wait up to 3 hours to tour the house. Accordingly, get here before opening time in the morning, and get in line at the house. Attendants at the ticket office, about halfway up the mountain (vans shuttle from there to the mansion), will tell you how long the wait will be. Once it gets to 30 to 40 minutes, timed tickets are given to those in line (they are not issued at the ticket office). You can use the wait to explore the gardens and outbuildings.

Off Va. 53. ℂ **434/984-9822** for information, 434/984-9844 on weekends, or 434/984-9800 daily for recorded information. www.monticello.org. Admission $13 adults, $6 children 6–11, free for children 5 and under. Mar–Oct daily 8am–5pm; Nov–Feb daily 9am–4:30pm. Closed Christmas Day. Mandatory 30-min. house tours run continuously. From the visitor center go south on Va. 20, turn left on Va. 53, then 2 miles to entrance.

THE UNIVERSITY OF VIRGINIA 👁👁

One of the world's most beautiful college campuses, Jefferson's **University of Virginia** is graced with spacious lawns, serpentine-walled gardens, colonnaded pavilions, and a classical rotunda inspired by the Pantheon in Rome. Jefferson regarded its creation as one of his three greatest achievements—all the more remarkable since it was started in his 73rd year. He was, in every sense, the university's father, since he conceived it, wrote its charter, raised money for its construction, drew the plans, selected the site, laid the cornerstone in 1817, supervised construction, served as the first rector, selected the faculty, and created the curriculum. His good friends, Monroe and Madison, sat with him on the first board, and Madison succeeded him as rector, serving for 8 years.

The focal point of the university is the **Rotunda** (on University Ave. at Rugby Rd.), restored as Jefferson designed it. Some 600 feet of tree-dotted lawn extends from the south portico to what is now Cabell Hall, designed at the turn of the 20th century by Stanford White. On either side of the lawn are pavilions still used for faculty housing, each of a different architectural style "to serve as specimens for the Architectural lecturer." Behind are large gardens (originally used by faculty members to grow vegetables and keep livestock) and the original student dormitories, used—and greatly coveted—by students today; though centrally heated, they still contain working fireplaces. The room Edgar Allan Poe occupied is furnished as it would have been in 1826 and is open to visitors.

Paralleling the lawn are more rows of student rooms called the Ranges. Equally spaced within each of the Ranges are "hotels," originally used to accommodate student dining. Each hotel represented a different country, and students would have to both eat the food and speak the language of that country. Although a wonderful idea on Jefferson's part, it lasted only a short while since everyone wanted to eat French but not German.

When school is in session, students lead 45-minute **campus tours** daily at 10 and 11am and 2, 3, and 4pm, usually from the Rotunda, but call ℂ **434/982-3200** to confirm. Self-guided walking tour brochures are available from the university's **Visitor Information Center** (ℂ **434/924-7166**), which is located not on campus but in the University Police Headquarters, on Ivy Road (U.S. 250 Business) just east of the U.S. 29/U.S. 250 bypass. The visitor center is open 24 hours a day. See "Getting Around," earlier, for parking information.

Note: The University is closed 3 weeks around Christmas.

MORE ATTRACTIONS IN TOWN

The center of Charlottesville's historic district is the **Downtown Mall,** a pedestrian-only section of Main Street between 2nd and 6th streets (ℂ **434/296-8548** or check www.cvilledowntown.org for mall events). It's handy for visitors because it's lined by a host of restaurants and boutiques, and there's parking (see "Getting Around," earlier). Fountains, park benches under shade trees, outdoor cafes, and buskers making music day and night, enhance it all. On the west end, you'll find a six-screen movie theater, the Charlottesville Omni Hotel (see "Where to Stay," earlier) and the **Charlottesville Ice Park** (ℂ **434/817-2400;** www.icepark.com), which offers an irregular schedule of ice-skating, skating lessons and pick-up hockey games.

Albemarle County Court House   The center of village activity in colonial days, the Court House in the historic downtown area features a facade and portico dating from the Civil War. There's no tour offered, but you can take a glance at Jefferson's will in the County Office Building. It's easy to imagine Jefferson, Madison, and Monroe talking politics under the lawn's huge shade trees.

501 E. Jefferson St. (at 5th St. E.). ℂ **434/296-5822.** Free admission. Mon–Fri 9am–5pm.

McGuffey Art Center   Local artists and craftspeople work in their studios in this early-20th-century school building a block north of the Mall. Their arts and crafts are displayed at monthly exhibits. The **Second Street Gallery,** which displays contemporary art from all over the United States, also is here.

201 2nd St. NW (between High and Market sts.). ℂ **434/295-7973.** www.avenue.org/mcguffey. Free admission. Tues–Sat 10am–5pm; Sun 1–5pm.

The Kluge-Ruhe Aboriginal Art Collection 𝄢   This museum, about 3 miles east of Charlottesville, houses one of the largest private collections of Australian Aboriginal art in the world. It includes the gatherings of wealthy American businessman John W. Kluge, who began collecting in 1988, and of the late Professor Edward L. Ruhe of Kansas University, who began collecting while visiting Australia as a Fulbright Scholar in 1965. Kluge bought Ruhe's collection and archives and later gave it all to the University of Virginia.

400 Peter Jefferson Place. ℂ **434/244-0234.** www.virginia.edu/kluge-ruhe. Free admission. Tues–Sat 9am–3pm; guided tour Sat 10:30am. Take U.S. 250 east to Pantops Mountain Dr. Take the first right after State Farm Blvd. Follow the driveway to the white house at the top of the hill.

Virginia Discovery Museum *Kids*   The Virginia Discovery Museum is a place of enchantment, offering numerous hands-on exhibits and programs for children. Here, kids can dress up as firefighters, soldiers, police, and other grownups. The Showalter Cabin, an authentic structure that once stood on a site in Mt. Crawford, Virginia, is outfitted with the simple furnishings appropriate to an early-19th-century lifestyle. A series of fascinating exhibits appeals to the senses, including the Fun and Games exhibit offering a wonderful array of games, including bowling and giant checkers. An arts and crafts studio, an active beehive, and a changing series of traveling and made-on-site exhibits round out the fun.

524 E. Main St. (east end of Downtown Mall). ℭ 434/977-1025. www.vadm.org. Admission $4 adults, $3 seniors and children 1–13. Tues–Sat 10am–5pm; Sun 1–5pm.

University of Virginia Art Museum   This nationally accredited museum has permanent exhibits of 17th- to 20th-century American and European art, and an active exhibition schedule items from its Asian, African, American Indian, and pre-Columbian collections. Nationally touring exhibits also appear here.

Thomas H. Bayly Building, 155 Rugby Rd. ℭ 434/924-7458. www.virginia.edu/artmuseum. Free admission (donations welcome). Tues–Sun 1–5pm. Guided tours Sat 10:30am.

JAMES MADISON'S MONTPELIER

Montpelier 𝕽𝕽   This 2,700-acre estate facing the Blue Ridge Mountains 25 miles northeast of Charlottesville was home to Pres. James Madison and his equally famous wife, Dolley. Madison was just 26 when he ensured that the 1776 Constitutional Convention in Williamsburg would include religious freedom in the Virginia Declaration of Rights, and his efforts at the federal Constitutional Convention in 1787 earned him the title "Father of the Constitution." Madison became secretary of state under his good friend Thomas Jefferson in 1801, and succeeded Jefferson as president in 1809. He and Dolley fled the White House in the face of advancing British troops during the War of 1812. The gracious Dolley served as White House hostess during bachelor Jefferson's two terms and as First Lady during her husband's two.

Madison inherited Montpelier which, at that time, was a modest two-story red-brick Georgian residence, from his father, who built it around 1760. With architectural advice from Jefferson, Madison expanded its proportions, including a wing just for Dolley. Two structures remain from their time: the main house and the "Ice House Temple" (built over a well and used to store ice).

William du Pont Sr. bought the estate in 1901. He enlarged the mansion and added barns, staff houses, a sawmill, a blacksmith shop, a train station, a dairy, and greenhouses, and his wife created a 2-acre formal garden. Daughter Marion du Pont Scott later built a steeplechase course and initiated the **Montpelier Hunt Races,** which are still held here on the first Saturday in November. The National Trust for Historic Preservation acquired the property following her death in 1984, and in 2003 launched a major, 4-year restoration, which will rip away the du Pont's additions to the mansion, reducing it from 55 rooms to the 22-room version the Madisons occupied in 1820s. The house will be open to the public during the project. In fact, you can actually visit seldom seen rooms on special "Behind the Scenes" guided tours of the construction areas, daily at 10am, 11am, 1pm, 2pm, and 3pm. "Insider Briefings," offered hourly starting at 9:30am, cover an overview of the restoration.

Also call ahead for a schedule of special events, such as the races in November, birthday celebrations for James (Mar 16) and Dolley (May 20), and the Montpelier Wine Festival in May.

11407 Constitution Hwy. (Va. 20), Montpelier Station. ℭ 540/672-2728. www.montpelier.org. Admission $11 adults, $10 seniors, $6 children 6–14, free for children 5 and under. Apr–Oct daily 9:30am–5:30pm); Nov–Mar daily 9:30am–4:30pm. Closed New Year's Day, Thanksgiving, Christmas Eve, Christmas, and New

Year's Eve. Montpelier is 25 miles northeast of Charlottesville. Take U.S. 29 north to U.S. 33 east at Ruckersville. At Barboursville, turn left onto Va. 20 north.

ON THE WINE TRAIL

There have been vineyards in the Piedmont since the 18th century, and Jefferson hoped to produce quality wines in Virginia. His dream has come true, and today Charlottesville is in the middle of one of Virginia's prime winemaking regions. Many wineries offer tours and tastings.

Jefferson Vineyards (✆ **434/977-3042;** www.jeffersonvineyards.com) is on Va. 53 between Monticello and Ash Lawn–Highland, so consider stopping for a taste after your day's sightseeing. **Oakencroft Vineyard** (✆ **434/296-4188;** www.oakencroft.com) is off Barracks Road, 3½ miles northwest of U.S. 29.

Near Montpelier, some 20 miles northeast of Charlottesville, award-winning **Horton Vineyards** (✆ **800/829-4633** or 540/832-7440; www.hvwine.com) is 8 miles east of U.S. 29 on U.S. 33 near Gordonsville. Between there and U.S. 29, **Barboursville Vineyards** (✆ **540/832-3824;** www.barboursvillewine.com), on C.R. 177 near the intersection of Va. 20 and Va. 33, was Virginia's first winery. On U.S. 29, 8 miles south of Culpepper, **Prince Michel and Rapidan River Vineyards** (✆ **800/869-8242** or 540/547-9720; www.princemichel.com) is one of the state's largest; it has a museum, a fine-dining restaurant, and bed-and-breakfast suites. Call the vineyards for hours and admission prices, or visit the Virginia Wine Country website at www.vawine.com.

ATTRACTIONS IN THE LYNCHBURG AREA

When Jefferson wanted to get away from it all, he headed south to Poplar Forest, his country retreat near the James River town of Lynchburg. Today, Lynchburg is a base from which to explore not just Poplar Forest but Patrick Henry's plantation home and the village of Appomattox Court House, where Robert E. Lee surrendered to Ulysses S. Grant. There's also a memorial to the D-day invasion during World War II.

Note that most of these attractions are closer to Roanoke (see chapter 8) than to Charlottesville.

Thomas Jefferson's Poplar Forest ★★ In 1806, while he was president, Jefferson himself assisted the masons in laying the foundation for this dwelling on what was then a 4,819-acre plantation and the source of much of his income. He designed the octagonal house to utilize light and air flow to the maximum in as economical a space as possible. It became his favorite place to escape from the parade of visitors at Monticello. Today, his final architectural masterpiece is again a work in progress, as it is being slowly and meticulously restored to the way it looked in the early 19th century. There are a few furniture reproductions (try the "siesta" chair). Outside, archaeologists dig about the grounds, trying to discover how Jefferson landscaped the gardens. You can see artifacts from the buildings and grounds as they are brought to light and exhibited. During summer a pavilion covers hands-on activities representing Jefferson's time. You can tour the property on your own, but it's much more rewarding to take a 45-minute guided tour.

Va. 661, Forest. ✆ 434/525-1806. www.poplarforest.org. House tour $7 adults, $6 seniors, $1 children 6–16, free for children 5 and under; self-guided grounds tour, $3 per person. Apr–Nov daily 10am–4pm (last tour begins at 4pm). Tent with hands-on activities, Memorial Day to Labor Day, daily 11am–2pm. Closed Thanksgiving and Dec–Mar. 45-min. house tours depart on the hour and half-hour. Entrance is about 6 miles southwest of Lynchburg. From Lynchburg take U.S. 221 south, go straight on Va. 811, turn left on Va. 661.

Appomattox Court House National Historical Park 👁👁👁   Here, in the parlor of Wilmer McLean's home 2 miles north of Appomattox, Robert E. Lee surrendered the Army of Northern Virginia to Ulysses S. Grant on April 9, 1865, thus ending the bitter Civil War. Today, the 20 or so houses, stores, courthouse, and tavern that made up the village then called Appomattox Court have been restored and you can explore them. You will need at least 2 hours to visit the restored houses and walk the country lanes in the rural stillness where these events took place. At the visitor center, pick up a map of the park and a self-guided tour booklet. Upstairs, slide presentations and exhibits include excerpts from the diaries and letters of Civil War soldiers. Allow at least 2 hours to do that and visit McLean's house, Clover Hill Tavern, Meeks' Store, the Woodson Law Office, the courthouse (totally reconstructed), jail, and Kelly House. Surrender Triangle, where the Confederates laid down their arms and rolled up their battle flags, is outside Kelly House. There's a full schedule of ranger programs during the summer months.

Va. 24 (P.O. Box 218), Appomattox. 🕐 434/352-8987. www.nps.gov/apco. Admission Memorial Day to Labor Day, $4 adults, free for children under 17 (maximum $10 per vehicle); rest of year, $2 adults, free for children under 17 (maximum $5 per vehicle). Daily 8:30am–5pm. Closed New Year's Day, Thanksgiving, and Christmas. From Lynchburg take U.S. 460 east 22 miles.

Booker T. Washington National Monument 👁   At this memorial to one of America's great African-American leaders, visitors can conjure up the setting of Booker T. Washington's childhood in reconstructed buildings and demonstrations of farm life and slavery in Civil War–era Virginia. Although Washington called his boyhood home a plantation, the Burroughs farm was small, at 207 acres and never with more than 11 slaves. His mother was the cook, and the cabin where he was born was also the kitchen. His family left the farm in 1865, when he was nine. He determinedly sought an education and walked most of the 500 miles from his home in West Virginia to Hampton Institute. He worked his way through school and achieved prominence as an educator, founder of Tuskegee Institute in Alabama, author, and advisor to presidents. In 1956, a century after he was born, this monument was established to honor his life and work. Begin at the visitor center, which offers a slide show and a map with a self-guided plantation tour and nature walks that wind through the original Burroughs property.

12130 Booker T. Washington Hwy. (Va. 122), Hardy. 🕐 540/721-2094. www.nps.gov/bowa. Free admission. Daily 9am–5pm. From Lynchburg, take U.S. 460 west to Va. 122 south. Park is 16 miles northeast of Rocky Mount.

National D-Day Memorial   On a hilltop with a splendid view of the Blue Ridge, this new memorial honors the American soldiers, sailors and airmen who fought and died in the invasion of Normandy on June 6, 1944. The town of Bedford was chosen for the monument because 19 of its young men were killed during the invasion and four more died during the Normandy campaign. The town had a population of 3,200, which meant that proportionally Bedford lost more men than any other town in the United States. Stunning in its architectural symbolism, the monument recalls the five landing beaches, the cliffs Allied soldiers climbed, and the contributions of the army, navy and air force. Be sure to pick up a brochure or take a 45-minute guided tour, either on foot.

U.S. 460 at Va. 122, Bedford. 🕐 540/587-3619. www.dday.org. Admission $10 per vehicle. Walking tours $2, free for children 5 and under. Riding tours $4 per person. Daily 10am–5pm. Closed New Years Day, Thanksgiving, and Christmas.

Red Hill, Patrick Henry National Memorial Fiery orator Patrick ("Give me liberty or give me death") Henry retired to Red Hill plantation in 1794 after serving five terms as governor of Virginia. Failing health forced him to refuse numerous posts, including chief justice of the United States, secretary of state, and minister to Spain and France. He died at Red Hill on June 6, 1799, and is buried in the family graveyard. Begin your tour at the visitor center, where you can see a 15-minute video about Henry's years here and visit the museum with the world's largest assemblage of Henry memorabilia. The centerpiece is Peter Rothermel's famous painting *Patrick Henry before the Virginia House of Burgesses,* depicting his "If this be treason, make the most of it" speech against the Stamp Act in 1765. The site contains his actual law office, an accurate reproduction of the main house, the carriage house, and other small buildings. You can't miss the most striking feature of the landscape: Standing 64 feet high and spanning 96 feet, the Osage Orange Tree is listed in the American Forestry Hall of Fame.

1250 Red Hill Rd., Brookneal. ✆ 434/376-2044. www.redhill.org. Admission $6 adults, $5 seniors, $2 students. Apr–Oct daily 9am–5pm; Nov–Mar daily 9am–4pm. Closed New Year's Day, Thanksgiving, and Christmas. Red Hill is 35 miles from Lynchburg. From Lynchburg take U.S. 501 south to Brookneal, then Va. 40 east and follow the brown signs.

5 Golfing, Canoeing & Ballooning

If you can afford it, the best golfing is at the Arnold Palmer-designed links at the private Keswick Club, which guests of Keswick Hall at Monticello can pay to play (see "Where to Stay," earlier). The University of Virginia's 18-hole **Birdwood Golf Course** (✆ 434/293-GOLF), adjacent to the Boar's Head Inn (see "Where to Stay," earlier), is one of the top 10 collegiate courses in the country. The 18-hole **Meadow Creek Golf Course,** 1400 Pen Park Rd. (✆ **434/977-0615**), is a short but challenging 18-holer. Call the courses to reserve tee times and get directions.

You can go canoeing on the James River at Scottsville, a quaint, 19th-century town 20 miles south of Charlottesville via Va. 20. The river can run swiftly here—class I or II if it has rained recently; tubing conditions if it hasn't. Contact **James River Runners,** 10082 Hatton Ferry Rd., Scottsville (✆ **434/286-2338;** www.jamesriver.com), for canoe and inner tube rentals.

You can go ballooning over the foothills with **Bear Ballooning** (✆ **800/932-0152** or 434/971-1757; www.2comefly.com). The sunrise flights last about an hour and end with champagne at the Boar's Head Inn (see "Where to Stay," earlier).

For hiking and other outdoor activities, remember you're less than an hour's drive from Shenandoah National Park (see chapter 7).

6 Charlottesville After Dark

The University of Virginia has a constant and ever-changing parade of concerts, plays, lectures, exhibits, and other events. For a complete schedule, pick up the free newspapers *C-Ville Weekly* (www.c-ville.com) and *The Hook* (www.readthehook.com) at the Monticello Visitors Center (see "Visitor Information," above).

You can see live performances at the **Culbreth and Helms Theatres of The University of Virginia** and the **Heritage Reperatory Theatre,** all at 109 Culbreth Rd. (✆ **434/924-3376;** www.virginia.edu), and at **Live Arts,** 609 E. Market St. (✆ **434/977-4177;** www.livearts.org), and **Old Michie Theatre,** 221 E. Water St. (✆ **434/977-3690;** www.oldmichie.com), both near the Downtown

Mall. It's only 40 miles via I-64 to Shakespeare in Staunton's marvelous Black-friars Playhouse (see section 7 in chapter 7).

Vinegar Hill Theatre, 220 W. Market St. (© **434/977-4911;** www.vinegar hilltheatre.com), a block north of the Downtown Mall, presents classic foreign and art films on the silver screen.

Like most college towns, Charlottesville sees numerous bands performing, especially on weekends. Even if you're hard of hearing, you can feel the music coming from the student-oriented bars around The Corner. On the more gen-trified Downtown Mall, there's nighttime jazz or blues at **Miller's,** 109 W. Main St. (© **434/971-8511**), and at **South Street Brewery,** 106 South St. (© **434/293-6550**).

7

The Shenandoah Valley

Extending north-south some 150 miles from Winchester to Natural Bridge, the famous Shenandoah Valley is one of the most beautiful areas of the eastern United States. The Blue Ridge Mountains flank it to the east. To the west rise the even taller Shenandoah and Allegheny ranges. Down on the rolling valley floor lie picturesque small towns steeped in American history dating from the early 1700s, when pioneers moved west from the Tidewater. Scotch-Irish and German emigrants arrived later from the north and built their farmhouses of stone, which makes the valley seem as much Pennsylvania as Virginia.

Most visitors come here to see the view from the Shenandoah National Park atop the Blue Ridge Mountains. The park offers spectacular landscapes and a plethora of hiking and riding trails, including a portion of the Maine-to-Georgia Appalachian Trial. The Skyline Drive—one of America's great scenic routes—runs the full length of the park and connects directly with the Blue Ridge Parkway, which continues south into North Carolina.

Down in the valley, outdoor enthusiasts can ride horses and go tubing, canoeing, or rafting.

In addition to its scenic grandeur and outdoor pursuits, history is a major reason to come here. Lord Fairfax sent George Washington west to survey the valley, and reminders of his visits are at Natural Bridge, where he carved his initials, and in Winchester, which has preserved the office he occupied during the French and Indian Wars.

During the Civil War, the Shenandoah's rich farmland served as the breadbasket for Robert E. Lee's Army of Northern Virginia, and Union armies staged several assaults to cut off Lee's supplies. Stonewall Jackson left Lexington's Virginia Military Institute to become one of the Confederacy's major generals. The entire VMI Corps of Cadets fought heroically in the legendary Battle of New Market. After the war, Lee settled in Lexington as president of what is now Washington and Lee University, and both he and Jackson are buried there.

Woodrow Wilson was born in Staunton in 1856, and a museum adjoining his birthplace pays tribute to this president's peace-loving ideals.

EXPLORING THE VALLEY

VISITOR INFORMATION   For information about attractions, accommodations, restaurants, and services in the entire region, contact the **Shenandoah Valley Travel Association (SVTA),** 277 W. Old Cross Rd. (P.O. Box 1040), New Market, VA 22844 (© **877/847-4878** or 540/740-3132; fax 540/740-3100; www.shenandoah.org). The SVTA operates a visitor center in New Market, just off I-81 at U.S. 211 (Exit 264). The center, open daily from 9am to 5pm, has a free phone line for hotel reservations.

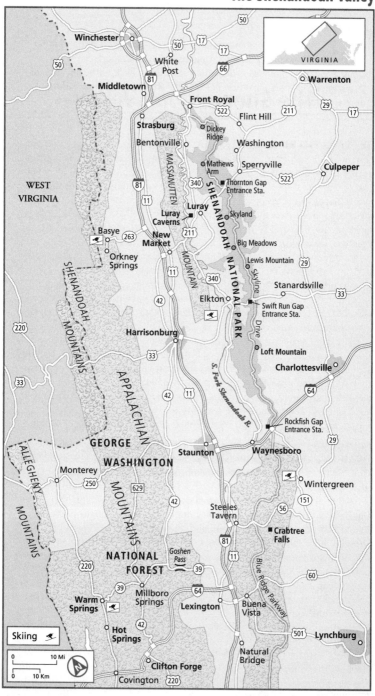

The Shenandoah Valley

VIRGINIA

Winchester

White Post

50

17

50

50

66

17

Warrenton

Middletown

81

Front Royal

522

Flint Hill

211

29

17

Strasburg

Dickey Ridge

Washington

Bentonville

Mathews Arm

Sperryville

Culpeper

WEST VIRGINIA

81

340

Thornton Gap Entrance Sta.

522

11

Luray Caverns

Luray

Skyland

Basye

263

New Market

211

Big Meadows

Orkney Springs

11

Lewis Mountain

29

Stanardsville

33

340

42

Elkton

Swift Run Gap Entrance Sta.

220

Harrisonburg

33

SHENANDOAH MOUNTAINS

APPALACHIAN MOUNTAINS

42

11

S. Fork Shenandoah R.

Loft Mountain

Charlottesville

64

Rockfish Gap Entrance Sta.

29

GEORGE WASHINGTON MOUNTAINS

Staunton

Waynesboro

Monterey

250

629

Wintergreen

151

ALLEGHENY MOUNTAINS

42

Steeles Tavern

56

NATIONAL FOREST

Goshen Pass

39

Crabtree Falls

81

11

Blue Ridge Parkway

60

220

39

Millboro Springs

64

Warm Springs

Lexington

Buena Vista

501

Lynchburg

Skiing

Hot Springs

42

Natural Bridge

0   10 Mi

0   10 Km

Clifton Forge

Covington

220

MASSANUTTEN MOUNTAIN

SHENANDOAH NATIONAL PARK

Skyline Drive

Tips Snow, Ice & Fog

Major highways in the Shenandoah Valley are kept open during winter, but snow, ice and fog can close secondary roads and especially the Skyline Drive and other mountain roads during winter. Check with the **Virginia Department of Transportation** (© 800/367-ROAD; www.virginiadot.org) or the **Weather Channel** (www.weather.com) for present conditions.

GETTING THERE & GETTING AROUND   Public transportation is non-existent in Shenandoah National Park, so you will need a **car.** The gorgeous scenery of the Shenandoah is best seen by private vehicle, anyway, so bring your own or rent one at the airport. At least part of your trip should include the park's spectacular Skyline Drive (see below). The fastest way to and through the region is via I-81, which runs the entire length of the valley floor and has been designated one of America's 10 most scenic interstates. Running alongside I-81, the legendary Valley Pike (U.S. 11) is like a trip back in time at least 50 years, with its old-fashioned gas stations, small motels, shops, and restaurants. Likewise, the old U.S. 340 follows the scenic western foothills of the Blue Ridge.

I-66 enters the valley from Washington, D.C., before ending at Strasburg. I-64 comes into the valley's southern end from both east and west, running contiguous with I-81 between Staunton and Lexington. Other major east-west highways crossing the valley are U.S. 50, 211, 33, 250, and 60.

The nearest major airport is Washington Dulles International, 50 miles east of Front Royal (see "Getting There & Getting Around" in chapter 2). **US Airways Express** (© 800/428-4322) has commuter flights to and from **Shenandoah Valley Regional Airport** (© 540/234-8304; www.flyshd.com), off I-81 between Harrisonburg and Staunton. There are also airports in Charlottesville (see chapter 6) and Roanoke (see chapter 8).

Amtrak (© 800/872-7245; www.amtrak) offers direct service to Staunton.

---

1 Shenandoah National Park & the Skyline Drive ✺✺✺

Running for 105 miles atop the spine of the Blue Ridge Mountains, Shenandoah National Park is a haven for plants and wildlife. Although long and skinny, the park encompasses some 300 square miles of mountains, forests, waterfalls, and rock formations. It has more than 60 mountain peaks higher than 2,000 feet, with Hawksbill and Stony Man exceeding 4,000 feet. Although high ozone levels frequently create obscuring smog during the summer, on many spring and fall days you will have panoramic views from overlooks along the Skyline Drive over the Piedmont to the east and the Shenandoah Valley to the west. The drive gives you access to the park's visitor facilities and to more than 500 miles of glorious hiking and horse trails, including the Appalachian Trail.

Europeans began settling these slopes and hollows in the early 18th century. Plans for establishment of a national park got under way 200 years later, and it was Pres. Franklin D. Roosevelt's Depression-era Civilian Conservation Corps that built the recreational facilities, guard walls, cabins, and many hiking trails. The corps completed the Skyline Drive in 1939, thus opening this marvelously beautiful area to casual visitors.

Today, over two-fifths of the park is considered wilderness. Animals like deer, bear, bobcat, and turkey have returned, and sightings of deer and smaller animals are frequent; the park also boasts more than 100 species of trees.

JUST THE FACTS

ACCESS POINTS & ORIENTATION   The park and its Skyline Drive have four entrances. Northernmost is at **Front Royal** on U.S. 340 near the junction of I-81 and I-66, about 1 mile south of Front Royal and 90 miles west of Washington, D.C. The two middle entrances are at **Thornton Gap,** 33 miles south of Front Royal on U.S. 211 between Sperryville and Luray, and at **Swift Run Gap,** 68 miles south of Front Royal on U.S. 33 between Standardsville and Elkton. The southern gate is at **Rockfish Gap,** 105 miles south of Front Royal at I-64 and U.S. 250, some 21 miles west of Charlottesville and 18 miles east of Staunton.

The Skyline Drive is marked with **Mile Posts,** starting at zero at the Front Royal entrance and increasing as you go south, with Rockfish Gap on the southern end at Mile 105.

DISTRICTS   The access roads divide the park into three areas: **Northern District,** between Front Royal and U.S. 211 at Thornton Gap (Mile 0 to Mile 31.5); **Central District,** between Thornton Gap and U.S. 33 at Swift Run Gap (Mile 31.5 to Mile 65.7); and **Southern District,** between Swift Run Gap and I-64 at Rockfish Gap (Mile 65.7 to Mile 105).

INFORMATION   For free information, call or write **Superintendent,** Shenandoah National Park, 3655 U.S. Hwy., 211 East, Luray, VA 22835 (© **540/999-3500;** www.nps.gov/shen). The headquarters is 4 miles west of Thornton Gap and 5 miles east of Luray on U.S. 211.

Aramark Virginia Sky-Line Co., the park's major concessionaire, maintains an informative website at **www.visitshenandoah.com.**

The **Shenandoah National Park Association** (© 540/999-3582; www.snp books.org), is the best source of maps, guidebooks, and other publications about the park's cultural and natural history. It has a bookstore at park headquarters, and many of its publications are available at the visitor centers.

For guide books and detailed topographic maps of the park's three districts, write or call the **Potomac Appalachian Trail Club (PATC),** 118 Park St., Vienna, VA 22180 (© **703/242-0315,** or 703/242-0965 for a recording of the club's activities; www.patc.net). The PATC helps build and maintain the park's portion of the Appalachian Trail, including trail cabins (see "Hiking & Other Sports," below). The PATC is part of the **Appalachian Trail Conference,** P.O. Box 807, Harpers Ferry, WV 25425-0807 (© **304/535-6331;** www.atconf.org), which covers the entire trail from Maine to Georgia.

EMERGENCIES   In case of emergencies, call the park headquarters (© **540/999-3500**).

Tips Your Indispensable Guide

In addition to the magnificent map brochure the ranger will hand you, be sure to get a copy of *Shenandoah Overlook* when you enter the park, or pick one up at a visitor center. This tabloid newspaper will be your Bible during your visit, since it tells you about ranger programs and everything else that's going on during your visit.

Tips **Avoiding the Crowds**

With its proximity to the Washington, D.C., metropolitan area, the park is at its busiest on summer and fall weekends and holidays. The fall-foliage season in October is the busiest time, and reservations for October accommodations in or near the park should be made as much as a year in advance. The best time to visit is during the spring and on weekdays from June through October. When the Central District around Big Meadows and Skyland is packed, there may be more space available in the Northern and Southern Districts.

FEES, REGULATIONS & BACKCOUNTRY PERMITS Entrance permits good for 7 consecutive days are $10 per car, $5 for each pedestrian or bicyclist. A Shenandoah Passport ($20) is good for 1 year, as is the National Park Service's Golden Eagle Passport ($50). Park entrance is free to holders of Golden Access (for disabled U.S. citizens) and Golden Age (U.S. citizens 62 or older) passports. The former is free; the latter is available at the entrance gates for $10.

Speed limit on the Skyline Drive is 35 mph, although given the number of camper vans and rubberneckers creeping along this winding, two-lane road, you'll be lucky to go that fast. This no place to have a fit of "road rage."

Plants and animals are protected; so all hunting is prohibited. Pets must be kept on a leash at all times and are not allowed on some trails. Wood fires are permitted only in fireplaces in developed areas. The Skyline Drive is a great bike route, but neither bicycles nor motor vehicles of any sort are allowed on the hiking trails.

Most of the park is open to backcountry camping. Permits, which are free, are required; get them at the entrance gates, visitor centers, or by mail from park headquarters (see "Information," above). Campers are required to leave no trace of their presence. No permits are necessary for backcountry hiking, but the same "no-trace" rule applies.

VISITOR CENTERS There are two park visitor centers, **Dickey Ridge Visitor Center,** at Mile 4.6, and **Byrd Visitor Center,** at Mile 51 in Big Meadows. Both are open daily 8:30am to 5pm from mid-April through October (to 6pm from July 4 to Labor Day) and on an intermittent schedule through Thanksgiving weekend in late November. Both provide information, maps of nearby hiking trails, interpretive exhibits, films, slide shows, and nature walks. There is a small information center at **Loft Mountain** (Mile Post 79.5), which is open daily from 9am to 5pm during the summer months.

In addition, the town of Waynesboro runs the **Rockfish Gap Information Center,** on U.S. 211 outside the park's southern gate (© **540/949-8203**). That's at Exit 99 off I-64. It has a terrific room-size topographical map of the region. Open daily from 9am to 5pm except Thanksgiving and Christmas.

SEASONS The park is most popular from mid- to late October, when the fall foliage peaks, and weekend traffic on the Skyline Drive can be bumper-to-bumper. Days also tend to be more clear in fall than in summer, when lingering haze can obscure the views. In spring, the green of leafing trees moves up the ridge at the rate of about 100 feet a day. Wildflowers begin to bloom in April, and, by late May, the azaleas are brilliant and the dogwood is putting on a show. Nesting birds abound, and the normally modest waterfalls are at their highest during spring, when warm rains melt the highland snows. You'll find the clearest views across the distant mountains during winter, but many facilities are closed then, and snow and ice can shut down the Skyline Drive. Also, parts of the drive are closed at night during Virginia's hunting season from mid-November to early January.

RANGER PROGRAMS The park offers a wide variety of ranger-led activities—nature walks, interpretive programs, cultural and history lectures, and campfire talks. Most are held at or near Dickey Ridge Visitor Center in the north; Byrd Visitor Center and the Big Meadows and Skyland lodges and campground in the center; and Loft Mountain campground in the south. Schedules are published seasonally in the Shenandoah Overlook, available at the entrance gates, visitor centers, and from park headquarters.

SEEING THE HIGHLIGHTS

The most interesting and beautiful section is the **Central District,** between Mile 31.5 and Mile 65.7 (that is, between U.S. 211 at Thornton Gap and U.S. 33 at Swift Run Gap). It has the highest mountains, best views, nearly half of the park's 500 miles of hiking trails, and its only stables and overnight accommodations. You can see the views in a day, but plan to spend at least 2 nights here if you're doing extensive hiking, riding, or fishing. The lodges at Big Meadows or Skyland are the best bases, but make your reservations as early as possible (see "Accommodations," below). If you can't get a room at Big Meadows or Skyland, Luray is the nearest town with accommodations (see section 5, later).

SCENIC OVERLOOKS Among the more interesting of the 75 designated overlooks along the drive are the **Shenandoah Valley Overlook** (Mile 2.8), with views west to the Signal Knob of Massanutten Mountain across the south fork of the river; **Range View Overlook** (Mile 17.1; elevation 2,800 ft.), providing fine views of the central section of the park, looking south; **Stony Man Overlook** (Mile 38.6), offering panoramas of Stony Man Cliffs, the valley, and the Alleghenies; **Thoroughfare Mountain Overlook** (Mile 40.5; elevation 3,595 ft.), one of the highest overlooks, with views from Hogback Mountain south to cone-shaped Robertson Mountain and the rocky face of Old Rag Mountain; **Old Rag View Overlook** (Mile 46.5), dominated by Old Rag, sitting all by itself in an eastern extremity of the park; **Franklin Cliffs Overlook** (Mile 49), offering a view of the cliffs and the Shenandoah Valley and Massanutten Mountain beyond; and **Big Run Overlook** (Mile 81.2), which looks down on rocky peaks and the largest watershed in the park.

WATERFALLS Only one waterfall is visible from the Skyline Drive, at Mile 1.4, and it's dry part of the year. On the other hand, 15 other falls are accessible via hiking trails (see "Hiking," below).

⌒ *Tips* Slow Down, You Move Too Fast . . .

Unless you're caught in heavy traffic on fall foliage weekends, you can drive the entire length of the **Skyline Drive** in about 3 hours without stopping. But why rush? Give yourself at least a day, so lovely are the views from its 75 designated scenic overlooks. Stop for lunch at a wayside snack bar, lodge, or one of seven official picnic grounds (any of the overlooks will do for an impromptu picnic). Better yet, get out of your car and take at least a short hike down one of the hollows to a waterfall.

HIKING & OTHER SPORTS

HIKING The number-one outdoor activity here is hiking. The park's 112 hiking trails total more than 500 miles, varying in length from short walks to a 101-mile segment of the Appalachian Trail running the entire length of the park. Access to the trails is marked along the Skyline Drive. There are parking lots at the major trailheads, but they fill quickly on weekends.

I strongly recommend that you get maps and trail descriptions before setting out—even before leaving home, if possible. Free maps of many trails are available at the visitor centers, which also sell the topographic maps, published by the Potomac Appalachian Trail Conference, as well as a one-sheet map of all of the park's walks published by Trails Illustrated. See "Information," above, for contact information.

Try to take at least one of the short hikes on trails at Dickey Ridge Visitor Center (Mile 4.6), Byrd Visitor Center/Big Meadows (Mile 51), and Loft Mountain (Mile 79.5). There's an excellent 1.6-mile hike at Stony Man (Mile 41.7).

Here are a few of the best trails:

- **Limberlost Accessible Trail:** At Mile 43 south of Skyland, Limberlost is accessible to visitors in wheelchairs. The 1.3-mile loop runs through an old-growth forest of ancient hemlocks. The trail has a 5-foot-wide, hard-packed surface; crosses a 65-foot bridge; and includes a 150-foot boardwalk.

- **White Oak Canyon** 🐾🐾: Beginning at Mile 42.6 just south of Skyland, this steep gorge is the park's scenic gem. The 7.3-mile trail goes through an area of wild beauty, passing no less than six waterfalls and cascades. The upper reaches to the first falls are relatively easy, but further down the track can be rough and rocky. Total climb is about 2,160 feet, so allow 6 hours.

- **Cedar Run Falls:** Several trails begin at Hawksbill Gap (Mile 45.6). A short but steep trail leads 1.7 miles round-trip to the summit of Hawksbill Mountain, the park's highest at 4,050 feet. Another is a moderately difficult 3.5-mile round-trip hike to Cedar Falls and back. You can also connect from Cedar Run to White Oak Canyon, a 7.3-mile loop that will take all day.

- **Dark Hollow Falls** 🐾: One of the park's most popular hikes is the 1.4-mile walk to Dark Hollow Falls, the closest cascade to the Skyline Drive. The trail begins at Mile 50.7 near the Byrd Visitor Center. Allow 1¼ hours for the round-trip.

- **Camp Hoover/Mill Prong** 🐾: Starting at the Milam Gap parking area (Mile 52.8), this 4-mile round-trip hike drops down the Mill Prong to the Rapidan River, where Pres. Herbert Hoover, an avid fisherman, had a camp during his administration (sort of the Camp David of his day). The park service has plans to restore Camp Hoover, so don't be surprised if construction is going on. The total climb is 850 feet; allow 4 hours.

- **South River Falls** 🐾🐾: Third-highest in the park, South River Falls drops a total of 83 feet in two stages. From the parking lot at South River Overlook (Mile 62.7), the trail is a moderately easy 2.6 miles round-trip, with a total climb of about 850 feet. Allow 2½ hours.

- **Doyles River Falls:** Starting at a parking lot at Mile 81.1, a trail drops to a small waterfall in a natural amphitheater surrounded by trees. Continue another .25 mile to see an even taller waterfall (63 ft.). This hike is 2.7 miles round-trip, with a few steep sections in its 850-foot climb; allow 3 hours.

- **Appalachian Trail:** Access points to the Appalachian Trail are well marked at overlooks along the Skyline Drive. Along the trail, five backcountry

Tips **It Gets Chilly Up Here**

It's much cooler on the mountaintops than in the valley, especially at night. In fact, it can get downright chilly in Shenandoah National Park even during July and August. Translated: Remember to bring long pants and a jacket or sweater. And comfortable walking shoes, too.

shelters for day use each offer only a table, fireplace, pit toilet, and water. The **Potomac Appalachian Trail Club,** 118 Park St. SE, Vienna, VA 22180 (*©* 703/242-0693; www.patc.net), maintains huts and fully enclosed cabins that can accommodate up to 12 people. Use of the huts is free, but they are intended for long-distance hikers only. Cabins cost $10 to $20 on weekdays, $15 to $40 on weekends. You can reserve cabins by contacting PATC Monday to Thursday between 7 and 9pm, Thursday and Friday from noon to 2pm Eastern time (*only* during these hours). You'll have to submit a signed form (available on PATC's website), so start the process as early as possible.

FISHING   The park's streams are short, with limited fishing, so it's hardly worth the time and effort. The park publishes a free recreational fishing brochure and an annual list of streams open for fishing, available at the Big Meadows and Loft Mountain waysides or at sporting-goods stores outside the park.

HORSEBACK RIDING   Horses are allowed only on trails marked with yellow, and only via guided expeditions with **Skyland Stables** (*©* 540/999-2210), on the Skyland Lodge grounds (Mile 41.8). Rides cost $20 per hour during the week, $22 per hour on weekends. Pony rides for children are $3 for 15 minutes, $6 for 30 minutes. Children must be 4 feet, 10 inches tall to ride the horses (otherwise they can take a pony ride); an adult must accompany those under 12. The stables operate from April to November. Call for reservations, which are accepted 1 day in advance.

CAMPING

The park has four campgrounds with tent and trailer sites (but no hookups anywhere). In the middle of the park's Central District, **Big Meadows** (Mile 51.2) has the best location and sites equipped for disabled campers. You can reserve Big Meadows sites in advance by calling *©* 800/365-2267 daily between 10am and 10pm Eastern time, or on the park service's reservation website at http://reservations.nps.gov. They cost $17 per night. Big Meadows is open from early April to the end of October.

Sites at **Mathews Arm** (Mile 22.2), **Lewis Mountain** (Mile 57.5), and **Loft Mountain** (Mile 79.5) are on a first-come, first-served basis at $14 per site per night. They are open from mid-May to late October. Lewis Mountain has only 31 sites and is often full during summer and early fall. Mathews Arm and Loft Mountain have 100 and 200 sites, respectively, and usually only fill on summer and fall weekends.

ACCOMMODATIONS

Situated on the Skyline Drive in the heart of the Central District, **Big Meadows Lodge** and **Skyland Lodge** (see below) are the only hotels in the park. They are managed by the park concessionaire, **Aramark Virginia Sky-Line Co.,** P.O.

Box 727, Luray, VA 22835 (© **800/999-4714** or 540/743-5108; www.visit shenandoah.com), which also operates food and other services for park visitors. Lodge reservations should be made well in advance—up to a year ahead for the peak fall season. In addition, cottages are available at Lewis Mountain.

Luray is the nearest town to the Central District (see section 5, later). The sections that follow describe accommodations in other Shenandoah Valley towns.

Big Meadows Lodge ⭐ *Value*   Big Meadows is what you expect a historic mountain lodge to be. Built of stone and timber, the rustic main building sports a large guest lounge with a roaring fireplace, and its window walls present a spectacular view over the Shenandoah Valley. Accommodations consist of rooms upstairs in the main lodge and in rustic cabins, and multi-unit lodges with suites spread out over the premises. Not all have the valley view, however, so request one of the six "terrace" rooms in the main lodge or a top-floor unit in the Doubletop or Rapidan buildings. The view is worth paying extra for, but make sure the reservation clerk understands that you don't want just any room. Whichever unit you get, you'll have a private bathroom but no air-conditioning (you won't need it up here), TVs, phones, or any other modern amenities in your unit. The main-lodge dining room features steaks, fried chicken, mountain trout, and pastas. Wine, beer, and cocktails are available. During the season, live entertainment keeps the Taproom busy. Big Meadows is a major recreational center. Many hiking trails start here, and it's also the site of the Byrd Visitor Center.

P.O. Box 727, Luray, VA 22835 (on Skyline Drive at Mile 51.2). © **800/999-4714** or 540/999-2221. Fax 540/ 999-2011. www.visitshenandoah.com. 97 units. $70–$121 double main lodge; $82–$111 double motel; $115–$146 double suite; $78–$90 double cabin. Highest rates charged weekends and in Oct. Packages available. AE, DISC, MC, V. Closed Nov to early May. **Amenities:** Restaurant, bar.

Skyland Lodge   Skyland was built by naturalist George Freeman Pollock in 1894 as a summer retreat almost atop Stony Man Mountain, the highest point on the Skyline Drive at 3,600 feet. The main building is smaller and less charming than Big Meadow Lodge's. The resort offers rooms in the main lodge as well as in rustic wood-paneled cabins and motel-type accommodations spread out over its 52 acres. Some have wonderful views; again, tell the reservations clerk you want a view. Like Big Meadows, you won't have TVs, phones, or other amenities. Some of the buildings are dark-brown clapboard, others fieldstone, and all nestle among the trees. The main building's restaurant has a view, and it offers breakfast, lunch, and dinner menus at reasonable prices. There's a fully stocked taproom.

P.O. Box 727, Luray, VA 22835 (on Skyline Drive at Mile 41.8). © **800/999-4714** or 540/999-2211. Fax 540/ 999-2231. www.visitshenandoah.com 177 units. $82–$123 double in lodge; $55–$108 double in cabin; $116–$185 suite. Highest rates charged weekends and in Oct. Packages available. Closed Nov to early May. AE, DISC, MC, V. **Amenities:** Restaurant; bar.

WHERE TO DINE

In addition to the lodges at Big Meadows and Skyland, there are daytime restaurants and snack bars at Big Meadows (Mile 51), Elkwallow Wayside (Mile 24.1), Panorama-Thornton Gap (Mile 31.5), and Loft Mountain (Mile 79.5).

Picnic areas with tables, fireplaces, water fountains, and restrooms are at Dickey Ridge (Mile 4.6), Elkwallow (Mile 24.1), Pinnacles (Mile 36.7), Big Meadows (Mile 51), Lewis Mountain (Mile 57.5), South River (Mile 62.8), and Loft Mountain (Mile 79.5).

2 Winchester: Apple Capital ⟨★

76 miles W of Washington, D.C.; 189 miles NW of Richmond

Winchester is Virginia's present-day "Apple Capital," so-called because of the number of apple orchards in the northern end of the Shenandoah Valley. It was the site of a Shawnee Indian campground before Pennsylvania Quakers settled it in 1732. Later, George Washington set up shop here during the French and Indian Wars. Thanks to its strategic location, Winchester changed hands no fewer than 72 times during the Civil War. Both Confederate Gen. Stonewall Jackson and Union Gen. Philip Sheridan made their headquarters here at one time or another.

Winchester is also the birthplace of novelist Willa Cather and hometown of country music great Patsy Cline. It's also famous for the **Shenandoah Apple Blossom Festival** in May, one of the region's most popular events.

You can spend a morning or afternoon here and see Washington's office and Stonewall Jackson's headquarters, Winchester's major attractions. And country music fans can visit Patsy Cline's gravesite on the edge of town.

ESSENTIALS

VISITOR INFORMATION The **Winchester/Frederick County Visitors Center,** 1360 S. Pleasant Valley Rd., Winchester, VA 22601 (© **800/662-1360** or 540/542-1326; fax 540/450-0099; www.visitwinchesterva.com), is open daily from 9am to 5pm; closed New Year's Day, Easter, Thanksgiving, and Christmas. The center shows an 18-minute video about the area and has a small exhibit about Patsy Cline, Winchester's contribution to country music (see box above). Take Exit 313 off I-81, go west on U.S. 50, and follow the signs.

GETTING THERE Winchester is on I-81, U.S. 11, U.S. 522, U.S. 50, and Va. 7.

⟨Fun Fact "Crazy" for Patsy Cline

Only die-hard country music fans know Winchester-native Virginia Hensley by her real name, for it was as Patsy Cline that Virginia Hensley sang "Walkin' After Midnight" on the nationally televised "Arthur Godfrey's Talent Scouts" in the 1950s. The record of that song sold a million copies.

Other tunes like "Crazy," "Leavin' on Your Mind," and "Imagine That" will forever be linked to Patsy Cline.

Her life came to an abrupt end in March 1963, when she, Hawkshaw Hawkins, and the Cowboy Copas died in a plane crash. Her body was brought home and buried in Shenandoah Memorial Park, 3 miles south of town on U.S. 522.

The Winchester/Frederick County Visitors Center (see "Essentials," below) has a Patsy Cline Corner that includes her very own jukebox. Pick up a brochure that points the way to important sites in her life, including her home, Gaunt's Drug Store (where she worked), the high school she attended, GNM Music (where she cut her first record), the house where she married second husband Charlie Dick, and her grave.

EXPLORING THE TOWN

Both visitor centers distribute free maps, walking-tour brochures of the Old Town historic district, and Patsy Cline driving tour maps (www.patsycline.com), and they sell a 90-minute **Follow the Apple Trail** audiotape driving tour ($5), which will guide you around Winchester and Frederick County.

The heart of Winchester's historic area is the **Old Town Mall,** a 4-block-long pedestrian mall along Loudon Street between Piccadilly and Cork streets. Here you can explore a number of boutiques and enjoy refreshment at a bookstore-cum-coffeehouse, a pastry shop, or several restaurants, some of which offer outdoor seating under shade trees in warm weather (see "Where to Dine," below). Facing the mall, the imposing **Frederick County Court House** was built in 1840 and is now home to the Old Court House Civil War Museum (see below).

While walking between the George Washington and Stonewall Jackson museums (see below), you can't miss the elaborate, beaux arts–style **Handley Library,** at the corner of Braddock and Piccadilly streets (© 540/662-9041). Built between 1907 and 1912, it's adorned with a full panoply of Classic Revival statues. A copper-covered dome covers the rotunda, which symbolizes the spine of a book, with the two flanking wings representing its open pages.

Across the street from the library is the white-columned **Elks Building,** headquarters of Union Gen. Philip Sheridan from 1864 to 1865.

If you don't believe this northern end of the valley was fought over during the Civil War, visit **Mt. Hebron Cemetery,** on Woodstock Lane, east of downtown. Some 8,000 men killed in the battles are buried here—the Rebels in Stonewall Confederate Cemetery on the south side of the street, the Yankees in the National Cemetery on the north side.

Abram's Delight   Adjoining the visitor center is this native-limestone residence built in 1754 by Quaker Isaac Hollingsworth on a site beside a lake. The oldest house in Winchester, served as the town's first Quaker Meeting House. Today, it's fully restored and furnished with simple 18th- and 19th-century pieces. Volunteers serve as guides, and, if you're lucky, one will be on hand to lead a tour.

1340 S. Pleasant Valley Rd. © 540/662-6519. www.winchesterhistory.org. Admission (without block ticket) $12 family, $5 adults, $4.50 seniors, $2.50 students 7–18, free for children 6 and under. Apr–Oct Mon–Sat 10am–4pm; Sun noon–4pm. Mandatory 45-min. house tours depart anytime a guide is available. Closed Nov–Mar.

Stonewall Jackson's Headquarters ⭐   Stonewall Jackson used this Victorian home, once owned by a great-grandfather of actress Mary Tyler Moore, as his headquarters in the winter of 1861–62. It's filled with maps, photos, and memorabilia. As you aren't allowed to just walk through, plan on taking a guided tour. Two guides are usually on hand, so there's seldom a wait.

415 N. Braddock St. (between Peyton St. and North Ave.). © 540/667-3242. www.winchesterhistory.org. Admission (without block ticket) $12 family, $5 adults, $4.50 seniors, $2.50 students 7–18, free for children 6 and under. Apr–Oct Mon–Sat 10am–4pm, Sun noon–4pm; Nov–Mar Fri–Sat 10am–4pm, Sun noon–4pm. Mandatory 30-min. house tours depart as needed.

Glen Burnie   On the western side of town, Glen Burnie is a lovingly restored, red-brick Georgian plantation home standing on the original homestead of Winchester founder James Wood. With sections dating to 1755, the house is appointed with a remarkable collection of 18th-century furniture and art—including paintings by Rembrandt Peale and Gilbert Stuart—amassed by the late Julian Wood Glass Jr., the last descendant of James Wood to live at Glen Burnie. A 14-minute film will set the stage for your tour of the house. Afterwards, you can easily spend another hour strolling though the magnificent

> ### *Value* Saving with a Block Ticket
>
> You can buy a **block ticket** to visit Abram's Delight, Washington's Office Museum, and Stonewall Jackson's Headquarters for $20 for a family, $10 adults, $9 seniors, and $4 students 7 to 18 (free for children under 7). Tickets are available at the museums or at the Winchester/Frederick County Visitors Center (see "Essentials," above).

formal gardens, which shouldn't be missed (there has been many a wedding among the flowers).

801 Amherst St. (U.S. 50 west). ✆ **888/556-5799** or 540/662-1473. Admission to house and gardens, $8 adults, $6 seniors and students, free for children 6 and under; gardens only, $5 per person. Apr–Oct Tues–Sat 10am–4pm; Sun noon–4pm. Closed Nov–Mar. Mandatory 30-min. house tours depart on hour and half-hour.

Old Court House Civil War Museum Housed in the 1840 Frederick County Court House, this new museum tells of Winchester's role in the Civil War, when it see-sawed between Union and Confederate hands. Both sides used the courthouse as a hospital and prison. The museum's most interesting exhibit is upstairs, where upwards of 500 prisoners were detained. Many of them carved graffiti into the walls, which you can see through windows in the walls. Note that the museum is only open Friday to Sunday.

20 N. Loudon St. (on Old Town Mall). ✆ **540/542-1145**. www.civilwarmuseum.org. Admission $3, free for children 4 and under. Fri–Sat 10am–5pm; Sun 1–4pm.

Washington's Office Museum 🖈🖈 George Washington used this small log cabin (since covered with clapboard) as his office in 1755 and 1756 when he was a colonel in the Virginia militia, charged with building Fort Loudon to protect the colony's frontier from the French and the Indians. The building itself is the highlight of this charming little museum, whose exhibits explain Washington's career from 1748 to 1758. You can see it all in 30 minutes. Informative staff members are on hand to answer questions and lead guided tours.

32 W. Cork St. (at Braddock St.). ✆ **540/662-4412**. www.winchesterhistory.org. Admission (without block ticket) $12 family, $5 adults, $4.50 seniors, $2.50 students 7–18, free for children 6 and under. Apr–Oct Mon–Sat 10am–4pm; Sun noon–4pm. Closed Nov–Mar.

WHERE TO STAY

If you decide to stay over, the area along Millwood Avenue (U.S. 50) at I-81 (Exit 313), on the southeast side of town, has Winchester's major shopping mall and several chain restaurants and motels. About half the rooms at the **Holiday Inn** (✆ **800/HOLIDAY** or 540/667-3300) face a courtyard with outdoor pool; the hotel's restaurant is one of the town's most popular lunch spots. Also nearby are the **Best Western Lee-Jackson Motor Inn** (✆ **800/528-1234** or 540/662-4154); **Comfort Inn** (✆ **800/228-5150** or 540/667-5000); **Hampton Inn** (✆ **800/ HAMPTON** or 540/667-8011); **Quality Inn East** (✆ **800/221-2222** or 540/ 667-2250); **Shoney's Inn** (✆ **800/222-2222** or 540/665-1700), which has an indoor pool; the inexpensive **Super 8** (✆ **800/800-8000** or 540/665-4450); and **Travelodge of Winchester** (✆ **800/255-3050** or 540/665-0685).

A NEARBY COUNTRY INN WITH A FRENCH FLAVOR

L'Auberge Provençale 🖈🖈 Master chef Alain Borel and his vivacious wife, Celeste, have managed to re-create the look, feel, and cuisine of Provence in a 1750s fieldstone farmhouse set on a hilltop with a view of the Blue Ridge. In the original main house are three intimate dining rooms and a parlor to which guests are invited for pre-dinner drinks in front of the fireplace. Three of the 11 guest rooms are in this building; antiques and beautiful fabrics complement the colonial farmhouse's fine features. The remaining cozy accommodations, in an adjoining gray-clapboard addition, are individually decorated with Victorian and European pieces and lovely French provincial–print fabrics. Exceptional works of fine art—including prints by renowned artists and a unique selection of carved wooden animals and small handcrafted bird sculptures—adorn the guest rooms. Alain uses the finest-quality ingredients, many from his own garden or local farmers, to create his superb five-course prix-fixe dinners (reservations required). Even breakfast is a splendid repast, and Alain will provide a gourmet picnic lunch on request. No children under 10 need apply for a room here.

U.S. 340 (P.O. Box 190), White Post, VA 22663. ℰ 800/638-1702 or 540/837-1375. Fax 703/837-2004. www.laubergeprovencale.com. 11 units, including 2 suites. $150–$275 double. Rates include full breakfast. AE, DC, MC, V. From I-81, take U.S. 50 east 7 miles, turn right on U.S. 340. The inn is 1 mile on the right. **Amenities:** Restaurant; heated outdoor pool; Jacuzzi; babysitting. No children under 10. *In room:* A/C, dataport, coffeemaker, iron.

WHERE TO DINE

Although One Block West isn't far behind, Winchester's finest cuisine is at L'Auberge Provençale (see above).

The Old Town Mall along Loudon Street in the heart of downtown has a number of coffeehouses, bakeries, and restaurants. Best are **Violino Ristorante Italiano** (ℰ 540/667-8006) and the publike **Brewbaker's** (ℰ 540/667-0429), both on the north end of the mall at Piccadilly Street. They offer outdoor seating in good weather. Around the corner on West Cork Street, the **Cork Street Tavern** (ℰ 540/667-3777) occupies an ancient building with small, dark rooms and a fireplace. A newer wing offers outdoor patio seating in warm weather.

One Block West ✶✶ ECLECTIC   You'll find Winchester's most refined dining in this small brick building almost hidden on Indian Alley, which runs north-south 1 block west of the Loudon Street mall (hence, the name of the restaurant). Although he changes the menu daily, owner Ed Matthews puts the grill to excellent use on steaks, lamb chops, pork loin, and bison. He might also offer rainbow trout stuffed with sautéed spinach and bacon.

25 S. Indian Alley (between Boscowen and Cork sts.). ℰ 540/662-1455. Reservations recommended. Main courses $16–$38. AE, DC, MC, V. Tues–Sat 11am–2pm and 5–10pm.

3 Middletown & Strasburg: Antiques Galore ✶

Middletown: 13 miles S of Winchester; 174 miles NW of Richmond; 76 miles W of Washington, D.C. Strasburg: 6 miles S of Middletown

Middletown's historic sites will interest both history and architecture buffs, while its Wayside Theatre will entertain anyone who loves live theater. An extraordinary collection of shops makes Strasburg a prime destination for antiquers and collectibles shoppers. Both hamlets have exceptional country inns offering antiques-filled accommodations and fine dining.

It was to Strasburg that Gen. Stonewall Jackson brought the railroad locomotives he stole from the Union during his daring Great Train Raid on Martinsburg, West Virginia. He rolled the iron beasts down the Valley Pike to the existing station at Strasburg, which is now a local museum.

ESSENTIALS

VISITOR INFORMATION   The **Winchester/Frederick County Visitors Center** (see "Essentials" in section 2, above) has in-depth information about Middletown. For Strasburg, contact the **Chamber of Commerce,** 132 W. King St., Strasburg, VA 22657 (© **540/465-9197;** www.strasburg.com). It's open Monday to Friday from 8am to 5pm.

GETTING THERE   From I-81, take Exit 302 west to U.S. 11 into Middletown. Take Exits 298 or 300 into Strasburg.

THE TOP ATTRACTIONS

Belle Grove Plantation ★★   One of the finest homes in the Shenandoah Valley, this beautiful stone mansion was built in 1794 by Maj. Isaac Hite, whose grandfather, Joist Hite, first settled here in 1732. At the request of James Madison, brother-in-law of Isaac Hite, Thomas Jefferson was actively involved in Belle Grove's design. The columns and Palladian-style front windows are just two examples of Jefferson's influence. Now owned by the National Trust for Historic Preservation, Belle Grove is at once a working farm, a restored 18th-century plantation house, and a center for the study and sale of traditional rural crafts. The interior is furnished with period antiques.

Belle Grove suffered considerable damage in 1864 during the Battle of Cedar Creek, fought on 4,000 acres surrounding the manor house. If you're here on a Sunday, visit the **Cedar Creek Battlefield Visitors Center** across U.S. 11 (© **888/628-1846** or 540/869-2064; www.cedarcreekbattlefield.org), which honors the fight with Civil War weapons and a diorama depicting the Napoleonic tactics. The battle is re-enacted each year on the weekend closest to October 19.

Although the plantation and battlefield visitor center will continue to operate independently, both are partners in the new **Cedar Creek & Belle Grove National Historical Park,** P.O. Box 229, Strasburg, VA 22657 (© **540/868-9176;** www.nps.gov/cebe), launched in 2003 to protect the surrounding battlegrounds. Call or check the website for developments.

336 Belle Grove Rd. (off U.S. 11), Middletown. © **540/869-2028.** www.bellegrove.org. Admission $7 adults, $6 seniors, $3 children 6–12, free for children 5 and under. Belle Grove, mid-Mar to Oct Mon–Sat 10:15am–3:15pm, Sun 1:15–4:15pm; Nov Sat 10:15am–3:15pm, Sun 1:15–4:15pm. Closed Dec to mid-Mar except candlelight tours at Christmas. Cedar Creek Battlefield, Apr–Oct Sun 1–4pm; Nov–Mar by appointment only. Mandatory 45-min. house tours depart 15 min. past the hour. From Winchester, take U.S. 11 south, or I-81 south to Exit 302 at Middletown, then U.S. 11 south 1 mile.

The Museum of American Presidents (Kids)   Leo M. Bernstein, a former Washington, D.C., lawyer and banker who restored the Wayside Inn (see "Where to Stay & Dine," below), displays his monumental collection of presidential memorabilia at this well-designed small museum in Strasburg. Among the highlights are a lock of George Washington's hair and James Madison's writing desk from his bedroom at Montpelier. Kids can don costumes and play games in a room set up like a Colonial-era schoolhouse, complete with a potbelly stove.

130 N. Massanutten St. (U.S. 11), Strasburg. © **540/465-5999.** www.waysideofva.com. Admission $3 adults, $2 children 6–16, free for children 5 and under. Combination tickets with Stonewall Jackson Museum at Hupp's Hill and Crystal Caverns $10 adults, $8 seniors and children 6–16. May–Oct Mon–Sat 10am–5pm, Sun noon–5pm; Nov–Apr Fri–Sat 10am–5pm.

Stonewall Jackson Museum at Hupp's Hill and Crystal Caverns (Kids)   Although not on the same level as the Stonewall Jackson House in Lexington (see below), this small museum does a good job of explaining the nine valley battles Stonewall Jackson commanded, including the Battle of Hupp's Hill fought on this site October 13, 1864. It does so from the common soldier's perspective, using Civil War photographs, excerpts from diaries of local residents, and videos. This is a particularly good museum for children, who can go on scavenger hunts and try on replicas of Civil War uniforms in a hands-on room. Brochures outline a walking tour of the battlefield. Also on site, Crystal Caverns are less commercialized than most others in the valley, with tours concentrating on the geology and history of the cave.

33229 Old Valley Pike (U.S. 11), Strasburg. © 540/465-5884. www.waysideofva.com. Museum admission $3 adults, $2 children 6–16, free for children 5 and under. Museum and caverns $8 adults, $6 seniors and children 6–12. Combination tickets with Museum of American Presidents $10 adults, $8 seniors and children 6–16. Daily 10am–5pm. Cavern tours 11am, 12:30, 2 and 3pm.

ANTIQUING

Antiques lovers will want to hunt in nearby Strasburg, which has a bevy of fine outlets at the intersection of U.S. 11 and Va. 55. The **Great Strasburg Antiques Emporium** ☆☆, 110 N. Massanutten St. (© 540/465-3711; www.wayside ofva.com/emporium), is one of the state's largest shops, an enormous warehouse with vendors selling both antiques and a plethora of collectibles. It's open Sunday to Thursday from 10am to 5pm, Friday and Saturday from 10am to 7pm.

You can't buy them, but there are plenty of antiques at the **Strasburg Museum,** 440 E. King St. (Va. 55) (© 540/465-3175), 2 blocks east of the emporium. It occupies the old train station where Stonewall Jackson brought his stolen locomotives. Admission is $3 for adults, $1 for teenagers, 50¢ for children under 12. The museum is open May through October, daily from 10am to 4pm.

WHERE TO STAY & DINE

Hotel Strasburg ☆   Strasburg likes to call itself the Antiques Capital of Virginia, and this restored Victorian hotel, built as a hospital in 1902, is furnished with an impressive collection of period pieces. Most units are in the main building, but three suites and a room are in the Chandler House, while the Taylor House holds four suites. Ten rooms have Jacuzzis. Known for excellent international fare, the dining room is open for all three meals. A first-floor pub offers friendly conversation and libation.

213 Holliday St., Strasburg, VA 22657. © 800/348-8327 or 540/465-9191. Fax 540/465-4788. www.hotel stasberg.com. 29 units. $79 double; $114–$175 suite. Weekend and other packages available. AE, DC, DISC, MC, V. From I-81, take Exit 298 and go south on U.S. 11 1½ miles to the first traffic light; turn right 1 block, left at the light onto Holliday St. **Amenities:** Restaurant; bar. *In room:* A/C, TV, dataport.

Wayside Inn ☆☆   This rambling roadside inn first offered bed and board to Shenandoah Valley travelers in 1797. It became a stagecoach stop some 20 years later when the Valley Pike was hacked out of the wilderness, and has continued to function as an inn ever since. In the 1960s, Washington financier and antiques collector Leo M. Bernstein restored it, and today, rooms are beautifully decorated with an assortment of 18th- and 19th-century pieces. Each room's decor reflects a period style, from colonial to elaborate Victorian Renaissance Revival. Expect to find canopied beds, armoires, highboys, writing desks, antique clocks, and stenciled or papered walls adorned with fine prints and oil paintings. Southern-style home cooking is served in seven antiques-filled dining rooms. Cocktails and light fare are served in the **Coachyard Lounge.**

7783 Main St., Middletown, VA 22645. © 877/869-1797 or 540/869-1797. Fax 540/869-6038. www. alongthewayside.com. 24 units. $105–$165 double. Weekend and theater packages available. AE, DC, MC, V. From I-81, take Exit 302 to U.S. 11 (Main St.). **Amenities:** Restaurant; bar. *In room:* A/C, TV.

MIDDLETOWN AFTER DARK

Since 1961, the **Wayside Theatre,** 7853 Main St. (U.S. 11) in Middletown (© **540/869-1776;** www.waysidetheatre.org), has staged fine productions by contemporary dramatists, including Peter Shaffer, Neil Simon, Wendy Wasserstein, and Alan Ayckbourn. Peter Boyle, Susan Sarandon, and Donna McKechnie began their careers here. Tickets range from $18 to $26. The box office is open Monday to Friday from 10am to 5pm.

4 Front Royal: A Spy's Home

20 miles SE of Strasburg; 174 miles NW of Richmond; 70 miles W of Washington, D.C.

At the northern end of the Skyline Drive, Front Royal offers easy access to the Shenandoah National Park's Northern District and is a good place to stay either before or after touring the park. It lacks the charm of Staunton, Lexington, and other valley towns, nor is it as convenient to the park's popular Central District, but this area has the valley's widest array of outdoor activities: golfing, horseback riding, and canoeing, rafting, kayaking, and inner-tubing on the sometimes lazy, sometimes rapid South Fork of the Shenandoah River (see "Rafting, Canoeing & Kayaking" box, below). And if you didn't disappear into the caverns down in Luray, you can go underground here.

Front Royal was named for a royal oak that stood in the town square during the Revolutionary War. In those days, it was a wild and woolly frontier waystation at the junction of the two trails that later became U.S. 340 and Va. 55. During the Civil War, it was home to the infamous Confederate spy Belle Boyd, whose close contact—to say the least—with Union officers led to Stonewall Jackson's surprise victory at the Battle of Front Royal in 1862.

Across the mountains to the east are two fine inns and dining choices, including a nationally famous, five-star inn and restaurant in "Little" Washington.

ESSENTIALS

VISITOR INFORMATION   Contact the **Front Royal/Warren County Visitors Center,** 414 E. Main St., Front Royal, VA 22630 (© **800/338-2576** or 540/635-5788; fax 540/622-2644; www.frontroyalchamber.com). The chamber's visitor center is located in the old yellow train station and is open daily from 9am to 5pm. From I-66, follow U.S. 340 into town and turn left on Main Street at the Warren County Courthouse. The center sells discounted tickets to Skyline Caverns (see "Exploring the Town & the Caverns," below).

GETTING THERE   From I-66, take Exit 6, U.S. 340/U.S. 522 south; it's 5 minutes to town. Front Royal is also easily reached from I-81 by taking I-66 east to Exit 6.

EXPLORING THE TOWN & THE CAVERNS

If you're interested in the Civil War, be sure to pick up a free driving tour brochure from the visitor center (see "Essentials," above). It will lead you to the key sites of the Battle of Front Royal, which Stonewall Jackson won in May of 1862.

In town, you'll find two mildly fascinating Civil War attractions on Chester Street, 1 block north of the visitor center. The **Warren Rifles Confederate Museum** (© **540/636-6982**) has a collection of Civil War firearms, battle flags, uniforms, letters, diaries, and other personal items. Admission is $4 for adults, free for students. Open April 15 through November 1, Monday to Saturday from 9am to 4pm, Sunday from noon to 4pm, by appointment the rest of the year. Next door is the restored **Belle Boyd Cottage** (© **540/636-1446**), where the Confederate spy pillow-talked with her unsuspecting Union lovers. It's open April through October, Monday, Tuesday, Thursday and Friday from 12:30 to 3pm, weekends by appointment. Admission is $2 per person, free for children under 12 accompanied by an adult.

Skyline Caverns *(Kids* Although neither as varied nor as interesting as Luray Caverns (see below), the highlights here are rock formations called anthodites—delicate white spikes that spread in all directions from their positions on the cave ceiling. Their growth rate is about 1 inch every 7,000 years. A sophisticated lighting system enhances formations like the Capitol Dome, Rainbow Trail, and Painted Desert. A miniature train covering about ½ mile is a popular attraction for kids. The cave temperature is a cool 54°F (12°C) year-round, and the tours take an hour, so bring a sweater, even in summer.

10344 Stonewall Jackson Hwy. (U.S. 340). ℂ 800/296-4545 or 540/635-4545. www.skylinecaverns.com. Admission $14 adults, $12 seniors, $7 children 7–13, free for children 6 and under. Train rides $3. June 15 to Labor Day daily 9am–6:30pm; Mar 15–June 14 and Labor Day to Nov 14 Mon–Fri 9am–5pm, Sat–Sun 9am–6pm; Nov 15–Mar 14, daily 9am–4pm. Mandatory 1-hr. tours run continuously. Entry is 2 miles south of downtown Front Royal, 1 mile south of the Shenandoah National Park's northern entrance.

SPORTS & OUTDOOR ACTIVITIES

GOLF   Front Royal has more golf courses than any other valley town. Duffers are welcome at the 27-hole **Shenandoah Valley Golf Club** (ℂ 540/635-3588; www.svgcgolf.com), the 36-hole **Bowling Green Country Club** (ℂ 540/635-2095; www.bowlinggreencountryclub.com), the 18-hole **Jackson's Chase** (ℂ 540/635-7814; www.jacksonschase.com), and the nine-hole **Front Royal Country Club** (ℂ 540/636-9062). Call for directions, starting times, and greens fees.

HORSEBACK RIDING   The Front Royal area also offers more horseback riding than anywhere else in the valley. The 4,500-acre **Marriott Ranch,** 5305 Marriott Lane, Hume, VA 22639 (ℂ 877/278-4574 or 540/364-2627; www.marriottranch.com), offers 1½-hour guided trail rides, buggy rides, summer sunset rides, and full-moon rides. Serious equestrians can stay over in the ranch's bed-and-breakfast inn (ℂ 540/364-3221), which has 10 rooms (7 with bathroom). Hume is on the eastern side of the Blue Ridge, about 15 minutes from Front Royal via U.S. 522, C.R. 635, and C.R. 726.

Other stables are **Indian Hollow Stables,** in Raymond R. "Andy" Guest Jr. Shenandoah River State Park on U.S. 340 between Front Royal and Luray (ℂ 800/270-8808 or 540/636-4756; www.frontroyalcanoe.com/horse.htm), and **Highlander Horses,** 5297 Reliance Rd., Front Royal (ℂ 540/636-4523; www.highlanderhorses.com).

WHERE TO STAY

On U.S. 522 east of U.S. 340, the **Quality Inn Skyline Drive** (ℂ 800/228-5151 or 540/635-3161) is the largest and best-equipped motel here. The inexpensive **Scottish Inn** (ℂ 800/251-1962 or 540/636-6168) and **Super 8** (ℂ 800/800-8000 or 540/636-4888) are both at the junction of U.S. 340 and Va. 55.

Also worth consideration is **Killahevlin,** 1401 N. Royal Ave. (ℂ 800/847-6132 or 540/636-7335; www.vairish.com), a bed-and-breakfast occupying a hilltop mansion built by William Edward Carson, an Irishman who came to the United States in 1885, when he was 15 years old, and amassed a fortune in the limestone business. Today, Susan O'Kelly, another Irish immigrant, operates it. Among its luxurious amenities is an Irish pub.

Rafting, Canoeing & Kayaking on the Shenandoah

The streams flowing west down from Shenandoah National Park end up in the South Fork of the Shenandoah River, which winds its way through a narrow valley between the Blue Ridge and Massanutten mountains. The switchbacks between Front Royal and Luray are the region's main center for river rafting, canoeing, and kayaking from mid-March to mid-November. The amount of recent rain will determine whether you go white-water rafting, canoeing, kayaking, or just lazily floating downstream in an inner tube.

About 5½ miles of the river skirts the **Raymond R. "Andy" Guest Jr. Shenandoah River State Park,** 8 miles south of Front Royal on U.S. 340 (© 540/622-6840; www.dcr.state.va.us/parks/andygues.htm). The park has 13 miles of hiking trails, fishing, horseback riding, picnic areas, and a primitive campground (© 800/933-PARK or 804/225-8367 to reserve a site). The park is open daily from 8am to dusk. Admission is $1 per vehicle weekdays, $2 on weekends and holidays.

Several rafting and canoe outfitters are based along U.S. 340, which parallels the river between Front Royal and Luray. All require advance reservations, and all are closed from November through April.

- **Front Royal Canoe Company** (© 800/270-8808 or 540/635-5440; www. frontroyalcanoe.com) provides equipment and guides from its location on U.S. 340 south of Front Royal.
- In Bentonville, a small village about 8 miles south of Front Royal, you'll find **Downriver Canoe Company** (© 800/338-1963 or 540/635-5526; www.downriver.com) and **Shenandoah River Trips** (© 800/RAPIDS-1 or 540/635-5050; www.shenandoah.cc).
- Near Luray, you can go with **Shenandoah River Outfitters** (© 800/6CANOE2 or 540/743-4159; www.shenandoah-river.com).

Chester House Inn   This B&B occupies a stately 1905 Italian Renaissance estate set on 2 pretty acres of century-old gardens adorned with a fountain, statuary, and brick walls. The premier accommodations are the two-story Garden Cottage, with its own fireplace, TV, kitchen, sleeping loft, and Jacuzzi. In the main house, the Royal Oak Suite is a spacious high-ceilinged unit with a fireplace, separate sitting room, and private bath; it overlooks the gardens. Another charmer is the Blue Ridge Room, which has a Shaker-style bed and an old coal stove. The inn has two TV parlors, but you won't have one (or a phone) in your room.

43 Chester St., Front Royal, VA 22630. © **800/621-0441** or 540/635-3937. Fax 540/636-8695. www.chester house.com. 6 units, 1 cottage. $120–$150 double room or suite; $220 cottage. Rates include full breakfast. Golf packages available. AE, MC, V. *In room:* A/C, kitchen (cottage only), coffeemaker (cottage only), no phone.

TWO FINE NEARBY COUNTRY INNS

The two places below are in the eastern foothills of the Blue Ridge Mountains, but within an easy (and picturesque) drive from Front Royal via U.S. 522.

Caledonia Farm–1812 🐾🐾   This 1812 Federal-style stone farmhouse, listed on the National Register of Historic Places, is a delightful B&B set on a 115-acre working cattle farm adjacent to the Shenandoah National Park. A scenic old barn, livestock, and open pastureland make for a bucolic setting. The common rooms are furnished with country charm. The upstairs suite has two bedrooms and a private bath. A breezeway connects the main house with the romantic two-and-a-half-room guesthouse. All accommodations offer working fireplaces and views of the Blue Ridge. TVs, VCRs, coffeemakers, and irons are available on request. There're bikes and a hot tub for guests' use. Host Phil Irwin, a retired broadcaster, will arrange hayrides and other activities.

47 Dearing Rd., Flint Hill, VA 22627. © 800/262-1812 or 540/675-3693. Manual-start fax on 540/675-3693. www.bnb1812.com. 2 units. $140 double. Rates include full breakfast. DISC, MC, V. From Front Royal, take U.S. 522 south 12 miles to Flint Hill and turn right onto C.R. 641, to C.R. 606 to C.R. 628; look for a sign indicating a right turn to the farm. **Amenities:** Jacuzzi; laundry service. *In room:* A/C, TV/VCR (on request), coffeemaker (on request), iron (on request).

Inn at Little Washington ★★★ Located in the one-gas-station village of Washington, Virginia (also known as "Little Washington"), which then-surveyor George Washington laid out in 1749, this is one of America's finest country inns. It was opened as a restaurant in 1978 by owners Patrick O'Connell, who is the chef, and Reinhardt Lynch, who serves as *maitre d'hôtel*. Rather than being an outstanding inn with a restaurant, theirs is an outstanding restaurant with rooms. O'Connell makes inventive use of regional products—trout, Chesapeake Bay seafood, wild ducks, local cheeses–for his fabulous fixed-price ($100-plus) dinners. For a real treat, reserve one of the two fireside tables back in the kitchen, where you can watch the master and his crew at work. The extraordinary 14,000-bottle wine cellar may leave you pondering before deciding from its 40-page list (trust the waiters; they know what they're doing even if you don't). Dinner reservations are essential. They begin taking them 30 days in advance, and Saturdays are often fully booked within 2 days.

English decorator Joyce Evans magnificently appointed the rooms, and her original sketches are framed and hanging in the inn's upstairs hallways. The two bi-level suites have loft bedrooms, balconies overlooking the courtyard garden, and bathrooms with Jacuzzi tubs. Sumptuous amenities include terry robes, thick towels, and elegant toiletries. Antiques and Oriental rugs add warmth to the rooms, distinguished by extravagantly canopied beds and hand-painted ceiling borders. O'Connell and Lynch recently had Ms. Evans turn a 1790s farmhouse into their luxurious President's Retreat, which sleeps six. It's 17 miles away, but the butler prepares your breakfast and picks you up for dinner at the inn, and a guide will teach you to fly-fish.

Middle and Main sts. (P.O. Box 300), Washington, VA 22747. © 540/675-3800. Fax 540/675-3100. www.relaischateaux.com/washington. 14 units. $340–$495 double; $550–$640 suite; $600–$2,400 farmhouse. Add $125–$225 for all Sat, major holidays, Oct. Rates include continental breakfast and afternoon tea. MC, V. From Front Royal, take U.S. 522 south 16 miles, then west on U.S. 211 to Washington. **Amenities:** Restaurant; bar; Jacuzzi; 24-hr. room service; massage; babysitting; laundry service. *In room:* A/C, safe.

WHERE TO DINE

Main Street Mill Restaurant and Pub AMERICAN Occupying a picturesque 1922 mill building, this establishment has massive supporting columns and ceiling beams of chestnut. Local artist Patricia Windrow executed the distinctive *trompe l'oeil* murals representing Front Royal's pioneer and 19th-century eras. Lunch fare includes soups, spicy chili, salads, and overstuffed deli sandwiches. Main courses range from pastas to bacon-wrapped filet mignon to a Virginia ham dinner.

500 E. Main St. (next to visitor center). © 540/636-3123. Reservations not needed. Sandwiches (lunch only) $5–$6; main courses $9–$20. AE, MC, V. Sun–Thurs 10:30am–9pm; Fri–Sat 10:30am–10pm.

5 Luray: An Underground Organ

6 miles W of Shenandoah National Park; 91 miles SW of Washington, D.C.; 135 miles NW of Richmond

Established in 1812, this small town is home to the famous Luray Caverns, the most visited caves in the eastern United States. Surrounded by the lush, rolling farmlands of a picturesque valley between the Blue Ridge and Massanutten Mountains, Luray's accommodations are the closest to the Shenandoah National Park's popular Central District. Thus, it is the most convenient base in the valley if you can't get a room at one of the park's inns. The park headquarters and the Thornton Gap entry are up U.S. 211 just a few miles east of town.

ESSENTIALS

VISITOR INFORMATION   Call or write the **Page County Chamber of Commerce,** 46 E. Main St., Luray, VA 22835 (© **888/743-3915** or 540/743-3915; fax 540/743-3944; www.luraypage.com). It's open Monday to Saturday 9am to 5pm, Sunday noon to 4pm. The chamber's visitor center is an excellent source of information—including trail maps—about Shenandoah National Park.

GETTING THERE   From Shenandoah National Park, take U.S. 211 west. From I-81, follow U.S. 211 east (this scenic road goes up and over Massanutten Mountain; see below). From Front Royal, take U.S. 340 south.

EXPLORING THE CAVERNS

Luray Caverns ✪   This U.S. Registered Natural Landmark is the most visited underground attraction in the eastern U.S., and with good reason, for these are the Shenandoah Valley's most interesting and entertaining caverns. In addition to monumental columns in rooms more than 140 feet high, they're noted for the beautiful cascades of natural colors found on the interior walls. They also combine the works of man and nature into an unusual organ with a sound system directly connected to stalactites. Music is produced when rubber-tipped plungers controlled by an organist or an automated system tap the stalactites. Guided tours follow a system of brick and concrete walkways and take about an hour. It's about 55°F (13°C) down here all the time, so bring a jacket or sweater.

Fun Fact **An Eight-Cylinder General Lee**

Drive 7 miles on U.S. 211 from the Skyline Drive down toward Sperryville and you'll spot a bright orange roadside garage with a 1969 Dodge Charger parked out front. Dubbed the "General Lee," the car played a leading role in the 1980s TV sitcom *The Dukes of Hazzard.*

Today, it's the star attraction at **Cooter's Place** ✪✪, 16692 Lee Hwy. (U.S. 211; © **540/987-8545;** www.cootersplace.com), the creation of Ben Jones, who played Cooter, the show's trusty mechanic. Jones later served two terms as a Democratic congressman from Georgia and today lives near Sperryville. Sometimes Jones and his band are among the musicians playing bluegrass at the garage on Saturday and Sunday afternoons.

The museum sells memorabilia from the show, and a snack bar serves burgers, hot dogs, and barbecue sandwiches. Admission is free. The garage is open April to October, daily from 10am to 6pm.

Admission to the caverns includes the **Car and Carriage Caravan Museum,** a collection of antique carriages, coaches, and cars—including actor Rudolph Valentino's 1925 Rolls-Royce. The complex also contains a snack bar, gift shop, and fudge kitchen. Separate admission is charged to get thoroughly confused in the outdoor **Garden Maze.**

Across U.S. 211 stands the **Luray Singing Tower,** a stone carillon with 47 bells. It was given to the town of Luray in 1937 as a memorial to one of its residents. Free concerts are given spring through autumn (pick up a schedule at the Luray visitor center or at the caverns).

U.S. 211 West (2 miles west of downtown). ℂ 540/743-6551. www.luraycaverns.com. Admission to caverns and car museum, $16 adults, $14 seniors, $7 children 7–13, free for children 6 and under; to Garden Maze, $5 adults, $4 children. June 15 to Labor Day daily 9am–7pm; Mar 15–June 14 and day after Labor Day to Nov 14 daily 9am–6pm; Nov 15–Mar 14 Mon–Fri 9am–4pm, Sat–Sun 9am–5pm. Mandatory 1-hr. tours depart every 20 min. Self-guided tour of car museum.

WHERE TO STAY

Just as bed-and-breakfasts proliferated during the 1980s and early 1990s, **mountain cabins** are the latest trend around Luray. Most require a 2-night minimum rental. The visitor center (see "Essentials," above) can provide information about the area's many rental cabins and B&Bs.

The **Days Inn,** on U.S. 211 northeast of town (ℂ **800/325-2525** or 540/743-4521), is surrounded by acres of farmland, giving most rooms mountain views. The **Best Western,** on West Main Street/U.S. 211 Business (ℂ **800/528-1234** or 540/743-6511), is an older motel in town. Both have outdoor swimming pools.

The Cabins at Brookside ★ Owners Bob and Cece Castle remodeled this 1940s service station/motel into a collection of log-look cabins with comfortable Williamsburg-style furnishings throughout. This is the closest accommodations to the Shenandoah National Park. Although located along busy U.S. 211, the rear of the cabins open to decks or sunrooms overlooking a bubbling brook, and road noise dies down after dark. Four "honeymoon" units have whirlpool tubs or hot tubs, four have gas fireplaces, and one has a kitchen (the others, refrigerators only). None has a TV or phone. Open for breakfast, lunch and dinner, the **Brookside Restaurant** on the premises serves inexpensive Southern-style home cooking.

2978 U.S. 211 East, Luray, VA 22835. ℂ **800/299-2655** or 540/743-5698. Fax 540/743-1326. www.brookside cabins.com. 9 cabins. $85–$195 double. AE, DC, DISC, MC, V. From Luray, go east 4½ miles) on U.S. 211. From Shenandoah National Park Headquarters, go west ½ mile on U.S. 211. **Amenities:** Restaurant. *In room:* A/C, fridge, coffeemaker, no phone.

Luray Caverns Motel West *(Value)* Sitting opposite Luray Caverns, which owns and spotlessly maintains it, this older one-story motel with a plantation facade is dated, but it got a thorough renovation in 2001. The spacious rooms have pleasant views across pastureland to the Blue Ridge Mountains. The choice unit is an apartment with full kitchen. A sister establishment, the equally clean **Luray Caverns Motel East** (ℂ **540/743-4531**), is a short distance east on U.S. 211 Business. Many of its 44 units are small but comfortable stone cottages. Rates are the same at both motels.

U.S. 211 West (P.O. Box 748), Luray, VA 22835. ℂ **540/743-4536.** www.luraycaverns.com. 19 units. $62–$79 double; $124 apt. Rates include continental breakfast. AE, DISC, MC, V. **Amenities:** Outdoor pool. *In room:* A/C, TV, coffeemakers.

The Mimslyn Inn This three-story, colonial-style country inn has been well maintained but not substantially changed since it was built in 1931 on 14 acres of lawns and trees west of the business district. Although wear shows here and there, the Mimslyn retains a kind of old-fashioned charm, and the rooms are clean and comfortable. A porch with tall white columns and high-back rockers fronts the brick building. Modern amenities such as TVs and phones have been added to the medium-size rooms, but they still have their original floor-to-ceiling windows and 1930s bathroom fixtures. A few suites have living rooms with two walls of paned windows, letting in lots of light. "Family units" have a single bath between two bedrooms. A stunning dining room with large fan-topped windows offers regional fare for breakfast, lunch, and dinner. On the third floor, you'll find a sunroom opening onto a rooftop deck. In the basement, the **Mimslyn Gallery** exhibits the works of noted artist P. Buckley Moss; it's open daily from 9am to 5pm.

401 W. Main St. (U.S. 211 Business), Luray, VA 22835. Ⓒ 800/296-5105 or 540/743-5105. Fax 540/743-2632. www.mimslyninn.com. 49 units. $69–$99 double; $99–$159 suite. AE, DISC, MC, V. **Amenities:** Restaurant; bar. *In room:* A/C, TV.

BED & BREAKFASTS

The Woodruff Collection ★★ (Value)

Owners Lucas and Deborah Woodruff have converted three Victorian houses into charming B&Bs. Their star is **The Victorian Inn,** on Main Street, which has three extremely romantic, Jacuzzi-equipped suites. All of these have sun-filled sitting rooms and balconies with private entries so you don't have to go through the house to get to your room. The master suite also has a fireplace—in the bathroom, of all places. Less expensive but nonetheless charming are rooms in the nearby **Woodruff House** and **The Victorian Rose.** They both have hot tubs in their gardens. All three houses are furnished with mid- to late-19th-century antiques. The Woodruff's also have riverside cottages for rent.

138 E. Main St., Luray, VA 22835. Ⓒ **540/743-1494.** Fax 540/743-1722. www.woodruffinns.com. 9 units. $155–$295. Rates include breakfast, afternoon tea, 4-course dinner. DISC, MC, V. **Amenities:** Jacuzzi; massage. *In room:* A/C, coffeemakers.

A NEARBY EQUESTRIAN INN

Jordan Hollow Farm Inn ★★

Horse lovers and hikers will enjoy this working farm and inn, which has a stable of horses and ponies and 5 picturesque miles of hiking trails in the foothills of the Blue Ridge. They don't rent horses, but you can stable your own here. Two types of guest quarters are offered. Those in the vine-entangled Arbor View are suites with separate living rooms and spacious, romantic bedrooms with a two-person whirlpool tub in one corner, a realistic-looking electric fireplace in another. The bedrooms open to a long porch with high-backed rockers for taking in the mountain view. The units in the log-sided, cabinlike Mare Meadow Lodge sport heavy pine furniture.

The Farmhouse Restaurant, in the original clapboard homestead with wrap-around porches upstairs and down, offers some of the area's best cuisine, along with fine vintages from Virginia wineries. The menu changes seasonally and features local products.

326 Hawksbill Park Rd., Stanley, VA 22851. Ⓒ **888/418-7000** or 540/778-2285. Fax 540/778-1759. www.jordanhollow.com. 15 units. $133–$199 double. Rates include full breakfast. AE, DC, DISC, MC, V. From Luray, take U.S. 340 south 6 miles, turn left on Hawksbill Park Dr. (C.R. 624), left on Marksville Rd. (C.R. 689), right on Hawksbill Park Rd. (C.R. 629). **Amenities:** Restaurant (American). *In room:* A/C, TV.

WHERE TO DINE

The **Farmhouse Restaurant,** at Jordan Hollow Farm Inn (see "A Nearby Equestrian Inn," above), serves some of the best cuisine in this area. For inexpensive country cooking, drive out to the **Brookside Restaurant,** at the Cabins at Brookside (see "Where to Stay," above).

A Moment to Remember Espresso Bar & Cafe AMERICAN   Across Main Street from the visitor center, this converted Victorian-era hardware store still has its pressed tin ceiling, oak counter, nail and screw drawers, and shelves, which now hold books and knick-knacks. It's the business district's favorite place for morning coffee, bagels and croissants, or for a lunch of freshly made salads and sandwiches ranging from a simple BLT to a tasty Thai chicken wrap.

55 E. Main St. ✆ **540/743-1121.** Reservations not accepted. Sandwiches $4.50–$7; main courses $9–$16. MC, V. Mon–Thurs 8am–6pm; Fri–Sat 8am–11pm.

The Victorian Inn ★★ REGIONAL   At night the first floor of this romantic member of The Woodruff Collection of B&Bs (see "Where to Stay," above) turns into Luray's only fine dining venue. The menu varies by season and availability of local produce. One autumn saw pork tenderloin with a spiced pear sauce and Cornish hen with an apple cider sauce. Summer might see salmon baked in a garlic wine sauce.

138 E. Main St. ✆ **540/743-1494.** Reservations highly recommended. Fixed-price 4-course dinners $30 per person. AE, DISC, MC, V. Mon–Tues 11:30am–3pm; Wed–Sat 11:30am–3pm and 5–9pm; Sun 5–9pm.

A MOUNTAIN RESORT WITH GOLF & SKIING

Primarily a time-share operation, **Massanutten Resort,** P.O. Box 1227, Harrisonburg, VA 22801 (✆ **800/207-MASS** or 540/289-9441; www.massresort.com), offers year-round outdoor activities. The property has 27 holes of golf, tennis courts, indoor and outdoor swimming pools, a half-dozen downhill ski slopes, and areas for snowboarding and snow tubing (riding inner tubes down a gentle slope). The 140 hotel rooms have a queen or two double beds, sitting areas, and balconies. Most of the 800-plus time-share units are equipped with kitchens, fireplaces, and decks, and many have whirlpools. There's a full-service restaurant, a pizzeria, bar, and grocery store on site. From I-81, take exit 247A and follow U.S. 33 east 10 miles to the resort entrance on the left.

6 New Market: A Civil War Battlefield & the Endless Caverns ★

16 miles W of Luray; 110 miles SW of Washington, D.C.

The little village of New Market holds a hallowed place in the hearts of Civil War buffs, for it was here in 1864 that the cadets of Virginia Military Institute distinguished themselves in battle against a much larger and more experienced Union force. New Market has been a waystation on the Valley Pike (U.S. 11) since frontier times, and many buildings from that era still stand along Congress Street, the main drag. Congress Street is also a good place to browse for antiques.

ESSENTIALS

VISITOR INFORMATION   The **Shenandoah Valley Travel Association,** 277 Old Cross Rd. (P.O. Box 1040), New Market, VA 22844 (✆ **877/847-4878** or 540/740-3132; fax 540/740-3100; www.shenandoah.org), operates a visitor center across I-81 from New Market (Exit 264). It has a free phone line for hotel reservations, and is open daily from 9am to 5pm. Closed New Year's Day and Christmas.

GETTING THERE   New Market is on U.S. 11 at the junction of U.S. 211 and I-81 (Exit 264).

EXPLORING THE BATTLEFIELD

Even if your knowledge of the Civil War doesn't extend much beyond distinguishing the blue from the gray, you'll be fascinated by what happened here in

May 1864. In a desperate move to halt Union troops advancing up the valley, Confederate Gen. John Breckenridge ordered 257 Virginia Military Institute cadets to New Market. The teenagers marched in the rain for 4 days to reach the front line. They charged the enemy on May 15, won the day, and returned home victorious, with only 10 cadets killed and 47 wounded. Hearing of the battle, Grant exclaimed, "The South is robbing the cradle and the grave."

The battle took place over a 6-mile-long stretch of ground now bisected by I-81. Only a small portion has been preserved, and it's on the western side of I-81 (the village of New Market is on the eastern side). From the village, go under I-81 (exit 264) and turn immediately right on Collins Drive (C.R. 305), which will take you to New Market Battlefield State Historical Park and its Hall of Valor Museum, which are operated by the Virginia Military Institute Museum in Lexington (see section 9, below). It's at the end of Collins Drive. Make this your first stop. Afterwards, you can stop at the New Market Battlefield Military Museum, which sits on part of the battlefield but is privately owned and operated. You'll need at least 2 hours to examine both museums.

New Market Battlefield Military Museum   In a structure built to resemble Robert E. Lee's Arlington House at Arlington National Cemetery (see chapter 4), this privately owned museum arranges its exhibits of photos, small arms, uniforms, personal gear, and other artifacts to follow the build up to the Civil War and the battle. Among the more interesting items: Stonewall Jackson's family Bible, a pair of spurs left behind when Gen. George Armstrong Custer was almost overrun by Confederate troops, and a bullet-pierced belt buckle worn by a Union soldier. Outside, monuments note troop placements on the battlefield. The museum does not offer guided tours. Give yourself at least 45 minutes here.

9500 Collins Dr. Ⓒ 540/740-8065. Admission $8 adults, $4 children 6–14, free for children 5 and under. Mid-Mar to Oct, daily 9am–5pm. Nov, Sat–Sun 9am–5pm. Closed Dec to mid-Mar.

New Market Battlefield State Historical Park/Hall of Valor Museum ⋆⋆⋆   Well worth a visit, this interesting museum sits in a lovely park on part of the battlefield. Begin at the Hall of Valor Museum, dedicated to the VMI cadets who fought here (see the introduction, above). You can watch two films, including the award-winning "Field of Shores (45 min.), then walk through the museum, which further explains the battle with paintings, uniforms, and small arms. Gen. Breckenridge's sword is among the exhibits. Outside on the rolling, grassy fields, students lead 1-hour tours three times daily during summer, or you can take a self-guided 1-mile walking tour along the final Confederate assault on the Union line. In the center of the battle line was the Bushong farmhouse, which served as a hospital. The farm today is a museum of 19th-century valley life. The battle is reenacted in mid-May each year. Note that the ticket booth is on Collins Drive near I-81, not at the park and museum.

8895 Collins Dr. Ⓒ 540/740-3101. www.vmi.edu/museum/nm. Admission $8 adults, $4 students grades 1–12, free for children 5 and under. Daily 9am–5pm. 1-hr. tours daily 10am, 1:30, and 3pm during summer. Closed New Year's Day, Thanksgiving, and Christmas.

Impressions

Gentlemen . . . I trust you will do your duty.
    —Gen. John Breckenridge, Battle of New Market, May 15, 1864
I look back upon that orchard as the most awful spot on the battlefield.
    —Cadet John C. Howard, Battle of New Market, May 15, 1864

EXPLORING THE TOWN & THE CAVERNS

Begin your visit at the Shenandoah Valley Travel Association's visitor center (see "Essentials," above), where you can pick up a walking-tour brochure. Most of the historic buildings, some of them dating to before 1800, are along Congress Street (U.S. 11), so you can walk down one side of the street and return on the other.

Be sure to poke your head into the many relic-filled shops you'll pass on Congress Street.

Endless Caverns   Extending into the western flank of the Blue Ridge, these caverns use dramatic lighting to display spectacular rooms, each with a variety of stalactites, stalagmites, columns, and limestone pendants orchestrated into brilliant displays of nature's work. Endless Caverns maintains a year-round temperature of 55°F (12°C), so bring a sweater or jacket. Camping is available here.

Endless Caverns Rd. (3 miles south of town off U.S. 11). © 540/740-3993. www.endlesscaverns.com. Admission $14 adults, $6 children 4–12, free for children 3 and under. Mar 15–June 14 daily 9am–5pm; June 15 to Labor Day daily 9am–6pm; day after Labor Day to Nov 14 daily 9am–5pm; Nov 15–Mar 14 daily 9am–4pm. Mandatory 1¼-hr. tours depart every 30–40 min. From New Market, go 2 miles south on U.S. 11, turn left on Endless Caverns Rd.

A ROUND OF GOLF

On the south end of town, off Fairway Drive, **The Shenvalee Golf Resort** was originally part of a plantation whose name is a contraction of Shenandoah, Virginia, and Lee. During World War II, the U.S. State Department used the manor house to keep Italian detainees who had diplomatic rank. The 18-hole golf course, built in 1926, is open to the public (© 540/740-8931; www.shenvalee.com).

WHERE TO STAY & DINE

Near exit 264 off I-81, the **Days Inn New Market** (© 800/325-2525 or 540/740-4100) is on Collins Drive next to the New Market Battlefield Military Museum and near the state park. On the town side of I-81 is the **Quality Inn Shenandoah Valley** (© 800/228-5151 or 540/740-3141).

Bed-and-breakfasts include **Cross Roads Inn,** 9222 John Sevier Rd. (© 540/740-4157; fax 540/740-4255; www.crossroadsinnva.com); **The Jacob Swartz House,** 574 Jiggady Rd. (© 540/740-9208; www.shenwebworks.com/jshouse); and **Red Shutter Farmhouse** (© 800/738-8BNB or 540/740-4281; www.bbhsv.org/redshutter), which is off Endless Caverns Road near the caves.

You'll find the usual national fast-food restaurants at the I-81 interchange.

Southern Kitchen SOUTHERN   You can get your arteries hardened in a hurry at this down-home restaurant sporting the same green leatherette booths and jukeboxes installed when it was built in the 1950s. Except for salads, there isn't a single non-fattening item on the menu, but the peanut soup, sandwiches, barbecue pork, steaks, and house-special pan-fried chicken warrant a caloric splurge.

9576 Congress St. (U.S. 11, ½ mile south of I-81 interchange). © 540/740-3514. Reservations not accepted. Sandwiches $2.50–$6.50; main courses $7.50–$13.50. DISC, MC, V. Daily 7am–9pm.

7 Staunton: A Presidential Birthplace & the Bard's Playhouse ⋆⋆⋆

42 miles S of New Market; 142 miles SW of Washington, D.C.; 92 miles NW of Richmond

Settled well before the Revolution, Staunton (pronounced "*Stan*-ton") was a major stop for pioneers on the way west. In the early 1800s, it was the eastern terminus of the Staunton-Parkersburg Turnpike (now U.S. 250), a major mountain road linking the Shenandoah Valley and the Ohio River. When the Central Virginia Railroad arrived in 1854, Staunton became even more of a regional center.

Today, the town is noted as the birthplace of Woodrow Wilson, our 28th president. Along with Wilson's first home, many of Staunton's 19th-century downtown buildings have been restored and refurbished, including the train station and its adjacent Wharf District, now a shopping and dining complex. Staunton is becoming equally known for the new Blackfriars Playhouse, a stunning replica of one of Shakespeare's theaters, has brought the Bard to the Shenandoah and made Staunton the valley's prime performing-arts center. On the outskirts of town is a living-history museum explaining the origins of the unique Shenandoah Valley farming culture.

ESSENTIALS

VISITOR INFORMATION   There are two walk-in visitor centers here. Downtown, the **Staunton Visitors Center,** 35 S. New St., at Johnson Street (© **540/ 332-3971;** www.stauntonva.org), provides information including free maps and walking-tour brochures to the historic district. It's open daily 9am to 6pm from April through December, to 5pm January through March.

At the Frontier Culture Museum, on U.S. 250 west of Exit 222 of I-81, the **Staunton/Augusta County Travel Information Center,** P.O. Box 810, Staunton, VA 24404 (© **800/332-5219** or 540/332-3972), is open daily from 9am to 5pm except New Year's Day, Thanksgiving, and Christmas.

GETTING THERE   Staunton is at the junctions of I-64 and I-81 and U.S. 11 and U.S. 250. **Amtrak** trains serve Staunton's station at 1 Middlebrook Ave. (© **800/872-7245;** www.amtrak).

GETTING AROUND   The free **Downtown Staunton Trolley** runs every 25 minutes Monday to Saturday from 10am to 10pm, passing all the key sights. Riding it all the way around will give you an informative 25-minute tour of the town. Board at the Staunton Visitors Center (see above), which has route maps.

EXPLORING THE TOWN

Downtown Staunton is a treasure trove of Victorian architecture, from stately residences to the commercial buildings downtown and in the adjacent Wharf District (actually along the railroad, not a river). Pick up a walking-tour brochure from one of the visitor centers (see "Essentials," above), and set out on your own. The brochure describes five tours, but be sure to take the "Beverly" and "Wharf" tours, which cover all of historic downtown.

Free 2-hour **guided tours** of downtown depart from in front of the Woodrow Wilson Presidential Library at His Birthplace at 10am on Saturday in May, Tuesday, Thursday and Saturday from June to October. Whether you do it yourself or take the guided tour, be prepared to work up a sweat: Staunton is built on the side of a steep hill, a la San Francisco.

Blackfriars Playhouse ★★★ *Finds*   Opened in 2001, this stunning re-creation of the first indoor theater in the English-speaking world, which William Shakespeare and his colleagues built on part of London's Blackfriars Monastery in 1642, is, in itself, a reason to visit Staunton. As in the Bard's time, the audience sits on three sides of the stage, most on benches (don't worry: you can rent cushions and seat backs). Members of Shenandoah Shakespeare, the theater's resident company, as well as touring companies perform Shakespeare's masterpieces, but the theater also hosts other classic plays and performances by modern day musicians. Be sure

---

Fun Fact Mr. Jefferson on the Run

Staunton served as Virginia's capital for 17 days during June 1781, when then-Governor Thomas Jefferson fled Richmond in the face of advancing British troops.

---

to take a guided tour, which sheds light not only on this theater but how plays were performed in The Bard's day.

10 S. Market St. (between Beverley and Johnson sts.). Box office at 35 S. New St. (at Johnson St.) ☎ 540/885-5588. www.shenandoahshakespeare.com. Tours $5. Tickets $10–$28. Box office Mon 10am–5pm; Tue 9:30am–5pm; Wed–Sat 10am–5pm and 6:30–7:30pm; Sun 1:30–4:30pm. 1-hr. tours usually Mon–Sat 11am; Mon–Fri 2pm (call for current schedule).

Frontier Culture Museum (Kids In light of its history as a major stopping point for pioneers, Staunton is a logical location for this museum, which consists of 17th-, 18th-, and 19th-century working farmsteads representing the origins of the Shenandoah's early settlers—Northern Irish, English, and German—and explaining how aspects of each were blended into a fourth farm, a typical colonial American homestead. Staff members in period costumes plant fields, tend livestock, and do domestic chores. A 15-minute film will set the stage for your self-guided exploration, which will take about 2 hours to thoroughly cover. Children will love seeing the animals, but bring them in warm weather, since many exhibits are outdoors.

Richmond Rd. (U.S. 250), ½ mile west of I-81. ☎ 540/332-7850. www.frontiermuseum.org. Admission $10 adults, $9.50 seniors, $6 children 6–12, free for children 5 and under. Mid-Mar to Dec, daily 9am–5pm; Jan to mid-Mar, daily 10am–4pm. Closed New Year's Day, Thanksgiving, and Christmas.

The Woodrow Wilson Presidential Library at His Birthplace ★★★ A National Historic Landmark, this handsome Greek Revival building, built in 1846 by a Presbyterian congregation as a manse for their ministers, stands beside an excellent library and museum detailing Wilson's life. As a minister, Wilson's father had to move often, and so the family left Staunton when the future president was only 2. The house is furnished with many family items, including the crib Wilson slept in and the chair in which his mother rocked him. The galleries of the museum next door trace Wilson's Scotch-Irish roots, his academic career as a professor and president at Princeton University, and, of course, his 8 presidential years (1913–21). America's entry into World War I and Wilson's unsuccessful efforts to convince the U.S. Senate to participate in the League of Nations are also explored. Don't overlook the beautiful Victorian garden or Wilson's presidential limousine, a shiny Pierce-Arrow, in the museum. You must take the 45-minute tour of the house, but you can wander through the museum and gardens on your own. About 1½ hours will be required to see it all.

24 N. Coalter St. (at Frederick St.). ☎ 888/496-6376 or 540/885-0897. www.woodrowwilson.org. Admission $6.50 adults, $4 students, $2 children 6–12, free for children 5 and under. Mar–Oct daily 9am–5pm; Nov–Feb Mon–Sat 10am–4pm, Sun noon–4pm. Mandatory 45-min. house tours depart continuously.

WHERE TO STAY

On U.S. 250 at Exit 222 off I-81, you'll find the **Best Western Staunton Inn** (☎ 800/528-1234 or 540/885-1112), **Comfort Inn** (☎ 800/228-5150 or 540/886-5000), the above-average **EconoLodge** (☎ 800/446-6900 or 540/885-5158), **Hampton Inn** (☎ 800/HAMPTON or 540/886-7000), **Shoney's Inn of**

Historic Staunton (✆ **800/222-2222** or 540/885-9193), and **Super 8** (✆ **800/ 800-8000** or 540/886-2888). Near Exit 225 (Woodrow Wilson Parkway), the **Holiday Inn Golf & Conference Center** (✆ **800/HOLIDAY** or 540/248-6020) is adjacent to the Country Club of Staunton, where guests can play. There also are several bed-and-breakfasts in the area; ask the visitor center for a list.

Belle Grae Inn ✮✮   This beautifully restored 1873 Victorian house, with white gingerbread trim and an Italianate wraparound front porch, sits well back from the street atop a sloping lawn. The property now occupies an entire city block, and most accommodations are in the adjoining 19th-century houses, all of them beautifully restored. Rooms are furnished with period antiques and reproductions, Oriental rugs, wicker pieces, and canopied four-poster, sleigh, and brass beds. All but two rooms have working fireplaces. Most, but not all, units have TVs, phones, refrigerators and coffeemakers, so discuss your needs with the clerk when making reservations. Two units have Jacuzzis. The restaurant here is Staunton's finest (see "Where to Dine," below).

515 W. Frederick St. (Va. 254, between Jefferson and Madison sts.), Staunton, VA 24401. ✆ **888/541-5151** or 540/886-5151. Fax 540/886-6641. www.bellegrae.com. 18 units, including suites and small cottage. $99–$249 double. Meal, golf, and other packages available. Rates include full breakfast. AE, DISC, MC, V. From I-81, take Exit 222 west and follow signs to Wilson Birthplace; once there, turn left on Frederick St. (Va. 254) to inn on right. **Amenities:** Restaurant, bar, access to nearby health club, limited room service, coin-op washers and dryers. *In room:* A/C, TV, dataport, kitchen, minibar, fridge, coffeemaker, iron, safe.

Frederick House ✮   Innkeepers Joe and Evy Harmon began converting these seven historic town houses—dating from between 1810 and 1910—into a low-key, European-style hotel back in 1984. The rooms and suites are individually decorated with authentic antiques and reproductions from the Victorian era. Most have hardwood floors covered by Oriental rugs, and seven units have fireplaces. All suites have separate living rooms, and three of them have two bedrooms. If you don't mind bright light early in the morning, the choice unit here is suite 35, whose bedroom once was a sun porch extending across the rear of one of the houses. Frederick House is across the street from Mary Baldwin College and just 2 blocks from the Wilson Presidential Library and the Blackfriars Playhouse. Joe and Evy recently added a sleek new restaurant featuring simple but stylishly prepared meals; organically grown local produce is used whenever possible.

28 N. New St. (at Frederick St.), Staunton, VA 24401. ✆ **800/334-5575** or 540/885-4220. Fax 540/885-5180. www.frederickhouse.com. 23 units, including 11 suites. $85–$125 double; $110–$200 suite. Theater packages available. AE, DC, DISC, MC, V. From I-81, take Exit 222 west and follow the signs to Wilson Birthplace; once there, turn left on Frederick St., left on Augusta St., and left into municipal parking lot to hotel entrance. **Amenities:** Restaurant; bar; access to nearby health club; laundry service. *In room:* A/C, TV, dataport.

Regency Inn *Finds*   Just 2 blocks north of the historic district, this former Holiday Inn–cum–Travelodge–cum–Best Value is downtown's only budget choice. It's not much to look at—a white four-story building with exterior walkways facing a parking lot—but extensive renovations have put it on an upward path after many years of decline. The rooms are moderately spacious and modestly comfortable. Three have Jacuzzi tubs, while another three sport kitchenettes. Not all rooms have coffeemakers and hairdryers, so request them when you make reservations.

268 N. Central Ave. (north of Frederick St.), Staunton, VA 24401. ✆ **540/886-5330**. Fax 540/886-5313. 104 units. $60–$90 double, $115 kitchen unit. Rates include continental breakfast and free local calls. AE, DISC, MC, V. **Amenities:** Outdoor pool. *In room:* A/C, TV, dataport, kitchen (3 units), coffeemaker.

BED & BREAKFASTS

Bed-and-breakfasts in Staunton include **Ashton Country House,** 1205 Middlebrook Ave. (© **800/296-7819** or 540/885-7819; www.bbhost.com/ashtonbnb); **Montclair,** 320 N. New St. (© **877/885-8823** or 540/885-8832; www.bbonline. com/va/montclair); **The Sampson Eagon Inn,** 238 E. Beverley St. (© **800/597-9722** or 540/886-8200; www.eagoninn.com); and **Thornrose House at Gypsy Hill,** 531 Thornrose Ave. (© **800/861-4338** or 540/885-7026; www.thornrose house.com). Unlike the others, the **Twelfth Night Inn,** 402 E. Beverly St. (© **540/885-1733;** www.12th-night-inn.com), accepts pets.

WHERE TO DINE

Staunton Station, the town's old railway depot on Middlebrook Avenue between Augusta and Lewis streets in the Wharf District, has been restored and converted into a dining/entertainment complex. Here you'll find **The Depot Grille** (© **540/885-7332**) and **The Pullman Restaurant** (© **540/885-6612**), both moderately priced, publike establishments worth checking out. Nearby in the Wharf District, **Byers Street Bistro** (© **540/887-8100**) is a lively restaurant-bar fronting a municipal parking lot on Byers Street at Central Avenue. Locals describe a visit to these three institutions as pub crawling.

On Beverly Street, in the heart of downtown, **Baja Bean & Co. Restaurant & Cantina,** 9 W. Beverly St. (© **540/885-9988**), uses fresh ingredients in its Southern California–influenced Mexican cuisine. Local young folk hang out at the **Clock Tower Tavern,** 27 W. Beverly St. (© **540/213-2403**), which serves American fare and provides live music after 9pm on weekends. It gets its name from the clock tower atop the building. For creative soups, salads and sandwiches, head for **The Pampered Palate Café,** 26–28 E. Beverly St. (© **540/886-9463**), which is open Monday from 9am to 5:30pm, Tuesday to Saturday 9am to 7:30pm.

Belle Grae Inn ✦✦✦ CONTINENTAL/REGIONAL   The living and dining rooms of this in-town country inn (see "Where to Stay," above), are the settings for Staunton's finest yet casual dining. "You can eat fried chicken at home," says proprietor Michael Organ. "Here you can have quail." Indeed, the kitchen puts out fine continental cuisine with regional influences and ingredients.

515 W. Frederick St. (Va. 254, between Jefferson and Madison sts.). © 888/541-5151 or 540/886-5151. Reservations recommended. Fixed-price 4-course dinner, $37.50 per person; 3-course $32.50 per person. Wed–Sun 5:30 and 9pm. AE, DISC, MC, V.

The Beverly Restaurant (Value AMERICAN   Family-owned and -operated since 1961, this storefront eatery in the heart of the business district hearkens back to that nearly bygone era when even hashhouse cooks made everything from scratch. The fresh fare is typically small-town Southern: rib-eye steaks,

---

⟨ **Fun Fact The 1950s Live**

The 1950s are still very much alive at **Wright's Dairy Rite,** 346 Greenville Ave. (U.S. 11), a block south of Richmond Road (© **540/886-0435**), a classic drive-in that has had carhop service since it opened in 1952. Even if you dine inside this brick building, or outside on the patio, you must lift a phone to place your order and wait for it to be delivered to your leatherette booth. Nothing here costs more than $7. MasterCard and Visa are accepted. It's open **Sunday** through **Thursday** from 9am to 10pm, **Friday** and **Saturday** from 9am to 11pm.

fried shrimp or fish, veal cutlets, and roast beef. It's the best place in town for an old-fashion cooked breakfast.

12 E. Beverly St. (between Augusta and New sts.). ℂ **540/886-4317**. Reservations not accepted. Breakfast $2–$6; sandwiches $4.50–$6.50; main courses $5–$7. MC, V. Mon–Fri 7am–7pm; Sat 7am–3pm.

L'Italia Restaurant and Pompeii Lounge ITALIAN   This pleasant establishment is run by accomplished cooks who moved here from Italy. You'll enter through a nondescript foyer in front of a small bar, but French doors lead to a sophisticated L'Italia, with modern art hung in lighted alcoves. Ceiling spotlights highlight the black tables and chairs set far apart for privacy. Upstairs, meanwhile, the Pompeii Lounge presents an urbane nightclub atmosphere, with comfy chairs and sofas for relaxing over drinks and outdoor dining on its rooftop patio, which also hosts live music from Thursday to Saturday nights during summer. The well-prepared offerings at both institutions range from Sicilian-style veal parmigiana to northern Italian veal piccata in a sauce of white wine, lemon, and capers.

23 E. Beverly St. (between Augusta and New sts.). ℂ **540/885-0102**. Reservations recommended. Main courses $9–$16. AE, DISC, MC, V. Tues–Thurs 11am–10pm, Fri–Sat 11am–11pm, Sun 11am–9pm.Pompeii Lounge Tues–Thurs 5pm–midnight, Fri–Sat 5pm–1am.

Mill Street Grill AMERICAN   In the basement of the old White Star mill, which produced Melrose flour from 1890 to 1963, this lively pub serves barbecued beef and pork ribs, steaks and prime rib with or without sauces, and seafood. The shrimp, steamed with spicy Old Bay seasoning, are worthy of a coastal town. You can also opt for dinner-size salads, a variety of sandwiches, a few chicken and pasta dishes, and vegetarian platters such as spicy Cajun-style vegetables over pasta. Heavy support beams, cozy tables and booths, and back-lit stained glass windows portraying chefs at work all contribute to a warm and friendly atmosphere.

1 Mill St. (south of Johnson St./U.S. 250). ℂ **540/886-0656**. Reservations not accepted. Sandwiches and salads $5.50–$9; main courses $8.50–$22. AE, DC, DISC, MC. V. Mon–Thurs 4–10pm; Fri–Sat 4–10:30pm; Sun 11:30am–9pm.

Mrs. Rowe's Restaurant and Bakery ⭐⭐ 𝒱𝑎𝑙𝑢𝑒 SOUTHERN   Opened in 1947 by Mildred Rowe and still run by her family, this is one of the best home-style restaurants in Virginia. Made from recipes from Mrs. Rowe's own cookbook, dishes here are very much in the Southern tradition, but lighter than the usual fare cooked elsewhere with ample portions of salt and lard. Grilled steaks, country ham, pork chops, and fried chicken lead the regular items, but you can also choose from daily specials such as meatloaf and gravy or fried flounder filet, served with two veggies (corn pudding, spoon bread, baked tomatoes, and cucumber-and-onion salads are notable). The fresh pies are so good that locals order slices along with their main courses, just to make sure they get their favorite flavors. So are the cookies: Mrs. Fields has nothing on Mrs. Rowe's chocolate chips.

74 Rowe Rd. (U.S. 250, just east of I-81). ℂ **540/886-1833**. Reservations not accepted. Sandwiches $5–$7; main courses $6–$14.50. DC, DISC, MC, V. May–Oct, Mon–Thurs 7am–8pm; Fri–Sat 7am–9pm; Sun 7am–7pm. Nov–Apr, Mon–Sat 7am–8pm; Sun 7am–7pm. Breakfast daily 7–10:45am year-round.

A PICNIC STOP

A good place to stop for a picnic lunch midway between Staunton and Lexington is the picturesque **Cyrus McCormick Farm** (ℂ **540/377-2255**). In a lovely rural setting, it contains a small blacksmith shop, a gristmill, and other log cabins, where exhibits include a model of McCormick's 1831 invention, the first reaper. Open daily from 8:30am to 5pm; admission is free. From I-81, Exit 205 is well marked to the village of Steele's Tavern and the McCormick Birthplace, but the scenic way to get there from Staunton is via U.S. 11 South.

STAUNTON AFTER DARK

Staunton's showpiece is the **Blackfriars Playhouse** (see above), where you can see performances of Shakespeare's plays as well as concerts.

The pubs in and around **Staunton Station,** the old railway depot on Millwood Avenue, as well as The Clock Tower Tavern and the Pompeii Lounge on East Beverly Street (see "Where to Dine," above), have live bands playing on weekend nights. The city has a summertime program of free outdoor concerts in Gypsy Hill Park and the Wharf District. Check with the visitor center for a schedule.

OVER THE MOUNTAINS TO MONTEREY

You can scoot along I-81 from Staunton to Lexington, but a scenic detour will take you west across the mountains into Highland County, whose rugged beauty has given it the nickname "Virginia's Switzerland." In fact, U.S. 250 from Staunton to the town of **Monterey** is one of the state's most scenic excursions. Carved out of the rocks in the early 1800s as the Staunton-Parkersburg (W.Va.) Turnpike, the two-lane highway climbs over four mountains on its way to Monterey. Don't be in a hurry: the 50-mile drive will take 1½ hours.

Be sure to stop at **Fort Edward Johnson,** a Confederate breastworks atop Shenandoah Mountain (elevation 3,760 ft.). Confederate Gen. Stonewall Jackson's army crossed the mountain here in 1862 on its way to victory in the Battle of McDowell, between here and Monterey. The little park has an interpretive trail and a magnificent view.

U.S. 250 then scales two more ridges and Bull Pasture Mountain (elevation 3,240 ft.) before descending into Monterey, whose white clapboard churches and Victorian homes conjure up images of New England hamlets. At more than 2,500 feet elevation, Monterey enjoys a refreshing, springlike climate during summer.

EXPLORING MONTEREY

Start your visit at the **Highland Chamber of Commerce,** P.O. Box 223, Monterey, VA 24465 (© **540/468-2550;** fax 540/468-2551; www.highlandcounty. org), in the Highland Center, an old school on Spruce Street (turn off U.S. 250 at the courthouse and go 3 blocks south). It's open Monday through Friday from 10am to 5pm. There's also an information board in front of the Highland County Court House on Main Street. The chamber has maps of **driving tours** of the area, including the extraordinarily scenic Bluegrass Valley, over the mountain west of Monterey.

Pick up a walking-tour brochure, and then stroll along picturesque Main Street (U.S. 250) past the likes of **H&H Cash Store,** a holdover from the days when general stores sold a little bit of everything, and **Landmark House,** built of logs around 1790. You can also poke your head into several good arts and crafts stores.

The best (and most crowded) time to be here is on the second and third full weekends in March, when Monterey hosts the **Highland Maple Festival,** one of Virginia's top annual events. A smaller version, the **Hands and Harvest Festival,** is held on Columbus Day weekend in October.

Outdoor enthusiasts can contact Rick Lambert of **Highland Adventures,** P.O. Box 151, Monterey, VA 24465 (© **540/468-2722;** fax 540/468-2724), who specializes in caving, rock climbing, mountain biking, and other outdoor adventures in the Allegheny Highlands of Virginia and West Virginia (reservations are essential).

Accommodations are available at the charming **Highland Inn,** on Main Street (P.O. Box 40) (© **888/466-4682** or 540/468-2143; fax 540/468-3143; www.highland-inn.com), a 17-unit, veranda-fronted hotel built in 1904, renovated and improved in the 1980s. Rooms and suites range from $75 to $125 and include continental breakfast. Dinner is served in the dining room and the Black Sheep Tavern from 6 to 8pm Wednesday through Saturday. Brunch is served on Sunday from 11:30am to 2pm. Less expensive is the **Montvalle Motel** on Main Street (© **540/468-2500**), a plain but comfortable 1950s facility. There are several B&Bs here (the chamber posts a list on its website).

High's Restaurant on Main Street (© **540/468-1600**), the town's oldest, and the **Maple Restaurant** on Spruce Street (© **540/468-2684**), behind the courthouse, both serve inexpensive, down-home Southern fare.

From Monterey, another marvelously scenic drive on U.S. 220 takes you 30 miles south along the Jackson River to Warm Springs (see below). From there, you can drive back across the mountains to Lexington via Va. 39 and the Goshen Pass.

8 Warm Springs & Hot Springs: Taking the Waters ⟨★

Hot Springs: 220 miles SW of Washington, D.C.; 160 miles W of Richmond

Warm Springs: 5 miles N of Hot Springs

At temperatures from 94°F to 104°F (35°C–40°C), thermal springs rise in appropriately named Bath County. This little valley has been a retreat since the 18th century, when Thomas Jefferson and other notables stopped at Warm Springs to "take the waters." The Homestead was founded in 1766 and is still one of the nation's premier spas and golf resorts (the nation's oldest tee is here). After you've soaked in the waters, played the links and had your pedicure, you can hear classical music at the Garth Newel Music Center.

Warm Springs today is a charming little hamlet that serves as the Bath County seat. The even smaller village of Hot Springs, 5 miles to the south, is virtually a company town: It lives to serve The Homestead. Hot Springs' Main Street begins where U.S. 220 circles around the resort and runs for 2 blocks south; here you'll find a country grocery store, several upscale art and clothing dealers (some in the old train depot), and a funky and very fine little restaurant that is not— surprisingly—part of The Homestead.

ESSENTIALS

VISITOR INFORMATION   The **Bath County Chamber of Commerce,** P.O. Box 718, Hot Springs, VA 24445 (© **800/628-8092** or 540/839-5409; www. bathcountyva.org), operates a visitor center 2 miles south of Hot Springs on U.S. 220 (it shares space with the U.S. Forestry Service's information center). The visitor center is open Monday, Wednesday, Friday and Saturday 9am to 4pm, Tuesday and Thursday 8am to 4pm, and Sunday 10am to 5pm. There's an unstaffed information kiosk, on U.S. 220 just south of the Va. 39 junction in Warm Springs. It usually has copies of a walking-tour brochure to the little village.

GETTING THERE   U.S. 220 runs north and south through Hot Springs and Warm Springs, with access to I-64 at Covington, 20 miles of winding mountain road south of Hot Springs. The scenic route is via Va. 39 from Lexington, a 42-mile drive that follows the Maury River through Goshen Pass. You can also take the scenic loop through "Virginia's Switzerland," described at the end of the Staunton section, above.

The nearest regular air service is at Roanoke Regional Airport. Clifton Forge has an Amtrak station (© **800/872-7245;** www.amtrak.com).

TAKING THE WATERS IN THE JEFFERSON POOLS ★★★

The most famous of the thermal springs are the **Jefferson Pools,** in a grove of trees in Warm Springs, just south of the intersection of U.S. 220 and Va. 39 (© **540/ 839-5346**). The crystal-clear waters of these natural rock pools circulate gently and offer a wonderfully relaxing experience. The octagonal white clapboard bathhouse covering the men's pool was built in 1761, and the women's building dates to 1836, so the only luxuries you'll get at the pools are a clean towel and a rudimentary changing room. The Homestead manages them, however, and provides massages in an adjacent building (at $100 per session). Use of the pools cost $12 an hour. Reservations aren't taken; just walk in. The pools are open from June to October, daily from 10am to 7pm. Call for winter hours.

There's music in the mountains on summer weekends at the **Garth Newel Music Center** ★★ on U.S. 220 between Warm Springs and Hot Springs (© **877558-1689** or 540/839-5018; fax 540/839-3154; www.garthnewel.org). The center's summer-long chamber music festival has been drawing critical acclaim since the 1970s, and concerts now go into the autumn months. Garth Newel also sponsors a series of Music Holiday Weekend Retreats in spring, fall, and winter, including Christmas and New Year's. Accommodations and dining at the on-site **Manor House** are part of the package. Call, write, or check the website for details.

WHERE TO STAY

The Homestead ★★★   With a prodigious reputation dating back to 1766, this famous spa and golf resort has been host to Presidents Jefferson, Wilson, Hoover, F.D.R., Truman, Eisenhower, Carter, and Reagan, plus social elites like the Henry Fords, John D. Rockefeller, the Vanderbilts, and Lord and Lady Astor. Two mountains flank its main building, which is built of red Kentucky brick with white-limestone trim. Guests enter via the Great Hall, lined with 16 Corinthian columns and a 211-foot floral carpet. Two fireplaces, wing chairs, Chippendale-reproduction tables with reading lamps, and deep sofas create a warm atmosphere. Afternoon tea is served daily to the classical music of the piano in the background.

Guests have a variety of accommodations in rooms and suites with a Virginia country-manor ambience and custom-designed mahogany furniture. Most units offer spectacular mountain views. Best are the 81 suites in the South Wing, which have working fireplaces, private bars, sun porches, two TVs, and two phones.

In addition to its three outstanding golf courses and 12 tennis courts, diversions include bowling, fishing, hiking, horseback and carriage rides, ice-skating on an Olympic-size rink, lawn bowling and croquet, billiards, sporting clays and skeet trap, downhill and cross-country skiing mid-December to March. Then you can ease the aches and pains in the springs-fed indoor pool or the full-service spa.

Tips Take a Stroll

Even if you don't "take the waters," get out of the car and spend a few minutes strolling around the lovely grounds of the Jefferson Pools. It's easy to imagine Thomas Jefferson sitting under the gazebo covering the "Drinking Pool."

Under the supervision of European-trained chefs, the historic **Dining Room** is a lush palm court, in which an orchestra performs every evening during six-course dinners and for dancing afterwards. The Homestead's signature restaurant, **The 1766 Grille,** is more casual, as is the **Casino Club.** Across Main Street from the hotel, **Sam Snead's Tavern** is a lively pub serving traditional American fare. Or you can dine at the golf clubs or at the ski slopes.

Guests may don casual resort wear during the day, including shorts of respectable length, but men must wear jackets and long pants after dark, with both jackets and ties required in the Dining Room.

This large property hosts conventions and other group meetings, so you'll have lots of company here.

P.O. Box 2000, Hot Springs, VA 24445. ✆ **800/838-1766** or 540/839-1776. Fax 540/839-7670. www.the homestead.com. 506 units. $129–$290 double per person, $203–$486 suites per person. Children staying in parent's room pay less. Rates include breakfast, dinner, and afternoon tea. Weekend, golf, and other packages available. AE, DC, DISC, MC, V. Main entrance is off U.S. 220 south of Main St. **Amenities:** 5 restaurants; 3 bars; indoor and outdoor pools; 3 golf courses; 12 tennis courts; health club; spa; children's programs; game room; concierge; shopping arcade; salon; limited room service; massage; babysitting; laundry service. *In room:* A/C, TV, dataport, minibar, iron, safe.

Inn at Gristmill Square ✦ Five restored 19th-century buildings, including an old mill, make up this unique hostelry in Warm Springs. It includes the Blacksmith Shop, which houses a country store; the Hardware Store, with seven guest units; the Steel House, with four units; and the Miller's House, with four rooms. Furnishings are period pieces, with comfortable upholstered chairs, brass chandeliers, quilts on four-poster beds and marble-top side tables, and many units have working fireplaces. Breakfast is served in your room in a picnic basket. Other facilities include an outdoor pool, three tennis courts, and sauna.

The rustic **Waterwheel Restaurant** and **Simon Kenton Pub** are cozy spots in the old mill building. The restaurant features notably good American cuisine. Wines are displayed among the gears of the waterwheel. The restaurant also serves Sunday brunch. Call for reservations.

C.R. 645 (Box 359), Warm Springs, VA 24484. ✆ **540/839-2231.** Fax 540/839-5770. www.gristmillsquare.com. 16 units, 1 suite. $85–$160 double. Rates include continental breakfast. Modified American Plan available. DISC, MC, V. From U.S. 220N, turn left onto C.R. 619 and right onto C.R. 645. **Amenities:** Restaurant; bar; outdoor pool; 3 tennis courts; health club; sauna; limited room service; massage; babysitting. *In room:* A/C, TV, fridge.

Roseloe Motel *Value* At the opposite extreme from the Homestead, Dave and Marcy Hodges' brick-fronted motel offers inexpensive, well-maintained, and clean rooms near the Garth Newel Music Center, between Warm Springs and Hot Springs. Four units have full kitchens, two have kitchenettes, and all have microwave ovens and refrigerators. It's very popular with leaf-watchers and deer hunters during fall, so book early. Small pets are welcome here.

Rte. 1, Box 590 (U.S. 220 N.), Hot Springs, VA 24445. ✆ **540/839-5373.** Fax 540/839-4625. www.roseloe. netfirms.com. 14 units. $60–$85 double. AE, DC, DISC, MC, V. Pets accepted ($10 fee). From Hot Springs, go north 3 miles on U.S. 220. *In room:* A/C, TV, kitchen, fridge, coffeemaker, iron.

BED & BREAKFASTS

Other bed-and-breakfasts in Warm Springs include **Three Hills Inn & Cottages** (✆ **888/23-HILLS** or 540/839-5381; fax 540/839-5199; www.3hills.com), which has its own amphitheater hosting summertime concerts; and **Warm Springs Inn** (✆ **540/839-5351;** www.warmsprings-inn.com), a converted court-house across the road from the Jefferson Pools; it has a restaurant. In Hot Springs,

Vine Cottage Inn (℗ **800/410-9755** or 540/839-2422; www.vinecottageinn. com) is a block from The Homestead.

Anderson Cottage Bed & Breakfast   One of Bath County's oldest buildings, this log-and-white-clapboard cottage has been in owner Jean Randolph Bruns' family since the 1870s. She has welcomed guests into her home since 1983, and still operates it as "private home B&B" (in contrast to the more commercial operations which have sprung up all over Virginia). The setting is an expansive lawn with a warm stream flowing through the property in the heart of the picturesque village. The house has country charm, with many family heirloom pieces and photos, wide-board floors, Oriental rugs, working fireplaces, and lots of loaded bookcases. Accommodations are individually decorated and exceptionally spacious. Originally an 1820s brick kitchen, the Guest Cottage is ideal for families, with two bedrooms, two baths, a full kitchen/dining/sitting room with fireplace, and a living room. Otherwise, the rooms are not air-conditioned (seldom needed at this altitude), nor do they have TVs, phones, or other amenities.

Old Germantown Rd. (P.O. Box 176), Warm Springs, VA 24484. ℗ **540/839-2975.** www.bbonline.com/va/anderson. 4 units (3 with bathroom). $70–$125 double. Rates include full breakfast. No credit cards. From Va. 39, turn left onto Old Germantown Rd. (C.R. 692), to 4th house on the left.

AN UNUSUAL COUNTRY INN

Fort Lewis Lodge ⭐⭐ *(Kids)*   You'll discover one of Virginia's most unusual country inns at John and Caryl Cowden's farm beside the Cowpasture River, which cuts a north-south valley over the mountain from Warm Springs. Most guest quarters are in a reconstructed barn, but an outside spiral staircase leads to three rooms inside the silo—yes, a silo. One end of the rough-look barn is now a comfortable lounge with stone fireplace and large windows looking out to a Jacuzzi-equipped deck to the farmland and mountains beyond. Other guests stay in hand-hewn log cabins, each with a fireplace, or in a restored farmhouse.

The Cowdens' summertime garden supplies flowers and vegetables for excellent meals served in the old Lewis Mill, whose upstairs has been turned into a game room. A screened porch to one side shelters **Buck's Bar,** which serves beer and wine. Activities include mountain biking, hiking, and swimming and fishing for trout in the Cowpasture River (don't count on eating your catch; you must throw it back into the river). Fort Lewis Lodge is popular with families getting away from Washington, D.C., and other nearby cities, so book early.

HCR 3, Box 21A, Millboro, VA 24460. ℗ **540/925-2314.** Fax 540/925-2352. www.fortlewislodge.com. 18 units. $165–$210 double. Rates include breakfast and dinner. MC, V. From Warm Springs, go 13 miles east on Va. 39, turn left on Indian Draft Rd. (C.R. 678) and drive north 10.8 miles, then turn left on River Rd. (C.R. 625) to entrance. **Amenities:** Restaurant; bar; Jacuzzi; bike rental, game room. *In room:* A/C.

WHERE TO DINE

Don't overlook the elegant dining rooms at The Homestead in Hot Springs and the rustic **Waterwheel Restaurant** at the Inn at Gristmill Square in Warm Springs (see "Where to Stay," above).

Part of a gasoline station 3½ miles north of Hot Springs, the clean and modern **Varsity Grill** (℗ **540/839-4000**) provides inexpensive breakfasts, salads, and deli sandwiches. It's open daily from 7am to 10pm.

Elliott's ⭐ *(Value)* ECLECTIC   This Main Street storefront, ½ block south of The Homestead, is the domain of chef Josh Elliott, who busily whips up fine, eclectic cuisine in a kitchen behind the meat chiller at the rear. For lunch he offers salads, sandwiches, and tasty wraps (go for the marvelous curry chicken salad), and two entrees, often grilled salmon and prawns, both a bargain. At night, Josh offers an eclectic menu drawing from a number of cuisines. Baked rainbow trout stuffed with crabmeat is but one example. The Homestead doesn't voluntarily tell its guests about this little gem.

3 Main St., Hot Springs. ℭ 540/839-3663. Reservations recommended at dinner. Lunch $4–$8; main courses $13.50–$20. MC, V. Tues–Sat 11am–2pm and 5:30–9pm.

9 Lexington: A College Town with a Slice of American History ★★★

36 miles S of Staunton; 180 miles SW of Washington, D.C.; 138 miles W of Richmond

A college atmosphere prevails in Lexington, one of America's best small towns. Fine old homes line tree-shaded streets, among them the house where Stonewall Jackson lived when he taught at Virginia Military Institute. A beautifully restored downtown looks so much like it did in the 1800s that scenes for the movie *Sommersby* were filmed on Main Street (Richard Gere was "hanged" behind the Jackson House). After the Civil War, Robert E. Lee came to Lexington to serve as president of what was then Washington College; he and his horse, Traveller, are buried here. And Gen. George C. Marshall, winner of the Nobel Peace Prize for his post–World War II plan to rebuild Europe, graduated from VMI, which has a fine museum in his memory.

Washington and Lee University has one of the oldest and most beautiful campuses in the country. Built in 1824, Washington Hall is topped by a replica of an American folk art masterpiece, an 1840 carved-wood statue of George Washington. Lee reputedly planted some of the massive trees dotting the campus.

Sometimes called the West Point of the South, VMI opened in 1839 on the site of a state arsenal, abutting the Washington and Lee campus (W&L's buildings are like brick Southern manses; VMI's look like stone fortresses). The most dramatic episode in VMI's history took place during the Civil War at the Battle of New Market on May 15, 1964, when the corps of cadets helped turn back a larger Union army (see earlier). A month later, Union Gen. David Hunter got even, bombarding Lexington and burning down VMI.

If you have time to stop in only one Shenandoah Valley town, make it lovely Lexington.

ESSENTIALS

VISITOR INFORMATION   The **Lexington & Rockbridge Area Visitor Center,** 106 E. Washington St., Lexington, VA 24450 (ℭ **877/453-9822** or 540/463-3777; fax 540/463-1105; www.lexingtonvirginia.com), is a block east of Main Street. Begin your tour of Lexington at this excellent source of information, for it offers museumlike displays about the town's history, has an accommodations gallery for making same-day hotel reservations, and distributes free walking-tour brochures (you can park in the center's lot while touring the town). The center is open daily from 8:30am to 6pm June through August, from 9am to 5pm the rest of the year. Closed New Year's Day, Thanksgiving, and Christmas.

GETTING THERE   Lexington is on both I-81 and I-64, and U.S. 60 and U.S. 11 go directly into town.

EXPLORING THE TOWN

Be sure to pick up a free **walking tour** brochure at the visitor center. It explains Lexington's historic buildings and contains one of the best maps of downtown.

For a good overview, take a ride with **Lexington Carriage Company** (© 540/ 463-5647), whose horse-drawn carriages depart from the visitor center for 45-minute narrated tours daily from 10am to 6pm during the summer, from 11am to 5pm during April, May, September, and October. Fares are $16 for adults, $14 for seniors, $7 for ages 7 to 13, free for kids under 7.

Haunting Tales of Historic Lexington (© 540/464-2250) conducts 1¼-hour nighttime walks through the streets, back alleys, and Stonewall Jackson Cemetery from Memorial Day weekend to Halloween. Cost is $8 for adults, $6 for children 4 to 10, and free for children under 4. Reservations are strongly recommended, so call ahead.

George C. Marshall Museum and Research Library ★★

Facing the VMI parade ground, this impressive stone structure houses the personal archives of General of the Army George C. Marshall, a 1901 graduate of VMI. Marshall had an illustrious career, including service in France in 1917, when he was aide-de-camp to General Pershing. As army chief of staff in World War II, he virtually directed that conflict (it was Marshall who chose Gen. Dwight D. Eisenhower to command all Allied forces in Europe). After the war he served as secretary of state and secretary of defense under President Truman. He is best remembered for the Marshall Plan, which fostered the economic recovery of Europe after the war. For his role in promoting post-war peace, he became the first career soldier to be awarded the Nobel Peace Prize, in 1956. The Nobel medal is on display. An electronic map charts the war and Marshall's decisions, and films explain his life. Allow at least an hour to explore the museum on your own.

VMI Parade Grounds. © 540/463-7103. www.marshallfoundation.org. Admission to museum $3 adults, $2 seniors, free for students and children; free admission to research library. Museum, daily 9am–5pm; research library, Mon–Fri 8:30am–4:30pm.

Lee Chapel and Museum ★★★

This magnificent brick and limestone Victorian-Gothic chapel on the Washington and Lee campus was built of brick and native limestone in 1867 at the request of General Lee. Begin by walking up on the auditorium stage and Edward Valentine's striking white-marble sculpture "Lee Recumbent." A docent will explain history of the building and the intricacies of the statue, which Valentine carved between 1871 and 1875, shortly after Lee's death. Charles Willson Peale's 1772 portrait of George Washington wearing the uniform of a colonel in the Virginia militia and Theodore Pine's painting of Lee in Confederate uniform flank the statue. Then climb down the narrow rear steps to the basement, where the remains of the general and many other members of the Lee clan (including "Light-Horse Harry" Lee of Revolutionary War fame) are entombed. Robert E. Lee's beloved horse, Traveller, is buried in a plot outside the museum. Across the vestibule, Lee's office remains just as he left it when he died on October 12, 1870. The museum itself is devoted to the history of the university and its two namesakes. It includes the impressive Washington-Custis-Lee collection of American portraits. Allow 30 minutes to see the statue, the crypt, and Lee's office, another 30 in the museum.

⸜ Fun Fact ⸝ Presidential Prototype

The George C. Marshall Museum and Research Library served as the prototype for modern presidential libraries, starting with President Truman's in Independence, Missouri.

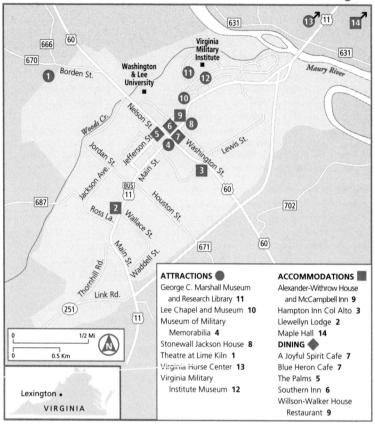

ATTRACTIONS ●

George C. Marshall Museum
   and Research Library **11**
Lee Chapel and Museum **10**
Museum of Military
   Memorabilia **4**
Stonewall Jackson House **8**
Theatre at Lime Kiln **1**
Virginia Horse Center **13**
Virginia Military
   Institute Museum **12**

ACCOMMODATIONS ■

Alexander-Withrow House
   and McCampbell Inn **9**
Hampton Inn Col Alto **3**
Llewellyn Lodge **2**
Maple Hall **14**

DINING ◆

A Joyful Spirit Cafe **7**
Blue Heron Cafe **7**
The Palms **5**
Southern Inn **6**
Willson-Walker House
   Restaurant **9**

Washington and Lee University. ℂ **540/458-8768**. http://leechapel.wlu.edu. Free admission. Apr 1–Oct 31 Mon–Sat 9am–5pm, Sun 1–5pm; Nov 1–Mar 31 Mon–Sat 9am–4pm, Sun 1–4pm. Limited free parking on Jefferson St. opposite west end of Henry St. Follow signs from parking lot.

Museum of Military Memorabilia   This small but fascinating museum displays a collection of military uniforms and various bits of soldiers' gear, with the oldest dating from 1740 in Prussia and the newest from the 1991 Persian Gulf War. The uniforms come from several different countries and represent a number of conflicts. You'll also see insignia, flags, a few weapons, trench art from World War I, and a piece of the Berlin Wall. If you miss the beginning, you can join the 45-minute guided tours in progress.

122½ S. Main St. (in the driveway beside the Presbyterian Church). ℂ **540/464-3041**. Admission $3 per person. Apr–Oct Wed–Fri noon–5pm; Sat 9am–5pm. Rest of year by appointment. 45-min. tours run continuously.

Stonewall Jackson House 🏠🏠   Maj. Thomas Jonathan Jackson came to Lexington in 1851 to take a post as teacher of natural philosophy (physics) and artillery tactics at VMI. Jackson lived here with his wife, Mary Anna Morrison, from early 1859 until he was summoned to Richmond in 1861; it was the only house he ever owned. Exhibits tell the story of the Jacksons' stay here, and many of the Jacksons' personal effects duplicate the items on the inventory of Jackson's estate made shortly after he died near Chancellorsville in 1863. His body was

Impressions

Let us cross the river and rest under the shade of the trees.
— Stonewall Jackson's last words, May 10, 1863

returned to Lexington and buried in **Stonewall Jackson Memorial Cemetery** on South Main Street. Also have a look at the backyard vegetable garden and the carriage house, which protects a Rockaway model Jackson owned.

8 E. Washington St. (between Main and Randolph sts.). ℂ 540/463-2552. www.stonewalljackson.org. Admission $5 adults, $2.50 children 6–18, free for children 5 and under. Mon–Sat 9am–6pm; Sun 1–6pm. Mandatory 30-min. tours depart on the hour and half-hour (last tour 30 min. prior to closing). Closed New Year's Day, Easter, Thanksgiving, and Christmas.

Virginia Horse Center   Sprawling across nearly 400 acres, the Virginia Horse Center offers educational seminars, and sales of fine horses, and it has a coliseum for concerts as well as horse shoes. Annual events include draft pulls, rodeos, various competitions, and competitive breed shows. For a full program of events, check the website or contact the center at P.O. Box 1051, Lexington, VA 24450.

Va. 39, west of U.S. 11 and north of I-64. ℂ 540/463-7060. www.horsecenter.org. Admission varies by event; most are free. Open year-round. From downtown, take U.S. 11 north, turn left on Va. 39 1/10 mile north of I-64. The center is 1 mile on the left.

Virginia Military Institute Museum ★★   This museum tracing VMI's history is well worth a visit, especially to see the raincoat Stonewall Jackson was wearing when his own men accidentally shot him at Chancellorsville (the bullet hole is in the upper left shoulder) and—thanks to taxidermy—Jackson's unflappable war horse, Little Sorrel. Also here are one of Gen. George S. Patton's pearl-handled pistols and his shiny helmet liner. Patton graduated from VMI in 1907. The museum is in the lower level of Jackson Memorial Hall, the school's auditorium. It was built in 1915 with federal funds paid in partial compensation for the Union army's burning the school after its cadets helped defeat federal troops at the Battle of New Market in May 1864 (see earlier). Be sure to step into the auditorium to see B. West Clinedinst's oversize oil painting of the cadets' heroic Civil War charge. It hangs over the stage. *Note:* Renovations were scheduled to begin in 2004 and last for 18 to 24 months.

Letcher Ave., VMI Parade (in Jackson Memorial Hall). ℂ 540/464-7232. www.vmi.edu/museum. Free admission. Daily 9am–5pm. Closed New Year's Day, Thanksgiving, and Christmas week.

THE NATURAL BRIDGE

Thomas Jefferson called this hugely impressive limestone formation "the most sublime of nature's works . . . so beautiful an arch, so elevated, so light and springing, as it were, up to heaven." The bridge was part of a 157-acre estate Jefferson acquired in 1774 from King George III. It was included in the survey of western Virginia carried out by George Washington, who carved his initials into the face of the stone. This geological oddity rises 215 feet above Cedar Creek; its span is 90 feet long and spreads at its widest to 150 feet. The Monacan Indian tribes worshipped it as "the bridge of God." Today, it is also the bridge of man, as U.S. 11 passes over it.

It's not all a tacky tourist trap, since the bridge itself and its **Monacan Indian Living History Village** are worth seeing, but "Natural Bridge" today includes a cavern (45-min. tours depart every 30 min.), department store–size souvenir shop, restaurant, hotel, and toy and wax museums. There's a small, independently operated zoo up the road, but you, the kids, and especially the animals will have more fun at the nearby Virginia Safari Park (see box).

There are no guided tours, but the bridge and the Monacan village are an easy ¼-mile walk from the visitor center. From there, the 1-mile-long **Cedar Creek Trail** descends past a cave, a waterfall, and a 1,500-year-old arbor vitae tree. The bridge is open daily from 8am to dusk. During summer, a 45-minute sound-and-light show begins at dusk beneath the bridge.

Admission to the bridge, Monacan village, and show is $10 for adults, $5 for children 6 to 15. Tickets to the wax or toy museum or caverns cost $8 for adults, $5 for children 6 to 15. Combination tickets to any two of the attractions are $14 adults, $7 children 6 to 15. Any three attractions cost $18 adults, $8.50 for kids 6 to 15. The attractions are open during summer daily from 8am to sunset; the rest of the year, daily from 8am to 5pm.

The bridge is 12 miles south of Lexington on U.S. 11 (take Exit 175 off I-81). For more information, or to book a hotel room or campsite here, contact Natural Bridge, P.O. Box 57, Natural Bridge, VA 24578 (© **800/533-1410** or 540/291-2121; fax 540/291-1896; www.naturalbridgeva.com).

OUTDOOR ACTIVITIES

The Lexington & Rockbridge Area Visitor Center (see "Essentials," above) publishes a useful guide, *Rockbridge Outdoors,* which gives a complete run-down of the area's active pursuits.

An avid outdoorsman, co-host John Roberts at **Llewellyn Lodge** organizes fly-fishing trips and hiking expeditions into the nearby hills and mountains (see "Where to Stay, below).

CANOEING, KAYAKING & RAFTING   The Maury River, which runs through Lexington, provides some of Virginia's best white-water rafting and kayaking, especially through the Goshen Pass, on Va. 39 northwest of town. The visitor center has information about several put-in spots, or you can rent equipment or go on expeditions on the Maury and James rivers with **James River Basin Canoe Livery,** U.S. 60 East (Route 4, Box 125), Lexington, VA 24450 (© **540/261-7334;** www.canoevirginia.com). Call, write, or check the website for schedules and reservations.

HIKING   Two linear parks connect to offer hikers and joggers nearly 10 miles of gorgeous trail between Lexington and Buena Vista, a railroad town 7 miles to the southeast. The major link is the **Chessie Nature Trail,** which follows an old railroad bed along the Maury River between Lexington and Buena Vista. No vehicles (including bicycles) are allowed, but you can cross-country ski the trail during winter. The Chessie trail connects with a walking path in **Woods Creek Park,** which starts at the Waddell School on Jordan Street and runs down to the banks of the Maury. Both trails are open from dawn to dusk. The visitor center has maps and brochures.

There are excellent hiking, mountain-biking, horseback-riding, and all-terrain-vehicle trails in the **George Washington National Forest,** which encompasses

---

Fun Fact **Big Age for Little Sorrel**

Stonewall Jackson's trusty horse, Little Sorrel, survived the Civil War and died in 1886 at the ripe old age of 32. He was stuffed and placed in the Virginia Military Institute Museum, where he stands to this day.

Kids On Safari in Virginia

It's a far cry from the real Serengeti Plain, but the **Virginia Safari Park,** at exit 180 off I-81 (© **540/291-3205**), has zebras, giraffes, antelopes, monkeys, emus, deer, elk and bison among more than 400 animals roaming the hills between Lexington and Natural Bridge. There's even a petting area with goats, lambs, and pigs. The best way to see the beasts is on a 90-minute wagon ride at 1 and 3pm on Saturday and Sunday. At other times you merely drive your own vehicle through the park. Admission is $8 for adults, $7 for seniors, and $6 for children 3 to 12. The park is open from mid-March to Thanksgiving weekend, daily from 9am to 5pm, to 6pm from Memorial Day to Labor Day.

much of the Blue Ridge Mountains east of Lexington. Small children might not be able to make it, but the rest of the family will enjoy the 3-mile trail up to **Crabtree Falls,** a series of cascades tumbling 1,200 feet down the mountain (it's the highest waterfall in Virginia). Heartier hikers can scale up to the Appalachian Trail at on the mountaintop. Crabtree Falls is on Va. 56 east of the Blue Ridge Parkway; from Lexington, go north on I-81 to Steeles Tavern (Exit 205), then east on Va. 56.

The National Forest Service has an **information office** at Natural Bridge (© **540/291-1806**), which offers free brochures and sells maps of trails and campgrounds. It's open April through November, daily from 9am to 4:30pm. Or you can contact the Glenwood Ranger District, George Washington and Jefferson National Forests, P.O. Box 10, Natural Bridge Station, VA 24579 (© **540/291-2188;** www.southernregion.fs.fed.us/gwj).

SHOPPING

Lexington's charming 19th-century downtown offers more than a dozen interesting shops and art galleries, most of them on Main Street and on the blocks of Washington and Nelson streets between Main and Jefferson streets. Among the best is **Artists in Cahoots,** a cooperative venture run by local artists and craftspeople in the Alexander-Withrow House, at the corner of Main and Washington (© **540/464-1147**). It features an outstanding selection of paintings, sculptures, wood and metal crafts, hand-painted silk scarves, handblown glass, Shaker-style furniture, photographs, prints, decoys, stained glass, and jewelry. **Virginia Born & Bred,** 16 W. Washington St. (© **540/463-1832**), has made-in-Virginia gifts. Collectible hunters will find an amazing array of old and not-so-old stuff literally stuffed into **The Second Hand Shop,** 7 S. Jefferson St. (© **540/463-7559**), between Washington and Nelson streets.

The **Lexington Antique & Craft Mall** (© **540/463-9511**) has space for 250 dealers in its 40,000 square feet of space. They offer country and formal furniture, glassware, books, quilts, folk art, and more. The mall is located in the College Square shopping center on U.S. 11, about ½ mile north of downtown. It's daily from 10am to 6pm.

ON THE WINE TRAIL

A renovated dairy houses the award-winning **Rockbridge Vineyard,** 30 Hillview Lane (C.R. 606) near I-81 and Raphine about halfway between Lexington and Staunton (© **888/511-WINE** or 540/377-6204; www.rockbridgevineyard.com).

The tasting room is open Wednesday through Saturday 11am to 5pm, Sunday noon to 5pm. From I-81, take exit 205 and follow Va. 606 west 1 mile to the vineyard on right.

WHERE TO STAY

Lexington has several chain motels, especially at the intersection of U.S. 11 and I-64 (Exit 55), 1½ miles north of downtown. The 100-unit **Best Western Inn at Hunt Ridge,** 25 Willow Springs Rd./Va. 39 (✆ **800/464-1501** or 540/464-1500; www.dominionlodging.com), is the only full-service hotel among them, offering a restaurant, bar, limited room service, indoor-outdoor pool, and fine mountain views. Try to get one of its six rooms with balconies.

Other nearby motels are: **Comfort Inn** (✆ **800/628-1956** or 540/463-7311), **Country Inn & Suites** (✆ **800/456-4000** or 540/464-9000), **EconoLodge** (✆ **800/446-6900** or 540/463-7371), **Holiday Inn Express** (✆ **800/HOLIDAY** or 540/463-7351), and **Super 8** (✆ **800/800-8000** or 540/463-7858).

Hampton Inn Col Alto ★★   This is no ordinary Hampton Inn: Col Alto is an 1827 manor house built on a plantation then on the outskirts of town. The carefully renovated mansion now houses 10 bedrooms comparable to deluxe country inns or B&Bs. An interior designer individually decorated these luxurious quarters with made-in-Virginia linens, reproduction antiques, and bright, vivid paints, wallpapers, and fabrics. Accommodations range in size from huge, light-filled rooms on the front of the house to smaller, more private ones in the rear. One unit even has a semi-round "fan" window of the style favored by Thomas Jefferson. Two formal parlors on the first floor are available for mansion guests only. Guests can also choose to have breakfast and the morning newspaper delivered to their rooms. Rooms in the new, L-shaped motel wing next door are somewhat larger than average and have microwave ovens, coffeemakers, robes, and irons and ironing boards; some have balconies overlooking a courtyard with outdoor swimming pool and whirlpool. There's a small exercise room here, too. Guests in both wings get complimentary continental breakfasts in the original dining room, but it's standard Hampton Inn fare and doesn't live up to the gourmet breakfasts served at most bed-and-breakfasts.

401 E. Nelson St., Lexington, VA 24450. ✆ **800/HAMPTON** or 540/463-2223. Fax 540/463-9707. www. hampton-inn.com/hi/lexington-historic. 86 units. $90–$125 double motel room; $180–$225 in manor house. Rates include continental breakfast. AE, DC, DISC, MC, V. **Amenities:** Outdoor pool; health club; Jacuzzi; concierge; babysitting; laundry service. In room: A/C, TV, coffeemaker, iron.

HISTORIC COUNTRY INNS

Make reservations for Alexander-Withrow House, McCampbell Inn, and Maple Hall through **Historic Country Inns,** 11 N. Main St., Lexington, VA 24450 (✆ **877/283-9680** or 540/463-2044; fax 540/463-7262; www.lexington historicinns.com).

Alexander-Witherow House and McCampbell Inn ★   The Alexander-Witherow House is a lovely late Georgian town house built in 1789 as a family residence over a store. Artists in Cahoots (see "Shopping," above) occupy the ground floor. Accommodations are all homey suites with separate living rooms and small kitchens. Comfortable furnishings include wing chairs, four-poster beds, and hooked rugs on wide-board floors. The McCampbell Inn, across Main Street, houses the main office for Historic Country Inns; guests at both hostelries eat breakfast here. Begun in 1809, with later additions in 1816 and 1857, it occupies a rambling building, with rooms facing both Main Street and the quieter back courtyard. Furnishings are a pleasant mix of antiques and reproductions; all units have wet bars and refrigerators, and one of the suites has a Jacuzzi.

11 N. Main St. ℂ **877/283-9680** or 540/463-2044. Fax 540/463-2044. www.lexingtonhistoricinns.com. 15 units, 8 suites. $105–$140 double; $165–$185 suite. Rates include extensive continental breakfast. DISC, MC, V. *In room:* A/C, TV, fridge, coffeemaker, iron.

Maple Hall ⚐ Set on 56 rolling acres, this handsome red-brick, white-columned 1850 plantation house offers a restful retreat. Old boxwoods surround the inn, which consists of a main house, a restored Guest House, and a Pond House. Rooms are individually furnished, many with antiques, Oriental rugs, and massive Victorian pieces; 10 units have gas fireplaces. The Guest House has a living room, kitchen, and three bedrooms with baths. The Pond House, added in 1990, contains four suites and two mini-suites. Guests relax on the shaded patio, on porches with rocking chairs, and on back verandas overlooking the fishing pond and nearby hills. A pool, tennis court, and 3-mile hiking trail are on-site. Elegant dining in pretty gardenlike surroundings attracts a good following to the Maple Hall restaurant, which is open daily for dinner.

3111 N. Lee Hwy. (U.S. 11), Lexington, VA 24450. ℂ **877/283-9680** or 540/463-6693. Fax 540/463-2044. www.lexingtonhistoricinns.com. 21 units. $105–$140 double; $165–$185 suite. Rates include breakfast. DISC, MC, V. Take U.S. 11, 7 miles north of town; house is near Exit 195 of I-81. **Amenities:** Restaurant; outdoor pool; golf course; tennis court. *In room:* A/C, TV.

BED & BREAKFASTS

In addition to those mentioned below, Lexington has several other B&Bs; the visitor center offers a complete list.

Llewellyn Lodge A half-century-old brick colonial-style house, the Llewellyn Lodge is within easy walking distance of all of Lexington's historic sites. On the first floor are a cozy sitting room with working fireplace and a TV room. Guest rooms are decorated in exceptionally attractive color schemes. All rooms have ceiling fans, and three have TVs. Co-host John Roberts has hiked just about every trail and fished every stream in the Blue Ridge Mountains; he organizes fly fishing and hiking expeditions (see "Outdoor Activities," above).

603 S. Main St., Lexington, VA 24450. ℂ **800/882-1145** or 540/463-3235. Fax 540/463-3235. www.llodge.com. 6 units. $65–$140 double. Rates include full breakfast. AE, DC, DISC, MC, V. *In room:* A/C, TV (4 rooms), iron.

WHERE TO DINE

While you're walking around town, stop in at Lexington's famous **Sweet Things,** 106 W. Washington St., between Jefferson Street and Lee Avenue (ℂ **540/463-6055**), for a cone or cup of "designer" ice cream or frozen yogurt. It's open Monday to Thursday noon to 9:30pm, Friday and Saturday noon to 10pm, and Sunday 2 to 9:30pm.

Get your caffeine fix at **Lexington Coffee Co.,** 9 W. Washington St. (ℂ **540/464-6586**), a quintessential, college-town coffeehouse with a selection of exotic brews plus bagels and pastries. It's open Monday to Friday 7:30am to 5pm, Saturday 8am to 5pm, Sunday 9 to 3pm.

A Joyful Spirit Cafe *Finds* DELI This bright, lively order-at-the-counter restaurant is the best place in town for hot coffee and pastries for breakfast and creative sandwiches with a joyful combination of flavors for lunch. Bagels with salmon, cream cheese, and capers are available all day. If you're lucky you can claim one of the two tables out on the sidewalk.

26 S. Main St. (between Washington and Nelson sts.). ℂ **540/463-4191**. Reservations not accepted. Breakfast $2–$4; sandwiches and salads $3.50–$5.50. AE, DC, DISC, MC, V. Mon–Fri 8:30am–5:30pm, Sat 10am–5pm, Sun 11am–4pm.

Blue Heron Cafe ⭐ _Finds_ VEGETARIAN   Owner Laurie Macrae is the "Food Goddess" at this fine vegetarian restaurant in an old office building with big double-hung windows on two sides (never mind the staff reaching over your table to grab a ripening tomato off the sill; that juicy morsel will soon be on your plate). Primary-color art also adds to a festive atmosphere. The wonderful aromas wafting from the open kitchen will tell you there are terrific flavors to be enjoyed here. Best lunch bets are the soup, salad, and pasta combos. Dinner on weekends presents three specials such as Japanese-style noodles in a miso sauce.

4 E. Washington St. (east of Main St.). ℂ **540/463-2800**. Reservations recommended for dinner. Sandwiches and salads $4–$6; main courses $8–$14. No credit cards. Mon–Thurs 11:30am–2:30pm, Fri–Sat 11:30am–2pm and 5:30–9pm.

The Palms   AMERICAN/PUB FARE   With neon palms in its storefront window, this popular pub draws town and gown alike with its substantial (if uninspired) fare, sports TVs, and friendly bar. At lunch or dinner, the hearty burgers will not disappoint. Deli sandwiches run the gamut from roast beef to smoked turkey. Dinner entrees, served with soup or salad, vegetable, and bread, include choices like baby back ribs, grilled mahimahi, and fettuccine Alfredo either plain or with shrimp, chicken, ham, or vegetables. Ask about dinner–and–Theater at Lime Kiln packages.

101 W. Nelson St. (at Jefferson St.). ℂ **540/463-7911**. Reservations not accepted. Sandwiches, burgers and salads $4.50–$7; main courses $7–$15. AE, DC, DISC, MC, V. Mon–Tues 11:30am–1am; Wed–Fri 11:30am–2am; Sat noon–2am; Sun noon–11pm.

Southern Inn ⭐⭐⭐ REGIONAL   Crisp linen adorns the plain wooden booths at this former down-home-style Southern restaurant (note the brass coat hooks between the booths and the 1950s neon sign out front). In its refined reincarnation, it gives the Willson-Walker House serious competition for Lexington's top dining spot. You can order excellent sandwiches such as Dijon and tarragon chicken salad, and the regular menu features comfort food such as an excellent rendition of Mom's meatloaf, but the real stars here are specials like sea scallops sautéed with garlic and herb butter and braised lamb shanks with herb risotto. There's an excellent wine list featuring Virginia vintages. The small but lively **Digger's Pub** next door serves the same fare and attracts a more affluent crowd than The Palms (see above). Digger's has live music on weekend nights.

37 S. Main St. (between Washington and Nelson sts.). ℂ **540/463-3612**. Reservations recommended. Sandwiches $9–$10.50; main courses $11–$26. AE, MC, V. Daily 11:30am–10pm.

Willson-Walker House Restaurant ⭐⭐⭐ REGIONAL   Occupying the first floor of an 1820 Greek Revival town house and furnished with period antiques, this distinctive restaurant offers some of the valley's finest cuisine. In good weather, the most popular tables are on the verandah behind two-story white columns. At lunch, the $5 chef's special includes choice of soup or salad, entree, homemade muffins and rolls, and beverage. Changing seasonally, the dinner menu offers such tempting main courses as potato-crusted North Carolina rainbow trout. The best of Virginia wines are available by the glass or bottle.

30 N. Main St. (between Washington and Henry sts.). ℂ **540/463-3020**. Reservations recommended. Lunch $5–$8; main courses $11–$20. AE, DISC, MC, V. Tues–Sat 11:30am–2:30pm and 5:30–9pm. Closed for Sat lunch Jan–Mar.

LEXINGTON AFTER DARK

The ruins of an old limestone kiln provide the backdrop for the open-air **Theater at Lime Kiln** ★★ on Borden Road off U.S. 60W, which presents musicals, plays, and concerts from March through September. Productions have ranged from a Civil War epic called Stonewall Country, based on Jackson's life, to Shakespeare, Appalachian folktales, and even water puppeteers from Vietnam. Tickets to the plays cost from $17 to $19; to concerts, $19 to $30. The in-town box office is at 14 S. Randolph St., between Nelson and Washington streets (© **540/463-3074;** www.theateratlimekiln.com). It's open Monday to Friday from 9am to 5pm. To reach the theater from downtown Lexington, take U.S. 11 south and turn right onto U.S. 60W.

You will pay as little as $4 for tickets to see both students and famous visiting artists in concerts, plays, and recitals in the **Lenfest Center for the Performing Arts,** on the W&L campus (© **540/458-8000;** www.wlu.edu). The schedule is released prior to each school year.

If you're here during the summer, catch a free **Friday Alive** concert in Davidson Park on East Nelson Street. Rock, reggae, and other bands make outdoor music on Fridays from 5:30 to 8:30pm. You can also relive the 1950s at **Hull's Drive-In,** 4 miles north of downtown on U.S. 11 (© **540/436-2621;** www. hullsdrivein.com), one of the nation's few remaining outdoor movie theaters. It shows double features Friday, Saturday, and Sunday nights from April through October.

8

Roanoke & the Southwest Highlands

You soon notice after leaving the vibrant, railroad-oriented city of Roanoke that I-81 begins climbing into the mountains as it heads into the Southwest Highlands, Virginia's increasingly narrow "tail" hemmed in by West Virginia, Kentucky, Tennessee, and North Carolina. You don't come down on the other side of the mountain, however, for I-81 will deposit you instead in the Great Valley of Virginia, whose floor averages 2,000 feet in altitude. Just as they delineate the Shenandoah Valley, the Blue Ridge Mountains form the eastern boundary of the Southwest Highlands. But while peaks above 4,000 feet are rare in the Shenandoah, here they regularly exceed that altitude, with Mount Rogers reaching 5,729 feet, the highest point in Virginia.

Thousands of acres of this beautiful country are preserved in the Jefferson National Forest and in Mount Rogers National Recreation Area, which rivals the Shenandoah National Park with 300 miles of hiking and riding trails, including a stretch of the Appalachian Trail. Two other major routes, the Virginia Creeper and New River Trails, lure hikers and bikers along old railroad beds by river banks.

The Highlanders are justly proud of their history, which includes Daniel Boone's following the Wilderness Road through the mountains, plateaus, and hollows to Cumberland Gap and on into Kentucky. Gorgeous Abingdon and other small towns still have log cabins from those frontier days.

The Highlanders have also preserved their traditional arts, crafts, and renowned mountain music. Abingdon hosts both Virginia's official state theater and the Highlands Festival, one of America's top annual arts and crafts shows. The famous Carter family makes mountain music at tiny Maces Spring, and fiddlers from around the world gather every August for their old-time convention at Galax.

Whether you love history, drama, music, arts, crafts, the great outdoors, or all of the above, you will be enchanted with Virginia's beautiful Southwest Highlands.

EXPLORING THE SOUTHWEST HIGHLANDS

VISITOR INFORMATION   A one-stop source for regional information is the **Highlands Gateway Visitor Center,** 975 Tazewell St., Wytheville, VA 24382 (© **800/446-9670;** www.virginiablueridge.org), which shares space with the Wytheville Convention and Visitors Bureau (see section 3, below). It offers brochures from all towns in the region and sells National Forest and Appalachian Trail topographical maps and guidebooks. The center is open Monday through Saturday from 9am to 5pm.

GETTING THERE & GETTING AROUND   Given the distances, the lack of public transportation, and the need to be able to explore the area's spectacular scenery at leisure, traveling by **car** is the only way to go. I-81 runs the entire length of the highlands and is its major thoroughfare. U.S. 11 follows I-81, and the Blue Ridge Parkway parallels it to the east. I-77 cuts north-south through the center of the region (the section from Wytheville north to Bluefield, West Virginia, is one of America's most scenic interstates). Otherwise, byways in the region are mountain roads—narrow, winding, and sometimes steep—so give yourself ample time to reach your destination.

The area's only air gateway is Roanoke Regional Airport (see "Getting There by Plane" under "Roanoke: City Below a Star," below). The nearest **Amtrak (© 800/ 872-7245;** www.amtrak.com) station is in Clifton Forge, 45 miles northwest of Roanoke on I-64. Amtrak has a bus connection from Clifton Forge to Roanoke.

1 The Blue Ridge Parkway ★

Maintained by the National Park Service, Blue Ridge Parkway, in effect, is a continuation of the 105-mile-long Skyline Drive in the Shenandoah National Park, running another 469 miles southwest through the Blue Ridge Mountains to the Great Smoky Mountains National Park in North Carolina. Magnificent vistas and the natural beauty of the forests, wildlife, and wildflowers combine with pioneer history to make this a scenic and fascinating route.

Unlike the Skyline Drive, which is surrounded by a national park, the parkway, for most of its route, runs through mountain meadows, farmland, and forests (some, but not all, national forests). Nature hikes, camping, and other activities are largely confined to the visitor centers and to more than 200 overlooks. There are about 100 **hiking trails** along the route, including the Appalachian Trail, which follows the parkway from Mile 0 to about Mile 103.

In Virginia, the 62-mile stretch between Otter Creek and Roanoke Mountain is the best part. It crosses the James River Gorge and climbs Apple Orchard Mountain, the highest parkway point in Virginia (elevation 3,950 ft.). At times, the road here follows the ridgeline, rendering spectacular views down both sides of the mountains at once. It also passes the peaceful Peaks of Otter Lodge, the only place actually on the parkway where you can spend the night (see "Accommodations," below).

South of Roanoke, the parkway runs through lower country, with more meadows and less mountain scenery.

JUST THE FACTS

ACCESS POINTS & ORIENTATION   The northern parkway entrance is near Waynesboro at the southern end of the Skyline Drive, on U.S. 250 at Exit 99 off I-64. The major access points in Virginia are U.S. 60 east of Buena Vista; U.S. 501 between Buena Vista and Lynchburg (Otter Creek and the James River Gorge); U.S. 460, Va. 24, U.S. 220 and the Mill Mountain Spur near Roanoke; U.S. 58 at Meadows of Dan; and I-77 at Fancy Gap.

Mile Posts on the west side of the parkway begin with Mile 0 at the northern Rockfish Gap entry and increase as you head south. The North Carolina border is at Mile 218.

INFORMATION   For general information, contact the **National Park Service (NPS),** 199 Hemphill Knob Rd., Asheville, NC 28801 (© **828/298-0398;** www.nps.gov/blri). Ask for a copy of the NPS's brochure with an excellent map of the parkway, and the *Parkway Milepost,* a quarterly tabloid newspaper with articles about the parkway and a schedule of events. Both are available at the visitor centers, which also sell books about the parkway.

The Southwest Highlands

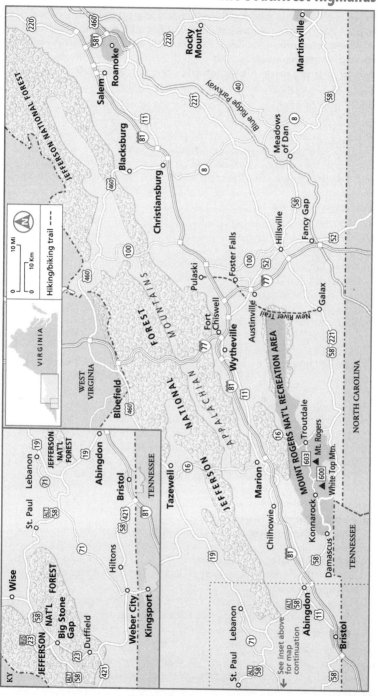

You can also get an information packet, including a copy of the indispensable *Blue Ridge Parkway Directory & Travel Planner,* from the **Blue Ridge Parkway Association,** P.O. Box 2136, Asheville, NC 28802 (© **828/298-0398;** www.blueridgeparkway.org).

EMERGENCIES Call © **800/PARK-WATCH** in case of emergencies anywhere along the parkway.

FEES, REGULATIONS & BACKCOUNTRY PERMITS There is no fee for using the parkway. Maximum speed limit is 45 mph in rural areas, 35 mph in built-up zones. Bicycles are allowed on paved roads and parking areas, not on any trails. Camping is permitted in designated areas (see "Camping," below). Fires are permitted in campgrounds and picnic areas only. Hunting is prohibited. Pets must be kept on a leash. No swimming is allowed in parkway ponds and lakes.

VISITOR CENTERS Several visitor centers along the parkway are the focal points of most visitor activities, including ranger programs. The **Rockfish Gap Visitor Center,** at the northern end (Mile 0), is open year-round. Others are closed from November to March. Hours for all are 9am to 5pm daily. Here's a run-down heading south:

Humpback Rocks Visitor Center (Mile 5.8) has picnic tables, restrooms, and a self-guiding trail to a reconstructed mountain homestead.

James River Visitor Center (Mile 63.6), near U.S. 501 northwest of Lynchburg, is worth a stop. It has a footbridge that crosses the river to the restored canal locks, exhibits, and a nature trail. The nearby Otter Creek wayside has a daytime restaurant and campground just up the road.

Peaks of Otter (Mile 85.9), at Va. 43 northwest of Bedford, is the most picturesque visitors center. It has a 2-mile hike to the site of a historic farm, wildlife and Native American exhibits, restrooms, and the Peaks of Otter Lodge (see "Accommodations," below), which sits beside a gorgeous lake wedged between two cone-shaped mountains—the Peaks of Otter. A trail leads to the top of Sharp Top, the tallest of the two at 3,875 feet, Weather permitting, a **shuttle bus** runs to within 1,500 feet of the peak. It's a strenuous 1.6-mile hike to the summit, so allow 3 hours for the total excursion. Needless to say, wear comfortable walking shoes and bring water. The bus runs May through October, daily from 10am to 4pm, every hour on the hour. Buy your tickets and water at the camp store (© **540/586-1614**) beside the visitor center. Round-trip fares are $4.50 for adults, $3 for children under 13.

Virginia's Explore Park (Mile 115) is on the grounds of the living history museum on the outskirts of Roanoke (see "Roanoke," below).

Rocky Knob (Mile 167.1), southeast of Va. 8, has some 15 miles of hiking trails (including the Rock Castle Gorge National Recreational Trail), a comfort station, and picnic area.

Mabry Mill (Mile 176), between Va. 8 and U.S. 58, has a picturesque gristmill with a giant wheel spanning a little stream. Displays of pioneer life, including crafts demonstrations, are featured, and the restored mill still grinds flour. A restaurant, open May through October, adjoins it.

SEASONS The parkway is at its best during spring, when the wildflowers bloom and leaves are multi-hued green, and during mid-October, when changing leaves are at their blazing best (and traffic is at its heaviest). Winter is not a good time, since most facilities are closed, and snow, ice, and fog can close the road.

ON THE WINE TRAIL   At Mile 171.5, between Va. 8 and U.S. 58 north of Mabry Mill, you can turn off on C.R. 726 and follow the signs to **Chateau Morrisette** (© 540/593-2865; www.chateaumorrisette.com), a vineyard which produces Black Dog and Our Dog Blue, two of Virginia's most popular red wines. It's open for tastings and sales Monday to Thursday 10am to 5pm, Friday and Saturday 10am to 6pm, Sunday 11am to 5pm. A restaurant on premises is open for lunch Wednesday to Sunday, for dinner on Friday and Saturday (it's open daily during the October leaf season).

CAMPING

The visitor centers at **Otter Creek,** Mile 60.8 (© 804/299-5125); **Peaks of Otter,** Mile 86 (© 540/586-4357); **Roanoke Mountain,** Mile 120.4 (© 540/982-9242); and **Rocky Knob,** Mile 174.1 (© 540/745-9664) all have campgrounds. The Roanoke Mountain campground is actually on Mill Mountain, about 1 mile west of the parkway above Roanoke (see "Roanoke: City Below a Star," below).

Campgrounds are open from about May 1 to early November, depending on weather conditions. Drinking water and restrooms are available, but shower and laundry facilities are not. There are tent and trailer sites, but none have utility connections. Sites cost $14 a night. Golden Age and Golden Access Passport holders are entitled to a 50% discount. Daily permits are valid only at the campground where purchased.

Cabins are available at **Rocky Knob Cabins,** Meadows of Dan, VA 24120 (© 540/593-3903).

ACCOMMODATIONS

Peaks of Otter Lodge ★ *Value*   Split-rail fences and small footbridges add to the picturesque beauty of this serene, lakeside lodge nestled in a gorgeous valley between two mountain peaks. The main lodge building has a restaurant, a crafts and gift shop, and a game and TV room with a view of the lake. On a grassy slope overlooking the lake, accommodations are in motel-like units a 600- to 900-foot walk from the main building (bring an umbrella and insect repellent). Virtually identical, the rooms have private balconies or terraces to maximize the splendid view, but you will not have a TV or phones (folks come up here to literally get away from it all). Reservations are accepted beginning October 1 for the *following* year's fall foliage season. Winter and early spring are not overly crowded, but reservations should be made 4 to 6 weeks ahead for all good-weather months. The parkway's Peaks of Otter visitor center, with its ranger programs and shuttle bus up Sharp Top Mountain, is within walking distance (see "Just the Facts," above).

Milepost 86 (P.O. Box 489), Bedford, VA 24523. © 800/542-5927 (in Virginia and North Carolina) or 540/586-1081. Fax 540/586-4420. www.peaksofotter.com. 63 units. $61–$93 double. MC, V. **Amenities:** Restaurant; bar. *In room:* A/C, no phone.

2 Roanoke: City Below a Star ★

54 miles SW of Lexington; 74 miles NE of Wytheville; 193 miles SW of Richmond; 251 miles SW of Washington, D.C.

Sprawling across the floor of the Roanoke Valley, Virginia's largest metropolitan area west of Richmond likes to call itself the "Capital of the Blue Ridge." It's also known as "Star City," for the huge lighted star overlooking the city from Mill Mountain, which stands between it and the Blue Ridge Parkway.

There was no star on the mountain when Colonial explorers followed the Roanoke River gorge through the Blue Ridge Mountains in the 17th century. They established several settlements in the Roanoke Valley, including one named Big Lick. When the Norfolk and Western Railroad arrived in the 1880s and laid out a town for future development, it decided that *Roanoke*—a Native American word for "shell money"—was a more prosperous-sounding name for the new city.

Although Roanoke is still a major railroad junction (as the many tracks running through downtown will attest), its economy suffered when the interstate highway system shifted most freight from boxcars to trucks in the mid–20th century. Milestones in its Renaissance have been the construction of the Civic Center and a convention and cultural complex, and the restoration of the Market Square area around the Historic City Market. With its museums, theater, and trendy restaurants, Market Square serves as the focal point for both daytime activities and lively after-dark entertainment.

With its zoo, its hands-on museums, and a fine living-history facility at Virginia's Explore Park, Roanoke also has special appeal for children. Families can easily spend a day and more exploring its sights.

ESSENTIALS
VISITOR INFORMATION
Contact the **Roanoke Convention and Visitors Bureau,** 101 Shenandoah Ave. NE, Roanoke, VA 24016 (© **800/635-5535** or 540/342-6025; fax 540/342-7119; www.visitroanokeva.com), in the recently restored Norfolk & Western train station just across the tracks from Market Square (which it shares with the new O. Winston Link Museum). The bureau's new visitor center is the best place to pick up maps and brochures for walking and biking tours before starting to explore Roanoke, and you can make same-day hotel reservations here. Be sure to watch the 8-minute video about the valley. The center is open daily from 9am to 5pm.

If you're arriving via the Blue Ridge Parkway, the **Blue Ridge Parkway Visitor Center** at Virginia's Explore Park, at Mile 115 (© **540/427-5871**), is open from May through mid-November, daily 9am to 5pm. See "Attractions on or near Mill Mountain," below.

GETTING THERE
BY PLANE   **Roanoke Regional Airport** (© **540/362-1999;** www.roanoke regionalairport.com), 5½ miles northwest of downtown off Hershberger Road (Exit 3E off I-581), is served by Delta Connection, Northwest Airlink, United Express, and US Airways. The major car-rental units have booths on-site. **Roanoke Airport Limousine Service** (© **800/228-1958** or 540/345-7710) runs vans to downtown and to points as far away as Abingdon (see section 5, below) and throughout the Shenandoah Valley (see chapter 7, "The Shenandoah Valley.")

BY CAR   From I-81, take I-581 (exit 143) south into the heart of Roanoke. I-581 becomes U.S. 220; together, they form an expressway that passes all the way through town. The Blue Ridge Parkway runs along the top of the mountains east of the city; the major Roanoke exits are at U.S. 460, Va. 24, the Mill Mountain Spur Road (at Mile 120), and U.S. 220.

BY TRAIN   Amtrak (© **800/872-7245;** www.amtrak.com) provides Thruway bus connections daily between Roanoke and its stations in Lynchburg to the east (see chapter 6, "Charlottesville") and to the west at Clifton Forge, on I-64 west of Lexington. Either is about an hour's bus ride away.

Roanoke

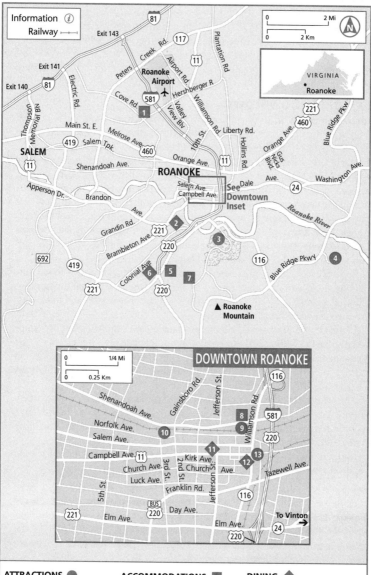

Information ⓘ
Railway ⊢——⊣

Exit 143

Exit 141
Exit 140
81

VIRGINIA
• Roanoke

81
117
Roanoke Airport
581

Peters Creek Rd.
Airport Rd.
Cove Rd.
Hershberger R
Williamson Rd.
Plantation Rd.

Electric Rd.
Thompson Memorial BN
Main St. E.
419 Salem Tpk.
Melrose Ave.
460
SALEM
11
Shenandoah Ave.
Liberty Rd.
Hollins Rd.
ROANOKE
Orange Ave.
Gus Nicks Blvd.
221
460
Blue Ridge Pkw

Apperson Dr.
Brandon
Salem Ave.
Campbell Ave.
See Downtown Inset
Dale Ave.
24
Washington Ave.
Orange Ave.

Grandin Rd.
Ave.
221
220
692
419
Colonial Ave.
221
220

Roanoke River
116
Blue Ridge Pkwy
4

▲ Roanoke Mountain

DOWNTOWN ROANOKE

0 1/4 Mi
0 0.25 Km

Shenandoah Ave.
Gainsboro Rd.
Jefferson St.
116
581

Norfolk Ave.
Salem Ave.
Williamson Rd.
220

Campbell Ave.
11
Kirk Ave.
3rd St.
2nd St.
Church Ave.
Luck Ave.
Church Ave.
Jefferson St.
Tazewell Ave.

5th St.
Franklin Rd.
116

221
Elm Ave.
BUS 220
Day Ave.
Elm Ave.
220

To Vinton →
24

ATTRACTIONS ●
Center in the Square **13**
Market Square **13**
Mill Mountain Park
  & Zoo **3**
O. Winston Link Museum **9**
Virginia Museum of
  Transportation **10**
Virginia's Explore Park **4**

ACCOMMODATIONS ■
Colony House
  Motor Lodge **5**
Hotel Roanoke &
  Conference Center **8**
Roanoke Mountain
  Campground **7**
Wyndham Roanoke Airport **1**

DINING ◆
Alexander's **11**
Buck Mountain Grille **6**
Corned Beef & Co.
  Bar & Grill **11**
Metro! **12**
The Roanoker Restaurant **2**

GETTING AROUND

Yellow Cab (© 540/345-7711) is the largest taxi company here. **Valley Metro** provides public bus service Monday through Saturday from 5:45am to 8:45pm. The downtown transfer point is Campbell Court, 17 W. Campbell Ave. Call © 540/982-2222 for schedules and fares. The visitor center distributes free Ride Guide route maps.

EXPLORING DOWNTOWN

Market Square ✪ in the center of downtown at Market Street and Campbell Avenue, is Roanoke's answer to Georgetown in Washington, D.C., and Shockoe Slip in Richmond. As they have for more than a century, stands and shops at the **Historic City Market** display plants, flowers, fresh fruits and vegetables, dairy and eggs, and farm-cured meats (Sat morning is the best time to visit). Nearby, restored Victorian-era storefronts house an eclectic mix of trendy restaurants, gift shops, tattoo parlors, art galleries, antiques dealers, an Orvis outdoor-wear outlet, and pawn shops. Of special note are two spiffed-up relics from the past: **Agnew Seed Store,** which still uses its old-fashioned oak drawers, and **Wertz's Country Store,** carrying a gourmet selection of local produce, which its restaurant puts to good use (see "Where to Dine," below).

Built of red brick in 1922, the **Market Building** now houses a food court offering the downtown lunch crowd an inexpensive international menu, from Chinese egg rolls to North Carolina–style barbecue. The market and food court are open Monday through Saturday.

Center in the Square, the big modern building on Market Square at Campbell Avenue (© 540/342-5700; www.centerinthesquare.org), is home to the Art Museum of Western Virginia, the History Museum of Western Virginia, and the Science Museum of Western Virginia (see below), as well as the Mill Mountain Theatre (see "Roanoke After Dark," later).

An enclosed walkway leads over the railroad tracks from Market Square to the visitor's center and the new O. Winston Link Museum, both in the city's recently restored train station. It sits in front of the Hotel Roanoke & Conference Center, itself a sightseeing attraction (see "Where to Stay," later).

Also from Market Square, you can follow the O. Winston Link Railwalk beside the tracks to the Virginia Museum of Transportation.

Art Museum of Western Virginia This fine regional museum focuses on 19th-and 20th-century American art and decorative arts, including works by artists from throughout the South. There's a very good museum store here. Call or check the website for special exhibits such as tours, gallery walks, and family days.

1 Market Square, in Center in the Square. © 540/342-5760. www.artmuseumroanoke.org. Free admission (docent-led tours available for a fee). Tues–Sat 10am–5pm; Sun 1–4:30pm.

History Museum of Western Virginia Documents, tools, costumes, and weapons tell the story of Roanoke from American Indian days 10,000 years ago through pioneer days 2 centuries ago to the present. The museum shop carries historic items, wooden and tin toys, and locally made quilts.

1 Market Square, in Center in the Square. © 540/342-5770. www.history-museum.org. Admission $2 adults, $1 seniors and children 6–12, free for children 5 and under. Tues–Fri 10am–4pm; Sat 10am–5pm; Sun 1–5pm.

O. Winston Link Museum In the restored art moderne Norfolk & Western railway station, this museum is devoted to the extraordinary black-and-white railroad photography of the late O. Winston Link. Born in Brooklyn, NY, in

---

Tips A Ford's-Eye View of Roanoke

Weather permitting, you can tool all the way up Mill Mountain in a 1924 Model-T truck owned and operated by Bob Hudson (✆ **540/389-4392**), who charges $8 per person. It's a good way to get a Ford's-eye view of Roanoke. Look for Bob outside the Virginia Museum of Transportation.

1914 of parents who hailed from Virginia and West Virginia, Link took his first photos of N&W locomotives in 1955 while on another assignment in Staunton. For the next 5 years, he traced the railroad's tracks, taking thousands of pictures of steam locomotives just before diesel-powered models replaced most of them. His most dramatic shots came at night. The museum, which he helped design, has 190 signed prints, 85 estate prints, and more than 2,400 of his negatives. Along with the Virginia Museum of Transportation (see below), this is a must-see for railroad buffs—and everyone else with an interest in photography.

101 Shenandoah Ave. (in old train station). ✆ 540/857-4394. www.linkmuseum.org. Admission $5 adults, $4 seniors, $3 children 3–7, free for children 2 and under. Includes admission to History Museum of Western Virginia through 2004. Mon–Sat 10am–5pm; Sun noon–5pm.

Science Museum of Western Virginia/Hopkins Planetarium   Children will be intrigued with the high-tech interactive exhibits here. A weather gallery features a tornado simulator and a Weather Channel–like studio. Other permanent galleries have hands-on exhibits in physics, geology, and the human body. The Hopkins Planetarium offers programs related to the stars, planets, and galaxies; the MegaDome Theatre shows large format 70mm films. The museum store on the ground level offers a fascinating collection of educational toys.

1 Market Square, in Center in the Square. ✆ 540/342-5710. www.smwv.org. Exhibits admission $7 adults, $6 seniors, $5 children 3–12, free for children 2 and under. Combination exhibits and planetarium shows $8 adults, $7 seniors, $6 children 3–12. Tues–Sat 10am–5pm; Sun 1–5pm.

Virginia Museum of Transportation ★★ *Kids*   In a restored freight depot 5 blocks west of Market Square, this wide-ranging museum has aviation, automotive, space, and canal exhibits, but it's best feature is an extraordinary collection of vintage locomotives, passenger and mail cars, and cabooses on display under the Claytor Pavilion's big roof out back. You can climb aboard some of them, get up close and personal with others, but the best way to see them is on a guided tour of the rail yard (call for times). Also out back, a playground will keep the kids occupied riding in model trains, cars, and a helicopter. Inside, they will get a kick out of a gargantuan and very real model railroad, and can learn about the effects of motion in the Star Station, which the museum best describes as "a petting zoo of transportation artifacts." You'll need an hour to 2½ hours to thoroughly digest all the exhibits.

303 Norfolk Ave. (at 3rd St.). ✆ 540/342-5670. www.vmt.org. Admission $7 adults, $6 seniors, $5 children 3–11, free for children 2 and under. Mon–Fri 11am–4pm; Sat 10am–5pm; Sun noon–5pm. Rail yard closes 30 min. earlier.

ATTRACTIONS ON OR NEAR MILL MOUNTAIN

Situated between the city and the Blue Ridge Parkway, Mill Mountain offers panoramic views over Roanoke Valley. The two main attractions are in **Mill Mountain Park,** on the Mill Mountain Parkway Spur, a winding road that leaves the Blue Ridge Parkway at Mile 120. From the city, take Walnut Avenue, which becomes the J.P. Fishburn Parkway and intersects the Mill Mountain Parkway Spur at the entry to Mill Mountain Park.

Local citizens know they're home when they see the white neon **Roanoke Star on the Mountain.** Erected in 1949 as a civic project, it stands 88½ feet tall, uses 2,000 feet of neon tubing, and is visible from most parts of the city. Stop at the base for a magnificent view over the city and valley.

Mill Mountain Zoo *(Kids)* One of the two accredited zoos in Virginia (the Virginia Zoo in Norfolk being the other; see chapter 11), this one is home to more than 50 animal species, including snow and clouded leopards, monkeys, prairie dogs, hawks, red pandas, Japanese macaques and a bald eagle. It's star is "Ruby," a solitary Siberian tiger. **ZooChoo,** an open-air, narrow gauge train, runs around the periphery, giving access to red wolves and deer, which the walking paths don't. You'll need about 1½ hours up here.

Mill Mountain Pkwy. Spur (in Mill Mountain Park). ℂ **540/343-3241.** www.mmzoo.org. Admission $6.50 adults, $5.85 seniors, $4.25 children 2–12, free for children 1 and under. Train rides $2. Daily 10am–5pm.

Virginia's Explore Park *(★)* It's a scenic 7-mile drive from Mill Mountain to this a 1,100-acre reserve astride the gorge cut by the Roanoke River on its way through the Blue Ridge. Like the Frontier Culture Museum in Staunton (see chapter 7), the Historic Areas of the park feature reconstructed settlements with costumed re-enactors who explain what life was like in these parts around 1671, 1740, and 1850. This is much more of an adventure, however, for the settlements are on the forested slopes of the steep gorge. If you and your small children are not up to the strenuous, 1¾-mile walk, staff-driven golf carts will take you up and down. In addition to the settlements, a crewman down by the river explains life on a bateau, a flat bottom boat used for river transport before railroads. Begin at the welcome center, where a 13-minute video will set the scene. Then allow about 2 hours for a self-guided tour of the historic areas. You can take a break at the moderately priced Brugh Tavern (appropriately pronounced "Brew"), which serves bag lunches.

More than 800 acres of the park's hills and wetlands have been set aside as a natural area. You can hike or mountain bike on 12 miles of trails, and canoe or fish on the river. On-site bike and canoe rentals are available.

Mile Post 115, Blue Ridge Pkwy. ℂ **800/842-9163** or 540/427-1800. www.explorepark.org. Museum admission $8 adults, $6 seniors, $4.50 children 3–11, free for children 2 and under. Recreation fee $3 per person. Grounds open year-round, daily 8am–sunset. Historic areas, May–Oct Wed–Sun 10am–5pm. Brugh Tavern, May–Oct Wed–Sun 11am–5pm. From Mill Mountain, take Mill Mountain Pkwy. Spur to Blue Ridge Pkwy., turn left, go to Mile Post 115, turn right on Roanoke River Pkwy. to park.

WHERE TO STAY

If you're coming off the Blue Ridge Parkway, convenient choices include the **Holiday Inn Tanglewood** (ℂ **800/HOLIDAY** or 540/774-4400) and **Hampton Inn Tanglewood** (ℂ **800/HAMPTON** or 540/989-4000), both on Franklin Road near U.S. 220 southeast of downtown. A **Sleep Inn** is between them at 4045 Electric Rd. (ℂ **800/628-1929** or 540/772-1500).

Near the airport, Hershberger Road (Exit 3 off I-581) has the **Best Western at Valley View** (ℂ **800/362-2410** or 540/362-2400), and **Clarion Hotel** (ℂ **800/ CLARION** or 540/362-4500). Farther out, Peters Creek Road (Exit 2 off I-581) has a new **Courtyard by Marriott** (ℂ **800/321-2211** or 540/563-5002), a **Hampton Inn** (ℂ **800/HAMPTON** or 540/265-2600), the **Holiday Inn Airport** (ℂ **800/HOLIDAY** or 540/366-8861), and an inexpensive **Super 8 Roanoke** (ℂ **800/800-8000** or 540/563-8888).

Colony House Motor Lodge *Value*   This clean, well-maintained motel enjoys a convenient suburban location in the Tanglewood shopping area, 2 miles south of downtown and 2 miles north of the Blue Ridge Parkway. A series of peaked roofs creates cathedral ceilings in some of the spacious rooms, all of which have louvered screen doors that let in fresh air without sacrificing privacy. About half the rooms are at the rear of the property; they face a steep hillside and get less light but also less traffic noise. About half the rooms have refrigerators and microwave ovens. A small roadside outdoor swimming pool has a view of the K-Mart across Franklin Road. Continental breakfast is served on the premises, and there's a 24-hour Waffle House next door. For lunch and dinner, the excellent Buck Mountain Grille is across the street (see "Where to Dine," below).

3560 Franklin Rd. (U.S. 220 Business), Roanoke, VA 24014. ✆ **866/203-5850** or 540/345-0411. Fax 540/345-1137. 72 units. $62 double. Rates include continental breakfast. AE, DC, DISC, MC, V. From I-581/U.S. 220, exit at Franklin Rd. (U.S. 220 Business), turn left at traffic signal to motel on right. From Blue Ridge Pkwy. take U.S. 220 Business west, exit on Franklin Rd. north to motel on right. **Amenities:** Outdoor pool; health club; business center; laundry service; coin-op washers and dryers. *In room:* A/C, TV, dataport, fridge (some units).

Hotel Roanoke & Conference Center ★★★   The Norfolk and Western Railroad built this grand Tudor-style hotel in 1882 on a hill overlooking its new town, even before it changed the name from Big Lick to Roanoke. Heated by steam from the railroad's maintenance shops and cooled by America's first hotel air-conditioning system (which cooled the rooms with circulating ice water), it became a resort as well as a stopover. Some 26 passenger trains a day rolled into the station at the foot of the hill, and virtually every celebrity passing though Roanoke stayed here, among them Elvis Presley and Presidents Eisenhower, Nixon, Ford, Reagan, and the elder Bush. For the locals, it was *the* place for wedding receptions, reunions, beauty pageants, and other special events.

The hotel fell on hard times and was closed from 1989 to 1995, when it reopened after a magnificent, $42 million restoration financed in part by local residents who dug into their pockets to save the venerable property. It's now recognized as a Historic Hotel of America, and Roanokers—who call it simply The Hotel—once again celebrate very special occasions in the elegant **Regency Room** (see "Where to Dine," below). Pub fare is available in the knotty **Pine Room,** which has a large bar, sports TV, and billiard table.

The building was gutted and rebuilt above the public areas, so all the rooms and suites are completely modern. Virginia Tech University, which along with the city of Roanoke owns the hotel, has installed high-speed and wireless Internet access throughout the building. Given the odd shape of the structure, there are now 92 room configurations, many with sloping ceilings and gable windows. Some have windows on two sides, while a few others seem like small cottages.

110 Shenandoah Ave., Roanoke, VA 24016. ✆ **800/222-TREE** or 540/985-5900. Fax 540/853-8264. www.hotelroanoke.com. 332 units. $84–$169 double; $159–$499 suite. Packages available. AE, DC, DISC, MC, V.

Tips **Worth a Look**

Even if you don't stay at the **Hotel Roanoke & Conference Center,** it's worth a walk over the railroad tracks just to see the rich, black walnut-paneled lobby with its Oriental rugs and leather lounge furniture. To the right, as you enter, is the oval-shaped Palm Court lounge with its four lovingly restored murals of colonial and Victorian Virginians dancing the reel, waltz, minuet, and quadrille.

Fun Fact   Dirty Dancing

Mountain Lake played the part of the Catskills resort in the movie *Dirty Dancing* starring Patrick Swayze.

Self-parking $5, valet parking $8. From I-581 south, take Exit 5, cross Wells Ave. into parking lot. **Amenities:** 2 restaurants; bar; outdoor pool; health club; concierge; business center; limited room service; laundry service; concierge-level rooms. *In room:* A/C, TV, dataport, coffeemaker, iron.

Wyndham Roanoke Hotel   With its hacienda-style public areas, the ambience at this eight-story hotel is more like Big Sur than Virginia. Its brick-accented lobby is adorned with decorative objects from Italy, France, and Spain, and Oriental rugs and a huge fireplace create a warm atmosphere. In two seven-story buildings, the spacious guest rooms are decorated with inlaid traditional furnishings of dark wood. Try to get an upper floor room, since they have great views of the valley. Also ask for one with sliding doors opening to a balcony. An inviting dining room with skylights and high ceilings is open for all meals, and there's a lobby bar and entertainment lounge. Your small pet can stay with you here.

2801 Hershberger Rd. NW, Roanoke, VA 24017. ℭ 800/WYNDHAM or 540/563-9300. Fax 540/366-5846. www.wyndham.com/roanoke. 320 units. $99–$159 double. Weekend rates available. AE, DC, DISC, MC, V. Free parking. Pets accepted ($25 fee). From I-581 south, take Exit 3, Hershberger Rd. west; make a right U-turn at the first light; the hotel is on the service road. **Amenities:** Restaurant; bar; indoor and outdoor pool; 2 tennis courts; health club; Jacuzzi; sauna; concierge; limited room service; concierge-level rooms. *In room:* A/C, TV, dataport, coffeemaker, iron.

A NEARBY MOUNTAIN RESORT

Mountain Lake Hotel   Surrounded by a 2,600-acre wildlife conservancy, this rustic mountaintop resort consists of a stately, rough-cut-stone lodge with clusters of small, white-clapboard summer cottages nearby. The lobby has thick rugs over a terra-cotta tile floor and comfortable seating in front of a massive fireplace. Complimentary tea and coffee are kept hot on the sideboard. A stone archway separates the lobby from the adjoining bar and lounge. The spacious, stone-walled dining room has large windows offering panoramic lake views—a romantic evening setting. There's also a snack bar in the Recreation Barn.

The popular parlor suites have Jacuzzis and fireplaces, and some rooms offer lake views. Dark-wood Chippendale-reproduction furnishings give the decor a traditional look. Cottages are more simply furnished, although guests enjoy kitchens and porches with rockers. Chestnut Lodge is a three-story gray-clapboard building set on the side of a hill. Rooms here are decorated in country style, with fireplaces and balconies. You'll have a phone and coffeemaker but no TV or other modern amenity in your unit.

Pembrooke, VA 24136. ℭ 800/346-3334 or 540/626-7121. Fax 540/626-7172. www.mountainlakehotel.com. 101 units, including 22 cottages. Main hotel $190 double; Chestnut Lodge $230 double. Children 12 and older in parent's unit are charged $35 per day; ages 4–11, $20; ages 3 and under free. Rates include breakfast and dinner. AE, DC, DISC, MC, V. Closed Nov–Apr. From I-81, take Exit 118B, U.S. 460 west; turn right onto C.R. 700 and go 7 miles to Mountain Lake. **Amenities:** Restaurant; bar; outdoor pool; tennis court; Jacuzzi; sauna; watersports equipment/rentals; bike rentals; game room; children's programs; shopping arcade; massage; coin-op washers and dryers. *In room:* Kitchen (cottages only), coffeemaker.

WHERE TO DINE

Roanoke is becoming one of Virginia's most interesting dining scenes, with exciting new restaurants opening their doors all over town. While you can still get good country cooking here (including the state's best biscuits), young chefs are using flavors their Southern ancestors probably never heard of, much less tasted.

DOWNTOWN RESTAURANTS

Market Square (see "Exploring Downtown," above) is Roanoke's dining center, with the 3 blocks of Campbell Avenue between Williamson Road and Jefferson Street, and the contiguous block of Jefferson Street, offering a host of restaurants catering to many tastes and all pocketbooks. A new establishment seems to join the ranks every month, so take a stroll and a see what's happening (most post their menus outside).

Behind the stalls on Market Street, **Wertz's Country Store, Restaurant & Wine Bar** (© 540/342-5133) uses the store's gourmet produce in sandwiches and salads at lunch, while tender, 21-day aged steaks appear along with seafood and pasta dishes at dinner. Its wine cellar is one of the city's best. And Virginia Tech's successful football coach Frank Beamer has opened a branch of his **Beamer's** steakhouse at the south end of the market at 315 Market St. (© 540/345-5000; www. beamerball.com).

Alexander's ⭐⭐ NEW AMERICAN   In operation since 1979, Alexander's was the first trendy restaurant to open during downtown's Renaissance, and it's still one of the best. The pinkish lighting, widely spaced tables, and extraordinarily attentive wait staff make this a great place for special occasions. The New American menu blends the classics with flavors from Louisiana, Asia, and the Mediterranean. Veal Alexander, with lump crab meat and a Hollandaise sauce, is a regular, as is shrimp *étouffée* with grits cakes, which will exercise your taste buds. On the way out, you can buy some of the special spices the chef uses, or perhaps a "Phantom of the Okra" T-shirt.

105 Jefferson St. (between Campbell and Salem aves.). © 540/982-6983. Reservations recommended. Main courses $15–$28. AE, MC, V. Wed 11am–2pm; Tues–Thurs 5–9pm; Fri–Sat 5–10pm.

Corned Beef & Co. Bar and Grill AMERICAN   A block west of Market Square, this lively sports-bar emporium—the largest one its kind I've ever seen—occupies half a city block. There's a sophisticated billiard parlor and beaucoup TV screens for watching every game being televised at the moment. You can even watch from a rooftop patio during warm weather. Having a good time is the main reason to come here (it literally overflows with young folk on Friday and Saturday nights). Nevertheless, the chow is better than average pub fare: deli sandwiches (including the namesake corned beef), salads, wood-fired pizzas, and main courses such as chicken "diablo" (a breast piqued with Texas Pete hot sauce).

107 Jefferson St. (between Campbell and Salem aves.). © 540/342-3354. Reservations accepted. Salads, sandwiches, burgers $5–$9; pizzas $8–$12; main courses $10–$16. AE, DC, DISC, MC, V. Mon–Sat 11:30am–midnight (bar open to 2am).

Metro! ⭐⭐ *Finds* ECLECTIC   The big city came to Roanoke when this sophisticated restaurant and lounge opened in 2003. You can watch the chefs scurrying around the open kitchen through the big storefront windows on Campbell Avenue, but wander on in for a drink and some sushi at the large martini bar, which dominates the main dining room. Most of the city's well-heeled young professionals will be here, especially on weekend nights, when the tables are pushed aside after 11pm and Metro! becomes a South Beach–style lounge with dancing. Beforehand, the kitchen provides a wide range of exciting fare, from sushi and sashimi to Thai-style shrimp whose coconut-curry sauce will bite the back of your palate. The teriyaki salmon wrapped in *nori* (seaweed), lightly breaded, sautéed, and served over a miso broth presents a marvelous fusion of Asian flavors. If the main courses are too dear for your credit card, the crab cake sandwich is less expensive way to sample this fine fare.

14 Campbell Ave. (between Market and Jefferson sts.). ℂ 540/345-6645. Reservations recommended, especially on weekends. Sandwiches $8–$14; sushi $4–$6; main courses $20–$28. Tasting menus $44–$77 per person. AE, DISC, MC, V. Mon–Sat 5–10pm (bar to 2am).

The Regency Room ★★★ INTERNATIONAL   The Hotel Roanoke & Conference Center's main dining room has long been Roanokers' favorite place for a special dinner, and with good reason. Fresh flowers adorn the widely spaced tables, and the wait staff wearing starched tunics provides the best service in town. The food lives up to the setting, too. The signature peanut soup has been around since 1940, and it provides a fitting—if fattening—entree to the crab cakes, which hold a half-pound of back-fin lumps, the best part of these tasty crustaceans. The chef makes some unusual uses of this and other Virginia produce, such as his Corn Cake Chesapeake, a cornbread cake under crabmeat, shrimp, oysters and scallops simmered in a Smithfield ham sauce. The Regency Room was 1 of only 58 winners of the 2002 Distinguished Restaurants of North America (DiRoNa) award. There's live music for dancing on Friday and Saturday nights.

In Hotel Roanoke & Conference Center, 110 Shenandoah Ave. ℂ 540/985-5900. Reservations recommended. Breakfast $6–$12; main courses $19–$33. AE, DC, DISC, MC. V. Daily 7–11:30am, noon–2pm, and 5–9pm.

OTHER RESTAURANTS

Buck Mountain Grille ★ INTERNATIONAL   Formerly located just off the Blue Ridge Parkway, but now closer to downtown, the Buck Mountain Grille still offers a mix of cuisine, with innovative new American and Mediterranean dishes predominating. Nightly specials feature Roanoke's freshest seafood, including outstanding crab cakes made with all back-fin meat. Vegetarians can choose from several offerings, and a children's menu is available. You'll find widely spaced tables and subdued lighting in its white building, which sits across Franklin Road from the Colony House Motor Lodge.

3603 Franklin Rd. (U.S. 220 Business; north of I-581/U.S. 220). ℂ 540/348-6455. Reservations recommended on weekends. Main courses $12–$25. AE, DC, DISC, MC, V. Mon–Sat 11am–10pm; Sun 11am–9pm. From downtown, take I-581/U.S. 220 south to 2nd Franklin Rd. exit; turn left to restaurant on left. From Blue Ridge Pkwy. take U.S. 220 west to 1st Franklin Rd. exit; turn right; restaurant is on left.

Roanoker Restaurant ★ (Value SOUTHERN   A popular local restaurant since 1941, the Roanoker occupies a colonial-style building surrounded by much-needed parking lots. Several dining rooms offer booth seating arranged to provide privacy. Antique signs from Roanoke businesses adorn the walls. At breakfast, the fluffy biscuits are Virginia's finest, either by themselves, wrapped around country ham or sausage, or covered in sausage gravy. Lunch and dinner specials change daily, depending on available produce. If you're lucky, the fresh vegetables will include skillet-fried yellow squash, a mouth-watering Southern favorite.

2522 Colonial Ave. (south of Wonju St.). ℂ 540/344-7746. Reservations not accepted. Breakfast $1.50–$7; sandwiches $3.50–$5; main courses $6–$12. MC, V. Mon–Thurs 7am–9pm; Fri–Sat 7am–10pm; Sun and holidays 8am–9pm. From downtown, go south on Franklin Rd., turn right on Brandon Ave., left on Colonial Ave. From I-581, go south to Colonial Ave. exit, turn left at traffic light on Colonial Ave. to restaurant on left.

ROANOKE AFTER DARK

Available at the visitor center (see "Essentials," earlier) and at many hotels and restaurants, the free *City Magazine* has a rundown of what's going on around town.

Mill Mountain Theatre, in the Center in the Square building on Campbell Avenue (© **800/317-6455** or 540/342-5740; www.millmountain.org), offers children's productions, free lunchtime readings (Oct–May), and year-round matinee and evening performances on two stages. Productions range from Shakespeare to minstrels. Recent performances have included *Joseph and the Amazing Technicolor Dreamcoat,* and *Keep on the Sunny Side.* Tickets prices range from $5 to $30, depending on performance and venue.

The **Roanoke Civic Center,** 710 Williamson Rd. NE (© **540/981-1201;** www.roanokeciviccenter.com), hosts visiting performers and concerts by **The Roanoke Symphony** (© **540/343-9127;** www.rso.com). From fall to spring you can watch the **Roanoke Express** (© **540/343-4500;** www.roanokeexpress.com), the city's minor-league hockey team, and the **Roanoke Dazzle** (© **540/266-1000;** www.roanokedazzle.com), a member of the National Basketball Association's developmental league.

Baseball fans can see the Class A **Salem Avalanche** (© **540/389-3333;** www.salemavalanche.com), an affiliate of the big-league Colorado Rockies, play in Salem, Roanoke's sister city.

The Market Square area running along Campbell Avenue to Jefferson Street is Roanoke's pub-crawling scene, especially on weekends when many restaurants and pubs have music and dancing. **Metro!** attracts the well-heeled young professional set, while **Corned Beef and Company** gets the sometimes rowdy masses (don't be surprised to see a cop or two across Jefferson St.). For a more refined experienced, **The Regency Room** in the Hotel Roanoke & Conference Center has live music and dancing on weekends.

3 Wytheville: Crossroads of the Highlands

74 miles SW of Roanoke; 49 miles NE of Abingdon; 306 miles SW of Washington, D.C.; 247 miles SW of Richmond

Situated on a relatively flat plateau, Wytheville's position in the center of the Highlands has made it a major crossroads since trappers and hunters came to the region in the early 1700s. After a treaty with hostile Native Americans opened Kentucky for settlement in 1775, Daniel Boone built the Wilderness Road through the Highlands to Cumberland Gap. Monroe Street in Wytheville was part of that route, and a few log cabins left over from those days still stand on Main Street.

An 1830s mayor decided Wytheville needed wide streets to keep fires from spreading, so while the town dates to 1757, the broad avenues deprive it of some quaintness and charm of other old towns like Lexington and Abingdon. But with I-81 and I-77 meeting here today, Wytheville has a motel room for every family in town, plus a host of chain restaurants to satisfy every taste. Since accommodations are relatively scarce elsewhere in this sparsely populated region, these facilities make Wytheville a well-equipped base from which to explore the New River Trail State Park, Mount Rogers National Recreation Area, and other sights in the central portion of the Highlands.

ESSENTIALS

VISITOR INFORMATION   For information, contact the **Wytheville Convention and Visitors Bureau,** 975 Tazewell St., Wytheville, VA 24382 (© **877/ 347-8307** or 276/223-3355; fax 276/223-3315; http://visit.wytheville.com), which supplies information about the town, including a walking-tour brochure to the historic district. To get here, take Exit 70 north off I-81, go north on 4th St. (U.S. 522), and turn left at the first traffic signal onto Tazewell Street. You'll find the Highlands Gateway Visitor Center here, too (see "Exploring the Southwest Highlands," above). Roadside tourist information gazebos are also located at all interstate exits leading into town.

GETTING THERE   I-81 and I-77 meet on the outskirts of Wytheville. To get into town, take Exits 67, 70, or 73 off I-81. U.S. 11 (Main St.) and U.S. 21 meet downtown.

EXPLORING THE TOWN

Stop at the convention and visitors bureau office for a walking-tour brochure about the town's historic buildings (see "Essentials," above).

With the South's only salt mine, and an important lead mine nearby (see "Outdoor Pursuits," below), Union troops attacked the crossroads village and burned many historic homes and businesses during the Civil War.

The Old Town area remained untouched, however, and you will want to examine its **Old Log Houses,** on Main Street (U.S. 11) between 5th and 7th streets. Some of them now house shops and an interesting restaurant (see "Where to Dine," below).

Another house that escaped Civil War destruction—but not bullet holes—was the **Rock House Museum,** at Monroe and Tazewell streets (© 276/223-3330). A National and State Historic Landmark, this Pennsylvania-style stone structure was built in 1820. The museum has a collection of historic artifacts from the region. Just behind the house on Tazewell Street, the **Thomas J. Boyd Museum** (same phone number) has exhibits on Wytheville's history, including an 1850s fire truck, Civil War relics, and farm equipment. Admission for either is $3 for adults, $1.50 for children 6 to 12, and free for children under 6. You can see them both for $5 adults, $2.50 for children. Both are open Tuesday through Friday from 10am to 4pm, Saturday from noon to 4pm, except that the Rock House Museum is closed during November.

Although it's not open to the public, upstairs in the building at 145 E. Main St., in the business district, was the **Birthplace of Edith Bolling Wilson,** second wife of Staunton-born President Woodrow Wilson.

Also, be on the lookout for the new **Homestead Museum,** which is scheduled to open next to the visitor center.

NEW RIVER TRAIL STATE PARK ★★

With its plethora of accommodations, Wytheville is an excellent base from which to hike, bike, or ride horses on the exceptional **New River Trail,** which runs for 57 miles between Galax and Pulaski. The trail follows an old railroad bed beside the New River, which, despite its name, is in geologic terms, one of the oldest rivers in the United States (it predates the Appalachian Mountains). The river flows toward the Mississippi River, on its way carving the New River Gorge in southeastern West Virginia, the best white-water rafting spot in the eastern U.S.

The park's headquarters are at **Foster Falls State Park,** a restored mining hamlet on Foster Falls Road (C.R. 608), about 20 miles northeast of Wytheville, or 2 miles north of U.S. 52 (take Exit 24 off I-77 and follow the signs). From April through November you can enter the trail here daily from 8am to 10pm. Parking costs $2 per vehicle during the week, $3 on weekends.

Other entries to the trail are at **Shot Tower Historical State Park** (see below); **Draper,** near Exit 92 off I-81; **Allisonia** and **Hiwassee,** both on C.R. 693; **Barren Springs,** on Va. 100; **Austinville,** on Va. 69; **Ivanhoe,** on Va. 94; **Byllesby Dam,** on C.R. 602; and **Galax,** on U.S. 58. There's also a branch trail to **Fries,** on Va. 94.

Operating as Foster Falls Livery, **New River Outdoors** (℃ **276/699-1034** or 276/228-8311 in Wytheville; www.newriveradventures.com) rents bicycles, canoes, kayaks, inner tubes, and horses at Foster Falls. Bikes cost $5 per hour or $20 per day. Canoes and kayaks start at $7 an hour or $30 per day. Tubes go for $10 per day. The adjacent stables (℃ **276/699-2460**) rents horses and has guided rides along the trail (call for prices and reservations). Overnight canoe and fishing trips are available, too. The livery is open from Memorial Day to Labor Day, Sunday to Thursday 8am to 5pm, Friday and Saturday 8am to 8pm; from April to Memorial Day and from Labor Day through October, Saturday and Sunday from 8am to 3pm. The company also provides shuttle service between the key points along the trail, so you don't have to walk, ride, or paddle back to your car.

For more information, write or call **New River Trail State Park,** 176 Orphanage Rd., Foster Falls, VA 24360 (℃ **276/699-6778;** www.dcr.state.va.us/parks/newriver.htm). The office is open Monday to Friday 8am to 4:30pm.

While in this area, you can stop at **Shot Tower Historical State Park,** on U.S. 52 near Exit 5 off I-77, which features a stone shot tower built about 1807. Molten lead, poured from the top of the tower, fell 150 feet into a kettle, thus cooling and turning into round shot. The lead was mined at nearby Austinville, birthplace of Stephen Austin, the "Father of Texas." (There's a monument to Austin at the New River Trail State Park in Austinville.) Admission to the park is free, but there's a $2 per vehicle parking fee. The park is open April to November from 8am to dusk. Rangers conduct tours of the tower from Memorial Day to Labor Day on weekends and holidays from 10am to 6pm.

SHOPPING

Three log cabins in Old Town Square, Main Street at 7th Street, now house the **Wilderness Road Trading Company** (℃ **276/223-1198**), purveyor of Appalachian crafts, pottery, toys, and a wide range of gifts.

Near Fort Chiswell, about 10 miles northeast of Wytheville on the service road between Exits 77 and 80 off I-81, you'll find **Snooper's Antique & Craft Mall** (℃ **276/637-6441**) and **Old Fort Emporium Antique Mall** (℃ **276/228-GIFT**). Both are cooperatives, with vendors selling a wide range of antiques, collectibles, and gifts. Both are open from Memorial Day to Labor Day, daily from 10am to 8pm, to 7pm in spring and fall, to 6pm in winter.

WHERE TO STAY

The Wytheville area has over 1,200 motel rooms. Most are in national chain establishments along I-81 and I-77.

The largest concentration is Exit 73 off I-81 (U.S. 11), where the **Holiday Inn Wytheville** (℃ **800/HOLIDAY** or 276/228-5483) is the only motel in town with its own restaurant. Also at Exit 73 is a **Days Inn** (℃ **800/325-2525** or 276/228-5500), **Motel 6** (℃ **800/446-8356** or 276/228-7988), and **Red Carpet Inn** (℃ **800/251-1962** or 276/228-5525). Some rooms in the Days Inn, Motel 6 and Red Carpet Inn are virtually beside I-81 and are subject to traffic noise. You can also take Exit 73 to reach a parking lot–surrounded **EconoLodge** (℃ **800/424-4777** or 276/228-5517), about 1 mile to the south on U.S. 11.

For less congested locations, consider Exit 70 off I-81 (N. 4th St.), which has the modern **Comfort Inn Wytheville** (℃ **800/228-5150** or 276/228-4488), and Exit 41 off I-77 (Peppers Ferry Rd.), where the **Best Western Wytheville Inn** (℃ **800/528-1234** or 276/228-7300), **Hampton Inn** (℃ **800/HAMPTON** or 276/228-6990), and **Ramada Inn** (℃ **800/2-RAMADA** or 276/228-6000) are far enough away from the interstate to escape the road noise.

Fun Fact Skeeter's World Famous Hotdogs

Housed in an ancient storefront, **Skeeter's E.N. Umberger Store,** 165 E. Main St., between 1st and Tazewell sts. (C 276/228-2611), has been serving "Skeeter's World Famous Hotdogs" since 1920. The wieners come Southern-style on squishy steamed buns, covered with mustard, onions and chili. They don't get any better for those of us who grew up eating our dogs this sloppy way. The diner hasn't changed since the 1940s, as the old ads and ripped counter seats attest. Skeeter's is open Monday to Friday from 8am to 5:30pm, Saturday from 8am to 5pm.

WHERE TO DINE

The Clinic *Value* *Finds* REGIONAL   Crutches, one-blip neon electrocardiograms, and drinks served on gauze pads instead of napkins set a clever medical theme for this restaurant/pub/billiard parlor in the heart of Wytheville's business district. The reason for all the medical paraphernalia is that these two storefront buildings served as a private clinic until the town built a modern hospital in 1973. This incarnation of The Clinic opened 30 years later and quickly became the town's favorite spot for a little medicinal whiskey. You'll find a long bar down one side and tables and booths on the other of the big front room. A small wine room in the middle of the building presents a good selection. The pool hall is in the rear. The fare consists of steaks, ribs, shrimp, scallops, and chicken dishes, none of them outstanding, but all passable, especially for the price.

95 W. Main St. C 276/228-9111. Reservations not accepted. Main courses $8–$15. AE, DISC, MC, V. Mon–Thurs 11am–11pm; Fri–Sat 11am–2am.

The Log House 1776 Restaurant *✿* AMERICAN   Although clapboard additions to this historic building were made in 1804 and 1898, the main dining room is in a log house built in 1776. Modern gas logs now burn in the fireplaces, but antiques augment the Colonial charm of the dining room. Offerings include Virginia fare such as peanut soup, Smithfield ham, Confederate beef stew (a sweet concoction of beef, vegetables, and apples that General Lee fed his troops), and Thomas Jefferson's favorite, chicken Marengo, which he brought home from his stint as ambassador to France. You should dine here for the colonial experience, as at The Tavern in Abingdon (see below) and the Colonial Williamsburg taverns (see chapter 10).

520 E. Main St. (U.S. 11) (at 7th St.). C 276/228-4139. Reservations recommended. Lunch sandwiches $3–$5; main courses $8–$18. AE, DISC, MC, V. Mon–Sat 11am–3pm and 4–10pm (to 9:30pm Jan–Apr). From I-81, take Exit 67 or 73 and follow U.S. 11 to the restaurant.

---

4 Mount Rogers National Recreation Area

Noted for its 300 miles of hiking, mountain biking, cross-country skiing, and horse trails, Mount Rogers National Recreation Area includes 117,000 forested acres running some 60 miles from the New River southwest to the Tennessee line. Included is its namesake, Virginia's highest peak at 5,729 feet. Nearby White Top is the state's second-highest point at 5,520 feet. Most of the land, however, flanks Iron Mountain, a long ridge running the area's length. Ranging the extensive upland meadows are wild ponies, introduced to keep the grasses mowed.

Not all of this expanse is pristine; as part of the Jefferson National Forest, it's subject to multiple uses such as hunting and logging. Nevertheless, you'll find three preserved wilderness areas and plenty of backcountry to explore, with mountain scenery that's some of the best in Virginia. The trails include the Virginia Creeper Trail, Virginia Highlands Horse Trail, and part of the Appalachian Trail. A spur off that trail leads to the summit of Mount Rogers.

JUST THE FACTS

ACCESS POINTS & ORIENTATION   Access roads from I-81 are U.S. 21 from Wytheville; Va. 16 from Marion; C.R. 600 from Chilehowie; Va. 91 from Glades Spring; and U.S. 58 from Damascus and Abingdon. C.R. 603 runs 13 miles lengthwise through beautiful highland meadows from Troutdale (on Va. 16) to Konnarock (on U.S. 58).

INFORMATION   Since the area is so vast and most facilities widespread, it's a good idea to get as much information in advance as possible. Contact the **Mount Rogers National Recreation Area,** 3714 Hwy. 16, Marion, VA 24354 (© 800/628-7202 or 276/783-5196; www.southernregion.fs.fed.us/gwj/mr). If you're driving from the north on I-81, stop at the **Highlands Gateway Visitor Center** in Wytheville (see "Exploring the Southwest Highlands" at the beginning of this chapter). Both offer free brochures describing the trails, campgrounds, and wilderness areas, and they sell a one-sheet topographic map of the area. The topographic map does not show the trails, however, so if writing or calling for information, specifically request brochures on trails, campgrounds, horseback riding, and recreation areas.

FEES, REGULATIONS & BACKCOUNTRY PERMITS   There is no charge to drive through the area, but parking fees of $3 per vehicle apply to specific recreational areas, payable on the honor system. Except for the Appalachian Trail and some others reserved for hikers, mountain bikes are permitted but must give way to horses. Bikers and horseback riders must walk across all bridges and trestles. Hikers must not spook the horses. Fishing requires a Virginia license. The "No-Trace Ethic" applies: Leave nothing behind, and take away only photographs and memories.

VISITOR CENTER   The area headquarters is at 3714 Va. 16, about 6 miles south of Marion (take Exit 45 off I-81 and go south on Va. 16). Exhibits and a 10-minute video describe the area. The center is open Memorial Day to October, Monday through Friday from 8am to 4:30pm, Saturday from 9am to 5pm, Sunday from 1 to 5pm. Off season, it's open Monday through Friday from 8am to 4:30pm, closed on federal holidays.

SEASONS   The area gets the most visitors on summer and fall weekends and holidays. Spring is punctuated by wildflowers in bloom (the calendars published by the Blue Ridge Parkway are generally applicable here), while fall foliage is at its brilliant best in mid-October. Cross-country skiers use the trails during winter. Summer thunderstorms, winter blizzards, and fog any time of the year can pose threats in the high country, so caution is advised.

SEEING THE HIGHLIGHTS

If you don't have time to camp and hike, you can still enjoy the scenery from your car. From Marion on I-81, take Va. 16 south 16 miles to the country store at Troutdale. Turn right on C.R. 603 and drive 13 miles southwest to U.S. 58. Turn right there and drive 20 miles down Straight Branch—a misnomer if ever there was one—through Damascus to I-81 at Abingdon.

An alternative route is to continue on Va. 16 south past Troutdale and turn west on U.S. 58. This will take you past Grayson Highlands State Park (see below). After you pass the park, turn right on C.R. 600 north. This road climbs almost to the summit of White Top Mountain. Up there, a dirt track known as Spur 89 branches off for 2 miles to the actual summit, it's the highest point in Virginia to which you can drive a vehicle and has great views. C.R. 600 then descends to a dead-end at C.R. 603; turn right there and drive down to U.S. 58, then west to Damascus and Abingdon, as described above.

OUTDOOR PURSUITS

HIGH-COUNTRY HIKING   Almost two-thirds of the area's 300 miles of trails are on these routes: the local stretch of the **Appalachian Trail** (64 miles), the **Virginia Highlands Horse Trail** (66 miles), and the **Iron Mountain Trail** (51 miles). Many of the other 67 trails connect to these main routes, and many can be linked into circuit hikes.

You can walk for days on the white-blaze Appalachian Trail without crossing a paved road, especially on the central stretch up and down the flanks of Mount Rogers between C.R. 603 and C.R. 600. A spur goes to the top of the mountain. The blue-blaze **Mount Rogers Trail,** a very popular alternate route, leaves C.R. 603 near Grindstone Campground; a spur from that track heads down into the pristine Lewis Fork Wilderness before rejoining the Appalachian Trail.

Running across the southern end of the area, the **Virginia Creeper Trail** offers a much easier, but no less beautiful, hike (and bike ride). This 34-mile route follows an old railroad bed from Abingdon to White Top Mountain (see "The Virginia Creeper Trail" under "Abingdon: A Town with Beauty & Charm," below).

HORSEBACK RIDING   Riders can use 150 miles of the area's trails, including Iron Mountain, New River, and the Virginia Highlands Horse Trail, which connects Elk Garden to Va. 94. Horse camps are at Fox Creek, on Va. 603; Hussy Mountain, near Speedwell; and Raven Cliff, about 4 miles east of Cripple Creek. They have toilets and drinking water for horses (but no water for humans).

GRAYSON HIGHLANDS STATE PARK   On the southern edge of the national recreation area, 8 miles west of Va. 16 on U.S. 58, the lovely **Grayson Highlands State Park** ⟨🎯⟩ sits almost at the summit of Haw Orchard Mountain (the visitors center is at 4,958-ft. altitude). Here you'll find nine short hiking trails to panoramic vistas, waterfalls, and a 200-year-old cabin; bridle paths; a picnic area near a rebuilt frontier homestead; 73 campsites; horse stables; hunting; and fishing. Admission is $1 weekdays, $2 on weekends. Call ⓒ **800/933-PARK** to reserve a campsite, which cost $23 a night with electricity, $18 without.

For info, contact the park at 829 Grayson Highland Lane, Mouth of Wilson, VA 24363 (ⓒ **276/579-7092;** www.dcr.state.va.us/parks/graysonh.htm).

CAMPING

In addition to the horse camps mentioned above, the recreation area has several other campgrounds; all open from mid-March through December. A limited number of sites can be reserved in advance by calling ⓒ **877/444-6777** or on the National Forest Service website (www.fs.fed.us).

On C.R. 603 between Troutdale and Konnaraock, **Grindstone** serves as a base camp for hikers heading up Mount Rogers. It has 100 sites with campfires, drinking water, a .5-mile nature trail, and weekend ranger programs during summer. **Beartree Recreation Area,** a popular site 7 miles east of Damascus on U.S. 58, features a sand beach on a 12-acre lake stocked with trout for fishing. Both Grindstone and Beartree have flush toilets and warm showers but no trailer hookups. Fees range from $7.50 to $19 per night.

WHERE TO STAY

There are no hotels, motels, or inns within Mount Rogers National Recreation Area. The nearest motels are in Wytheville on the north end (see above); Abingdon on the south (see below); and Marion in the center, where the **Best Western Marion** (© 800/528-1234 or 540/783-3193) and the **EconoLodge Marion** (© 800/55-ECONO or 540/783-6031) stand side by side on U.S. 11 north of downtown. Both are well maintained. Opposite them on U.S. 11 is the **Virginia House Inn** (© 800/505-5151 or 276/783-5112; fax 276/783-1007), a one-story motel built in 1952 but still in fine shape. It has an outdoor pool for cooling off after all that hiking. The rooms are small but clean and comfortable. Rates range from $43 to $60 for a double, including continental breakfast.

Fox Hill Inn   Situated on a secluded, 3,200-foot-high hilltop and surrounded on three sides by mountain views, this comfortable country home offers spacious rooms and suites furnished in simple country style with no phones, TVs, or other modern amenities. The inviting living room has a fireplace and a TV. There's a CD player in the library, and a basement gameroom has Ping-Pong. Guests can use the country kitchen (the nearest restaurant is 20 miles away in Marion, so bring groceries). The inn also has cabins for rent. This is a working farm, where sheep graze the meadows in the summer. The innkeepers will arrange canoe trips on the New River, horseback riding, and mountain biking, and they will pick you up if you're hiking the Appalachian Trail. Children are welcome.

8568 Troutdale Hwy. (Va. 16), Troutdale, VA 24378. © 800/874-3313 or 540/677-3313. Fax 815/550-5490. www.bbonline.com/va/foxhill. 7 units, 1 suite. $80–$90 double; $160 suite. Rates include full breakfast. DISC, MC, V. From I-81, take Exit 45 at Marion, then Va. 16 south 20 miles. Inn is on the left, 2 miles south of C.R. 603 at Troutdale.

5 Abingdon: A Town with Beauty & Charm *(★(★(★

49 miles SW of Wytheville; 133 miles SW of Roanoke; 437 miles SW of Washington, D.C.; 315 miles SW of Richmond

While on his first expedition to Kentucky in 1760, Daniel Boone tramped across the 2,000-foot-high Holston Valley and camped at the base of a hill near a small settlement known as Black's Fort. When wolves emerged from a cave and attacked his dogs, Boone named the place Wolf Hill. Boone and other pioneers opened the area for settlement, and by 1778, a thriving community named Abingdon had grown up around Black's Fort and Wolf Hill. The Washington County Court House has replaced the fort, but Boone's cave is still behind one of the historic homes on tree-shaded Main Street. Indeed, Abingdon today looks much as it did in those early years, making it one of Virginia's best small towns to visit.

Abingdon's beauty and historic charm have attracted more than its share of actors, artists, craftspeople, and even a few writers. Visitors drive hundreds of miles to attend shows at the Barter, Virginia's official state theater, and the town is crowded the first 2 weeks of August for the popular Virginia Highlands Festival, a display of the region's best arts and crafts.

You can spend a fascinating weekend here walking around the beautiful town, seeing two plays, and literally coasting on your bike down White Top Mountain on the Virginia Creeper Trail, one of the country's great bicycle paths.

ESSENTIALS

VISITOR INFORMATION   Contact the **Abingdon Convention & Visitors Bureau,** 335 Cummings St., Abingdon, VA 24210 (© 800/435-3440 or 276/676-2282; fax 276/676-3076; www.abingdon.com/tourism). Located in a restored Victorian house, the **Abingdon Visitors Center** is on the left as you drive into town on U.S. 58. It's open daily from 9am to 5pm.

GETTING THERE & GETTING AROUND   American, Delta, Northwest, and US Airways have commuter service to **Tri Cities Regional Airport** (✆ **423/ 325-6000;** www.triflight.com), about 30 miles southwest of Abingdon between Bristol and Kingsport, Tennessee. You can rent a car there, or call **Bob's Limo Service** (✆ **423/325-6379**).

By road, Abingdon is at the junction of I-81 and U.S. 11, U.S. 19, and U.S. 58. From I-81, take Exit 17 and follow U.S. 58 west directly into town. U.S. 11 runs east-west along Main Street (which has a phenomenal amount of traffic for such a small town). Both the **Greyhound/Trailways** bus station (✆ **800/231-2222;** www.greyhound.com) and the local **taxi depot** are at 495 W. Main St. (✆ **276/628-4409**).

WHAT TO SEE & DO

Stop at the visitor center (see "Essentials," above) and pick up a walking tour brochure and map. With advance notice, the center can also arrange guided tours. Lined with brick sidewalks, the historic part of Main Street runs for about ¾ mile. It goes up and down two hills, so wear comfortable walking shoes.

Begin your tour at the **Fields-Penn 1860 House Museum,** at the corner of Main and Cummings streets (✆ **800/435-3440** or 276/676-0216), which depicts how Abingdon's elite lived in the mid–19th century. The museum is open from April through December, Wednesday 11am to 4pm, Thursday through Saturday from 1 to 4pm. Admission is free (donations requested).

From there, head west on Main Street through Abingdon's 3-block-long business district. Several antiques and collectibles emporia will vie for your attention, but keep going to Depot Square. Turn left there to the **Abingdon Passenger Train Station,** which has been restored as home to the **Historical Society of Washington County** (✆ 276/628-8761). One end of the building is used for exhibitions; if it's still here, don't miss the dramatic railway photographs of O. Winston Link, he of the Roanoke museum (see section 2, above). The old freight depot next door is now the **Abingdon Arts Depot** ⭐ (✆ **276/628-9091;** www.abingdonartsdepot.org), where you can watch artists at work in their studios Thursday, Friday, and Saturday from 11am to 3pm.

Now backtrack east along lovely Main Street, where the Martha Washington Inn, the Barter Theatre, and 30 other buildings and homes—with birth dates ranging from 1779 to 1925—wait to be observed.

Past the Washington County Court House, you'll head downhill past **The Tavern,** considered the oldest building in town. Built around 1779 and used as a stagecoach inn and tavern, it's now home to one of the town's better restaurants

---

⸢Fun Fact⸥ The Wolves & Daniel Boone's Dogs

After walking over Abingdon's second hill—where the 1869 Washington County Court House stands—you'll come to the **Cave House,** now home to a fine crafts shop (see "Shopping," below). Behind the house is the cave from whence emerged the wolves that attacked Daniel Boone's dogs. It's not marked, but find it, take the alley to the left of the house to a stop sign, and turn right. You can peer through a lattice fence into the mouth of the cave, which is below a rickety old barn.

(see "Where to Dine," below). You can still see the mail slot in the original post office, in an addition on the east side of the building.

Art lovers can head to the west side of town and the **William King Regional Arts Center,** 415 Academy Dr. (© **276/628-5005;** www.wkrac.org), where three galleries host rotating exhibits showcasing regional and world art. One gallery focuses on regional heritage. There's also a good museum shop. Admission is free. The center is open Tuesday 10am to 9pm; Wednesday, Thursday and Friday 10am to 5pm, Saturday and Sunday 1 to 5pm. The center is in an old school building (turn uphill off West Main St. on Academy Dr. at the Chevron station and follow the signs for arts-center parking).

NEARBY ATTRACTIONS

A scenic 3½-mile drive leads from Abingdon through a picturesque valley to **White's Mill** (© **276/628-2960**), built in 1790 and now on the National Register of Historic Places. The 22-foot diameter steel wheel and original grinding stone should be restored and in operation by the time you arrive. Admission is by donation. Open Wednesday through Sunday from 10am to 6pm. You can buy meal from the mill and hand-made brooms from a shop across the road. From East Valley Street in Abingdon, turn north onto White's Mill Road (C.R. 692).

Stock-car racing fans will enjoy a stop at the **Morgan-McClure Motorsports Museum and Souvenir Gift Shop,** 26460 Newbanks Rd., at Exit 22 (Va. 75) off I-81 (© **888/346-3289** or 276/628-1289; www.77sports.com), about 5 miles north of town. The museum, which resembles an auto parts store, is home to the Kodak No. 4 NASCAR Winston Cup team. Highlights include a car in which driver Bobby Hamilton escaped injury during a serious crash in Japan (it gives new meaning to the term "rear-ender"). Admission is free. Open Monday to Saturday 10am to 5pm.

THE VIRGINIA CREEPER TRAIL ✹✹✹

Take Pecan Street south off Main Street to the western head of the **Virginia Creeper Trail** (www.vacreepertrail.org). This fabulously beautiful 34-mile hiking, biking, and horseback-riding route follows an old railroad bed between Abingdon and White Top Station, at the North Carolina line on the southern flank of White Top Mountain, just inside Mount Rogers National Recreation Area. Now on display at the Abingdon trail head is the old steam engine, which had such a tough time with this grade that it became facetiously known as the "Virginia Creeper."

Beginning 2 miles east of Damascus, the stretch between Green Cove Station and Iron Bridge crosses High Trestle (about 100 ft. high) and has swimming holes in the adjacent stream. Green Cove is a seasonal Forest Service information post with portable toilets.

The trail starts at an elevation of 2,065 feet in Abingdon, drops to 2,000 feet at Damascus (11 miles east on U.S. 58), then climbs to 3,675 feet at White Top. No one I know is about to ride a bike *up* that mountain, so the secret is to take a shuttle bus to the top and coast for 17 of the 23 gorgeous miles downhill to Damascus. If you can ride a bike, this is one of Virginia's top outdoor excursions.

In an old store building on Pecan Street near the trail head, **Virginia Creeper Trail Bike Shop** (© **888/BIKEN4U** or 276/676-2552; www.vacreepertrail bikeshop.com) rents bikes and provides shuttle service to Damascus and White Top Station. Prices are $13 adults, $8 for children for the shuttle, or $21 adults, $15 for children for both shuttle and rental. The shop is open Monday to Friday 9am to 7pm, weekends 8am to 7pm. Reservations are advised.

In Damascus, contact **Blue Blaze Bike & Shuttle Service** (© 800/475-5905 or 276/475-5095; www.blueblazebikeandshuttle.com), **Adventure Damascus Bicycles** (© 888/595-2453; www.adventuredamascus.com), or **The Bike Station,** 501 E. Third Street (© 276/475-3629; www.thebike-station.com).

Black's Fort Stable, on Greenspring Road (© 276/628-6263; www.blacks fortstable.com), has guided horseback rides along the trail, beginning at $10 for 30 minutes. Reservations are recommended.

If you don't want to hike or bike up to the heights, you can get a bird's-eye view of the highlands from the basket under a hot-air balloon. **Balloon Virginia** (© 276/628-6353) flies just after-sunrise and just before-dusk rides. Call for prices and reservations, which are essential.

SHOPPING

Mountain arts and crafts are for sale in the **Cave House Crafts Shop** ★★, 279 E. Main St. (© 276/628-7721), a 130-member cooperative in the 1858 Victorian home built in front of the famous wolf cave. The handmade quilts here are extraordinary. Open January and February, Thursday to Saturday 10am to 5:30pm; March to mid-April, Monday to Saturday 10am to 5:30pm; mid-April through December, Monday to Saturday 10am to 5:30pm, Sunday 1 to 5pm.

Main Street has no fewer than 10 **antiques shops,** which you will pass during your walking tour.

Your hunter-gather instincts will get a workout at **Dixie Pottery,** 5 miles south of Abingdon on U.S. 11 (½ mile south of Exit 13 off I-81). This warehouse-style store sells decorative objects and housewares from around the world. You'll find both cheap and high-quality china, porcelain figurines, candles, dried and artificial flower arrangements, and baskets. They also offer brass, copper, pewter, enamel, and cast-iron pots and cookware. It's open Monday to Saturday 9:30am to 6pm, Sunday 1 to 6pm.

WHERE TO STAY

I-81 has four chain motels: **Comfort Inn** at Exit 14 (© 800/221-2222 or 276/ 676-2222), **Hampton Inn** (© 800/HAMPTON or 276/619-4600) and **Super 8** (© 800/800-8000 or 276/676-3310) at Exit 17, and **Holiday Inn Express** (© 800/HOLIDAY or 276/676-2929) at Exit 19. The Hampton Inn is the newest and best of them.

The Martha Washington Inn ★★ Across Main Street from the Barter Theatre in the heart of the historic district, this is one of Virginia's best in-town country inns. The stately Greek Revival portico creates a formal facade for this two and a half-story red-brick hotel. Its center portion was built as a private residence in 1832. White-wicker rocking chairs give the front porch the look of an old-time resort. With loudly creaking floors, the lobby and adjoining parlors are elegantly decorated, with original marble fireplaces and crystal chandeliers. Choose from regular or deluxe rooms, the latter larger and more lavishly appointed with rich fabrics and fine antiques. Two premium suites have museum-quality furnishings, two fireplaces, whirlpool tubs, and steam showers. Another has a small private balcony off the anteroom between its sleeping and living parlors. Decanters of sherry, down duvets, plush robes, and Caswell-Massey toiletries add to the luxuries. Although a notch below the Peppermill and the Starving Artist Cafe (see "Where the Dine," below), the formal **dining room** serves good American fare amid Victorian elegance at breakfast, lunch, and dinner, and **Martha's Gourmet Market** offers excellent made-to-order sandwiches and salads weekdays from 10am to 3pm

150 W. Main St., Abingdon, VA 24210. © **800/555-8000** or 276/628-3161. Fax 276/628-8885. www.camberleyhotels.com. 61 units. $169–$174 double; $199–$375 suite. AE, DC, DISC, MC, V. **Amenities:** 2 restaurants (American); 1 bar; business center; limited room service; babysitting; laundry service; concierge-level rooms. *In room:* A/C, TV, dataport, iron.

BED & BREAKFASTS

In addition to the Summerfield Inn listed below, B&B accommodations are available at **The Love House** (© **800/475-5494** or 276/623-1281; www.abingdon-virginia.com); **The Shepherd's Joy** (© **276/628-3273;** www.shepherdsjoy.com), which is on a working sheep farm; **Abingdon Boarding House** (© **276/28-9344** or 276/608-1263; www.abingdonboardinghouse.com), the oldest operating boarding house in the area; **Victoria and Albert Inn** (© **888/645-5636** or 276/676-2797; www.abingdon-virginia.com), in an 1892 Victorian home; and **White Birches Inn** (© **800/BIRCHES** or 276/676-2140; www.whitebirchesinn.com), with a gazebo in its gardens.

Summerfield Inn Bed & Breakfast ★★ Just 1 block from Main Street and the Barter Theatre, this gracious 1920s Colonial Revival residence is set back from the street on an expansive lawn. The wrap-around front porch, bright with flower boxes, white wicker rockers, and an old-fashion swing is inviting. A spacious foyer leads to a cozy library where guests can relax and watch TV. The living room is furnished with a player piano and plush Regency-style sofas flanking the fireplace. The guest rooms offer both the ambience of a private home and the luxurious comfort of a fine hotel; each is elegantly furnished with antique pieces and reproductions. The real stars are the three units in the "Carriage House" beside the main building, especially the Rose Room with its two-person hot tub. In fact, five of the seven units here have whirlpool tubs. Hosts Janice and Jim Cowan serve full breakfasts in the formal dining room or, in warm weather, on the porch.

101 W. Valley St., Abingdon, VA 24210. © **800/668-5905** or 276/628-5905. Fax 276/628-7515. www.summerfieldinn.com. 7 units. $125–$165 double. Rates include full breakfast. AE, MC, V. *In room:* A/C, TV, dataport, iron.

WHERE TO DINE

The Cafe at Barter Theater Stage II DELI   Big window walls let lots of light into this delightful, gardenlike room attached to the Barter Theater's Stage II. Theater posters add an artsy touch, while easy chairs and sofas make this seem like a coffeehouse. In fact, you can get your morning latte or espresso here, plus high-cholesterol pastries. Big deli sandwiches are the lunchtime specialty—Black Forest ham, salami, turkey, or vegetarian options on a choice of breads. Everything is made from scratch, so don't be in a rush. Order at the counter and they'll call an actor's name when your order is ready (I did love being called Harrison Ford).

110 Main St. (actually on Church St.). © **276/619-5462.** Reservations not accepted. Salads and sandwiches $2.50–$6. AE, DISC, MC, V. Mon prior to performance; Tues–Sat 8:30am to after show; Sun 11:30am–9pm.

Caroline's ★ REGIONAL   This restored general store at the eastern end of the historic district houses one of Abingdon's newest fine-dining venues. The setting is not as charming as The Tavern's 1779 building (see below), but the food is first rate. Your choices will include traditional crab cakes and trout amandine, but there are some interesting twists, too, such as char-grilled salmon accompanied by North Carolina barbecue sauce.

301 E. Main St. (at Tanner St.). 🕐 **276/739-0042.** Reservations recommended. Main courses $16–$32. AE, DISC, MC, V. Tues–Sat 11am–2pm and 5pm–9pm.

Peppermill ⭐⭐ SEAFOOD/INTERNATIONAL   It may not look like it from the outside, but this chic restaurant is a favorite hangout of local "foodies" who appreciate exciting flavors. Chef Jack Barrow honed his skills in Charleston, SC, and he brings a deft touch to Low Country specialties such as crab cakes. Lightly breaded oysters and scallops are other favorites. Three outdoor tables are available for al fresco dining in warm weather.

967 W. Main St. 🕐 **276/623-0530.** Reservations recommended. Main courses $14–$24. AE, DISC, MC, V. Mon–Fri 11am–2:30pm and 5–9pm; Sat noon–9pm. Restaurant is 1½ miles west of historic district, ½ mile west of railroad overpass.

Starving Artist Cafe ⭐⭐ AMERICAN   Despite its unpretentious location at Depot Square, this charming cafe lacks nothing in the way of culinary sophistication. The food is innovative and delicious and is prepared using the freshest ingredients. The setting is low-key: The walls are adorned with a changing display of artists' work, all for sale. In summer, there's outdoor dining in the alley-turned-patio. At lunch, the menu bestows artists' names on a gallery of sandwiches: The Leonardo da Vinci, for example, features spicy Italian meatballs on a hoagie roll with fresh tomato-basil sauce and melted provolone. The chef makes superb pan-blackened prime rib with Cajun spices (Fri–Sat nights), steaks, and seafood such as Norwegian salmon Oscar. Keep your eye on the specials board, too. Freshly baked desserts are excellent. The cafe doesn't lack for customers, and the small dining room is usually full; arrive off-hours or prepare for a wait—it's worth it.

134 Wall St. (Depot Sq.). 🕐 **276/628-8445.** Reservations not accepted. Main courses $13–$21. AE, MC, V. Mon 11am–2pm; Tues–Sat 11am–3pm and 5–9pm.

The Tavern ⭐ INTERNATIONAL   The oldest building in Abingdon, the Tavern was built in 1779 as an inn for stagecoach travelers. Exposed brick and stone walls, log beams, and hand-forged locks and hinges make for a rustic setting. Despite the indoor charm, choice warm weather tables are on an upstairs porch or on the brick terrace under huge shade trees. The menu reflects the well-traveled owners' backgrounds, with Wiener schnitzel, baked salmon sprinkled with Thai spices, chicken *saltimbocca,* and medallions of beef with a French influence. Forget the over-spiced jambalaya. Lunch offers bratwurst with German potato salad, as well as a Reuben sandwich, and a smoked-turkey club sandwich.

222 E. Main St. 🕐 **276/628-1118.** Reservations recommended for outdoor seating at dinner. Main courses $15–$25. AE, MC, V. Mon–Sat 11am–3pm and 5–10pm; Sun 4–9pm. Closed New Year's Day, Thanksgiving, and Christmas.

Wither's Hardware Restaurant AMERICAN   This building housed a hardware store from 1885 until 1983, and the pressed-tin ceiling, rolling ladder, brick walls, and the oak counter (now a long bar) remain. The walls are hung with hardware-store memorabilia. Although not in the same league as other restaurants here, the menu offers a variety of piled-high sandwiches and burgers and makes a stab at fine dining with the likes of rack of lamb, herb-crusted trout and salmon, and sesame-crusted tuna. Asian flavors appear in the shrimp or pork curry. Smokers can light up in the lively bar at the rear of the building.

260 W. Main St. 🕐 **276/628-1111.** Reservations not accepted. Sandwiches and burgers $7–$9; main courses $15–$22. AE, DISC, MC, V. Daily 11am–10pm (bar open to 2am).

ABINGDON AFTER DARK

Barter Theatre ✿✿✿   Official policy still permits barter for admission (with prior notice), but theatergoers now pay cash to attend the State Theater of Virginia, America's longest-running professional repertory theater. The building was built around 1832 as a Presbyterian church, and later served as a meeting hall for the Sons of Temperance. It functioned as the town hall and opera house when Robert Porterfield brought his unemployed actors here in 1933 (see box). Recent productions, now performed by a professional company, have included *The Tempest; 1776; Steel Magnolias;* and *The Lion in Winter.* The theater's alumni include Hume Cronyn, Patricia Neal, Fritz Weaver, Ernest Borgnine, Gregory Peck, and Ned Beatty. Across Main Street, the **Barter's Stage II** specializes in the classics. The season for both stages runs from February through December.

127 W. Main St. (at College St.). ✆ 276/628-3991. www.bartertheatre.com. Tickets $18–$36, depending on show and time.

Carter Family Fold Music Shows ✿✿   If you have the slightest interest in mountain music, make the 78-mile round-trip from Abingdon to the Carter Family Music Center, where you will see and hear the best regional artists every Saturday night. The music is as pure as it gets, for the descendants of country music royalty A. P. Carter, wife Sara, and sister-in-law Maybelle won't allow the musicians to use any electric equipment. The unpretentious auditorium occupies a huge shed, and local residents are likely to get up and buck dance and clog on a small dance floor in front of the stage. An annual festival during the first weekend in August (the same time as the Virginia Highlands Festival in Abingdon) draws well-known singers and music groups, clog-dance performers, and local artisans who sell crafts. A family museum in A. P. Carter's country store is open from 6 to 7pm, before the show.

C.R. 614, Maces Spring. ✆ 276/386-9480. www.fmp.com/orthey/carter. Music show tickets $5 adults, $1 children 6–12, free for children 5 and under. Shows Sat 7:30pm. Doors open 6pm. From Abingdon, take I-81 south 17 miles to Bristol, U.S. 58 west 19 miles to Hiltons, C.R. 614 east 3 miles to auditorium.

(*Fun Fact*   **Hams for Hamlet**

The career of an aspiring, Virginia-born actor named Robert Porterfield came to a screeching halt during the Great Depression. Giving up on Broadway, he and 22 other unemployed actors came to Abingdon during the summer of 1933 and began putting on plays and shows.

Their first production was John Golden's *After Tomorrow,* for which they charged an admission of 40¢, or the equivalent in farm produce— thus did their little operation become known as the Barter Theatre.

Playwrights who contributed—among them Noel Coward, Thornton Wilder, Robert Sherwood, Maxwell Anderson, and George Bernard Shaw—were paid with a Virginia ham. Shaw, a vegetarian, returned the smoked delicacy and requested spinach instead; Porterfield and his crew obliged.

The first season ended with a profit of $4.30, two barrels of jelly, and a collective weight gain of 300 pounds!

9

Richmond

Now a sprawling metropolitan area flanking the James River in the center of the state, Richmond has been Virginia's capital since 1780 and has been the stage for much history. It was in Richmond's St. John's Church that Patrick Henry concluded his address to the second Virginia Convention with the stirring words "Give me liberty, or give me death!" During the Revolution, turncoat Gen. Benedict Arnold led British troops down what is now Main Street in 1781 and set fire to many buildings, including tobacco warehouses—in those days, the equivalent of banks. Cornwallis briefly occupied the town, and Lafayette came to the rescue.

But it was in the role as capital of the Confederate States of America that Richmond left an indelible mark on American history. Jefferson Davis lived in the Confederate White House here while presiding over the rebel government, and Robert E. Lee accepted command of the Army of Northern Virginia. For 4 years the Union army tried unsuccessfully to capture the city. Troops often battled on its outskirts, its tobacco warehouses overflowed with prisoners of war, its hospitals with the wounded, and its cemeteries with the dead. Richmond didn't fall into Union hands until Lee abandoned Petersburg—an easy excursion to the south—a week before surrendering at Appomattox.

The city has a host of other attractions, including fine old homes, an excellent fine arts museum, a hands-on science museum with state-of-the-art planetarium, and a botanical garden. But its prime attractions are the monuments, battlefields, and museums that recall the nation's bloodiest conflict. If you have any interest in the Civil War, Richmond is an essential stop.

1 Orientation & Getting Around

VISITOR INFORMATION
The **Richmond Visitors Center,** 405 N. Third St. (between Clay and Marshall sts.), Richmond, VA 23219 (© **800/RICHMOND;** www.richmondva.org), provides information and operates a hotel reservation service. The center is in the Greater Richmond Convention Center and is open Monday through Friday from 8:30am to 5pm. Park in the municipal garage at Marshall and Third streets.

In addition, the **Richmond International Airport Visitors Center** (© **804/ 236-3260**) is open Monday to Friday 9:30am to 4:30pm. It will make same-day hotel reservations.

The state operates a visitor information center in the **Bell Tower** (© **804/ 786-4485**), on the State Capitol grounds near 9th Street and Marshall Avenue. It's open Monday to Friday 9am to 5pm.

GETTING THERE
BY PLANE   Richmond International Airport, Airport Drive off I-64, I-295, and Williamsburg Road (U.S. 60) (© **804/226-3052;** www.flyrichmond.com),

---

Impressions

Broad-streeted Richmond . . . The trees in the streets are old trees used to living with people. Family trees that remember your grand- father's name.

—Stephen Vincent Benet, *John Brown's Body*

---

known locally as Byrd Field, is about 15 minutes east of downtown. American, Continental, Delta, Northwest, TWA, United, and US Airways fly there. The major car-rental companies have desks at the airport.

Groome Transportation (© 804/222-7222; www.groometransportation. com) offers 24-hour van service to Richmond, Petersburg, Fredericksburg, and Williamsburg. Per-person fares range from $16.25 to downtown Richmond to $40 to Williamsburg. Public bus service is available during weekday morning and evening rush hours, but the savings are hardly worth the time and trouble.

BY CAR   Richmond is at the junction of **I-64,** traveling east-west, and **I-95,** traveling north-south. **I-295** bypasses the city on its east and north sides. **U.S. 60** (east-west) and **U.S. 1** and **U.S. 301** (north-south) are other major arteries.

BY TRAIN   Several daily **Amtrak** trains pull into the station at 7519 Staples Mill Rd., north of Exit 185 off I-64 (© 800/872-7245; www.amtrak.com).

BY BUS   The **Greyhound/Trailways** bus terminal is at 2910 N. Boulevard (© 800/231-2222; www.greyhound.com).

CITY LAYOUT

Richmond is located at the fall line of the James River. Instead of growing away from the river, the original city spread westward along the north shore. Thus, the main streets run east-west for several miles from the original settlement, in today's Shockoe Bottom. Although Richmond now has suburbs sprawling across the surrounding countryside, most of the hotels, restaurants, and historic sites of interest to visitors are in the old part of the city.

A series of bridges crosses the river, and there's also access to two islands, Brown's Island and Belle Isle, from the **Richmond Riverfront Canal Walk,** a promenade extending along the downtown riverfront beside the **James River & Kanawha Canal** (see "What to See & Do," later).

Foushee Street divides street numbers east and west, while **Main Street** divides them north and south. **Broad Street** is the major east-west thoroughfare, and it's one of the few downtown streets with two-way traffic.

NEIGHBORHOODS IN BRIEF

As you explore the neighborhoods described below (moving from east to west), you'll get a good sense of Richmond's history.

CHURCH HILL   Named for St. John's Church, its major landmark, this east Richmond neighborhood is largely residential, with many 19th-century Greek Revival resi- dences. Bordering Church Hill is:

TOBACCO ROW   Paralleling the James River for some 15 blocks

between 20th and Pear streets, this is the latest urban redevelopment area. Handsome redbrick ware- houses are being turned into apart- ment houses. The Edgar Allan Poe and Virginia Holocaust museums are here.

SHOCKOE BOTTOM Shockoe Bottom is roughly bounded by Dock and Broad streets and 15th and 20th streets, with the heart at the 17th Street Farmer's Market between East Main and East Franklin streets. Richmond's first business district, it once encompassed tobacco factories, produce markets (farmers still sell produce at stands on N. 17th St.), slave auction houses, warehouses, and shops, and it retains much of its original character. Today, old-fashioned groceries with signs in their windows for fresh chitterlings stand alongside trendy shops, restaurants, and noisy nightclubs aimed primarily at 20-somethings. Its old train station has a spectacular clock tower that is visible to motorists passing above it on I-95.

SHOCKOE SLIP Bordering downtown roughly between 10th and 14th streets and Main and Canal streets, this warehouse and commercial area was reduced to rubble in 1865 and rebuilt as a manufacturing center after the war. Today it's the city's most urbane (and expensive) dining and entertainment section. With its cobblestones restored and old-fashioned street lamps providing light, East Cary Street features renovated warehouses containing restaurants, galleries, nightspots, shops, and two major hotels. The Richmond Riverfront Canal Walk boat rides begin here.

DOWNTOWN West and north of Shockoe Slip, downtown is Richmond's governmental and financial center. It includes the old and new city halls, the state capitol, and government buildings of **Capitol Square;** and the historic homes and museums of the **Court End** area, notably the Valentine Richmond History Center, Museum and White House of the Confederacy, and John Marshall House. It also encompasses the Coliseum, the city's convention center, and the Carpenter Center for the Performing Arts.

JACKSON WARD Home to many free African Americans before the Civil War ended slavery, Jackson Ward, north of Broad Street, is a National Historic District. Its famous residents have included the first woman bank president in the United States, Maggie Walker, and legendary dancer Bill "Bojangles" Robinson, who donated a stoplight for the safety of children crossing the

---

⌒ Fun Fact   From Swords to Tennis Racquets

Since it fell to Grant's army in 1865, Richmond has changed in many ways—especially in its demographics. Many descendants of the defeated Confederate soldiers have fled to Richmond's sprawling suburbs, while descendants of the slaves those soldiers fought so hard to keep in bondage now make up a majority of the city's population—and the city council.

The council set the city's old-line white residents on their ears a few years ago by voting to place a statue of the late Arthur Ashe—the great African-American tennis star and Richmond's most famous modern son—among those of the Civil War heroes along Monument Avenue. It was a hard-fought battle, but today at the corner of Monument Avenue and Roseneath Road stands Ashe's bronze likeness, holding not a sword, but a tennis racquet.

Metropolitan Richmond

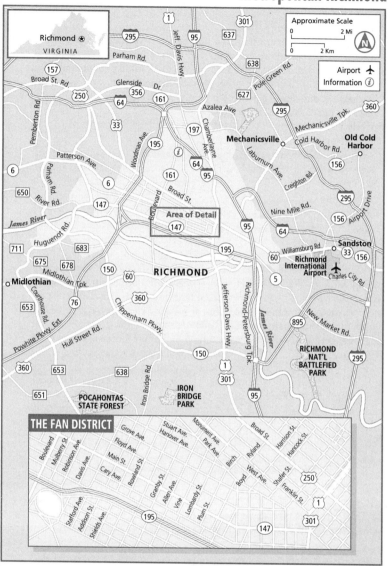

intersection of Leigh Street and Chamberlayne Avenue (where a monument to him stands today). Notable, too, is the fine ornamental ironwork gracing the facades of many Jackson Ward residences.

THE FAN Just west of downtown, the Fan is named for the shape of the streets, which more or less "fan" out from downtown. Bordered by West Broad and Boulevard and West Main and Belvidere, this gentrified area of turn-of-the-20th-century town houses includes Virginia Commonwealth University and many restaurants and galleries. Monument Avenue's most scenic blocks, with the Civil War statues—and one of

---

Tips   Safety in Richmond

As in any city, it's wise to stay alert and be aware of your surroundings, whatever the time of day. Ask at the visitor centers or at your hotel desk if a neighborhood you intend to visit is safe. Most neighborhoods described in this chapter are generally safe during the day, and Shockoe Slip and Shockoe Bottom are safe during the evening when their restaurants are open. Avoid all deserted streets after dark.

African-American tennis star Arthur Ashe—down its median strip, are in the Fan.

CARYTOWN Just west of Boulevard, affluent Carytown has been called Richmond's answer to Georgetown. Cafes, restaurants, boutiques, antiques shops, and the Byrd Theater, a restored movie palace, bring Saturday-afternoon crowds to West Cary Street between Boulevard and Nasemond Street.

GETTING AROUND

BY PUBLIC TRANSPORTATION   The Greater Richmond Transit Company (GRTC; 𝄪 804/358-GRTC; www.ridegrtc.com) operates the **public bus** system throughout the metropolitan area. Base bus fare is $1.25 (exact change only). Service on most bus routes begins at 5am and ends at midnight. GRTC also has express bus service between Richmond and Petersburg.

If you're here on a weekend, the motorized **Richmond Cultural Connection Shuttle** (𝄪 804/783-7450 weekdays, 804/266-8100 weekends) runs downtown on Saturday and Sunday from June until early September. Call or check with the visitor center for the schedule. The **Orange Line** goes from Chimborazo Park, on East Broad Street at 33rd Street, across town to the Science Museum of Virginia, on West Broad Street at Robinson Street. It stops at all attractions in between. From the science museum, the **Blue Line** runs along Boulevard to Maymount, passing Carytown on the way. Trolley fare is $1 with free re-boarding.

BY CAR   Richmond is fairly easy to navigate by car, although all but a few streets are one-way. Left turns from a one-way street onto another one-way street may be made at red lights after a full stop.

BY TAXI   Call **Yellow Cab Service Inc.** (𝄪 804/222-7300) or **Veterans Cab Association** (𝄪 804/329-1414). Fares are approximately $1.50 per mile.

2 Where to Stay

The **Richmond Visitors Center** operates a free hotel reservation service (𝄪 800/ RICHMOND; see "Essentials," above). If you arrive without a reservation, the center will make same-day reservations for walk-in visitors, often at a discount. See "Visitor Information" above. Note that rooms can be scarce here on NASCAR weekends at Richmond International Raceway (see "Sports & Outdoor Activities," below).

Chain motels are scattered throughout the suburbs. The Executive Center area, on West Broad Street (U.S. 33/250) at I-64 (Exit 183), about 5 miles west of downtown is a campuslike area convenient to the major attractions. The best of its hotels is the redwood-and-brick **Sheraton Richmond** (𝄪 800/325-3535 or

Downtown Richmond Accommodations & Dining

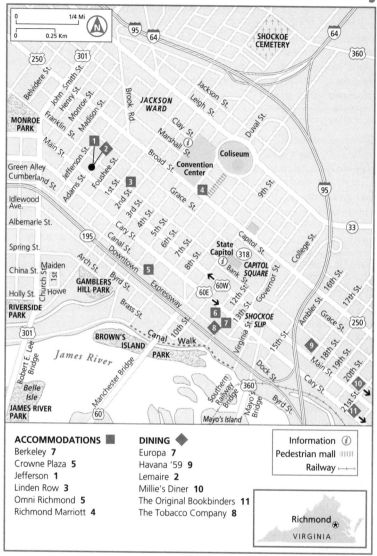

ACCOMMODATIONS ■
Berkeley **7**
Crowne Plaza **5**
Jefferson **1**
Linden Row **3**
Omni Richmond **5**
Richmond Marriott **4**

DINING ◆
Europa **7**
Havana '59 **9**
Lemaire **2**
Millie's Diner **10**
The Original Bookbinders **11**
The Tobacco Company **8**

Information ⓘ
Pedestrian mall ▦
Railway ├──┤

Richmond ⊛
VIRGINIA

804/285-1234). Nearby are the Colonial-look **Comfort Inn Executive Center** (✆ **800/228-5150** or 804/672-1108), a **Courtyard by Marriott** (✆ **800/321-2211** or 804/282-1881), a **Days Inn** (✆ **800/DAYS-INN** or 804/282-3300), an **Econolodge** (✆ **800/55-ECONO** or 804/672-8621), the **Hampton Inn West** (✆ **800/HAMPTON** or 804/747-7777), the **Holiday Inn West** (✆ **800/HOLIDAY** or 804/285-9951), a **Shoney's Inn** (✆ **800/222-2222** or 804/672-7007), and a **Super 8** (✆ **800/800-8000** or 804/672-8128).

The Berkeley Hotel ★★ At this elegant inn, on the border of downtown and Shockoe Slip, a handsome redbrick facade opens into a seemingly Old World interior. Although established in 1988, the hotel creates the illusion that it was built long ago. A cozy ambience and attentive service prevail. Rooms are residential in feel and luxuriously appointed with period reproduction furnishings and walls hung with botanical prints; some have whirlpool tubs. The Berkeley has one of Richmond's finest hotel dining rooms. Virginia ingredients are used extensively in the excellent fare. **Nightingale's Lounge** adjoins.

1200 E. Cary St. (at 12th St.), Richmond, VA 23219. (*C*) **888/780-4422** or 804/780-1300. Fax 804/648-4728. www.berkeleyhotel.com. 55 units. $185–$200 double. Weekend and other packages available. AE, DC, DISC, MC, V. Valet parking $12. **Amenities:** Restaurant; bar; access to nearby health club; laundry service. *In room:* A/C, TV, dataport, coffeemaker, iron, safe.

Crowne Plaza Hotel   You won't mistake this Crowne Plaza for any other building in town—it's a starkly modern, triangular 16-story high-rise with reflecting glass windows. A recent renovation has spiffed up the rooms, which offer stunning river and city views. Some of the units here are bi-level suites. It's less expensive than the Berkeley and the Omni Richmond, and it's a few blocks to Shockoe Slip. The mezzanine-level **Pavilion Cafe** serves all three meals, while the **Canal Club** off the lobby offers drinks and light fare with a view of Canal Walk.

555 E. Canal St. (at 6th St.), Richmond, VA 23219. (*C*) **800/227-6963** or 804/788-0900. Fax 804/788-7087. www.crowneplazarichmond.com. 299 units. $129–$169 double. AE, DC, DISC, MC, V. Self-parking $7; valet parking $10. **Amenities:** Restaurant; bar; indoor pool; access to nearby health club; exercise room; Jacuzzi; sauna; business center; limited room service; laundry service; concierge-level rooms. *In room:* A/C, TV, dataport, coffeemaker, iron.

The Jefferson Hotel 🌟🌟🌟   This stunning six-story beaux arts building is the creation of Maj. Lewis Ginter, a founder of the American Tobacco Company who in addition to the Lewis Ginter Botanical Garden (see "What to See & Do," later) succeeded in giving his city one of America's finest hotels. In 1895 he hired the firm of Carriere & Hastings, which had designed the New York Public Library. The magnificent limestone-and-brick facade is adorned with Renaissance-style balconies, arched porticos, and an Italian clock tower. Two-story faux-marble columns, embellished with gold leaf, encircle the Rotunda, the original lobby, which has a small museum explaining the hotel's history. From there, the marble Grand Staircase, wide and red-carpeted, leads up to reception in the Palm Court lobby. There Edward Valentine's statue of Thomas Jefferson stands directly under a stained-glass domed skylight, 9 of its 12 panes original Tiffany glass.

Furnished with custom-made 18th-century reproduction pieces, the well-equipped rooms come in 57 different configurations, including two-room suites with a multitude of phones (politicians make good use of them when the state legislature is in session). It's worth an extra $20 a night to get one of the "Deluxe" rooms, which have more space and charm—some have their original

---

(Fun Fact **Mr. Jefferson's Ascot**

With its Rotunda, grand marble staircase, sky-lit Palm Court, and small museum dedicated to itself, The Jefferson Hotel is an attraction in its own right. Take a close look at Edward Valentine's stunning statue of Thomas Jefferson standing in the middle of the Palm Court. In an effort to save it during a 1902 fire, Valentine and others lassoed the statue and pulled it down on some mattresses. Unfortunately the fall decapitated Mr. Jefferson. Valentine added the ascot to conceal T.J.'s scar.

fireplace mantels—than the "Superior" models. Despite the building's ornate balconies, only the Presidential suite opens to one of them.

Lemaire (as in the real T.J.'s maitre d') is one of the state's finest dining rooms (see "Where to Dine," below). Basically a lounge, **The Rotunda** (as in the University of Virginia) is put to use for outstanding, if pricey, Sunday brunches ($38 per person, including champagne; reservations suggested). Off the Rotunda, the recently remodeled **T.J.'s** (as in Thomas Jefferson) offers good food in an informal setting. The hotel's bar is almost hidden behind The Rotunda's original reception windows. Other notable amenities include a state-of-the-art health club and a resorty indoor pool under a skylight.

Note that your pets can enjoy the luxuries here, too.

101 W. Franklin St. (at Adams St.), Richmond, VA 23220. © 800/484-8014 or 804/788-8000. Fax 804/225-0334. www.jefferson-hotel.com. 264 units including 36 suites. $265–$315 double; $365–$650 suite. Weekend and other packages available. AE, DC, DISC, MC, V. Self-parking $10; valet parking $15. Pets accepted ($35 per day fee). **Amenities:** 2 restaurants; bar; indoor pool; health club; access to nearby YMCA; children's programs; concierge; business center; salon; 24-hr. room service; massage; babysitting; laundry service. *In room:* A/C, TV, dataport, minibar, iron, safe.

Linden Row Inn ⊕ (*Value* Not only the facades of this row of seven mid-19th-century Greek Revival town houses, but their garden dependencies (small, separate buildings) have remained intact. Despite a major renovation in 2003, original interior features such as fireplaces, marble mantels, and crystal chandeliers still grace the inn, which the National Trust for Historic Preservation has officially designated a Historic Hotel of America. Rooms in the main houses, all with windows nearly reaching the 12-foot ceilings, have a mix of late-Empire and early-Victorian pieces, with marble-top dressers. Back rooms overlook a walled garden and patio, and the garden dependencies of the town houses offer accommodations with private entrances, country-look furniture, and handmade quilts. The cozy dining room serves continental breakfast to guests, lunch and dinner to all comers. Cheese, crackers, and wine are laid out during the early evening in two parlors with working fireplaces. Limo service within a 3-mile radius is available.

100 E. Franklin St. (at 1st St.), Richmond, VA 23219. © 800/348-7424 or 804/783-7000. Fax 804/648-7504. www.lindenrowinn.com. 70 units. $99–$149 double; $149–$189 suite. Rates include continental breakfast. AE, DC, MC, V. Valet parking $9.75. **Amenities:** Restaurant; bar; access to nearby health club; limited room service; laundry service. *In room:* A/C, TV, dataport, coffeemaker, iron, safe.

Omni Richmond Hotel ⊕ Although not on a par with The Jefferson or even The Berkeley Hotel across the street, the Omni enjoys a terrific location next to Shockoe Slip's boutiques, restaurants, and clubs. It boasts a handsome pink-marble lobby, with green velvet–upholstered chairs and sofas around a working fireplace. Rooms are decorated in soft pastels, and some have spectacular views of the nearby James River. Club-floor rooms offer access to a private lounge, where a complimentary continental breakfast and afternoon refreshments are served on weekdays. **Barlow's Terrace,** the hotel's casual restaurant, opens to the James Center office tower's atrium.

100 S. 12th St. (at E. Cary St.), Richmond, VA 23219. © 800/THE-OMNI or 804/344-7000. www.omnihotels.com. Fax 804/648-6704. 361 units. $189 double; $239–$299 suite. Weekend and other packages available. AE, DC, DISC, MC, V. Valet parking $15. **Amenities:** Restaurant; bar; indoor-outdoor pool; access to nearby health club; concierge; limited room service; babysitting; laundry service; concierge-level rooms. *In room:* A/C, TV, dataport, minibar, coffeemaker, iron.

Richmond Marriott Although it's too far away to safely walk to Shockoe Slip after dark, the recently renovated Marriott is ideally located for conventioneers, since it sits next door to the new Richmond Metropolitan Convention Center. Many of the exceptionally spacious accommodations offer panoramic city views.

500 E. Broad St. (at 5th St.), Richmond, VA 23219. ℂ 800/228-9290 or 804/643-3400. Fax 804/788-1230. 402 units. $89–$159 double. Weekend and other packages available. AE, DC, DISC, MC, V. Self-parking $9; valet parking $12. **Amenities:** Restaurant; bar; indoor pool; health club; concierge; limited room service; coin-op washers and dryers; concierge-level rooms. *In room:* A/C, TV, dataport, coffeemaker, iron.

3 Where to Dine

I've arranged the restaurants by neighborhood, running from east to west across the city in the order they're described under "Neighborhoods in Brief," earlier.

CHURCH HILL

Millie's Diner ★★ ECLECTIC   Once Millie's really was a diner, and although it's been renovated, the counter, booths with juke boxes, and open kitchen from those days are still here. It's not a diner anymore; now talented young chefs work the gas stove, turning out a variety of tasty dishes. The spicy Thai shrimp with asparagus, red cabbage, shiitake mushrooms, cilantro, lime, peanuts, and hot chiles over fettuccine is usually on the menu, which changes every few weeks. Whatever you order, it will be made from scratch—as you watch, if you grab a counter seat. Excellent fare, an entertaining wait staff, and hearty portions make this noisy eatery highly popular among Richmond's young professionals. You can dine outside at lunch during warm weather but not at dinner.

2603 E. Main St. (at 26th St.). ℂ 804/643-5512. Reservations accepted only for seating before 6:30pm. Main courses $19–$27. AE, DC, DISC, MC, V. Tues–Fri 11am–2:30pm and 5:30–10:30pm; Sat 10am–3pm (brunch) and 5:30–10:30pm; Sun 9am–3pm (brunch) and 5:30–9:30pm.

TOBACCO ROW

The Old Original Bookbinder's ★★ SEAFOOD/STEAKS   On the first floor of River Lofts, one of the old Tobacco Row warehouses converted into condos, this branch of the Philadelphia institution is Richmond's best place for seafood. The warehouse's brick walls and the exposed air ducts overhead add a certain rustic charm to this chic but casual spot, which is so popular you should book as soon as possible. The chef takes his own approach to crab imperial and other traditional Chesapeake dishes and adds more inventive fare such as pan-seared sea scallops with snow peas and andouille sausage in a bacon and port wine sauce. For landlubbers, steaks range from 8- to 24-ounces. There's validated parking in the lot across the street, plus valet parking on weekends.

2306 E. Cary St. (between 23rd and 24th sts.). ℂ 804/643-6900. Reservations highly recommended. Main courses $18–$40. AE, MC, V. Mon–Sat 5–10pm; Sun 5–9pm.

SHOCKOE BOTTOM

Havana '59 CUBAN   This lively theme restaurant presents a strange sight across the street from the covered stalls of Richmond's ancient Farmer's Market, especially during warm weather when its big, garage-style storefront windows roll up to let fresh air in—and cigar smoke out. Then you might swear you're in Havana in 1959. Fake palms, ceiling fans, string lights, Cuban music, and adobe walls with gaping holes (where plaster ought to be) set a festive scene. The Cuban-accented cuisine lives up to the ambience. The menu changes frequently, so you never know what will be marching into Havana any given day. There's validated parking in the lot at Franklin and 17th streets.

16 N. 17th St. (between Main and Franklin sts.). ℂ 804/649-2822. Reservations recommended. Salads and sandwiches $6–$10; main courses $20–$25. AE, DC, DISC, MC, V. Mon–Sat 4:30–10pm.

SHOCKOE SLIP

East Cary Street between 12th and 15th streets is Richmond's premier dining mecca, with a bevy of good-to-excellent restaurants. In addition to those listed below, you can get sushi at **Hana Zushi Japanese,** 1309 E. Cary St. (© **804/225-8801**); excellent Italian at **La Grotta Restaurant,** 1218 E. Cary St. (© **804/644-2466**); Chinese at **The Peking Pavilion,** 1302 E. Cary St. (© **804/649-8888**); fresh, raw bar fare at **The Hard Shell,** 1411 E. Cary St. (© **804/643-2333**); upscale American at **Sam Miller's Warehouse,** 1210 E. Cary St. (© **804/643-1301**); and French-Moroccan at **Rivah Bistro,** 1417 E. Cary St. (© **804/344-8222**).

Steak lovers with extra cash can grill it at a branch of **Morton's of Chicago** at 111 Virginia St. (© **804/648-1662**), a block south of East Cary Street.

Consistently popular with young professionals as a watering hole, **Siné Irish Pub & Restaurant,** 1327 E. Cary St. (© **804/649-7767**), is anything but a typical Irish pub, offering a wide selection of seafood, steaks, and chicken in addition to the usual corned beef and cabbage. In warm weather you can dine and drink on the deck out back.

Europa ✿ MEDITERRANEAN   This casual, brick-walled restaurant offers tasty if not exceptional paella from Spain, vegetable risotto from Italy, braised lamb shanks from Morocco, and other fare from around the Mediterranean. The best choices here are the tapas, often eaten by a crowd of 30-somethings gathered at the long bar. The morsels range from marinated olives to a selection of Spanish meats and cheeses. The salmon tartare is worth a try, too.

1409 E. Cary St. (between 14th and 15th sts.). © 804/643-0911. Reservations recommended. Tapas $4–$8; main courses $15–$20. AE, DC, DISC, MC. V. Mon–Thurs 11:30am–2:30pm and 5:30–10:30pm; Fri 11:30am–2:30pm and 5:30–11pm; Sat 5:30–11pm.

The Tobacco Company AMERICAN   Appropriately, this dining-entertainment complex is in a former tobacco warehouse that's been converted to a sunny, plant-filled three-story atrium. It was a pioneer in Shockoe Slip's renaissance and always draws its share of tourists and the expense-account crowd. It's a fun place, nonetheless. An antique elevator carries you from the first-floor cocktail lounge to the two dining floors above. Nostalgic touches abound—brass chandeliers, Tiffany-style lamps, a cigar-store Indian, even an old ticket booth that now serves as the hostess desk. Exposed-brick walls are festooned with antique collectors' items. Contemporary American cuisine is featured. Lunch specialties could be as light as a vegetarian burger or as hearty as crab cakes. At dinner, you might begin with crab croquets, then move on to slow-roasted prime rib with seconds on the house. There's live music in The Club downstairs Tuesday through Saturday nights, with dancing Thursday through Saturday.

1201 E. Cary St. (at 12th St.). © 804/782-9431. Reservations accepted. Main courses $18–$30. AE, MC, V. Mon–Thurs 11:30am–2:30pm and 5:30–10pm; Fri–Sat 11:30am–2:30pm and 5–10:30pm; Sun 10:30am–2:30pm and 5–9:30pm.

DOWNTOWN

Lemaire ✿✿✿ FRENCH   Named for Thomas Jefferson's maitre d', Lemaire is one of Virginia's finest hotel dining rooms. With a pianist on the grand, waiters providing gracious service, and tables widely spread through several areas including a glass-enclosed room along Franklin Street, it also is Richmond's favorite restaurant for very special occasions. Although French in origin, the cuisine relies heavily on local produce such as Chesapeake Bay rockfish (sea bass) with country bacon, tomatoes and shitake mushroom succotash; glazed pork chop with braised collard greens; and shrimp and clams with Surry sausage and stone-ground grits. Both breakfast and lunch see extensive buffets in addition to the regular menus.

In The Jefferson Hotel, 101 W. Franklin St. (at Adams St.). ℂ **804/788-8000.** Reservations highly recommended. Breakfast $7–$18; lunch $8–$19; main courses $23–$34. AE, DC, DISC, MC. V. Mon–Thurs 6:30–10am, noon–2pm, and 5:30–9pm; Fri 6:30–10am, noon–2pm, and 5:30–10pm; Sat 6:30–11am and 5:30–9pm; Sun 6:30am–1pm.

THE FAN

You pay a premium in the Shockoes for ambience and location. You get equally as good but less expensive fare by driving out to The Fan, where the two neighborhood restaurants below have been feeding the locals for years. You'll get a good look at The Fan's gentrified row houses, too, as you drive around hunting for a parking space.

Joe's Inn (Value ITALIAN   This popular neighborhood hangout has been serving Greek-accented Italian fare since 1952, including veal parmigiana, fish, pizzas, and pasta. The house specialty is gargantuan portions of spaghetti. Two can easily share an order of somewhat rubbery spaghetti a la Joe, which is served steaming hot en casserole, bubbling with a layer of baked provolone between the pasta and heaps of rich meat sauce. Soups, salads, omelets, and sandwiches are also options. Stop by anytime for a mouth-watering stack of hotcakes or French toast at breakfast. Joe's occupies two storefronts: a dining room side and a bar side with sleek mahogany booths and ornate brass-trimmed ceiling fans.

205 N. Shields Ave. (between Grove and Hanover sts.). ℂ **804/355-2282.** Reservations not accepted. Breakfast $4–$12; sandwiches $3.50–$6.50; main courses $6–$13. AE, MC, V. Mon–Thurs 9am–midnight; Fri–Sat 8am–2am; Sun 8am–midnight.

Strawberry Street Café ☆ (Value AMERICAN   This chic but casual cafe is decorated in turn-of-the-20th-century style, with a beautiful oak bar, *Casablanca*-inspired fan chandeliers, and a gorgeous stained glass room divider. Flower-bedecked tables (candlelit at night) add a cheerful note. At lunch or dinner, you can help yourself to unlimited offerings from an extensive salad bar nestled in a claw-foot bathtub. At lunch, you might get a broccoli quiche or a 6-ounce burger. At dinner, the menu offers pastas plus London broil, steaks, spicy Southwestern-style pork chops, and homemade chicken potpie with a flaky crust. There's luscious chocolate cake for dessert. The weekend brunch bar lets you create a memorable meal from an assortment of fresh fruits, yogurt, baked ham, pastries, hot entree, salads, homemade muffins, and beverage.

421 N. Strawberry St. (between Park and Stuart aves.). ℂ **804/353-6860.** Reservations needed only for large groups. Sandwiches and burgers $6–$11; main courses $8–$18; weekend brunch buffet $10. AE, MC, V. Mon–Thurs 11:30am–3pm and 5–10:30pm; Fri 11:30am–3pm and 5pm–midnight; Sat 11am–midnight; Sun 10am–10:30pm.

CARYTOWN

Acacia ☆☆ REGIONAL   You can't miss this fine restaurant as you stroll through Carytown, for it occupies the front portico and part of the 19th-century First Baptist Church, now converted into a shopping complex. It's the domain of chef Dale Reitzer and wife Aline, who honed their skills at The Frog and The Redneck, once one of Richmond's finest restaurants. Dale presides over the kitchen and concocts a nightly dinner menu to reflect the produce they've procured from the region's farmers and fishers that day. He always prepares one vegetarian and one chicken main course. In autumn, look for venison and buffalo. Lunch doesn't reflect the quality of the dinner fare, but you'll still enjoy the sandwiches, wraps, soups, and salads aimed at Carytown's office workers and shoppers.

3325 W. Cary St. (at Dooley Ave.). © 804/354-6060. Reservations strongly recommended at dinner. Lunch $4–$8; main courses $13–$25. AE, DC, MC, V. Mon–Sat 11:30am–2:30pm (to 4pm in summer) and 5:30–9:30pm, Sun 5:30–10pm.

Ristorante Amici ⊛ NORTHERN ITALIAN   This delightful restaurant has been serving Richmond's best northern Italian cuisine since 1991. On the street floor is a small bar and seating at several additional tables for dinner, and during good weather, patrons vie for seats on a covered sidewalk patio. The owners of Amici (which means "friends" in Italian) hail from Cervinia, a resort in the Italian Alps, where they perfected their craft—and perfection in the culinary arts is certainly what they have achieved here. The menu changes seasonally, but you might begin with grilled portobello mushroom caps with garlic, basil, and olive oil; and thin slices of veal loin with delicate tuna sauce. Among the entree highlights is a Black Angus tenderloin steak with a Gorgonzola cheese sauce. From the grill also come fresh salmon, sea bass, jumbo shrimp and scallops, chicken breast, lamb chops, and bison. Stunning desserts include a wicked tiramisu. The wine list, with many Italian vintages, is surprisingly affordable.

3343 W. Cary St. (between Freeman Rd. and S. Dooley St.). © 804/353-4700. Reservations recommended. Main courses $14–$28. AE, DISC, MC, V. Mon–Thurs 11:30am–2:30pm and 5:30–10pm; Fri–Sat 11:30am–2:30pm and 5:30–11pm; Sun 5:30–10pm.

PICNIC FARE

In Carytown, **Coppola's Delicatessen,** 2900 W. Cary St., at South Colonial Avenue (© **804/359-NYNY**), evokes New York's Little Italy with an aromatic clutter of cheeses, sausages, olives, pickles, and things marinated. Behind-the-counter temptations include pasta salads, antipasti, cannoli, specialty sandwiches, and pasta dinners. Coppola's is so New York that it "imports" Thuman's low-fat, low-salt deli meats from New Jersey. Prices are low; this is a down-to-earth deli, not a pretentious gourmet emporium, though the fare is as good as any the latter might offer. Hours are Monday through Wednesday from 10am to 8pm, Thursday through Saturday from 10am to 9pm, Sunday from 11am to 4pm. There's a branch a block north of Shockoe Slip at Main and 12th streets (© **804/225-0454**), which is open Monday to Friday from 10am to 4pm.

4 What to See & Do

The best way to see the downtown sights is on foot, but a narrated trip with **Richmond Tours** (© **877/913-0151** or 804/213-0151; www.richmondtours. com) is a good way to get the lay of the land before striking out on your own. The 3-hour "Discover Richmond" tour departs daily at 9:45am and gives an overview of the city. Fares are $23. The 2-hour "Richmond at a Glance" tour hits the highlights. It runs from April through October daily at 2pm and costs $21. Children under 12 get a $2 discount on all tours. They'll pick you up at your hotel if you book at least a day in advance.

RICHMOND RIVERFRONT CANAL WALK ⊛

George Washington envisioned a system of canals that would link America's eastern seaboard with the Ohio and Mississippi rivers in the west. In Richmond, construction began in 1789 on the James River & Kanawha Canal, which was to run alongside the James River and connect it to the Kanawha River. It reached as far as Buchanan, Virginia, before the railroads made canal transportation obsolete in the early 19th century (its towpath was later sold to the Richmond and Allegheny Railroad, which laid tracks along it).

The city has restored more than 1 mile of the canal between Tobacco Row and the Tredegar Iron Works, at the foot of 5th Street, and turned it into the **Richmond Riverfront Canal Walk** (✆ **804/648-6549**). Brochures are available at the city's visitor centers (see "Orientation & Getting Around," earlier).

The ends of the walk are the most interesting parts. Near the eastern end, at the foot of Virginia Street in Shockoe Slip, you can take a 35-minute ride on the canal in a bateau operated by **Richmond Canal Cruises** (✆ **804/649-2800; www.richmondriverfront.com**). Weather permitting, the motorized passenger boats run Wednesday to Saturday from noon to 7pm, Sunday from noon to 5pm, in summer. Spring and fall schedules are usually Friday and Saturday from noon to 7pm, Sunday from noon to 5pm, but call to confirm. Rides are $5 for adults, $4 seniors and children 5 to 12, free for kids under 5. Buy tickets at the booth at the foot of Virginia Street.

You can cross the canal on the 14th Street Bridge, a block away, and see the **Floodwall Picture Gallery,** whose mural of Robert E. Lee stirred up nearly as much controversy as the statute of Arthur Ashe on Monument Avenue (see "From Swords to Tennis Racquets", earlier). The wall was built after the James flooded during Hurricane Agnes in 1972, causing some $350 million in damages in the area (whose restoration led to their emerging as dining-entertainment areas).

At the western end of the walk, at the foot of 5th Street, the **Tredegar Iron Works** on Brown's Island was the South's largest industrial complex during the Civil War, producing about half of the Confederacy's armaments. The restored brick building now houses the National Park Services' **Richmond Civil War Visitor Center at Tredegar Iron Works** (see "Top Historical Attractions," below). Opposite the visitor center, **Brown's Island** is the scene of festivals and free outdoor concerts and movies (see "Fun Freebies," later).

TOP HISTORICAL ATTRACTIONS

Edgar Allan Poe Museum ⭐   The poet Edgar Allan Poe was orphaned at age 2 and taken into the home of John and Frances Valentine Allan, thus his middle name. As a young man, Poe worked as an editor, critic, and writer for the *Southern Literary Messenger*. The desk and chair he used are among the memorabilia, photographs, portraits, and documents that tell the story of his rather sad life and career. Consisting of four buildings, the museum complex centers on the Old Stone House, the oldest building in Richmond, dating to about 1736. Poe didn't live here, but as a 15-year-old he was part of a junior honor guard that escorted Lafayette here when the aging general visited in 1824. Today the Old Stone House is the starting point for tours of the complex. The other buildings were added to house the collection of Poe artifacts and publications, the largest in existence. Most fascinating is the Raven Room's illustrations of "The Raven" by Edouard Manet and James Carling. You must take a guided tour, but you can examine its Enchanted Garden containing evergreens and flowers on your own. (The Poe Museum is only a block from the Virginia Holocaust Museum, so park once to see both attractions.)

1914–1916 E. Main St. ✆ **888/21E-POE** or 804/648-5523. www.poemuseum.org. Admission $6 adults, $5 seniors and students, free for children 7 and under. Tues–Sat 10am–5pm; Sun 11am–5pm. Mandatory 45-min. tours depart on the hour (last tour departs 4pm).

John Marshall House ⭐   This historic property is the restored home of John Marshall, a giant in American judicial history. As its chief justice from 1801 to

Downtown Richmond Attractions

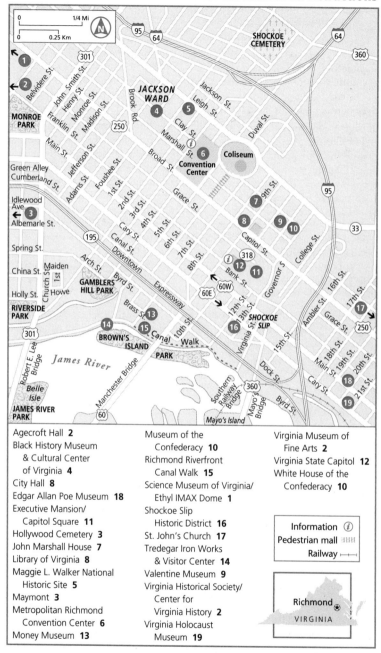

Agecroft Hall **2**
Black History Museum
& Cultural Center
of Virginia **4**
City Hall **8**
Edgar Allan Poe Museum **18**
Executive Mansion/
Capitol Square **11**
Hollywood Cemetery **3**
John Marshall House **7**
Library of Virginia **8**
Maggie L. Walker National
Historic Site **5**
Maymont **3**
Metropolitan Richmond
Convention Center **6**
Money Museum **13**

Museum of the
Confederacy **10**
Richmond Riverfront
Canal Walk **15**
Science Museum of Virginia/
Ethyl IMAX Dome **1**
Shockoe Slip
Historic District **16**
St. John's Church **17**
Tredegar Iron Works
& Visitor Center **14**
Valentine Museum **9**
Virginia Historical Society/
Center for
Virginia History **2**
Virginia Holocaust
Museum **19**

Virginia Museum of
Fine Arts **2**
Virginia State Capitol **12**
White House of the
Confederacy **10**

Information *i*
Pedestrian mall
Railway

Richmond
VIRGINIA

Tips View from Above

For a fine bird's-eye view of the city, go up to the observation deck of the **New City Hall,** 900 Broad St. at 9th Street. You can see for miles over Richmond and the James River.

1835, Marshall essentially established the power of the U.S. Supreme Court through his doctrine of judicial review, under which federal courts can overturn acts of Congress. Earlier, Marshall served in the Revolutionary Army, argued cases for his close friend George Washington, served as ambassador to France under John Adams, and had a brief term as secretary of state. He was a political foe of his cousin, Thomas Jefferson. Largely intact, the house he built between 1788 and 1790 is remarkable for many original architectural features—exterior brick lintels, interior wide-plank pine floors, wainscoting, and paneling. Period antiques and reproductions supplement Marshall's own furnishings and personal artifacts. You must take a guided tour to see the house. If you have to wait, spend the time checking out the museum shop and the gardens.

818 E. Marshall St. (at 9th St.). (ⓒ 804/648-7998. www.apva.org. Free admission to museum. Tours $5 adults, $4 seniors, $3 students, free for children 6 and under. Tues–Sat 10am–4:30pm, Sun noon–5pm. Mandatory 1-hr. house tours run as necessary Tues–Fri, on the hour and half-hour Sat–Sun.

Maggie L. Walker National Historic Site   The daughter of a former slave, Maggie L. Walker was a gifted woman who achieved success in the world of finance and business and rose to become the first woman bank president in the country. Originally a teacher, Walker, after her marriage in 1886, became involved in the affairs of a black fraternal organization, the Independent Order of St. Luke, which grew under her guidance into an insurance company, then into a full-fledged bank, the St. Luke Penny Savings Bank. The bank continues today as the Consolidated Bank and Trust, the oldest surviving African-American-operated bank in the United States. Walker also became editor of a newspaper and created and developed a department store. Her residence from 1904 until her death in 1934, this house remained in her family until 1979. The National Park Service has restored it to its 1930 appearance. Park rangers lead 30-minute guided tours.

600 N. 2nd St. (between 1st and 2nd sts.). (ⓒ 804/771-2017. www.nps.gov/malw. Free admission. Mon–Sat 9am–5pm. Closed New Year's Day, Thanksgiving, and Christmas. 30-min. tours depart as necessary.

The Museum and White House of the Confederacy ✦✦✦   One of Virginia's top attractions, and a must for Civil War buffs, this excellent museum houses the largest Confederate collection in the country, much contributed by veterans and their descendants. All the war's major events and campaigns are documented, and exhibits include period clothing and uniforms, a replica of Lee's headquarters, the role of African-Americans in the Civil War, Confederate memorabilia, weapons, and art. When the rebels moved their capital to Richmond, the city government leased the 1818 mansion next door as a temporary home for Pres. Jefferson Davis. As the White House of the Confederacy, it was the center of wartime social and political activity in Richmond. Formal dinners, luncheons, and occasional cabinet meetings were held in the dining room, a Victorian chamber with ornate ceiling decoration; some of the furniture in this room is original to the Davis family. The entrance hall is notable for its classical Comedy and Tragedy figures holding exquisite gas lamps. Guests were received in the center parlor, interesting now for its knickknacks produced by captured Confederate soldiers and for an 1863 portrait of Davis. Upstairs are the bedrooms and the office in which Davis conducted the business of war. You can explore the museum on your own, but you must take a guided tour to see the house (tours depart from the museum lobby). Allow at least 2 hours to see both. There is validated parking in MCVH patients parking deck next door at end of Clay Street.

1201 E. Clay St. (at 12th St.). © 804/649-1861. www.moc.org. Museum admission $7 adults, $6 seniors, $3 children 7–18, free for children 6 and under. White House admission $7 adults, $6 seniors, $4 children 7–18. Combination ticket (White House and museum) $10 adults, $9 seniors, $5 children 7–18. Mon–Sat 10am–5pm (tours 11:30am–4pm); Sun noon–5pm (tours 12:30–4pm). Mandatory 45-min. White House tours depart continuously. Closed New Year's Day, Thanksgiving, and Christmas.

Richmond National Battlefield Park ★★★   As the political, medical, and manufacturing center of the South and the primary supply depot for Lee's Army of Northern Virginia, Richmond was a prime Union target throughout the Civil War. In 1862 Gen. George McClellan's Peninsula Campaign attacked from the southeast, and in 1864 Gen. Ulysses S. Grant advanced from the north. Neither succeeded in capturing Richmond, but Grant won the war by laying siege to Petersburg, thus cutting off Richmond's supplies from the south. The bloody battlefields of those campaigns ring Richmond's eastern side, now mostly suburbs, for some 80 miles.

Stop first at the **Richmond Civil War Visitor Center at Tredegar Iron Works,** at the foot of 5th Street on the Richmond Riverfront Canal Walk (see above). Here, a 22-minute video about the battles will get you oriented. Upstairs, the "Richmond Speaks" exhibit poignantly tells the city's story with photos, artifacts, and readings from letters soldiers wrote to their families. Outside stands a touching statue of Pres. Abraham Lincoln and son Todd, a depiction of their visit to Richmond shortly after it fell in 1865. The visitor center and Chimborazo Medical Museum (see below) are open daily 9am to 5pm; closed New Year's Day, Thanksgiving, and Christmas.

If you're planning to drive around the battlefields, be sure to get the free park service brochure, which has an excellent map outlining the route, and buy an audio tape or CD tour at the bookshop ($10 tape, $16 CD), which also carries a wide array of Civil War books. You will need an at least an hour at the visitor center and another 3 to complete the battlefield tour without stops, so give yourself at least half a day, more to do it in comfort.

Your first stop heading out of town will be the **Chimborazo Medical Museum,** on East Broad Street at 33rd Street. This was the site of one of the Confederacy's largest hospitals (about 76,000 patients were treated here). Park headquarters are located here.

There are visitor centers at **Cold Harbor** to the northeast and at **Fort Harrison** and **Glendale/Malvern Hill** to the southeast. Cold Harbor was the scene of a particularly bloody 1864 encounter during which 7,000 of Grant's men were

---

Impressions

As the sun rose on Richmond, such a spectacle was presented as can never be forgotten by those who witnessed it . . . All of the horrors of the final conflagration, when the earth shall be wrapped in flames and melt with fervent heat, were, it seemed to us, prefigured in our capital.

—An observer, April 3, 1865

Tips   Keep Going

It's convenient to combine a tour of the Civil War battlefields east of Richmond with the James River plantations (see chapter 10), since the Fort Harrison and Glendale/Malvern Hill visitor centers are near Va. 5, the plantations route.

---

killed or injured in just 30 minutes. Programs with costumed Union and Confederate soldiers re-enacting life in the Civil War era take place during the summer. The Cold Harbor visitor center is open year-round, daily 9am to 5pm, and rangers lead 45-minute walking tours of the battlefield during summer. The Fort Harrison and Glendale/Malvern Hill visitor centers are open daily 9am to 5pm in summer, on weekends during spring and fall.

For more information, contact the park at 3215 E. Broad St. at 33rd St. (© **804/ 226-1981;** www.nps.gov/rich). Admission to all visitor centers is free, but there's a $4 parking fee at Tredegar Iron Works.

St. John's Episcopal Church ✶✶   Originally known simply as the "church on Richmond Hill," St. John's dates to 1741, but its congregation was established in 1611. Alexander Whitaker, the first rector, instructed Pocahontas in Christianity, baptized her, and married her to John Rolfe. The building is best known as the 1775 meeting place of the second Virginia Convention. In attendance were Thomas Jefferson, George Wythe, George Mason, Benjamin Harrison, George Washington, Richard Henry Lee, and many other historic personages. In support of a bill to assemble and train a militia to oppose Great Britain, Patrick Henry stood up and delivered his incendiary speech: "Is life so dear, or peace so sweet, as to be purchased at the price of chains or slavery? Forbid it, Almighty God! I know not what course others may take; but as for me, give me liberty, or give me death!"

You'll see the original 1741 entrance and pulpit, the stained-glass windows, and the pew where Patrick Henry sat during the convention. From Memorial Day through Labor Day weekends, there's a living-history program at 2pm re-creating the Second Virginia Convention (admission is free but donation plates are passed).

2401 E. Broad St. (at 24th St.). © 804/648-5015. www.historicstjohnschurch.org. Admission $5 adults, $4 seniors, $3 children 7–18, free for children 6 and under. 25-min. tours given Mon–Sat 10am–3:30pm; Sun 1–3:30pm; services Sun at 8:30 and 11am.

The Valentine Richmond History Center ✶   This museum takes its name from Mann S. Valentine II, a 19th-century businessman and patron of the arts whose fortune was based on a patent medicine called Valentine's Meat Juice, and his brother, the noted sculptor Edward Valentine, whose extraordinary image of Thomas Jefferson adorns The Jefferson Hotel. Documenting the history of Richmond from the 17th to the 20th centuries, it includes the Federal-style Wickham House, built in 1812 by attorney John Wickham, Richmond's wealthiest citizen, who had helped defend Aaron Burr against treason charges in 1807. Wickham assembled the finest talents of his day to design and decorate his mansion and entertained Richmond's social elite here, along with such visiting notables as Daniel Webster, Zachary Taylor, John Calhoun, Henry Clay, and William Thackeray. Highlights include spectacular wall paintings, perhaps the rarest and most complete set in the nation; the Oval Parlor, designated as "one of the hundred most beautiful rooms in America"; and the circular Palette Staircase.

Even more interesting to art lovers is the **Edward Valentine Sculpture Studio,** in a carriage house behind the Wickham House. It contains Edward Valentine's personal effects and plaster models of his work, including an early version of "Lee Recumbent," his magnificent statue of Robert E. Lee now at the Lee Chapel Museum in Lexington (see chapter 7).

Wickham's Garden Café is a good place to refresh during your walking tour. It's open Monday to Friday from 8am to 3pm.

1015 E. Clay St. © 804/649-0711. www.valentinemuseum.com. Admission $7 adults, $6 seniors and students, $4 children 7–12, $1 children 3–7, free for children 2 and under. Tues–Sat 10am–5pm; Sun noon–5pm. Mandatory 30-min. tours depart on the hour 11am–4pm.

Virginia State Capitol ★★
Thomas Jefferson was minister to France when he was commissioned to work on a capitol building for Virginia. He patterned the Classical Revival building on the Maison Carrée, a Roman temple built in Nîmes during the 1st century A.D., which he greatly admired. The colonnaded wings were added between 1904 and 1906. Today the building is the second-oldest working capitol in the United States, in continuous use since 1788.

The central portion is the magnificent Rotunda, its domed skylight ceiling ornamented in Renaissance style. The room's dramatic focal point is Houdon's life-size statue of George Washington, said to be a perfect likeness. "That is the man, himself," said Lafayette. "I can almost realize he is going to move." A Carrara-marble bust of Lafayette by Houdon is also displayed in the Rotunda, along with busts of the seven other Virginia-born presidents.

Resembling an open courtyard, the old Hall of the House of Delegates, where the Virginia House of Delegates met from 1788 to 1906, is now a museum. Here, in 1807, Washington Irving took notes while John Marshall tried and acquitted Aaron Burr of treason. The room was also a meeting place of the Confederate Congress. In the former Senate chamber, now used for occasional committee meetings, Stonewall Jackson's body lay in state after his death in 1863.

Like most government buildings these days, access is restricted and you must pass through a metal detector at the visitor's entrance on the western side of the building. Casual visitors are now required to take a 30-minute guided tour in order to see inside the building. After the tour, explore the **Capitol grounds.** To the east is the **Executive Mansion,** official residence of governors of Virginia since 1813. Another historic building is the old **Bell Tower,** built in 1824, often the scene of lunch-hour entertainment in summer. The Bell Tower houses a visitor center, where you can get information about Virginia destinations.

Note: The capitol complex is scheduled to be undergoing renovation from 2004 through 2006, so call ahead to make sure tours will be given when you're here.

9th and Grace sts. © 804/698-1788. www.virginia.org. Free admission. 30-min. tours depart continuously Mon–Fri 9am–4:30pm, Sat 10am–3pm.

Fun Fact Thick Walls

While walking around downtown, stop into the **Old City Hall,** on Broad Street between 9th and 10th streets. Built in 1894, it is a dramatic Victorian Gothic with gray-stone walls 3 feet thick. Now a private office building, it has an interior courtyard that's a three-story marvel of painted cast iron. Visitors are welcome to enter the first floor during business hours. It's well worth the stop.

Fun Fact **A Lifelike Washington**

The Houdon statue of George Washington in the Rotunda of the Virginia State Capitol is the only one ever made of the first president from life.

THE "BOULEVARD MUSEUMS"

The following museums are either on or near Boulevard, a major north-south avenue. On weekends the city's **Blue Line** trolley operates along Boulevard between the science museum and Maymount (see "Getting Around," earlier).

Science Museum Of Virginia/Ethyl Corporation IMAX Dome & Planetarium *Kids*   There are few "do not touch" signs here; hands-on exhibits are the norm in this science museum with state-of-the-art planetarium, making it ideal for youngsters. For example, in "Computer Works," visitors create programs, discuss their problems with a computer shrink, and play "assistant" for a computer magician. One wing features exhibits on aerospace technology, energy and electricity, chemistry, and physics. Elsewhere, you'll learn about optical illusions inside a giant kaleidoscope, try to get your bearings in a full-size distorted room, crawl into a space capsule, and learn about DNA in the Bioscape. Not to be missed are the shows at the 250-seat Ethyl Corporation IMAX Dome & Planetarium, which shows Omnimax films as well as the most sophisticated special-effects multimedia planetarium shows.

The building itself merits attention: It's the beaux arts former Broad Street Station, designed in 1919 by John Russell Pope (architect of the Jefferson Memorial, the National Archives, and the National Gallery of Art) as the city's train station. With a soaring rotunda, classical columns, vaults, and arches, Pope created it to evoke a sense of wonder—very fitting for a museum of science. Free parking.

2500 W. Broad St. (3 blocks east of Boulevard). © 800/659-1727 or 804/864-1400. www.smv.org. Admission $7 adults, $6.50 seniors, $6 children 4–12. Tickets to films, $7 per person, free for children 2 and under. Exhibits, summer Mon–Thurs 9:30am–5pm, Fri–Sat 9:30am–7pm, Sun 11:30am–5pm; winter Mon–Sat 9:30am–5pm, Sun 11:30am–5pm. Theater, Mon–Thurs 10:30am–5pm; Fri–Sat 10:30am–9pm; Sun noon–5pm. Call or check website for daily show times.

Virginia Historical Society/Museum of Virginia History *★*   Housed in the neoclassical Battle Abbey, built in 1913 as a shrine to the state's Civil War dead, the South's oldest historical society (founded in 1831) has the world's largest collection of Virginia artifacts. Touring the major exhibit, "The Story of Virginia, an American Experience," is like rummaging through the state's attic: You'll see gold buttons from Pocahontas's hat, Patrick Henry's eyeglasses, and much, much more. Changing exhibits cover a range of subjects, from Civil War armaments to the civil rights movement in Virginia. Genealogists will find a treasure trove of family histories in the library of some 125,000 volumes and seven million manuscripts.

428 N. Boulevard (at Kensington Ave.). © 804/358-4901. www.vahistorical.org. Admission $4 adults, $3 seniors, $2 students and children. Free admission to galleries on Mon. Mon–Sat 10am–5pm; Sun 1–5pm.

Virginia Museum of Fine Arts *★★*   Any city would be proud of this museum, noted for the largest public Fabergé collection outside Russia—more than 300 objets d'art created at the turn of the century for Tsars Alexander III and Nicholas II. The Imperial jewel-encrusted Easter eggs evoke what art historian Parker Lesley calls the "dazzling, idolatrous realm of the last czars." Other highlights include the Goya portrait *General Nicholas Guye,* a life-size marble statue of Roman emperor Caligula, Monet's *Iris by the Pond,* and six magnificent Gobelin *Don Quixote* tapestries. That's not to mention the works of de Kooning, Gauguin, van Gogh, Delacroix, Matisse, Degas, Picasso, Gainsborough, and others; antiquities from China, Japan, Egypt, Greece, Byzantium, Africa, and South America; art from India, Nepal, and Tibet; and an impressive collection of contemporary American art. The museum also has an inexpensive cafeteria overlooking a waterfall cascading into a pool with a Maillol sculpture.

2800 Grove Ave. (at Boulevard). (C) 804/340-1400. www.vmfa.state.va.us. Free Admission ($5 donation suggested). Wed–Sun 11am–5pm. Closed New Year's Day, July 4th, Thanksgiving, and Christmas.

HOUSES, GARDENS & CEMETERIES

Agecroft Hall   In an elegant neighborhood overlooking the James River, Agecroft Hall is a late-15th-century Tudor manor house built in Lancashire, England, brought here piece by piece in the 1920s. Today it serves as a museum portraying the social history and material culture of an English gentry family of the late-Tudor and early-Stuart eras. Typical of its period, the house has ornate plaster ceilings, massive fireplaces, rich oak paneling, leaded and stained glass windows, and a two-story great hall with a mullioned window 25 feet long. Furnishings authentically represent the period. Adjoining the mansion are a formal sunken garden, resembling one at Hampton Court Palace, and a formal flower garden, an Elizabethan knot garden, and an herb garden. Visitors see a brief video about the estate before taking the tour. Plan time to explore the gardens as well.

4305 Sulgrave Rd. (C) 804/353-4241. www.agecrofthall.com. Admission $7 adults, $6 seniors, $4 students; half-price for gardens only. Tues–Sat 10am–4pm; Sun 12:30–5pm. Mandatory 30-min. house tours depart on hour and half-hour.

Hollywood Cemetery   Perched on the bluffs overlooking the James River not far from Maymont (see below), Hollywood Cemetery is the serenely beautiful resting place of Presidents Monroe and Tyler, Confederate president Jefferson Davis, six Virginia governors, and 18,000 Confederate soldiers, including J.E.B. Stuart and 21 other Confederate generals. Designed in 1847, it was conceived as a place where nature would remain undisturbed. A 90-foot granite pyramid, a monument constructed in 1869, marks the Confederate section. A 20-minute film about the cemetery is shown in the office.

412 S. Cherry (at Albemarle St.). (C) 804/648-8501. www.hollywoodcemetery.org. Free admission. Cemetery, daily 8am–5pm; office, Mon–Fri 8:30am–4:30pm.

Lewis Ginter Botanical Garden ★★   In the 1880s, self-made Richmond millionaire, philanthropist, and amateur horticulturist Lewis Ginter (a founder of the American Tobacco Company and creator of The Jefferson Hotel) built the Lakeside Wheel Club as a playground for the city's elite. The resort boasted a lake, a nine-hole golf course, cycling paths, and a zoo. At Ginter's death in 1897, his niece, Grace Arents, converted the property to a hospice for sick children. An

---

Kids **More Cool Stuff for Kids**

Next door to the Science Museum Of Virginia, the **Children's Museum of Richmond,** 2626 W. Broad St. ((C) 877/295-CMORB or 804/424-CMOR; www. c-mor.org), has more innovative hands-on exhibits for kids age 6 months to 12 years. Admission is $7 per person. Open Tuesday to Saturday from 9:30am to 5pm, Sunday from noon to 5pm.

ardent horticulturist herself, she imported rare trees and shrubs and constructed greenhouses. Grace died in 1926, leaving her estate to the city to be maintained as a botanical garden and public park. Today it's one of the finest botanical gardens in the state. Start at the visitor center and give yourself plenty of time here. In addition to the greenhouses and 30 acres of gardens, you can tour the Bloemendall House (named for Ginter's ancestral home in The Netherlands), visit the conservatory and library-education complex, have lunch at the **Garden Cafe** or refreshments in the **Robins Tea House,** and browse the garden shop. Anyone with a green thumb will love it all.

1800 Lakeside Ave. ℂ 804/262-9887. www.lewisginter.org. Admission $8 adults, $7 seniors, $4 children 3–12, free for children 2 and under. Daily 9am–5pm. Take I-95N to Exit 80 (Brook Rd.) and turn left at Hilliard Rd. to Lakeside.

Maymont ⭐ *(Kids)*   In 1886, Maj. James Henry Dooley, one of Richmond's self-made millionaires, purchased a 100-acre dairy farm and built this 33-room Romanesque Revival–style mansion surrounded by beautifully landscaped grounds. The house has a colonnaded sandstone facade, turrets, and towers. The details of the formal rooms reflect various periods, most notably 18th-century French. The dining room has a coffered oak ceiling; the library, a stenciled strapwork ceiling. A grand stairway leads to a landing from which two-story-high stained-glass windows rise. The house is elaborately furnished with pieces from many periods chosen by the Dooleys—Oriental carpets, an Art Nouveau swan-shaped bed, marble and bronze sculpture, porcelains, tapestries, and Tiffany vases.

The Dooleys lavished the same care on the grounds. They placed gazebos wherever the views were best, laid out Italian and Japanese gardens, and planted horticultural specimens and exotic trees culled from the world over. The **Nature and Visitor Center** has interactive exhibits interpreting the James River. There are outdoor animal habitats for birds, bison, beaver, deer, elk, and bear. At the **Children's Farm,** youngsters can feed chickens, piglets, goats, peacocks, cows, donkeys, and sheep. A collection of late-19th- and early-20th-century horse-drawn carriages— surreys, phaetons, hunting vehicles—is on display at the **Carriage House.** Carriage and hayrides are a weekend afternoon option during summer.

You can see everything else on your own, but you must take a guided tour in order to visit Maymont house (enter the park via the visitor center). There's a parking lot off Spottswood Road near the Children's Farm, and another at Hampton Street and Pennsylvania Avenue near the gardens.

2201 Shields Dr. (north of the James River between Va. 161 and Meadow St.). ℂ 804/358-7166. www.maymont.org. Free admission (donations suggested). Tues–Sun noon–5pm (last house tour 4:30pm). Mandatory 25-min. house tours depart every half-hour. Go south to the end of Boulevard; follow signs to the parking area.

Wilton House   Originally built on the James River about 14 miles below Richmond, this 1753 Georgian mansion was painstakingly dismantled and reconstructed on this bluff overlooking the river in 1933. Most of the original brick, flooring, and paneling were saved. Wilton's design has been attributed to Williamsburg architect Richard Taliaferro. It was part of a 2,000-acre plantation where William Randolph III entertained many of the leading figures of the day, including George Washington, Thomas Jefferson, and Lafayette. The house has a fine collection of period furnishings based on an 1815 inventory. All rooms feature pine paneling, some with fluted pilasters and denticulated cornices.

215 S. Wilton Rd. (off W. Cary St.). ℂ 804/282-5936. www.wiltonhousemusuem.org. Admission $5 adults, $4 seniors and students, free for children 5 and under. Tues–Fri 1–4:30pm; Sat 10am–4pm, Sun 1:30–4:30pm; Feb by appointment only. Closed national holidays. Mandatory 45-min. tours depart continuously. Take Va. 147 (W. Cary St.) west and turn south on Wilton Rd.

SPECIAL INTEREST MUSEUMS

In Jackson Ward, the **Black History Museum & Cultural Center of Virginia,** 00 Clay St. (yes, that's the address), at Foushee Street (© **804/780-9093;** www.blackhistorymuseum.org), houses documents, limited editions, prints, art, and photos emphasizing the history of the state's African-American community. It's in a Federal–Greek Revival–style house built in 1832 and purchased a century later by the Council of Colored Women under the leadership of Maggie L. Walker. Admission is $4 for adults, $3 seniors, $2 for children under 12. Open Tuesday to Saturday 10am to 5pm, Sunday 11am to 5pm.

Built by Richmond's Jewish community, one of the oldest in the United States, **Virginia Holocaust Museum,** 2000 E. Cary St. (© **804/257-5400;** www. va-holocaust.com), in Tobacco Row between 20th and 21st streets, honors those who died in or lived through the Holocaust. Local survivors tell their stories in the moving Survivors' Room. There's also a mock ghetto surrounded by barbed wire and a model of an underground hiding place. Admission is free but donations are encouraged. It's open Monday to Friday from 9am to 5pm, Saturday and Sunday from 11am to 5pm.

Numismatists will enjoy the small but interesting **Money Museum,** in the Federal Reserve Bank lobby, 701 E. Byrd St., between 7th Street and the Manchester Bridge (© **804/679-8108;** www.rich.frb.org). Exhibits trace the history of money, from the bartering of corn to an uncut sheet of $100,000 gold certificates. You can see it all in 20 minutes. Admission is free. Open Monday to Friday from 9:30am to 3:30pm.

The lobby of the **Library of Virginia,** 800 Broad St., between 8th and 9th streets (© **804/692-3919;** www.lva.lib.va.us), has changing exhibits of state documents and published works, some of them more than 400 years old. The library is open Monday through Saturday from 9am to 5pm; admission is free.

Anyone who loves old airplanes can see some beautifully restored craft at the small but impressive **Virginia Aviation Museum,** 5701 Huntsman Rd. (© **804/236-3622;** www.vam.smv.org), on the grounds of Richmond International Airport. The planes date from 1916 to 1946, often called the golden age of aviation. Included is a World War I Spad, one of the few still airworthy. The museum is a division of the Science Museum of Virginia (see above). Admission is $5.50 adults, $4.50 seniors, $3 for kids 4 to 12. It's open Monday to Saturday 9:30am to 5pm, Sunday noon to 5pm. Closed Thanksgiving and Christmas.

A RIVERBOAT CRUISE

Modern technology's answer to an 1850s riverboat, the paddle wheeler *Annabel Lee* (© **866/211-3810** or 804/664-5700; www.annabellee.com) offers a variety of lunch, dinner, and sightseeing cruises down the James River, some as far as the plantations. She operates from April to mid-October. Call or check the website for prices and departure times. Reservations are a must, especially on weekends.

NEARBY ATTRACTIONS

About 14 miles north of Richmond on I-95, the communities of **Ashland** and **Hanover** have deep historical roots. Patrick Henry once tended bar at Hanover Tavern, built in 1723, and argued cases in the Hanover County Courthouse, dating from 1735. For more information contact the Ashland/Hanover Visitor Center, 112 N. Railroad Ave. in Hanover (© **800/897-1479** or 804/752-6766; www.town.ashland.va.us). Open daily 9am to 5pm except major holidays.

Scotchtown ⭐ One of Virginia's oldest plantation houses, Scotchtown is a charming one-story white-clapboard home in a parklike setting of small

---

Tips **Overseeing the Dominion**

Paramount's Kings Dominion theme park has a host of activities on many acres of land, so arrive early, pick up a park guide, and spend your first half-hour carefully planning how to spend the rest of the day.

---

dependencies and gardens. Charles Chiswell of Williamsburg built the house around 1719, but it's best known as a residence of Patrick Henry, who bought it in 1770 and lived here from 1771 to 1778 with his wife, Sarah, and their six children. Henry served as governor of Virginia during those years, but sadly, Sarah was mentally ill during much of that time and eventually confined to a room in the basement. Although Henry last lived at Red Hill near Lynchburg (see chapter 6), this is the only house he ever occupied which is still standing. It has been beautifully restored and furnished with 18th-century antiques, some associated with the Henry family. In the study, Henry's mahogany desk-table still bears his ink stains, and bookshelves hold his law books. Scotchtown has associations with another historical figure, Dolley Madison, whose mother was a first cousin to Patrick Henry. Dolley and her mother lived here while their family moved back to this area from North Carolina. Unlike so many historic houses, none of the rooms here are roped off, so you can go into all of them during the leisurely and informative guided tours, which give an overview of 18th-century plantation life in Virginia, in addition to the specific Henry story.

16120 Chiswell Lane, Beaverdam. © 804/227-3500. www.apva.org. Admission $7 adults, $5 seniors, $4 students 6–18, free for children 5 and under; grounds only, $3 per person. Apr–Oct Tues–Sat 10am–4:30pm, Sun 1:30–4:30pm; Nov Sat 10am–4:30pm, Sun 1:30–4:30pm; Dec–Mar by appointment only. Closed Easter, Mother's Day, July 4th. Mandatory 1-hr. house tours depart on demand. From Ashland, follow Va. 54 west, right on Scotchtown Road (C.R. 671) north, take right fork on C.R. 685.

Paramount's Kings Dominion *Kids* One of the most popular theme parks in the East, this 400-acre fanciful facility offers a variety of rides and entertainment, many with themes from Paramount movies and TV shows. It's especially famous for having the tallest drop ride in North America and one of the largest roller coaster collections on the east coast (you can spend all day here just being jolted up and down). The shows change from year-to-year so as not to bore the locals, but you can count on several from the Nickelodeon and Country Music Television cable channels, both Paramount properties. Almost like its own theme park, the splash-happy **WaterWorks** features Big Wave Bay, a 650,000-gallon wave pool. White Water Canyon is a wet-and-wild ride simulating whitewater rafting.

Doswell, VA. © 804/876-5000. www.kingsdominion.com. Admission changes from year to year, usually about $35 adults and children 3 and over. Parking $7. Season passes available. Hours may vary a bit from year to year, but generally park is open Memorial Day to Labor Day, daily 9:30am–8 or 10pm; Apr–May and Labor Day to early Oct, Sat–Sun 9:30am–8pm. Take Va. 30 (Exit 98) off I-95.

5 Sports & Outdoor Activities

SPECTATOR SPORTS

AUTO RACING See NASCAR racing at **Richmond International Raceway,** between Laburnum Avenue and the Henrico Turnpike/Meadowbridge Road (© 804/329-6796; www.rir.com). The Raceway is Virginia's largest sports facility, attracting crowds of 70,000 or more. (Check the website and avoid being in Richmond on race weekends, when accommodations are scarce.)

BASEBALL The **Richmond Braves** (© 804/359-4444; www.rbraves.com), the top minor league club in the Atlanta Braves' organization, compete in the AAA International League from April to mid-September. All home games are played at the 12,500-seat Diamond, 3001 N. Boulevard.

COLLEGE SPORTS The **University of Richmond**'s Spiders play football and basketball in the **Colonial Athletic Association** (© 804/289-8388; www. richmondspiders.com). **Virginia Commonwealth University**'s Rams, play basketball at the **Coliseum** (© 804/282-7267; www.vcurams.vcu.edu).

HORSE RACING Virginia's only parimutuel racetrack, **Colonial Downs,** is on Va. 155, between I-64 (Exit 205) and U.S. 60 in New Kent County, 25 miles east of Richmond (© 888/4VA-TRAC or 804/966-7223; www.colonialdowns.com). Call or check the website for schedule and ticket prices.

SOCCER The **Richmond Kickers** play professional soccer games at the **University of Richmond Stadium** (© 804/282-6776; www.richmondkickers. com).

OUTDOOR ACTIVITIES

GOLF Golf courses abound in the Richmond area. Among them are the public **Belmont Park Recreation Center,** 1800 Hilliard Rd. (© 804/266-4929; www.vwc.edu), and semi-private **Glenwood Golf Club,** Creighton Road (© 804/226-1793).

WHITE-WATER RAFTING You don't have to trek to the mountains to ride the rapids, for **Richmond Raft Company,** 4400 E. Main St., at Water Street (© 804/222-7238; www.richmondraft.com), offers trips on the James through the heart of Richmond. Water levels aren't always predictable, but the James is usually high and fast enough from March to November, with spring best for fast water.

6 Shopping

Richmond's neighborhoods have a number of specialty shops, including those mentioned below. The visitor centers provide brochures that cover these and many other stores around the city and out in the suburbs.

For distinctive souvenirs, don't forget museum gift shops, especially those at the Science Museum, Art Museum, Museum and White House of the Confederacy, Valentine Richmond History Museum, and the Virginia Children's Museum.

There are upscale shops along East Cary Street in Shockoe Slip, but the best place in town for a pleasant shopping stroll is in **Carytown,** the 7 blocks of West Cary Street between Boulevard and Nasemond Street, which is lined with a mix of small stores and interesting cafes. The old **First Baptist Church,** 3325 W. Cary St., has been transformed into an inviting retail complex, with the high-fashion **Annette Dean Apparel** and the fine Acadia restaurant (see "Where to Dine," earlier). Antiques hunting is good here, especially at **Thomas-Hines Antiques,** 3027 W. Cary St. (© 804/355-2782), and **Mariah Robinson Antiques and Fine Art,** 3455 W. Cary St. (© 804/355-1996). **Ten Thousand Villages,** 3201 W. Cary St. (© 804/358-5170), carries international handcrafts, with lots of baskets and primitive pottery.

You'll also find gourmet food shops, ethnic restaurants, secondhand clothing stores, and the landmark **Byrd Theater,** which shows second-run films at discount prices.

7 Richmond After Dark

Richmond is no New York or London, so you won't be attending internationally recognized theaters and music halls. Nevertheless, you might be able to catch visiting productions and artists at several venues. The city has its own ballet company and theater groups, and pierced-set bands rock Shockoe Bottom.

Current entertainment schedules can be found in the Thursday "Weekend" section of the *Richmond Times-Dispatch* (www.timesdispatch.com), the city's daily newspaper. The free tabloid *Style Weekly* (www.styleweekly.com) has details on theater, concerts, dance performances, and other happenings. It's widely available at the visitor centers and in hotel lobbies.

MAJOR CONCERT HALLS & ALL-PURPOSE AUDITORIUMS

Built in 1928 as a Loew's Theater, the **Carpenter Center for the Performing Arts,** 600 E. Grace St., at 6th Street (© 804/782-3900; www.carpentercenter.org), was restored in 1983 to its Moorish splendor, complete with twinkling stars and clouds painted on the ceiling overhead. The center hosts national touring companies for dance, orchestra, and theater performances. The Richmond Ballet, the Virginia Opera, and the Richmond Symphony perform here as well (see "The Performing Arts," below).

In the summer months, Richmond goes outdoors to **Dogwood Dell Festival of the Arts,** in Byrd Park, Boulevard and Idlewild Avenue (© 804/780-8683; www.dogwooddell.org), for free music and drama under the stars in this tiered grassy amphitheater. Bring the family, spread a blanket, and enjoy a picnic.

Built in 1927 adjacent to the bustling campus of Virginia Commonwealth University, the 3,500-seat **The Mosque,** Main and Laurel streets (© 804/780-4213), is decorated with exotic mosaics and pointed-arch doorways. Offerings range from stage productions to nationally known musicians. Next to the new Richmond Metropolitan Convention Center, the **Richmond Coliseum,** 601 E. Leigh St. (© 804/780-4970; www.richmondcoliseum.org), hosts everything from the Ringling Bros. and Barnum & Bailey circus to rock concerts. It's the largest indoor entertainment facility in Virginia and seats about 12,000. Major sporting events—wrestling, ice hockey, and basketball—are also scheduled here.

THE PERFORMING ARTS

You can catch family plays and musicals at **Theatre IV,** 114 W. Broad St. (© 804/344-8040; www.theatreiv.org), which stages family-oriented performances in the Empire Theater, at Broad and Jefferson streets.

The **Richmond Ballet** (© 804/359-0906; www.richmondballet.com), the official State Ballet of Virginia, performs from mid-October to May. Their productions run the gamut from classical to modern, from *The Nutcracker* to commissioned world premieres. The ballet, the **Virginia Opera** (© 804/643-6004;

Tips Fun Freebies

A non-profit organization called **City Celebrations** (© 804/788-6466; www.citycelebrations.org) keeps Richmond hopping with a series of free outdoor concerts, beer blasts, and street festivals from May through September. Regular freebies include a "Midweek MoJo" Wednesday evenings on the Richmond Riverfront Canal Walk, Thursday night outdoor movies on the riverfront, and Friday Cheers on Brown's Island.

www.vaopera.org), and the **Richmond Symphony** (© 804/788-1212; www. arts.state.va.us/richsymp.htm) all perform in the Carpenter Center for Performing Arts.

Tickets for most events are available through **Ticketmaster** (© 804/262-8003; www.ticketmaster.com).

THE CLUB & MUSIC SCENE

Shockoe Bottom is the city's funky nightlife district. It occupies the square block beginning with the 17th Street Farmer's Market going east along East Main and East Franklin streets to 18th Street. Its joints attract the "let's see your ID" crowd, and they go up and down in popularity, so those I visited recently may not be in vogue when you get here. If you can find a parking space, you can see for yourself what's going on by bar-hopping around Shockoe Bottom's busy block (but *do not* wander off onto deserted streets). Note that many Shockoe Bottom establishments are closed on Sunday and Monday.

Up Cary Street in the more affluent (and well-behaved) Shockoe Slip, several restaurants and pubs have live music, including **The Tobacco Company,** 1201 E. Cary St. (© **804/782-9555**), which has acoustic jazz upstairs Tuesday through Saturday and dancing downstairs Wednesday through Saturday from 8pm to 1am.

8 An Easy Excursion to Petersburg

In the 1860s, Petersburg was a vital rail junction, which Grant recognized as the key to his quest to take Richmond. When every effort to capture the Confederate capital failed, Grant, in an inspired move, crossed the James River south of Richmond and advanced on Petersburg. Lee's forces weren't cooperative, however, and a tragic 10-month siege ensued. Finally, on April 2, Grant's all-out assault smashed through Lee's right flank, and that night Lee retreated west. A week later came the surrender at Appomattox Court House.

Today, Petersburg is a quiet southern town on the banks of the Appomattox River 23 miles south of Richmond on I-95. Its downtown has a few museums of the Civil War period, which you can see in a few hours. The more interesting sights are on the outskirts, where the battles took place.

VISITOR INFORMATION   When you arrive, take Washington Street (Exit 52) west and follow the Petersburg Tour signs to the **Petersburg Visitor Center,** 425 Cockade Alley, Petersburg, VA 23804 (© **800/368-3595** or 804/733-2400; www.petersburg-va.org), where you can get maps and literature and buy a block ticket to local museums (see below). The center is open daily from 9am to 5pm.

There's also a visitor information center at the **Carson Rest Area** on I-95 (© **434/246-2145**), 18 miles south of the city. It's open daily from 9am to 5pm.

EXPLORING THE TOWN

Begin at the visitor center, in the basement of the 1815 McIlwaine House, which sells **block tickets** to the Siege Museum, Centre Hill Mansion, and Old Blandford Church for $11 adults, $9 seniors and children 7 to 12. Otherwise, admission to each is $5 adults, $4 seniors and children. Active-duty military personnel pay the seniors/children rate.

The **Siege Museum,** 15 W. Bank St. (© **804/733-2404**), tells the story of everyday life in Petersburg up to and during the siege in displays and an interesting 18-minute film narrated by the late Joseph Cotten, whose family lived in

---

Moments **The First Memorial Day**

After the Civil War, a group of Petersburg schoolgirls and their teacher came to Old Blandford Church to decorate the graves of the soldiers' buried in the churchyard. The ceremony inspired Mary Logan, wife of Union Gen. John A. Logan, who was head of the major organization of Union army veterans, to campaign for a national Memorial Day, which was first observed in 1868.

Petersburg during the Civil War. It's shown on the hour. Give yourself another 30 minutes to see the museum, in the old Merchant Exchange, a magnificent Greek Revival temple-fronted building. It's open daily from 10am to 5pm.

Centre Hill Mansion, 1 Centre Hill Circle (© 804/733-2401), between Adams and Tabb streets, is a nicely restored 1823 mansion furnished with Victorian pieces. Hours are daily from 10am to 5pm. You'll have to take a 30-minute tour (departing every hour from 10:30am to 4:30pm).

THE CIVIL WAR BATTLEFIELDS

Together, the sites below will take most of a day to tour. Start in the morning at the national battlefield's visitor center east of town and follow the one-way tour to the Crater. You'll come out of the national battlefield at Crater Road (U.S. 301), where Old Blandford Church is ¼ mile north. Have lunch at King's Barbecue No. 2, which is also nearby on Crater Road (see "Where to Dine," below). Spend the afternoon at Pamplin Historical Park.

Old Blandford Church 🔎   About 2 miles south of downtown, this ancient church boasts one of the largest collections of Tiffany-glass windows in existence and is noted for the first observance of Memorial Day. The church was constructed in 1735 but abandoned in the early 1800s when a new Episcopalian church was built closer to the town center. During the Civil War, the building became a hospital for wounded soldiers, and many were later buried in the church graveyard. The 13 Confederate states each sponsored one of the Tiffany windows as a memorial to its Confederate dead. The local Ladies Memorial Association commissioned the 14th window. The artist himself, Louis Comfort Tiffany, gave the church the 15th window, a magnificent "Cross of Jewels" that is thrillingly illuminated at sunset.

319 S. Crater Rd. (U.S. 301; at Rochelle Lane). © 804/733-2396. Admission $5 adults, $4 seniors and children. Daily 10am–5pm. 30-min. tours depart every 45 min. 10am–4pm. From downtown, take Bank St. east and turn right on Crater Rd. (U.S. 301).

Pamplin Historical Park & The National Museum of the Civil War Soldier 🔎   The battleground where Union troops actually broke through the Confederate lines on April 2, 1865, to end the siege is in this fine, privately owned park, where more than a mile of interpretive trails lead through some of Petersburg's best-preserved Confederate earthen-work fortifications. There's a re-created Military Encampment with costumed interpreters, and a Battlefield Center with high tech displays explaining the final conflict. Guides lead 45-minute guided walking tours of the battlefield twice a day; call for times. The park also includes Tudor Hall, a plantation home built in 1812, which you can see on your own or via a 2-hour guided tour. You start all this at The National Museum of the Civil War Soldier, which is dedicated to the common foot soldier (no famous generals need apply). The Field Quarter interprets what slave life was like in the 19th century. The museum is best explored with an audio-tour (which you can rent from the museum), which will explain the exhibits and what a soldier's life was like from 1861 to 1865. Allow an hour in the museum, another 2 to see the battlefield and Tudor Hall.

6125 Boydton Plank Rd. (U.S. 1). © 877/PAMPLIN or 804/861-2408. www.pamplinpark.org. Admission $14 adults, $12 seniors, $7 children 6–11, free for children 5 and under. Daily 9am–5pm (to 6pm Memorial Day to Labor Day). Closed New Year's Day, Thanksgiving, and Christmas. Park is 6 miles south of downtown, 1 mile south of I-85.

Petersburg National Battlefield Park ✦✦   Encompassing some 2,646 acres, this park preserves the key sites of the siege that lasted from mid-June 1864 to early April 1865. A 17-minute multimedia presentation at the visitor center tells the story, and a one-way 4-mile battlefield driving tour has wayside exhibits; some stops have short walking trails. The last and most fascinating is the site of the Crater, literally a huge depression blown into the ground when a group of Pennsylvania volunteer infantry, including many miners, dug a passage beneath Confederate lines and exploded 4 tons of powder, creating the 170-foot by 60-foot crater. The explosion killed 278 Confederates, and, during the ensu-ing battle, thousands more men on both sides were killed or wounded. Stop at the Taylor Home before you get there for a view down over the Crater. If you have more time, an extended driving tour follows the entire siege line from the visitor center 26-miles to Five Forks Battlefield in Dinwiddie County.

1539 Hickory Hill Rd. (Va. 36; 2½ miles east of downtown via E. Washington St.). © 804/732-3531. www.nps.gov/pete. Admission $5 per vehicle; $3 per pedestrian or bicyclist. Open year-round daily 9am–5pm.

ATTRACTIONS AT FORT LEE

Fort Lee is home to the U.S. Army Quartermaster Corps and its **Quartermaster Museum** (© 804/734-4203; www.qmmuseum.lee.army.mil), which has uni-forms and equipment from all of America's wars. Stars of the show are the World War II Jeep with a Mercedes car seat specially installed for Gen. George S. Patton and one of the armored "Circus Wagons" in which Gen. Dwight D. Eisenhower lived when on the road in Europe during the war. The museum is open Tuesday to Friday 10am to 5pm, Saturday and Sunday 11am to 5pm. Admission is free.

Next door is the **U.S. Army Women's Museum** (© 804/734-4327; www.awm.lee.army.mil), which tells the story of the women in the U.S. Army. It's open Tuesday through Friday from 10am to 5pm and Saturday, Sunday, and fed-eral holidays from 11am to 4:30pm. Admission is free.

The gate into Fort Lee is a mile east of the national battlefield visitor center on Va. 36. This is an active U.S. army post, so visitors must show valid photo identification and are subject to being searched. Tell the guards at the gate that you want to visit the Quartermaster Museum and the U.S. Army Women's Museum, and they'll tell you how to get there.

WHERE TO STAY

National chain motels near I-95 and Washington Street (Exit 52) include **Best Western** (© 800/528-1234 or 804/733-1776), **Howard Johnson** (© 800/654-2000 or 804/732-5950), **Knights Inn** (© 800/843-5644 or 804/732-1194), **Ramada Inn** (© 800/272-6232 or 804/733-0730), **Super 8** (© 800/800-8000 or 804/861-0793), and **Travelodge** (© 800/578-7878 or 804/733-0000).

Mayfield Inn ✦   You'll think you're in Williamsburg at this stately Georgian-style brick manse, built as a plantation home around 1750 by a member of the

House of Burgesses and moved to this 4-acre plot of land in 1969. General Lee is thought to have spent the night in the house before going on to Appomattox. The present owners acquired it in 1979 and spent 5 years restoring it and furnishing it with antiques and period reproductions. Much of the interior is original, including seven working fireplaces. Rooms are spacious and luxurious; the largest has a four-poster canopied bed, dormer windows, a loveseat, and a small table with a pewter tea service cozily set in front of the fireplace. Hearty country breakfasts are served downstairs in a formal dining room. Guests can stroll in a lovely colonial herb garden or lounge at the pool or in the gazebo.

3348 W. Washington St. (P.O. Box 2265), Petersburg, VA 23804. © **800/538-2381** or 804/861-6775. Fax 804/863-1971. www.mayfieldinn.com. 4 units. $100–$120 double. Rates include full breakfast. AE, MC, V. From I-95 take Exit 52 and go west 3 miles on Washington St. (U.S. 1) to inn on the left. **Amenities:** Outdoor pool. *In room:* A/C.

WHERE TO DINE

King's Barbecue 🛱 *Value* AMERICAN   Open since 1946, this Petersburg institution supplies some of the best barbecue in the South. The setting is a pine-paneled room with colonial-style tables and Windsor chairs. Notice the shelves over the lunch counter and booths: They're lined with an extraordinary collection of pig dolls and figurines, including a Miss Piggy bank. Pork, beef, ribs, and chicken smoke constantly in an open pit right in the dining room. Unlike most other barbecue emporia, the pork and beef are served just as they come from the pit. Aficionados can enjoy the smoked flavor *au naturel* or apply vinegary sauce from squeeze bottles. The menu also offers such Southern standbys as crispy fried chicken, ham steak, and seafood items like salmon cakes and fried oysters.

If you're going to the Crater and Old Blandford Church, **King's Barbecue No. 2,** 2910 S. Crater Rd. (© **804/732-0975**), has the same menu and is just as good.

3221 W. Washington St. (U.S. 1 South). © **804/732-5861.** Main courses $5–$10. AE, MC, V. Tues–Sun 7am–9pm. Follow U.S. 1 south 3 miles from downtown.

10

Williamsburg, Jamestown & Yorktown

Known as "the Peninsula," the strip of land stretching southeast from Richmond between the James and York rivers saw the beginnings of Colonial America and the rebellion that created the United States. Today the Peninsula is rightly one of the most visited parts of Virginia, especially the "Historic Triangle" of Williamsburg, Jamestown, and Yorktown.

You can get an extensive history lesson at the beautifully restored 18th-century town of Colonial Williamsburg. You can see where the first permanent English settlers in North America landed at Jamestown in 1607 and visit re-creations of the ships they came in and the village they built. At Yorktown you can walk the ramparts where Washington defeated Cornwallis, turning the colonists' dream of a new nation into a reality. Along the James River you can tour some of the tobacco plantations that created Virginia's first great wealth.

At the eastern end of the Peninsula, where it meets Hampton Roads and the Chesapeake Bay, Hampton is America's oldest continuously English-speaking town, but it also has a modern air and space museum. In the shipbuilding city of Newport News, one of the country's finest maritime museums owns part of the USS *Monitor,* whose Civil War battle with the CSS *Merrimac* was the world's first engagement between ironclad ships.

More than history makes this one of America's family vacation meccas, for there's also the Busch Gardens Williamsburg theme park with entertainment and rides, and Water Country USA provides watery rides and attractions in the summer. Golfers can play some of the country's finest courses, and there's plenty of shopping, too, especially for bargain hunters at numerous factory outlet stores west of Williamsburg.

1 Williamsburg ⭐⭐⭐

150 miles S of Washington, D.C.; 50 miles E of Richmond

"I know of no way of judging the future," said Patrick Henry, "but by the past." That particular quotation couldn't be more fitting as an introduction to Williamsburg, since Henry played a very important role here when, as a 29-year-old backcountry lawyer, he spoke out against the Stamp Act in the House of Burgesses in 1765. Many considered him an upstart and called the speech traitorous; others were inspired to revolution.

If he was right, you'll never have a better opportunity to examine the past than in Colonial Williamsburg, as the town's restored Historic Area is known. Unlike most other historic attractions in Virginia, Williamsburg has not just been meticulously re-created to look exactly as it did in the 1770s, while the town served as Virginia's capital. Today, Williamsburg's central Historic Area is, for all practical purposes, one of the world's largest and best living-history museums.

Tips 21st-Century Changes in an 18th-Century Town

Visitors to Colonial Williamsburg have dropped to about 850,000 a year from more than one million since before the September 11, 2001, terrorist attacks. While some attractions have been closed, including the nearby Carter's Grove plantation, fewer visitors mean shorter lines to get into the main buildings.

To help counter the drop, Colonial Williamsburg, Busch Gardens Williamsburg, Jamestown Settlement, and Yorktown Victory Center have come up with money-saving "Flex" vacation packages including accommodations and discounted admission to all four attractions. See the individual listings for each destination for more information.

Here the British flag flies most of the year over the Capitol building. Women wear long dresses and ruffled caps, and men don powdered wigs. Taverns serve colonial fare, blacksmiths and harness-makers use 18th-century methods, and the local militia drills on Market Square. Clip-clopping horses draw carriages just as their ancestors did when George Washington rode these cobblestone streets. Your impromptu banter with "Thomas Jefferson" in the Kings Arms Tavern will seem so authentic you won't even notice it's really Bill Barter, an exceptional actor who has been bringing Jefferson to life since 1976.

Regardless of age, anyone who visits Williamsburg will come away with an understanding and appreciation of how life was lived in 18th-century Virginia.

ESSENTIALS
VISITOR INFORMATION

For information specific to the Historic Area, contact the **Colonial Williamsburg Foundation,** P.O. Box 1776, Williamsburg, VA 23187 (© **800/HISTORY** or 757/220-7645; www.colonialwilliamsburg.org). Open 365 days a year, the foundation's visitors center is both a font of information and the beginning of any visit here (see "Exploring the Historic Area," below).

The best source for general information about the hotels, restaurants, and activities not operated by the foundation is the **Williamsburg Area Convention & Visitor Bureau,** 421 N. Boundary St., Williamsburg, VA 23187 (© **800/368-6511** or 757/253-0192; fax 757/253-1397; www.visitwilliamsburg.com). The bureau sells one of the best maps of the area. It shares offices, on Boundary Street between Lafayette and Scotland streets, 2 blocks north of the Historic Area, with the Williamsburg Area Chamber of Commerce. Open Monday to Friday 9am to 5pm.

The **Williamsburg Hotel/Motel Association** (© **800/446-9244;** www.my williamsburgvacation.com) publishes "Williamsburg Great Entertainer Magazine," a quarterly visitors guide. It also operates a hotel and motel reservation service (see "Where to Stay," later).

GETTING THERE

BY PLANE   **Newport News/Williamsburg International Airport** (© **757/ 877-0221;** www.nnwairport.com), 14 miles east of Williamsburg, is served by AirTran, United Express, and US Airways Express. **Avis** (© 800/331-1212), **Budget** (© 800/527-0700), **Hertz** (© 800/654-3131), and **National** (© 800/ 328-4567) have desks at the airport.

More flights arrive at **Richmond International Airport** (see chapter 9), about 45 miles west of town via I-64. **Norfolk International Airport** (see chapter 11) is about the same distance to the east, but traffic on I-64 can cause delays in ground transport to Williamsburg during rush hours, and especially on summer weekends when beach traffic funnels through the Hampton Roads Bridge Tunnel.

BY CAR   Williamsburg is on I-64 about halfway between Richmond and Norfolk. For the historic area, take Exit 238 (Va. 143) off I-64 and follow the signs south to Va. 132 and Colonial Williamsburg. The visitor center will be on your left as you approach the town. U.S. 60 is the old highway paralleling I-64; it's known as Richmond Road west of the Historic Area, and as York Street/Pocahontas Trail to the east. The scenic John Tyler Highway (Va. 5) runs between Richmond and Williamsburg, passing the James River plantations (see section 4, later). Va. 199, which forms a beltway around the southern side of the city, joins I-64 at Exit 242 east of town; this is the quickest way to get to Busch Gardens Williamsburg and Water Country USA. The Colonial Parkway, one of Virginia's most scenic routes, connects Williamsburg to Jamestown and Yorktown. It runs through a tunnel under the Historic Area. You can get on and off the parkway at the Colonial Williamsburg visitor center.

BY TRAIN & BUS   Amtrak trains (© 800/872-7245; www.amtrak.com) and **Greyhound/Trailways** buses (© 800/231-2222; www.greyhound.com) arrive at the local **Transportation Center** (© 757/229-8750), at Boundary and Lafayette streets, within walking distance of the historic area.

ORIENTATION & GETTING AROUND

CITY LAYOUT   The 1-mile long by ½-mile wide restored **Historic Area** is at the center of Williamsburg. The 99-foot-wide **Duke of Gloucester Street** is this area's principal east-west artery, with the Capitol building at the eastern end, and the Wren building of the College of William and Mary at the west end. **Merchant Square** shops and services are on the western end of Duke of Gloucester Street, next to the college. The visitor center is north of the Historic Area.

Richmond Road (U.S. 60 West) runs northwest from the Historic Area and is Williamsburg's main commercial strip, with a selection of motels, restaurants, and shopping centers, including the area's outlet malls. On the east side of town, **York Street/Pocahontas Trail** (U.S. 60 East) goes out to Busch Gardens Williamsburg. **ByPass Road** joins these two highways on the north side of the Historic Area.

GETTING AROUND   Since few cars are allowed into the Historic Area between 8am and 10pm, you must park elsewhere. The Colonial Williamsburg Visitor Center (see "Exploring the Historic Area," below) has ample free parking and operates shuttle buses to and around the Historic Area.

Since traffic as well as the heat can be stifling during the summer, the easiest way to get around outside the Historic Area is by public bus service operated by **Williamsburg Area Transport** (© 757/259-4093; www.williamsburgtransport. com). The buses run Monday through Saturday, about every hour from 6am to 8pm, to 10pm during the summer months. Fare is $1 for adults and students, 50¢ for seniors, free for children under 6. Exact fare is required. For visitors, the Blue, Gray, and Yellow lines are the most useful. The **Blue Line** runs west from the Transportation Center to the Williamsburg Soap & Candle Factory via Richmond Road (U.S. 60 West), thus passing a majority of the area's motels, chain restaurants, and shopping centers. The **Gray Line** operates east from the Transportation Center to Busch Gardens via Lafayette Street and Pocahontas Trail

(U.S. 60 East). During summer, the **Yellow Line** links the Colonial Williamsburg Visitor Center to the Transportation Center and Busch Gardens.

The land is flat here, so getting around via bicycle is a great idea. **Bike and stroller rentals** are available from **Tazewell Club Fitness Center,** at the Williamsburg Lodge (© **757/220-7690**). It's open year-round, daily 9am to 5pm. An outdoor stand is open from Easter through October at the Williamsburg Woodlands Hotel & Suites, at the Colonial Williamsburg Visitor Center (© **757/229-1000**). Bikes start at $8 an hour or $28 a day at both stands, including helmets, baskets, and locks.

Yellow Cab (© **757/722-1111**) and **Williamsburg Taxi** (© **757/566-3009**) are based at the Transportation Center (see "Getting There," above).

HISTORY & BACKGROUND

In 1699, after nearly a century of famine, fevers, and battles with neighboring American Indian tribes, the beleaguered Virginia Colony abandoned the mosquito-infested swamp at Jamestown for a planned city 6 miles inland and about halfway to Yorktown, which had developed as a major seaport. They named it Williamsburg for the reigning British monarch, William of Orange.

Royal Gov. Francis Nicholson laid out the new capital on a grid with public greens and ½ acre of land for every house on the main street. People used their lots to grow vegetables and raise livestock. Most houses were whitewashed wood frame (trees being more abundant than brick), and kitchens were in separate structures to keep the houses from burning down. A "palace" for the governor was finished in 1720.

The town prospered and became the major cultural and political center of Virginia. The government met here four times a year during "Publick Times," when rich planters and politicos (one and the same, mostly) converged on Williamsburg and the population, normally about 1,800, doubled. Shops displayed their finest wares, and there were balls, horse races, fairs, and auctions.

Until the government was moved to Richmond in 1780 to be safer from British attack, Williamsburg played a major role as a seat of royal government and later as a hotbed of revolution. Many of the seminal events leading up to the Declaration of Independence occurred here. Thomas Jefferson and James Monroe studied at the College of William and Mary, the nation's second oldest university behind Harvard. Jefferson was the second state governor and last occupant of the Governor's Palace before the capital moved to Richmond (Patrick Henry was the first). During the Revolution, Williamsburg served as the wartime capital for 4 years and was the headquarters of Generals Washington (he planned the siege of Yorktown in George Wythe's house), Rochambeau, and Cornwallis.

Fun Fact **Learning Lord's Lines**

You'll see a familiar face in *Williamsburg—the Story of a Patriot,* the 35-minute film shown at the Colonial Williamsburg Visitor Center—and on TVs in hotels operated by the Colonial Williamsburg Foundation. It's Jack Lord, who later became famous as the detective in the 1970s TV show *Hawaii Five-0.* Students at the College of William and Mary consider the 1950s film so campy that they learn every one of Lord's lines by heart.

Williamsburg Area

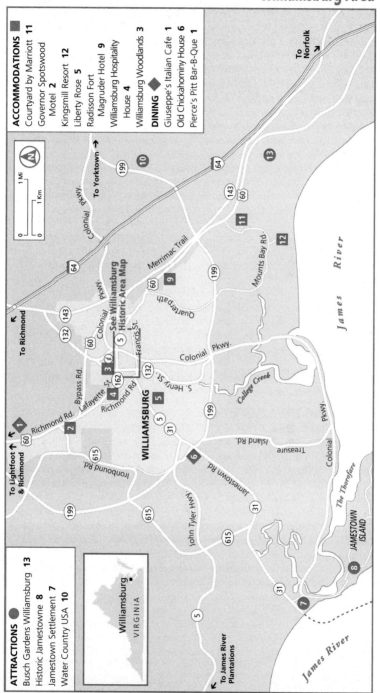

ATTRACTIONS ●
Busch Gardens Williamsburg **13**
Historic Jamestowne **8**
Jamestown Settlement **7**
Water Country USA **10**

ACCOMMODATIONS ■
Courtyard by Marriott **11**
Governor Spotswood Motel **2**
Kingsmill Resort **12**
Liberty Rose **5**
Radisson Fort Magruder Hotel **9**
Williamsburg Hospitality House **4**
Williamsburg Woodlands **3**

DINING ◆
Giuseppe's Italian Cafe **1**
Old Chickahominy House **6**
Pierce's Pitt Bar-B-Que **1**

WILLIAMSBURG

To Richmond
To Norfolk
To Yorktown →
← To Lightfoot & Richmond
To James River Plantations

Williamsburg
VIRGINIA

See Williamsburg Historic Area Map

James River
Jamestown Island
The Thorofare

247

A REVEREND, A ROCKEFELLER & A REBIRTH

Williamsburg ceased to be an important political center after 1780, but remained a charming Virginia town for another 150 years or so, changing little. As late as 1926, the colonial town plan was virtually intact, including numerous original buildings. Then the Reverend W.A.R. Goodwin, rector of Bruton Parish Church, envisioned restoring the entire town to its colonial appearance as a symbol of our early history. He inspired John D. Rockefeller Jr., who during his lifetime contributed some $68 million to the project and set up an endowment to help provide for permanent restoration and educational programs. Today gifts and bequests by thousands of Americans sustain the project Goodwin and Rockefeller began.

Today, the Historic Area covers 301 acres of the original town. A mile long, it encompasses 88 original buildings and several hundred reconstructed houses, shops, taverns, public buildings, and outbuildings, most on their original foundations after extensive archaeological, architectural, and historical research.

Williamsburg set a very high standard for other Virginia restorations. Researchers investigated international archives, libraries, and museums and sought out old wills, diaries, court records, inventories, letters, and other documents. The architects studied every aspect of 18th-century buildings, from paint chemistry to brickwork. Archaeologists recovered millions of artifacts while excavating 18th-century sites to reveal original foundations. The Historic Area also includes 90 acres of gardens and greens, and 3,000 surrounding acres serve as a "greenbelt" against commercial encroachment.

The Colonial Williamsburg Foundation, a nonprofit organization, owns most of the Historic Area, conducts the ongoing restoration, and operates the Historic Area and its visitor center. A profit-making subsidiary owns and operates the foundation's hotels and taverns. Needless to say, "CW" exerts enormous influence over tourism, the town's main income earner.

EXPLORING THE HISTORIC AREA
FIRST STOP: THE VISITOR CENTER

You and the million or so other people who come here every year will begin your visit at the **Colonial Williamsburg Visitor Center,** on Va. 132 south of U.S. 60 Bypass (© **800/HISTORY** or 757/220-7645; www.colonialwilliamsburg.com). You can't miss it; bright green signs point the way from all access roads to Williamsburg. The center is open 365 days a year, from 8:30am to 7pm in summer, to 5pm the rest of the year.

It has a bookstore, a coffee shop, and two **reservations services:** one for Colonial Williamsburg Foundation **hotels** (© **800/HISTORY** or 757/220-7645), the other for its four colonial **taverns** (© **800/TAVERNS** or 757/229-2141). It's advisable to make these reservations well in advance anytime, and it's essential every day during the summer and on weekends during spring and fall.

The center continuously shows a free 8-minute video about Williamsburg, and once you've bought your ticket, you can watch the 35-minute orientation film, *Williamsburg—the Story of a Patriot,* which also runs throughout the day.

Parking at the visitor center is free. (You can park for $1 an hour in the **Merchants Square** daily lot on Francis St. between Henry and Boundary sts. in the Historic Area.)

TICKETS It costs nothing to stroll the streets of the Historic Area, and perhaps debate revolutionary politics with the actors playing Thomas Jefferson or Patrick Henry, but you will need a **ticket** to enter the key buildings and all the

---

Tips **Planning Your Time in Williamsburg**

There is so much to see and do in the Historic Triangle that you can easily spend a week in this area. Colonial Williamsburg itself requires a
minimum of 2 days to explore, preferably 3. It will take another day to
see Jamestown and Yorktown. If you have kids in tow, they'll want to
spend at least another day at Busch Gardens Williamsburg or Water
Country USA.

Spend at least an hour planning your visit at the Colonial Williamsburg Visitor Center. Historic Area programs change frequently, so it's
imperative to pick up the *Colonial Williamsburg Companion,* a weekly
newspaper which gives the hours the attractions are open and the
times and places of the week's presentations, exhibits, plays, and
events. It also has a detailed map. It is the single most valuable tool in
planning the best use of your time.

---

museums, to see the 35-minute orientation film at the visitor center, use the
Historic Area shuttle buses, and take a 30-minute Orientation Walk through the
restored village.

The Colonial Williamsburg Foundation is notorious for frequently changing
its system of tickets and passes, so what follows may be outdated by the time you
arrive. You should *definitely* call the visitor center or check the Colonial
Williamsburg website for the latest information. With that caveat, this was the
pass structure at press time.

A 1-day **General Admission** ticket to the museums, Historic Area exhibits,
walking tours, and interpretive programs cost $37 for adults, $19 for children 6
to 14, free for children 5 and under. It is good for the day you buy it, regardless
of the time you purchased it. You can add a second consecutive day for an additional $3 adults, $1.50 for children—a most prudent investment since you'll
want to spend at least 2 days here.

If you were going to be here for 3 days or more, it was worth paying $49 per
person (regardless of age) for a **Freedom Pass,** which is good for one year and
includes 50% discount on the night-time performances.

Tickets are available at the Colonial Williamsburg Visitor Center, a **ticket
booth** at the Merchants Square shops on Henry Street at Duke of Gloucester
Street, and **Lumber House** on Duke of Gloucester Street opposite the Palace
Green.

American Express, Diners Club, MasterCard, and Visa credit cards are accepted
at Colonial Williamsburg ticket outlets, attractions, hotels, and taverns.

GETTING TO THE HISTORIC AREA   Once you have a plan of action and
have your tickets in hand, a **Red Line** bus will shuttle you between the visitor
center and the **Gateway Building,** behind the Governor's Palace, where guides
conduct a 30-minute Orientation Walk. It's a good way to get an overview of the
village. From there, **Blue Line** buses make a circle around the circumference of
the Historic Area. The buses begin operating at 8:50am, with frequent departures
until 10pm. The two lines merge into one after 5pm, forming one loop around
the area. They are free to holders of tickets to the Historic Area attractions.

Note that the Colonial Williamsburg buses are not the same as those operated by Williamsburg Area Transport (see "Orientation & Getting Around," earlier).

You can also walk to the Historic Area, a 20-minute stroll via a footpath.

HOURS   You can stroll the Historic Area streets anytime, but in general, its attractions are open from April to October daily 9am to 5pm, to 6pm from Memorial Day to Labor Day. Some places are closed on specific days, and hours can vary, so check the *Colonial Williamsburg Companion* for current information.

THE COLONIAL BUILDINGS
Bassett Hall

Though colonial in origin (built between 1753 and 1766 by Col. Philip Johnson), Bassett Hall was the mid-1930s residence of Mr. and Mrs. John D. Rockefeller Jr., and it is restored and furnished to reflect their era. The mansion's name derives from the ownership of Burwell Bassett, a nephew of Martha Washington who lived here from 1800 to 1839. The Rockefellers moved into a restored two-story dwelling on 585 acres in 1936. In spite of changes they made, much of the interior is original, including woodwork, paneling, mantels, and yellow pine flooring. Much of the furniture is 18th- and 19th-century American in the Chippendale, Federal, and Empire styles. There are beautifully executed needlework rugs made by Mrs. Rockefeller, and early 19th-century prayer rugs adorn the morning room. Hundreds of examples of ceramics and china are on display, as are collections of 18th- and 19th-century American and English glass, Canton enamelware, and folk art. Reservations are required; make them at the visitor center.

Brush-Everard House ⟨★

One of the oldest buildings in Williamsburg, the Brush-Everard House was built in 1717 as a residence-cum-shop by Public Armorer and master gunsmith John Brush. The most distinguished owner was Thomas Everard, two-time mayor of Williamsburg. Though not as wealthy as George Wythe and John Randolph, he was in their elite circle. He enlarged the house, adding the two wings that create a U shape. Today, the home is restored and furnished to its Everard-era appearance. The smokehouse and kitchen out back are original. Special programs here focus on African-American life in the 18th century.

The Capitol ★★★

Virginia legislators met in the H-shaped Capitol at the eastern end of Duke of Gloucester Street from 1704 to 1780. America's first representative assembly, it had an upper house, His Majesty's Council of State, of 12 members appointed for life by the king. Freeholders of each county elected Members of the lower House of Burgesses (there were 128 burgesses by 1776). The Burgesses became a training ground for patriots such as George Washington, Thomas Jefferson, Richard Henry Lee, and Patrick Henry. As 1776 approached, the Burgesses passed petitions and resolutions against acts of Parliament: the Stamp Act and the levy on tea—in Henry's immortal words, "taxation without representation," a phrase which became a motto of the Revolution.

The original Capitol burned down in 1747, was rebuilt in 1753, and succumbed to fire again in 1832. This reconstruction is of the 1704 version, complete with Queen Anne's coat-of-arms adorning the tower and the Great Union flag flying overhead. The Secretary's Office next door is original. You must take a 30-minute **tour** to get inside the Capitol.

Williamsburg Historic District

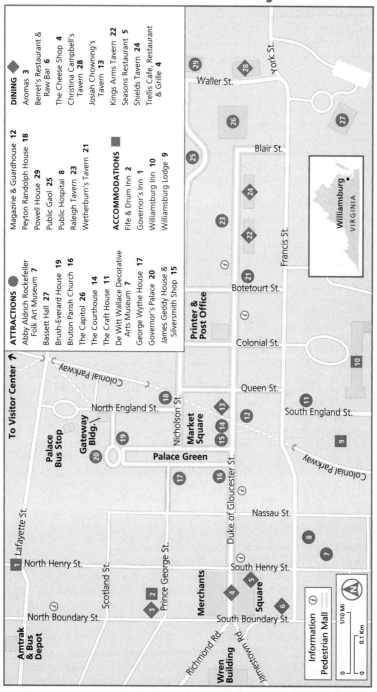

ATTRACTIONS ●
Abby Aldrich Rockefeller
  Folk Art Museum **7**
Bassett Hall **27**
Brush-Everard House **19**
Bruton Parish Church **16**
The Capitol **26**
The Courthouse **14**
The Craft House **11**
De Witt Wallace Decorative
  Arts Museum **7**
George Wythe House **17**
Governor's Palace **20**
James Geddy House &
  Silversmith Shop **15**

Magazine & Guardhouse **12**
Peyton Randolph House **18**
Powell House **29**
Public Gaol **25**
Public Hospital **8**
Raleigh Tavern **23**
Wetherburn's Tavern **21**

ACCOMMODATIONS ■
Fife & Drum Inn **2**
Governor's Inn **1**
Williamsburg Inn **10**
Williamsburg Lodge **9**

DINING ◆
Aromas **3**
Berret's Restaurant &
  Raw Bar **6**
The Cheese Shop **4**
Christina Campbell's
  Tavern **28**
Josiah Chowning's
  Tavern **13**
Kings Arms Tavern **22**
Seasons Restaurant **5**
Shields Tavern **24**
Trellis Cafe, Restaurant
  & Grille **4**

The Courthouse ★★★

An intriguing window on colonial life's criminal justice division is offered in the courthouse, which dominates Market Square. An original building, the courthouse was the scene of proceedings ranging from criminal trials to the issuance of licenses. Wife beating, pig stealing, and debtor and creditor disputes were among the cases tried here. You can participate in the administration of colonial justice at the courthouse by sitting on a jury or acting as a defendant. In colonial times, convicted offenders were usually punished immediately after the verdict. Punishments included public flogging at the whipping post (conveniently located just outside the courthouse) or being locked in the stocks or pillory, where they were subjected to public ridicule. Jail sentences were very unusual—punishment was swift and drastic, and the offenders then returned to the community, often bearing lifelong evidence of their conviction.

George Wythe House ★

On the west side of the Palace Green is the elegant restored brick home of George Wythe (pronounced "with"), classics scholar, noted lawyer and teacher (Thomas Jefferson, Henry Clay, and John Marshall were his students), and member of the House of Burgesses. A close friend of royal governors, Wythe nevertheless was the first Virginia signer of the Declaration of Independence. Wythe did not sign the Constitution, however, because it did not contain a Bill of Rights or antislavery provisions. His house was Washington's headquarters prior to the siege of Yorktown and Rochambeau's after the surrender of Cornwallis. Open-hearth cooking is demonstrated in the outbuilding.

Governor's Palace ★★★

This meticulous reconstruction is of the Georgian mansion that was the residence and official headquarters of royal governors from 1714 until Lord Dunmore fled before dawn in the face of armed resistance in 1775, thus ending British rule in Virginia. The final 5 years of British rule is the period portrayed in the palace. Though the sumptuous surroundings, nobly proportioned halls and rooms, 10 acres of formal gardens and greens, and vast wine cellars all evoke splendor, the king's representative was, by that time, little more than a functionary of great prestige but limited power. He was more apt to behave like a diplomat in a foreign land than an autocratic colonial ruler.

Tours, given continuously through the day, end in the gardens, where you can explore the elaborate geometric parterres, topiary work, bowling green, pleached allées, and a holly maze patterned after the one at Hampton Court. Plan at least 30 minutes to wander the stunning grounds and visit the kitchen and stable yards.

James Geddy House & Silversmith Shop ★

This two-story L-shaped 1762 home (with attached shops) is an original building. Here you can see how a comfortably situated middle-class family lived in the 18th century. Unlike the fancier abodes, the Geddy House has no wallpaper

---

> **Fun Fact   Hang 'Em High**
>
> In colonial times, all civil and criminal cases (the latter punishable by mutilation or death) were tried in the General Court. Since juries were sent to deliberate in a third-floor room without heat, light, or food, there were few hung juries. Thirteen of Blackbeard the Pirate's crew were tried here and sentenced to hang.

The College of William & Mary

Standing at the western end of Duke of Gloucester Street, the stately **Sir Christopher Wren Building** may not be part of Colonial Williamsburg, but it is the oldest restored structure here. It's also America's oldest college building. Constructed between 1695 and 1699, even before there was a Williamsburg, it's the campus centerpiece of the **College of William and Mary,** the country's second oldest college behind only Harvard University. King William III and Queen Mary II chartered the school in 1693, and over the next century it was the alma mater of many of the country's early leaders, including Thomas Jefferson. Fire gutted the Wren building in 1705, 1859, and 1862. Its exterior walls remained intact, and in 1928 John D. Rockefeller Jr. restored it to its colonial appearance. The college still uses its upstairs classrooms and offices, but the first-floor Grammar School, Great Hall, and Chapel are open to the public Monday to Friday from 10am to 5pm, Saturday 9am to 5pm, and Sunday from noon to 5pm. Admission is free. The college's **visitor information office** in the rear of the building (© **757/221-4000**) has campus maps.

or oil paintings; a mirror and spinet from England, however, indicate relative affluence.

James Getty Sr. was a gunsmith and brass founder who advertised in the *Virginia Gazette* of July 8, 1737, that he had "a great Choice of Guns and Fowling Pieces, of several Sorts and Sizes, true bored, which he will warrant to be good; and will sell them as cheap as they are usually sold in England." A younger son, James Jr., became the town's foremost silversmith; he imported and sold jewelry, and was a member of the city's Common Council involved in furthering the patriot cause. At a foundry on the premises, craftsmen cast silver, pewter, bronze, and brass items at a forge.

The Magazine & Guardhouse 𝒜𝒜

Another original building, this sturdy octagonal brick structure was constructed in 1715 to house ammunition and arms for the defense of the colony. In colonial Williamsburg every able-bodied freeman belonged to the militia from the ages of 16 to 60 and did his part in protecting hearth and home from attack by local tribes, riots, slave uprisings, and pirate raids. The high wall and guardhouse were built during the French and Indian War to protect the magazine's 60,000 pounds of gunpowder. Today the building is stocked with 18th-century equipment—flintlock muskets, cannons and cannonballs, barrels of powder, bayonets, and drums, the latter for communication purposes. Children can join the militia here during the summer (see "Especially for Kids," later).

Peyton Randolph House 𝒜

The Randolphs were one of the most prominent and wealthy families in colonial Virginia. Sir John Randolph was a respected lawyer, Speaker of the House of Burgesses, and Virginia's representative to London, where he was the only colonial-born Virginian ever to be knighted. When he died he left his library to a 16-year-old Peyton, "hoping he will betake himself to the study of law." When Peyton Randolph died in 1775, his cousin, Thomas Jefferson, purchased his books at auction; they eventually became the nucleus of the Library of Congress. Peyton Randolph followed in his father's footsteps, studying law in London after attending the College of William and Mary. He served in the House of Burgesses from 1744 to 1775, the last 9 years as Speaker. Known as the great mediator, he was unanimously elected president of 1774's First Continental Congress in Philadelphia, and though he believed in nonviolence and hoped the colonies could amicably settle their differences with England, he was a firm patriot.

The house (actually, two connected homes) dates to 1715. It is today restored to reflect the period around 1770. Robertson's Windmill, in back of the house, is a post mill of a type popular in the early 18th century. The house is open to the public for self-guided tours with period-costumed interpreters in selected rooms.

The Public Gaol ☞

As noted above, imprisonment was not the usual punishment for crime in colonial times, but persons awaiting trial and runaway slaves sometimes spent months in the Public Gaol. In winter, the cells were bitterly cold; in summer, they were stifling. Beds were piles of straw; leg irons, shackles, and chains were used frequently; and the daily diet consisted of "salt beef damaged, and Indian meal." In its early days, the gaol doubled as a madhouse, and during the Revolution redcoats, spies, traitors, and deserters swelled its population.

The gaol opened in 1704. Debtors' cells were added in 1711 (though the imprisoning of debtors was virtually eliminated after a 1772 law made creditors responsible for their upkeep), and keeper's quarters were built in 1722. The thick-walled redbrick building served as the Williamsburg city jail through 1910. The building today is restored to its 1720s appearance.

The Public Hospital ☞

Opened in 1773, the "Public Hospital for Persons of Insane and Disordered Minds" was America's first asylum. From 1773 to about 1820, "treatment" involved solitary confinement and a grisly course of action designed to "encourage" patients to "choose" rational behavior (it was assumed back then that patients willfully chose a life of insanity). So-called therapeutic techniques included the use of drugs, submersion in cold water for extended periods, bleeding, blistering salves, and an array of restraining devices. On a self-guided tour, you'll see a 1773 cell, with a straw-filled mattress on the floor, ragged blanket, and manacles.

Raleigh Tavern ☞☞

This most famous of Williamsburg taverns was named for Sir Walter Raleigh, who launched the "Lost Colony" which disappeared in North Carolina some 20 years before Jamestown was settled. After the Governor's Palace, it was the social and political hub of the town, especially during Publick Times. Regulars included George Washington and Thomas Jefferson, who met here in 1774 with Patrick Henry, Richard Henry Lee, and Francis Lightfoot Lee to discuss revolution. Patrick Henry's troops gave their commander a farewell dinner here in 1776.

The original tavern was destroyed by fire in 1859. Reconstructed on the original site in 1932, its facilities include two dining rooms; the famed Apollo ballroom,

---

Tips **Carriage Rides**

A fun way to see the Historic District is on horse-drawn carriage rides, which depart from a horse post in front of The Magazine & Guardhouse (see above). Check with the visitor center for schedule and prices.

> **Fun Fact Stocks & Bondage**
>
> The swift punishments meted out in 18th-century Williamsburg included public ridicule. The convicted had their neck, arms and legs bound in stocks and pillories. Passersby added to the ridicule by tossing rotten tomatoes at the convicts.

scene of elegant soirees; a clubroom that could be rented for private meetings; and a bar where ale and hot rum punch were the favored drinks. In the tavern bakery you can buy 18th-century confections like gingerbread and Shrewsbury cake as well as cider to wash them down.

Wetherburn's Tavern

Though less important than the Raleigh, Wetherburn's also played an important role in Colonial Williamsburg. George Washington occasionally favored the tavern with his patronage. And, like the Raleigh, it was mobbed during Publick Times and frequently served as a center of sedition and a rendezvous of Revolutionary patriots. The heart of yellow-pine floors are original, so you can actually walk in Washington's footsteps; windows, trim, and weatherboarding are a mixture of old and new; and the outbuildings, except for the dairy, are reconstructions. Twenty-five-minute **tours** are given throughout the day.

THE MUSEUMS AT COLONIAL WILLIAMSBURG

Plans were afoot at press time to combine Colonial Williamsburg's two museums—the Abbey Aldrich Rockefeller Folk Art Museum and the DeWitt Wallace Decorative Arts Museum—into one facility occupied at present by the Wallace museum. They will maintain their separate identities but collectively will be known as The Museums at Colonial Williamsburg. A museum cafe also was on the drawing board.

Abby Aldrich Rockefeller Folk Art Museum ☆☆☆

The folk art displayed at Bassett Hall (see above) are just a small sampling of enthusiast Abby Aldrich Rockefeller's extensive collection. This delightful museum contains more than 2,600 folk-art paintings, sculptures, and art objects. Mrs. Rockefeller was a pioneer in this branch of collecting in the 1920s and 1930s. Folk art is of interest not only aesthetically, but as visual history; since colonial times, untutored artists have creatively recorded everyday life. The collection includes household ornaments and useful wares (hand-stenciled bed covers, butter molds, pottery, utensils, painted furniture, boxes), mourning pictures (embroideries honoring departed relatives and national heroes), family and individual portraits, shop signs, carvings, whittled toys, calligraphic drawings, weavings, quilts, and paintings of scenes from daily life.

DeWitt Wallace Decorative Arts Museum ☆☆

This 62,000-square-foot museum houses some 10,000 17th- to 19th-century English and American decorative art objects. You'll see period furnishings, ceramics, textiles, paintings, prints, silver, pewter, clocks, scientific instruments, mechanical devices, and weapons.

In the upstairs Masterworks Gallery, you will see a coronation portrait of George III of England and a Charles Willson Peale study of George Washington. Surrounding the atrium are some 150 objects representing the highest achievement of American and English artisans from the 1640s to 1800. At the

---

To the Poorhouse!
Before the advent of Williamsburg's Public Hospital in 1773, the mentally ill were often thrown in jail or confined to the poorhouse.

---

east end of the museum, a 6,000-square-foot area with four galleries around a sky-lit courtyard is used for changing exhibits. On the first level you'll see small exhibits of musical instruments, objects related to European conquest and expansion in the New World, and 18th-century dining items. A small cafe here offers light fare, beverages, and a limited luncheon menu.

The museum's Lila Acheson Wallace Garden is scheduled to be sacrificed to make room for the Abby Aldrich Rockefeller Folk Art Museum.

SHOPS, CRAFTS & TRADE EXHIBITS
Numerous 18th-century crafts demonstrations occur throughout the Historic Area. Such goings-on were a facet of everyday life in this pre-industrial era. Dozens of crafts are practiced by over 100 master craftspeople. They're an extremely skilled group, many having served up to 7-year apprenticeships both here and abroad. The program is part of Williamsburg's efforts to present an accurate picture of colonial society, portraying the average man and woman as well as more illustrious citizens. Crafts displays are open 5 to 7 days a week, with evening tours of candlelit shops available (visitors carry lanterns).

You can see a cabinetmaker, a wig maker, a silversmith, a printer and bookbinder, a maker of saddles and harnesses, a blacksmith, a shoemaker, a gunsmith, a milliner, a wheelwright, housewrights, and a candlemaker—all carrying on—and explaining—their trades in the 18th-century fashion.

Interesting in a morbid way is the apothecary shop, where sore feet were treated with leeches between the toes, a headache with leeches across the forehead, and a sore throat with leeches on the neck.

ESPECIALLY FOR KIDS
In addition to the excitement at Busch Gardens Williamsburg and Water Country USA (see below), families can enjoy many hands-on activities in the Historic Area. A fun activity is at the **Governor's Palace,** where the dancing master gives lessons. During the summer kids can "enlist" in the militia and practice marching and drilling at the **Magazine and Guardhouse** (I still have a snapshot of myself holding a flintlock when I was a boy). If they get unruly, you can lock them in the stocks in front of **The Public Gaol.** Inquire at the Visitor Center for special themed tours in areas of your children's specific interests.

Busch Gardens Williamsburg (*Kids*)   At some point you may need a break from early American history, especially if you have kids in tow, and head over to Busch Gardens Williamsburg, a 360-acre family entertainment park. Here you can get a peek at European history, albeit fanciful, in authentically detailed 17th-century hamlets from England, Ireland, Scotland, France, Germany, and Italy. Little mental effort is required to enjoy the villages, shows, festivities, and more than 50 rides, including the world-class roller coasters Apollo's Chariot and Alpengeist.

The usual starting place is the Elizabethan hamlet of **Banbury Cross,** where you can watch "R.L. Stine's Haunted Lighthouse," a 3-D movie with sound effects. From there you proceed to **Heatherdowns,** Scotland, home of the famous Anheuser-Busch Clydesdale horses and the serpentine Loch Ness Monster, a terrifying roller coaster with two interlocking 360-degree loops and a 130-foot drop. Back on ground, proceed to **Killarney,** Ireland, where you can go to Budweiser beer school and see animals at Jack Hanna's Wild Reserve.

Next comes **Aquitaine,** New France, where you and the kids can test your driving skills on the hairpin turns of Le Mans Raceway. The Royal Theatre is the venue for the park's nighttime entertainment and special events. In an odd juxtaposition, New France is home to Trappers Smokehouse, a Southern-style barbecue joint. Now it's on to **Rhinefeld,** Germany, where Land of the Dragons lets the kids explore a three-story tree house and ride a flume and a dragon-themed Ferris wheel. Both you and kids can drop your hearts on the Alpengeist inverted roller coaster. Dancers and an oompah band entertain in the Das Festhaus, a 2,000-seat festival hall where Oktoberfest never ends. It's the best place to take a break, cool off, and have a cold drink.

From Germany, a 300-foot bridge crosses the "Rhine River" to **Fiesta Italia,** a Renaissance-style Italian village where the water ride Escape from Pompeii will whisk you to the smoldering ruins of the ancient Italian city destroyed by a volcano, and Roman Rapids will speed you to a watery splash in front of the ruins. Also here is Apollo's Chariot, a "hypercoaster" with nine vertical drops of up to 210 feet. Tamer rides pay tribute to Leonardo da Vinci's inventions.

During October, the park switches to a "Howl-O-Scream" theme after 6pm on weekends, with blood-curdling screams splitting the artificial fog, which fills the night air. It's a fun time for young ghouls to be out and about.

1 Busch Gardens Blvd. (3 miles east of Williamsburg on U.S. 60). ℂ **800/343-9746** or 757/253-3350. www. buschgardens.com. Admission and hours vary, so call ahead, check website, or get brochure at visitor centers. Admission $45 adults, $38 children 3–6, children 2 and under free for unlimited rides, shows, and attractions. "Bounce" multi-day passes with Water Country USA available. Late Mar to mid-April Fri and Sun 10am–6pm; Sat 10am–10pm. Mid-Apr to mid-May Sun–Thurs 10am–7pm; Fri 10am–9pm; Sat 10am–10pm. Mid-May to mid-June Mon–Thurs 10am–6pm; Fri 10am–9pm; Sat 10am–10pm; Sun 10am–7pm. Mid-June to mid-Aug daily 10am–10pm (to 11pm July 4th weekend). Mid-Aug to Sept 1 Mon–Fri 10am–6pm (to 10pm weekends). Sept Fri 10am–6pm; Sat–Sun 10am–7pm; Oct Fri–Sun 10am–10pm. Closed Nov to late Mar. Parking $7–$10.

Water Country USA *Kids* Virginia's largest water-oriented amusement park features exciting water slides, rides, and entertainment set to a 1950s and '60s surf theme. The largest ride—Big Daddy Falls—takes the entire family on a

Fun Fact **Strange Bedfellows**

Williamsburg's taverns were crowded establishments during the busy Publick Times, when they offered accommodations, food, and libation to the wealthy planters and others who thronged the town.

Some things are almost like they were when Thomas Jefferson wrote after a night at the Raleigh Tavern: "Last night, as merry as agreeable company and dancing with Belinda in the Apollo the Raleigh's ballroom could make me, I never could have thought the succeeding Sun would have seen me so wretched."

On the other hand, the degree of comfort found at Williamsburg's hostelries has changed immeasurably since then. In those days, the taverns' upstairs bedrooms offered nothing in the way of privacy. Often five or more grown men would share a bed, sleeping crossways in a half-sitting position. A smelly pig farmer might sleep next to a wealthy planter, thus giving rise to the expression, "Politics makes strange bedfellows."

colossal river-rafting adventure. Or, they twist and turn on giant inner tubes through flumes, tunnels, water "explosions," and down a waterfall to "splash-down." And there's much more, all of it wet and sometimes wild. It's a perfect place to chill out after a hot summer's day in the Historic District.

176 Water Country USA Pkwy. (off Va. 199, north of Exit 242 off I-64). © **800/343-SWIM** or 757/229-9300. www.watercountryusa.com. Admission, hours vary; call ahead, check website, or get brochure at visitor centers. Admission at least $30 adults, $23 children 3–6, free for children 2 and under. "Bounce" multi-day passes with Busch Gardens Williamsburg available. Mid-May to late May Fri–Sun 10am–6pm; Late-May to mid-June daily 10am–6pm. Mid-June to mid-Aug daily 10am–10pm. Mid-Aug to late Aug daily 10am–7pm. Late Aug to Labor Day daily 10am–6pm. Closed Labor Day to mid-May. Parking $7. Take Va. 199 north of I-64 and follow signs.

OUTDOOR ACTIVITIES

BICYCLING   Not only is a bike the easiest way to get around the Historic Area, the 23-mile-long **Colonial Parkway** between Jamestown and Yorktown is one of Virginia's most scenic bike routes. You'll peddle along the banks of the James and York Rivers (where there are picnic areas) and through a tunnel under Colonial Williamsburg. The 7 miles between Williamsburg and Jamestown are fairly flat, but you'll have more car traffic to contend with than on the more rolling 13-mile journey to Yorktown. Rentals are available at the Williamsburg Lodge and Williamsburg Woodlands (see "Orientation & Getting Around," earlier).

GOLF   The Williamsburg area is *the* place to play golf in Virginia—if you can afford it, since a round here can cost $100 and up during the prime summer months. It all started in 1947 with the noted Golden Horseshoe course at the **Williamsburg Inn** (© **757/229-1000**), which has two additional 18-holers to play. On the James River, **Kingsmill Resort** (© **800/832-5665** or 757/253-3998) has three top-flight 18-hole courses of its own, including the world-famous River Course, home of the LPGA Michelob Light Open. See "Where to Stay," below, for more about the Williamsburg Inn and Kingsmill Resort.

  Ford's Colony (© **800/334-6033** or 757/258-4130; www.fordscolony.com) has two Dan Maples-designed courses, the challenging Blue-Gold (12 of 18 holes bordered by water) and the more forgiving White-Red. Another Maples-designed course is in the works. Golf carts here have satellite global positioning equipment, so you know exactly how long you have to hit your next shot. **Williamsburg National Golf Club** (© **800/826-5732** or 757/258-9642; www.wngc.com) has Virginia's only Jack Nicklaus-designed course, which *Golf Digest* magazine considers one of the state's top 10 links.

  Royal New Kent Golf Club (© **888/253-4363** or 804/966-7023) has "a succession of you've-never-seen-this-before holes," according to *Golf Digest*. Its sister course at **Stonehouse Golf Club** (© **888/253-4363** or 757/566-1138) is more like a mountain course, with great vistas to please your eyes and deep bunkers to test your skills. Also pleasing to the eye, **Kiskiack Golf Club** (© **800/989-4728** or 757/566-2200), has two lakes nestled among its rolling hills.

  Call the courses for current greens fees, directions, and tee times.

Tips Coin of the Realm

Rather than have your children walking around with real loot, you can purchase "Colonial Currency" at the Colonial Williamsburg Visitor Center. The scrip looks like 18th-century money but can only be spent at Historic Area shops and restaurants.

(*Tips* **How to See Busch Gardens**

Each village in Busch Gardens Williamsburg has its own shops, crafts demonstrations, restaurants, rides, shows, and other entertainment such as top-quality musicals and bird shows. The entertainment changes from day to day, so before you strike out into the park, get a show schedule when you come in and spend some time planning your day. The park is laid out in a circle. Since most visitors tend to go clockwise, you can beat some of the crowds turning left at the entrance and going around in the opposite direction. You might even start at the back of the park, since visitors tend to stop at the first attraction they come to. Sky rides and trains connect the villages, so you can easily skip around.

SHOPPING
IN THE HISTORIC AREA

Duke of Gloucester Street is the center for 18th-century wares created by craftspeople plying the trades of our forefathers. The goods include hand-wrought silver jewelry from the Sign of the Golden Ball, hats from the Mary Dickenson shop, pomanders to ward off the plague from McKenzie's Apothecary, hand-woven linens from Prentis Store, books bound in leather and hand-printed newspapers from the post office, gingerbread cakes from the Raleigh Tavern Bake Shop, and everything from foods to fishhooks at Greenhow and Tarpley's, a general store. In fine weather, check out the outdoor market next to the Magazine.

Not to be missed is **Craft House**, also run by the Colonial Williamsburg Foundation. There are two locations, one in Merchants Square and one at the Williamsburg Inn (note, however, that the latter is slated to be turned into a spa and health evaluation center). Featured at Craft House are exquisite works by master craftspeople and authentic reproductions of Colonial furnishings. There are also reproduction wallpapers, china, toys, games, maps, books, prints, and souvenirs aplenty.

The modern, independently owned and operated **Merchants Square** "shoppes" at the west end of Duke of Gloucester Street offer a wide range of merchandise: antiques, antiquarian books and prints, 18th-century-style floral arrangements, candy, toys, handcrafted pewter and silver items, needlework supplies, country quilts, and Oriental rugs. It's not all of the "ye olde" variety, however, for national chains such as Chico's, Williams-Sonoma, and Barnes & Noble (disguised as the William and Mary Bookstore) are here, too. Merchants Square has free 2-hour parking for its customers.

ON RICHMOND ROAD

Shopping in the Historic Area is fun, but the biggest draws are along Richmond Road (U.S. 60) between Williamsburg and Lightfoot, an area 5 to 7 miles west of the Historic Area. If you like outlet shopping, Richmond Road is for you.

Driving west from town (or taking Williamsburg Visitors Shuttle during summer), you'll come first to **Patriot Plaza Premium Outlets** (© **757/258-0767; www.premiumoutlets.com**), between Ironbound and Airport roads. It's a more up-market mall, with Dansk, Donna Karan, Lenox china and crystal, Polo Ralph Lauren, Villeroy & Boch, WestPoint Stevens, Leather Loft and more. Shops here are open Monday to Saturday 10am to 9pm, Sunday 10am to 6pm.

Next comes **Prime Outlets Williamsburg** ✿, between Airport and Lightfoot roads (© **877/GO-OUTLETS** or 757/565-0702; www.primeoutlets.com/p.cfm/centers/Williamsburg). The largest and best outlet mall here, it has a wide selection of more than 85 shops including Bass, Bose, Brooks Brothers, Coach Leather, Crabtree & Evelyn, Eddie Bauer, Etienne Aigner, Harvé Bernard, J. Crew, Jones New York, Jos. A. Bank, L'eggs/Hanes/Bali, Maidenform, Mikasa, Naturalizer, Nike, Reebok/Rockport, Royal Doulton, Seiko, Van Heusen, and Waterford Wedgwood. It's open Monday to Saturday 10am to 9pm, Sunday 10am to 6pm.

Patriot Plaza and Prime Outlets have eclipsed **The Williamsburg Outlet Mall** (© **888/SHOP-333** or 757/565-3378), at the intersection of U.S. 60 Lightfoot Road (C.R. 646), where Levi's and Bass Shoes are the only major stores in residence. Its saving grace is that it's enclosed in an air-conditioned mall. It's open Monday to Saturday 10am to 9pm, Sunday 10am to 6pm.

Across the highway you can browse for collectibles and perhaps find a priceless piece of antiquity at the **Williamsburg Antique Mall,** 500 Lightfoot Rd. (© **757/565-3422;** www.antiqueswilliamsburg.com), with 45,000 square feet of dealer space. It's open Monday to Saturday 10am to 6pm, Sunday noon to 5pm.

Just up the road is the famous **Williamsburg Pottery Factory** (© **757/564-3326;** www.williamsburgpottery.com), a 200-acre shopping complex with over 31 tin buildings selling an eclectic collection of merchandise from all over the world. Shops sell Christmas decorations, garden furnishings, lamps, art prints, dried and silk flowers, luggage, linens, baskets, hardware, glassware, cookware, candles, wine, toys, crafts, clothing, food, jewelry, plants (there's a greenhouse and nursery)—even pottery. There's plenty of quality and plenty of kitsch. It even has its own **Pottery Factory Outlets,** but do your discount shopping at Patriot Plaza and Prime Outlets. The complex is open daily from 8am to 7pm in summer, daily from 9am to 5pm the rest of the year.

Continue west 1½ miles on U.S. 60, and you'll come to the **Williamsburg Doll Factory** (© 757/564-9703; www.dollfactory.com), with limited-edition porcelain collector's dolls. You can observe the doll-making process and buy parts to make your own. Other items available are stuffed animals, dollhouses and miniatures, clowns, and books on dolls. Open daily from 9am to 5pm.

Lastly you'll come to the **Williamsburg Soap & Candle Company** (© 757/564-3354; www.candlefactory.com). You can see a video on candle making while watching the process through windows that look out on the factory. There are shops adjoining, and a cozy country-style restaurant on the premises. It's open daily from 9am to 5pm, with extended hours in summer and fall.

⌒Tips "Bounce" Between the Parks

If you're going to spend more than a day at Busch Gardens Williamsburg and Water Country USA, consider buying a **Bounce Ticket,** which permits unlimited admission to both parks. Prices are $64.95 for 2 days; $74.95 for 3 days. Also, during the hot summer months, Busch Gardens offers a **Night Time Pass,** which permits unlimited visits after 4pm. They cost the same as 1-day tickets, but are handy if you plan to tour the area's other attractions during the day and spend the cooler evenings at the park. Remember, however, that prices and ticketing arrangements change from year to year, so call ahead or check the websites for current deals.

ON THE WINE TRAIL

In 1623, the Jamestown settlers were required to plant "20 vines for every male in the family above the age of 20." By doing so, it was thought, the fledgling colony would develop a profitable wine industry. As it turned out, the profitable industry was tobacco, not grapes, and winemaking never took off.

Until the 1980s, that is, when **The Williamsburg Winery,** 5800 Wessex Hundred (© **757/229-0999;** www.williamsburgwinery.com), Virginia's first modern vineyard, proved that good grapes could be grown on the peninsula. *Wine Spectator* magazine's critics have twice cited its vintages for excellence. Its Governor's White is the most widely purchased of Virginia's wine, although you'll find the Vintner's Reserve and John Adlum blended Chardonnays much better wines. You can try them daily from 11am to 4pm. Tastings and 45-minute tours cost $7 per person. Plan to have a bite of lunch along with your Two Shilling Red in the winery's Gabriel Archer Tavern. From the Historic Area, take Henry Street (Va. 132) south, turn right on Va. 199, left on Brookwood Drive, and another left on Lake Powell Road to the winery.

WHERE TO STAY
COLONIAL WILLIAMSBURG FOUNDATION HOTELS

The Colonial Williamsburg Foundation operates four hotels in all price categories: Williamsburg Inn (very expensive), Williamsburg Lodge (expensive), Woodlands Hotel & Suites (moderate), and the Governor's Inn (inexpensive), in the Historic Area. For advance reservations, call the **Visitor Center reservations service** (© **800/HISTORY;** www.colonialwilliamsburg.com). You also can make walk-in reservations at the Colonial Williamsburg Visitor Center. See "Just for Guests" for money-saving tips.

Governor's Inn   Least expensive of the foundation's hotels, the Governor's Inn is a two- and three-story brick motel surrounded by parking lots. Natural wood furniture brightens the standard motel-style rooms. There's a small outdoor pool for cooling off. It's near the visitor center on the northwest edge of the Historic Area. Some rooms are "pet friendly." Note that the Governor's Inn is near the Transportation Center, which means that trains come by during the night.

506 Henry St. (Va. 132), at Lafayette St., Williamsburg, VA 23185. © **800/HISTORY** or 757/229-1000. Fax 757/220-7480. www.colonialwilliamsburg.com. 200 units. $60–$100 double. Rates include continental breakfast. AE, DC, DISC, MC, V. Pets accepted (no fee). **Amenities:** Outdoor pool; access to nearby health club; babysitting; laundry service. *In room:* A/C, TV, iron.

Williamsburg Inn ★★★   One of the nation's most distinguished hotels, this rambling white-brick Regency-style inn has played host to heads of state from 17 countries including Queen Elizabeth II; U.S. presidents Truman, Eisenhower, Nixon, Ford, Reagan and Clinton; and lesser lights such as Shirley Temple. With giant floor-to-ceiling windows overlooking the renowned Golden Horseshoe golf course, the Regency Dining Room features classic American cuisine (coats and ties required after 6pm). An extensive 2001 renovation cut the number of rooms and suites by a third, enlarging all of them (suites now range up to 600 sq. ft.). They have marble bathrooms with double hand basins and separate tubs and showers. All are exquisitely furnished with reproductions, books, and photos of famous prior guests. This is also a great golf resort, with three top-flight courses to play, including the noted Golden Horseshoe (see "Outdoor Activities," above). The inn shares the Tazewell Club fitness center and spa at the Williamsburg Lodge, which is across the side street. Plans call for the adjacent building now occupied by the Craft House to be converted into a comprehensive spa and health evaluation center.

Value Just for Guests

There are certain advantages to staying at one of the Williamsburg Foundation's hotels. For example, guests can purchase discounted Colonial Williamsburg admission tickets valid for the length of their stay (recently $29 adults, $2 children). They also get breaks on other fees, have free access to the Tazewell Club Fitness Center, and can use their room keys to charge Historic Area expenses to their hotel bill.

Room rates at the foundation's accommodations can vary widely, depending on the season and how many guests may be booked on a given night. Try to reserve as far in advance as possible for the busy summer season. You might get a bargain during other times, especially if business is slow. You also can make walk-in reservations at the Colonial Williamsburg Visitor Center—at discounted rates if the hotels have rooms to spare (don't expect to get a deal on weekends and holidays). Also be sure to ask about holiday, golf, family, and other package deals.

Rooms in a modern building called **Providence Hall,** adjacent to the inn, are furnished in a contemporary blend of 18th-century and Oriental style, with balconies or patios overlooking tennis courts and a beautiful wooded area. The Inn provides the same services at Providence Hall that they do in the Williamsburg Inn. Rates range from $300 to $350.

136 Francis St., Williamsburg, VA 23187. (©) **800/HISTORY** or 757/229-1000. Fax 757/220-7096. www.colonial williamsburg.com. 63 units. $425–$750 double, $750 suite. AE, DC, DISC, MC, V. **Amenities:** Restaurant; bar; 2 outdoor pools; 3 golf courses; 8 tennis courts; access to nearby health club; spa; bike rentals; children's programs; concierge; 24-hr. room service; babysitting; laundry service. *In room:* A/C, TV, dataport, minibar, iron, safe.

Williamsburg Lodge ★★   Across the street from the Williamsburg Inn, the foundation's second-best hotel shares the inn's sports facilities. The flagstone-floored lobby is indeed lodgelike, with cypress paneling and a large working fireplace. Outside a covered verandah with rocking chairs overlooks two pools and the inn's Golden Horseshoe golf course. Accommodations are contemporary but warm and homey, with polished wood floors, handcrafted furniture inspired by pieces in the Abby Aldrich Rockefeller Folk Art Museum, and American folk Art Deco—decoys, samplers, and such. West Wing rooms have window walls overlooking duck ponds or a wooded landscape, and 12 have working fireplaces. Rooms in the Tazewell Wing have balconies facing landscaped courtyards; those in the West Wing do not have balconies.

310 S. England St., Williamsburg, VA 23185. (©) **800/HISTORY** or 757/229-1000. Fax 757/220-7685. www. colonialwilliamsburg.com. 264 units. $179–$235 double. AE, DC, DISC, MC, V. Free parking. **Amenities:** 2 restaurants; bar; 2 outdoor pools; 8 tennis courts; health club; spa; bike rentals; children's programs; game room; concierge; business center; limited room service; babysitting; laundry service; coin-op washers and dryers. *In room:* A/C, TV, dataport, minibar (suites only), coffeemaker, iron.

Williamsburg Woodlands Hotel & Suites ★ *Kids*   Beside the visitor center, this is the foundation's newest and third-best hotel. A separate building with a peaked roof and skylights holds the lodgelike lobby, where guests are treated to continental breakfast in a room with a fireplace. Interior corridors lead to the guest quarters, which are in a U-shaped building around a courtyard. The more expensive suites have separate living and sleeping rooms divided by the bathroom and a wet bar with coffeemaker, fridge and microwave oven (you won't have these extra amenities in the moderately spacious rooms). All units have Colonial-style pine furniture and photos of the Historic Area on their walls. The hotel has its own family restaurant (think Applebee's). There's plenty to keep kids occupied around the complex. Couple that with the pullout sofa beds in the suites, and it's a good choice for families of moderate means.

105 Visitors Center Dr. (P.O. Box 1776), Williamsburg, VA 23187. ℂ 800/HISTORY or 757/229-1000. Fax 757/229-7079. www.colonialwilliamsburg.com. 300 units. $99–$190 double. Rates include continental breakfast. AE, DC, DISC, MC, V. **Amenities:** Restaurant; bar; outdoor pool; access to nearby health club; bike rentals; children's programs; concierge; babysitting; coin-op washers and dryers. *In room:* A/C, TV, dataport, fridge (suites only), coffeemaker (suites only), iron.

COLONIAL HOUSES 🐾🐾

The foundation also has 77 rooms in the Historic Area in its **Colonial Houses.** Tastefully furnished with 18th-century antiques and reproductions, they all are variously equipped with canopied beds, kitchens, living rooms, fireplaces, and/or sizable gardens. Many of these are former laundries, workshops, small homes and stand-alone kitchens that have been converted into one- and two-bedroom bungalows. Others are rooms in taverns, some of which have as many as 16 units. Some rooms are tiny; tell the reservation clerk precisely what size room and what bed configuration you want. Some units are close to Francis Street, whose traffic noise can easily penetrate the non-insulated walls.

Rates range from $185 to $525. Williamsburg Inn manages the houses, but call the Visitor Center's reservations service (ℂ **800/HISTORY;** www.colonial williamsburg.com).

OTHER HOTELS & MOTELS

The area has more than 80 hotels and motels, including Best Western, Comfort Inn, Days Inn, EconoLodge, Hampton Inn, Holiday Inn, Marriott, Motel 6, Quality Inn, Ramada Inn, and Travelodge. You should be able to find a room on short notice except during the peak holiday periods.

The **Williamsburg Hotel and Motel Association** (ℂ **800/446-9244** or 757/220-3330; www.mywilliamsburgvacation.com) operates a very good free reservations service. Its clerks will help you to find the best rates. Their listings include most of the accommodations mentioned below.

Courtyard By Marriott *(Value)* This four-story member of the fine chain designed by business travelers (and very comfortable for the rest of us) enjoys a quiet setting of trees and shrubs on the eastern side of town near Busch Gardens. A plant-filled lobby looks out to the courtyard and its good-size pool. Furnished with substantial oak pieces, the guest quarters feature large desks, separate seating areas, and long phone cords. Suites have full sofa-bedded living rooms with extra phones and TVs, plus wet bars with small refrigerators. The lobby restaurant offers a full breakfast buffet but no other meals.

470 McLaws Circle, Williamsburg, VA 23185. ℂ 800/321-2211 or 757/221-0700. Fax 757/221-0741. www.courtyard.com. 151 units. $109–$159 double; $129–$199 suite. Weekend rates available. AE, DC, DISC, MC, V. Free parking. From Williamsburg, follow U.S. 60 east about 2 miles to Busch Corporate Center, turn right at light and bear right on McLaws Circle. **Amenities:** Restaurant (breakfast only); outdoor pool; exercise room; Jacuzzi; game room; business center; laundry service; coin-op washers and dryers. *In room:* A/C, TV, dataport, fridge, coffeemaker, iron.

Tips Avoiding the Noise

The main railroad line between Richmond and Norfolk runs along the north side of Richmond Road (U.S. 60), which translates into train noise. For a quiet night's sleep stay at a hotel on the south side of the highway.

Tips **Saving Money with a "Flex" Vacation**

One way to save money on accommodations and admission fees is through a **Williamsburg Flex Vacation** package organized by the Williamsburg Area Convention and Visitors Bureau. For example, a recent offering included 3 nights accommodations and 4 days unlimited admission to Colonial Williamsburg, Busch Gardens Williamsburg, Water Country USA, Jamestown Settlement, and the Yorktown Victory Center for $527, double occupancy. Call © **800/465-5563** or click on www.williamsburgflex.com for current packages.

Governor Spottswood Motel *Value* Owned and operated by the same family for two generations, this older but well-maintained motel is the best inexpensive property here. It offers rooms in one-story buildings facing a parking lot, but more charming are cottages set back among magnolias, camellias, and towering pines on the property's 10 acres. Capable of accommodating up to seven persons, each of the cottages has two bedrooms, a living room, kitchen, and bath. The smallish but comfortable rooms have tub-shower combination baths; some sport brass or canopy beds, and 19 of them have kitchens. There's a playground area for kids.

1508 Richmond Rd. (just east of Ironwood Rd.), Williamsburg, VA 23185. © **800/368-1244** or 757/229-6444. Fax 757/253-2410. www.govspottswood.com. 78 units, including 7 cottages. $32–$160 double. AE, DISC, MC, V. **Amenities:** Outdoor pool; coin-op washers and dryers; concierge-level rooms. *In room:* A/C, TV, kitchen (cottages only).

Radisson Fort Magruder Hotel *Kids* Sitting between the Historic Area and Busch Gardens, this modern hotel draws lots of conventions and meetings but is also a good choice for families with children who want a location convenient to both attractions. Two-story glass walls create an atrium lobby, but lots of brick and antique-look furniture remind you that this is Williamsburg. Guest rooms are spacious, with wing chairs, desks, and balconies, most looking out on gardens that surround the swimming pool and lighted tennis courts.

6545 Pocahontas Trail (U.S. 60), Williamsburg, VA 23185. © **800/333-3333** or 757/220-2250. Fax 757/220-9059. 303 units. $89–$169 double, $175–$300 suites. AE, DC, DISC, MC, V. From I-64, take Va. 199 west to U.S. 60 west. **Amenities:** Restaurant; bar; indoor and outdoor pools; 2 tennis courts; exercise room; Jacuzzi; sauna; concierge; business center; limited room service; babysitting; laundry service; coin-op washers and dryers; concierge-level rooms. *In room:* A/C, TV, dataport, fridge, coffeemaker, iron.

Williamsburg Hospitality House Just 2 blocks west of the Historic Area and opposite the College of William and Mary, this four-story brick hotel is as convenient to the major sights as any non-foundation hotel. It's built around a central courtyard with flowering trees and plants and umbrella tables. Spacious guest rooms and public areas are appointed with a gracious blend of 18th-century reproductions. The 415 Grill offers contemporary fare. Suites here have either one or two bedrooms.

415 Richmond Rd., Williamsburg, VA 23185. © **800/932-9192** or 757/229-4020. Fax 757/220-1560. www.williamsburghosphouse.com. 295 units. $79–$185 double; $375–$475 suite. AE, DC, DISC, MC, V. **Amenities:** Restaurant; bar; outdoor pool; exercise room; game room; concierge; limited room service. *In room:* A/C, TV, dataport, coffeemaker, iron.

BED & BREAKFAST INNS

In addition to those below, Williamsburg has at least 16 more B&Bs, including **Williamsburg Sampler,** 922 Jamestown Rd., Williamsburg, VA 23185 (© **800/ 722-1169** or 757/253-0399; www.williamsburgsampler.com), a 1976-vintage replica of an 18th century plantation manse. The Williamsburg Area Convention & Visitors Bureau has a list (see "Essentials," earlier).

Liberty Rose ★★ Williamsburg's most romantic B&B, Brad and Sandra Hirz's 1920s two-story white-clapboard home enjoys a premier location on a wooded hilltop 1¼ miles from the Historic Area. An overall feeling of graciousness makes it a refuge from the rigors of sightseeing. Throughout you'll find Victorian, French- and English-country, and 18th-century antiques and reproductions—and fresh roses in every room. The elegant parlor, complete with grand piano that guests may play, has a working fireplace and comfortable chairs for relaxing. The accommodations are luxurious, each distinctively decorated. Bathrobes and a bowl of chocolates are *de rigeur,* as are telephones in each room. A full breakfast is served on the morning porch or in the courtyard.

1022 Jamestown Rd., Williamsburg, VA 23185. © **800/545-1825** or 757/253-1260. Fax 757/253-8529. www. libertyrose.com. 4 units. $195–$275 double. Rates include full breakfast. AE, MC, V. *In room:* A/C, TV.

The Fife & Drum Inn ★★ *(Finds* Occupying upstairs quarters in one of the Merchants Square buildings, this relaxed and interesting charmer is the only privately owned accommodations in the Historic Area. "Colonial Williamsburg is your front yard," says Billy Scruggs, who with wife Sharon opened the inn in 2000. Guests gather under the cathedral ceiling of the common room complete with fireplace, big TV with VCR, and a small library of books about Williamsburg. Sharon and Billy, who grew up here, put out a full breakfast every morning, including Virginia country ham biscuits. A sky-lit hallway with faux brick floor and clapboard siding (you will swear it's a street) leads to the seven medium-size rooms and two suites, some of which have dormer windows. The suites open to a narrow balcony out back. Collages of old Williamsburg postcards hanging on the walls overlook an eclectic mix of furniture, including birdhouses hiding a few of the TVs. The Conservancy room is the most romantic, with a canopied double bed and a claw-foot bathtub. The inn has its own parking lot.

441 Prince George St., Williamsburg, VA 23185. © **888/838-1783** or 757/345-1776. Fax 757/253-1676. www.fifeanddruminn.com. 9 units. $145–$165 double. Rates include full breakfast. AE, DISC, MC, V. Free parking. *In room:* A/C, TV, dataport, iron.

A NEARBY RESORT WITH CHAMPIONSHIP GOLF

Kingsmill Resort ★★★ Nestled in a peaceful setting on beautifully landscaped grounds beside the James River, the luxurious, country clublike Kingsmill Resort is the centerpiece of a 2,900-acre residential development. It's one of Virginia's most complete resorts, offering three golf courses, a sports complex with 15 tennis courts, and the Williamsburg area's only full-service spa. Highlight is the world-famous River Course, home of the LPGA Michelob Open golf championship. Accommodations consist of guest rooms and one-, two-, and three-bedroom suites in gray clapboard buildings overlooking the James River (most expensive), golf-course fairways, or tennis courts. The suites are individually owned and furnished condos, so decor varies from Colonial reproductions to contemporary settings. They have complete kitchens and living rooms with fireplaces.

Daily housekeeping service, including fresh linens, is included. Kingsmill's main dining room offers fine cuisine with a terrific view of the James, while the golf club's Eagles Steakhouse overlooks the River Course. Guests can take a complimentary shuttle to Colonial Williamsburg and Busch Gardens Williamsburg.

1010 Kingsmill Rd., Williamsburg, VA 23185. © 800/832-5665 or 757/253-1703. Fax 757/253-3993. www. kingsmill.com. 400 units. $139–$299 double, $219–$997 suites. Golf, tennis and spa packages available. AE, DC, DISC, MC, V. From I-64, take Exit 242 and follow Va. 199 west past U.S. 60 to sign for Kingsmill on the James. **Amenities:** 3 restaurants; 3 bars; indoor and outdoor pools; 3 golf courses; 15 tennis courts; health club; spa; Jacuzzi; sauna; bike rentals; children's programs; concierge; business center; limited room service; babysitting. *In room:* A/C, TV, kitchen (suites only), coffeemaker, iron.

WHERE TO DINE

Williamsburg abounds in restaurants catering to tourists. Most national chain, fast food, and family restaurants have outlets on Richmond Road (U.S. 60) west of town.

COLONIAL WILLIAMSBURG FOUNDATION TAVERNS 🎭🎭

The Colonial Williamsburg Foundation runs four reconstructed 18th-century "ordinaries" or taverns. They aim at authenticity in fare, ambience, and costuming of the staff. Although they are all relatively expensive, dinner at one of the taverns is a necessary ingredient of the Williamsburg experience.

Except for Josiah Chowning's Tavern, which serves pit-cooked barbecue, they offer colonial-style fare such as peanut soup, Brunswick stew, sautéed back-fin crabmeat and ham topped with butter and laced with sherry, Sally Lunn bread, and deep-dish Shenandoah apple pie. They all have al fresco dining in good weather on brick patios under grape arbors. Children's menus are available.

Their seasonal hours and menus are posted out front and at the ticket booth on Henry Street at Duke of Gloucester Street, and are available at the visitor center, so you can see what's being served before making your reservations.

Christina Campbell's Tavern Almost hidden behind the Capitol, Christina Campbell's Tavern is "where all the best people resorted" around 1765. George Washington recorded in his diary that he dined here 10 times over a 22-month period. After the capital moved to Richmond, business declined and operations ceased. In its heyday, the tavern was famous for seafood, and today that is once again the specialty. Campbell's is an authentic reproduction with 18th-century furnishings, blazing fireplaces, and flutists and balladeers to entertain diners.

302B E. Francis St. © 757/229-2141. Reservations required at dinner. Lunch $8.50–$11; main courses $22–$28. AE, DC, DISC, MC, V. Daily 11:30am–2:30pm and 5–9pm.

Josiah Chowning's Tavern In 1766, Josiah Chowning announced the opening of a tavern "where all who please to favour me with their custom may depend upon the best of entertainment for themselves, servants, and horses, and good pasturage." It's charming, with low-beamed ceilings, raw pine floors, and

---

Tips The Early Bird Gets the Reservation

Advance reservations for dinner at the taverns are essential during the summer and on weekends during spring and fall. Except at Josiah Chowning's Tavern, which does not accept reservations, you can book tables up to 60 days in advance by dropping by or calling the visitor center (© 800/ TAVERNS or 757/229-2141). Lunch reservations are only accepted for major holidays.

country-made furnishings. There are two working fireplaces, and at night one dines by candlelight. These days the fare is strictly pit-cooked Virginia-style barbecue. One of the best things to do here after 9pm is to take in the 18th-century music, magic, and games, when the tavern becomes Gambols Pub. This is the only tavern that does not accept reservations.

Duke of Gloucester St. 🕐 **757/229-2141.** Reservations not accepted. Lunch $7–$10; main courses $19–$21. Gambols Pub, free with dinner, otherwise $3 cover charge. AE, DC, DISC, MC, V. Mon–Sat 11am–4pm and 5–9pm; Gambols pub, daily 9pm–midnight.

Kings Arms Tavern   On the site of a 1772 establishment, Kings Arms Tavern is a re-creation of the tavern and an adjoining home. Stables, a barbershop, laundry, smokehouse, kitchen and other outbuildings have also been reconstructed. The original proprietress, Mrs. Jane Vobe, was famous for her fine cooking, and her establishment's proximity to the Capitol made it a natural meeting place during Publick Times. Today the 11 dining rooms (8 with fireplaces) are painted and furnished following early Virginia precedent. The Queen Anne and Chippendale pieces are typical appointments of this class of tavern, and the prints, maps, engravings, aquatints, and mezzotints lining the walls are genuine examples of period interior decorations. Balladeers wander the rooms during dinner. There's outdoor dining in the Garden during warm weather.

409 E. Duke of Gloucester St. 🕐 **757/229-2141.** Reservations required at dinner. Lunch $7–$10; main courses $24–$32. AE, DC, DISC, MC, V. Lunch daily 11:30am–3pm. Dinner seatings every 15 min. daily 5–9pm. Garden, daily 11:30am–dark.

Shields Tavern _Value_   With 11 dining rooms and a garden under a trumpet-vine-covered arbor that seats 200, Shields is the largest of the Historic Area's tavern/restaurants. It's named for James Shields who, with his wife, Anne, and family, ran a much-frequented hostelry on this site in the mid-1700s. Based on a room-by-room inventory of Shields' personal effects, the tavern has been furnished with items similar to those used in the mid–18th century, and many rooms have working fireplaces. Upstairs serves an a la carte menu, while down in the wine cellar, the cook offers a fixed-price, all-you-can-eat "bountiful feast" of Colonial fare. It's a good value compared to prices at the other taverns.

422 E. Duke of Gloucester St. 🕐 **757/229-2141.** Reservations required at dinner. Lunch $7–$12; main courses $27–$30; fixed-price dinner $30 adults, $13 children 9 and under. AE, DC, DISC, MC, V. Lunch daily 11:30am–3pm. Dinner seatings every 15 min. daily 5–9pm. Garden, daily 11:30am–dusk.

RESTAURANTS IN MERCHANTS SQUARE

The Merchants Square commercial area at the west end of the Historic Area has several restaurants and bars to satisfy your appetite and slake your thirst.

Berret's Restaurant & Tap House Grill 𝆕 SEAFOOD   A congenial, casual place, Berret's has a popular outdoor Tap House Grill that seems to be busy all day in warm weather, especially on weekends. It's the best place in town to slake a thirst after schlepping around the Historic Area all day. The adjoining restaurant is bright and airy, with several dining rooms. Canvas sailcloth shades, blue-trimmed china, and marine artifacts on the walls make an appropriate backdrop for the excellent seafood. Oysters or clams raw or steamed on the half shell do nicely as starters inside or out. For a main course, the crab cakes are pan-fried with country bacon—a far cry from those dished up at fried seafood joints. The Tap House serves sandwiches at night. There's a good selection of microbrews and Virginia wines by the glass.

199 S. Boundary St. (at Francis St.). 🕐 **757/253-1847.** www.berrets.com. Reservations recommended for dinner. Sandwiches and salads (Tap House Grille only) $8–$15; main courses $15–$25. AE, DISC, MC, V.

(Value Mmmm . . . Aromas

The local branch of **Aromas,** 431 Prince George St. in Merchants Square (© **757/221-6676**), is Williamsburg's favorite town-and-gown coffee house, with gourmet sandwiches and pastries, too. You can get cooked breakfasts before 10:30am, and tapas and meals such as seared scallops or shrimp with grits after 5pm. With no item over $10, it's a very good value. Aromas is open Monday to Thursday 7am to 10pm, Friday and Saturday 7am to 11pm, Sunday 8am to 8pm. MasterCard and Visa cards accepted.

Restaurant, Apr–Oct daily 11:30am–3:30pm and 5:30–9pm (extended hours in summer). Tap House Grill, Apr–Nov, daily 5–10pm.

The Cheese Shop *(Value* DELI   This gourmet deli is the best place in Williamsburg for take-out salads, sandwiches, and other fixings. Head to the rear counter and place your order for ham, roast beef, turkey, chicken, and barbecue sandwiches on a choice of fresh bread. The cheese counter has a wide selection of domestic and imported brands plus fresh salads. You can eat your meal at wrought iron umbrella tables out front. (The owners were building an adjoining bistro-style restaurant during my visit; it'll be worth checking out.)

410 Duke of Gloucester St. (between Henry and Boundary sts.). © **757/220-0298**. Most items $4–$6. AE, DC, DISC, MC, V. Mon–Sat 10am–8pm, Sun 11am–6pm.

Seasons Restaurant AMERICAN   If you have trouble slaking your thirst at Berret's outdoor Tap House Grille, the large patio behind this pleasant restaurant is the next best place. For food, it offers a mixed lot of beef, ribs, lamb chops, salmon, fried catfish, and house specialties such as lemon-garlic flavored stir-fried beef, chicken and shrimp. Each dining room is decorated to match one of the seasons, but try for a table on the patio out back.

110 S. Henry St. (at Duke of Gloucester St.). © **757/259-0018**. Reservations not accepted but call ahead to get on the waiting list. Main courses $16–$21. AE, DC, DISC, MC, V. Mon–Thurs 11am–10pm; Fri–Sat 11am–11pm; Sun 10am–10pm (brunch 10am–3pm).

Trellis Cafe, Restaurant & Grill ✦✦✦ AMERICAN   Executive chef Marcel Desaulniers has brought national recognition to this restaurant, whose decor evokes delightful establishments in California's wine-country. He was the first chef from the South to be honored by the James Beard Foundation, whose awards are considered the Oscars of the culinary world, and was named to *Food & Wine* magazine's honor roll of American chefs and to *Who's Who of Cooking in America*. Marcel changes the menu every season to take advantage of local produce, which he imaginatively combines with the best in foods from different regions of the United States. If it's offered, try his exciting combination of grilled fish, thinly sliced Virginia country ham, pine nuts, and zinfandel-soaked raisins.

A highlight is a complete, fixed-price dinner, which might consist of a salad or a bowl of hearty, sage-laced sausage and corn chowder; a mixed grill of duck's leg, chicken breast, and country sausage with a side of perfectly steamed green beans and onions; and ice cream or sorbet. You can upgrade the dessert to Marcel's sinful Death by Chocolate, which is the title of one of several cookbooks he has authored.

If weather is fine, you might dine on the planter-bordered brick terrace.

Duke of Gloucester St. (between Henry and Boundary sts.). © **757/229-8610**. Reservations recommended at dinner. Sandwiches $7–$10; main courses $16–$30; fixed-price dinners $26. AE, DC, DISC, MC, V. Daily 11am–3pm and 5–9:30pm.

NEARBY DINING

Giuseppe's Italian Cafe *Value* ITALIAN   This pleasant local favorite may be difficult to see from Richmond Highway (it's at the end of a strip mall with a Food Lion supermarket at its center), but it's a great place for a meal during or after a shopping expedition. The chef's lentil-and-andouille soup won justified raves from *Bon Appetit* magazine, and he's also adept at the likes of chicken Antonio in a subtly spicy pepper pesto sauce. Also on the menu: heaping plates of spaghetti, a page full of vegetarian pastas, and single-size pizzas with some unusual toppings such as smoked oysters. All entrees come with a salad or a bowl of the hearty soup. There are two dining rooms here plus heated sidewalk seating.

5601 Richmond Rd. (U.S. 60 at Airport Rd.), in Ewell Station Shopping Center. ✆ **757/565-1977.** Reservations not accepted, call for preferred seating. Main courses $5–$17. AE, DISC, MC, V. Mon–Thurs 11:30am–2pm and 5–9pm; Fri–Sat 11:30am–2pm and 5–9:30pm. From Historic District, go 4 miles west on U.S. 60 to shopping center on left.

Old Chickahominy House ★★ TRADITIONAL SOUTHERN   One of the great places to sample traditional, down home Virginia cooking, the Old Chickahominy House is a reconstructed 18th-century house with mantels from old Gloucester homes and wainscoting from Carter's Grove. Floors are bare oak, and walls, painted in traditional colonial colors, are hung with gilt-framed 17th- and 18th-century oil paintings. Three adjoining rooms house an antiques/gift shop. The entire effect is cozy and charming. Before making my rounds, I always opt for the plantation breakfast of real Virginia ham with two eggs, biscuits, cured country bacon and sausage, grits, and coffee or tea. At lunch, Miss Melinda's special is a cup of Brunswick stew with Virginia ham on hot biscuits, fruit salad, homemade pie, and tea or coffee. After dining it's fun to roam through the warren of antiques-filled rooms. Also check out the Shirley Pewter Shop next door.

1211 Jamestown Rd., at Va. 199. ✆ **757/229-4689.** Reservations not accepted. Breakfast $3–$8; lunch $2.50–$8. MC, V. Daily 8:30–10:15am and 11:45am–2:15pm. Closed 2 weeks in Jan, Easter, July 4th, Thanksgiving, and Christmas.

Pierce's Pitt Bar-B-Que BARBECUE   Visible from I-64, this gaudy yellow-and-orange barbecue joint has been dishing up pulled pork, chicken, and smoked ribs since 1961, as the walls hung with old photos of the owners and their family and staff will attest. The pulled pork is better than the ribs here, but unlike the unadulterated version at King's Barbecue in Petersburg (see section 8 in chapter 9), here it comes soaked in a smoky-flavored, tomato-based sauce. Order at the counter and take your meal (served in plastic containers) to a table inside or outdoors under cover. No alcoholic beverages are served here.

447 E. Rochambeau Dr., Lightfoot (beside I-64). ✆ **757/565-2955.** Reservations not accepted. Sandwiches $2–$4; main courses $5.50–$16. MC, V. Mon–Thurs 7am–8pm (to 9pm in summer); Fri–Sun 7am–9pm (to 10pm in summer). From Historic Area, go west on Richmond Rd. (U.S. 60), right on Airport Rd. (C.R. 645) 2 miles toward I-64, follow signs to restaurant on Rochambeau Dr., about 2 miles.

WILLIAMSBURG AFTER DARK

You should spend at least one evening taking in a little 18th-century nightlife in Colonial Williamsburg. The colonial taverns have evening entertainment, but don't miss an **18th Century Play** staged in and around the historic buildings. For example, "Jumping the Broom" deals with the difficulties of love and romance among Williamsburg's slaves in 1774. It's performed in and out of the Powell House, one of the 88 buildings surviving from the 18th century. When it's over, you get to discuss slavery with the young African-American cast.

Colonial Williamsburg also conducts nighttime tours and other activities in the Historic Area. Check the schedule in the *Colonial Williamsburg Companion,* the weekly newspaper that tells what's going on and when. Copies are available at the Visitor Center (see "Exploring the Historic Area," earlier).

Another great way to spend a warm-weather evening is with **The Original Ghosts of Williamsburg Tours** (© 877/62-GHOST or 757/565-4821), which entertainingly blends ghost stories and local folklore with historical fact. Children will enjoy them, too. The candlelight tours are based on L.B. Taylor's 1983 book, *The Ghosts of Williamsburg,* which sold more than 100,000 copies. Call for reservations, which are essential.

The Kimball Theater, on Duke of Gloucester Street in Merchants Square (© 757/565-8588), hosts concerts, special lectures by W&M professors, puppet shows, second-run movies, and other events. Call or drop by the theater to see what's going on. William and Mary drama department students refine their skills in the **William and Mary Theater** (© 757/221-2676; www.wm.edu). The college also has an active calendar of concerts and lectures.

The Music Theatre of Williamsburg, 7575 Richmond Rd. in Lightfoot (© 888/MUSIC-20 or 757/564-0200; www.musictheatre.com), presents revues by its own resident company and hosts performances by touring musicians. The shows change frequently, so call or check the website to find out who's on stage.

For more ideas pick up a copy of *Williamsburg* magazine or check its website at www.williamsburgmag.com.

2 Jamestown: The First Colony

9 miles SW of Williamsburg

The story of Jamestown, the first permanent English settlement in the New World, is documented here in a national park on the Jamestown Island site where they landed. Here you'll learn the exploits of Capt. John Smith, the colony's leader, rescued from execution by the American Indian princess Pocahontas; the arrival of the first African-American slaves; and how life was lived in 17th-century Virginia. Archeologists have excavated more than 100 building frames, evidence of manufacturing ventures (pottery, winemaking, brick-making, and glass blowing), wells, and roads, as well as hundreds of thousands of artifacts of everyday life—tools, utensils, ceramic dishes, armor, keys, and the like.

Next door at Jamestown Settlement, a state-run living-history museum complex, you can see recreations of the three ships in which the settlers arrived in 1607, the colony they built, and a typical American Indian village of the time.

Allow at least half a day for your visit and consider packing a lunch. There is a cafe at Jamestown Settlement, but you may want to take advantage of the picnic areas at the National Park Service site.

The scenic way here from Williamsburg is via the picturesque Colonial Parkway, or you can take Jamestown Road (Va. 31).

Historic Jamestowne   Now part of the Colonial National Historical Park and jointly administered by the National Park Service and the Association for the Preservation of Virginia Antiquities (APVA; www.apva.org), this is the site of the actual colony. It was an island then; now an isthmus separates it from the mainland. After entering the park, stop first at the reconstructed **Glasshouse,** where costumed interpreters make glass in the ancient way used by the colonists in 1608 during their first attempt to create an industry (it failed). Remains of the original glass furnaces are nearby. Then proceed to the visitors center, where a museum and a 15-minute film telling the story of Jamestown from its earliest days to 1699, when the capital of Virginia moved to Williamsburg, will get you oriented. Inquire at the reception desk about audiotape tours and ranger-led walking tours, costumed interpretive programs, and other programs offered during your visit.

The visitor center stands at the actual site of **"James Cittie,"** as the colonists called their new village. The brick foundations outside aren't original, but they do stand on the actual locations of the 17th-century homes as determined by extensive and very much on-going archaeological work. You're welcome to view the digging, and APVA archaeologists and volunteers will answer your questions. Most of what's left of James Cittie is now about 18 inches below ground, but the tower of one of the first brick churches in Virginia (1639) still stands. Behind the tower, **Memorial Church** is a 1907 re-creation built by the Colonial Dames of America on the site of the structure (note the glass panels along the sides of the floor, which show some of the original foundation). In 1619, the church housed the first legislative assembly in English-speaking North America. A wooden stockade fence stands above the triangular borders of the 1607 **James Fort,** part of which has eroded into the James River.

A short walk along the seawall past Confederate breastworks—built during the Civil War to protect this narrow part of the river—will take you to the **Dale House,** which displays a resin cast reproduction of the skeleton of one of the original settlers. Unearthed by archaeologists in 1996, the actual bones are at the Smithsonian Institution in Washington, D.C. Apparently the young man was killed by a musket shot to the right knee, giving rise to the theme of the interactive display: "Who Shot J.R.?"

A fascinating **5-mile loop drive** begins at the Visitor Center parking lot and winds through 1,500 wilderness acres of woodland and marsh that have been allowed to return to their natural state in order to approximate the landscape as 17th-century settlers found it. Illustrative markers interpret aspects of daily activities and industries of the colonists—tobacco growing, lumbering, silk and wine production, pottery making, farming, and so on.

Allow at least 2 hours for this special attraction

Southern end of Colonial Pkwy., at Jamestown Rd. (Va. 31). © **757/898-2410** or 757/229-1773. www.nps.gov/colo. Admission $6 adults, free for children 16 and under. Combination ticket with Yorktown Battlefield $9 adult, free for children 16 and under. Both admissions good for 7 days. National Park Service passports accepted. Main gate, daily 8:30am–4:30pm; visitor center daily 9am–5pm; glasshouse daily 8:30am–5pm. Extended hours in summer. Closed Christmas.

Jamestown Settlement ⚐⚐ (Kids)   Built in 1957 by the Commonwealth of Virginia to celebrate Jamestown's 350th anniversary, this living history museum is being enlarged and improved in preparation for the 400th anniversary in 2007. It shows you what the settlers' three ships, their colony, and a typical Powhatan Indian village looked like, and costumed interpreters will show you how they lived in the early 1600s.

The entrance building shows a 15-minute video about Jamestown and has museum galleries featuring artifacts, documents, decorative objects, dioramas,

---

Fun Fact **A Helping Hand**

Legend says you'll have good luck if you shake hands with the statue of Pocahontas standing outside the old church at Historic Jamestowne.

and graphics relating to the Jamestown period. Don't miss the exact reproduction of the deerskin-and-seashells cape worn by Chief Powhatan, father of Pocahontas (the Ashmolean Museum in Oxford, England, has the original). Leaving the museum complex, you'll come directly into the **Powhatan Indian Village,** representing the culture and technology of a highly organized chiefdom of 32 tribes that inhabited coastal Virginia in the early 17th century. There are several mat-covered lodges, which are furnished as dwellings, as well as a garden and a ceremonial dance circle. Historical interpreters tend gardens, tan animal hides, and make bone and stone tools and pottery.

Triangular **James Fort** is a re-creation of the one constructed by the Jamestown colonists in the spring of 1607. Inside the wooden stockade are primitive wattle-and-daub structures with thatched roofs representing Jamestown's earliest buildings. Interpreters are engaged in activities typical of early-17th-century life, such as agriculture, military activities (including firing muskets), carpentry, blacksmithing, and meal preparation.

A short walk from James Fort are reproductions of the three **ships,** the *Susan Constant, Godspeed,* and *Discovery,* that transported the 104 colonists to Virginia. Boarding and exploring the ships will give you an appreciation of the hardships they endured even before they reached the hostile New World.

The exhibits are interactive, assigning such activities as having you use a shell to scrape the fur off deerskin. Children are more likely to enjoy a visit here than to Historic Jamestowne.

Jamestown Rd. (Va. 31), at James River. ℂ 888/593-4682 or 757/253-4838. www.historyisfun.org. Admission $11 adults, $5.25 children 6–12; free for children 5 and under. Combination ticket with Yorktown Victory Center $16 adults, $7.75 children 6–12. Daily 9am–5pm (to 6pm June 15–Aug 15). Closed New Year's Day and Christmas.

3 Yorktown: Revolutionary Victory ★★★

14 miles NE of Williamsburg

Although the 13 American colonies declared their independence from England on July 4, 1776, their dream of freedom from King George III actually came to fruition here at Yorktown in October of 1781, when Gen. George Washington won the last major battle of the American Revolution. "I have the Honor to inform Congress that a Reduction of the British Army under the Command of Lord Cornwallis is most happily effected," Washington wrote to the Continental Congress on October 19, 1781. Though it would be 2 years before a treaty was signed and sporadic fighting would continue, the Revolution, for all intents and purposes, was over.

Today the decisive battlefield is a national park, and the Commonwealth of Virginia has built the Yorktown Victory Center, an interpretive museum explaining the road to revolution, the war itself, and the building of a new nation afterwards. Predating the revolution and overlooking the picturesque York River, the old town of Yorktown itself is worth a visit.

To get here from Williamsburg, drive to the eastern end of the Colonial Parkway. From Norfolk, take I-64 west to U.S. 17 north and follow the signs to Yorktown.

You'll need at least half a day to digest all this history.

HISTORY

Though tourist attention focuses to a large degree on the town's role as the final Revolutionary battlefield, Yorktown is also of interest as one of America's earliest colonial towns.

BEFORE THE REVOLUTION   Yorktown's history dates to 1691, when the General Assembly at Jamestown passed the Port Act creating a new town on the York River, which unlike the James River, has a shoal-free, deep-water channel to the Chesapeake Bay. Yorktown quickly became a principal mid-Atlantic port and a center of tobacco trade. By the time of the American Revolution, it was a thriving town with several thousand planters, innkeepers, seamen, merchants, craftsmen, indentured servants, and slaves. Water Street, paralleling the river, was lined with shops, inns, and loading docks.

THE VICTORY AT YORKTOWN   After a rather fruitless and exhausting march through the Carolinas, Cornwallis brought his army to Yorktown in hopes of being moved to New York by the British navy. Marching quickly from the north, Washington's army of 17,600 American troops and their French allies laid siege to Yorktown on September 28, 1781. Meanwhile, a French fleet sailed up from the Caribbean and defeated the British navy off the Virginia Capes, thereby cutting off Cornwallis' escape route.

On October 9 the allies began bombarding the British positions. The French were the first to fire. Two hours later, George Washington personally fired the first American round. At 8pm on October 14, the French stormed Redoubt 9 while the Americans made short work of Redoubt 10. The Americans broke through in 10 minutes; the French, whose target was stronger, took half an hour.

Two days later a desperate Cornwallis tried to escape with his troops across the York River to Gloucester Point, but a violent storm scattered his boats. On October 17 at 10am, a British drummer appeared on the rampart. He beat out a signal indicating a desire to discuss terms with the enemy. A ceasefire was called, and a British officer was led to American lines where he requested an armistice. On October 18, commissioners met at the house of Augustine Moore and worked out the terms of surrender.

At 2pm on October 19, 1781, the French and Continental armies lined Surrender Road, each stretching for over a mile on either side. About 5,000 British soldiers and seamen, clad in new uniforms, marched out of Yorktown to a large field, where they laid down their weapons and battle flags. Gen. Charles O'Hara of the British Guards represented Cornwallis who, pleading illness, did not surrender in person.

THE TOP ATTRACTIONS

Yorktown Battlefield ★★★   Today, most of Yorktown and the surrounding battlefield areas are included in this 4,300-acre section of the Colonial National Historical Park. You can drive around the key battle sites, which have interpretive markers, but begin at the visitor center, where the 16-minute documentary film *Siege at Yorktown* is shown on the hour and half-hour. Not to be missed among the museum displays is Washington's actual sleeping and dining tent, now preserved in a hermetically sealed room (it's really cool to actually walk into his tent without entering the glass-enclosed room). There's also a replica (which you can board and explore) of the quarterdeck of HMS *Charon;* additional objects recovered during excavations; exhibits about Cornwallis's surrender and the events leading up to it; and dioramas detailing the siege. Upstairs, an "on-the-scene" account of the Battle of Yorktown is given by a 13-year-old soldier in the Revolutionary army, his taped narrative accompanied by a sound-and-light show.

National Park Service Rangers are on hand to answer questions. They give free **tours** of the British inner defense line seasonally (call the visitor center for times).

⟨*Tips*⟩ Best Battlefield Strategies

You'll enjoy the 90-minute audio driving tour tape or CD of the Yorktown battlefield. Narrated by "British and American colonels" whose polite hostilities to each other are most amusing, the taped commentary further elucidates the battlefield sites. Listen to the introduction in the parking lot; it will tell you when to depart. Tape or not, drive the Battlefield Route first; then if time permits, the Encampment Route.

To make it easy to follow what happened, the park is divided into two routes. You won't stay in your car the whole time; it's frequently necessary to park, get out, and walk to redoubts and earthworks. A lot of the drive is very scenic, winding through woods and fields abundant with bird life. The Encampment route is especially beautiful.

On the 7-mile **Battlefield Route** you'll see the **Grand French Battery,** where French soldiers manning cannons, mortars, and howitzers fired on British and German mercenary troops; the **Moore House,** where British and American representatives hammered out the surrender on October 18, 1781; and **Surrender Field,** where the British laid down their arms at the end of the siege.

Note that the Moore House usually is open daily from 10am to 4:30pm during summer, weekends from 1 to 4pm in spring and autumn, but check with the visitor center to be sure. The 10.2-mile **Encampment Route** takes you to the sites of Washington's and Rochambeau's headquarters, the French cemetery and Artillery Park, and allied encampment sites.

North end of Colonial Pkwy. ⟨✆⟩ **757/898-2410** or 757/898-3400. www.nps.gov/colo. Admission $5 per person 17 and over, free for children under 17. Combination ticket with Jamestown Island $9 per person 17 and over, free for children under 17. Both admissions good for 7 days. Audio tape tours $2. National Park Service passports accepted. Battlefield daily 8:30am–dusk. Visitor center Apr to mid-June and mid-Aug to Oct daily 8:30am–5pm; mid-June to mid-Aug daily 8:30am–5:30pm; Oct–Mar daily 9am–5pm. Visitor center closed Christmas.

Yorktown Victory Center ⟨✸⟩ This state-operated multimedia museum offers an excellent orientation to Yorktown, and coming here first will prepare you for your battlefield tour. You'll start with an open-air timeline walkway known as the "Road to Revolution," which illustrates the relationship between the colonies and Great Britain beginning in 1750. Aspects of the American Revolution are explored in its gallery exhibits. "Witnesses to Revolution" focuses on ordinary individuals who recorded their observances of the war and its impact on their lives. The "Converging on Yorktown" gallery and "A Time of Revolution" film focus on the military campaign. "Yorktown's Sunken Fleet" uses artifacts recovered from British ships sunk during the siege of Yorktown to describe shipboard life.

Outdoors, costumed interpreters in the Continental army encampment re-create the lives of men and women who took part in the American Revolution. There are presentations on weaponry, military drills and tactics, medicine, and cookery. Nearby, an 18th-century farm site demonstrates how "middling" farmers—no wealthy plantation owners here—lived and worked. Interpreters lead 1-hour tours of the living history several times a day; ask at reception when you enter.

Colonial Pkwy., ½ mile west of Yorktown. ⟨✆⟩ **888/593-4682** or 757/253-4838. www.historyisfun.org. Admission $8.25 adults, $4 children 6–12; free for children 5 and under. Combination ticket with Jamestown Settlement $16 adults, $7.75 children 6–12. Daily 9am–5pm. Closed New Year's Day and Christmas.

TOURING THE TOWN

Though it is doubtful that Yorktown would have recovered from the destruction and waste that accompanied the Siege of 1781, it received the coup de grace in the "Great Fire" of 1814 and declined steadily over the years, becoming a quiet rural village. In fact, like Williamsburg, it changed so little that many of its picturesque old streets and buildings have survived intact to this day.

Self-guided or ranger-led walking tours of historic Yorktown—which includes some places of interest not related to the famed battle—are available at the Yorktown Battlefield visitor center (call for times; see listing above). From the battlefield visitor center, take the path to:

THE VICTORY MONUMENT   News of the allied victory at Yorktown reached Philadelphia on October 24, 1781. On October 29, Congress resolved "that the United States . . . will cause to be erected at York, in Virginia, a marble column, adorned with emblems of the alliance between the United States and his Most Christian Majesty; and inscribed with a succinct narrative of the surrender of Earl Cornwallis to his excellency General Washington, Commander in Chief of the combined forces of America and France."

So much for government intentions: The cornerstone of the symbolic 98-foot marble shaft with Lady Liberty atop was laid a century later to open the Yorktown Centennial Celebration. The podium is adorned with 13 female figures hand in hand in a solemn dance to denote the unity of the 13 colonies; beneath their feet is the inscription "One Country, One Constitution, One Destiny"—a moving post-Civil War sentiment.

A footpath leads from the monument into town, where you can explore:

CORNWALLIS CAVE   According to legend, Cornwallis lived here in two tiny "rooms" during the final days of the siege when he hoped to cross the river and escape overland to New York. Various occupants of the cave—which may at one time have included the pirate Blackbeard—carved out the two rooms. Confederate soldiers later enlarged the shelter and added a roof. The cave is at the foot of Great Valley Road, right on the river.

THE DUDLEY DIGGES HOUSE   This 18th-century weather-board house on Main Street at Smith Street is the only wood-frame house to survive the siege. Owner Dudley Digges was a Revolutionary patriot who served with Patrick Henry, Benjamin Harrison, and Thomas Jefferson on the Committee of Correspondence.

⟨Moments Of Bug-Eyes & Skipjacks

On Water Street beside the river, Yorktown's **Watermen's Museum** (ⓒ 757/887-2641) displays a bug-eye, a skipjack, a dug-out canoe, and other working boats unique to the Chesapeake Bay, plus oyster harvesting tools and other equipment used by the region's famous "watermen" to earn their livings. Admission is $3 for adults, $1 for children. It's open Tuesday to Saturday 10am to 4pm, Sunday 1 to 4pm.

You can get out on the water with **Yorktown Lady Cruises** (ⓒ 757/229-6244; www.yorktowncruises.com), whose narrated trips get underway from the museum's pier. The 2½-hour narrated cruises depart Tuesday, Wednesday, and Thursday at 12:30pm and cost $16 for adults, $11 for children under 13. Boxed lunches are available for $9. The company also has "haunted" and sunset cruises.

Bring your bathing suit: There's a white sand beach at the museum.

After the war he was rector of the College of William and Mary. It's still a private residence, not open to the public.

THE NELSON HOUSE   Scottish merchant Thomas Nelson made three voyages between Great Britain and Virginia before deciding to settle in Yorktown in 1705. He became co-operator of a ferry, charter member of a trading company, builder of the Swan Tavern, and a large-scale planter. In 1729 he built this house, at Main and Nelson streets, which is considered one of the finest examples of Georgian architecture in Virginia. His grandson, Thomas Nelson Jr., signed the Declaration of Independence, served as governor of Virginia during the war, and marched the 3,500-man state militia to Yorktown to help Washington win the victory. The Revolution ruined his health and fortune, however, and he died in 1789.

Though damaged (cannonballs remain embedded in the brickwork), the house survived the Battle of Yorktown, and the Nelson family continued to live in it until 1907. The National Park Service acquired the house in 1968 and restored it to its original appearance.

It's usually open daily from 10am to 4:30pm in summer, daily from 1 to 4pm the rest of the year.

THE SESSIONS HOUSE   Just across from the Nelson House, this is the oldest house in Yorktown, built in 1692 by Thomas Sessions. At least five U.S. presidents have visited the house, today a private residence.

THE CUSTOMHOUSE   Dating to 1720, this brick building at the corner of Main and Read was originally the private storehouse of Richard Ambler, collector of ports. It became Gen. J. B. Magruder's headquarters during the Civil War. The Daughters of the American Revolution maintain it today as a museum.

GRACE EPISCOPAL CHURCH   On Church Street near the river, Grace Church dates to 1697 and has been an active house of worship since then. Its first rector, the Rev. Anthony Panton, was dismissed for calling the secretary of the colony a jackanapes. Gunpowder and ammunition were stored here during the siege of Yorktown. During the Civil War, the church served as a hospital. It's open to visitors daily from 9am to 5pm. The communion silver, made in England in 1649, is still in use. Thomas Nelson Jr. is buried in the adjacent graveyard.

THE SWAN TAVERN   For over a century the Swan Tavern, at the corner of Main and Ballard streets ((C) **757/898-3033**), was Yorktown's leading hostelry. Originally owned by Thomas Nelson, it was in operation 20 years before Williamsburg's famous Raleigh. The Swan was demolished in 1863 by an ammunition explosion at the courthouse across the street, rebuilt, and destroyed again by fire in 1915. Today it is reconstructed as per historical research, and the premises house a fine 18th-century antiques shop. It's open Tuesday to Saturday 10am to 5pm, Sunday noon to 5pm.

THE POOR POTTER   Constructed on the site of Yorktown's original pottery factory on Read Street, inland from the Customhouse, this new re-construction shows how the locals produced pottery of better quality than their English cousins were making back home.

WHERE TO DINE

The town's favorite watering hole is the **Yorktown Pub,** 112 Water St. ((C) **757/886-9964**), on the waterfront. It's a fun place if you can stand the smoke, with draft brew served in Mason jars and bands making music on Saturday nights. The sandwiches, burgers, and other pub fare are passable, while the main courses

Moments **Virginia Is for Gardens**

Garden Week in Virginia, during the last week in April, is the ideal time to visit the plantations. All the grounds are at their magnificent, full-bloom best then. It's also the only time that the manor house at **Westover,** which shares Berkeley's lane off Va. 5 (© **804/829-2882**), is open to the public. Richmond's founder, William Byrd II, built this beautiful Georgian manor house in the 1730s directly on the banks of the James. You can walk around the grounds and gardens year round, daily from 9am to 6pm. Admission is an honorary $2.

are mostly broiled or fried seafood (avoid the crab cakes). Open Monday to Thursday from 11am to 10pm, Friday and Saturday 11am to 11pm. Bring cash; no credit cards are accepted.

Families can get inexpensive sandwiches, burgers, salads, and pizza plus moderately priced meals next door at **Water Street Landing,** 114 Water St. (© **757/ 886-5890**). It's open Sunday to Thursday from 11am to 9pm, weekends from 11am to 10pm. It accepts MasterCard and Visa.

Carrot Tree *Finds* SANDWICHES/SALADS   Occupying the Cole Diggs House, Yorktown's oldest brick residence (1720), this sandwich shop is a good place for refreshment during your walking tour of town. The house was restored by the National Park Service, which won't allow a stove inside for safety reasons. Accordingly, many items are prepared in Williamsburg and heated in a microwave oven here. It's good stuff nevertheless. Check out the pastries in the chiller box by the front door; they make a fine breakfast or snack. Lunch sees salads, barbecue, Brunswick stew, and made-to-order sandwiches.

411 Main St. © 757/246-9559. Reservations recommended. Most items $4–$7.50. DISC, MC, V. Mon–Sat 8am–5pm, Sun 9am–5pm.

4 James River Plantations

While Williamsburg was the political capital of Virginia during the 18th century, its economic livelihood depended on the great tobacco plantations like Carter's Grove. Several more of the mansions built during that period of wealthy landowners still stand today along the banks of the James River between Williamsburg and Richmond, some occupied to this day by the same families which have produced generals, governors, and two presidents. They provide an authentic feel for 18th-century plantation life.

SEEING THE PLANTATIONS

The plantations are on John Tyler Highway (Va. 5) between Williamsburg and Richmond. From Williamsburg, take Jamestown Road and bear right on Va. 5. From Richmond, take Main Street east, which becomes Va. 5.

This so-called Plantation Route covers a distance of 55 miles between Williamsburg and Richmond and makes an excellent scenic driving tour between the two cities. Allow a full day to visit all the plantations and to take a break for lunch. I list them here east-to-west as you come to them from Williamsburg. If you're driving from Richmond, start at Shirley and work backwards.

The plantations' **mailing address** is Charles City, VA 23030.

Evelynton   Adjacent to and part of the original 1619 Westover Plantation land grant, this tract was named for William Byrd's daughter Evelyn (pronounced

"*Eve*-lyn"). She is said to have died of a broken heart because her father refused to let her marry her chosen suitor. According to legend, her ghost still roams both houses. Since 1847, Evelynton has been home to the Ruffin family, whose patriarch, noted agriculturist Edmund Ruffin, fired the first shot of the Civil War at Fort Sumter, SC. The original house was destroyed in 1862, when Gen. George McClellan's Union troops skirmished with Confederates led by J. E. B. Stuart and John Pelham in the fierce but short-lived Battle of Evelynton Heights. The present structure, a magnificent example of Colonial Revival style, was designed by renowned Virginia architect Duncan Lee and built in 1935.

6701 John Tyler Hwy. (Va. 5), 25 miles west of Williamsburg. ⓒ 800/473-5075 or 804/829-5075. Admission $11 adults, $7 students, $4 grounds only. Daily 9am–5pm. Closed New Year's Day, Thanksgiving, and Christmas. Mandatory 30-min. house tours on demand.

Berkeley ⓡⓡ The aristocratic Harrison family bought Berkeley in 1691. Benjamin Harrison III made it a prosperous operation, and in 1726 his son, Benjamin Harrison IV, built the three-story Georgian mansion. Benjamin Harrison V was a signer of the Declaration of Independence and thrice governor of Virginia. The next generation produced William Henry Harrison, the frontier fighter whose nickname "Old Tippecanoe" helped him get elected as our ninth president. His grandson, another Benjamin Harrison, took the presidential oath 47 years later. George Washington was a frequent guest, and every president through Tyler enjoyed Berkeley's gracious hospitality.

Berkeley was twice occupied by invading troops. A British army under Benedict Arnold burned the family portraits, practiced target shooting on the cows, and went off with 40 slaves. Gen. George McClellan's Union army trampled the gardens and chopped up the elegant furnishings for firewood. After the war, the Harrisons never returned to live at Berkeley.

John Jamieson, a Scottish-born New Yorker who had served as a drummer in McClellan's army, purchased the disfigured manor house and 1,400 acres in 1907. His son, Malcolm, has completely restored the house and grounds to their appearance in the early days of the Harrisons tenure. Allow at least an hour to see a 10-minute slide presentation, take a 30-minute guided tour of the house, and explore the magnificent grounds and gardens. The **Coach House Tavern,** appropriately in the carriage house, serves lunch daily and dinner on weekends.

12602 Harrison Landing Rd. (off Va. 5), 30 miles west of Williamsburg. ⓒ 888/466-6018 or 804/829-6018. www.berkeleyplantation.com. Admission $11 adults, $7 children 13–16, $5.50 children 6–12, free for children 5 and under. Daily 9am–5pm. Closed Christmas. Mandatory 30-min. house tours on demand.

Shirley ⓡⓡⓡ The oldest plantation in Virginia, Shirley was founded in 1613 and has been in the Carter family since 1660—thus making it the oldest family business in North America. The present mansion, built by Elizabeth Hill and John Carter, dates to 1723. Since that time two distinguished Virginia families—the

---

⌒Tips Taking a Break

You can break your driving tour of the plantations at Berkeley's **Coach House Tavern,** or at **Indian Fields Tavern,** 9220 John Tyler Hwy. (Va. 5), between Sherwood Forest and Evelynton (ⓒ 804/829-5004). In a restored Victorian farmhouse, with screened porches open during warm weather, this fine restaurant is open for lunch and dinner from Monday to Saturday, and for dinner daily.

Fun Fact Taps

It was during the Yankee occupancy of Berkeley Plantation during the Civil War that Gen. Dan Butterfield composed "Taps."

Hills and the Carters—have occupied Shirley. Because of this continuous ownership, many original furnishings, portraits, and memorabilia remain, making this one of the most interesting plantations open to public view. The carved-walnut staircase, rising three stories with no visible means of support, is the only one of its kind in America. The house survived the Revolution, the Civil War, and Reconstruction, as did the dependencies—seven superb brick outbuildings, forming a Queen Anne forecourt that was unique in this country, that include a large two-story kitchen, a laundry house, and two barns. Other original structures are the stable, smokehouse, and dovecote. After the tour, allow at least another 30 minutes to explore the grounds and dependencies.

501 Shirley Plantation Rd. (off Va. 5), Charles City, 35 miles west of Williamsburg. © **800/232-1613** or 804/ 829-5121. www.shirleyplantation.com. Admission $11 adults, $7 children 6–18, free for children 5 and under. Daily 9am–5pm. Closed Thanksgiving and Christmas. Mandatory 45-min. house tours depart continuously.

5 An Easy Excursion to Hampton & Newport News

Jamestown was barely 2 years old when Capt. John Smith sent a contingent of men to build America's first fort on the Hampton River, strategically located on the western shore of Hampton Roads. There's been a town here since 1610, making Hampton the nation's oldest continuously English-speaking settlement. It was the colony's first seaport, and it was here in 1718 that British troops displayed the head of Edward Teach, better known as Blackbeard the Pirate, whom they killed during a furious battle on the North Carolina Outer Banks (his captured crew were tried and hanged in Williamsburg).

Unfortunately, there are few remaining structures from those early days other than the U.S. Army's **Fort Monroe,** for during the Civil War a Confederate general ordered the town burned to the ground rather than permit Union forces holding the fort to quarter troops and former slaves here. You can visit the dank Fort Monroe room where Confederate Pres. Jefferson Davis was imprisoned after the war, the fine museum at Hampton University, and the very modern Virginia Air and Space Center, a smaller but excellent rendition of the Smithsonian Institution's National Air and Space Museum in Washington, D.C.

Named for Christopher Newport, skipper of the *Discovery,* which brought some of the Jamestown settlers to Virginia, Newport News dates back to the early 1600s and has a long maritime tradition. The city is home to the Mariners' Museum, the largest maritime museum in the Western Hemisphere.

Hampton has enough interesting sights to take up most of a day trip from Williamsburg. The Mariners' Museum is on the way to Hampton, so you can spend part of the morning there on the way. You can also visit both cities on day excursions from Norfolk and Virginia Beach.

ESSENTIALS

VISITOR INFORMATION   For advance information contact the **Hampton Convention and Visitor Bureau,** 1919 Commerce Dr., Hampton, VA 23666 (© **800/800-2202** or 757/727-1102; fax 757/727-6712; www.hamptoncvb.com).

The bureau's visitor center shares quarters with the **Hampton History Museum,** where you can learn of the city's past. Open daily 9am to 5pm except New Year's Day, Thanksgiving, and Christmas.

For information about Newport News, contact the **Newport News Tourism Development Office,** 700 Town Center Dr., Suite 320, Newport News, VA 23606 (© **888/493-7386** or 757/926-1400; fax 757/926-1441; www.newport-news.org). The walk-in **Newport News Visitor Center** is in Newport News Park, 13560 Jefferson Ave., west of Fort Eustis Boulevard near exit 250 off I-64 (© **888/493-7386** or 757/886-7777). It's open daily from 9am to 5pm.

Newport News Park, 13560 Jefferson Ave. (© **757/888-3333;** www.nngov.com/parks), is the largest municipal park east of the Mississippi River and has one of the best campgrounds in Virginia.

GETTING THERE   From Williamsburg, take I-64 east. To reach downtown Hampton, take Exit 267 and turn right on Settlers Landing Road and cross the Hampton River to the visitor center (a left turn at the exit will take you to Fort Monroe and the Casemate Museum via the village of Poquoson). To reach the Mariners' Museum, take Exit 258 and follow J. Clyde Morris Boulevard (U.S. 17) south; the museum is at the southern end of the boulevard. From Norfolk and Virginia Beach, take I-64 west through the Hampton Roads Bridge Tunnel to these exits.

Amtrak (© **800/872-7245;** www.amtrak.com) has daily service to its station in Newport News.

ATTRACTIONS IN HAMPTON

The Casemate Museum ⊀   The Casemate Museum is a must-see for Civil War buffs, for Confederate Pres. Jefferson Davis was imprisoned in the bowels of this stone fort in 1865 after being captured in Georgia. The accusation that he had participated in Lincoln's assassination was disproved, and Davis was released in 1867. Located at the tip of a peninsula and surrounded by a moat, the fort was built between 1819 and 1834. Robert E. Lee served as second in command of the construction detachment in 1831 when he was a young officer in the Army Corps of Engineers, and Edgar Allen Poe spent 16 months here in 1828–29 as an enlisted man. The dungeonlike *casemates,* or rooms, were designed as storage for seacoast artillery. After 1861, they were modified to serve as living quarters for soldiers and their families. You'll need about 45 minutes in the museum to view displays of military memorabilia and Davis' sparsely furnished quarters (his intricately carved pipe—an egg-shaped bowl clinched in an eagle's claw—is outside the door). **Tours** can be arranged in advance by contacting the museum. Note that you'll need to show a picture ID in order to get into Fort Monroe.

Fort Monroe. © 757/727-3391. http://fort.monroe.army.mil/museum. Free admission. Daily 10:30am–4:30pm. Closed New Year's Day, Thanksgiving, and Christmas. From downtown Hampton take Settlers Landing Rd. east across Hampton River bridge and under I-64 (Exit 267) into Phoebus, take right fork onto County St., turn right on Mallory St., left on Mellen St., straight into Fort Monroe. Follow signs to museum.

(*Fun Fact* **The First Thanksgiving**

On December 4, 1619, 38 English settlers sent by the Berkeley Company put ashore after a 3-month voyage. They fell on their knees in a prayer of thanksgiving. If you're here the first Sunday of November, you can participate in the annual commemoration of that first Thanksgiving in the New World.

Hampton University Museum   Across the river from downtown, Hampton University was founded in 1868 to provide an education for newly freed African Americans. Its graduates include Booker T. Washington, who founded Tuskegee Institute in Alabama and whose birthplace is preserved near Lynchburg (see chapter 6). Four landmarks are nearby, including the imposing Memorial Chapel (1886). The museum is noted for its collection of more than 2,700 African art objects and artifacts representing 887 ethnic groups and cultures. Rivaling the African collection in quality and importance, the Native American collection includes works from 93 tribes; it was established in 1878, when the federal government began sending Native Americans from reservations in the West to be educated at Hampton. The museum also has notable holdings in works by Harlem Renaissance artists, and a number of Oceanic and Asian objects.

Huntington Building, Hampton University. ℂ 757/727-5308. www.hamptonu.edu. Free admission. Mon–Fri 8am–5pm; Sat noon–4pm. From downtown Hampton, take Settlers Landing Rd. across the Hampton River and follow signs to the university and museum.

Virginia Air & Space Center ★★ *Kids*   A stunning glass-fronted futuristic structure on the edge of Hampton's riverfront, this museum chronicles the history of aviation and space travel and also serves as the official visitor center for NASA's Langley Research Center. The interior is separated into bays that hold individual exhibits on rockets, satellites, space exploration, ham radio, Mars, weather, and the Tuskegee Airmen, the famous World War II squadron of African-American fighter pilots. There's also a rock brought back from the moon by Apollo 17 in 1969. In the main gallery, about 10 air vehicles are suspended from the 94-foot vaulted ceiling, and below sits the *Apollo 12* command module—complete with reentry burn marks. In the Space Gallery, you can don an astronaut's helmet and see yourself on a TV monitor. An IMAX theater shows 45-minute films about flying and space as well as full-length features. There are no guided tours; allow at least 2 hours to explore it all on your own.

600 Settlers Landing Rd. (at King St.). ℂ 757/727-0900. www.vasc.org. Admission $7 adults, $5.50 seniors and military, $5 children 3–11, free for children 2 and under. Combination tickets including the IMAX film $3 additional. Memorial Day to Labor Day, Mon–Wed 10am–5pm, Thurs–Sat 10am–7pm, Sun noon–7pm; off season, Mon–Sat 10am–5pm, Sun noon–5pm.

HARBOR CRUISES

The most popular harbor cruises in Virginia are on the *Miss Hampton II,* 764 Settlers Landing Rd. (ℂ **888/757-BOAT** or 757/722-9102; www.misshampton cruises.com), a 65-foot passenger boat which sails from downtown across Hampton Roads and within sight of the huge U.S. Naval Base at Norfolk. You'll pass the landing site of the Jamestown settlers and Blackbeard's Point, where the pirate's head was displayed in 1718. Weather permitting, you'll go ashore for a 45-minute guided tour of the pre-Civil War **Fort Wool,** on a 15-acre island out in the Chesapeake. The narrated 3-hour cruises depart from the town dock, on Settlers Landing Road beside Radisson Hampton hotel. Departures usually are daily at 10am and 2pm from Memorial Day to Labor Day, at 10am only in April, May, September and October. Fares are $17 for adults, $15 for seniors and military, $9 for children 6 to 12, free for kids under 6. The company also has sunset and daylong Intercoastal Waterway cruises.

A MARITIME MUSEUM IN NEWPORT NEWS

Mariners' Museum ★★   Dedicated to preserving the culture of the sea and its tributaries, this is the largest maritime museum in the Western Hemisphere. It's in a pleasant 550-acre park setting, with a lake, picnic areas, and walking trails. Inside, handcrafted ship models, scrimshaw, maritime paintings, decorative arts, working steam engines, and more are displayed in spacious galleries. A highlight of any visit is the museum's USS *Monitor* conservation area, where the turret, engine, propeller and hundreds of other artifacts—including handwritten letters—recovered from the Union ironclad are being preserved. The *Monitor* sank off Cape Hatteras in 1862; divers located her in the 1990s. Shown on the hour and half-hour, an 18-minute film narrated by actor James Earl Jones discusses maritime activity the world over. There usually are two guided tours a day Monday to Friday (call for schedule). Otherwise, allow about 2 hours here.

100 Museum Dr. ⓒ 757/596-2222. www.mariner.org. Admission $7 adults, $8 children 6–17, free for children 5 and under. Daily 10am–5pm. Closed Thanksgiving and Christmas. From I-64, take Exit 258A, follow J. Clyde Morris Blvd. (U.S. 17) south to intersection with Warwick Blvd. (U.S. 60), go straight on Museum Dr.

11

Norfolk, Virginia Beach & the Eastern Shore

The Jamestown colonists set foot in the New World in 1607 on the sandy shores of Cape Charles. Although they didn't stay on the banks of Hampton Roads, one of the world's largest natural harbors, later generations did. Norfolk and Portsmouth became major seaports—they were fought over often during the Civil War, including the famous battle between the ironclads, USS *Monitor* and CSS *Merrimac*, out on Hampton Roads. Today, the cities of Norfolk, Virginia Beach, Portsmouth, and Chesapeake create a sprawling megalopolis on the southern shores.

The area's population swells significantly during the summer, when the sand and surf of Virginia Beach draw vacationers from around the globe. With a host of activities, a multitude of hotels, and close proximity to the other cities, "The Beach" makes a fine base of operations for a visit to this area.

The population here also goes up and down depending on deployments by the U.S. Navy; this area has America's largest concentration of naval bases. The sailors once made Norfolk a bawdy seaport, but the city has rebuilt its downtown into a vibrant center of shopping, dining, and sightseeing. A ferry crosses the Elizabeth River to the neighboring city of Portsmouth, whose architecturally rich Olde Town may remind you of Charleston and Savannah.

From Virginia Beach, the 17-mile long Chesapeake Bay Bridge-Tunnel whisks visitors north to a different world: Virginia's rural Eastern Shore. The Delmarva Peninsula hosts an ancient fishing village on Chincoteague Island, a wildlife refuge and seashore teeming with birds and the famous wild ponies of Assateague.

1 Norfolk ✶

190 miles SE of Washington, D.C.; 93 miles E of Richmond; 17 miles W of Virginia Beach

Although it's still a major seaport and naval base, Norfolk has replaced its notorious sailor bars (they're in suburban strip malls now) with a vibrant, modern downtown of high-rise offices, condominiums, marinas, museums, shops, nightspots, and a 12,000-seat minor league baseball park. The MacArthur Center, a shopping mall just a few blocks from the riverfront, now dominates downtown.

Interspersed are reminders of Norfolk's past, such as historic houses and the old City Hall, now a museum and memorial to World War II hero Gen. Douglas MacArthur. Here also is Virginia's finest art museum, the state's official zoo, and a beautiful botanical garden. And for foodies, hip restaurants have brought great tastes to downtown and the gentrified residential neighborhood known as Ghent.

ESSENTIALS

VISITOR INFORMATION

For advance information, contact the **Norfolk Convention & Visitors Bureau,** 232 E. Main St., Norfolk, VA 23510 (© **800/368-3097** or 757/441-1852; fax 757/622-3663; www.norfolkcvb.com). The bureau dispenses walking-tour brochures and other information at its offices (open Mon–Fri 8:30am–5pm), which are across Main Street from the Norfolk Marriott. The main downtown walk-in information center, however, is at NAUTICUS (see "The Top Attractions," below).

If you're arriving from the west via I-64, the **Norfolk Visitor Center** is on Fourth View Street at Exit 273 in the Ocean View section (© **757/441-1852**). It's open daily from 9am to 5pm.

GETTING THERE

BY PLANE   **Norfolk International Airport,** on Norview Avenue 1½ miles north of I-64 (© **757/857-3351;** www.norfolkairport.com), is served by American, Continental, Delta, Northwest, Southwest, and US Airways. The major car-rental firms have desks here. **Norfolk Airport Express** (© **757/857-3991**) runs vans to points between Williamsburg and Virginia Beach. It has a booth outside baggage claim area no. 3. Fares to downtown Norfolk are $19 for one person, $15 a person for two or more.

BY CAR   From the west, I-64 runs from Richmond to Norfolk, then swings around the eastern and southern suburbs, where it meets I-664 to form a beltway around the area. U.S. 460 also runs the length of Virginia to Norfolk, and U.S. 13 and 17 lead here from north or south. If you're coming from Virginia Beach, I-264 goes through downtown and Portsmouth. Norfolk is linked to Portsmouth by ferry, bridge, and tunnel, and to Hampton and Newport News by the Hampton Roads Bridge-Tunnel (I-64) and Monitor-Merrimac Bridge-Tunnel (I-664).

BY TRAIN & BUS   **Amtrak** (© **800/872-7245;** www.amtrak.com) has bus connections to and from its station in Newport News. **Greyhound** (© **800/231-2222;** www.greyhound.com) has bus service to downtown Norfolk.

CITY LAYOUT   Norfolk occupies two peninsulas formed by the Chesapeake Bay and the Elizabeth and Lafayette rivers. **Downtown** is on the southern side of the city, on the north bank of the Elizabeth River. Bordering downtown to the northwest, **Freemason** is Norfolk's oldest residential neighborhood, with most of its 18th- and 19th-century town houses restored as private homes, businesses, and restaurants. You'll still find a few cobblestone streets here. Northwest of Freemason, across a semicircular inlet known as The Hague, **Ghent** was the city's first subdivision and is now its trendiest enclave. Most houses in "old"

> ⌒ **Tips**   **Avoiding Gridlock**
>
> Hampton Roads has some of Virginia's most congested traffic. Lengthy backups can occur anytime on I-64 at the Hampton Roads Bridge-Tunnel, and especially during weekday rush hour and all day on summer weekends. If you're approaching on I-64 from the west, an alternative is to take I-664 and the Monitor-Merrimac Bridge-Tunnel, then Va. 164 east to Portsmouth and the Midtown Tunnel (U.S. 58) into Norfolk. Tune your radio to 610AM or call © **800/792-2800** on your cellphone to check on current conditions.

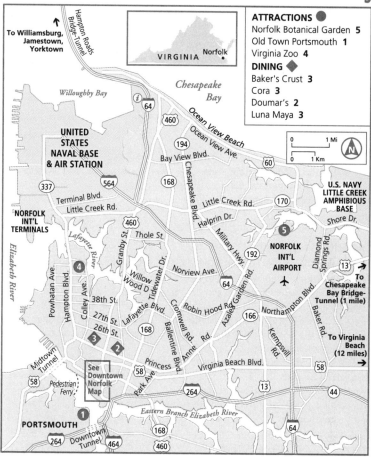

Ghent, near The Hague and the Chrysler Museum of Art (see "The Top Attractions," below), were built between 1892 and 1912. Now thoroughly gentrified, it's home to everyone from well-heeled professionals to writers, artists, and college students. The heart of Ghent's business district runs along **Colley Avenue** between Baldwin Avenue and 21st Street, and along **21st Street** from Colley Avenue east to Granby Street. Here you'll find antiques shops, restaurants, and the artsy NORA Cinema.

GETTING AROUND

A car is the easiest way to get around this spread-out area, although as noted, traffic can back up in the Hampton Roads Bridge-Tunnel. **Parking** is available downtown at the MacArthur Center and in four municipal garages (the most convenient is on Atlantic Ave. between Waterside Dr. and Main St.).

Once you're downtown, the free **Norfolk Electric Transit (NET)** trolleys are the most convenient way to get around Monday to Friday from 6:30am to 11pm, Saturday from noon to midnight, Sunday from noon to 8pm. The Blue Line runs from Harbor Park across downtown and north via Granby Street to the Harrison Opera House. The Orange Line makes loops around the

Tips **Safety in Norfolk**

Downtown Norfolk had a serious street-crime problem before 1998, when the MacArthur Center began bringing crowds of shoppers and diners to the area. You should be safe if you stick to the busy main streets between the mall and The Waterside, but don't take unnecessary risks like wandering off into deserted or ill-lit side streets. Volunteer **Public Safety Ambassadors** now patrol the streets and will escort you back to your car (© 757/478-7233).

downtown shopping-and-dining area. The routes are shown on city maps distributed at the visitor centers (see "Essentials," earlier). The NET is operated by the city's parking department (© **757/441-2661;** www.norfolk.gov/visitors/net.asp).

For taxis, call **Yellow Cab** (© **757/622-3232**).

SEEING THE SIGHTS

Downtown Norfolk's centerpiece is the **MacArthur Center** ★★, a $300 million shopping mall covering the 9 square blocks bordered by Monticello and City Hall avenues, Freemason Street, and St. Paul's Boulevard (© **757/627-6000;** www.shopmacarthur.com). The main entry is on Monticello Avenue at Market Street. Anchored by Nordstrom and the largest Dillard's department store in existence, it has most of the mall regulars, an 18-screen cinema, a food court, and full-service restaurants.

Built in 1983 between Waterside Drive and the Elizabeth River, **The Waterside Festival Marketplace** (© 757/627-3300; www.watersidemarketplace.com), which everyone calls simply "The Waterside," was the catalyst for downtown Norfolk's revitalization, like Baltimore's Inner Harbor, Boston's Faneuil Hall, and New York's South Street Seaport. The Elizabeth River Ferry and harbor cruises leave from the dock outside this glass-and-steel pavilion. With so much of its shopping business now going to the MacArthur Center, The Waterside now is primarily an after-dark dining and entertainment center (see "Norfolk After Dark," later).

In **Town Point Park,** between The Waterside and NAUTICUS, don't miss **The Homecomer,** a statue of a returning sailor greeted by his wife and child, and the moving **Armed Forces Memorial,** where bronze letters written home by sailors litter the ground. The park's amphitheater features a full schedule of free events all year—concerts, children's theater, magic shows, puppetry, and more.

East of the Elizabeth River bridges, **Harbor Park,** a 12,000-seat stadium, is home to the **Norfolk Tides,** a Class AAA International League baseball team affiliated with the New York Mets (© **757/622-2222;** www.norfolktides.com).

THE TOP ATTRACTIONS

The Chrysler Museum of Art ★★★   Originally built in 1932 as the Norfolk Museum of Art, this imposing Italian Renaissance building on The Hague inlet was renamed in 1971 when Walter P. Chrysler Jr. gave a large portion of his collection to the city. Today it's Virginia's finest art museum. It spans artistic periods from ancient Egypt to the present and includes one of the finest and most comprehensive glass collections in the world. Adjoining is an outstanding collection of Art Nouveau furniture. Other first floor galleries exhibit ancient Indian, Islamic, Oriental, African, and pre-Columbian art. Most second-floor galleries are devoted to painting and sculpture, particularly Italian baroque and

Downtown Norfolk

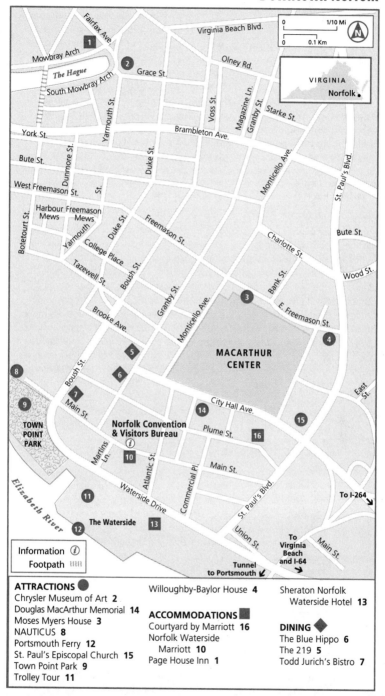

ATTRACTIONS ●
Chrysler Museum of Art **2**
Douglas MacArthur Memorial **14**
Moses Myers House **3**
NAUTICUS **8**
Portsmouth Ferry **12**
St. Paul's Episcopal Church **15**
Town Point Park **9**
Trolley Tour **11**

Willoughby-Baylor House **4**

ACCOMMODATIONS ■
Courtyard by Marriott **16**
Norfolk Waterside
   Marriott **10**
Page House Inn **1**

Sheraton Norfolk
   Waterside Hotel **13**

DINING ◆
The Blue Hippo **6**
The 219 **5**
Todd Jurich's Bistro **7**

French, including works by Monet, Renoir, Matisse, Braque, Bernini, and Rouault. American art holdings include 18th- and 19th-century paintings by Charles Willson Peale, Benjamin West, John Singleton Copley, and Thomas Cole, and 20th-century works by Thomas Hart Benton, Calder, Kline, Warhol, Rauschenberg, and Rosenquist. A permanent gallery is devoted solely to photography, showcasing everyone from Walker Evans to Diane Arbus.

Pick up a free audio tour at the desk, which will explain some of the key items as you see them. Allow at least 2 hours here, half a day to do it complete justice.

The museum administers the Moses Myers and Willoughby-Baylor houses (see below) and sells economical combination tickets covering all three places.

245 W. Olney Rd. (at Mowbray Arch). © 757/644-6200. www.chrysler.org. Admission $7 adults, $5 seniors and students, free for children 11 and under. Combination tickets with Moses Myers/Willoughby houses $10 adults, $6 seniors and students, free for children under 5. Wed 10am–9pm; Thurs–Sat 10am–5pm; Sun 1–5pm. Closed New Year's Day, July 4th, Thanksgiving, and Christmas.

Douglas MacArthur Memorial ★★ Gen. Douglas MacArthur's immortal words "I shall return" are engraved on a bronze plaque, along with excerpts from his other speeches, at his final resting place in Norfolk's old city hall, an imposing domed structure with a columned front portico. In a scene a bit reminiscent of the Taj Mahal in India, the dome towers over the side-by-side marble crypts of the general and his wife, Jean. Shown every half-hour in a theater next door, a 22-minute film will give you a perspective on MacArthur's life and help you understand the exhibits. Filled with his personal memorabilia, the chronologically arranged galleries trace U.S. history during MacArthur's life and his role in events up to his ringing "Old Soldiers Never Die" speech to Congress after President Truman fired him during the Korean War. Of particular interest: MacArthur's famous corncob pipe, his omnipresent sunglasses, his field cap with its sides rolled down, and a replica of the plaque marking the spot on the USS *Missouri* where MacArthur presided over the surrender of Japan. A short film of the surrender ceremony includes his famous remark, "These proceedings are closed."

MacArthur Sq. (between City Hall Ave. and Plume St., at Bank St.). © 757/441-2965. http://sites.communitylink.org/mac. Free admission (donations encouraged). Mon–Sat 10am–5pm; Sun 11am–5pm. Closed New Year's Day, Thanksgiving, and Christmas. Validated 3-hr. parking at MacArthur Center South Garage or any City of Norfolk lot.

Moses Myers House and Willoughby-Baylor House It has the MacArthur Center as its backyard these days, but this handsome early-Federal brick town house was in Norfolk's oldest residential neighborhood when it was built by Moses Myers and his wife, Eliza, who came to Norfolk in 1787. They were the first Jews to settle here, and programs in observance of Jewish holidays are among the museum's annual events. Some 70% of the furniture and decorative arts displayed are original to the first generation of the family, which lived here until 1930. Two Gilbert Stuart portraits of Mr. and Mrs. Myers hang in the drawing room, which

---

(*Fun Fact* **He Liked Ike**

On display in Norfolk's Douglas MacArthur Memorial is a yellowing copy of an army "efficiency report" filled out by Gen. Douglas MacArthur in 1937. In it, he grades the performance of a member of his staff and recommends that in time of war, the subordinate should be immediately promoted to general. The staffer was Lt. Col. Dwight D. Eisenhower.

contains some distinctive Empire pieces. The fireplace surround has unusual carvings depicting a sun god—with the features of George Washington.

Also administered by The Chrysler Museum of Art, the **Willoughby-Baylor House,** a block away at 601 E. Freemason St., was built in 1794 and is furnished with Georgian and Federal pieces. One-hour tours covering both houses depart from the **Freemason Street Reception Center,** between the houses at 401 E. Freemason St. (🕿 **757/441-1526**).

331 Bank St. (at E. Freemason St.). 🕿 **757/333-6283.** www.chrysler.org. Admission $5 adults, $3 seniors and students, free for children 12 and under. Combination tickets with The Chrysler Museum of Art $10 adults, $6 seniors and students, free for children 11 and under. Wed–Sat 10am–5pm; Sun noon–5pm. Last tour daily 4pm. Mandatory 1-hr. tours of both houses depart on the hour. Closed New Year's Day, July 4th, Thanksgiving, and Christmas.

NAUTICUS, The National Maritime Center *(Kids)*

This large gray building designed like an artist's rendering of a futuristic battleship is a multi-faceted museum dedicated to the U.S. Navy and the sea over which it rules. It's actually three attractions in one. You must pay to enter the third-floor **NAUTICUS,** a very good children's museum with a plethora of movies and hands-on interactive exhibits aimed at families with kids ages 8 to 14. The youngsters will get a kick out of petting a live nurse shark in a touch tank. Arranged in three areas, other educational exhibits explain economic power, naval power, and natural power (you can record yourself forecasting the weather). After a morning here, your school-age kids may be ready to enlist—or apply for a job at The Weather Channel.

Admission is free to the second floor **Hampton Roads Naval Museum** ★ (🕿 **757/444-8921;** www.hrnm.navy.mil), in which the U.S. Navy tells the story of its presence here. The exhibit describing the Civil War battle between the ironclads USS *Monitor* and CSS *Merrimac* out on Hampton Roads is worth seeing.

The naval museum also has the star adult attraction here: the real battleship **USS *Wisconsin* ★★★.** Berthed alongside on the Elizabeth River, the mighty 888-foot ship was built in 1943 and saw duty in the Pacific during World War II. It was recalled from mothballs to fight in the Korean and Gulf wars. It is once again on inactive reserve status, meaning it can be recalled to duty within 3 months. You cannot go inside, since the innards are hermetically sealed, but you can walk on board and stare up at the enormous 16-inch guns overhanging its teak main deck. It's quite a sight.

Moored on the other side of the building is the **Tugboat Museum** (🕿 **757/627-4884**), actually the *Huntington,* a tug built in 1933 and used by the navy to dock its ships for more than 50 years. It's an interesting 30-minute tour, but you'd better take some Dramamine if you're prone to seasickness, since the tug rolls whenever a passing boat churns up a wake.

Save a pill for the ***Victory Rover*** cruises to the naval station, which leave from here (see "Harbor Cruises to Where the Ironclads Fought," below).

1 Waterside Dr. (at Boush St.). 🕿 **800/664-1080** or 757/664-1000. www.nauticus.org. Free admission to 1st deck, naval museum and battleship. Admission to NAUTICUS exhibits and theaters $9.95 adults, $8.95 seniors, $7.50 children 4–12, free for children 3 and under. Tugboat Museum, $2 adults, $1 children 11 and under. Battleship audiotape tour $5 ($3 with NAUTICUS admission). NAUTICUS and Naval Museum, Memorial Day to Labor Day daily 10am–6pm; rest of year Tues–Sat 10am–5pm, Sun noon–5pm. Tugboat Museum, Memorial Day to Labor Day daily 11am–5pm; rest of year Tues–Sun 11am–5pm (closed Jan–Mar). Entire complex closed Thanksgiving and Christmas.

Norfolk Botanical Garden ★★

The grounds of this botanical garden, on Lake Whitehurst about 4 miles northeast of downtown, are brilliantly abloom with one of the East Coast's largest display of azaleas from early April to mid-June—the best

> **Tips Stop, Look & Listen**
>
> Before you go on board the USS *Wisconsin,* take a few minutes to view the Hampton Roads Naval Museum's "City at Sea" exhibit, a multi-media exhibit in which seamen reminisce about their experiences aboard the battleship. Then rent a 45-minute audiotape tour. Although docents, many of them veterans of the ship, are on duty to explain what's what, the tape is the best way to see the Goliath. Otherwise you'll be staring at a lot of gray steel and teak decking.

time to visit. This quiet beauty can be seen by 25-minute tram tour, by 45-minute canal boat tour, or by foot over more than 12 miles of floral pathways. The Statuary Vista is a beautiful setting for Moses Ezekiel's heroic-size statues of great painters and sculptors—Rembrandt, Rubens, Dÿrer, and da Vinci, among others. Notable, too, are the rose garden, with more than 450 varieties among its 3,000 bushes; a classic Japanese hill-and-pond garden; a fragrance garden; and an Italian Renaissance garden with terraces, statuary, a fountain, and a reflecting pool. Behind the pool is the Hofheimer Camellia Garden and Renaissance Court, where April's Azalea Festival queen is crowned. Garden lovers can easily spend half a day here. You can grab a bite at the Azalea Café and browse for gifts in the garden shop.

6700 Azalea Garden Rd. (off Norview Ave., near airport). ⓒ 757/441-5385. www.norfolkbotanicalgarden. org. Admission $6 adults, $5 seniors, $4 children 6–16, free for children 5 and under. Boat tours $3. Mid-Apr to Labor Day, daily 9am–7pm. Sept to mid-Apr, daily 9am–5pm. Tram tours mid-Mar to Oct daily 10am–4pm. Boat tours Apr–Sept, Mon–Fri 11:45am–1:45pm, Sat–Sun 11:45am–3:45pm. Cafe, mid-Mar to mid-Nov, daily 10am–5pm. Take I-64 to Exit 279 (Norview/Airport), go east on Norview Ave., turn left on Azalea Garden Rd.

St. Paul's Episcopal Church ✸
The only building to survive when the British burned Norfolk in 1776, the main chapel of this lovely brick Anglican church was constructed in 1739 to serve a parish which had been in existence since about 1637. The tower was added in 1902, and the interior was restored to its present state in 1913. Take a moment to reflect inside the church, then examine the ancient tombstones in the shady churchyard. The earliest original stone is from 1748; three others dating from 1673, 1687, and 1681 were brought here. One of them, now affixed to the south wall of the church, proclaims: "Here lyeth y Body of William Harris Who Dep'ted This Life Ye 8th day of March 1687/8. Aged 35 years." The skull-and-crossbones on the stone were a symbol of mortality, not that Ye William was a pirate. There's also a cannonball lodged in the southwest wall. The church museum upstairs in the Parish House definitely is worth a visit just to see the chair in which John Hancock sat when he affixed his famous signature to the Declaration of Independence.

201 St. Paul's Blvd. (at City Hall Ave.). ⓒ 757/627-4353. Free admission (donations suggested). Mon–Fri 9am–5pm. Sun services 8 and 10am summer, 8 and 10:30am winter.

The Virginia Zoo ✸
On 53 acres adjacent to Norfolk's Lafayette Park and bordered by the Lafayette River, Virginia's state zoo is noted for its new Okavango Delta African plains exhibit. Ten years in the making, it added zebras, lions, giraffes, and meerkats to the nearly 400 animals who already lived here. You'll also see monkeys, baboons, elephants, rhinos, reptiles, and colorful birds.

3500 Granby St. (at 35th St.). ⓒ 757/441-5227. www.virginiazoo.org. Admission $3.50 adults, $3 seniors, $1.75 children 2–11. Daily 10am–5pm. Closed New Year's Day, Thanksgiving, and Christmas. From downtown, go north on Monticello Ave., which merges with Granby St., to the zoo on the right.

HARBOR CRUISES TO WHERE THE IRONCLADS FOUGHT

Three cruise boats docked at The Waterside or NAUTICUS offer cruises on the Elizabeth River, Hampton Roads, and the Chesapeake Bay. You will pass the naval base with nuclear subs and aircraft carriers and cross the site of the Civil War battle between the *Monitor* and the *Merrimac*.

Departing from NAUTICUS, the *Victory Rover* (© 757/627-7406; www. navalbasecruises.com) cruises to the Norfolk Naval Station—or as close thereto as security will permit. It has at summertime trips departing at 11am, 2 and 5:30pm, and at least one trip a day (usually departing at 2pm) the rest of the year. Fares are $14 adults, $9 for children.

Departing from the Waterside, the sleek but less charming *Spirit of Norfolk* (© 866/211-3803 or 757/625-3866; www.spiritofnorfolk.com) is like an oceangoing cruise ship, complete with dancing, good food, and entertainment. Offerings include lunch cruises starting $25 per person, dinner cruises from $43, and moonlight party cruises with cocktails from $24. Call for the schedule and to make reservations.

From April to October, there are cruises on the *American Rover* (© 757/627-7245; www.americanrover.com), a graceful schooner modeled after 19th-century Chesapeake Bay schooners. Prices for the 2-hour sail-powered cruises along the Elizabeth River are $15 for adults, $10 for children under 12. It also does 3-hour and adults-only cruises.

From mid-April to October, the *Carrie B* (© 757/393-4735; www.carrieb cruises.com), a reproduction of a 19th-century Mississippi riverboat, offers daily 1½- and 2½-hour cruises departing at noon and 2pm, respectively, from the Waterside. They pick up passengers at Portsmouth's North Landing 10 minutes later. Fares start at $14 for adults, $7 for children. There's also a 2½-hour sunset cruise. Call for the schedule and reservations.

SHOPPING FOR ANTIQUES ★★

Norfolk is one of the better places in Virginia to search for antiques, with at least 32 shops selling a range of furniture, decorative arts, glassware, jewelry, and other items, from both home and overseas. The best place to look is in Ghent, where several shops sit along the 4 blocks of West 21st Street between Granby

---

Tips Trolley Tours of the Naval Station

In these days of tight security at military bases, the **Naval Station Norfolk Tour** operated by Hampton Roads Transit (HRT) (© 757/222-6100; www. hrtransit.org) is the best way to see the aircraft carriers and other ships moored at the huge naval complex. The tours depart from the Naval Station Tour Center, 9079 Hampton Blvd., every 30 minutes or every hour, depending on time of year. Fares are $7.50 for adults, $5 for seniors, children under 12, and disabled persons. All persons 18 and over will need a picture ID to get on the base.

For a view of downtown, HRT's **Norfolk Destination Tour** will take you past all the sites. You can get off at any attraction and reboard the next tour. They run from Memorial Day to Labor Day, daily at 11am, 1 and 3pm. Fares are $10 for adults, $8 for seniors, children under 12, and disabled passengers. You can get schedules and tickets between Memorial Day and Labor Day at HRT's ticket kiosk on Waterside Drive in front of The Waterside.

A Ferry Ride to Olde Town Portsmouth

Across the Elizabeth River from downtown Norfolk, Portsmouth's **Olde Town** section traces its roots back to 1752. Like those in Charleston and Savannah, Olde Town's homes present a kaleidoscope of architectural styles: colonial, Federal, Greek Revival, Georgian, and Victorian. Plaques mounted on imported English street lamps point out their architectural and historical significance.

Until the 1950s, ferries were the main means of getting across the river. Operated by Hampton Roads Transit (© 757/222-6100), the paddlewheel **Elizabeth River Ferry** still makes the short but picturesque trip. It departs the Waterside marina every 30 minutes Monday through Thursday from 7:15am to 9:45pm, Friday from 7am to 11:35pm, Saturday and Sunday from 10am to 11:35pm. Fare is 75¢ for adults, 50¢ for children, and 35¢ for seniors and disabled passengers (exact change required).

Get off at Portsmouth's **North Landing Visitor Center,** on Harbor Court (© 800/PORTS-VA or 757/393-5111; www.portsva.com), and pick up a walking tour brochure and map. Ask about a **Key Museums Pass,** which admits you to most city museums for $9 per person. The center is open during summer Monday to Saturday 9am to 7pm, Sunday 9am to 5:30pm; off season, daily 9am to 5pm.

At the **Lightship Museum,** in Riverfront Park at the foot of London Boulevard (© 757/393-8741), you can tour the *Portsmouth,* built in 1915 and anchored offshore until the 1980s to warn mariners of the dangerous shoals on the approach to Hampton Roads. Also in the park, the **Portsmouth Naval Shipyard Museum,** 2 High St. (© 757/393-8591), houses many ship models and relics of Portsmouth's military past, including a cannon mount possibly from the Confederate ironclad *Merrimac,* which fought the Union's turret-topped *Monitor* on Hampton Roads during the Civil War. Admission to either is $3 per person. Both are open June to Labor Day, Monday to Saturday 10am to 5pm, Sunday 1 to 5pm; rest of the year, Tuesday to Saturday 10am to 5pm, Sunday 1 to 5pm.

You can keep the kids busy at a number of interactive exhibits in **Children's Museum of Virginia,** 221 High St. (© 757/393-8393; www.portsva.com/childrensmuseumva), but you must supervise them at all times. Admission is $6 per person. Open during summer from Monday to Saturday 9am to 5pm, Sunday 11am to 5pm. Closed Monday off season.

Also here is the **Virginia Sports Hall of Fame,** 420 High St. (© 757/393-8031), whose most famous members are golfers Sam Sneed and Lanny Wadkins, tennis pro Arthur Ashe, and basketball players Ralph Sampson and Nancy Lieberman Cline. Admission is free. Open Tuesday to Saturday 10am to 5pm, Sunday 1 to 5pm.

Street and Colonial Avenue, especially at the corner of Llewellyn Avenue. Granby Street has another 13 shops of its own, including the **Ghent Market & Antique Center,** which occupies an entire city block between 14th and 15th streets and Monticello Avenue (*©* **757/625-2897;** www.ghentmarket.com). The "market" part of this huge establishment is actually a farmer's market, where you can load up on fresh produce. Open Monday and Wednesday to Saturday from 10am to 6pm, Sunday from 11am to 6pm.

The visitor centers have a complete list and description of the shops.

WHERE TO STAY
DOWNTOWN
Courtyard by Marriott *★* *Value*   Downtown's first modern, moderately priced hotel, this Courtyard opened in 2002 almost next door to the MacArthur Center. Compared to it's suburban sisters, this prototype of a new breed of city-center Courtyards has a larger lobby with fireplace, a bar open nightly, and a restaurant serving both breakfast and dinner. Dark-wood trim and thick carpets also help give it an upscale ambience. The comfortable rooms and suites are typical Courtyard, with big desks, high-speed dataports, and other amenities aimed at business travelers. Unlike the other downtown hotels, here you can open the windows to let in fresh air.

520 Plume St. (between Court St. and St. Paul Blvd.), Norfolk, VA 23510. *©* **800/321-2211** or 757/963-6000. Fax 757/963-6001. www.courtyard.com. 140 units. $89–$159 double; $159–$179 suite. AE, DC, DISC, MC, V. Valet parking $15. **Amenities:** Restaurant; bar; heated indoor pool; Jacuzzi; exercise room; business center; limited room service (dinner only); laundry service; coin-op washers and dryers. *In room:* A/C, TV, high-speed dataport, fridge, coffeemaker, iron.

Norfolk Waterside Marriott *★★*   One of Norfolk's two convention hotels (the Sheraton is the other) and its most elegant, this 24-story high-rise is connected to The Waterside via a covered skywalk. Its mahogany-paneled lobby is a masterpiece of 18th-century European style, with fine paintings, crystal chandelier, potted palm trees, comfortable seating areas with gleaming lamps, and one-of-a-kind antiques. A magnificent staircase leads to the main restaurant, lounge and meeting rooms on the second floor. There's a deli and second bar downstairs off the lobby. Guest rooms are sumptuously furnished with Marriottesque dark-wood pieces. Although the rooms do not have balconies, ask for an upper floor unit with a river view. The indoor pool here opens to a sun deck overlooking the river.

235 E. Main St. (between Atlantic St. and Martins Lane), Norfolk, VA 23510. *©* **800/228-9290** or 757/627-4200. Fax 757/628-6452. 405 units, including 8 suites. $179–$199 double. Weekend packages available. AE, DC, DISC, MC, V. Valet parking $22; self-parking $17. **Amenities:** 2 restaurants; 2 bars; heated indoor pool; health club; concierge; business center; limited room service; laundry service; coin-op washers and dryers; concierge-level rooms. *In room:* A/C, TV, dataport, coffeemaker.

Sheraton Norfolk Waterside Hotel *★★*   Next door to The Waterside and overlooking busy Norfolk Harbor, this contemporary 10-story hotel recently underwent extensive renovation, which has made it competitive with the more traditionally styled Marriott 2 blocks away. A three-story, light-filled atrium lobby gives way to two restaurants with outdoor seating and a bar with 30-foot windows overlooking the river. The spacious guest quarters are furnished with dark wood furniture. About a third of the units facing the river have small balconies (they're allotted on a first-come, first-served basis). Although the Sheraton draws groups and conventions, its location and facilities make it a good choice for individuals, couples and families, too.

777 Waterside Dr., Norfolk, VA 23510. *©* **800/325-3535** or 757/622-6664. Fax 757/625-8271. www.sheraton norfolk.com. 445 units. $209–$239 double. Weekend and other packages available. AE, DC, DISC, MC, V. Valet parking $20, self-parking $9. Small pets accepted free with advance notice. **Amenities:** 2 restaurants; bar; outdoor heated pool; exercise room; concierge; business center; babysitting; laundry service; concierge-level rooms. *In room:* A/C, TV, dataport, coffeemaker, iron.

IN GHENT

Page House Inn ⭐⭐   Centrally located in the historic Ghent district and across the street from The Chrysler Museum, this grand three-story brick Colonial Revival mansion with a dormered roof and double columns punctuating the expansive veranda was built in 1899 by Herman L. Page, a Welsh immigrant. You'll find golden-oak paneling, sliding doors, and moldings plus a hand-carved fireplace in the living room and a soaring staircase ascending to the rooms upstairs. Guest quarters are beautifully furnished with four-poster beds and one-of-a-kind antiques. Five units have gas-log fireplaces. The most expensive also has a sunken whirlpool tub and a steam shower with his-and-her heads. A gourmet European-style breakfast is served in the large dining room set with Lenox china.

323 Fairfax Ave. (at Mowbray Arch), Norfolk, VA 23507. © **800/599-7659** or 757/625-5033. Fax 757/623-9451. www.pagehouseinn.com. 7 units, including 2 suites. $130–$220 double. Rates include full breakfast. MC, V. *In room:* A/C.

WHERE TO DINE
DOWNTOWN

The downtown renaissance has turned the 200 block of **Granby Street** into Norfolk's Restaurant Row, as hip new dining rooms open all the time. Here you'll find The Blue Hippo and The 219 (see below). In addition, you'll get excellent tapas at the fast-paced **Empire Little Bar & Bistro,** 245 Granby St. (© **757/626-3100**), open daily until 2am. **Domo Sushi,** 273 Granby St. (© **757/628-8282**), serves just that, plus other Japanese fare. **Havana,** 255 Granby St. (© **757/627-5800**), serves Cuban-influenced fare. **Wraps,** 271 Granby St. (© **757/623-5635**), has sidewalk tables for enjoying Southwestern and Caribbean wraps. And you'll get your fill of corned beef and cabbage at **Jack Quinn's Irish Pub,** 241 Granby St. (© **757/274-0024**).

To catch the games, head to **AJ Gator's Sports Bar & Grill,** 244 Granby St. (© **757/622-5544**). For a caffeine fix and inexpensive food to go with it, there's a branch of **Aromas** at 233 Granby St. (© **757/625-4888**).

In the MacArthur Center, on Monticello Avenue at Market Street, is a branch of the elegant but informal **Kincaid's Fish, Chop, & Steak House** (© **757/622-8000**), offering exactly what its name says. Downtown professionals turn the bar into a favorite Friday evening "meet" market. There's a very good and inexpensive **food court** up on the third floor.

The Waterside also has a food court and a branch of **Joe's Crab Shack** (© **757/625-0655**), which has patio tables and a non-supervised children's playroom (don't worry, there's only one way the little rascals can get out, and the staff will see them trying to escape). There are branches of Outback Steakhouse and Hooters in The Waterside. See "Norfolk After Dark," below.

The Blue Hippo ⭐ ECLECTIC   "Life is too short to eat boring food" is the motto of this urbane bistro, a block from the MacArthur Center and The Waterside. Indeed, the food that is anything but boring, creatively blending local produce with flavors from Thailand, Jamaica, and other spice-oriented locales. The menu changes frequently and always has a couple of surprises. For example, the crab cakes are served over a snap peas, apple, and carrot slaw. The dining room is nicely decorated with colorful works by local artist Tom Barnes. This is more a fine dining spot than the more casual The 219 (see below).

147 Granby St. (between City Hall Ave. and Plume St.). © **757/533-9664.** Reservations recommended. Main courses $20–$29. AE, MC, V. Mon–Thurs 11:30am–2:30pm and 5:30–10pm; Fri 11:30am–2:30pm and 5:30–11pm; Sat 5:30–11pm; Sun 5–9pm.

The 219 ★★ *Value* PIZZAS/ECLECTIC A block north of The Blue Hippo, this storefront cafe also offers an eclectic mix of cuisines but with more noise—and less expense. A hit here is the pecan-crusted Chesapeake Bay rockfish (sea bass) baked in butter and finished with a tomato *concassé* (fresh ripe tomatoes that have been peeled, seeded, and coarsely chopped) and accompanied by garlic mashed potatoes. Asian flavors crop up in fresh tuna subjected to a sauce of soy, ginger, and chives. You also can opt for one-person pizzas with usual and unusual toppings. There's always a vegetarian selection such as tofu fried in a spicy chili and garlic sauce.

219 Granby St. (at Brooke Ave.). ℂ 757/627-2896. Reservations recommended. Pizzas $10; main courses $13–$22. AE, DC, DISC, MC, V. Mon–Fri 11:30am–2:30pm and 5–10pm; Sat 11:30am–2:30pm and 5–11pm; Sun 5–9pm.

Todd Jurich's Bistro ★★★ CREATIVE AMERICAN Todd Jurich's urbane bistro is the top restaurant in Hampton Roads. You'll see why when you partake of Todd's creative twists on Southern traditions, such as his all-lump-meat crab cakes with lemon mayonnaise—a far cry, indeed, from the fried cakes dispensed at many Chesapeake Bay seafood shacks. Todd uses only fresh produce, drawn whenever possible from local farms that practice "ecologically sound agriculture." His "Signature Menu" is good value, offering three courses for $30 per person, $60 with wine pairings. For lunch, you can choose from sandwiches made with such filling as crab cakes or from smaller portions of the nighttime mains.

150 Main St. (at Boush St., opposite NAUTICUS). ℂ 757/622-3210. Reservations recommended. Main courses $18–$32; fixed-price menu $30 ($60 with wine). AE, DC, DISC, MC, V. Mon–Thurs 11:30am–2pm and 5:30–10pm; Fri 11:30am–2pm and 5:30–10pm; Sat 5:30–10pm.

IN GHENT

Baker's Crust ★★ *Value* INTERNATIONAL/BAKERY This lively restaurant is both the best place in town for breakfast and one of the better values for lunch and dinner. From the bakery on one side of the warehouselike room, comes fresh pastries to start your day, or you can opt for specialty omelets, pancakes, waffles, sausage biscuits, granola, fresh fruit, or sweet crepes. The bakery also supplies the bread for a variety of meal-size salads and sandwiches at lunch and dinner. Rotisserie chicken and a few other lunchtime main courses are joined after 5pm by the terrific likes of Jamaican-style rotisserie chicken and shrimp with andouille sausage and grits. Don't ignore the desserts here. The jellyrolls with Bavarian cheese and fresh strawberries will add a few inches to your girth.

330 W. 21st St. (in Palace Shops, between Llewellyn and DeBree sts.). ℂ 757/625-3600. Reservations not accepted. Breakfast $4.50–$7; sandwiches and salads $6.50–$10; main courses $11–$17. AE, DC, DISC, MC, V. Daily 8am–11pm.

Cora ★★ *Value* CREATIVE SOUTHERN You might say I have a conflict of interest since my cousin Nancy Cobb owns and does most of the cooking at this casual but sophisticated restaurant. Be that as it may, you will thoroughly enjoy this accomplished young chef's "refined Southern chow." For example, Nancy uses chunks of Smithfield country ham and lumps of Chesapeake crabmeat to give her James River Caesar salad an extraordinary combination of flavors. Breaded with Japanese crumbs, her fried shrimp and okra is anything but down home. "Ed Cobb's Como North Carolina fishmuddle" is a rich seafood stew (think bouillabaisse) originally concocted by Nancy's father, who grew up in the hamlet of Como, NC. Nancy named the restaurant for her great-grandmother—that's her with great-grandpa in the 1940s photo on the back wall. There's always

---

Fun Fact **Cones & Carhops**

Some of the wafflelike ice cream cones made at **Doumar's,** an old-fashioned drive-in with carhops and curb service at 19th Street and Monticello Ave. (© 757/627-4163), come from the original cone-making machine invented by Abe Doumar at the St. Louis Exposition in 1904. Abe's descendants keep his invention oiled and working, and descendants of his barbecue sandwiches, burgers, hot dogs, sundaes, and milkshakes round out the extremely inexpensive menu. Doumar's has been around since the 1930s, which makes it a hip historical attraction. Open Monday to Thursday from 8am to 11pm, Friday and Saturday 8am to 12:30am.

---

a vegan choice here. For dessert, try the "shallow" chocolate cake—so named because a restaurant reviewer said it "lacked depth."

723 W 21st St. (between Colley and Colonial aves.). © 757/625-6100. Reservations recommended. Main courses $10–$18. AE, DISC, MC, V. Mon–Thurs 11am–2pm and 5–10pm; Fri 11am–2pm and 5–11pm; Sat 5–11pm; Sun 11am–3pm.

Luna Maya ★ *Finds* LATIN AMERICAN This little creation of Bolivian-born sisters Karla and Vivian Montano brings the delightful flavors of Latin America to Ghent. Although burritos and tamales outnumber dishes from Bolivia and Argentina, this is no refried-bean joint. Try a shrimp or chorizo burrito, and you'll see what I mean. The flavors leap from the fresh ingredients. I would say start with their own concoction of a Bolivian salad—a mix of fresh greens, fried and fresh tomatoes, and boiled potatoes with a spicy peanut sauce—but it's apt to fill you up before the main course arrives. You won't get linens and silver here, but the food is interesting and very good.

2000 Colonial Ave. (at 21st St. in Corner Shops). © 757/622-6986. Reservations not accepted. Main courses $10–$14. AE, MC, V. Tues–Sat 5:30–10pm.

NORFOLK AFTER DARK

For a rundown on events, pick up a copy of *Port Folio* (www.portfolioweekly.com), a weekly paper free at the visitor information offices, most hotel lobbies, and The Waterside. The "Daily Break" section in the local rag, *The Virginian-Pilot* (www.pilotonline.com), is also a good source.

THE PERFORMING ARTS

In addition to outdoor entertainment during the summer in Town Park, between The Waterside and NAUTICUS on the Elizabeth River, you may be here during performances by several outstanding companies.

The **Virginia Stage Company** (© 757/627-1234; www.vastage.com) puts on productions from October through April in the **Wells Theatre,** a restored Beaux-Arts gem (it's on the National Register of Historic Places) on Monticello Avenue opposite the MacArthur Center (© 757/627-1234).

The **Norfolk SCOPE** complex (© 757/441-2161; www.norfolkscope.com), consists of several venues. The futuristic **Norfolk SCOPE Arena,** Brambleton Avenue and St. Paul's Boulevard, seats 12,000 for major events—including the circus, ice shows, sports, and concerts (Cher brought her Living Proof Farewell show here in 2003). **Chrysler Hall,** Charlotte Street and St. Paul's Boulevard, is home to the **Virginia Symphony** (© 757/892-6366; www.virginiasymphony.org) and the annual Pops series. And the **Harrison Opera House,** 160 E. Virginia

Beach Blvd. at Llewellyn Avenue (© 757/623-1223), is home to the Virginia Opera (www.vaopera.org).

THE BAR & CLUB SCENE

With more than 37 bars, restaurants and stores, **The Waterside Festival Marketplace** (see "Seeing the Sights," earlier) is the center of downtown's bar and music scene. Upstairs is dominated by a branch of **Jillian's** (© 757/624-9100), a noisy emporium with a Japanese hibachi steakhouse, a huge sports bar, billiards and electronic games, and a dance club featuring DJ-spun blues, acid jazz and rock. Through it all blares the steady thump of rock music to soothe the soul of any 20-year-old. A bit more refined are the dueling pianos at **Crocodile Rocks** (© 757/478-1138). You can get your laughs at the **Comedy Zone** (© 757/627-HAHA). And there's more in The Waterside—just follow your ears.

2 Virginia Beach ★

20 miles E of Norfolk; 110 miles E of Richmond; 207 miles S of Washington, D.C.

Given its more than 20 miles of unbroken sand and surf, it's not surprising that Virginia Beach comes alive during the summer. Although big hotels line the beachfront and block off ocean views from everywhere except their own rooms, the 59-block-long Boardwalk (it's actually concrete) boasts immaculate landscaping, wood benches, small parks, a bike-skating path, public restrooms, and attractive white colonial-style street lamps.

Adding to Virginia Beach's allure as a family vacation destination is the **Virginia Marine Science Museum,** the most popular museum in the state. History lovers will find several sites of interest, including the **First Landing Cross** where the Jamestown settlers came ashore. Nature lovers can drive a few miles south to the **Back Bay National Wildlife Refuge,** which attracts migrating birds and protects several miles of beach and marshlands from development.

Thousands of families from throughout Virginia and the nearby states take their annual beach vacations here. Many of them are of modest means, and the oceanfront area has scores of cheap motels catering to them. It's not unfair to say that the area takes on a certain "Redneck Riviera" flavor from Memorial Day to Labor Day. It's also a popular beach with African-Americans—not surprising since the population of nearby Norfolk, Hampton, and Newport News is approximately 40% black.

ESSENTIALS
VISITOR INFORMATION

For information on planning your trip, or assistance while you're here, contact the **Visitor Information Center,** 2100 Parks Ave., Virginia Beach, VA 23451 (© 800/VA-BEACH; www.vbfun.com). A large board has phones connected to the reservations desks of major hotels and resorts. Particularly helpful is a free **map** showing public restrooms and municipal parking lots in the resort area. The center's annual "Vacation Guide" is a no-nonsense listing of every hotel, restaurant, and activity here. The center is at the eastern end of I-264. It's open daily from 9am to 5pm, to 8pm from Father's Day through Labor Day weekend.

A satellite office is in First Landing State Park's **Chesapeake Bay Center,** 2500 Shore Dr. (U.S. 60) (© 757/412-2316). It's open daily 9am to 5pm.

There are **information kiosks** at the beach on Atlantic Avenue at 17th, 24th, and 30th streets from late spring through October. (*Note:* These are the only official visitor information booths at the beach; most others with "tourist information" signs are come-ons for time-share sales operations.)

Racks at the visitor information center and elsewhere contain several slick give-away tourist publications packed with information and money-saving coupons.

GETTING THERE

BY PLANE   Virginia Beach is served by **Norfolk International Airport,** about 30 minutes (15 miles) west of the oceanfront resort area (see "Essentials" in "Norfolk," earlier).

BY CAR   Follow I-64 to I-264 east. I-264 ends near the heart of the oceanfront resort area. Also from the west, U.S. 60 becomes the scenic Shore Drive, which dead-ends at Atlantic Avenue on the northern end of the ocean beach; a right turn takes you along this main north-south drag through the resort area. From the north or south, U.S. 13 and 17 will take you to I-64.

CITY LAYOUT

The city of Virginia Beach covers a huge geographic area between the Chesapeake Bay and the North Carolina line. There's no real downtown; instead, most of the action is at the **Oceanfront,** the prime resort area where you'll find a solid line of big hotels, restaurants, beachwear and souvenir shops, video-game arcades, and the **Boardwalk** and its adjacent bike/skating path, which run along the beach. The resort area extends from 1st Street at Rudee Inlet north to 42nd Street (the boardwalk ends at 39th St.). Behind the beachfront hotels, **Atlantic Avenue** runs north-south between Rudee Inlet and Cape Henry. A block inland, the wider **Pacific Avenue** is a much speedier way through the resort area. At Rudee Inlet, Pacific Avenue gives way to **General Booth Boulevard,** which runs southwest past the Virginia Marine Science Museum.

The Chesapeake Bay and the Atlantic Ocean meet at Cape Henry, home to **Cape Henry Lighthouse, Fort Story,** and **First Landing State Park.**   On the Chesapeake Bay 3 miles west of Cape Henry is **Lynnhaven Inlet,** a less congested area where you'll find more local residents than tourists at restaurants and marinas along Shore Drive (U.S. 60). Lynnhaven Inlet is about a 15-minute drive from the Oceanfront.

Some 12 miles south of the resort area, **Sandbridge** is an oceanfront enclave of cottages and a relatively undeveloped public beach. From Sandbridge south to the North Carolina line, the **Back Bay National Wildlife Refuge** and **False Cape State Park** offer undisturbed beach and marshland for hikers, bikers, birdwatchers, and sun worshippers.

⎛Tips   No Bad Behavior

By and large Virginia Beach is a safe place to visit, but you should take the same precautions you would in any city. Although youths congregating along Atlantic Avenue on the oceanfront late on weekend nights, and especially on long holiday weekends, can make this seem like a rowdy spring break in Florida, the police strictly enforce—some critics say heavy-handedly—the city's so-called "No Bad Behavior" Ordinance. Public drunkenness, lewdness, loud car stereos, and any other behavior "which is likely to intimidate, harass or disrupt the peaceful enjoyment of others" is strictly prohibited. Nevertheless, it's best to simply stay away from the oceanfront after 10pm on weekends, especially if you have children in tow.

Virginia Beach

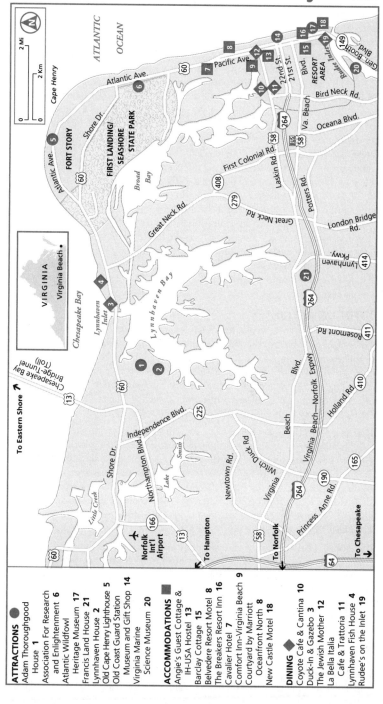

ATTRACTIONS ●
Adam Thoroughgood
  House **1**
Association For Research
  and Enlightenment **6**
Atlantic Wildfowl
  Heritage Museum **17**
Francis Land House **21**
Lynnhaven House **2**
Old Cape Henry Lighthouse **5**
Old Coast Guard Station
  Museum and Gift Shop **14**
Virginia Marine
  Science Museum **20**

ACCOMMODATIONS ■
Angie's Guest Cottage &
  IH-USA Hostel **13**
Barclay Cottage **15**
Belvedere Resort Motel **8**
The Breakers Resort Inn **16**
Cavalier Hotel **7**
Comfort Inn-Virginia Beach **9**
Courtyard by Marriott
  Oceanfront North **8**
New Castle Motel **18**

DINING ◆
Coyote Cafe & Cantina **10**
Duck-In & Gazebo **3**
The Jewish Mother **12**
La Bella Italia
  Cafe & Trattoria **11**
Lynnhaven Fish House **4**
Rudee's on the Inlet **19**

GETTING AROUND

Between mid-June and Labor Day, especially on weekends, parking spaces near the beach can be as scarce as hen's teeth. Try the **municipal parking garages** on Atlantic Avenue at 9th, 19th, 25th and 31st streets, or a few private pay lots along Pacific Avenue (the visitor information center has free maps that show them).

Your best bet is to stay at the shore and get around on the **Atlantic Avenue Trolley,** which runs from May 1 to October 1, about every 15 minutes from 8am to 2am along the entire length of the avenue. The **Museum Express Trolley** runs daily during the summer, about every 15 minutes from 8am to 2am between Atlantic Avenue at 40th Street and the Virginia Science Museum and Ocean Breeze Amusement Park on General Booth Boulevard.

Fare on any of these trolleys is $1 per ride except for children under 38 inches tall, who ride free. You can also buy a 3-day **Trolley Pass** for $5 or a 5-day pass for $8. Both permit unlimited rides. You can get free trolley passes if you park in the municipal garages on Atlantic Avenue.

The trolleys are operated by **Hampton Roads Transit** (© **757/222-6100;** www.hrtransit.org), which also provides public bus service in the region. HRT has a **ticket kiosk** on the oceanfront at Atlantic Avenue and 24th Street, where you can also buy tickets to its trolley tour of the Oceana naval air station (see "Thundering Overhead," p. 304.

For a taxi, call **Andy's Cab Co.** (© **757/495-3300**).

OUTDOOR ACTIVITIES

Virginia Beach offers a wonderful variety of water sports, starting, of course, with its fine-sand beach. But note that between Memorial Day and Labor Day, no ball playing, fishing, and other sports are allowed on the beach between 2nd Street and 42nd Street from 10am to 5pm.

Boating and fishing are centered at marinas at **Rudee Inlet,** which empties into the ocean, and at **Lynnhaven Inlet,** where the Lynnhaven River meets the Chesapeake Bay.

BIKING, JOGGING & SKATING You can walk, jog, or run on the Boardwalk, or bike and skate on its adjoining bike path. There are biking and hiking trails in **First Landing State Park** (which rents bikes) and in **Back Bay National Wildlife Refuge** (see "Parks & Wildlife Refuges," below).

You can rent wheels from early March to October from **Cherie's Bicycle & Blade Rental** (© **757/437-8888**), which has stations on the Boardwalk, at 2nd, 8th, 10th, 13th, 19th, 22nd, 23rd, 24th, 35th, and 39th streets. Rentals start at $6 an hour, $59 a week.

FISHING Deep-sea fishing aboard a party boat can be an exciting day's entertainment for novices and dedicated fishermen alike. Both party and private charter boats are based at the **Virginia Beach Fishing Center,** 200 Winston-Salem Ave. (© **757/422-5700;** www.virginiafishing.com), at the Rudee Inlet bridge. At Lynnhaven Inlet, party boats leave from the **D and M Marina,** 3311 Shore Dr. (© **757/481-7211**).

You can also drop a line from several piers. The **Virginia Beach Fishing Pier,** between 14th and 15th streets, oceanfront (© **757/428-2333**), open April through October, has bait for sale and rods for rent. On the Chesapeake Bay, **Lynnhaven Inlet Fishing Pier,** Starfish Road off Shore Drive (© **757/481-7071**), open 24 hours a day in summer, rents rods and reels and sells crab cages.

GOLF Next to Williamsburg, Virginia Beach offers more good golfing than any other Virginia destination. Sand, water, and wind make up for the area's flat

---

Tips **Good Golf Packages**

You don't have to be Tiger Woods to take advantage of golf packages organized by **Virginia Beach Golf Getaways** (© 866-4-VB-GOLF; www. vbgolf.com). Recent offerings started at $199 for 2-night accommodations and three rounds of golf. They're listed in the annual "Virginia Beach Golf Vacation Guide," available from the visitor center (see "Essentials," earlier). The guide also describes the city's courses.

---

terrain to provide plenty of challenges at the **TPC of Virginia Beach** (© 877/ 484-3872 or 757/563-9440; www.tpc.com), designed by Pete Dye and Curtis Strange for the Professional Golfer's Association (PGA), which owns and operates it. The course opened in 1999.

Elevated tees and strategically placed water and bunkers pose problems at **Heron Ridge Golf Club** (© 757/426-3800; www.heronridge.com), another new course. Sharp fairway angles at the Rees Jones-designed **Hell's Point Golf Course** (© 757/721-3400; www.hellspoint.com) have been described as "devilish." Another Rees Jones project, **Honey Bee Golf Course** (© 757/471-2768; www.honeybeegolfclub.com) is shorter (par-70) but presents challenges for beginners and experts alike. You can also play the **Red Wing Lake Municipal Golf Course** (© 757/437-4845; www.vbgov.com/dept/parks).

Call the courses for greens fees, tee times, and directions.

KAYAKING **Tidewater Adventures** (© 888/669-8368 or 757/480-1999; www.tidewateradventures.com) rents kayaks from May to September in front of the Cavalier Hotel, on the oceanfront at 42nd Street. Rentals range from $12 per hour to $65 for a full day. They also lead dolphin-watching trips and guided tours of Back Bay National Wildlife Refuge and to other nearby locations. Tour prices range from $40 to $75.

SCUBA DIVING The Atlantic Ocean off Virginia Beach is colder and less clear than it is below Cape Hatteras, NC, but that's not to say you can't dive here. For information about dive trips, contact **Lynnhaven Dive Center,** 1413 Great Neck Rd. (© 757/481-7949; www.ldcscuba.com).

SWIMMING During the summer season, lifeguards are on duty along the resort strip from 2nd to 42nd streets; they also handle raft, umbrella, and beach-chair rentals. Despite their presence, you should always be careful when swimming in the surf, particularly if a northeast wind is kicking up a dangerous undertow. When in doubt, ask the lifeguard.

You can get away from the summer crowds—and the lifeguards—by driving 12 miles south of Rudee Inlet to **Little Island City Park,** in the residential beach area of Sandbridge. To really escape the crowds, take the tram from there to **False Cape State Park** (see "Parks & Wildlife Refuges," below).

WAVE RUNNING & PARASAILING You can rent exciting wave runners from **Rudee Inlet Jet Ski Rentals** next to the Virginia Beach Fishing Center at Rudee Inlet (© 757/428-4614).

PARKS & WILDLIFE REFUGES

One of the best things about Virginia Beach is that you don't have to go far from the busy resort to find open spaces for hiking, biking, camping, and bird watching.

First Landing State Park ✿✿✿ Its 2,270 preserved acres run between the Lynnhaven River and the Chesapeake Bay to within 2 blocks of the ocean. Rabbits, squirrels, and raccoons are among the many species in this urban park, which boasts 19 miles of hiking trails. The main entrance is on Shore Drive (U.S. 60), where the visitor information center is open daily 9am to 5pm. The grounds and trails are open daily from 8am to sunset. The 64th Street entry, off Atlantic Avenue, leads to a quiet-water beach on Broad Bay. Admission to the park during summer is $3 per vehicle on weekdays, $4 on weekends. Bikes are prohibited except on the gravel, 6-mile Cape Henry Trail, which runs between the 64th Street entrance and the visitor center.

Twenty 2-bedroom cabins can be rented here. Rates vary by season, and bookings are essential, so call the state park reservations center (✆ **800/933-PARK**). A bayside campground in a wooded area beside a fine beach has 221 sites for tents and RVs (no hookups) for $22 a night. The park store (✆ **757/412-2302**) rents bicycles and beach equipment and supplies.

For more information, contact the park at 2500 Shore Dr., Virginia Beach, VA 23451 (✆ **757/412-2320;** www.dcr.state.va.us/parks/1stland.htm).

Next to the campground, the **Chesapeake Bay Center** (✆ **727/412-2316**) has an exhibit about the Jamestown settlers' landing here in 1607. It also shows a short video and has an exhibit about the local ecology, both put together by the Virginia Marine Science Museum; it's interesting but not as good as the main museum (see "The Top Attractions," below). There's a visitor information desk here. A beachside amphitheater hosts concerts during the summer (call for a schedule). The center is open daily 9am to 5pm.

Back Bay & False Cape ✿✿ Especially inviting for bird-watchers is **Back Bay National Wildlife Refuge,** in the southeastern corner of Virginia near the North Carolina line. Its 8,800 acres of beaches, dunes, marshes, and backwaters are on the main Atlantic Flyway for migratory birds. No swimming or sunbathing is allowed on the pristine beach here, but you can collect shells, surf-cast for fish, and bird watch. There are also nature trails and a canoe launching spot with marked trails through the marshes. Daily admission from April through October is $5 per vehicle, $2 per pedestrian or biker; free from November through March. The **visitor contact station** (✆ **757/721-2412**) is open Monday through Friday from 8am to 4pm, weekends from 9am to 4pm. It offers nature programs by reservation only. From Rudee Inlet, go south on General Booth Boulevard and follow the signs 12 miles to Sandbridge and the refuge. For more information, contact the Refuge Manager, 4005 Sandpiper Rd., Virginia Beach, VA 23456 (✆ **757/721-2412;** http://backbay.fws.gov).

Swimming and sunbathing are permitted on the beach in **False Cape State Park,** 4 miles south of the Back Bay visitor contact station via hiking and biking trail. You'll find 6 miles of beachfront (to the North Carolina line), an interpretive

---

Tips **The Thong Law**

You don't have to completely cover up when out on the beach here, but a certain degree of modesty is in order when selecting your bathing suit. It's illegal for women to swim or sunbathe topless. The same law doesn't apply to men, but Virginia Beach's Ordinance 22-10 is even-handed. It prohibits both men and women from exposing their "buttocks, with less than a fully opaque covering." Locals call it their Thong Law.

trail and more than 3 miles of hiking trails. Primitive camping is by permit only, which you can get by calling ✆ **800/933-PARK.** The park has no other visitor facilities, so bring your own drinking water. It's open daily from sunrise to sunset.

You can't park in the national wildlife refuge lot while visiting False Cape State Park, so leave your vehicle at Little Island City Park in Sandbridge. From there, you can either hike or bike the 6 miles to False Cape, or take the "Terra Gator," a specially built tram that inches its way down the beach daily from April through October, weekends only from November through March. It departs at 9am and returns at 1pm and stops for about 1 hour at the park's visitor contact station. Volunteers operate the tram, so call ✆ **800/933-PARK** to make sure it's running and to make reservations, which are essential. Fares are $8 per person.

For more information contact the park at 4001 Sandpiper Road, Virginia Beach, VA 23456 (✆ **757/426-7128;** www.dcr.state.va.us/parks/falscape.htm).

Sandbridge Eco Sports, at 577 Sandbridge Rd. (✆ **800/695-4212** or 757/721-6210; www.sandbridgeecosports.com), 2 miles inland from the beach, rents sea kayaks and has guided kayak trips.

THE TOP ATTRACTIONS

Association for Research and Enlightenment (A.R.E.)
If you're the least bit psychic, you'll enjoy a visit to this center carrying on the work of the late Edgar Cayce, whose own psychic talent manifested itself when he found he could enter into an altered state of consciousness and answer questions on any topic. His answers, or "discourses," now called "readings," number some 14,305. If you don't know about Cayce, show up at 2pm for a 30-minute movie about his life, followed by a 30-minute guided tour. The A.R.E. Bookstore on the first floor has an excellent selection of books and videos about holistic health, parapsychology, life after death, dreams, and even cooking. The Meditation Room on the third floor offers a spectacular view of the ocean and is painted with colors chosen because Cayce readings suggest they can help attain higher consciousness. Outside the center is the Meditation Garden. Inside, the health services department offers steam baths, facials, and massages to the public.

215 67th St. (at Atlantic Ave.). ✆ 757/428-3588. www.edgarcayce.org. Free admission. Mon–Sat 9am–8pm; Sun noon–8pm. 30-min. film, daily 2pm. 30-min. guided tours depart daily 2:30pm. Closed Thanksgiving and Christmas.

Atlantic Wildfowl Heritage Museum ★★
This small but excellent museum displays a collection of carved decoys—some of them a century old—and decorative wildlife, plus paintings of ducks, geese, and other wildfowl. It occupies the white-brick-and-clapboard DeWitt beach cottage built in 1895 by Virginia Beach's first mayor. The oldest structure on the waterfront, the cottage alone is worth a stop as you stroll the Boardwalk. It's operated by the Back Bay Wildfowl Guild, which applies the donations and profits from the gift shop (which carries excellent decoys) to its conservation efforts.

1113 Atlantic Ave. (at 12th St.). ✆ 757/437-8432. www.awhm.org. Free admission (donations encouraged). Summer, Mon–Sat 10am–5pm; Sun noon–5pm; closed Mon in the off season. Closed New Year's Day, Thanksgiving, Christmas, and New Year's Eve.

Old Cape Henry Lighthouse ★★
Built in 1791–92, this picturesque brick structure was the first lighthouse authorized by the U.S. Congress. It marked the southern entrance to Chesapeake Bay until 1881, when a new lighthouse nearby took over. If you're in shape, you can climb the 189 steps to the top for a spectacular view over Cape Henry, the bay, and ocean. The gift shop carries a plethora of lighthouse-themed items.

Tips **Thundering Overhead**

The U.S. Navy's airbase at Oceana is home to those low-flying F-14 Tomcat and F/A-18 Hornet fighter planes whose thundering jets disturb the peace over the beach (the "sound of freedom" to patriotic locals). The only way for us civilians to see them up close is on a **Naval Air Station Oceana Tour** offered by Hampton Roads Transit (© 757/222-6100; www.hrtransit.org). The tours depart from the HRT kiosk at Atlantic Avenue and 24th Street during the summer, Monday to Friday at 9:30 and 11:30 am, Saturday and Sunday at 9:30am. Fares are $7.50 for adults, $5 for seniors, children under 12, and disabled persons. You will need a picture ID to get on the base.

Across the road, the Jamestown colonists' **First Landing Site** is marked by a cross and plaque where they "set up a Crosse at Chesapeake Bay and named that place Cape Henry" for Henry, Prince of Wales. Also here are a monumental relief map showing the French and British naval engagement off Cape Henry during the Revolutionary War and a statue of the French commander. Now known as the **Battle of the Capes,** this decisive battle effectively trapped Cornwallis at Yorktown and helped end British dominion in America.

Note: This is all part of the U.S. Army's Fort Story, so you'll need a photo ID to get a permit allowing access to the fort's historic area.

583 Atlantic Ave. (in Fort Story). © 757/422-9421. www.apva.org. Admission $2 adults, $1 seniors and students. Mar 16–Oct 31 daily 10am–5pm; Nov 1–Mar 15 daily 10am–4pm. Closed Thanksgiving and Dec 5–Jan 4.

Old Coast Guard Station Museum and Gift Shop 👤 In the heart of the oceanfront resort area, this small museum is housed in the white-clapboard building constructed in 1903 as a life-saving station. Its exhibits recall rescue missions and shipwrecks along the coast. You can see it all in 30 minutes. An excellent gift shop carries clocks, drawings, books, and other things nautical.

24th St. and Atlantic Ave. © 757/422-1587. www.oldcoastguardstation.com. Admission $3 adults, $2.50 seniors, $1 children 6–18, free for children 5 and under. Summer Mon–Sat 10am–5pm; Sun noon–5pm; closed Mon in off season. Closed New Year's Day, Thanksgiving, Christmas, and New Year's Eve.

Virginia Marine Science Museum ★★★ *Kids* This entertaining, educational facility focusing on Virginia's marine environment is a wonderful place to take the kids, especially on a rainy day. It's 45 acres are beside Owls Creek salt marsh, a wildlife habitat in its own right. You can easily spend half a day here, a full day to see—and learn—it all. Plan to spend at least half of your time in the main building, where touch tanks will fascinate you and the kids (bet you don't know a horseshoe crab's mouth feels like a toothbrush). Rays willingly swim over in one tank to have their leathery hides petted. Kids will love playing with the switches and dials in a dark room designed like a submarine, complete with sonar "pings." The sub looks out into one of several room-size aquariums holding a myriad of sea turtles, sharks, rays, and other species found in Virginia waters.

As you leave the main building, take a look at the salt marsh room, which will prepare you for a .3-mile nature hike along the creek. There's an observation tower out here, from which you might see some of the wild animals living on an island across the creek. The boardwalk nature trail leads to the smaller Owl Creek Marsh Pavilion, were river otters play in an outdoor tank and more than 50 species of birds fly about an aviary (the big noisy birds passing overhead are fighters taking off and landing at nearby Oceana Naval Air Station). It also houses the fascinating "Macro Marsh" display in which everything is enlarged 10 times normal size to give you a crab's eye view of the world.

The Museum Trolley stops at both buildings, so you can get on at the pavilion; otherwise, you'll have to walk back to your car outside the main building.

717 General Booth Blvd. (southwest of Rudee Inlet). © 757/425-FISH. www.vmsm.com. Admission $11 adults, $9.95 seniors, $6.95 children 4–11, free for children 3 and under. IMAX tickets $7.25 adults, $6.25 children 4–11. Combination museum-IMAX tickets $16 adults, $15 seniors, $12 children 4–11. Daily 9am–5pm (with extended summer hours). Closed Thanksgiving and Christmas.

HISTORIC HOMES

While the beachfront resort area is a modern development, settlers carved out inland homesteads and plantations starting in the 1600s. Dating to circa 1680 and 1725, respectively, the Adam Thoroughgood and Lynnhaven houses are interesting because they were both built in the fashion of English farm cottages of Elizabethan times, 150 years before the Georgian architecture prevalent elsewhere in colonial Virginia. Allow half a day to see them all, including driving times.

Adam Thoroughgood House ⓧ   One of the oldest homes in Virginia and the most interesting of the trio, this medieval English-style cottage sits on 4½ acres of lawn and garden overlooking the Lynnhaven River. It was built around 1680 by one of Adam Thoroughgood's grandsons (historians believe its namesake didn't live in the house). The interior has exposed wood beams and whitewashed walls, and though the furnishings did not belong to the Thoroughgoods, they are original to the period and reflect the family's English ancestry.

1636 Parish Rd. (at Thoroughgood Lane). © 757/460-0007. Admission $4 adults, $4 seniors, $3 children 13–18, $2 children 6–12, free for children 5 and under. Tues–Sat 10am–4:30pm; Sun 1–4:30pm. Mandatory 30-min. tours available on demand (last tour 4:30pm). From oceanfront, take I-264 west to Exit 3, go north on Independence Blvd. (Va. 225), turn right on Pleasure House Rd., right on Thoroughgood Sq., left on Thoroughgood Dr., follow the very small signs to house at Parish Rd.

Francis Land House   Built as a plantation manor in the mid–18th century (now beside one of the region's busiest highways), this Georgian-style brick house is a restoration work in progress. Some rooms are furnished with antiques and reproductions. The highlights here are 7 acres of herb, vegetable and pleasure gardens and a .1-mile wetlands nature trail.

3131 Virginia Beach Blvd. (just west of Kings Grant Rd.). © 757/431-4000. Admission $4 adults, $4 seniors, $3 children 13–18, $2 children 6–12, free for children 5 and under. Tues–Sat 9am–5pm; Sun noon–5pm. Mandatory 30-min. house tours depart on demand (last tour 4:30pm).

Lynnhaven House   Built in 1725, this medieval cottage still doesn't have running water or electricity. When it took the house over in 1971, the Association for the Preservation of Virginia Antiquities stripped away plaster and discovered the Champford ceiling beams to be in original condition (note the chalk marks carpenters made in 1725). Tours led by costumed docents explain the house and

---

Tips **Dolphin- & Whale-Watching**

The Virginia Marine Science Museum offers offshore **dolphin-watching cruises** (daily June–Sept, Fri and Sat in spring and fall), **whale-watching cruises** (daily in late Dec, Wed–Sun Jan to mid-March), and **sea life collecting trips** (noon Wed June–Aug). They cost $12 to $15 for adults, $10 to $13 for children under 12. The cruises leave from Rudee Inlet, and reservations are required (© 757/437-BOAT).

interpret colonial lifestyles. We moderns won't find Lynnhaven oysters as gigantic as the shells excavated from the trash pit and displayed in the kitchen.

4405 Wishart Rd. (off Independence Blvd.). © **757/460-1688**. www.apva.org. Admission $4 adults, $2 students 5–16, free for children 4 and under. May–Oct, Tues–Sun noon–4pm. Mandatory 45-min. tours depart on demand. From the beach, take I-264 west to Exit 3, then north on Independence Blvd. (Va. 225), right on Wishart Rd.

WHERE TO STAY

The hotels and B&Bs listed below are just the tip of the iceberg in Virginia Beach, which has more than 11,000 hotel rooms. Even with that many places to stay, you should reserve as far in advance as possible for the busy summer season, from mid-June through Labor Day weekend. Room rates can more than double then, so both summer and off-season rates are listed below. Late spring and early fall are good times to visit; both have warm weather and lower rates.

Most of the major chains are represented here. There are three high-rise Holiday Inns on the oceanfront, including the **Holiday Inn Sunspree Resort on the Ocean,** Atlantic Avenue at 39th Street (© **800/HOLIDAY** or 757/428-1711), which is away from the crowds at the north end of the boardwalk. Nearby is the **Sheraton Oceanfront Hotel,** at 36th Street (© **800/325-3535** or 757/425-9000), which offers whirlpool tubs in some rooms. Even more removed from the resort scene is the **Ramada Plaza Resort,** sitting by itself at Atlantic Avenue and 57th Street (© **800/365-3032** or 757/428-7025). If you're on a tight budget, there are two **EconoLodges** on the oceanfront, at 21st Street (© **800/999-3360** or 757/428-2403) and 28th Street (© **800/228-3970** or 757/428-3970).

HOTELS

Belvedere Resort Motel ★★ *Value* This five-story building is the crown jewel of the less expensive, family-operated oceanfront hotels here. It justifiably attracts lots of repeat guests, so book early. Like the nearby Courtyard by Marriott Oceanfront North (see below), it's far enough north to avoid the rowdy crowds. The motel-style rooms have screen doors that swing open to balconies facing the ocean. The combo tub-shower bathrooms are small, but compensate with separate sinks and vanities. A few rooms have king-size beds (most have two doubles). The 10 units on the ends of the building are somewhat larger and have cooking facilities. There's a small swimming pool, sun deck, and the Belvedere Coffee Shop (see "Where to Dine," below). Guests also get free use of bicycles.

Oceanfront at 36th St. (P.O. Box 451), Virginia Beach, VA 23458. © **800/425-0612** or 757/425-0612. Fax 757/425-1397. 50 units. Summer $120–$130 double; off season $54–$95 double. AE, MC, V. Closed late-Oct to Mar. **Amenities:** Coffee shop; outdoor pool; free bicycles; limited room service. *In room:* A/C, TV, kitchen (efficiencies only), fridge, coffeemaker (efficiencies only).

The Breakers Resort Inn Another reasonably priced, family-operated oceanfront hotel, The Breakers occupies a white boxlike nine-story building. Its rooms are comfortably furnished with contemporary pieces. All have oceanfront balconies; some rooms with king-size beds contain hot tubs. Efficiency apartments have a bedroom with two double beds, a living room with a Murphy bed, and a full kitchen. Additional amenities include free bicycles. The on-site cafe serves breakfast and lunch.

1503 Atlantic Ave. (oceanfront at 16th St.), Virginia Beach, VA 23451. © **800/237-7532** or 757/428-1821. Fax 757/422-9602. www.breakersresort.com. 57 units. Summer $160–$225 double; off season $50–$210 double. Packages available. AE, DC, DISC, MC, V. **Amenities:** Restaurant (breakfast and lunch); heated outdoor pool; free bicycles; coin-op washers and dryers. *In room:* A/C, TV, dataport, kitchen (efficiencies only), fridge, coffeemaker, iron.

⌐Tips Finding the Best Room

With so many hotels offering so many rooms, choosing the right one can be a daunting task. The Virginia Beach visitor information center (see "Essentials," earlier) maintains a **reservations service** (© **800/VA-BEACH**) that will help you find accommodations in any price range. The center's annual "Vacation Guide" lists all the local hotels and their current rates. It also distributes an annual accommodations directory published by the **Virginia Beach Hotel/Motel Association** (www.va-beach-hotels.com). The association's website has brochures for many of the hotels, most of which give their current room rates.

Cavalier Hotel ⌐★   This venerable resort actually consists of two hotels—the original Cavalier built in 1927 on the hill across Atlantic Avenue from the beach, and the Cavalier on the ocean, which opened in 1973. Although it's not directly on the beach, and it's open only during the summer, the original building has all the charm. Its enclosed verandah with white wicker furnishings, potted plants, and great ocean views evoke images of the days when F. Scott and Zelda Fitzgerald danced here and lunches were black-tie. Its recently renovated guest rooms have Williamsburg-quality Chippendale reproductions, colonial-print fabrics, gilt-framed artwork, and museum-quality decorative objects. Some feature European-style baths with black and white tile, pedestal sinks, whirlpools, lighted makeup mirrors, and bidets. The heated indoor Olympic-size pool is magnificently tiled and illuminated by a skylight. Open all year, the newer beachside building has nicely decorated contemporary-style rooms, all with oceanfront balconies.

Oceanfront at 42nd Street, Virginia Beach, VA 23451. © **800/446-8199** or 757/425-8555. Fax 757/428-7957. www.cavalierhotel.com. 425 units, including 25 suites. Summer $140–$315 double; off season $85–$205 double. Weekend and other packages available. AE, DC, DISC, MC, V. Parking $5. **Amenities:** 5 restaurants; 3 bars; 1 indoor pool; 2 outdoor pools (full-size, children's); 3 tennis courts; exercise room; watersports equipment/rentals; bike rentals; children's programs; concierge; activities desk; business center; limited room service; babysitting; laundry service; concierge-level rooms. *In room:* A/C, TV, dataport, minibar (suites and oceanfront rooms), coffeemaker, iron.

Comfort Inn-Virginia Beach ⌐Value   One way to save money here, especially during the high summer season, is to stay a block off the beach, as opposed to on the oceanfront. This seven-story Comfort Inn is the best choice around in that respect. It offers a host of free amenities—a bountiful full breakfast buffet, local phone calls, daily newspaper delivery, high-speed Internet access in every room, and use of bicycles (albeit for an hour at a time)—which make it a very good value, especially for families. You won't have a balcony, since interior corridors lead to the well-equipped if moderately spacious rooms, all of which have microwave ovens as well as refrigerators.

2800 Pacific Ave. (at 28th St.), Virginia Beach, VA 23451. © **800/441-0684** or 757/428-2203. Fax 757/422-6043. www.choicehotels.com. 137 units. Summer $109–$189; off season $59–$109. Rates include full breakfast. AE, DC, DISC, MC, V. **Amenities:** Heated indoor and outdoor pools; Jacuzzi; exercise room; free bikes; game room; coin-op washers and dryers. *In room:* A/C, TV, dataport, fridge, coffeemaker, iron, safe, microwave.

Courtyard by Marriott Oceanfront North ⌐★★ ⌐Value   This 11-story oceanfront hotel, one of the first Courtyards designed as much as a resort as for business travelers, opened on the oceanfront in 2002 at 37th Street. Making this a good family choice is the oceanfront's largest outdoor pool, with waterfalls, bridges, a lifeguard on duty, and its own bar. The beach substitutes for an actual courtyard here, and big window walls look out to the boardwalk from the plush lobby and bright, casual dining room, which provides good hotel fare for breakfast, lunch, and dinner (you can dine outside in fine weather). Marriott's standard furniture prevails in the spacious guest quarters, all of which have balconies overlooking the ocean. Ten units have whirlpool tubs. The eight huge suites have bedrooms and living rooms, which come equipped with wet bars, microwave ovens, and refrigerators. A small indoor pool and a fitness room look out to the beach.

Its older sister, the **Courtyard by Marriott Oceanfront South,** 2501 Atlantic Ave., at 25th Street, (© **800/321-2211** or 757/491-6222; www.courtyardocean front.com), lacks an outdoor pool, but, otherwise, is identical.

3737 Atlantic Ave. (oceanfront at 37th St.), Virginia Beach, VA 23451. © **800/321-2211** or 757/437-0098. Fax 757/437-4272. www.courtyardoceanfrontnorth.com. 160 units. Summer $209–$329; off season $99–$189. AE, DC, DISC, MC, V. **Amenities:** Restaurant; bar; outdoor and indoor pools; exercise room; Jacuzzi; limited room service, coin-op washers and dryers. *In room:* A/C, TV, dataport, fridge, coffeemaker, iron.

New Castle Hotel   Situated beside the Atlantic Wildfowl Heritage Museum (see "The Top Attractions," above), the 10-story, family-operated New Castle offers the most unusual mix of rooms on the beach, ranging from standard motel units to romantic deluxe models with canopy beds, gas fireplaces, his-and-her shower heads, and wooden Venetian blinds to keep passersby from watching you frolic in big whirlpool tubs. All units have balconies, refrigerators, microwave ovens, and spa tubs. Guests get free bicycles in summer. The seasonal **Cabana Cafe** to one side offers reasonably priced meals under a big, beachside awning.

1203 Atlantic Ave. (oceanfront at 12th St.), Virginia Beach, VA 23451. © **800/346-3176** or 757/428-3981. www.newcastlehotelvb.com. Fax 757/491-4394. 83 units. Summer $199–$229; off season $49–$179. Off-season rates include continental breakfast. Packages available. AE, DC, DISC, MC, V. **Amenities:** Restaurant; indoor pool; exercise room; concierge; limited room service; coin-op washers and dryers. *In room:* A/C, TV, kitchen (2 units), fridge, iron, safe, microwave.

BED & BREAKFASTS

Angie's Guest Cottage and HI-USA Hostel ★ *Value*   You'll find a delightful mix of American and international folks at innkeeper Barbara Yates's quaint white-clapboard cottage. a block from the beach. It was built in 1918 as family housing for the nearby life-saving station, now the Old Coast Guard Station Museum and Gift Shop (see "Top Attractions," above). An addicted traveler herself, Barbara keeps her guest rooms spotlessly clean and freshly painted. The cottage is operated as a B&B, with guests being treated to breakfast. The front room upstairs is the choice, with a door opening to a deck (other guests can climb up there before 9pm, after which it's all yours). There's also a large family room with private access to the rear. Next door is The Lacy Duplex, with two kitchen-equipped units with porch and deck. Also here, one of Virginia's few official Hostelling International hostels offers men's, women's, and co-ed dorm rooms plus a communal kitchen. If space is available, HI members can rent private rooms at hostel rates. Barbara rents linens to her dorm guests. You had better check in by 9pm or you'll be sleeping on the porch.

302 24th St. (between Pacific and Arctic aves.), Virginia Beach, VA 23451. © **757/428-4690.** www.angies cottage.com. 8 units (3 with bathroom), 34 dorm beds. $66–$132 double room; $12–$18 dorm bed. Rates for rooms include continental breakfast. No credit cards. Free on-street parking with $20 refundable deposit for permit. *In room:* A/C, TV (duplex units only), fridge (upstairs units only), kitchen (duplex units only).

Barclay Cottage ⭐ This two-story, white-clapboard Victorian with wrap-around verandas is *very* coastal Southern, with rocking chairs on the porches and green shutters trimming tall windows hung with lace curtains. It was used as a boarding house and school for many years before being converted into a B&B. The guest rooms are adorned with Victorian pieces, including feather beds. Innkeepers Stephen and Marie-Louise LaFonde serve a full family-style breakfast in the lounge promptly at 9am. The heart of the oceanfront is a 2-block walk away.

400 16th St. (at Arctic Ave.), Virginia Beach, VA 23451. ℂ 757/422-1956. www.barclaycottage.com. 5 units (3 with bathroom). $96–$130 double. Rates include full breakfast. AE, MC, V. *In room:* A/C.

WHERE TO DINE

Just as Virginia Beach has thousands of hotel rooms, so it also has hundreds of restaurants, especially establishments serving up bountiful harvests of seafood. We've picked a few of the best to get you started.

For breakfast by the sea, head for the **Belvedere Coffee Shop,** an old-fashioned, greasy-spoon diner at the Belvedere Motel, Oceanfront at 36th Street (ℂ 757/425-1397). It's small, noisy, and busy, with cooks scurrying around the stove behind the counter, but big windows look right out on the boardwalk, beach, and surf. You'll have local company for eggs, omelets, pancakes, made-to-order sandwiches, salads, and a few inexpensive hot meals such as crab cakes. Prices range from $3 to $9, but don't plan to pay by credit card. It's open daily in summer from 7am to 3pm, off season, daily from 7:30am to 2:30pm.

For more refined breakfast, lunch and dinner fare, there's a branch of Norfolk's **Baker's Crust** (ℂ 757/422-6703) in the North Hilltop Shopping Center on Laskin Road 2 miles from the oceanfront. See "Where to Dine" in section 1, earlier.

I have organized the restaurants by those at or near the oceanfront, and those at or near Lynnhaven Inlet, on Shore Drive (U.S. 60) about a 15-minute drive from the beach.

AT THE OCEANFRONT

The oceanfront strip has scores of restaurants, many open only during the summer season when they cater to masses of tourists. Of those actually on the beach, best of the lot is **MahiMahi's Seafood Restaurant and Sushi Saloon,** in the Ramada on the Beach, 6th Street at the Oceanfront (ℂ 757/437-8030). It has live entertainment on the deck during summer.

The following establishments are slightly removed from the beach. They are open year-round and thus have thriving local trades.

Coyote Cafe & Cantina ⭐⭐ SOUTHWESTERN The best Southwestern-style food in Virginia is influenced by Mexico, but here the beef and chicken in the fajitas are grilled over mesquite and flamed with tequila. The menu offers lots more, all of it served in gargantuan portions. The front dining room is refined, with long benches down the walls, overstuffed booths in the center, and eclectic art on the walls. The back room is more like a Texas roadhouse, with wooden tables and chairs, a big bar on one side, and open kitchen in the rear. The Coyote is in a shopping center (look for Eckerd's Drugs) on the north side of Laskin Road about a mile from the oceanfront.

972 Laskin Rd. (in Linkhorn Shops, 1 block east of Birdneck Rd.). ℂ 757/425-8705. Reservations strongly recommended for dinner. Lunch $6–$9; main courses $12–$19. AE, DC, DISC, MC, V. Sun–Thurs 11:30am–2:30pm and 5–10:30pm; Fri 11:30am–2:30pm and 5–midnight; Sat 5pm–midnight; Sun 5–10:30pm.

The Jewish Mother DELI/AMERICAN The Jewish Mother has been a fixture on the Virginia Beach dining and nightlife scene since 1975. The decor is charmingly dilapidated, like a down-at-the-heels bar. In fact, it's now better known for nightly entertainment than for its deli sandwiches, oversize egg and omelet platters, fresh salads, bagels, blintzes, and potato latkes. Live music performances run the gamut from rock and blues to country, bluegrass, and zydeco. Depending on the performers, there may be a cover, especially on weekends. A huge bar offers a wide selection of microbrews on tap.

3108 Pacific Ave. (between Laskin Rd. and 32nd St.). 🅒 **757/422-5430.** Reservations not accepted. Breakfast $3–$7; sandwiches $4.50–$7; main courses $9–$13. AE, DISC, MC, V. Daily 8:30am–3am.

La Bella Italia Cafe & Trattoria 🟊 *Value* ITALIAN On Laskin Road near the Coyote Cafe & Cantina (see above), the deli is an excellent place to pick up sandwiches or Italian breads, pastries, and cookies for a day at the beach. After dark, you had best reserve a table, for a mesquite-fired oven produces the area's best pizzas, and locals flock here for bowls of homemade pasta. You'll recognize a few Southern Italian favorites such as spaghetti Bolognese, but others are more creative. For starters, try the bruschetta, fried calamari, or in summer when the tomatoes are ripe and sweet, the caprese salad with homemade mozzarella.

1065 Laskin Rd. (1 block east of Birdneck Rd.). 🅒 **757/422-8536.** Reservations highly recommended for dinner. Sandwiches $6–$8; pizza $7–$8; main courses $10–$16. AE, MC, V. Mon–Thurs 11:30am–2:30pm and 5–10pm; Fri–Sat 11:30am–2:30pm and 5–11pm.

Rudee's on the Inlet 🟊 SEAFOOD/STEAKS Inside this popular restaurant, occupying a replica of an old Coast Guard station, is dark and cozy, with big louvered windows overlooking Rudee Inlet. But that's not where you want to dine in good weather. Instead, walk across the parking lot to the marina-side sun deck and grab one of the gliding booths (that's right: you, the booth, and its green canopy actually slide back and forth). They serve a full menu out here until 6pm, then light fare, for the deck is a popular after-work watering hole for the locals. Although steaks and other fare are offered, seafood is the highlight. Everything is prepared to order, so kick back and enjoy the waterside setting while the chef fries or broils your fish, shrimp, scallops, above-average crab cakes, and oysters (best when they are being harvested during months spelled with an "r": Sept–Apr). Many fresh-off-the-boat items are market priced.

277 Mediterranean Ave. (at Rudee Inlet). 🅒 **757/425-1777.** Reservations not accepted but call ahead for preferred seating. Sandwiches $6–$11; main courses $12–$24. AE, DC, DISC, MC, V. Mon–Thurs 11am–midnight; Fri–Sat 11am–12:30am; Sun 10am–11pm.

AT LYNNHAVEN INLET

The restaurants listed below are on the eastern side of the Lynnhaven Inlet Bridge. From the resort area, follow Shore Drive (U.S. 60). Local residents avoid

---

Tips **"Da Bomb" for Sunsets, Ships & Hard Bodies**

The Gazebo at the Beach, at the **Duck-In & Gazebo,** is far and away the best place in this area to sip a cold drink and watch the sun set over the bay. During the day, aircraft carriers steam by on their way in and out of Hampton Roads, and at night, twinkling lights line the 17-mile-long Chesapeake Bay Bridge-Tunnel. If that's not enough to get your eyes working overtime, hard-bodies play volleyball tournaments on the beach here on summer weekends.

the oceanfront like the plague during summer and come here instead for their beaching, boating, and waterside dining.

Duck-In & Gazebo *(Value)* SEAFOOD   Starting as a shack on the beach, the Duck-In has been a local favorite since 1952. What draws them here is not so much the food as the bayside Gazebo at the Beach, a big open-air, tin-roofed gazebo sitting on stilts over a lovely white sand beach with a gorgeous view of the Chesapeake Bay Bridge-Tunnel. The gazebo offers a limited menu, since it's mostly a watering hole, especially after work and on summer weekends, when this becomes the most popular local beach hangout of all. (Happy hour takes place Mon–Thurs 4–7pm, but go to the bar inside the restaurant, where draft beers are even less expensive.) A DJ spins tunes for dancing Saturday night and Sunday afternoon. As for the food, it's mostly down-home fried or broiled seafood, but you can dine outside. If you're starved, the nightly seafood and Sunday brunch buffets are a good value.

3324 Shore Dr. (at Ocean Shore Ave.). © 757/481-0201. Reservations not accepted. Sandwiches $6–$9; main courses $10–$22; seafood buffet $22 adults, $12 children 5–10, $7 children 4 and under. Sun brunch buffet $8 adults, $5 children 5–10. Free for kids under 5. AE, DISC, MC, V. Mon–Thurs 11am–10pm; Fri–Sat 11am–midnight; Sun 9am–11pm. Gazebo open Apr–Oct. From the resort area, take Shore Dr. (U.S. 60) west to traffic signal before Lynnhaven Inlet Bridge; turn right on Ocean Shore Ave. and bear left. Restaurant is on east side of Lynnhaven Inlet.

Lynnhaven Fish House *(★★)* SEAFOOD/STEAKS   Perched over the beach on Lynnhaven Fishing Pier, this traditional Chesapeake Bay fish house has fabulous bay views from its wraparound windows. They don't accept reservations, so come early, grab a drink, and watch the setting sun cast its colors over the bay. The dinner menu starts off with oysters Rockefeller and selections from the chowder pots. Fresh fish of the day is offered broiled, grilled, steamed, or poached, accompanied by one of nine sauces. You won't go away hungry, since all dinners come with a choice of "smashed" potato (a lumpy but light Southern rendition of mashed spuds), sweet potato, steak fries, or black beans and rice; coleslaw, house salad, or Caesar salad; and corn muffins and hush puppies. A cafe to the side has outdoor dining beside the fishing pier.

2350 Starfish Rd. (on Lynnhaven Fishing Pier). © 757/481-0003. Reservations not accepted. Main courses $14–$24. AE, DC, DISC, MC, V. Daily 11:30am–10:30pm. Closed Thanksgiving and Christmas. From the resort area, take Shore Dr. (U.S. 60) west; turn right on Starfish Rd. to Lynnhaven Fishing Pier, east of Lynnhaven Inlet Bridge.

VIRGINIA BEACH AFTER DARK

The prime performing arts venue is the 20,000-seat, open-air **Verizon Wireless Virginia Beach Amphitheater,** inland at Princess Anne and Dam Neck roads (© 757/368-8888 for schedule, Ticketmaster at © 757/671-8100 for tickets, 757/368-3000 for trolley info; www.verizonwirelessamphitheater.com/vabeach). Big-name singers and bands appear here as well as more highbrow acts like the Virginia Symphony. About 7,500 seats are under cover, with some 12,500 spaces out on the lawn. Big TV screens and a state-of-the-art sound system let everyone see and hear what's going on. The season runs from April through October.

During summer there are frequent outdoor concerts on stages at 7th, 17th, and 24th streets along the Boardwalk (the visitor information center can tell you when and where). The biggest is the annual **Verizon Wireless American Music Festival,** over Labor Day weekend on the beach at 5th Street. You might catch the Beach Boys or Randy Travis on one stage, the Average White Band or Wilson Pickett on another. Contact the visitor center or call © 757/491-7866.

Hotels and restaurants all along the beach have live music for nighttime dancing during the summer. Just follow your ears along the Boardwalk—but remember, some pubs along Atlantic Avenue can get rough late at night.

3 Chincoteague & Assateague Islands ⋆⋆⋆

83 miles N of Virginia Beach and Norfolk; 185 miles SE of Washington, D.C.

Miles of deserted beaches, waterways, abundant wildlife, and down-home cooking and hospitality welcome visitors to Virginia's tranquil Eastern Shore. The Atlantic Ocean and the Chesapeake Bay border the state's 70-mile long end of the Delmarva Peninsula—so-called because it's shared by **Delaware, Maryland,** and **Virginia**. The ocean side is shielded by a string of barrier islands, most of them preserved in their natural state by the Nature Conservancy, making them impossible to visit without a boat. But you can visit two of Virginia's jewels: Chincoteague and Assateague Islands.

Chincoteague sits just south of the Maryland line and is surrounded by bays full of flounder, oysters beds, and clam shoals. Settled by the English in the late 1600s, it is famous as the setting of Marguerite Henry's children's book, *Misty of Chincoteague.* Later made into a film, the book aroused wide interest in the annual pony penning and swim on the last Wednesday in July, when pony-size wild horses are rounded up on Assateague Island, forced to swim across to Chincoteague, and sold to benefit the local fire department.

While the town of Chincoteague has its share of tourist facilities, it retains much of its old fishing-village charm. Rickety old piers still jut out into the water next to modern motels, and watermen in workboats still outnumber tourists on jet skis. Few nationally recognized chain names are on this quaint island.

A short bridge away, wonderful Assateague Island is the site of the Chincoteague National Wildlife Refuge and Assateague Island National Seashore, which together protect the wild ponies' habitat and 37 miles of pristine beach. Assateague is on the main Atlantic Flyway, and its population of both migratory and resident birds is simply astounding.

ESSENTIALS
VISITOR INFORMATION

The **Chincoteague Chamber of Commerce,** 6733 Maddox Blvd., Chincoteague Island, VA 23336 (© **757/336-6161;** fax 757/336-1241; www.chincoteague chamber.com), operates a visitor center in the traffic circle on Maddox Boulevard, about a mile before the Assateague Bridge. It's open Monday through Saturday from 9am to 4:30pm.

There's a **Virginia Welcome Center** on U.S. 301 just south of the Maryland state line. It's open daily from 9am to 5pm.

GETTING THERE

There is neither airport nor public transportation on the Eastern Shore, so you'll need a **car.** From Norfolk and Virginia Beach take U.S. 13 north across the Chesapeake Bay Bridge-Tunnel, a beautiful 17½-mile drive across and under the bay ($10 toll per car). U.S. 13 runs north-south down the center of the Eastern Shore. To reach Chincoteague, turn east on Va. 175, about 65 miles north of the bridge-tunnel and 5 miles south of the Maryland line.

The Eastern Shore

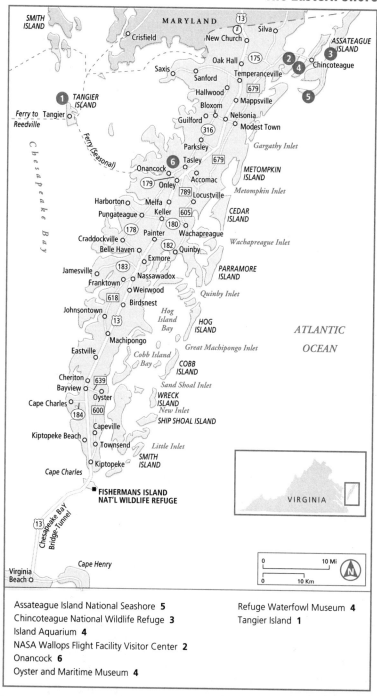

Assateague Island National Seashore **5**
Chincoteague National Wildlife Refuge **3**
Island Aquarium **4**
NASA Wallops Flight Facility Visitor Center **2**
Onancock **6**
Oyster and Maritime Museum **4**

Refuge Waterfowl Museum **4**
Tangier Island **1**

AREA LAYOUT

Va. 175 crosses the Chincoteague Channel and dead-ends in the old village at **Main Street,** which runs north-south along the island's western shore. Turn right at the stoplight to reach the motels, marinas, and bait shops that line Main Street south of the bridge. Turn left at the light for **Maddox Boulevard,** which heads east from Main Street 9 blocks north of the bridge and goes to Assateague Island. Maddox Boulevard is Chincoteague's prime commercial strip, with a plethora of shops, restaurants, and motels. **Church Street** goes east 2 blocks north of the bridge and turns into **East Side Drive,** which runs along the island's eastern shore. **Ridge Road** and **Chicken City Road** (yes, it's really named Chicken City) together run north-south down the middle of the island. On Assateague, there's only one road other than a wildlife drive, and it goes directly to the beach.

GETTING AROUND

These flat islands are great for biking, and you can rent bicycles at several shops on Maddox Boulevard. **The Bike Depot,** at the Refuge Motor Inn (© 757/ 336-5511), and **Jus' Bikes,** 6727 Maddox Blvd. (© 757/336-6700), are closest to Assateague Island. Rates start at $3 an hour, $10 a day.

ASSATEAGUE ISLAND 🐾🐾🐾

A barrier island protecting Chincoteague Island from the Atlantic, Assateague Island has over 37 miles of pristine **beaches** on its east coast, the northern 25 miles of which are in Maryland. The island is administered by two federal agencies, with the highest degree of protection afforded to wildlife on the Virginia side.

Bird-watchers know Assateague Island as a prime Atlantic Flyway habitat where sightings of peregrine falcons, snow geese, great blue heron, and snowy egrets have been made. The annual Waterfowl Week, generally held around Thanksgiving, takes place when a large number of migratory birds use the refuge.

The famous **wild horses**—called "ponies"—have lived on Assateague since the 17th century. Legend says their ancestors swam ashore from a shipwrecked Spanish galleon, but most likely English settlers put the first horses on Assateague, which formed a natural corral. Separated by a fence from their cousins in Maryland, the Virginia horses are owned by the Chincoteague Volunteer Fire Department, which rounds them up and sells the foals at auction on the last Wednesday in July.

THE WILDLIFE REFUGE

You first enter the **Chincoteague National Wildlife Refuge,** which is open May 1 to September 30, daily from 5am to 10pm; April and October, daily from 6am to 8pm; November 1 to March 31, daily from 6am to 6pm. Owned and managed by the U.S. Fish and Wildlife Service, the refuge accepts the annual

---

Kids Pony Rides

You can't bring a child to Chincoteague without letting him or her ride a pony—perhaps one of Misty's descendants—at the **Chincoteague Pony Centre,** 6417 Carriage Dr. (© 757/336-2776; www.chincoteague.com/pony centre), off Chicken City Road south of Maddox Boulevard. This small-scale equestrian center is open daily from 9am to 9pm, with pony rides ($5) from 3:30 to 6pm and a pony show at 8pm daily except Sunday during summer.

> ## *Tips* Assateague's Cars Quota
>
> It's best to go to the Chincoteague National Wildlife Refuge's visitor cen-
> ter early in the morning for two reasons. First, you can find out what
> guided walks and other interpretive programs are scheduled. Second, and
> most important, only a certain number of vehicles are allowed on
> Assateague Island at any one time. When that number is reached, park
> rangers stop traffic before the bridge to the island and allow one vehicle
> to cross only when another departs.

entrance passes issued at national parks; otherwise, admission is $10 per car for
1 week, free for pedestrians and bikers.

The refuge's visitor center (© **757/336-3696**), on the left, ¼-mile east of the
bridge, shows a video about the refuge on request and is the departure point for
the paved **Wildlife Drive,** which runs through the marshes and is the best place
to see the horses. This one-lane, one-way road is open to pedestrians and bicyclists all day, to motorized vehicles after 3pm. The visitor center is open daily
from 9am to 5pm except New Year's Day and Christmas.

An excellent way to see the multitudinous wildlife—minus mosquitoes—is to
take a **Wildlife Tour** in an air-conditioned bus. The 1¾-hour narrated rides
depart the visitor center daily at 10am, 1 and 4pm from Memorial Day weekend through Labor Day and cost $12 for adults, $8 for children 2 to 12. Buy
your tickets at the visitor center.

Built in 1867, the **Assateague Island Lighthouse,** near the visitor center, is
open to the public 1 weekend each month during the summer. Call the local
U.S. Coast Guard station (© **757/336-2822**) for the schedule.

For **information** about the refuge and visitor-center seasons and programs,
contact the Refuge Manager, Chincoteague National Wildlife Refuge, P.O. Box
62, Chincoteague Island, VA 23336 (© **757/336-6122;** http://chinco.fws.gov).

THE NATIONAL SEASHORE

The beach itself is in the **Assateague Island National Seashore,** operated by the
National Park Service. You'll find a visitor center, bathhouses, and summertime
lifeguards. In addition to swimming and sunning, activities at the beach include
shell collecting (most productive at the tip of the Tom's Cove spit of land, on the
island's southern tip) and hiking. Biking is allowed on the paved roads and along
a bike path beside the road from Chincoteague to the refuge visitor center, then
along Wildlife Drive to the **Tom's Cove Visitor Center,** which is open daily
from 9am to 6pm in summer, 9am to 5pm spring and autumn, 9am to 4pm in
winter. Closed Thanksgiving and Christmas.

Several **regulations** apply. Pets and alcoholic beverages are prohibited, even in
your vehicle. In-line skating is not allowed, and off-road vehicles are permitted
only at Tom's Cove. Surf fishing with a Virginia state license is allowed except
on the lifeguard beach at Tom's Cove. Climbing and digging in the sand dunes
is illegal. No overnight sleeping is allowed anywhere (backcountry camping is
permitted on the Maryland end, a 12-mile hike from the Virginia-side visitor
centers). And finally, thou shalt not feed the horses.

For information about the national seashore, contact the Superintendent,
Assateague Island National Seashore, 8586 Beach Rd. (P.O. Box 38), Chincoteague Island, VA 23336 (© **757/336-6577;** www.nps.gov/asis).

A Cruise to Tangier Island

The genteel town of Onancock, off U.S. 13 south of Chincoteague, is the departure point for cruises to quaint **Tangier Island** ✶✶✶ and its picturesque village of 650 souls out in the Chesapeake Bay. There are few cars on Tangier's narrow lanes, appropriate on this unspoiled island, discovered by Capt. John Smith in 1608 and permanently settled in 1686. In fact, the local accent hearkens back to the Elizabethan English of their ancestors. Out here, when someone says "Hoi toide onda soun soide tonoit," they mean there's high tide on the sound side tonight.

This is no glitzy resort. Entertainment consists of poking around the island, seeing some wildlife with **RB's Island Nature Cruises** (© 757/891-2240), and watching the mail boat arrive at 1:15pm—Tangier's biggest daily event. That's not say that tourism hasn't made some inroads in recent years. Local citizens now await the ferries to take you on 15-minute island tour by oversized golf cart. It's worth the $3 fare to get an overview of the island. You can rent golf carts and bikes at the wharf, although most of the island is within a 20-minute walk of the dock.

The island also has three restaurants, although you'll want to join the other day-trippers at **Hilda Crockett's Chesapeake House** (© 757/891-2331), where $15.50 will buy an all-you-can-eat (except crab cakes) lunch from mid-April to mid-October. You can stay overnight at Mrs. Crockett's for $90 double, including breakfast and dinner. MasterCard and Visa cards accepted.

Other overnight options include **Shirley's Bay View Inn** (© 757/891-2396; www.tangierisland.net), where owner Shirley Pruitt rents two bedrooms upstairs in her 1904 Victorian home and nine small cottages in motel-style structures flanking her backyard. Shirley charges $75 to $95 double but does not accept credit cards. Or you can opt for the **Sunset Inn Bed & Breakfast** (© 757/891-2535; www.tangierislandsunset. com), where host Grace Brown offers rooms in the main house plus cottages and an apartment. She charges $80 double, including breakfast, and she accepts MasterCard and Visa.

If you elect to stay over, remember that not all units here have a private bathroom, so if that's your preference, make sure to ask for one when you reserve.

Weather permitting, the **Tangier Island Ferry** (© 757/891-2240) leaves Onancock from May 15 to October 15, daily at 10am, returning at 3:30pm. Round-trip fare is $22 for adults, $11 for children 6 to 11, and free for children 5 and under. Reservations are not accepted. You can also get here from Reedville on the Northern Neck (see chapter 5).

Plan to look around Onancock while you're here. The **Hopkins & Bro. General Store** was built in 1842 on Onancock's Town Dock and has been fixed up into the Eastern Shore's largest bait-and-tackle shop. Many retirees and others have settled in Onancock, bringing with them other good restaurants, boutiques and craft shops (search along Market St., the main drag). If you like old houses, visit **Kerr Place** (© 757/787-8012), a stately Federal mansion built in 1799.

OUTDOOR ACTIVITIES

CRUISES   While most visitors head for the beach on Assateague, don't overlook the broad bays and creeks that surround Chincoteague. A good way to get out on them is with **Captain Barry's Back Bay Cruises** ★★ (© **757/336-6508;** www.captainbarry.bigstep.com), which depart Landmark Plaza on Main Street. Barry Frishman moved from upstate New York to Chincoteague and set about learning everything he could about the water and what's in it. Now he shares his knowledge by taking guests out on his pontoon boat for 1½-hour early-morning bird-watching expeditions ($20 per person); 4-hour morning or afternoon "Back Bay expeditions" in search of crabs, fish, shells, and clams ($40 per person); champagne sunset cruises ($30); moonlight excursions ($10); and just plain old "Fun Cruises" in spring and fall ($20). Call for Barry's schedule and reservations, which are required.

Another excellent option is Chincoteague native Mark Colburn's **Assateague Explorer** ★★ (© **866/PONY-SWIM** or 757/990-1795; www.assateagueisland. com/explorer.htm). His 1½-hour Pony Express Nature Tours ($20 per person) go up along the calm backwaters off Assateague in search of ponies and other wildlife to observe. He also has a 3-hour cruise around Chincoteague Island, flounder fishing trips and sunset cruises (all $30 per person). He will also do private fishing and hunting charters off season. Mark's grandfather, by the way, had a role in the movie version of *Misty of Chincoteague.*

FISHING   Before it became a tourist mecca, Chincoteague was a fishing village for centuries—and it still is. Both work and pleasure boats prowl the back bays and ocean for flounder, croaker, spot, kingfish, drum, striped bass, bluefish, and sharks, to name a few species.

You can go flounder fishing with Mark Colburn's *Assateague Explorer* (see "Cruises," above).

You can get to it yourself, either from a rented boat or by throwing your line from a dock. For charter boats, equipment, supplies, free tide tables, and advice, check in at **Barnacle Bill's Bait & Tackle** (© **757/336-5188**) or **Capt. Bob's** (© **757/336-6654**), both on South Main Street.

KAYAKING   The waters around Chincoteague are ideal for sea kayaking, and **Oyster Bay Outfitters,** 6332 Maddox Blvd. (© **888/732-7108** or 757/336-0700; www.oysterbayoutfitters.com), has half- and full-day trips ranging from $40 to $80. The company also rents kayaks for $40 to $50 a day.

MUSEUMS

You'll pass a large airstrip as you drive to Chincoteague on Va. 175, it's part of NASA's **Wallops Flight Facility,** a research and testing center for rockets, balloons, and aircraft. The facility also tracks NASA's spacecraft and satellites, including the space shuttles. Across the highway is the **NASA Visitor Center** (© **757/824-1344;** www.wff.nasa.gov), one of the best places to park the kids on a rainy day. The center's exhibits and entertaining 20-minute film explain the facility's history and role in the space program. Kids will get a kick out of seeing a practice space suit from Apollo 9. Admission is free. The visitor center is open from July 4 to Labor Day, daily from 10am to 4pm; March to June and September to November, Thursday through Monday from 10am to 4pm; winter Monday to Friday 10am to 4pm. The center is 5 miles west of Chincoteague.

On Maddox Boulevard, between the traffic circle and the bridge to Assateague, are two small marine-themed museums. The **Oyster and Maritime**

Museum (© 757/336-6117) tells the area's history and the role played by the vital seafood industry from the 1600s to the present, with examples of marine life (some of them live). The highlight is the original lens from the Assateague Lighthouse, which mariners could see 23 miles offshore from 1865 to 1961. Open Memorial Day to Labor Day, Monday to Saturday 10am to 5pm, Sunday noon to 4pm. Admission is $3 for adults, $1.50 for children 12 and under.

Virtually next door, the **Refuge Waterfowl Museum** (© 757/336-5800) has a variety of antique decoys, boats, traps, art, and carvings by outstanding crafts-people, some of whom do their carving here. There's very good shopping here, although it's difficult to tell what's for sale and what's not. Open Memorial Day to Labor Day, Thursday through Monday from 10am to 5pm. Call for off-season hours. Admission is $3 for adults, $1.50 for children under 12.

In the Landmark Plaza on North Main Street, the small **Island Aquarium** (© 757/336-6508) contains a marsh exhibit and touch tanks, where children can handle some of the marine life from local waters. It's a good place for kids on a rainy day, but you'll learn much, much more at the Virginia Marine Science Museum in Virginia Beach (see section 2, above). Admission is $4 for adults, $3 for children under 15. Open Memorial Day to Labor Day, Monday to Friday 5 to 9pm, Saturday 9am to 5pm, and Sunday 10am to 5pm. Call for off-season hours.

WHERE TO STAY

If you plan to stay a week or more, renting a cottage may be more economical than staying at a hotel. Among several companies handling cottage rentals are **Chincoteague Resort Realty,** 6378A Church St., Chincoteague Island, VA 23336 (© 800/668-7836 or 757/336-3100; www.chincoteagueresort.com) and **Chincoteague Vacation Rentals,** 7038 Maddox Blvd., Chincoteague, Virginia 23336 (© 757/336-1236; www.igetaway.net).

MOTELS

Until recently Chincoteague's only accommodations were small, family-run motels and bed-and-breakfasts. The small motels are still here, and by and large possess more charm and hands-on attention that the island's two chain motels: the **Comfort Suites,** 4195 Main St. (© 800/228-5150 or 757/336-3700; fax 757/336-5452; www.chincoteaguechamber.com/comfortsuites), and the **Hampton Inn & Suites,** 4179 Main St. (© 800/HAMPTON or 757/336-1616; www.hamptoninnsuiteschincoteague.com). These new motels are next to each other beside Chincoteague Channel. Both have heated indoor pools but neither has a restaurant.

Driftwood Motor Lodge   Along with the Refuge Inn across the road (see below), this gray, three-story shiplap building is the closest accommodations to Assateague Island. Entered from the rear, the motel-style rooms all have balconies facing the road (those on the third floor overlook the marshes). Most contain two double beds, tables and chairs, and full tiled baths. The one suite has two bedrooms, one bath, and a microwave, refrigerator, and coffeemaker.

7105 Maddox Blvd. (P.O. Box 575), Chincoteague Island, VA 23336. © 800/553-6117 or 757/336-6557. Fax 757/336-6558. www.driftwoodmotorlodge.com. 52 units, 1 suite. Summer $109–$145 double, $146 suite; off season $77–$95 double, $97–$149 suite. AE, DC, DISC, MC, V. From the bridge, turn left on Main St., right on Maddox Blvd. **Amenities:** Heated outdoor pool. *In room:* A/C, TV, dataport (3rd-floor rooms), fridge, coffeemaker.

Island Motor Inn Resort ★★   The best-equipped motel here, the Inn sits on Chincoteague Channel just north of the business district, giving its spacious rooms great views across the bay to the mainland. Reception is in a three-story building whose rooms are better appointed than the standard units in an older, two-story motel block adjoining. Rooms on the ends of this new building have bay windows on their sides, giving them two-way views. All rooms have private balconies. On the water side of the property, you'll find a 600-foot boardwalk and boat dock, a covered barbecue area with hammock for lounging, an outdoor pool, and glass-enclosed indoor pool and fitness center (with a trainer on duty during summer). On the road side, owners Reggie and Anna Stubbs have built a landscaped garden with lily ponds and benches for relaxing. The **Island Cafe** only serves breakfast, but it's exceptionally good (see box below). Also note that the mini-suites are reserved for honeymoons and other special celebrations.

4391 N. Main St., Chincoteague Island, VA 23336. ℂ **757/336-3141.** Fax 757/336-1483. www.islandmotorinn. com. 60 units. Summer $105–$175; off season $68–$140. AE, DC, DISC, MC, V. From the bridge, turn left on Main St. to motel on left. **Amenities:** Restaurant; indoor/outdoor pool; 2 exercise rooms; Jacuzzi; limited room service (breakfast only); babysitting; free washers and dryers; concierge-level rooms. *In room:* A/C, TV, dataport, fridge.

Refuge Inn ★★ *Kids*   Between the traffic circle and the bridge to Assateague, this charming motel with weathered gray siding nestles on beautifully land-scaped grounds shaded by tall pines. Like the Driftwood Motor Lodge across the street (see above), this is as close to Assateague Island as you can stay. You won't have to go across the bridge to see the ponies, however, for several live in a small corral on the grounds. The care and attention that sisters Donna Leonard and Jane Wolffe have lavished on the decor are evident everywhere. Furnishings are charming: Some rooms have country inn–style colonial pieces, bleached-pine headboards, decoys, handmade wall hangings, and all the elements of country style. First-floor rooms facing the back have sliding doors to private patios where guests can use outdoor grills. One of the two suites is a one-bedroom apartment with a fully equipped kitchen, a screened porch across the front, a bathroom with whirlpool tub, and a spiral staircase leading to a loft with a double bed-size convertible futon (the unit can sleep up to six people). Other facilities include an observation sun deck on the roof, a glass-enclosed pool and whirlpool, a chil-dren's playground, and an excellent gift/crafts shop. Note that suites are rented on a weekly basis in summer. The Bike Depot is here, so you can rent a cycle virtually at your front door, and the island's McDonald's is a few steps away.

7058 Maddox Blvd., Chincoteague Island, VA 23336. ℂ **888/868-6400** or 757/336-5511. Fax 757/336-6134. www.refugeinn.com. 72 units. Summer $98–$130 double, call for weekly suite rates; off season $60–$105 double, suites $150–$250. AE, DC, DISC, MC, V. **Amenities:** Heated indoor/outdoor pool; exercise room; Jacuzzi; sauna; watersports equipment rentals; bike rentals; coin-op washers and dryers. *In room:* A/C, TV, dataport, fridge, coffeemaker.

Waterside Motor Inn ★   All the accommodations at this three-story prop-erty feature private wooden balconies overlooking Chincoteague Channel, guar-anteeing some breathtaking sunset views. Shingle-look siding gives the property a Victorian appearance. The spacious rooms are decorated in comfortable con-temporary style, and some have a king- or queen-size bed and a pullout sofa bed. Four other condo units in a nearby Victorian house have two bedrooms and kitchens. The Waterside has its own fishing and crabbing pier.

3761 Main St. (P.O. Box 347), Chincoteague Island, VA 23336. ℂ **757/336-3434.** Fax 757/336-1878. www. watersidemotorinn.com. 49 units. Summer $99–$160 double; off season $72–$105 double. Rates include morning coffee and muffins in room. AE, DC, DISC, MC, V. At the bridge entering Chincoteague, turn right; the motel is on the right, about ½ mile from the bridge. **Amenities:** Heated outdoor pool; tennis court; exercise room; Jacuzzi; coin-op washers and dryers. *In room:* A/C, TV, kitchen (in condo units only), fridge, coffeemaker.

BED & BREAKFASTS

Cedar Gables Seaside Inn ★★   Innkeeper Claudia Greenway offers Chincoteague's most luxurious accommodations at her modern house, which looks out to Assateague Island from beside a marsh-lined creek (this is the only B&B here that enjoys a waterfront location). The building doesn't actually have gables, although an irregularly shaped roof creates gablelike ceilings in the guest quarters. Each guest room has a gas fireplace, ceiling fan, TV with VCR, refrigerator, phone with dataport, individual heating and air-conditioning controls, embroidered robes and Egyptian-cotton bed linens, and a bathroom with whirlpool tub and its own phone. Most intriguing is the Captain's Quarters, a spacious top-level room with a deck and winding stairs leading up to a private cupola with 360-degree views over the waterways and islands. Every unit has both inside and outside entries, so you don't have to go through the house to get in and out of your room. Served on a screened porch in good weather, three-course breakfasts begin with fresh fruit and Claudia's homemade granola. On the lawn, a swimming pool is completely surrounded by screens to keep the mosquitoes away. Claudia also has a canoe and a kayak to rent. *Note:* One child 14 and older can stay in the one downstairs room; otherwise, this is an all-adult establishment.

6095 Hopkins Lane (P.O. Box 1006), Chincoteague Island, VA 23336. ℂ 888/491-2944 or 757/336-6860. Fax 757/336-1291. www.cedargable.com. 4 units. $145–$180 double. Rates include full breakfast. AE, DISC, MC, V. From the bridge, turn left on Main St., right on Maddox Blvd., left on Deep Hole Rd., right on Hopkins Lane. **Amenities:** Outdoor pool; Jacuzzi; watersports equipment rentals. *In room:* A/C, TV/VCR, dataport, fridge, coffeemaker.

Inn at Poplar Corner   This three-story house with wraparound veranda looks like it's been here since Victorian times, but it was built from scratch by Tom and Jacque Derrickson, owners of the Watson House across the street (see below). Floral wallpaper, antiques, and lace curtains add to the atmosphere. A central hallway is flanked by a parlor and a dining room, whose French doors open to the verandah, permitting guests to enjoy gourmet breakfasts outside during good weather. The room on the front of the second story has bay windows, while the one to the rear has its own private balcony. But the star here is the third story, which has a unique lounge (you have to stoop under the roof to reach a small reading area) and a bedroom with three gables and French doors leading to a huge bathroom. All rooms have window air-conditioning units, ceiling fans, and whirlpool tubs, but none has a phone or TV.

Tom and Jacque also operate **The Watson House** across the street (ℂ **800/ 336-6787** or 757/336-6115; www.poplarcorner.com). Unlike its newer sibling, the Watson House actually dates back to the Victorian era, having been built before 1874.

4248 Main St. (at Poplar St.), Chincoteague Island, VA 23336. ℂ 800/336-6787 or 757/336-6115. Fax 757/ 336-5776. www.poplarcorner.com. 4 units. Summer $129–$159; off season $109–$149. Rates include full breakfast and afternoon tea. MC, V. From the bridge, turn left on Main St. to inn on right. **Amenities:** Free bikes. *In room:* A/C, fridge, no phone.

Island Manor House   This B&B consists of two white-clapboard houses joined by a magnificent one-story, light-filled garden room with fireplace. It opens to a brick patio and fountain, where guests enjoy breakfast in good weather. Originally, there was only one house, built before the Civil War by two young men. They eventually married sisters, who did not enjoy living under the same roof, so they split the structure and moved one half next door. Today, both have been handsomely restored and are furnished in Federal style, along with

17th-, 18th-, and 19th-century pieces collected by owners Charles and Carol Kalmykow. In the two first-floor sitting rooms are fireplaces and telephones for guest use.

4160 Main St., Chincoteague Island, VA 23336. ℂ 800/852-1505 or 757/336-5436. Fax 757/336-1333. www. islandmanor.com. 8 units (6 with bathroom). $80–$140 double. Rates include full breakfast. AE, MC, V. From the bridge into Chincoteague, turn left onto Main St. and continue about 1½ blocks; the inn is on the right. *In room:* A/C.

CAMPGROUNDS

Chincoteague has several family-oriented campgrounds. Most convenient to Assateague is the **Maddox Family Campground,** 6742 Maddox Blvd. (at the traffic circle), (ℂ **757/336-3111;** fax 757/336-1980; www.chincoteague.com/ maddox), which has 550 campsites, some with views of the Assateague Lighthouse. On the grounds are a pool, playground, pavilion, a grocery store with RV supplies, laundry room, bathhouses, dump station, and propane filling station. Rates range from $27 for a tent site to $35 for full hookup. Discover, MasterCard, and Visa are accepted.

WHERE TO DINE

You won't find fine dining here, but you will be served seafood fresh from the boat. The famous Chincoteague oysters are harvested from September to March. The area is also known for flounder, caught year-round.

Winter is not a good time for dining here, for most restaurants close well before Christmas and reopen just before Easter weekend the following spring.

AJ's on the Creek ✷ SEAFOOD/STEAKS   The island's most romantic restaurant, AJ's offers dining either on a screened-in patio beside a narrow creek or inside, where candles and dried-flower arrangements adorn a mix of tables and booths. Most romantic of all is the one private table in a corner. The menu offers a mix of Italian-style pastas—Chincoteague oysters in a champagne cream sauce is a house specialty—and traditional dishes such as fried or steamed shrimp and oysters, plus char-grilled steaks. A popular local hangout, the friendly and cozy bar offers sports TVs and its own lunch and snack menu (including sandwiches, shrimp, and small orders of pasta).

6585 Maddox Blvd. ℂ 757/336-5888. Reservations not accepted. Lunch $3–$10; main courses $11–$25. AE, DC, DISC, MC, V. Summer Mon–Sat 11:30am–10pm (to 9:30pm in winter). Closed mid-Jan to mid-Feb.

Chincoteague Inn/P.T. Pelican's Intercoastal Deck Bar ✷ SEAFOOD Sitting beside the channel, the Chincoteague Inn has been a mainstay here for generations, offering traditional preparations and fine water views from big window walls. The delicately seasoned crab cakes are first rate, with large lumps of back-fin meat. But the fun part of this establishment is outside at P.T. Pelican's rustic and funky deck bar right on the Intercoastal Waterway. It's right out of Key West: well-weathered lean-to tin roof, spacious bar with well-weathered

---

⸜Tips⸝ Best Breakfast in Chincoteague

The best breakfast place in town is the **Island Cafe,** a cottage in front of the Island Motor Inn, 4391 Main St. ((ℂ **757/336-3141**). The big front porch is ideal for enjoying the house specialty, French toast laced with Grand Marnier, Amaretto, and Bailey's Irish Cream. Open year-round, daily from 6:30 to 11am.

stools, and real mouse traps to keep your money from blowing away. It's an interesting place for a lazy waterside lunch or for whiling away an afternoon chatting with the watermen who take libation here after crabbing and oystering. You can sit by the water at mix-and-match plastic patio tables and order from the Inn's dinner menu or from the all-day bar menu, which features burgers, crab cake sandwiches, soft-shell crabs, steamed or raw oysters and clams on the half shell, small pizzas, and tasty shrimp and crab salads.

Marlin St. (off Main St., south of the bridge). ⓒ **757/336-6110.** Reservations not accepted. Sandwiches and salads $4–$9; main courses $10–$19. DISC, MC, V. Easter to mid-Oct, deck bar daily 11am–10pm, dining room daily 4–10pm. Closed mid-Oct to Easter.

Village Restaurant SEAFOOD The gardenlike Village Restaurant, with white trellises and floral wallpaper, is one of the fanciest restaurants here. It enjoys a fine view of Assateague Island over a creek and a marsh. You'll enjoy some of the best traditionally prepared seafood in town here, whether you choose fried oysters, or flounder or shrimp stuffed with crab imperial. The house seafood platter is piled with fish filet, shrimp, scallops, oysters, clams, and lobster tail. Avoid the blackened fish, which is simply coated with Cajun spices. Non-seafood main dishes include veal or chicken Parmesan, fried chicken, and filet mignon. All entrees are served with home-baked bread, either potato or rice, and a choice of slaw, salad, or vegetable of the day.

7576 Maddox Blvd. ⓒ **757/336-5120.** Reservations recommended. Main courses $10–$20. AE, DISC, MC, V. Daily 5–9pm. Closed Mon off season.

Appendix:
Virginia in Depth

Below, we take a look at modern Virginia and examine the state's illustrious past. The history of English-speaking America began here, the fires of independence were flamed here, the American Revolution was won here, and much of the Civil War was fought here. Virginia's history will play a very important role in your visit, for many of the state's major attractions are houses, buildings, monuments, sites, and battlefields marking 3 centuries of America's past.

1 Virginia Today

The memory of the state's past still exerts its influence, as it surely must in towns where descendants of America's first patriots still live and where the homes, monuments, and battlefields that shaped the country's history comprise their daily landscape. So revered is history here that sometimes you would think George Washington still stands siege outside Yorktown, Thomas Jefferson still writes great political prose up at Monticello, and Robert E. Lee and Stonewall Jackson still ride at Fredericksburg and Chancellorsville.

Of all the memories, the Civil War lives strongest here, as witnessed by the recent civic battle in Richmond—whose population is now mostly African-American—over whether to place a statute of Pres. Abraham Lincoln and his son, Todd Lincoln, outside the National Park Services' new Richmond battlefields visitor center. Earlier, the city agonized about the statute of tennis star Arthur Ashe that stands among those of Civil War generals along Monument Avenue.

Prominent in Virginia Tidewater plantation society since the 1600s, the Byrd family dominated the state's politics from World War I until the 1980s. Under their conservative control, the "Mother of Presidents" virtually withdrew from national leadership. The state government fought federally mandated public school integration in the 1950s, with one county actually closing its schoolhouse doors rather than admit African-Americans to previously all-white institutions. Although racial relations have improved greatly since then, the old animosities still raise their ugly heads from time to time, as they have in Richmond.

Back in 1989, Virginians chose Democrat L. Douglas Wilder as the nation's first elected African-American governor, but Virginia still leans politically to the right of center. Conservative Republicans won two-thirds of the state legislature in 2001 while a Democrat, moderate high-tech businessman Mark Warner, laid claim to the governor's mansion.

Economically, the state did very well during the 1990s, thanks in large part to the growth of northern Virginia's high-tech corridor. The bloom came off the rose with the bursting of the Internet bubble in 1999, however, and the state economy has been limping along since then.

Although colonist John Rolfe is best remembered for marrying Indian princess Pocahontas, the tobacco industry he helped found is still important to Virginia's economy. Farm income also sprouts from apple orchards in the Shenandoah Valley; livestock, dairies, and poultry in the Piedmont; the state's famous Smithfield hams and peanuts from the Tidewater country; and seafood from the Chesapeake Bay. Industry includes the manufacturing of clothes, chemicals, furniture, and transportation equipment, plus shipbuilding at Newport News.

2 History 101

Virginia's recorded history began on April 26, 1607, when 104 English men and boys arrived at Cape Henry on the Virginia coast aboard the *Susan Constant,* the *Godspeed,* and the *Discovery.* The expedition—an attempt to compete with profitable Spanish encroachments in the New World— was sponsored by the Virginia Company of London and supported by King James I.

A MODEST BEGINNING

Although the colonists were heartened to find abundance of fish and game, if not streets paved with gold, their optimism was short-lived, for American Indians attacked them on their first day in the New World. Fleeing Cape Henry, they settled on Jamestown Island, which offered greater protection from the Spanish and the Indians but was a lousy, mosquito-infested place to live. They also had arrived in the midst of an extended drought. As one on-the-scene chronicler described it, "a world of miseries ensued." Only 50 settlers were alive by autumn.

When Capt. John Smith tried to barter for corn and grain, the Indians took him prisoner and carried him to Chief Powhatan. According to legend, they would have killed him, but Powhatan's teenage daughter, the beautiful princess Pocahontas, interceded and saved his life. However, Smith was not much of a diplomat in dealing with natives; he helped sow seeds of dissension that would result in centuries of hostility between the tribes and the European settlers.

In 1613, John Rolfe (who later married Pocahontas) brought from the New World a new aromatic tobacco that proved popular in England. The settlers had discovered not the glittery

Dateline

- **1607** First permanent English settlement in New World established at Jamestown.
- **1612** John Rolfe begins cultivation of tobacco for export.
- **1619** House of Burgesses—first representative legislative body in New World—meets in Jamestown. First Africans arrive at Jamestown as indentured servants.
- **1624** Virginia becomes a royal colony.
- **1652** Burgesses affirm that only they have right to elect officers of Virginia colony.
- **1682** Tobacco riots protest falling crop prices.
- **1699** Virginia's government moves to Williamsburg.
- **1754** French and Indian War begins as George Washington leads Virginia troops against French in Ohio Valley.
- **1755** Washington takes command of Virginia army on frontier.
- **1765** Patrick Henry protests Stamp Act, saying, "If this be treason, make the most of it."
- **1774** Virginia Convention meets, sends delegates to Continental Congress.
- **1775** Patrick Henry incites rebellion with "Liberty or Death" oration at Virginia Convention. Continental Congress chooses Washington to lead army.
- **1776** Patrick Henry elected first governor of self-declared Free State of Virginia. Thomas Jefferson's wording for Declaration of Independence adopted by Congress.
- **1779** State capital moved to Richmond.
- **1781** Cornwallis surrenders at Yorktown.
- **1787** Washington elected president of Constitutional Convention.
- **1788** Virginia ratifies Constitution.
- **1789** Washington inaugurated as first president. Virginia cedes area to U.S. for seat of government.
- **1801** Thomas Jefferson inaugurated president.

gold they expected, but the "golden weed" that would be the foundation of Virginia's fortunes.

In 1619, The Virginia Company sent a shipload of 90 women to suitors who had paid their transportation costs; 22 burgesses were elected to set up the first legislative body in the New World; and 20 Africans arrived in a Dutch ship to work as indentured servants, a precursor of slavery.

In 1699, the capital of the colony was moved from Jamestown, which had suffered a disastrous fire, to the planned town of Williamsburg. It was from Williamsburg that colonial patriots launched some of the first strong protests against Parliament.

UNREST GROWS The French and Indian War in the 1750s proved to be a training ground for America's Revolutionary forces. When the French built outposts in territory claimed by Virginia, Governor Dinwoody sent George Washington to protect Virginia's claims. In the field Washington acquitted himself with honor, and after General Braddock's defeat, he was appointed commander-in-chief of Virginia's army on the frontier.

Expenses from the war and economic hardships led the British to increase taxes in the colonies, and protests in Virginia and Massachusetts escalated. The 1765 Stamp Act met with general resistance. Patrick Henry inspired the Virginia General Assembly to pass the Virginia Resolves, setting forth colonial rights according to constitutional principles. The young orator exclaimed, "If this be treason, make the most of it." The Stamp Act was repealed in 1766, but the Revenue Acts of 1767, which included the hated tax on tea, exacerbated tensions.

Ties among the colonies were strengthened when Virginia's burgesses, led by Richard Henry Lee, created a committee to communicate their problems in dealing with England to similar

- **1803** Jefferson sends James Monroe to France for purchase of Louisiana Territory.
- **1809** James Madison inaugurated president.
- **1814** President and Dolley Madison flee to Virginia as British enter Washington.
- **1831** Nat Turner's slave rebellion.
- **1832** House of Delegates bill to abolish slavery in Virginia loses by seven votes.
- **1859** John Brown hanged after failed raid on Harper's Ferry Arsenal.
- **1861** Richmond chosen Confederate capital. First battle of Manassas.
- **1862** First ironclad ships, *Monitor* and *Merrimac*, battle in Hampton Roads harbor. Confederate victories at Second Manassas, Fredericksburg.
- **1863** Stonewall Jackson fatally wounded at Chancellorsville.
- **1864** Confederacy wins Battle of the Wilderness at Spotsylvania Court House near Fredericksburg. Grant's siege of Petersburg begins.
- **1865** Richmond evacuated. Lee surrenders at Appomattox.
- **1867** Virginia put under military rule of Reconstruction Act. Confederate President Jefferson Davis imprisoned for treason in Fort Monroe.
- **1870** Virginia readmitted to Union.
- **1900** Legislature passes "Jim Crow" segregation laws.
- **1902** Poll tax in new state constitution effectively keeps African-Americans from voting.
- **1913** Woodrow Wilson inaugurated president.
- **1917** Wilson leads America into war against Germany. Growth of Hampton Roads naval and military installations.
- **1954** Supreme Court school integration ruling leads to school closings to avoid compliance with law.
- **1989** L. Douglas Wilder, nation's first African-American governor, takes office in Richmond.
- **1994** Senator Charles Robb defeats challenge from controversial Republican Oliver North.
- **1999** Republicans gain historic majority in state legislature.

Continues

committees in the other colonies. When the Boston Post Bill closed that harbor in punishment for the Boston Tea Party, the Virginia Assembly moved swiftly. Although Governor Dunmore had dissolved the legislature, they met at Raleigh Tavern and recom-

- **2000** Robb loses U.S. Senate seat to Republican former Gov. George Allen.
- **2001** State economy enters recession; Republican legislative majority grows to two-thirds but Democrat Mark Warner is elected governor.

mended that a general congress be held annually. Virginia sent seven representatives to the First Continental Congress in 1774, among them Lee, Patrick Henry, and George Washington.

The following year, Patrick Henry made a plea for arming Virginia's militia. He concluded his argument in these words, "Is life so dear or peace so sweet as to be purchased at the price of chains and slavery? Forbid it, Almighty God! I know not what course others may take, but, as for me, give me liberty, or give me death!"

Later in 1775, upon hearing news of the battles of Lexington and Concord, the Second Continental Congress in Philadelphia voted to make the conflict near Boston a colony-wide confrontation and chose Washington as commander of the Continental Army. War had begun.

BIRTH OF THE NATION

Meeting in Williamsburg on June 12, 1776, the Virginia Convention adopted George Mason's Bill of Rights and instructed Virginia's delegates to the Continental Congress to propose independence for the colonies. Mason's document stated that "all power is vested in, and consequently derived from, the people," and that "all men are created free and independent, and have certain inherent rights . . . among which are the enjoyment of life and liberty, with the means of acquiring and possessing property . . . ." He also firmly upheld the right of trial by jury, freedom of the press, and freedom of religion. When the Congress meeting in Philadelphia adopted Thomas Jefferson's Declaration of Independence (based on Mason's bill) on July 4, 1776, the United States of America was born.

The Revolution was a bloody 7-year conflict marked by many staggering defeats for the patriots. Historians believe it was only the superb leadership and pertinacity of Gen. George Washington that inspired the Continental Army (a ragtag group of farmers, laborers, backwoodsmen, and merchants) to continue so long in the face of overwhelming odds.

VICTORY AT YORKTOWN   The turning point came in March 1781, when British General Lord Cornwallis arrived with his army at Yorktown. At the end of a long and rather fruitless march through the southern colonies, Cornwallis waited for the British navy to evacuate him and his men to New York.

While Cornwallis waited, Washington received word that a French admiral, the Comte de Grasse, was taking his squadron to the Chesapeake and would be at Washington's disposal through October 15. After conferring with the Comte de Rochambeau, commander of the French troops in America, Washington marched his 17,000-man allied army 450 miles to Virginia in hopes of trapping Cornwallis.

On September 5, 1781, a fleet of 19 British ships under Adm. Thomas Graves appeared at the entrance to Chesapeake Bay to evacuate Cornwallis. By coincidence, De Grasse's 24 French ships arrived at the same time. The naval battle ended in a stalemate, but Graves was forced to return to New York without Cornwallis. The French remained to block further British reinforcements or their escape by water, while Washington arrived at Yorktown. The trap had worked.

After 2 weeks of bombardment, Cornwallis waved the white flag. Although the war didn't officially end until the Treaty of Paris 2 years later, the colonists had won.

FRAMING THE CONSTITUTION   At first the new country adopted the Articles of Confederation, which created a weak and ineffectual national government. To remedy the situation, a Constitutional Convention met in Philadelphia in 1781. Washington was elected the convention's president. He and fellow Virginian James Madison fought to have the new Constitution include a Bill of Rights and gradual abolition of the slave trade. Although both measures were defeated, the two Virginians voted to adopt the Constitution.

In 1788, Virginia became the 10th state to ratify the Constitution, and by 1791 the first 10 amendments—the Bill of Rights—had been added. Madison was author of the first 9 amendments, Richard Henry Lee the 10th.

THE COUNTRY'S EARLY VIRGINIAN PRESIDENTS

Washington was elected president under the new Constitution and took office on April 30, 1789. Although he could have stayed in office, he stepped down after two terms, thus setting a precedent that ruled until Franklin D. Roosevelt was elected to a fourth term in 1940.

As third president of the United States, Jefferson nearly doubled the size of the country by purchasing the Louisiana Territory from Napoleon.

James Madison took office as president in 1809. Unable to maintain Jefferson's peacekeeping efforts in the face of continued provocations by England, Madison was swayed by popular demand for armed response, and in 1812, Congress declared war. Although British warships attacked some coastal plantations, the only suffering Virginia witnessed was the burning of nearby Washington, D.C.

James Monroe followed, and during his two terms, the nation pushed westward, and he faced the first struggle over slavery (which resulted in the Missouri Compromise), established the Monroe Doctrine, and settled the nation's boundary with Canada.

THE CIVIL WAR

It was not long before the United States became a nation divided. The issues were states' rights, slavery, and the conflicting economic goals of an industrial North and an agricultural South. In the election of 1860, the Republicans nominated Abraham Lincoln, whom the South vowed it would not accept; but the Democrats split and Lincoln was elected. Seven states soon seceded—Texas, Louisiana, South Carolina, Alabama, Georgia, Florida, and Mississippi. On April 12, 1861, guns sounded at Fort Sumter in Charleston harbor. Secession had become war.

FIRST MANASSAS   In May 1861, the Confederate capital was transferred to Richmond, only 100 miles from Washington, dooming Virginia to be the major battleground of the Civil War. The Union strategy was to advance south and capture Richmond. The first of six attempts was decisively repulsed on July 21, 1861, at the battle of First Manassas (Bull Run), where a stonewall-like stand by the Virginia Brigade of Gen. Thomas J. Jackson swept Union forces back to Washington. In addition to the victory, the South had found a new hero—"Stonewall" Jackson. Total casualties in this first major engagement of the war—4,828 men—made it apparent that this would be a long and bitter conflict.

THE PENINSULA CAMPAIGN   The second major offensive against Richmond, the Peninsula Campaign, devised by Union Gen. George B. McClellan, was the setting for a famous naval engagement. On March 9, 1862, two iron-clad vessels, the USS *Monitor* and the CSS *Virginia* (formerly the *Merrimac*) pounded each other with cannon. Although the battle was a draw, the advent of ironclad warships heralded a new era in naval history.

Two months later Yorktown was reduced to rubble and the Union army advanced up the peninsula. The Confederates retreated until taking a stand only 9 miles from Richmond. The Confederate leader, Gen. Joseph Johnson, was badly wounded during the battle. Robert E. Lee, grandson of colonial patriot Richard Henry Lee, was appointed head of the Army of Northern Virginia. Personally opposed to secession, Lee had sadly resigned his commission in the U.S. Army when Virginia joined the Confederacy, saying, "My heart is broken, but I cannot raise my sword against Virginia." In a series of victories beginning on June 26, 1862, Lee defeated McClellan and Richmond was saved.

SECOND MANASSAS, FREDERICKSBURG & CHANCELLORSVILLE
The third Union drive against Richmond was repulsed at the Second Battle of Manassas, where Lee's 55,000 men soundly defeated 70,000 Union troops under Gen. John Pope. On December 13, 1862, Gen. Ambrose Burnside, newly chosen head of the Army of the Potomac, crossed the Rappahannock and struck Fredericksburg while Lee's army was in northern Virginia. The federal advance was so slow that by the time the Union armies moved, Lee's forces were entrenched on a hill south of the city. The result was a Union massacre, and the fourth Union drive against Richmond was turned back.

Gen. Joseph Hooker took command of the Union army early in 1863, and, once again, federal forces crossed the Rappahannock. Fighting raged for 4 days. The Union army retreated, and the fifth drive on Richmond failed. But Lee's victory was costly. In addition to heavy casualties, Stonewall Jackson was wounded by his own troops and died of complications resulting from the amputation of his arm. Jackson's loss was costly, as Lee learned in July 1863 at the small Pennsylvania town of Gettysburg.

A WAR OF ATTRITION   In March 1864, Grant was put in command of all federal armies. His plan for victory called for total unrelenting warfare that would put constant pressure on all points of the Confederacy. The first great confrontation between Lee and Grant, the Battle of the Wilderness, resulted in a Confederate victory, but instead of retreating back to Maryland, Grant kept advancing toward Richmond. The campaign was the heaviest fighting of the Civil War. Three times Grant tried and failed to interpose his forces between Lee and Richmond. More than 80,000 men were killed and wounded.

LAYING SIEGE TO PETERSBURG   Unable to capture Richmond, Grant secretly moved his army across the James River toward Petersburg, an important rail junction south of Richmond and the city's main supply line. Improvised Southern forces managed to hold Petersburg until Lee arrived. Grant then resorted to ever-tightening siege operations. If he left his trenches, Lee would be abandoning Petersburg and Richmond. Subjected to hunger and exposure, the Confederate will began to wane and periodic skirmishes weakened Confederate morale.

Lee, hoping to divert Grant, dispatched a small army under Jubal Early to the menaced Shenandoah Valley, Virginia's "Bread Basket." Grant instructed Union Gen. Philip Sheridan: "The Shenandoah is to be so devastated that crows flying across it for the balance of the season will have to bring their own provender." The second valley campaign resulted in the destruction of Early's army and Lee's main source of food.

LEE'S RETREAT   Back in Petersburg, Grant launched his inevitable onslaught on April 1, 1865, when federal forces smashed through Confederate lines at Five Forks. Petersburg fell, and Richmond was soon occupied by federal forces. Lee's last hope was to rendezvous with Joe Johnson's army, which was retreating northward through North Carolina before Sherman's advance. However, on April 8, the vanguard of Grant's army succeeded in reaching Appomattox Court House ahead of Lee, thus blocking the Confederates' last escape route.

On April 9, 1865, the Civil War ended in Virginia at Appomattox in Wilbur McLean's farmhouse. Grant, uncompromising in war, proved compassionate in peace. Confederate soldiers were permitted to return home on parole, cavalrymen could keep their horses, and officers could retain their sidearms. Rations were provided for the destitute southerners. Speaking to his 28,000 soldiers, the remnants of the once-mighty Army of Northern Virginia, Lee said, "I earnestly pray that a merciful God will extend to you his blessing and protection. With an unceasing admiration of your constancy and devotion to your country, and a grateful remembrance of your kind and generous consideration for myself, I bid you all an affectionate farewell."

RECOVERY & RENEWAL & THE 20TH CENTURY

To a state devastated by a conflict that pitted brother against brother, recovery was slow. Besides the physical and psychological damages of the conflict, the Reconstruction era brought Virginia under federal military control until 1870.

However, by the turn of the century, new railroad lines connecting remote country areas in the west with urban centers characterized Virginia's economic growth. Factories were bringing more people to the cities, and the economy, once based entirely on agriculture, now had a growing industrial base. The Hampton Roads ports enjoyed growing importance as steamship traffic carried an increasing volume of commercial freight (today, it's the world's largest coal port). During this period the great scholar, author, and educator Booker T. Washington, who had been born in slavery, studied at Virginia's Hampton Institute and achieved fame as an advisor to presidents.

Although he was serving as governor of New Jersey at the time, Virginian-born Woodrow Wilson was elected president in 1912. Noted for his peace-loving ideals, Wilson nevertheless led the United States into World War I in 1917. War brought prosperity to Virginia with new factories and munitions plants and the expansion of military-training camps throughout the state.

World War II brought a population explosion, with men and women of the armed forces flocking to northern Virginia suburbs near Washington, D.C., and the port area of Hampton Roads. Many of these people stayed after the war, and by 1955 the majority of Virginians were urban dwelling. Today, the state's population is about seven million.

Index

FROMMER'S® MEMORABLE WALKS

Chicago
London

New York
Paris

San Francisco

FROMMER'S® WITH KIDS GUIDES

Chicago
Las Vegas
New York City

Ottawa
San Francisco
Toronto

Vancouver
Washington, D.C.

SUZY GERSHMAN'S BORN TO SHOP GUIDES

Born to Shop: France
Born to Shop: Hong Kong,
  Shanghai & Beijing

Born to Shop: Italy
Born to Shop: London

Born to Shop: New York
Born to Shop: Paris

FROMMER'S® IRREVERENT GUIDES

Amsterdam
Boston
Chicago
Las Vegas
London

Los Angeles
Manhattan
New Orleans
Paris
Rome

San Francisco
Seattle & Portland
Vancouver
Walt Disney World®
Washington, D.C.

FROMMER'S® BEST-LOVED DRIVING TOURS

Britain
California
Florida
France

Germany
Ireland
Italy
New England

Northern Italy
Scotland
Spain
Tuscany & Umbria

HANGING OUT™ GUIDES

Hanging Out in England
Hanging Out in Europe

Hanging Out in France
Hanging Out in Ireland

Hanging Out in Italy
Hanging Out in Spain

THE UNOFFICIAL GUIDES®

Bed & Breakfasts and Country
  Inns in:
  California
  Great Lakes States
  Mid-Atlantic
  New England
  Northwest
  Rockies
  Southeast
  Southwest
Best RV & Tent Campgrounds in:
  California & the West
  Florida & the Southeast
  Great Lakes States
  Mid-Atlantic
  Northeast
  Northwest & Central Plains

Southwest & South Central
  Plains
  U.S.A.
Beyond Disney
Branson, Missouri
California with Kids
Central Italy
Chicago
Cruises
Disneyland®
Florida with Kids
Golf Vacations in the Eastern U.S.
Great Smoky & Blue Ridge Region
Inside Disney
Hawaii
Las Vegas
London
Maui

Mexio's Best Beach Resorts
Mid-Atlantic with Kids
Mini Las Vegas
Mini-Mickey
New England & New York with
  Kids
New Orleans
New York City
Paris
San Francisco
Skiing & Snowboarding in the West
Southeast with Kids
Walt Disney World®
Walt Disney World® for
  Grown-ups
Walt Disney World® with Kids
Washington, D.C.
World's Best Diving Vacations

SPECIAL-INTEREST TITLES

Frommer's Adventure Guide to Australia &
  New Zealand
Frommer's Adventure Guide to Central America
Frommer's Adventure Guide to India & Pakistan
Frommer's Adventure Guide to South America
Frommer's Adventure Guide to Southeast Asia
Frommer's Adventure Guide to Southern Africa
Frommer's Britain's Best Bed & Breakfasts and
  Country Inns
Frommer's Caribbean Hideaways
Frommer's Exploring America by RV
Frommer's Fly Safe, Fly Smart

Frommer's France's Best Bed & Breakfasts and
  Country Inns
Frommer's Gay & Lesbian Europe
Frommer's Italy's Best Bed & Breakfasts and
  Country Inns
Frommer's Road Atlas Britain
Frommer's Road Atlas Europe
Frommer's Road Atlas France
The New York Times' Guide to Unforgettable
  Weekends
Places Rated Almanac
Retirement Places Rated
Rome Past & Present

Fly.
Sleep.
Save.

Now you can book your flights and hotels together, so you can get even better deals than if you booked them separately.

Travelocity

Visit www.travelocity.com
or call 1-888-TRAVELOCITY